MATHEMATICAL
STRUCTURES FOR
COMPUTER GRAPHICS

MATHEMATICAL STRUCTURES FOR COMPUTER GRAPHICS

STEVEN J. JANKE

WILEY

Published by John Wiley & Sons, Inc., Hoboken, New Jersey
Published simultaneously in Canada

For general information on our other products and services or for technical support, please contact our
Customer Care Department within the United States at (800) 762-2974, outside the United States at
(317) 572-3993 or fax (317) 572-4002.

Wiley also publishes its books in a variety of electronic formats. Some content that appears in print may
not be available in electronic formats. For more information about Wiley products, visit our web site at
www.wiley.com.

Library of Congress Cataloging-in-Publication Data:

Janke, Steven J., 1947- author.
 Mathematical structures for computer graphics / Steven J. Janke, Department of Mathematics,
Colorado College, Colorado Spring, CO.
    pages cm
  Includes bibliographical references and index.
 ISBN 978-1-118-71219-1 (paperback)
1. Computer graphics–Mathematics. 2. Three-dimensional imaging–Mathematics. I. Title.
 T385.J355 2014
 006.601′51–dc23   2014017641

Printed in the United States of America

10 9 8 7 6 5 4 3 2 1

To Deborah

CONTENTS

5 Orientation   124

6 Polygons and Polyhedra   164

PREFACE

Computer graphics includes a large range of ideas, techniques, and algorithms extending from generating animated simulations to displaying weather data to incorporating motion-capture segments in video games. Producing these images requires an array of artistic, technical, and algorithmic skills. Software can help by offering a flexible user interface, but under the hood, mathematics is orchestrating the images. Not everything in graphics begins with a mathematical result, but nearly everything is founded on mathematical ideas, because ultimately algorithms direct the computer to light up specified pixels on the screen.

The evolution of computer graphics started in the early 1970s, and since then key mathematical ideas and techniques have risen to the surface and have proved their worth in solving graphics problems. This text tries to lay out these ideas in a way that is easily accessible to those interested in a sound footing in the field and to those software engineers eager to fill in gaps where their understanding faltered.

Organized to mimic the flow of a standard graphics course, this manuscript grew from the notes for an undergraduate graphics course taught regularly over a span of 20 years. Appropriate mathematical ideas are introduced along with the details of various techniques. The style is more informal than formal, yet the approach includes thorough derivations in the hope that context and careful arguments will build confidence in constructing new approaches and new algorithms.

One or two courses in calculus should give the readers sufficient mathematical maturity to work through the text, and even if their linear algebra background is limited to matrix multiplication, they should be able to develop some useful algebraic and geometric tools. Standard mathematics courses rarely have the time to cover all the important mathematical constructs used in graphics such as the description of curves necessary for surface design, or homogeneous coordinates necessary for affine transformations. This text fills in those gaps and looks behind the results enough to understand how they fit into the rest of mathematics. It does not rely on the rigorous theorem/proof format, and instead uses intuition and example to develop careful results. Although the mathematics is interesting in its own right, the text hopefully does not lose sight of the ultimate goal which is to produce interesting and useful images.

There are plenty of examples and exercises to help fix the ideas and several suggestions of other directions to investigate. At the end of each chapter (except the last), there is a section titled *Complements and Details* that collects a few historical notes, several calculation details, and occasionally some ideas which may lead to interesting tangents. The text is independent of any particular graphics system, but it does have OpenGL in mind when presenting details of the viewing frustum in the chapter on visibility. Otherwise, there are programming exercises throughout, which can be done with almost any language and graphics interface.

Chapters 1–3 carefully develop vector geometry assuming very little background. They highlight the difference between vectors and points and emphasize the connection between geometry and algebra. Coordinate-free expressions and homogeneous coordinates are both introduced.

Chapters 4 and 5 examine transformations, both linear and affine. Along the way, they develop basic matrix algebra, construct various transformations including the perspective transformation, examine coordinate systems (world, local, and camera), unravel Euler angles and quaternions, and consider alternate coordinate systems.

Chapters 6 and 7 develop modeling techniques through an exploration of polygons (particularly triangles), polyhedra, parametric description of curves, Lagrange interpolation, Bézier curves, splines, nonuniform rational B-splines (NURBS), and surface construction.

Rendering is covered in Chapters 8 and 9, starting with a look at the view frustum, hidden surface algorithms, and simple ray tracing. Then an elementary lighting model is examined in detail before introducing shading, shadows, the bidirectional reflectance distribution function (BRDF), the basics of radiosity, and texture mapping.

The final chapter collects three separate mathematical techniques that represent arguably different paradigms. Bresenham's algorithm starts a discussion of pixel-based mathematics, Perlin's noise prompts a visit to random distributions, and L-systems offer an alternative algebraic description of organic forms.

When used as a course text, the first five chapters as well as selections from the last five could serve to cover an appropriate amount of material. The idea is to rely on the text for the mathematics and supplement it with algorithms perhaps specific to the available graphics systems. There are both mathematical and programming exercises in each chapter. Throughout the examples in the text, the calculation results are rounded to two or three decimal places. This still leads to round-off error, and a good exercise for the student is to reconcile any perceived discrepancies in the results.

In the way of acknowledgement, first note that most of the figures in the text were prepared using Mathematica®. Second, many thanks go to my graphics students over the years who prompted me to learn the nuances of the subject and who offered constructive feedback on my courses. Thanks also go to Cory Scott whose comments on the completed manuscript were essential and to Craig Janke for cover ideas along with continued encouragement. Finally, without my wife Deborah and her unending support, this project would have dissolved on the screen.

STEVEN J. JANKE
Colorado College, 2014

1

BASICS

It is rather amazing that a finite rectangular array of colored dots (called *pixels* as an abbreviation of picture elements) is sufficient to display the nearly limitless collection of images we recognize as realistically or symbolically representing portions of our world. The power of combinatorics helps us to explain the situation (millions of possible colors for each pixel in the large display array), but we can hardly conceive of all the images we have already seen let alone those that are yet to be seen. From this reductionist viewpoint, the whole idea of computer graphics is to set the right pixels to the right color. Easier said than done. Yes, a plain red square is easy, but one that looks like it is made of bricks is tougher, and one that includes a human face taxes the best of known algorithms.

Of course, the computer graphics enterprise includes any and all manipulations of images. We can start from scratch and produce a photo-realistic image of a new airliner or perhaps construct a landscape design complete with a variety of plants. Maybe the challenge is to translate CAT (computerized axial tomography) scan data into an image of the brain or correct the color balance in a photo being readied for publication. To bring some order to the very long list of possibilities, it is helpful to consider two main categories: either we are generating images, or we are processing existing images. Both require mathematical tools, but the first category encompasses the broad mathematical approaches necessary to understand three-dimensional descriptions of objects and their interactions with light. The second category starts with an image and draws on the mathematics of transformations and filters necessary to convert it into a more useful visual representation. In this survey of mathematical tools that are

Mathematical Structures for Computer Graphics, First Edition. Steven J. Janke.
© 2015 John Wiley & Sons, Inc. Published 2015 by John Wiley & Sons, Inc.

useful in computer graphics, we will focus on the first category where we can start with the basics of mathematical descriptions and work through the generation and manipulation of objects in space.

1.1 GRAPHICS PIPELINE

As we examine the steps necessary to produce a new image on the computer screen, we are tracing what is often called the *graphics pipeline*. The pipeline analogy is intended to highlight the stages we go through both in designing images and in processing them on the computer to produce the final properly colored array of pixels on the display screen. As one frame is being completed, the next is making its way down the pipeline. Most modern hardware includes the main microprocessor (central processing unit, CPU), the graphics microprocessor (graphics processing unit, GPU), and various associated memory banks. The CPU and GPU work in parallel, as the CPU supplies descriptions of objects to the GPU which in turn processes the descriptions to determine which pixels on the screen need to be turned on. The exact order of all the required steps depends on the hardware and on the graphics software we use. However, we can make a more general description of the pipeline to enumerate the stages of image generation and set the context for understanding the associated mathematics. Our pipeline then looks like this:

1. *Modeling*. We need a mathematical description of objects, background, and light sources as well as a description of their placement in a scene. For more primitive objects such as buildings which are more or less constructed out of simple plane surfaces, the description includes a list of vertices and a list showing which vertices determine individual faces. For curved surfaces, we may attempt an accurate description (e.g., a sphere) or rely on an approximation with small flat triangles. These descriptions are, of course, just the beginning, as we need also to know the details of how the objects are placed in a scene and how light will interact with them. Mathematically, a geometric description including vertices and faces (surfaces) forms the kernel of our model, but certainly if the object is a tree or if there is fog affecting the lighting, the description may well require a deeper extension of the standard high school geometry. This modeling stage can be done with design software, allowing artists to manipulate the scene to reach the desired effect.

2. *Transformation*. Building a scene requires positioning objects relative to each other and includes rotation, scaling, and translation. Transformations reposition an object and convert its coordinate descriptions appropriately. Then, to view the scene, imagine a camera placed somewhere in space looking in a particular direction. (Alternatively, imagine your eye positioned in space looking at the scene.) Another transformation adjusts the mathematical descriptions so that they are relative to the camera position.

3. *Visibility*. Depending on where the camera is, we may not see the entire scene. Rather, some parts are outside the field of view and consequently can be ignored

when generating the image. Even those objects within the field of view usually have some surfaces that are facing away from the camera and need not be considered. Some objects in the scene may be only partially visible since they fall both inside and outside the field of view. These objects are clipped (often after projection) so that only the relevant pieces continue down the graphics pipeline. Dealing with only the visible portions of a scene improves the efficiency of image generation because the calculations necessary to determine pixel color are computationally expensive.

4. *Projection.* Once we position the camera (or our eye), the actual image of the scene is produced on a two-dimensional surface in the camera (or on our retina). The three-dimensional scene is projected onto a two-dimensional screen. It is somewhat easier to imagine that there is a window placed just in front of our eye or camera and the scene itself is painted on this window. Positions of points in the scene, including how far away from the window they are, determine where on the window they are projected. Done correctly, the projection preserves the perspective in the scene and adds realism. If the dimensions of the window do not match the display screen, yet another transformation is necessary to convert window coordinates to display coordinates.

5. *Rasterize.* Mathematical descriptions of objects are usually continuous, allowing line segments, for example, to have an infinite number of points. At some stage of the graphics pipeline, the continuous line must be approximated by a finite set of screen pixels. This process requires some care to avoid distorting the line and introducing unintended artifacts, but then we have a finite set of pixels rather than an infinite set of points. The task of determining the colors of the pixels is now manageable and, if done appropriately, can maintain the illusion of a continuous image.

6. *Shading.* Light determines the exact shade of color that an object reflects, and that light depends on the position of light sources, their intensity, and their color. Some objects may be casting shadows and others may actually be reflecting light onto the rest of the scene. The geometry of light rays is essential for making these shading calculations. Positioning light sources and determining the material properties of objects occurs early in the pipeline, but it is late in the process when color calculations are actually completed for individual pixels.

7. *Texturing.* Describing the surface of an object as mathematically planar indicates that it is flat and smooth. Yet surfaces can be rough or covered with patterns of color. For example, in a computer game, the walls of a room may well be made of stone, so it becomes important to determine how light reflects off stone. In the texturing stage, this type of surface detail is added somewhat artificially by either copying the detail from existing images (e.g., taking a picture of real stone) or generating it mathematically with functional descriptions (e.g., some function describing how bumpy stone really is). To determine final colors for pixels, textures need to be generated and mapped to individual pixels.

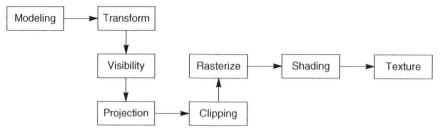

Figure 1.1   Graphics pipeline

This is the general notion of a graphics pipeline. The first stage, modeling, is often done interactively and builds the contents of the image, while all the rest of the stages taken together *render* the image on the screen. Depending on the hardware and software, the order of the rendering stages may be slightly permuted, but the scope of the process indicates the range of mathematical tools we need to explore (Figure 1.1).

1.2   MATHEMATICAL DESCRIPTIONS

To generate an image, we need to mathematically describe a scene. For a simple object such as a cube, we can list the position of its vertices and then list which vertices anchor each face. This is easy enough, but the positions of the vertices depend on the coordinate system we are using and it is not obvious which one we should use. Putting the origin of our coordinate system at the center of the cube makes describing the vertex positions easier, but there may be other objects in the scene which are good candidates for the origin. The answer may well be to use many coordinate systems and develop means of combining them into an all-inclusive scene.

If next to the cube there is a more organic object such as a flower, then we have an added difficulty because a flower is probably not well described by giving vertices and faces. There could be such a description, but there is also a special system of symbols (L-system) that was designed to capture the way plants grow, making a description both easier and more succinct.

The cube may be made of wood, making the faces more bumpy than smooth and making light reflect in a way that shows the grain. The scene description is now moving further and further from a simple list of vertices, and we will need additional means of describing the detail.

The larger goals are to make the mathematical description as simple as possible, as easy as possible to alter during the design process, and as independent of any fixed coordinate system as possible. Then the resulting computer code will be general and flexible.

To draw an object on the computer screen, we need to identify which pixels to light up (and what color to make them). Since most computer monitors are rectangular, locating a pixel usually means specifying its horizontal and vertical position in the rectangular array of pixels which make up the entire screen. This seems simple enough, but our common descriptions of objects are not usually in terms of the horizontal and vertical distances to each point. A cartoon character's head might be described as "oval, with a button nose, and beady eyes." And a tree may be "conical with short drooping branches covered with folded, heart-shaped leaves." To draw these objects on the screen, there is no escape from determining the horizontal and vertical positions of appropriate pixels, but the challenge for the graphics programmer is to find ways of describing the objects that are between the intuitive common way and the hard-core quantitative way that lists the horizontal and vertical positions of all the points. Unfortunately, qualitative descriptions of objects are not easily incorporated into computer programs, so it makes sense, at least at first, to concentrate on more quantitative descriptions.

1.3 POSITION

In the geometry of Euclid, there are no coordinates. Instead, geometric objects are compared to each other in order to understand their features; lines are compared to other lines, and triangles to triangles. This approach is not sufficient for computer graphics because we eventually need the absolute position of an object in order to determine which pixels on the screen to turn on. In the seventeenth century, Descartes, the philosopher and mathematician, made attempts to connect algebra and geometry, and although he did not develop coordinate systems as we know them now, we still refer to the rectangular coordinate system as the *Cartesian* coordinate system. This is the default coordinate system for computer graphics and the one we are all familiar with from high school (Figure 1.2).

In two dimensions, we have two perpendicular axes, the horizontal one labeled x and the vertical one labeled y. They cross at a unique origin labeled 0. Each is a number line increasing either to the right or up. Any point in the plane has a coordinate representation which is a pair of numbers (x, y) indicating how far to go horizontally (negative distance indicates left of the origin) and then how far to go vertically (negative here means down from the origin). Note that this is a unique representation; any pair of numbers determines exactly one point in the plane and any point determines exactly one pair of numbers.

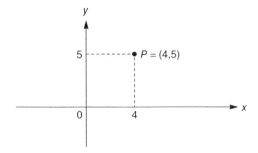

Figure 1.2 2D Cartesian coordinate system

In computer graphics, the fundamental task is to locate points in a scene, and to make that process easier and perhaps more intuitive, we define a new mathematical object called a *vector*.

Definition 1.1 *A two-dimensional vector is an object representing a displacement in the plane. It has a length and a direction.*

A vector is intended to describe how to get from one point to another. If our vector has a length of five units and is pointing to the right, then it represents moving from an arbitrary point to a point five units to the right. It is important to note that the vector is not positioned at any particular place in the plane. It represents displacement, not position. Once we apply the displacement to a point, we reach another point that is positioned in the plane. Visually, vectors are represented as arrows; they have length and direction. As we will soon see, a convenient way of describing a two-dimensional vector mathematically is to give two numbers indicating its displacement in the horizontal and vertical directions. Often the representative arrow is drawn with its tail at the origin, say, and its head (the end with the arrow) positioned to show the displacement. This can be a little confusing because the vector is really not positioned at any particular point in the plane; setting the tail at the origin is just a default approach to representing the vector visually (Figure 1.3).

We now can give a slightly different perspective on the standard Cartesian coordinate system. To describe a two-dimensional (2D) coordinate system, we specify a unique origin and two vectors. For the standard system, these vectors both have the same unit length and are perpendicular to each other. The vector with direction along the positive x-axis is usually referred to as $\vec{i}$, and the one in the direction of the positive y-axis is denoted as $\vec{j}$. Describing any point in the plane is now a matter of indicating how many unit steps in the direction of $\vec{i}$ and how many in the direction of $\vec{j}$ we need to take to reach the point. For example, the point $(4, 1.5)$ is the point we reach when starting at the origin, then taking 4 unit steps in the x-direction, and finally 1.5 unit steps in the y-direction. As you may have guessed, since $\vec{i}$ and $\vec{j}$ have unit length, the algebra of vectors allows us to represent the point as $4\vec{i} + 1.5\vec{j}$. This will prove to be useful in making geometric calculations (Figure 1.4).

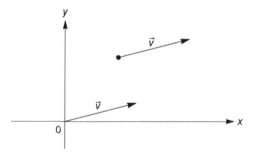

Figure 1.3   Vectors indicating displacement

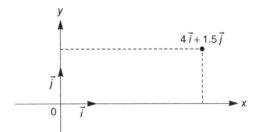

Figure 1.4 Vectors $\vec{i}$ and $\vec{j}$

Without much effort, we can move to three-dimensional space by adding a third axis labeled z perpendicular to the x- and y-axes. With our vector perspective, we have added a new vector, often called $\vec{k}$. Now each point in space is represented by a unique triple of numbers, or in terms of vectors as a combination of the three vectors $\vec{i}, \vec{j}$, and $\vec{k}$.

The nature of the Cartesian coordinate system depends on the direction of the unit vectors. The standard two-dimensional system has vector $\vec{i}$ pointing to the right along the positive x-axis and the perpendicular vector $\vec{j}$ pointing up. However, we might also let $\vec{j}$ point down. This is actually the default coordinate system for the computer screen when using some standard programming languages. An easy transformation can get us back to the standard system with $\vec{j}$ pointing up, and usually this is desirable. As we will see later, we could pick the two vectors for a system so that they are not perpendicular. These systems may prove useful in describing some objects, so we will have to develop transformations that allow us to easily move between all these various possibilities.

In three dimensions, there is one, often troubling, complication. There are two geometrically different ways to add a third vector and this time the mathematical consequences are not trivial. Basically, the third vector $\vec{k}$ could point in the direction designated in Figure 1.5 or in the opposite direction. To standardize, we designate a *right-handed* system to be one where if we position our right hand with the fingers pointing in the direction of $\vec{i}$ and adjust so that when we curl our fingers they point

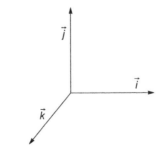

Figure 1.5 Right-handed coordinate system

in the direction of $\vec{j}$, then our thumb points in the direction of $\vec{k}$. Figure 1.5 shows a right-handed coordinate system. It is important to distinguish right-handed from left-handed systems in order to keep track of whether vectors point out of or into an object.

1.4   DISTANCE

Now that we have set up a coordinate system, we turn to the fundamental problem of determining the distance between two points. This is a job for the venerable Pythagorean theorem, named after an itinerant teacher of ancient Greece who led his devoted followers through a wide range of ideas drawn from topics as diverse as number theory and vegetarian diets. He is credited for the famous theorem about right triangles, but the result was undoubtedly known much earlier by at least Babylonian scholars if not others [1].

Theorem 1.1 (Pythagorean Theorem).   *In a right triangle, the sum of squares of the two legs equals the square of the hypotenuse.*

Proof Sketch.   First remember that a right triangle is one with a 90° angle. Figure 1.6 shows four identical right triangles with legs a and b. They are arranged in a large square on the left and then rearranged in the same large square on the right. On the left, the area not taken up by triangles is equal to c^2, the area of the labeled square in the middle. On the right, the area outside the triangles is in two pieces equaling $a^2 + b^2$. Hence the Pythagorean theorem: $a^2 + b^2 = c^2$.   □

This result allows us to calculate the distance between any two points on the screen or in an arbitrary plane. Simply, the distance is the length of the hypotenuse of a right triangle. The two points are the opposite corners of a rectangle with sides parallel to the vectors $\vec{i}$ and $\vec{j}$ which determine the coordinate system. The distance between the corners of the rectangle is the length of the hypotenuse of a right triangle. The legs of the right triangle are easy to find by taking differences of the Cartesian coordinates for the two points. If one point has coordinates (x_1, y_1) and the other (x_2, y_2), then the

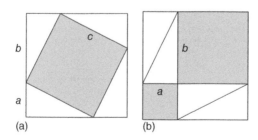

Figure 1.6   (a,b) Visual proof of the Pythagorean theorem

Pythagorean theorem gives

$$Distance = \sqrt{(x_1 - x_2)^2 + (y_1 - y_2)^2}$$

In three dimensions, the distance between points is not much harder to find once we visualize two right triangles. Suppose the two points are labeled P_1 and P_2. This time, they can be thought of as the opposite corners of a rectangular box where the faces of the box are parallel to the three coordinate planes (Figure 1.7). The distance between the points is the length of the hypotenuse of the right triangle $\Delta P_1 Q P_2$. The leg QP_2 is just one edge of the box, called a in the figure. The leg $P_1 Q$ is a diagonal of one face of the box and hence the hypotenuse of triangle $\Delta P_1 R Q$. By the Pythagorean theorem,

$$(P_1 Q)^2 = b^2 + c^2.$$

Since $(P_1 P_2)^2 = (P_1 Q)^2 + (QP_2)^2$, we finally have

$$(P_1 P_2)^2 = a^2 + b^2 + c^2$$

where a, b, and c are all edges of the rectangular box.

The Pythagorean theorem is essential to computer graphics. Dropping perpendiculars and forming right triangles is one of the most useful tools in the mathematics toolbox. Triangles are everywhere in graphics, and, in fact, they are central to all of geometry. Projections and visibility questions invariably involve drawing a triangle usually including the eye position as a vertex. Complicated objects are usually built from triangles because triangular faces are guaranteed to be planar; they can be drawn in a plane. (This is unlike quadrilateral faces which might be twisted so that the four vertices do not all lie in a plane.) So calculations with triangles are central to computer graphics and we rely both on the Pythagorean theorem and on a generalization that covers triangles of arbitrary angles. To reach this generalization, we use the cosine function (reviewed in Appendix A).

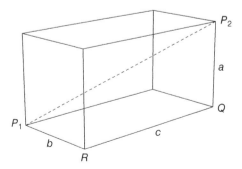

Figure 1.7 Distance in three dimensions

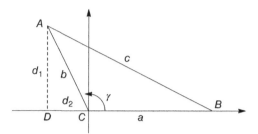

Figure 1.8   Law of cosines

Theorem 1.2 (Law of Cosines).   *In a triangle with sides $a, b,$ and c, let the angle γ be opposite the side c. Then we have $c^2 = a^2 + b^2 - 2ab\cos\gamma$.*

Proof Sketch. Note that γ is an angle inside the triangle, so we know it is less than $180°$. When $\gamma = 90°$, then $\cos\gamma = 0$ and we have a right triangle so the Pythagorean theorem applies and the law of cosines reduces to it. In general, we try making right triangles out of the original triangle to see why the law holds. There are actually two cases: $\gamma > 90°$ and $\gamma < 90°$. Figure 1.8 shows the first case.

In the figure, the side AD is perpendicular to the baseline CB. Then we have three triangles: the given triangle $\triangle ABC$ and two right triangles $\triangle ADC$ and $\triangle ADB$. With the lower case letters indicating lengths, apply the Pythagorean theorem to the triangle $\triangle ADC$ to get

$$b^2 = d_1^2 + d_2^2.$$

Applying the Pythagorean theorem to the second right triangle, $\triangle ADB$ gives

$$c^2 = d_1^2 + (d_2 + a)^2 = d_1^2 + d_2^2 + 2d_2 a + a^2 = a^2 + b^2 + 2d_2 a$$

Notice that $\angle ACD$ is the supplement of γ (i.e., they add to $180°$). This means $\cos(\angle ACD) = -\cos\gamma$, and since $\cos(\angle ACD) = d_2/b$, we now have the result $c^2 = a^2 + b^2 - 2ab\cos\gamma$.

For the second case where $\gamma < 90°$, we proceed just as above by drawing a new side and building new right triangles. The algebra is just a little different (Section 1.5).

□

Example 1.1 (Triangles in 3D).   Suppose we have three vertices in three dimensions complete with coordinates $A = (3, 5, 4), B = (6, 2, -3), C = (-4, 6, 3)$. Although we are in three dimensions, the triangle does lie in a single plane, so using the tools we developed we can completely describe it. Applying the Pythagorean theorem, first we get the lengths of all the sides:

$$|AB| = \sqrt{(3-6)^2 + (5-2)^2 + (4-(-3))^2} = \sqrt{67} \approx 8.185$$

$$|AC| = \sqrt{(3 - (-4))^2 + (5 - 6)^2 + (4 - 3)^2} = \sqrt{51} \approx 7.141$$

$$|BC| = \sqrt{(6 - (-4))^2 + (2 - 6)^2 + (-3 - 3)^2} = \sqrt{197} \approx 14.036$$

Comparing the squares of the lengths, we can determine whether each angle is larger or smaller than a right angle. For example, since $67 + 51 < 197$, we know that $\angle ABC$ must be larger than a right angle. That makes the other two smaller than a right angle because the sum of all angles must be $180°$ (or π radians).

Now, an application of the law of cosines gives us the actual angle:

$$197 = 67 + 51 - 2\sqrt{67}\sqrt{51}\cos(\angle BAC) \implies \cos(\angle BAC) \approx -0.676.$$

This indicates that $\angle BAC \approx 132.53°$. The same procedure gives the other two angles: $\angle ACB \approx 25.46°$ and $\angle ABC \approx 22.03°$. □

Once we can completely describe the triangle, we should be able to determine whether a light ray hits it. This is a common problem that we will solve later by first finding where the light ray hits the plane of the triangle and then deciding whether the intersection point is inside or outside the triangle. In order to solve this problem, it helps to translate the tools we are using to the language of vectors, and this we do in the next chapter.

1.5 COMPLEMENTS AND DETAILS

1.5.1 Pythagorean Theorem Continued

No one knows how Pythagoras proved his theorem because even the basic facts of his life (about 500 BCE) are a bit sketchy. Since then, there have been many proofs devised including a somewhat complicated one given by Euclid in Proposition 47 of Book I of his Elements (about 300 BCE). Just a little later, the illustrated square on the left in Figure 1.6 appeared in a Chinese manuscript, and in 1876 a New England education journal published a proof apparently constructed by James A. Garfield who later became President of the United States. Most of the proofs involve constructing geometric figures in one way or another. (A more complete history of the theorem is given in [1].)

For a slightly more algebraic approach to the proof in Figure 1.6, notice that the area of the large square in the left half of the figure is $(a + b)^2$. Yet, this must be equal to the area of four triangles plus the area of the square in the middle (c^2).

$$(a + b)^2 = 4\left(\frac{1}{2}ab\right) + c^2,$$
$$a^2 + 2ab + b^2 = 2ab + c^2$$
$$a^2 + b^2 = c^2$$

One important number-theoretic consequence of the theorem emerges when we draw the right triangle with both legs equal to 1. Then the hypotenuse is $\sqrt{2}$ and this number was important to the Greeks because it was *incommensurable*. To us now, this means the number is irrational; it cannot be represented as the quotient of two integers. The discovery of irrational numbers was both progress and an annoyance to the Greeks.

Other right triangles are equally surprising. If the legs are 3 and 4, then the hypotenuse is 5. This set of three integers is called a *Pythagorean triple* and is used frequently by carpenters to quickly construct a right angle. There are infinitely many of these Pythagorean triples and a detailed theory surrounding them (see Exercises for further examples).

1.5.2   Law of Cosines Continued

To derive the law of cosines, we noted that, if we do not have a right triangle, there are two cases: one where $\gamma > 90°$, and one where $\gamma < 90°$. The first case was covered in Figure 1.8, so now we consider the second case.

When $\gamma < 90°$, our triangle looks like the one in Figure 1.9. We have constructed two right triangles by adding the perpendicular AD. The Pythagorean theorem says

$$c^2 = h^2 + a_2^2$$

$$b^2 = h^2 + a_1^2$$

Note that $a = a_1 + a_2$ and $a_1 = b \cos \gamma$. By adding a^2 to both sides of $b^2 = h^2 + a_1^2$, we have

$$b^2 + a^2 = h^2 + a_1^2 + a^2 = h^2 + a_1^2 + a_1^2 + 2a_1a_2 + a_2^2$$
$$= c^2 + 2a_1(a_1 + a_2)$$
$$= c^2 + 2(b \cos \gamma)a$$

Rearranging just a little gives the law of cosines.

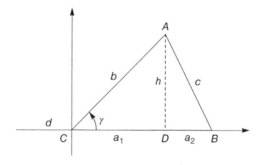

Figure 1.9   Law of cosines: $\gamma < 90°$

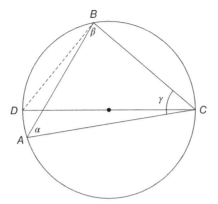

Figure 1.10   Law of sines

1.5.3   Law of Sines

Yes, there is a law of sines as well as a law of cosines.

Theorem 1.3 (Law of Sines). *In a triangle $\triangle ABC$, where the angles at the vertices are, respectively, $\alpha, \beta, and \gamma$, and the sides opposite the vertices are $a, b, and c$, respectively, we have*

$$\frac{\sin \alpha}{a} = \frac{\sin \beta}{b} = \frac{\sin \gamma}{c} = \frac{1}{d},$$

where d is the diameter of the circumcircle for the triangle.

Proof Sketch. Any triangle can be inscribed in a circle so that the three vertices are on the circle (Appendix A). Figure 1.10 shows one such arbitrary triangle, $\triangle ABC$. Draw diameter CD and dotted line DB. Since $\triangle CDB$ is inscribed in a semicircle, it is a right triangle. The sine of $\angle CDB$ is $\frac{a}{CD}$. But angle α equals angle $\angle CDB$ because they cut the same arc from the circle. Hence $\sin A = \frac{a}{CD}$ or $\frac{\sin A}{a} = \frac{1}{CD}$. The same argument for each angle shows the ratio of the sine to the side opposite is always the reciprocal of the diameter.

The diameter in Figure 1.10 cuts through the triangle. There is a second case where the diameter is outside the triangle. The argument changes only slightly (see Exercises).   □

The common ratio of the sine to the side opposite is equal to the reciprocal of the diameter of the circumcircle for the triangle.

1.5.4   Numerical Calculations

One slight hitch for the graphics programmer is the fact that calculating the square root and trigonometric functions (e.g., sine, cosine, and tangent) takes time. Modern processors incorporate floating point operations much more efficiently that they once did, but still, floating point arithmetic is slower than integer arithmetic. Making graphics programs run quickly requires attention to the length of calculations.

Consider the square root first. If the task is to simply compare distances, using the square of the distances works equally well. However, if the square root is actually needed, then often an approximation can work. To illustrate, suppose we need to calculate $\sqrt{x}$. Start with a guess, say g_0. Then x/g_0 should be g_0 if it is the square root. It probably is not, so take a next guess $g_1 = (g_0 + \frac{x}{g_0})/2$; this is the mean of the first guess and the quotient. Similarly, we can define successive guesses. For example, to find $\sqrt{120}$, let 10 be the first guess. Then $g_1 = 11$ and $g_2 = 10.95$. This last guess is accurate to two decimal places. (This algorithm for square root is actually Newton's method applied to the square root function.) Of course, this approximation is useful only if the time required to execute it is reasonably short.

Calculating the sine and cosine causes similar timing issues. One solution is to precalculate a table of common values and simply look up the answer when needed. For example, we could calculate the sine and cosine for all angles of radian measure $2\pi/n$ where $1 \leq n \leq 64$. If we need more accuracy, we can recall the Taylor series expansion (from calculus) of sine and cosine for small angles. The first few terms of these expansions (for radian measure) give

$$\sin(\theta) \approx \theta - \frac{\theta^3}{6} + \frac{\theta^5}{120}$$

$$\cos(\theta) \approx 1 - \frac{\theta^2}{2} + \frac{\theta^4}{24}$$

The Taylor series approximations are more accurate for small angles, so one scheme is to precalculate a table as before, let θ be the difference between the desired angle and the closest angle in the table (say α), approximate the sine or cosine of θ, and then use the addition formulas for sine and cosine to get $\sin(\alpha + \theta)$ or $\cos(\alpha + \theta)$.

1.6 EXERCISES

1. The standard Cartesian coordinate system has the vectors $\vec{i}, \vec{j}$, and $\vec{k}$ positioned to form a right-handed system. We can replace any or all of these vectors with one pointing in the opposite direction. This gives us a total of eight different coordinate systems. Determine which of these are right-handed systems.

2. Consider an isosceles right triangle. (This is one where both legs are equal.) Construct a square on each of the three sides. The Pythagorean theorem says that the sum of the areas of the two smaller squares equals the area of the larger square. By dividing each square into triangles equal to the initial triangle, establish the theorem in this special case.

3. For another proof of the Pythagorean theorem, consider Figure 1.11. Triangle $\triangle ABC$ is a right triangle with the right angle at C. Each of the smaller triangles

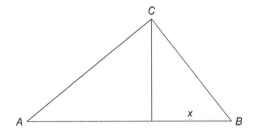

Figure 1.11   Alternate proof of Pythagorean theorem

is a right triangle and each is similar to $\triangle ABC$. This means that the ratio of sides in one triangle equals the ratio of sides in another. Find two of these equations which when added together give the Pythagorean theorem.

4. The vertices $(1, 0, 0)$, $(0, 1, 0)$, and $(0, 0, 1)$ form a triangle. Find the perpendicular distance from the origin $(0, 0, 0)$ to this triangle using right triangles.

5. Find the three angles of the triangle with vertices $A = (-1, 1, 2)$, $B = (5, 3, 1)$, $C = (2, 6, -4)$.

6. The four vertices $(2 + \sqrt{2}, 2 + \sqrt{2}, 2)$, $(1 - 3\sqrt{2}, 1 + 3\sqrt{2}, 1)$, $(-6, -6, -2)$, and $(2, 1, -6)$ form four triangles in space. Determine which of the four, if any, are right triangles.

7. Given two points in the plane, where are all the points that are at the same distance from both these selected points? Given three points in the plane that are not on a line, where are all the points equidistant from all three?

8. Describe all points that are at a fixed distance from a solid square in the plane. (The distance from a point to the square is the minimum distance between the point and any point on the square.)

9. For some right triangles, the two legs and the hypotenuse are all integers. For example, sides 3, 4, 5 form a right triangle. We call the triple $(3, 4, 5)$ a Pythagorean triple. Of course, any multiple of these three numbers [such as $(6, 8, 10)$] also forms a Pythagorean triple. Find two Pythagorean triples that are not multiples of $(3, 4, 5)$ or of each other.

10. Pick two positive integers s and t such that one is odd, one is even, and $s > t$. Show that $x = 2st$, $y = s^2 - t^2$, and $z = s^2 + t^2$ form a Pythagorean triple as defined in the previous exercise. If, in addition, s and t do not have a common divisor greater than 1, the triple is said to be primitive and all primitive triples can be found in this way.

11. The vectors $\vec{i}$ and $\vec{j}$ define the two-dimensional coordinate system. Suppose we replace $\vec{j} = (0, 1)$ with the vector $w = (\frac{1}{\sqrt{2}}, \frac{1}{\sqrt{2}})$. In this new coordinate system, what are the coordinates of the point with old coordinates $(2, 3)$?

12. If we use the vectors $2\vec{i}$ and $3\vec{j}$ to define a Cartesian coordinate system and we move the origin to the point $(-1, 6)$ in the original coordinate system, what are coordinates of the point with old coordinates $(4, 7)$? Give equations showing how to convert from old coordinates to new coordinates.

13. Referring to Figure 1.10, the diameter for the circle passes through the triangle. It could have passed outside the triangle. Complete the proof of the law of sines in this second case.

14. By drawing a perpendicular from the vertex A to the opposite side in a triangle, form two right triangles and show that $a = b\cos\gamma + c\cos\beta$. Then use the law of sines to show $\sin(\beta + \gamma) = \sin\beta\cos\gamma + \sin\gamma\sin\beta$.

1.6.1 Programming Exercises

1. Write a program displaying a right triangle along with squares drawn on each of the three sides in order to illustrate the Pythagorean theorem. Allow the user to dynamically change the shape of the right triangle.

2. The left diagram in Figure 1.6 has a square in the middle turned at an angle. We can replicate the same diagram inside this smaller square by drawing four more right triangles. To construct the new triangles, divide the side of the smaller square in the same ratio $(a : b)$ as the division on the side of the larger square. The process can be repeated many times to give an image of spiralling squares. Write a program to produce this image with as many spiralling squares as the user wishes. Also allow input for the ratio $(a : b)$. The key is to find the vertices of each smaller square.

2

VECTOR ALGEBRA

Vectors are essential for computer graphics. As we saw in Chapter 1, they represent displacement as we describe an object by moving from point to point. If we wish to move from point A to point B, an arrow drawn starting at point A and ending at point B tells us which direction to go and how far to go. This arrow is the vector and has both direction and length.

Displacement alone is not sufficient reason to develop the notion of a vector. It turns out that we can define operations between vectors that connect with geometric operations. For example, adding two vectors means adding two displacements and we can geometrically understand what it should mean to add displacements. Although not as intuitive, we can also define the multiplication of two vectors in such a way that there are geometric interpretations of the result. The plan then is to develop an algebra of vectors that corresponds to geometric operations and may make the task of describing geometric objects for images just a little easier.

Vectors are especially useful because they are independent of any particular coordinate system. A displacement in a given direction makes sense regardless of which coordinate system we use. It may be that in a particular coordinate system the displacement description is "two units to the left and one unit up" while in another system, perhaps one rotated relative to the first, the description is very different. The vector description might change, but the direction and length of the vector does not. So there is some hope that vector algebra will be general enough to help describe objects without the added detail of which coordinate system we are in. This can make graphics programs more efficient, even though at some stage of a calculation actually

Mathematical Structures for Computer Graphics, First Edition. Steven J. Janke.
© 2015 John Wiley & Sons, Inc. Published 2015 by John Wiley & Sons, Inc.

finding the direction and length of a vector does require settling on some coordinate system.

2.1   BASIC VECTOR CHARACTERISTICS

When we talk about points and vectors more abstractly, we will keep them separate symbolically by using upper case letters (e.g., A) for points and a small arrow over lower or upper case letters (e.g., $\vec{v}$ or $\vec{V}$) for vectors. When we need to describe a particular point or a particular vector, we simply use Cartesian coordinates for a default description and use ordered pairs (x, y) in two dimensions and ordered triples (x, y, z) in three dimensions. With this notation, there is still ambiguity between points and vectors, but usually the context resolves the confusion.

For studying geometric transformations, matrices play an essential role, and it makes sense to represent vectors and points as columns of numbers (just small matrices). So in two dimensions, a vector $\vec{v}$ which represents a displacement of five units to the left and three units up is represented as a column matrix with two entries.

$$\vec{v} = \begin{bmatrix} -5 \\ 3 \end{bmatrix}$$

A point with x coordinate -5 and y coordinate 3 is represented exactly the same way. Since it is awkward to write columns of coordinates in normal text, we will use the ordered pair or ordered triple notation as well as the column matrix notation depending on which is clearer.

Starting in two dimensions, let point A have coordinates $(3, 2)$ and B $(7, 4)$. Then let $\vec{v}$ be the vector from point A to point B.

$$\vec{v} = \begin{bmatrix} 7 \\ 4 \end{bmatrix} - \begin{bmatrix} 3 \\ 2 \end{bmatrix} = \begin{bmatrix} 4 \\ 2 \end{bmatrix}$$

Here, we take the coordinates of B and subtract the coordinates of A, component by component, to get $(4, 2)$. The vector $\vec{v}$ is the displacement: four units in the x-direction and two units in the y-direction. The description is relative to a default Cartesian coordinate system.

To find the length and direction of the vector $\vec{v}$, consider the vector as the hypotenuse of a right triangle (Figure 2.1) with angle α describing the direction. The length of $\vec{v}$ is denoted by $|\vec{v}|$, and using the Pythagorean theorem we get $|\vec{v}| = \sqrt{4^2 + 2^2} = \sqrt{20}$. We find the direction angle from the sine or cosine (or both). For $\vec{v}$, $\sin(\alpha) = \frac{2}{\sqrt{20}}$ and hence $\alpha \approx 26.57°$ (measured counterclockwise from the horizontal direction which points to the right).

It is important to note that the vector $\vec{v}$ denotes a displacement and therefore could represent the displacement between two other points, say $A_1 = (2, 1)$ and $B_1 = (6, 3)$. That is, the vector is not tied down in space.

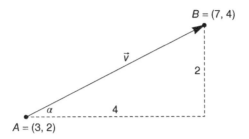

Figure 2.1   Vector length

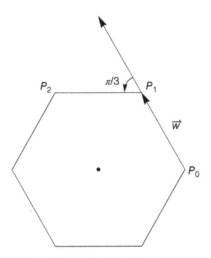

Figure 2.2   Regular polygon

Example 2.1 (Building a Regular Polygon).   To see how vectors might prove useful in describing objects, imagine an image of a regular hexagon. It is not too hard to calculate the coordinates for the six vertices especially if the hexagon is centered at the origin in a coordinate system. However, it is also easy to see how we could move from vertex to vertex regardless of where we place the first vertex. Let the vector $\vec{w}$ be the displacement indicated in Figure 2.2. When added to our initial point, say P_0, this will give us the next vertex P_1.

Now, if we can rotate the vector $\vec{w}$ counterclockwise by 60° ($\pi/3$ radians), then adding it to P_1 will give us vertex P_2. Repeating this procedure produces all the other vertices. Notice that this approach can build the hexagon image no matter where we begin and no matter what original direction we choose. Yes, we do need to learn how to rotate a vector, but that turns out to be relatively straightforward and will be addressed in a later chapter.   □

2.1.1 Points Versus Vectors

To define $\vec{v}$ above, we subtracted two points (A from B). With Cartesian coordinates for the points, it does make sense to subtract the coordinates component-wise to get the displacement. However, adding two points is another matter. Adding the coordinates together gives another point, but this resulting point does depend on which coordinate system we are using. For example, adding the two points A and B from above gives the point $C = A + B = (3, 2) + (7, 4) = (10, 6)$. Now imagine the coordinate system is shifted two units to the left to give a second Cartesian coordinate system. In this system, $A = (5, 2)$ and $B = (9, 4)$, giving $C^* = (14, 6)$. This point C^* has coordinates $(12, 6)$ in the first coordinate system, so it is definitely a different point from the original C. Addition depends on which coordinate system we are in, so addition of two points is not well defined if we want to stay independent of coordinate systems.

However, adding a point and a vector does make sense because we are starting at a location (which is dependent on the coordinate system) and moving in the direction of the vector by an amount equal to the vector length. This does give us a unique point regardless of which coordinate system we are in. If we start with point $A = (3, 2)$ in the first coordinate system and add vector $\vec{v} = (4, 2)$, then the result is point $B = (7, 4)$. In the second coordinate system, $A = (5, 2)$, and when we add $\vec{v} = (4, 2)$, we get $B = (9, 4)$. The coordinates of this B relative to the first coordinate system are indeed $(7, 4)$. We have the same point (Figure 2.3).

As we will see in the next section, adding two vectors together makes sense algebraically and geometrically. The two approaches coincide by giving the same answers once we interpret them algebraically and geometrically. With points, however, it is not immediately obvious how to define addition, for example, so that the algebraic sum agrees with a geometric sum. This is the advantage of vector algebra, where algebraic calculations coincide with geometric operations allowing numerical computations to result in graphical transformations.

2.1.2 Addition

Intuitively, the idea of adding two vectors is to follow one displacement with the other. The result will be the sum of the two displacements. Using Cartesian coordinates, an

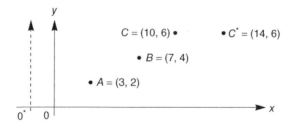

Figure 2.3 Adding points

algebraic addition of $\vec{E} = (2, 8)$ and $\vec{F} = (5, 1)$ is done component-wise to give

$$\vec{E} + \vec{F} = \begin{bmatrix} 2 \\ 8 \end{bmatrix} + \begin{bmatrix} 5 \\ 1 \end{bmatrix} = \begin{bmatrix} 7 \\ 9 \end{bmatrix}$$

Geometrically, this corresponds to starting at some point, say A, and placing the vector $\vec{E}$ so that it starts at A; the tail of the arrow is at A. The head of the arrow then ends at B. Placing the tail of $\vec{F}$ at B leaves the head of $\vec{F}$ pointing to C. The geometric sum, $\vec{E} + \vec{F}$, is the vector beginning at A and pointing to C.

Giving coordinates to A, say $A = (-1, 6)$, and placing the vector $\vec{E}$ so that it starts at A determines gives the coordinates $B = (1, 14)$. Then positioning $\vec{F}$ gives coordinates $C = (6, 15)$. The geometric sum, $\vec{E} + \vec{F}$, is the vector beginning at A and pointing to C; this is a displacement of $(7, 9)$. The algebraic and geometric definitions of addition coincide.

Another way of visualizing the vector $\vec{E} + \vec{F}$ is to imagine both $\vec{E}$ and $\vec{F}$ in what we might call the default position where the tails of both vectors start at $(0, 0)$. Then form a parallelogram with $\vec{E}$ and $\vec{F}$ as two adjacent sides. The sum, $\vec{E} + \vec{F}$, is the diagonal of the parallelogram starting at $(0, 0)$.

Both the algebraic and geometric approaches make it clear that $\vec{E} + \vec{F} = \vec{F} + \vec{E}$ (Figure 2.4).

2.1.3 Scalar Multiplication

If we position the vector $\vec{v}$ in its default position starting at $(0, 0)$ and ending at $(4, 2)$, then by recalling analytic geometry, the slope of the line containing the vector is $2/4 = 0.5$; slope is the change in y over the change in x. The ratio of the vector coordinates determines the slope, which in turn gives the direction when in two dimensions. (The slope is the tangent of the direction angle.) Therefore, if we multiply each coordinate by the same number, we do not change the vector's direction although we do

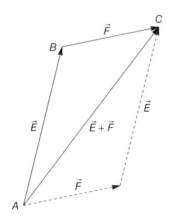

Figure 2.4   Vector addition

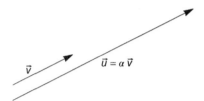

Figure 2.5   Scalar multiplication

change its length. The vector $\vec{u} = (12, 6)$ points in the same direction as $\vec{v}$. We use the notation $\alpha\vec{v}$ to denote multiplication of each component of $\vec{v}$ by α, some real number. This is called *scalar multiplication* (Figure 2.5).

Geometrically, scalar multiplication simply changes the length of the vector. If $\alpha < 0$, then scalar multiplication also changes the vector direction to the opposite direction; the vector $-2\vec{v}$ points in the opposite direction from $\vec{v}$.

2.1.4   Subtraction

Subtraction actually follows from addition. To find the difference of two vectors, say $\vec{G} - \vec{H}$, think of subtracting the two displacements. Algebraically, we notice that $\vec{G} - \vec{H} = \vec{G} + (-1)\vec{H}$. We are really adding a scalar multiple of $\vec{H}$ (giving $-\vec{H}$, a vector in the opposite direction) to the vector $\vec{G}$. Geometrically, $\vec{G} - \vec{H}$ is the vector we can add to $\vec{H}$ to get $\vec{G}$ (Figure 2.6).

If $\vec{G}$ and $\vec{H}$ are in their default positions and we again imagine a parallelogram with $\vec{G}$ and $\vec{H}$ as adjacent sides, then $\vec{G} - \vec{H}$ is a diagonal of the parallelogram going from the end of $\vec{H}$ to the end of $\vec{G}$.

2.1.5   Vector Calculations

So far, we have defined vectors and developed an arithmetic on vectors which includes addition and scalar multiplication. The point of this arithmetic using displacements is to more efficiently find various points on graphics objects. So, often we do some calculation using vectors and then apply the resulting displacement to an actual point to get another point.

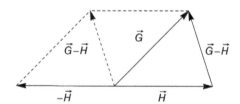

Figure 2.6   Vector subtraction

Example 2.2 (Midpoint of a Line Segment). Finding the midpoint of a line segment is not a hard calculation; it is almost intuitive that we simply want the average of the Cartesian coordinates at the two ends of the segment. However, we need to be careful because, as we have seen, adding two points together is not a well-defined operation. With vectors, it becomes a little clearer what we are actually doing. Let $\vec{v}$ be the vector from point A to point B. Then $\frac{1}{2}\vec{v}$ represents half the displacement from A to B, so if we add it to the point A, we will have the midpoint of the line segment between A and B. Let $A = (1.2, 4.5)$ and $B = (3.3, 6.1)$. Then $\vec{v} = (2.1, 1.6)$ and $\frac{1}{2}\vec{v} = (1.05, 0.8)$. Therefore, the midpoint M is

$$M = A + \frac{1}{2}\vec{v} = \begin{bmatrix} 1.2 \\ 4.5 \end{bmatrix} + \begin{bmatrix} 1.05 \\ 0.8 \end{bmatrix} = \begin{bmatrix} 2.25 \\ 5.3 \end{bmatrix}$$

Notice that the coordinates of M are indeed the averages of the coordinates of the end points (A and B). Actually, other scalar multiples of the displacement $\vec{v}$ will give other points on the line segment. If we let $0 \le \alpha \le 1$ and use $\alpha\vec{v}$ as our displacement, then the resulting point $P = A + \alpha\vec{v}$ will be on the line segment. If α is outside this range, P is on the line containing the line segment, but not inside the segment. Algebraically, we get

$$P = A + \alpha\vec{v} = A + \alpha(B - A) = (1 - \alpha)A + \alpha B,$$

where we replaced $\vec{v}$ with the difference of the coordinates for B and A, since this is how we calculate displacement. The resulting formula for P is what we call an *affine combination* of the points A and B. For α unrestricted, we get all the points on the line through A and B. For α restricted between 0 and 1, we get all the points on the line segment from A to B. With $\alpha = \frac{1}{2}$, we get the midpoint $P = \frac{1}{2}A + \frac{1}{2}B$ and it is the average of the coordinates for the two points (Figure 2.7).

The formula $P = (1 - \alpha)A + \alpha B$ makes some intuitive sense and we derived it from simply adding a vector to a point. However, it pays to be careful here because the formula looks as though we added multiples of two points together and we know that addition of two points is not well defined. It turns out that, in this case, where the scalar multiples add to one $[(1 - \alpha) + \alpha = 1]$, the addition is well defined. For

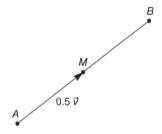

Figure 2.7 Midpoint

more detail on when these expressions are algebraically and geometrically correct, see Section 2.3. □

Example 2.3 (Normalized Vectors). Sometimes the interesting feature of a vector is its direction, not its length. For example, we usually only need to know the direction of a light source, not how far away it is. We can find a vector in the right direction by subtracting the coordinates of a point on the object of interest from the coordinates of the light source. Calculating with this vector is often more efficient if it has length 1, in other words, if it is a *unit vector*. Since the original length of the vector is not important to us, we can multiply by a scalar to get another vector in the same direction, but of a different length. What scalar should we use to guarantee that the result is a unit vector? Well, we use the reciprocal of the original length. Let $\vec{v}$ be the original vector. Then letting $\alpha = 1/|\vec{v}|$, we have a new vector $\alpha\vec{v}$ with

$$|\alpha\vec{v}| = \frac{1}{|\vec{v}|}|\vec{v}| = 1$$

We have used the fact that $|\alpha\vec{v}| = \alpha|\vec{v}|$, which follows from the definition of vector length. The process of converting a vector to a unit vector in the same direction is called *normalization*, and we simply multiply the original vector by the reciprocal of its length. The vector $\vec{w} = (3, 4)$ has length $|\vec{w}| = \sqrt{3^2 + 4^2} = 5$, and normalizing it gives a new vector $\vec{n} = \frac{1}{5}(3, 4) = \left(\frac{3}{5}, \frac{4}{5}\right)$. The length of $\vec{n}$ is $\sqrt{\left(\frac{3}{5}\right)^2 + \left(\frac{4}{5}\right)^2} = 1$ and, because it is a positive multiple of $\vec{w}$, it has the same direction as $\vec{w}$. □

2.1.6 Properties

The definitions of addition and scalar multiplication give us two operations on vectors. (As we noted, subtraction is a special case of addition: $\vec{v} - \vec{w} = \vec{v} + (-1) \cdot \vec{w}$.) There are some important properties of the two key operations between vectors that are somewhat intuitive and can be proved from the relevant definitions.

Result 2.1 *Let $\vec{v}$ and $\vec{w}$ be vectors, and let α and β be scalars. Then the following properties hold for vector addition and vector scalar multiplication:*

1. *Commutativity:* $\vec{v} + \vec{w} = \vec{w} + \vec{v}$
2. *Associativity:* $(\vec{u} + \vec{v}) + \vec{w} = \vec{u} + (\vec{v} + \vec{w})$
3. *There is a unique vector $\vec{0}$ such that $\vec{v} + \vec{0} = \vec{v}$*
4. *For each $\vec{v}$ there is a vector $-\vec{v}$ such that $\vec{v} + (-\vec{v}) = \vec{0}$*
5. $1 \cdot \vec{v} = \vec{v}$
6. $(\alpha\beta)\vec{v} = \alpha(\beta\vec{v})$
7. *Distributivity I:* $\alpha(\vec{v} + \vec{w}) = \alpha\vec{v} + \alpha\vec{w}$
8. *Distributivity II:* $(\alpha + \beta)\vec{v} = \alpha\vec{v} + \beta\vec{v}$.

These properties along with our definitions of vector, vector addition, and vector scalar multiplication form a mathematical object called a *vector space*. In computer graphics, our more geometric definition of a vector is key, but mathematical results from general vector spaces can come into play to extend how useful vectors are in describing images.

2.1.7 Higher Dimensions

Nothing we have done is specific to two dimensions. We can define vectors in an analogous manner for any number of dimensions. In three dimensions, for example, the vector $\vec{s} = (-1, 5, 2)$ indicates a displacement that decreases x by one unit, increases y by five units, and increases z by two units. This time the direction of the vector is a direction in space, so two direction angles (or two cosines) are necessary to describe the direction of $\vec{s}$. There are several ways of specifying angles, but one way is to position the vector so that its tail is at the origin and then specify an angle around the z-axis. Finally, give the angle between the vector and the z-axis. (This is the idea behind spherical coordinates.)

It takes two applications of the Pythagorean theorem to determine that the length of $\vec{s}$ is $\sqrt{(-1)^2 + 5^2 + 2^2} = \sqrt{30}$, and we normalize $\vec{s}$ by multiplying each component by $1/\sqrt{30}$, giving the unit vector $\frac{1}{\sqrt{30}}(-1, 5, 2) \approx (-0.18, 0.92, 0.37)$.

2.2 TWO IMPORTANT PRODUCTS

2.2.1 Dot Product

The power of vectors starts to become even more convincing when we notice that a simple calculation gives the cosine of the angle between two vectors. To see this, let $\vec{v} = (x_1, y_1)$ and $\vec{w} = (x_2, y_2)$. Place $\vec{v}$ and $\vec{w}$ in their default positions with their tails at $(0, 0)$. Let θ be the angle between $\vec{v}$ and $\vec{w}$ (Figure 2.8).

To find the cosine of θ, use the law of cosines: $c^2 = a^2 + b^2 - 2ab \cos \theta$. In the current situation, $a = |\vec{v}|$ and $b = |\vec{w}|$. For c, notice that it is the length of the vector $\vec{v} - \vec{w}$. (It is also the length of $\vec{w} - \vec{v}$.) Considering the vector coordinates and the Pythagorean theorem, we have

$$a = |\vec{v}| = \sqrt{x_1^2 + y_1^2}$$

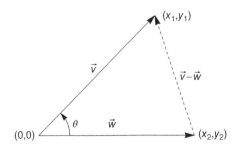

Figure 2.8 Angle between vectors

$$b = |\vec{w}| = \sqrt{x_2^2 + y_2^2}$$

$$c = |\vec{v} - \vec{w}| = \sqrt{(x_1 - x_2)^2 + (y_1 - y_2)^2}$$

Now we can apply the law of cosines and simplify.

$$c^2 = a^2 + b^2 - 2ab\cos\theta$$

$$(x_1 - x_2)^2 + (y_1 - y_2)^2 = (x_1^2 + y_1^2) + (x_2^2 + y_2^2) - 2|\vec{v}||\vec{w}|\cos\theta$$

$$\cos\theta = \frac{x_1 x_2 + y_1 y_2}{|\vec{v}||\vec{w}|}$$

For example, if $\vec{v} = (1, 1)$ and $\vec{w} = (1, 0)$, then $|\vec{v}| = \sqrt{2}$ and $|\vec{w}| = 1$. The cosine of the angle θ between the two vectors is

$$\cos\theta = \frac{1 \cdot 1 + 1 \cdot 0}{\sqrt{2} \cdot 1} = \frac{1}{\sqrt{2}}$$

This corresponds to an angle of $\pm 45°$ (or $\pm\pi/4$ radians).

The following definition draws on the geometry of two vectors.

Definition 2.1 (Dot Product). *If θ is the angle between two vectors $\vec{v}$ and $\vec{w}$, then the dot product, $\vec{v} \cdot \vec{w}$, is the quantity $|\vec{v}||\vec{w}| \cos(\theta)$.*

This definition encapsulates the geometric idea that the dot product is proportional to the cosine of the angle between the vectors, but with the previous derivation we have a theorem that gives an algebraic meaning to the dot product if we have Cartesian coordinates for the vectors. The result is a convenient way to compute the dot product.

Theorem 2.1 (Formula for Dot Product). *Let $\vec{v} = (x_1, y_1)$ and $\vec{w} = (x_2, y_2)$. Then $\vec{v} \cdot \vec{w} = x_1 x_2 + y_1 y_2$.*

The theorem depends on a coordinate system and can be thought of as an algebraic definition of dot product whereas Definition 2.1 does not depend on a coordinate system and is a geometric definition.

Example 2.4 (Perpendicular Vectors). We can use the dot product to find vectors perpendicular to others. We know that the cosine of $\pi/2$ radians (90°) is 0. If we have a vector $\vec{C} = (x, y)$, then it is easy to see that the vector $\vec{D} = (-y, x)$ is perpendicular to it. Since $\vec{C} \cdot \vec{D} = x(-y) + yx = 0$, the cosine of the angle between the vectors is 0 (as long as the vectors do not have zero length). This implies the angle between the vectors is $\pi/2$. Of course, there are many choices for $\vec{D}$ that make it perpendicular to $\vec{C}$; we just selected a convenient one.   □

In Chapter 1, we applied the law of cosines to a triangle in three dimensions. Indeed, in three dimensions, triangles still lie in a plane. This means that we can use the derivation of dot product to deal with three dimensional vectors and the angles between them. The dot product simply gets generalized to three coordinates. If $\vec{v} = (x_1, y_1, z_1)$ and $\vec{w} = (x_2, y_2, z_2)$, then the dot product is defined to be $\vec{v} \cdot \vec{w} = x_1 x_2 + y_1 y_2 + z_1 z_2$ (see Exercises).

Example 2.5 (Angle between Vectors in Space). Let $\vec{A} = (2, 1, 5)$ and $\vec{B} = (-1, 3, 1)$. These are vectors in three dimensional space and, if we imagine both with their tails at the origin, they determine a plane through the origin. In that plane, we can consider the angle between the two vectors and calculate the cosine.

$$\vec{A} \cdot \vec{B} = (2 \cdot (-1)) + (1 \cdot 3) + (5 \cdot 1) = 6$$

$$|\vec{A}| = \sqrt{2^2 + 1^2 + 5^2} = \sqrt{30}$$

$$|\vec{B}| = \sqrt{(-1)^2 + 3^2 + 1^2} = \sqrt{11}$$

$$\cos(\theta) = \frac{\vec{A} \cdot \vec{B}}{|\vec{A}| \cdot |\vec{B}|} = \frac{6}{\sqrt{30 \cdot 11}} \approx 0.33$$

Now, the inverse cosine function gives us $\theta \approx 1.23$ radians (or $70.7°$). There are two minor sources of ambiguity here. First, angles are positive or negative depending on whether we move counterclockwise or clockwise. With the angle between vectors, the sign of the angle is usually irrelevant. If one vector did move toward or away from the other, we need to look at other information to determine the sign. Second, there are really two angles between two vectors: one less than (or equal to) $\pi/2$ rad, and one greater than (or equal to) $\pi/2$ radians. When we take the inverse cosine, we can always take θ to be less than or equal to $\pi/2$ and this is usually the one we are interested in. Simply subtract from π if the other choice is needed. Finally, note that in this example we measured angles in radians; trigonometric functions in programming languages usually expect radians and to convert from degrees, we multiply by $\pi/180$.																□

By using the definition of the dot product and applying a little algebra, we can discover some useful properties when calculating with the vector dot product:

Result 2.2 (Properties of the Dot Product). *Let α be a scalar. Then the following properties hold for the dot product.*

1. $\vec{v} \cdot \vec{w} = \vec{w} \cdot \vec{v}$
2. $\vec{v} \cdot (\vec{r} + \vec{s}) = \vec{v} \cdot \vec{r} + \vec{v} \cdot \vec{s}$

3. $\vec{v} \cdot (\alpha \vec{w}) = \alpha(\vec{v} \cdot \vec{w})$

4. $\vec{v} \cdot \vec{v} = |\vec{v}|^2$.

Example 2.6 (Snowflake Curve). A snowflake curve (or Koch curve) is a fractal constructed by starting with an equilateral triangle and recursively replacing segments. Each edge in the triangle is replaced by a segment with part of a smaller equilateral triangle positioned in the middle third of the original edge (Figure 2.9). The smaller triangle is one-third the size of the original.

Once each of the three segments of the original triangle are replaced in this manner, the new figure has 12 edge segments. (In the figure, the original segment *AB* has been replaced by segments *AC*, *CD*, *DE*, and *EB*.) Now, each of the 12 new segments is replaced in a similar manner with a yet smaller equilateral triangle, and the process is repeated ad infinitum.

To design an algorithm for this construction, we need to find the coordinates of points *C*, *D*, *E* once we know the coordinates of *A* and *B*. As an example, take *A* to be the point $(1, 1)$ and let *B* be the point $(7, 2)$. Then the vector from *A* to *B* is $\vec{V}_{AB} = (6, 1)$. But the point *C* is one-third of the way from *A* to *B* because we wanted the smaller equilateral triangle to be one-third the size of the larger. This means the displacement from *A* to *C* is $\frac{1}{3}(6, 1)$, and hence we add this to *A* in order to get the coordinates of *C*.

$$C = \begin{bmatrix} 1 \\ 1 \end{bmatrix} + \frac{1}{3} \begin{bmatrix} 6 \\ 1 \end{bmatrix} \approx \begin{bmatrix} 3 \\ 1.33 \end{bmatrix}$$

Similar reasoning shows that *E* is two-thirds of the way from *A* to *B*, so $E = \left(5, \frac{5}{3}\right) \approx (5, 1.67)$.

To find *D*, we let *X* be the point half way between *A* and *B*. Hence, $X = (4, 1.5)$. The point *D* is on a line through *X* that is perpendicular to the segment *AB*. The distance from *D* to *X* is the height of the smaller triangle. The strategy for finding *D*

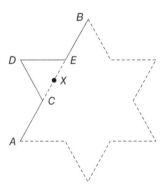

Figure 2.9   Constructing the snowflake curve

is to find the displacement from X. We need a vector with the right length and the right direction.

The direction is such that the vector should be perpendicular to $\vec{V}_{AB}$. That means the dot product of $\vec{V}_{AB}$ with the new vector must be zero. By careful guessing, we notice the vector $(-1, 6)$ fits the bill. So does $(1, -6)$, but this vector points below the segment AB and the point D is above the segment. So $(-1, 6)$ is the vector we want. (Later, we will develop a method using rotations to guarantee we pick the right direction without having to think about whether it points above or below a segment.)

The vector $(-1, 6)$ is in the right direction, but its length is not correct; it has length $\sqrt{37}$. Normalizing gives us a vector in the same direction with length 1: $\frac{1}{\sqrt{37}}(-1, 6)$. The final length of the vector we seek is the height of the small equilateral triangle. From geometry, this is $\frac{\sqrt{3}}{2}$ times the side of the triangle which is one-third of the distance from A to B. Hence, the height is $h = \frac{\sqrt{3}}{2} \cdot \frac{1}{3} \cdot \sqrt{37}$. We now have our displacement vector: $\vec{V}_{XD} = h \cdot \frac{1}{\sqrt{37}}(-1, 6) \approx (-0.29, 1.73)$. The coordinates of D are found by adding the displacement vector $\vec{V}_{XD}$ to the coordinates of X.

$$D = X + \vec{V}_{XD} \approx (4, 1.5) + (-0.29, 1.73) = (3.71, 3.23)$$

As a final check, we can compute the angle between $\vec{V}_{CD}$ and $\vec{V}_{CE}$. Since these vectors should be the sides of an equilateral triangle, the angle between them should be $\pi/3$ radians (60°) with a cosine of 0.5. From the previous calculations, $\vec{V}_{CD} \approx (3.71, 3.23) - (3, 1.33) \approx (0.71, 1.90)$ and $\vec{V}_{CE} = \frac{1}{3}(6, 1) \approx (2, 0.33)$. The dot product is $\vec{V}_{CD} \cdot \vec{V}_{CE} \approx 2.05$. Dividing by the lengths of the two vectors (which should be equal) gives $\cos \alpha \approx 0.5$.   □

2.2.2 Cross Product

With a little ingenuity, we can create a variety of operations between two vectors. Yet, an operation is most useful if it has a geometric interpretation. The dot product that we just defined is an operation between two vectors that gives a real number as the result and that real number has some geometric meaning; it is connected with the cosine of the angle between the vectors. Another operation called the *cross product* produces a new vector rather than a real number. In fact, the new vector is perpendicular to each of the original two vectors. The geometric interpretation here makes this operation a useful one.

We are now considering vectors in three dimensions, and if we start with two such vectors, say $\vec{A}$ and $\vec{B}$, then we would like to produce a new vector $\vec{C}$ that is perpendicular to both $\vec{A}$ and $\vec{B}$. Note that this means $\vec{C}$ is perpendicular to the plane determined by $\vec{A}$ and $\vec{B}$. Using the symbol $\times$ to denote the cross product, we have $\vec{C} = \vec{A} \times \vec{B}$. We now have to figure out how to determine $\vec{C}$.

To start, take the vector $\vec{i}$ which is a unit vector pointing in the direction of the positive x-axis. This vector has coordinates $(1, 0, 0)$. Similarly, $\vec{j} = (0, 1, 0)$ and

$\vec{k} = (0, 0, 1)$ are unit vectors along the y- and z-axes, respectively. We originally defined these vectors to be perpendicular to each other, and now we can verify this because the dot product of any two of them is zero. It seems reasonable that the cross product of $\vec{i}$ and $\vec{j}$ should be the vector $\vec{k}$. But notice that $-\vec{k}$, a unit vector in the opposite direction from $\vec{k}$, is also a vector perpendicular to both $\vec{i}$ and $\vec{j}$. So in defining the cross product, we need to use the order of the product to determine which of two directions is the correct one. This will allow us to distinguish, for example, a direction pointing into an object from one pointing out (Figure 2.10).

To fix the direction we want for the cross product, we use the right-hand rule introduced for the three-dimensional Cartesian coordinate systems. If we point the fingers of our right hand in the direction of the first vector and curl them toward the second vector, then our thumb points in the direction of the cross product. This leads us to the following:

$$\vec{i} \times \vec{j} = \vec{k} \qquad \vec{j} \times \vec{i} = -\vec{k}$$
$$\vec{j} \times \vec{k} = \vec{i} \qquad \vec{k} \times \vec{j} = -\vec{i}$$
$$\vec{k} \times \vec{i} = \vec{j} \qquad \vec{i} \times \vec{k} = -\vec{j}$$

There is a somewhat degenerate case when the two vectors are equal. Since a single vector does not lie in a unique plane, so we cannot decide on a perpendicular vector, we say $\vec{A} \times \vec{A} = \vec{0}$. This may seem like an arbitrary choice, but as we will see, it turns out to have a consistent geometric interpretation. We now have $\vec{i} \times \vec{i} = \vec{0}, \vec{j} \times \vec{j} = \vec{0}$, and $\vec{k} \times \vec{k} = \vec{0}$.

For the mutually perpendicular unit vectors, $\vec{i}, \vec{j}, \vec{k}$, we might agree that the cross products should have unit length, but in general it is not obvious what we would like the length of the cross product to be. Instead of worrying about this right now, we focus first on how the algebra of vectors should work with the cross product. Consider two vectors $\vec{A} = (2, 4, -1)$ and $\vec{B} = (3, -2, 5)$. We can decompose these into the unit vectors $\vec{i}, \vec{j}, \vec{k}$, as follows:

$$\vec{A} = 2\vec{i} + 4\vec{j} - 1\vec{k}$$
$$\vec{B} = 3\vec{i} - 2\vec{j} + 5\vec{k}$$

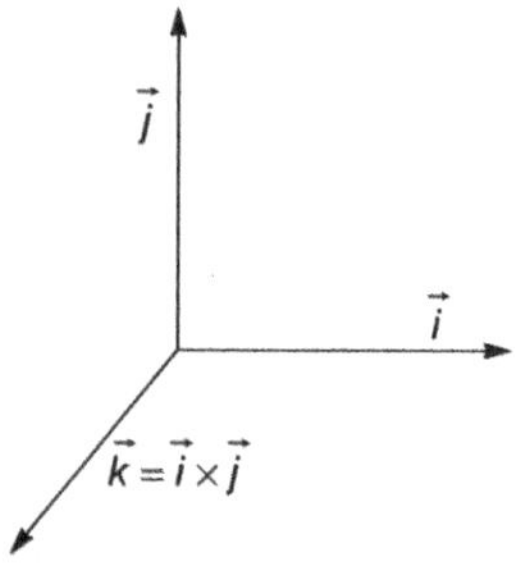

Figure 2.10   Vectors $\vec{i}, \vec{j}, \vec{k}$

Suppose we take the cross product just like we were multiplying two algebraic expressions together. This means we will use the distributive property for an algebra, the cross products for the unit vectors $(\vec{i}, \vec{j}, \vec{k})$, and also the fact that $\vec{A} \times \vec{A} = \vec{0}$ to get:

$$\vec{A} \times \vec{B} = (2\vec{i} + 4\vec{j} - 1\vec{k}) \times (3\vec{i} - 2\vec{j} + 5\vec{k})$$

$$= (2 \cdot 3)(\vec{i} \times \vec{i}) + (2 \cdot (-2))(\vec{i} \times \vec{j}) + (2 \cdot 5)(\vec{i} \times \vec{k})$$

$$+ (4 \cdot 3)(\vec{j} \times \vec{i}) + (4 \cdot (-2))(\vec{j} \times \vec{j}) + (4 \cdot 5)(\vec{j} \times \vec{k})$$

$$+ ((-1) \cdot 3)(\vec{k} \times \vec{i}) + ((-1) \cdot (-2))(\vec{k} \times \vec{j}) + ((-1) \cdot 5)(\vec{k} \times \vec{k})$$

$$= (-4)\vec{k} + 10(-\vec{j}) + 12(-\vec{k}) + 20\vec{i} + (-3)\vec{j} + 2(-\vec{i})$$

$$= 18\vec{i} - 13\vec{j} - 16\vec{k}$$

$$= (18, -13, -16)$$

This new vector $(18, -13, -16)$ should be perpendicular to both $\vec{A}$ and $\vec{B}$, so check the dot products:

$$\vec{A} \cdot \vec{C} = (2, 4, -1) \cdot (18, -13, -16) = 36 - 52 + 16 = 0$$

$$\vec{B} \cdot \vec{C} = (3, -2, 5) \cdot (18, -13, -16) = 54 + 26 - 80 = 0$$

Since the cosine of the angle between the vectors is zero, the angle is $\pi/2$ radians (90°). This new vector, the cross product, is perpendicular to both $\vec{A}$ and $\vec{B}$! When working with a flat face of some three-dimensional object, we now have a way of finding a vector that is perpendicular to that face. Just find two vectors that are parallel to the face and take their cross product.

If we carry out the same computation as we did above with two general vectors (and their Cartesian coordinates), we get an algebraic definition of the cross product (Figure 2.11).

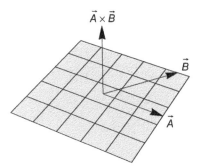

Figure 2.11 Perpendicular vectors

Definition 2.2 (Algebraic Definition of Cross Product). *Let* $\vec{A} = (x_1, y_1, z_1)$ *and* $\vec{B} = (x_2, y_2, z_2)$. *Then* $\vec{A} \times \vec{B}$ *is a new vector with coordinates* $((y_1 z_2 - z_1 y_2), (z_1 x_2 - x_1 z_2), (x_1 y_2 - y_1 x_2))$.

Example 2.7 (3D Triangle). Suppose $A = (1, 3, -1)$, $B = (4, 5, 8)$, $C = (2, 2, 6)$ are the vertices of a triangle in space. Then $\vec{V}_{AB} = (3, 2, 9)$ and $\vec{V}_{AC} = (1, -1, 7)$ are two vectors parallel to the plane of the triangle. (Note: There are many ways to find two such vectors.) Now,

$$\vec{V}_{AB} \times \vec{V}_{AC} = ((2 \cdot 7 - 9 \cdot (-1)), (9 \cdot 1 - 3 \cdot 7), (3 \cdot (-1) - 2 \cdot 1)) = (23, -12, -5)$$

The vector $(23, -12, -5)$ is perpendicular to the triangle $\triangle ABC$. □

Calculating with the cross product differs from calculating with real numbers in one notable way. The vector $\vec{A} \times \vec{B}$ is not the same as the vector $\vec{B} \times \vec{A}$. That is, the cross product operation is not commutative. We also chose $\vec{A} \times \vec{A} = \vec{0}$, which still seems arbitrary. This choice does mean that any two parallel vectors have a cross product equal to the zero vector. For, if two vectors are parallel, then one is a multiple of the other and when we apply the definition of cross product, all three coordinates of the result are zero. This will make more geometric sense once we interpret the length of the cross-product vector.

The following facts summarize the algebra of cross products.

Result 2.3 (Facts about the Cross Product). *Let α and β be scalars and let $\vec{A}$, $\vec{B}$, $\vec{C}$ be vectors. Then the following relationships hold:*

1. $\vec{A} \times \vec{B} = -(\vec{B} \times \vec{A})$
2. $\vec{A} \times \vec{A} = \vec{0}$
3. $(\alpha \vec{A}) \times (\beta \vec{B}) = (\alpha \beta)(\vec{A} \times \vec{B})$
4. $\vec{A} \times (\vec{B} + \vec{C}) = (\vec{A} \times \vec{B}) + (\vec{A} \times \vec{C})$.

So far, we understand $\vec{A} \times \vec{B}$ as a vector perpendicular to $\vec{A}$ and $\vec{B}$. Now we need to focus on the length of $\vec{A} \times \vec{B}$. Since we know the Cartesian coordinates for the cross product, we can calculate the length and then use some algebra to make things a little more understandable. Keep in mind that α is the angle between the vectors $\vec{A}$ and $\vec{B}$.

$$\begin{aligned}
|\vec{A} \times \vec{B}|^2 &= (y_1 z_2 - z_1 y_2)^2 + (z_1 x_2 - x_1 z_2)^2 + (x_1 y_2 - y_1 x_2)^2 \\
&= (x_1^2 + y_1^2 + z_1^2)(x_2^2 + y_2^2 + z_2^2) - (x_1 x_2 + y_1 y_2 + z_1 z_2)^2 \\
&= |\vec{A}|^2 |\vec{B}|^2 - (\vec{A} \cdot \vec{B})^2 \\
&= |\vec{A}|^2 |\vec{B}|^2 - |\vec{A}|^2 |\vec{B}|^2 cos^2(\alpha) \\
&= |\vec{A}|^2 |\vec{B}|^2 (1 - cos^2(\alpha)) \\
&= |\vec{A}|^2 |\vec{B}|^2 sin^2(\alpha)
\end{aligned}$$

Now we have it. The length of the cross product is related to the angle between the vectors as summarized in the following theorem.

Theorem 2.2 $|\vec{A} \times \vec{B}| = |\vec{A}||\vec{B}| \sin(\alpha)$ *where* α *(*$0 \leq \alpha \leq \pi$ *radians) is the angle between* $\vec{A}$ *and* $\vec{B}$.

We have the actual length of $\vec{A} \times \vec{B}$, but what does it represent? Geometrically, $\vec{A}$ and $\vec{B}$ form adjacent sides of a parallelogram. Interestingly enough, the length of $\vec{A} \times \vec{B}$ is the area of this parallelogram. To see this, notice that $|\vec{A}|$ is the length of the base of the parallelogram and $|\vec{B}| \sin(\alpha)$ is the height of the parallelogram (Figure 2.12). Now our assumption that $\vec{A} \times \vec{A} = \vec{0}$ makes more sense because, if $\vec{A} = \vec{B}$, then the parallelogram collapses and the area is zero. We can now think of the cross product in geometric rather than algebraic terms.

Definition 2.3 (Geometric Definition of Cross Product). *The cross product* $\vec{A} \times \vec{B}$ *is a vector perpendicular to both* $\vec{A}$ *and* $\vec{B}$ *with length equal to the area of the parallelogram formed by* $\vec{A}$ *and* $\vec{B}$.

Compare this definition with the algebraic one (Definition 2.2) and notice that there are no coordinates mentioned in the geometric definition. The geometry is independent of any coordinate system. Theorem 2.2 actually highlights the equivalence between the geometric and algebraic definitions; the algebraic definition leads to the same length for the cross product as claimed in the geometric definition.

Remembering how to calculate the cross product can be annoying, but there is a compact mnemonic rule that might help. When solving linear equations, the determinant of a matrix can play a key role, and here it serves as a template for the cross product. Simply, for a 2×2 matrix of numbers, the difference of the products on the diagonals is the determinant. Using vertical lines to denote the determinant, we have

$$\begin{vmatrix} a & b \\ c & d \end{vmatrix} = a \cdot d - b \cdot c$$

Each coordinate in the definition of cross product looks like a determinant of some 2×2 matrix. We can keep track of which matrix is appropriate by starting with a

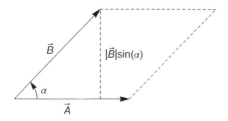

Figure 2.12   Cross product and area

3×3 matrix. Put the unit coordinate vectors in the first row, the coordinates of the first vector in the second row, and the coordinates of the second vector in the third row. So if we want to calculate $\vec{A} \times \vec{B}$, where $\vec{A} = (x_1, y_1, z_1)$ and $\vec{B} = (x_2, y_2, z_2)$, we can use the following determinants:

$$\begin{vmatrix} \vec{i} & \vec{j} & \vec{k} \\ x_1 & y_1 & z_1 \\ x_2 & y_2 & z_2 \end{vmatrix} = \begin{vmatrix} y_1 & z_1 \\ y_2 & z_2 \end{vmatrix} \vec{i} - \begin{vmatrix} x_1 & z_1 \\ x_2 & z_2 \end{vmatrix} \vec{j} + \begin{vmatrix} x_1 & y_1 \\ x_2 & y_2 \end{vmatrix} \vec{k}$$

This formula is one way for finding the 3×3 determinant by breaking it into 2×2 determinants. Notice that to find the smaller matrices, we delete the first row of the larger matrix and then one of the columns. For example, the second smaller matrix is the larger one with the first row and second column deleted. Finally, take special notice of the minus sign in front of the second determinant on the right; the first determinant is added, the second subtracted, and third added. The use of determinants for the cross product just gives a more visual way of remembering the cross product calculations.

Example 2.8 (Area of a Triangle). Let $P = (1, 0, 1)$, $Q = (2, 2, 4)$, and $R = (3, -4, 6)$ be the vertices of a triangle in space. Define the vectors $\vec{A} = Q - P = (1, 2, 3)$ and $\vec{B} = R - P = (2, -4, 5)$. Then the length of $\vec{A} \times \vec{B}$ is the area of the parallelogram formed by the vectors. So the area of the triangle $\triangle PQR$ is one-half of the cross product length. Using the determinant method to find the cross product, we find the square of the length as follows:

$$|\vec{A} \times \vec{B}|^2 = \begin{vmatrix} 2 & 3 \\ -4 & 5 \end{vmatrix}^2 + (-1)^2 \begin{vmatrix} 1 & 3 \\ 2 & 5 \end{vmatrix}^2 + \begin{vmatrix} 1 & 2 \\ 2 & -4 \end{vmatrix}^2$$

$$= 22^2 + 1^2 + 8^2 = 549$$

So the length of the cross product is $\sqrt{549} \approx 23.43$ and the area of the triangle is one-half of this which is about 11.72.   □

2.3   COMPLEMENTS AND DETAILS

2.3.1   Vector History

The connection between algebra and geometry has been an enduring thread throughout the development of mathematics. Once the Pythagorean theorem came into view, the conceptual relationship between the sides of a right triangle and the equation $a^2 + b^2 = c^2$ was ready to be exploited. Although the Greeks certainly understood that the hypotenuse of a right triangle with two sides equal to 1 was related to the solution of the equation $x^2 = 2$, it took a while, of course, for the general connection between algebraic equations and geometric constructions to come into focus. The Greeks can also be credited with the beginning notions of vectors because, when considering the velocities of objects, they began thinking in terms of a parallelogram of velocities. The algebraic notion of addition was tentatively connected with the physical (geometric) notion of velocity and this concept evolved throughout the sixteenth and seventeenth century when those struggling to understand physics considered quantities such as forces.

Descartes in the seventeenth century furthered the algebra–geometry connection with his ideas for coordinates and their algebraic manipulation. Although he did not quite invent modern analytic geometry (the study of geometric objects using coordinates), he did make strides in drawing the appropriate connections. Both Leibnitz and Newton in quite different ways continued the thread when they grappled with spatial problems in the natural world.

In the beginning of the nineteenth century, several mathematicians, including Gauss and Argand, developed geometrical interpretations of the complex numbers which bordered on the algebra of vectors. Although the term *radial vector* was in common use at the time, the actual term *vector* in its modern connotation was not introduced until 1844 when the famous Irish mathematician Sir William Rowan Hamilton published a paper on his newly discovered quaternions, an algebraic generalization of the complex numbers. (Quaternions turn out to be useful in graphics and are detailed in a later chapter.) Hamilton split the quaternion into two parts, the *scalar part* and the *vector part*, and the terminology endured as part of the mathematical vocabulary.

The study of vectors spread in fits and starts until a book published in 1901 offered a comprehensive look at the new vector analysis. This book was written by Edwin B. Wilson, a student of the well-known Yale physicist J. Willard Gibbs who was instrumental in the development of vectors analysis. Gibbs had given several courses on the subject and earlier in 1881 printed up some of his notes for circulation. Wilson based his book on these notes and on lectures that Gibbs gave in a Yale course. This was the first generally available book entirely devoted to vectors and their algebra.

Physicists took the lead in developing vector analysis, but the connection between algebra and geometry branched in several mathematical directions. Projective geometry had already taken a decidedly algebraic turn, and a field now called *algebraic geometry* became focused on studying special points and curves. Drawing on the work of Hermann Grassmann in the mid-nineteenth century, a field called *geometric algebra* grew to include the study of several specialized algebras which again have geometrical significance particularly in physics. Some of the basics of geometric algebra prove promising for work in computer graphics.

2.3.2 More about Points Versus Vectors

As noted earlier, the addition of two vectors makes sense, but the addition of two points does not. Adding two vectors gives us a unique vector, but adding two points gives a point that is dependent on the coordinate system we use. We were able to make sense of adding a vector to a point by starting at the point and applying the displacement described by the vector. The result was a unique point. However, now we are in an awkward situation because finding the midpoint M of a line segment from A to B gave us the following expression.

$$M = A + \frac{1}{2}(B - A) = \frac{1}{2}A + \frac{1}{2}B$$

The midpoint is the sum of a point and a vector, but it equals an expression that looks like the sum of two points (multiplied by scalars). A sum of scalar multiples of vectors, $\sum_{i=1}^{n} \alpha_i \vec{v}_i$, always makes sense in vector algebra, but a sum of scalar multiples of points, $\sum_{i=1}^{n} \alpha_i P_i$, only makes sense when it can be rewritten as a point plus a vector. Take the simpler case of three terms and put it in the correct form: point plus vector.

$$\alpha_1 P_1 + \alpha_2 P_2 + \alpha_3 P_3 = (\alpha_1 + \alpha_2 + \alpha_3)P_1 + \alpha_2(P_2 - P_1) + \alpha_3(P_3 - P_1)$$

The right-hand side of the equality is the sum of a multiple of P_1 and scalar multiples of two vectors; this has the form $\beta P_1 + \vec{w}$. The result will be a unique point if we can make sense of βP_1. Unfortunately, this scalar multiple of a point does not make sense for arbitrary values of β because, for example, when $\beta = 2$, we are really adding two points (both equal to P_1). It does make sense if $\beta = 1$, for then we simply have the point P_1 and the sum becomes P_1 plus a vector. In this case, $\alpha_1 + \alpha_2 + \alpha_2 = 1$. When the sum of the coefficients, α_i, is 1, the expression is an affine combination. Generalizing to an arbitrary number of points and coefficients gives the following result:

Result 2.4 (Affine Combination of Points). *If $\sum_{i=1}^{n} \alpha_i = 1$ where the α_i are scalars, then $P = \sum_{i=1}^{n} \alpha_i P_i$ is a well-defined point.*

Our combination of points can also make sense if $\beta = 0$. In this case, βP_1 can be interpreted either as the origin or as the zero vector. In both cases, the coordinates are all zero, but if we interpret the result as the origin, then it is a point with coordinates dependent on the coordinate system. So we choose to interpret βP_1 as the zero vector and then our original sum reduces to a sum of vectors which is another vector. If $\sum_{i=1}^{n} \alpha_i = 0$, we interpret $\sum_{i=1}^{n} \alpha_i P_i$ as a vector.

This diversion into the interpretation of a sum of multiples of points gives us a more solid footing to work with both vectors and points in describing geometric objects.

2.3.3   Vector Spaces and Affine Spaces

The properties listed in Result 2.1 came from the definition of vectors as displacements and from the definitions of vector addition and scalar multiplication. Mathematically, we have a set of objects (vectors) and two operations (addition and scalar multiplication). We can take one step up the abstraction stairway and say that, whenever we have a set of objects and two operations such that all the properties from Result 2.1 hold, we have what is called a *vector space*. The properties (along with others such as the existence of a zero vector) are really axioms which along with the objects and operations form a system that acts like the vectors we have been exploring. By studying vector spaces in general, any structure we uncover then applies to our particular flavor of a vector space where vectors are displacements.

As an example of another vector space, consider the quadratic polynomials: $a_2x^2 + a_1x + a_0$. We can add two such polynomials and multiply any one of them by a scalar in the obvious way. In fact, the notation (a_2, a_1, a_0) serves to completely describe a quadratic polynomial, so they indeed look like vectors. The properties we have noted for displacements hold similarly for polynomials, and any result that follows from these properties holds equally for either set of objects. The study of linear algebra is largely focused on finding properties of abstract vector spaces and many of these properties arise from understanding how we might transform vectors, perhaps by rotation, into other vectors. Some of these transformations (linear transformations) can be represented by matrix multiplication; multiplying a vector by a matrix gives a new vector. The study of matrices and their effect on vectors gives a more detailed view of vector spaces in general.

One key idea in the study of vector spaces starts with independent vectors. A set of vectors is independent if no vector in the set can be written as a linear combination (sum of scalar multiples) of the others. For example, in two dimensions, the displacement vectors $(1, 2)$ and $(-1, 5)$ are independent because neither is a multiple of the other. However, the set $\{(1, 2), (-1, 5), (-1, 12)\}$ is not independent because $(-1, 12) = (1, 2) + 2(-1, 5)$.

In two dimensions, the particular set $\{(1, 0), (0, 1)\}$ is independent and it has the distinction that any other two-dimensional vector is a linear combination of these two. For example, $(5, -3) = 5(1, 0) + (-3)(0, 1)$. The set $\{(1, 0), (0, 1)\}$ is a *basis* for the vector space of two dimensional vectors. It is not quite as easy to see that $\{(1, 2), (-1, 5)\}$ is also a basis. In two dimensions, any two nonzero vectors that are not multiples of each other form a basis. In three dimensions, bases must have three vectors and none of the three can be combinations of the other two.

In computer graphics, we consider both points and vectors. Starting with a set of points, the subtraction of any two gives a vector, and the collection of points and vectors forms an *affine space*. We can take an affine combination of points to get another point and we can define an affinely independent set of points analogous to the way we define an independent set of vectors. No point in an affinely independent set is an affine combination of the others. As we will see a little later, these kinds of point sets are very useful in defining *barycentric* coordinates which give a particularly important way to locate points.

Comparing affine spaces and vector spaces adds to both the theoretical and practical foundations of computer graphics. We have already noticed the similarities and differences between combinations of points and combinations of vectors. For one more example, consider the roles of the zero point and the zero vector. The zero vector is unique in that when added to any vector it gives the same vector back. On the other hand, a zero point depends on the coordinate system and is therefore not unique; it does not stand out from any other point. It may be a little hard to understand how these theoretical distinctions can affect the more practical side of graphics, but they do offer a broader perspective on the nature of graphics descriptions and transformations.

2.4 EXERCISES

1. Using vectors, find the midpoint of the line segment from $A = (50, 100)$ to $B = (170, 150)$.

2. Find four points that divide the line segment from $A = (80, 300)$ to $B = (450, 60)$ into five equal parts.

3. Let $D = (4, 1), E = (-3, 6)$, and $F = (2, -3)$ be vertices of a triangle. Find the length of each side and the three angles in this triangle.

4. The vectors $\vec{v} = (1, 1)$ and $\vec{w} = (\sqrt{2}, 0)$ form two adjacent sides of a parallelogram. Show first that the two vectors have the same length. Find vectors representing the two diagonals and show that they are perpendicular to each other.

5. The four points $A = (3, 1), B = (13, 3), C = (12, 8), D = (2, 6)$ are the vertices of a quadrilateral. Show that the quadrilateral is a rectangle.

6. With the vertices from Exercise 5, use vectors to find the point in the center of the rectangle and show that the coordinates are just the average of the coordinates for the four vertices.

7. A triangle has vertices A, B, and C. Let M be a point on the median two-thirds of the way from A to the midpoint of the opposite side. By expressing M as a point plus a vector, show that $M = \frac{1}{3}A + \frac{1}{3}B + \frac{1}{3}C$.

8. Using the algebraic definition of the dot product, prove Property 2 of Result 2.2.

9. The vector $\vec{w} = (3, 4)$ can be expressed as the sum of scalar multiples of the vectors $(6, 0)$ and $(0, 12)$. That is, $\vec{w} = \frac{1}{2}(6, 0) + \frac{1}{3}(0, 12)$. Show that $\vec{w}$ can also be written as the sum of scalar multiples of the vectors $(2, 7)$ and $(8, 1)$.

10. Using vectors, show that for any rhombus (a parallelogram with equal sides), the two diagonals are perpendicular.

11. Let $\vec{u} = (x_1, y_1, z_1)$ and $\vec{w} = (x_2, y_2, z_2)$ be two three-dimensional vectors. With the vectors in their default position, consider the triangle formed by the origin and the ends of the two vectors. Apply the law of cosines to show that $\vec{u} \cdot \vec{w} = x_1 x_2 + y_1 y_2 + z_1 z_2$.

12. Imagine you have placed your eye at position $(3, 1, 3)$ in space and you can barely see the entire line segment from $K = (8, 5, 12)$ to $L = (9, 5, -8)$ without moving your head. Find the angle the line segment extends at your eye. We can call this the *viewing angle*.

13. Let $S = (5, 1, -2), T = (-1, 2, 7)$, and $U = (2, -4, 3)$ be vertices of a triangle in three dimensions. Find the length of each side and the three angles in this triangle.

14. The triangle with vertices $(2,0,0), (0,2,0), (0,0,2)$ is symmetrically placed with respect to the coordinate axes. Using the cross product, find a vector perpendicular to the triangle and also find the area of the triangle. Show that the perpendicular vector you found has the same direction as the vector $(1,1,1)$.

15. Using the vectors $\vec{A} = (2,2,5), \vec{B} = (-1,4,2)$, and $\vec{C} = (-3,-1,6)$, verify Property 4 of Result 2.3.

16. The vector $\vec{A} \times (\vec{B} \times \vec{C})$ is called the *vector triple product*. Argue geometrically that this vector must be in the plane formed by $\vec{B}$ and $\vec{C}$. In fact, show algebraically that $\vec{A} \times (\vec{B} \times \vec{C}) = (\vec{A} \cdot \vec{C})\vec{B} - (\vec{A} \cdot \vec{B})\vec{C}$.

2.4.1 Programming Exercises

1. Write a program to draw the snowflake curve described in Example 2.6. Starting with an equilateral triangle, the first iteration replaces each line segment in the triangle with the pattern shown in the example. Allow the user to specify how many iterations to perform. As an added option, change the replacement pattern so that the smaller triangle points inside instead of outside the current figure.

3

VECTOR GEOMETRY

Much, if not most, of the graphics pipeline relies on asking geometric questions about objects in a scene. At the modeling stage, it is helpful to know where the middle of a face is or whether four vertices lie in a plane. If we think of light as traveling in rays, then asking where a ray intersects an object is key to understanding the shade of the object and the shadow it casts. The task now is to take the notion of a vector and use it as efficiently as possible to make geometric calculations. The goal is threefold: express the calculations simply so that producing an algorithm is relatively easy, make the calculations general so that the algorithms are easily extended, and keep an eye on the number of elementary arithmetic operations in each larger calculation so that the resulting computer code runs quickly.

Vectors fit Euclidean geometry particularly well, which means that linear structures such as lines and planes along with circular structures (with fixed radii) are the focus of attention. We certainly want to eventually extend our reach to more organic shapes, so we look for ways that vector calculations change our perspective in describing nonlinear forms.

3.1 LINES AND PLANES

3.1.1 Vector Description of Lines

One way to describe a line is to say it contains two particular points, say P_0 and P_1. This allows us to construct the line (actually draw it on a piece of paper), but it does

Mathematical Structures for Computer Graphics, First Edition. Steven J. Janke.
© 2015 John Wiley & Sons, Inc. Published 2015 by John Wiley & Sons, Inc.

not say much about the other points on the line. Analytic geometry takes the Cartesian coordinates of the points and produces a more complete description. Assuming the line is two dimensional and the coordinates are $P_0 = (-1, 2)$ and $P_1 = (5, 6)$, then the point-slope form of the line yields

$$\frac{y - 2}{x - (-1)} = \frac{6 - 2}{5 - (-1)} \implies y = \frac{2}{3}x + \frac{8}{3}$$

This description gives the coordinates for all the points on the line and hence is more useful when having to plot pixels on the display screen. A version of the line equation, $3y - 2x = 8$, gives what we call an *implicit* description of the line, because it does not explicitly describe how to calculate one coordinate from another (although a little algebra is all that is needed). There is not a single implicit equation for three-dimensional lines, so we turn to vector descriptions which generalize easily.

For two-dimensional lines, the vector description is simple. First, calculate the vector $\vec{v} = P_1 - P_0 = (6, 4)$. The direction of this vector is parallel to the line and any multiple, $t\vec{v}$, is also parallel. We call $\vec{v}$ the *direction vector* for the line. Starting at point P_0 and adding the direction vector gives us a point, $P_0 + t\vec{v}$, on the line. If $0 \le t \le 1$, then the point is on the line segment between P_1 and P_2; for $t = 0$, we get P_0 and for $t = 1$, we get P_1. For values of the parameter t that are larger than 1 or less than 0, the points are on the extension of the line segment. If P is an arbitrary point on the line, we can write

$$\boxed{\text{Line equation: } P = P_0 + t\vec{v}} \tag{3.1}$$

We can split this parametric description into two coordinate equations. If we let $P = (x, y)$, then using the coordinates of P_0, we have

$$x = -1 + 6t$$

$$y = 2 + 4t$$

Solving for t in the first equation and substituting in the second gives the implicit form we saw before, $3y - 2x = 8$. In the parametric descriptions, t is the multiplier for $\vec{v}$ and tells us where we are on the line. The implicit line equation, on the other hand, does not directly describe relative locations on the line. Instead, the ratio of the coefficients for y and x in the implicit equation gives the slope of the line.

Still thinking in terms of vectors, the direction vector $\vec{v} = (6, 4)$ is, of course, parallel to the line and therefore $\vec{n} = (4, -6)$ is perpendicular to the line because $\vec{n} \cdot \vec{v} = 0$. Every vector parallel to the line must be perpendicular to $\vec{n}$. In particular, if $P = (x, y)$ is a point on the line, the vector $\vec{w} = (P - P_0)$ is parallel to the line and perpendicular to $\vec{n}$. (Figure 3.1.)

$$\vec{n} \cdot \vec{w} = 0 \implies 4 \cdot (x - (-1)) + (-6) \cdot (y - 2) = 0$$

$$\implies 3y - 2x = 8$$

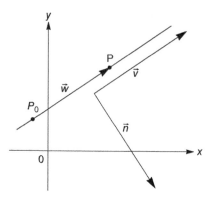

Figure 3.1   Vectors on a line

Again, we get the implicit form of the line equation, but we can also see that the coefficients $(3, -2)$ describe a vector perpendicular to the line.

We now have two vector descriptions of the two-dimensional line:

1. With two points, take $\vec{v} = (P_1 - P_0)$, then any point on the line takes the form $P_0 + t\vec{v}$;
2. With a single point P_0 and a vector $\vec{n}$ perpendicular to the line (called a *normal vector*), we know $\vec{n} \cdot (P - P_0) = 0$ describes any point P on the line.

Example 3.1 (Line Perpendicular to a Line Segment). Imagine we are drawing a tilted rectangle where the base edge is the line segment from $P_0 = (3.5, -2.2)$ to $P_1 = (8, 1.5)$. The vector $\vec{v} = P_1 - P_0 = (4.5, 3.7)$ is parallel to this line segment. The two edges perpendicular to the base are both in the same direction, which is represented by a vector $\vec{n}$ perpendicular to $\vec{v}$. There are many choices for $\vec{n}$, but one choice is $\vec{n} = (-3.7, 4.5)$ because then $\vec{n} \cdot \vec{v} = 0$. Vector $\vec{n}$ is normal to the base line segment. The equation of the line representing an edge through P_0 perpendicular to the base is

$$P = P_0 + t\vec{n} = \begin{bmatrix} 3.5 \\ -2.2 \end{bmatrix} + t \begin{bmatrix} -3.7 \\ 4.5 \end{bmatrix}$$

The other edge is through the point P_1.

$$P = P_1 + t\vec{n} = \begin{bmatrix} 8 \\ 1.5 \end{bmatrix} + t \begin{bmatrix} -3.7 \\ 4.5 \end{bmatrix}$$

The point P_2 is on the second edge, so $P_2 = P_1 + t\vec{n}$. Suppose we wanted the edge from P_1 to P_2 to be five units long. Then, the length of the vector $t\vec{n}$ needs to be five

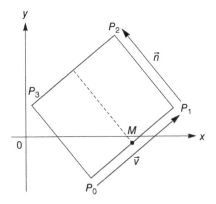

Figure 3.2   Tilted rectangle

units. Since $|\vec{n}| = \sqrt{(-3.7)^2 + 4.5^2} \approx 5.83$, we conclude that $t = \frac{5}{5.83} \approx 0.86$.

$$P_2 = \begin{bmatrix} 8 \\ 1.5 \end{bmatrix} + 0.86 \begin{bmatrix} -3.7 \\ 4.5 \end{bmatrix} \approx \begin{bmatrix} 4.82 \\ 5.37 \end{bmatrix}$$

To find the equation of the dotted line in the middle of the rectangle, we find the midpoint M of the base by setting $M = P_0 + 0.5 \cdot \vec{v} = (5.75, -0.35)$. Then the equation of the line is

$$P = M + t \cdot \vec{v} = \begin{bmatrix} 5.75 \\ -0.35 \end{bmatrix} + t \begin{bmatrix} -3.7 \\ 4.5 \end{bmatrix}$$

The final vertex P_3 of the rectangle is left for the exercises (Figure 3.2).   □

The vector description generalizes easily to three-dimensional lines. In fact, the equation $P = P_0 + t\vec{v}$ makes no mention of how many coordinates we have. If there are three coordinates, then $\vec{v}$ is a three-dimensional vector instead of a two-dimensional vector and we can split the vector equation into three parametric equations, one for each coordinate. If $P_0 = (5, -2, 1)$ and $P_1 = (3, 3, 4)$, then $\vec{v} = P_1 - P_0 = (-2, 5, 3)$. The vector equation is split into the following coordinate equations:

$$x = 5 - 2t$$

$$y = -2 + 5t$$

$$z = 1 + 3t$$

We can solve each of these equations for t to get the two equations:

$$\frac{x-5}{-2} = \frac{y+2}{5} = \frac{z-1}{3}$$

This is the analog of the single implicit equation we saw for two-dimensional lines.

We were able to give a perpendicular vector for two-dimensional lines and calculate the direction vector by knowing that the dot product of the two had to be zero. In three dimensions, there are an infinite number of vectors perpendicular to any vector. This means we need to specify at least two perpendicular vectors that are not multiples of each other before we have described a direction vector.

Example 3.2 (Three-dimensional Line). Suppose $P_0 = (-7, 5, 8), P_1 = (-3, 9, 0)$, and $P_2 = (1, 6, 8)$ are three points in space. To find the equation of the line through P_0 perpendicular to both segments $P_0 P_1$ and $P_0 P_2$, we find vectors $\vec{u} = P_1 - P_0 = (4, 4, -8)$ and $\vec{w} = P_2 - P_0 = (8, 1, 0)$. Then, since the direction vector $\vec{v}$ is perpendicular to $\vec{u}$ and $\vec{w}$, it is parallel to $\vec{u} \times \vec{w} = (8, -64, -28)$. We can take $\vec{v} = (2, -16, -7)$ because it is a multiple of the cross product. The equation of the line is then

$$P = P_0 + t\vec{v} = \begin{bmatrix} -7 \\ 5 \\ 8 \end{bmatrix} + t \begin{bmatrix} 2 \\ -16 \\ -7 \end{bmatrix}$$

The parametric coordinate equations are

$$\frac{x+7}{2} = \frac{y-5}{-16} = \frac{z-8}{-7}$$

If $z = 0$, then we are on the xy plane and solving the last equality for y gives $y \approx -13.29$. Similarly, $x \approx 4.71$. The line intersects the xy plane at the point $(4.71, -13.29, 0)$. □

3.1.2 Vector Description of Planes

A similar vector approach works to describe planes in three dimensions. Two points determine a line, and a single vector (parallel to the line) determines its direction. It takes three points to determine a plane and two vectors (parallel to the plane) to determine its orientation. Start with three points on the plane, P_0, P_1, P_2. The two vectors $\vec{v}_1 = P_1 - P_0$ and $\vec{v}_2 = P_2 - P_0$ determine the position of the plane (as long as the three points are not collinear). The cross product $\vec{n} = \vec{v}_1 \times \vec{v}_2$ is a vector that is perpendicular to the plane; $\vec{n}$ is a normal vector. This perpendicular vector alone determines the plane's orientation, whereas it takes two vectors parallel to the plane to do the same job (Figure 3.3).

Since every vector in the plane must be perpendicular to the normal, we take an arbitrary vector in the plane, say $\vec{w} = P - P_0$, where P_0 is a given point on the plane and $P = (x, y, z)$ is an arbitrary point in the plane. Then the dot product with the normal must be zero.

| Plane equation: $\vec{n} \cdot (P - P_0) = 0$ | (3.2) |

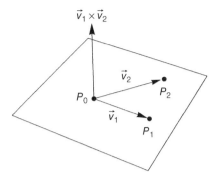

Figure 3.3   Vectors determine a plane

Example 3.3 (Plane Containing Three Points). With the three points, $P_0 = (1, 1, 1)$, $P_1 = (4, -2, 5)$, and $P_2 = (3, 8, -1)$, form the vectors $\vec{A} = P_1 - P_0 = (3, -3, 4)$ and $\vec{B} = P_2 - P_0 = (2, 7, -2)$. Then

$$\vec{n} = \vec{A} \times \vec{B} = \begin{vmatrix} -3 & 4 \\ 7 & -2 \end{vmatrix} \vec{i} - \begin{vmatrix} 3 & 4 \\ 2 & -2 \end{vmatrix} \vec{j} + \begin{vmatrix} 3 & -3 \\ 2 & 7 \end{vmatrix} \vec{k} = (-22, 14, 27)$$

This vector by itself describes the plane's orientation, so one point on the plane and a normal vector should also describe the plane.

Taking $P_0 = (1, 1, 1)$ and $P = (x, y, z)$ gives the vector $\vec{w} = P - P_0$. This should be perpendicular to the normal $\vec{n}$, so we have $\vec{n} \cdot \vec{w} = 0$.

$$\vec{n} \cdot \vec{w} = (-22, 14, 27) \cdot (x - 1, y - 1, z - 1) = 0$$
$$\implies -22x + 14y + 27z = 19$$

This is the implicit equation of a plane.   □

Using any of the three points to form vector $\vec{w}$ in the last example gives exactly the same equation. The coefficients in front of the variables x, y, and z are, of course, the coordinates of the normal vector. Since any multiple of a normal vector is still normal, these coefficients could differ but the resulting equation is equivalent.

Example 3.4 (Plane Perpendicular to a Line). To find a plane containing $P_0 = (-10, 3, 5)$ and perpendicular to the line through P_0 and $P_1 = (2, 7, 2)$, note that the vector $\vec{n} = P_1 - P_0 = (12, 4, -3)$ is normal to the plane. So the vector equation is $(12, 4, -3) \cdot (P - (-10, 3, 5)) = 0$ and the implicit coordinate equation is

$$12x + 4y - 3z = -123$$

Notice that the constant term in the implicit equation is calculated by considering the vector from the origin to P_0 and taking the dot product of this vector with the normal.   □

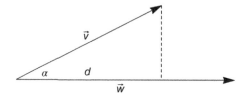

Figure 3.4   Projection of one vector onto another

3.2   DISTANCES

Finding the distance between two objects in a scene, whether they are two space ships or a player's foot and a boulder, can be reduced to finding distances between various combinations of points, lines, and planes. To design algorithms using vectors, it turns out that determining the projection of one vector onto another is a key step. In Figure 3.4, the dotted line from the head of $\vec{v}$ is perpendicular to $\vec{w}$. We can imagine that the distance d in the figure is the length of the shadow of vector $\vec{v}$ when the light source is directly overhead. More accurately, we say d is the length of the projection of $\vec{v}$ onto $\vec{w}$.

If α is the angle between the two vectors, then $\cos \alpha$ is the ratio of d to the length of $\vec{v}$. Figure 3.4 shows the situation when α is less than $\pi/2$ radians. If the angle is larger than $\pi/2$ radians, then the cosine will be negative and we will take the absolute value. Using the definition of the dot product, we have

$$| \cos \alpha | = \frac{d}{|\vec{v}|} \implies d = |\vec{v}| \cdot | \cos \alpha | \implies d = \frac{|\vec{v} \cdot \vec{w}|}{|\vec{w}|} \tag{3.3}$$

3.2.1   Point to a Line

To find the distance between a point and a line, we need the distance along a perpendicular to the line. So the idea in two dimensions is to find any vector from the point and the line and project it on the normal vector.

Example 3.5 (Distance from a Point to a Line in Two Dimensions). To find the distance between the point $P_2 = (3, 4.6)$ and the line between $P_0 = (-2.1, 5)$ and $P_1 = (7, 9)$, first find the vector $P_1 - P_0$; subtracting coordinates gives $(9.1, 4)$ and therefore the vector $\vec{n} = (-4, 9.1)$ is normal to the line. Next, the vector from P_2 to the point P_0 is $\vec{v} = (-5.1, 0.4)$. Now, the length of the projection of $\vec{v}$ onto $\vec{n}$ is the distance from the point P_2 to the line. That distance is

$$d = \frac{|\vec{v} \cdot \vec{n}|}{|\vec{n}|} = \frac{24.04}{\sqrt{98.81}} \approx 2.42$$

Notice that $\vec{v}$ is the vector from P_2 to P_0. If we had taken the vector from P_0 to P_2, then the dot product would have been negative. The negative cosine means that angle

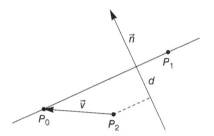

Figure 3.5   Point to 2D line

α would have been greater than $\pi/2$ radians. The length of the projection is really the absolute value of the quantity calculated (Figure 3.5).   □

A line in space has many normal vectors, so when we are looking for the distance between a point and a three dimensional line, it is not immediately obvious how to find an appropriate normal. Instead, we first describe the line with its equation: $P = P_0 + t\vec{v}$. Figure 3.6 shows the point P_0 on the line with a vector from the line to the point P_2, $\vec{a} = P_2 - P_0$. The vector $\vec{v}$ is in the direction of the line. If we project $\vec{a}$ onto $\vec{v}$, we will have the distance from P_0 to Q, where Q is at the foot of the perpendicular from P_2 to the line. The points P_0, Q, and P_2 determine a right triangle and since we can find the length of the hypotenuse, $|\vec{a}|$, and the length of the leg from projection, $(\vec{a} \cdot \vec{v})/|\vec{v}|$, the distance d follows from the Pythagorean theorem.

Example 3.6 (Distance from a Point to a Line in Three Dimensions). Suppose $P_0 = (3, -1, 5)$ is on a line and the vector $\vec{v} = (4, 2, 1)$ is in the direction of the line. If we want the distance between the line and the point $P_2 = (-2, 2, 6)$, then we calculate $|\vec{a}| = |(-2, 2, 6) - (3, -1, 5)| = \sqrt{35}$. The projection of $\vec{a}$ onto $\vec{v}$ is

$$\frac{\vec{a} \cdot \vec{v}}{|\vec{v}|} = \frac{|(-5, 3, 1) \cdot (4, 2, 1)|}{\sqrt{4^2 + 2^2 + 1^2}} = \frac{13}{\sqrt{21}}$$

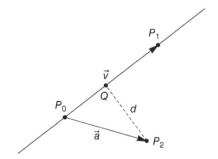

Figure 3.6   Vectors on plane

Now, we can find the second leg, d, of the right triangle. We have

$$d = \sqrt{(\sqrt{35})^2 - \left(\frac{13}{\sqrt{21}}\right)^2} \approx 5.19$$

This is the distance from the point to the line.   □

For another approach, look again at Figure 3.6. Let $\vec{b}$ be the vector from P_0 to Q. The length $|\vec{b}|$ is just the projection length that we calculated in the example. The vectors $\vec{a}$ and $\vec{b}$ form a parallelogram, and the area of that parallelogram is $|\vec{a} \times \vec{b}|$. For the base of the parallelogram, we have $|\vec{b}|$, which when multiplied by the height d gives the area. So,

$$d = \frac{|\vec{a} \times \vec{b}|}{|\vec{b}|} \tag{3.4}$$

Although this is a concise formula for the distance, the calculation of the cross product requires six multiplications and we still need to take the square root for the length. When compared to the way we calculated d in the example, it appears that this second approach takes more computational effort.

3.2.2   Point to a Plane

Turning now to a plane, a single normal vector determines the orientation, and consequently finding the distance to a point is easy. Take a vector from any point on the plane, say P_0, to a given point P_1 off the plane. Then, the projection of this vector onto the normal vector for the plane gives the distance from the point to the plane.

Example 3.7 (Distance from a Point to a Plane). To find the distance from the plane $x - y + 3z = 10$ to the point $P_1 = (4, -7, 1)$, first find a point P_0 on the plane. Any point on the plane will work, so, for example, take $y = 0$ and $z = 0$, which easily gives $x = 10$. Since the vector $(1, -1, 3)$ is normal to the plane, we project the vector from P_0 to P_1 onto it.

$$d = \frac{|((4, -7, 1) - (10, 0, 0)) \cdot (1, -1, 3)|}{|(1, -1, 3)|} = \frac{4}{\sqrt{11}} \approx 1.21$$

If, instead of the implicit equation for a plane, we are given the vector equation or just a point and a normal, we can immediately calculate d using the formula above (Figure 3.7).   □

3.2.3   Parallel Planes and Line to a Plane

We can count the various situations that might arise when finding distances between points, lines, and planes. There are six cases: point to point, point to line, point to

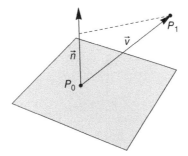

Figure 3.7 Point to plane

plane, line to line, line to plane, and plane to plane. We have covered distances from a point so what is left are those three cases with lines and planes. These cases make sense only if the two objects (lines or planes) do not intersect; that is, they are parallel.

For example, two planes are parallel if their normal vectors are parallel, and we can determine this if their normals are multiples of each other. Similar to what we have done before, projecting a vector (from the first plane to the second) onto the common normal gives the distance between the planes.

The same idea works for a line and a plane. If the direction vector for the line is perpendicular to the normal to a plane, then the line and plane do not intersect. Projecting a vector (from the line to the plane) onto the normal vector again gives the distance between the line and the plane.

Example 3.8 (Distance between Two Parallel Planes). We have two parallel planes with a common normal vector $\vec{n} = (8, 2, -5)$. One plane contains the point $P_0 = (1, 1, 2)$ and the other contains the point $P_1 = (7, -2, 1)$. To find the distance between the planes, we calculate the coordinates of $\vec{v} = P_1 - P_0 = (6, -3, -1)$ and then project it onto the normal vector $\vec{n}$.

$$d = \frac{|(6, -3, 1) \cdot (8, 2, -5)|}{|(8, 2, -5)|} = \frac{37}{\sqrt{93}} \approx 3.84$$

Notice that the order we subtract the points to get $\vec{v}$ does not matter (Figure 3.8). □

If we are thinking about computation efficiency, notice that, if we normalize the vector $\vec{n}$ so that it has length 1, then no division is required to calculate the projection and hence the distance. Of course, it takes three divisions to normalize a vector, but if we will be using it many times, it might be worth it.

Example 3.9 (Distance from a Line to a Plane). Instead of two planes, suppose we have one containing the point $P_0 = (1, 1, 2)$ with normal $\vec{n} = (8, 2, -5)$. Consider now the line $P = (5, 11, 3) + t(1, -4, 0)$. The direction vector $\vec{v} = (1, -4, 0)$ is perpendicular to the normal and hence parallel to the plane. By projecting a vector from P_0

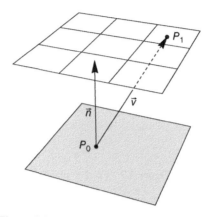

Figure 3.8   Distance between parallel planes

to a point on the line, say $P_1 = (5, 11, 3)$, we can find the distance between the line
and the plane. This time, normalize the vector $\vec{n}$ first, giving $\vec{n}^* = \frac{1}{\sqrt{93}}(8, 2, -5) \approx$
$(0.83, 0.21, -0.52)$

$$d = \frac{|(5 - 1, 11 - 1, 3 - 2) \cdot \vec{n}^*|}{|\vec{n}^*|} = |(4, 10, 1) \cdot (0.83, 0.21, -0.52)| \approx 4.9$$

In this case, picking any point on the line gives the same distance. If the line was not
parallel to the plane, this would not be true.   □

3.2.4   Line to a Line

In two dimensions, two lines either intersect or they are parallel. In three dimensions,
it is also possible that they do not intersect and they are not parallel; these are skew
lines. Suppose that for two nonintersecting lines we have found exactly where the
lines come closest to each other. That is, we have a point Q_1 on the first line and a
point Q_2 on the second line such that the distance between the two points is as close
as possible for any points on the lines. Then the vector $\vec{w} = Q_2 - Q_1$ must be perpendicular to each line. If it is not, then suppose it is not perpendicular to the second line.
Find a point P on the second line such that the vector $\vec{v} = P - Q_1$ is perpendicular.
Considering the triangle $\triangle Q_1 P Q_2$, it is clear that segment $Q_1 P$ is shorter than $Q_1 Q_2$,
so Q_2 should be repositioned.

The procedure for finding the shortest distance will be to take any vector from the
first line to the second and project it onto a vector perpendicular to both lines. As you
no doubt guessed, the cross product will give us the perpendicular vector. The cross
product of the two direction vectors for the lines gives the normal to both lines.

Example 3.10 (Distance between two Skew Lines). Let two lines have direction
vectors $\vec{v}_1 = (-1, 5, 1)$ and $\vec{v}_2 = (0, 2, 6)$. The point $P_1 = (4, 3, 5)$ is on the first line

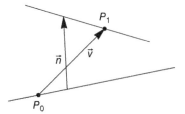

Figure 3.9 Two skew lines

and the point $P_2 = (8, -2, 10)$ is on the second. We need the cross product to find a vector normal to both lines.

$$\vec{v}_1 \times \vec{v}_2 = \begin{vmatrix} 5 & 1 \\ 2 & 6 \end{vmatrix} \vec{i} - \begin{vmatrix} -1 & 1 \\ 0 & 6 \end{vmatrix} \vec{j} + \begin{vmatrix} -1 & 5 \\ 0 & 2 \end{vmatrix} \vec{k} = (28, 6, -2)$$

Then projection of the vector $P_2 - P_1 = (4, -5, 5)$ onto this normal gives the distance (Figure 3.9).

$$d = \frac{|(4, -5, 5) \cdot (28, 6, -2)|}{|(28, 6, -2)|} = \frac{72}{\sqrt{824}} \approx 2.51$$

If the distance turned out to be zero, then the lines actually intersect (Figure 3.9). □

The last example used the power of vector geometry to find the distance between the two lines with only a modest amount of calculation, but it did not identify the points Q_1 and Q_2 that actually give us this distance. In some applications, it can be necessary to actually find these points. There are a few different algorithms we can design for locating the points, and most start by finding a vector between any two arbitrary points on the two lines. Let P_1 and P_2 be given points on the two lines, respectively, and let R_1 and R_2 be arbitrary points on the two lines. We calculate the vector $\vec{w}$ between R_1 and R_2.

$$R_1 = P_1 + t_1 \vec{v}_1$$
$$R_2 = P_2 + t_2 \vec{v}_2$$
$$\vec{w} = (R_2 - R_1) = (P_2 - P_1) + t_2 \vec{v}_2 - t_1 \vec{v}_1$$

The vector $\vec{w}$ is a function of the two parameters t_1 and t_2. One way then to find the vector of shortest length is to use calculus to minimize this function of two variables. Another way is to use the fact that the vector $\vec{w}$ must be perpendicular to both lines. Consequently, the dot product of $\vec{w}$ with each of the direction vectors must be zero. This leads to two linear equations for t_1 and t_2, which we can solve directly. (An equivalent way to proceed is to calculate the cross product of the two direction vectors and note that $\vec{w}$ must be parallel to it. That is, the coordinates of $\vec{w}$ must be in the same ratio as the cross product coordinates.)

Example 3.11 (Two Skew Lines Continued). Referring to Example 3.10, we have

$$\vec{w} = (4, -5, 5) + t_2(0, 2, 6) - t_1(-1, 5, 1)$$

$$\vec{w} \cdot \vec{v}_1 = -24 + 16t_2 - 27t_1 = 0$$

$$\vec{w} \cdot \vec{v}_2 = 20 + 40t_2 - 16t_1 = 0$$

Solving these last two equations gives $t_1 \approx -1.553$ and $t_2 \approx -1.121$. Plugging these in to the line equations gives the two points that are closest together.

$$Q_1 = (4, 3, 5) + (-1.553)(-1, 5, 1) \approx (5.55, -4.77, 3.45)$$

$$Q_2 = (8, -2, 10) + (-1.121)(0, 2, 6) \approx (8, -4.24, 3.27)$$

It is straightforward to check that the distance between these points is approximately 2.51 as we calculated before.   □

3.3   ANGLES

A light ray strikes plane faces of an object at a particular angle and this angle helps us to determine the brightness and color of the face. From our perspective of lines and planes, we need to calculate the angle between a line and a plane. First, to clarify which angle is the appropriate one, we draw the normal to the plane. The angle α between the line and the normal is determined by the dot product of the line's direction vector and the normal. If the direction vector is oriented as in Figure 3.10, the dot product will be positive and $\alpha \leq \pi/2$ radians. The complement, $\pi/2 - \alpha$, gives the angle β between the line and the plane. If the direction vector is in the opposite direction, then the dot product will be negative and we adjust to get $\alpha \leq \pi/2$. Looking at Figure 3.10, the normal vector and the line's direction vector along with the point of intersection P form a second plane, and it is in this plane that we see the normal, the line, and hence the angles α and β.

Example 3.12 (Angle with the Coordinate Axes). Consider the plane given by the point $P_0 = (-1, 3, 4)$ and the normal vector $(2, 8, 5)$. We wish to find the angles each coordinate axis makes with this plane. The x-axis has direction vector $\vec{i} = (1, 0, 0)$, so letting α_x be the angle with the normal, we have

$$\cos(\alpha_x) = \frac{(1, 0, 0) \cdot (2, 8, 5)}{\sqrt{1^2 + 0 + 0}\sqrt{2^2 + 8^2 + 5^2}} = \frac{2}{\sqrt{93}} \approx 0.207$$

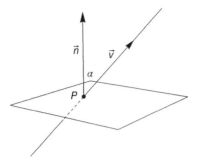

Figure 3.10   Angle line to plane

This means α_x is about 1.36 radians (77.91°), giving $\beta_x \approx 0.21$ radians (12.09°). Since the y-axis has direction vector $(0, 1, 0)$, we have $\cos \alpha_y \approx 0.830$, $\alpha_y \approx 0.59$ radians, and $\beta_y \approx 0.98$ radians. Finally, for the z-axis, $\cos \alpha_z \approx 0.518$, $\alpha_z \approx 1.03$, and $\beta_z \approx 0.54$.

The special simple form of the direction vectors in this example leads to a somewhat surprising result. The sum of the squares of the three cosines equals 1: $0.207^2 + 0.830^2 + 0.518^2 \approx 1.0$ Indeed, the three dot products we calculate just give the three coordinates of the normal vector and when we square them and add them up we get the square of the normal vector's length. This is exactly the square of the denominator, $\sqrt{93}$. □

The normal determines the orientation of a plane, so to find the angle between two planes, we just find the angle between their normals (Figure 3.11). This is a dot product calculation. It is important to note here that the angle we are calculating is the angle we see when we cut the two planes with another plane perpendicular to the line of intersection for the original planes. It is not the angle between any two vectors where one comes from each plane. (By choosing carefully, we can find two such vectors with an arbitrarily small angle between them.)

When we address shading of object surfaces in a later chapter, we will use our angle calculations to determine both the appropriate color for a face and whether we can even see the face at all.

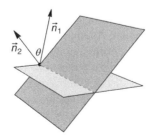

Figure 3.11   Angle plane to plane

3.4 INTERSECTIONS

It is important to be able to calculate intersections between various objects. The main idea is simple: intersection points must satisfy each equation defining the intersecting objects. A point of intersection for two lines, for example, is on both lines and therefore satisfies the two equations, one for each line.

3.4.1 Intersecting Lines

Lines in a plane or in space have the same vector description. The expression $P = P_0 + t\vec{v}$ serves to describe any line. If the point P_0 and the vector $\vec{v}$ have only two coordinates, then we are describing lines in the plane. With three coordinates, we have lines in space. To find the intersection of two lines, we simply set the two descriptions equal to each other:

$$P = P_1 + t_1 \vec{v}_1$$
$$P = P_2 + t_2 \vec{v}_2$$
$$P_1 + t_1 \vec{v}_1 = P_2 + t_2 \vec{v}_2 \implies t_1 \vec{v}_1 - t_2 \vec{v}_2 = P_2 - P_1$$

The two line descriptions have two different parameters, t_1 and t_2, because there is no guarantee that the same value for both parameters would work to describe the point P in the context of each line. If our lines are in a plane, the last equation above can be split into two linear equations (one for the x coordinates and one for the y coordinates) with the two parameters as unknowns. Of course, if our lines are in space, there are three equations.

For two-dimensional lines, the two linear equations in two unknowns are easy to solve with one of the linear algebra techniques. Cramer's rule (Appendix B) gives a little more formal approach, which in this two-variable case can easily be turned into a decent algorithm. Whichever technique we use, a little adjustment can usually reduce the number of arithmetic operations to improve efficiency. There are really three cases any complete algorithm needs to identify. The two lines may be parallel and hence not intersect, or they may actually coincide and hence give rise to an infinite number of intersection points, or they may intersect in a single point.

For three-dimensional lines, there are three equations because there are three coordinates, but only two unknowns, parameters t_1 and t_2. The fact that lines in space can be skew (neither parallel nor intersecting) results in an over-constrained system of equations with possibly no solution. Another vector approach avoids this complication and draws on the techniques for finding the distance between lines. If the lines do indeed intersect, then the two closest points (one on each line) will actually coincide. Searching for the smallest distance between two points is a job for calculus, and there is in fact an approach to finding the intersection that uses calculus to first find the closest points (see Exercises). However, we earlier saw that the closest points must form a vector perpendicular to both lines. Using this geometric observation, we can build a purely vector approach to the problem.

Start with the equation $t_1 \vec{v}_1 - t_2 \vec{v}_2 = P_2 - P_1$, and, since each side is a vector, the cross products of each side with the vector $\vec{v}_2$ must be equal. Hence, recalling that the cross product of a vector with itself is zero,

$$(t_1 \vec{v}_1 - t_2 \vec{v}_2) \times \vec{v}_2 = t_1 (\vec{v}_1 \times \vec{v}_2) = (P_2 - P_1) \times \vec{v}_2$$

Now, to turn the vector equation into an equation with real numbers, we take the dot product of each side with the vector $(\vec{v}_1 \times \vec{v}_2)$.

$$t_1 (\vec{v}_1 \times \vec{v}_2) \cdot (\vec{v}_1 \times \vec{v}_2) = ((P_2 - P_1) \times \vec{v}_2) \cdot (\vec{v}_1 \times \vec{v}_2)$$

$$t_1 = \frac{((P_2 - P_1) \times \vec{v}_2)) \cdot (\vec{v}_1 \times \vec{v}_2)}{|\vec{v}_1 \times \vec{v}_2|^2} \tag{3.5}$$

If we had crossed both sides with $\vec{v}_1$ in the beginning, then we would have an expression for t_2. A full geometric interpretation of the final expression for t_1 is somewhat elusive, but we can bring a little understanding to the numerator. Notice that if the two lines are actually in the same plane, then $(P_2 - P_1) \times \vec{v}_2$ and $\vec{v}_1 \times \vec{v}_2$ are parallel vectors. The cosine of the angle between them is 1 and the dot product is just the product of their lengths. A little algebra shows that this is just Cramer's formula for t_1.

If it turns out that $\vec{v}_1 \times \vec{v}_2 = 0$, then the lines are parallel. Otherwise, we will find the parameters for points that are closest together. From there, we can determine if the lines intersect.

Example 3.13 (Intersection of Two Three-Dimensional Lines). Begin with two direction vectors $\vec{v}_1 = (1, 1, 2)$ and $\vec{v}_2 = (0, 2, 3)$ along with the respective points $P_1 = (1, 0, 3)$ and $P_2 = (-1, 1, 0)$. Then $\vec{v}_1 \times \vec{v}_2 = (-1, -3, 2)$ and $\vec{v}_1 \cdot \vec{v}_2 = 8$. The vector $(P_2 - P_1) = (-2, 1, -3)$ and $(P_2 - P_1) \times \vec{v}_2 = (9, 6, -4)$. Now we can use the formula to find t_1.

$$t_1 = \frac{(9, 6, -4) \cdot (-1, -3, 2)}{14} = -2.5$$

To get t_2, we use $(P_2 - P_1) \times \vec{v}_1 = (5, 1, -3)$ and calculate

$$t_2 = \frac{(5, 1, -3)) \cdot (-1, -3, 2)}{14} = -1.0$$

We return to the original lines to find the two points closest together.

$$P_1 + t_1 \vec{v}_1 = (1, 0, 3) + (-2.5)(1, 1, 2) = (-1.5, -2.5, -2)$$

$$P_2 + t_2 \vec{v}_2 = (-1, 1, 0) + (-1.0)(0, 2, 3) = (-1, -1, -3)$$

We conclude that the lines do not intersect because the two calculated points are different. The vector $\vec{n} = (-1, -1, -3) - (-1.5, -2.5, -2) = (0.5, 1.5, -1)$ should be

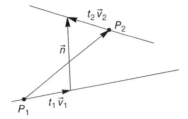

Figure 3.12   Two skew lines labeled

perpendicular to both lines and, indeed, the dot product with each of the line direction vectors is zero. The length of $\vec{n}$ is $\sqrt{3.5} \approx 1.87$, so the two lines are this far apart (Figure 3.12).

If we now move the first line in the direction of $\vec{n}$ by a distance 1.87, the two lines should intersect. We can move the line simply by moving P_1 because the direction vector stays the same. So let $P_1^* = P_1 + \vec{n} = (1.5, 1.5, 2)$. We should recalculate with this new line, but since we moved the first line in the direction of $\vec{n}$, we should not have changed the positions of the two closest points. The parameters t_1 and t_2 should be exactly as before. Therefore, the two new points are

$$P_1^* + t_1 \vec{v}_1 = (1.5, 1.5, 2) + (-2.5)(1, 1, 2) = (-1, -1, 3)$$

$$P_2 + t_2 \vec{v}_2 = (-1, 1, 0) + (-1.0)(0, 2, 3) = (-1, -1, -3)$$

The two lines now intersect at the point $(-1, -1, 3)$.

Turning this procedure for finding an intersection into an algorithm is not hard, but as with all algorithms dealing with floating point numbers (real numbers, not just integers), calculations are approximations. Consequently, determining whether the distance between the lines is zero involves checking if the distance is less than some small number.   □

3.4.2   Lines Intersecting Planes

To determine the light intensity reflecting off a surface, we only need to know the angle between a line (or vector) to the light source and the plane of the particular object face. Ray tracing (detailed in a later chapter), however, is different. There we need to know precisely where on a flat polygonal face the light ray strikes, and hence is either reflected or refracted. For a line and a plane, we know that an intersection point P must be on the line, and therefore $P = P_0 + t\vec{v}$ for some value of t. The point P is also on the plane, so we have $\vec{n} \cdot (P - Q_0) = 0$, where $\vec{n}$ is the normal to the plane and Q_0 is a given point on the plane. Substituting the first expression for P into the second equation gives

$$\vec{n} \cdot (P - Q_0) = \vec{n} \cdot (P_0 + t\vec{v} - Q_0) = \vec{n} \cdot ((P_0 - Q_0) + t\vec{v}) = 0$$

We solve this equation for t, giving

$$t = \frac{-\vec{n} \cdot (P_0 - Q_0)}{\vec{n} \cdot \vec{v}} \tag{3.6}$$

Now all we need is to substitute back into the line equation to find P.

Example 3.14 (Intersection of a Line and Plane). Consider the line given by $P_0 = (1.2, 4, -1.8)$ and $\vec{v} = (7, 5.5, 2)$. To find where it intersects the plane described by the point $Q_0 = (2, 1, 1)$ and normal $\vec{n} = (3.4, 3, 5)$, we first calculate t.

$$t = \frac{-(3.4, 3, 5) \cdot ((1.2, 4, -1.8) - (2, 1, 1))}{(3.4, 3, 5) \cdot (7, 5.5, 2)} = \frac{7.72}{50.3} \approx 0.153$$

The point of intersection is then calculated from the line equation

$$P = (1.2, 4, -1.8) + (0.153)(7, 5.5, 2) \approx (2.27, 4.84, -1.49)$$

We can verify that the point is indeed on the plane by subtracting Q_0 to get a vector that should be perpendicular to the normal. Taking the dot product should give zero (approximately). □

There is one more step if we are trying to determine where on a face the light ray intersects. It is possible that the ray misses the face entirely. That is, it intersects the plane of the face, but it is not inside the polygonal boundary of the face. Checking to see whether the point of intersection is actually inside the face requires a little more analysis, which we will begin to do later in this chapter.

3.4.3 Intersecting Planes

Two planes can intersect in two ways. They can either intersect in a line, or they can intersect everywhere (if they are identical). Of course, there is a third possibility—they may be parallel and not intersect at all. Parallel planes are easy to detect because their normals are parallel; that is, the normals are multiples of each other. If the planes are parallel, then checking the distance between them determines if they intersect. A distance of zero indicates they coincide, and any positive distance indicates they do not intersect (Figure 3.13).

When two planes do intersect to form a line, we notice immediately that the direction vector for that line is parallel to both planes and therefore must be perpendicular

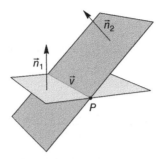

Figure 3.13   Two planes intersect

to the normal to each plane. Once again, the cross product proves its worth. Taking the cross product of the two normals gives a vector in the direction of the line. We then know the line has the form

$$P = P_0 + t(\vec{n}_1 \times \vec{n}_2) \tag{3.7}$$

All we need to finish the description of the line is the point P_0. This is just any point on the line. Since there are an infinite number of points on the line, it should not be that hard to explicitly find one, but it is a little awkward computationally. First, note that since the line of intersection is in both planes, our point P_0 must be on both planes. In short, it satisfies the equation for each plane. If the planes have normals $\vec{n}_1$ and $\vec{n}_2$ with points Q_1 and Q_2 on the respective planes, we have the following two relations:

$$\vec{n}_1 \cdot (P_0 - Q_1) = 0$$
$$\vec{n}_2 \cdot (P_0 - Q_2) = 0$$

These are vector equations and, if we replaced the points with their coordinate representations, we would have two equations with three unknowns, the coordinates of P_0. Now if we knew the line of intersection is not parallel to the xy plane, then there has to be a point on the line with $z = 0$. (If it is parallel, there must be a point with coordinate $y = 0$ or $x = 0$.) Setting $z = 0$ reduces the two equations to two variables and we can solve them.

Example 3.15 (Two Intersecting Planes). Suppose the normals to two planes are $\vec{n}_1 = (1, 0, 5)$ and $\vec{n}_2 = (3, -2, 2)$ with respective points $Q_1 = (1, 6, -2)$ and $Q_2 = (2, 1, 0)$. First, find the direction vector for the line by taking the cross product.

$$\vec{v} = (1, 0, 5) \times (3, -2, 2) = (10, 13, -2)$$

Then look for a point on the line. Since $\vec{v}$ is not parallel to the xy plane [i.e., it is not perpendicular to the normal vector $(0, 0, 1)$], we set the z coordinate of P_0 to zero.

$$\vec{n}_1 \cdot ((x, y, 0) - (1, 6, -2)) = (x - 1) + 10 = 0$$

$$\vec{n}_2 \cdot ((x, y, 0) - (2, 1, 0)) = 3(x - 2) - 2(y - 1) = 0$$

Solving gives $P_0 = (-9, -15.5, 0)$ and the line of intersection is $P = (-9, -15.5, 0) + t(10, 13, -2)$.   □

Our calculations for finding a point on the line may seem a little *ad hoc*, even though it can be turned into an algorithm. For a more general approach, we could pick a third plane guaranteed to intersect our line by taking the plane perpendicular to the line direction vector and containing the origin $(0, 0, 0)$. Then, finding the intersection of three planes (next example) will find a point on the line.

Three planes can intersect in various ways. We can have no intersections (at least two planes are parallel or they intersect in three parallel lines), or infinite intersections (the planes coincide or intersect in a line), or a single point of intersection (Figure 3.14). For the first two possibilities, checking the normals determines the situation. For the last possibility, the vector approach supplies three equations:

$$\vec{n}_1 \cdot (P - P_1) = 0$$

$$\vec{n}_2 \cdot (P - P_2) = 0$$

$$\vec{n}_3 \cdot (P - P_3) = 0$$

The point $P = (x, y, z)$ has three unknown coordinates, which turns the three vector equations into three linear equations in x, y, and z. The equations can be solved with any of the techniques from linear algebra. In particular, we can convert the three equations to a single matrix equation if we let M be the matrix with the normal vectors as rows. (Details of the conversion and solution are given in Section 3.7.) Using the matrix inverse to solve the matrix equation yields a vector formula for the point of intersection.

$$P = \frac{1}{\det M}[(\vec{n}_1 \cdot P_1)(\vec{n}_2 \times \vec{n}_3) + (\vec{n}_2 \cdot P_2)(\vec{n}_3 \times \vec{n}_1)$$

$$+ (\vec{n}_3 \cdot P_3)(\vec{n}_1 \times \vec{n}_2)] \qquad (3.8)$$

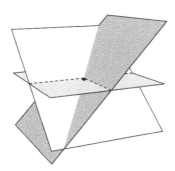

Figure 3.14   Three planes intersect

The points P_1, P_2, P_3 are not vectors, so the dot products in the formula look suspicious. Yet if we consider P_1, P_2, P_3 as vectors from the origin to the points, then the calculations make sense.

Example 3.16 (Intersection of Three Planes). Let us take an example where it is relative easy to watch the calculations evolve. We will pick the following three unit normals along with points on the associated planes:

$$\vec{n}_1 = \left(0, \frac{1}{\sqrt{2}}, \frac{1}{\sqrt{2}}\right) \qquad P_1 = (1, -1, 2)$$

$$\vec{n}_2 = \left(\frac{1}{\sqrt{3}}, \frac{1}{\sqrt{3}}, \frac{1}{\sqrt{3}}\right) \qquad P_2 = (0, 2, 1)$$

$$\vec{n}_3 = \left(\frac{1}{\sqrt{2}}, 0, \frac{1}{\sqrt{2}}\right) \qquad P_3 = (4, 0, -2)$$

The dot products turn out to be $(\vec{n}_1 \cdot P_1) = \frac{1}{\sqrt{2}}$, $(\vec{n}_2 \cdot P_2) = \sqrt{3}$, and $(\vec{n}_3 \cdot P_3) = \sqrt{2}$. The determinant of M, the matrix with the normals in the rows, can be calculated as follows:

$$\det M = \begin{vmatrix} 0 & \frac{1}{\sqrt{2}} & \frac{1}{\sqrt{2}} \\ \frac{1}{\sqrt{3}} & \frac{1}{\sqrt{3}} & \frac{1}{\sqrt{3}} \\ \frac{1}{\sqrt{2}} & 0 & \frac{1}{\sqrt{2}} \end{vmatrix} = -\frac{1}{\sqrt{2}} \cdot (0) + \frac{1}{\sqrt{2}} \cdot \left(-\frac{1}{\sqrt{6}}\right) = -\frac{1}{2\sqrt{3}}$$

The point of intersection is then found from Formula 3.8.

$$P = -(2\sqrt{3}) \left[\frac{1}{\sqrt{2}} \left(\frac{1}{\sqrt{6}}, 0, \frac{-1}{\sqrt{6}}\right) + \sqrt{3} \left(\frac{-1}{2}, \frac{-1}{2}, \frac{1}{2}\right) + \sqrt{2} \left(0, \frac{1}{\sqrt{6}}, \frac{-1}{\sqrt{6}}\right) \right]$$

$$= (2, 1, 0)$$

The first plane in this example has the implicit equation $\frac{1}{\sqrt{2}}(y + z - 1) = 0$. The point $P = (2, 1, 0)$ does satisfy the equation and hence lies on the plane. It is easy to check that the point also lies on the other two planes and is the point of intersection for all three planes. The vector viewpoint really did not give any special insight into this problem. Although the final formula for the point of intersection can be given in terms of vectors, it is not clear how to interpret it in a way that gives geometric insight. In Section 3.6, a new coordinate system (homogeneous) gives another view of this problem that does bring a little more insight. □

3.5   ADDITIONAL KEY APPLICATIONS

3.5.1   Intersection of Line Segments

In a graphics context, lines can represent light rays, but the edges of objects are usually line segments, not fully infinite lines. This means that two lines may intersect, but line segments on those lines may not. Determining whether two segments intersect is key, for instance, in deciding whether two-dimensional objects collide or not. Looking deeper into this problem does highlight a few more useful techniques in the associated vector geometry.

To set up the situation, suppose we have two lines L_1 and L_2 with segments on each. The first segment has end points P_0 and P_1 while the segment on the second line has end points Q_0 and Q_1. Once we form vectors $\vec{v}_1 = (P_1 - P_0)$ and $\vec{v}_2 = (Q_1 - Q_0)$, we can describe each line. L_1 has equation $P = P_0 + t_1\vec{v}_1$, and line L_2 has equation $P = Q_0 + t_2\vec{v}_2$.

We know that if $0 \leq t_1 \leq 1$, then the point P is actually on the first line segment. Assuming the two lines actually do intersect, using the earlier techniques will find t_1 and t_2 for the point of intersection. If both these parameters are between 0 and 1, then the intersection point is on both segments and the segments do intersect. This will work, but there is a bit of computation necessary to find the parameters and cover the various cases. Another more efficient approach can decide whether the segments intersect without actually finding the intersection.

Focus first on two dimensions. A line divides the two-dimensional space into two regions, one above the line and one below the line. (For a nearly vertical line, perhaps left and right are better directions.) For the line L_1, we have a normal vector $\vec{n}_1$. The normal "points" to one side of the line. Any multiple of the normal vector is still perpendicular to the line, so the normal may be pointing above the line or it may be pointing below the line. Once we pick the normal, we have distinguished between the two sides of the line (Figure 3.15).

A point R that is not on the line is on one side or the other. The vector $\vec{w} = R - P_0$ is not necessarily perpendicular to L_1, but it does point to one side of the line or the other. The dot product $\vec{w} \cdot \vec{n}_1$ is positive if R is on the side of the line pointed to by the normal vector $\vec{n}_1$. If it is on the other side, the dot product is negative.

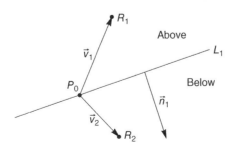

Figure 3.15   Side of line

The key idea here is that, if we take the end points of a segment on the second line L_2 and form vectors with P_0, the dot products with normal $\vec{n}_1$ will determine if they are on the same side of L_1 or not. If the two dot products are both positive or both negative, they are on the same side of the line. Otherwise, they are on opposite sides.

Result 3.1 *If the vectors from a point on a line to two points R_1 and R_2 are $\vec{v}_1$ and $\vec{v}_2$, then the two points are on the same side of the line if and only if the dot products $\vec{v}_1 \cdot \vec{n}$ and $\vec{v}_2 \cdot \vec{n}$ have the same sign. If either dot product is zero, then the corresponding point is on the line.*

Example 3.17 (Intersection of Two Line Segments (2D)). Consider two line segments with end points, direction vectors, and normals as given below:

$$P_0 = (1,4) \quad P_1 = (6,2) \quad \vec{v}_1 = (5,-2) \quad \vec{n}_1 = (2,5)$$

$$Q_0 = (4,3) \quad Q_1 = (5,5) \quad \vec{v}_2 = (1,2) \quad \vec{n}_2 = (-2,1)$$

Note that we could have taken the direction vectors and the normals in the opposite directions as well.

To determine whether the two line segments intersect, we first check if P_0 and P_1 are on the same side of line L_2.

$$\vec{n}_2 \cdot (P_0 - Q_0) = 7 > 0$$

$$\vec{n}_2 \cdot (P_1 - Q_0) = -5 < 0$$

Since the dot products have different signs, they are on different sides of the line containing the second segment. It is still possible that the segments intersect. Now, checking Q_0 and Q_1 against line L_1 gives

$$\vec{n}_1 \cdot (Q_0 - P_0) = 1 > 0$$

$$\vec{n}_1 \cdot (Q_1 - P_0) = 13 > 0$$

These end points are on the same side of L_2 and consequently the segments do not intersect. The algorithm here hinges on the fact that the segments intersect only if the two end points of each segment are on opposite sides of the line containing the other segment.

Just to check the result, we can find the intersection of the two lines. We have

$$L_1 : P = (1,4) + t_1(5,-2)$$

$$L_2 : P = (4,3) + t_2(1,2)$$

Setting the two line equations equal to each other gives a system of two equations in t_1 and t_2. Using Cramer's rule gives

$$t_1 = \frac{\begin{vmatrix} 3 & -1 \\ -1 & -2 \end{vmatrix}}{\begin{vmatrix} 5 & -1 \\ -2 & -2 \end{vmatrix}} = \frac{7}{12} \qquad t_2 = \frac{\begin{vmatrix} 5 & 3 \\ -2 & -1 \end{vmatrix}}{\begin{vmatrix} 5 & -1 \\ -2 & -2 \end{vmatrix}} = \frac{-1}{12}$$

Since t_1 is between 0 and 1, the intersection point is inside the first line segment, but t_2 is negative, indicating the intersection is outside the segment. The two segments do not intersect. This second approach finds the intersection and then compares with each segment; this requires more computation that the first algorithm.   □

A three-dimensional line does not split space into two regions but a plane does, and the same technique we have just discovered works to determine if two points are on the same side of a plane. Form vectors from a fixed point on the plane to the two points and take dot products with a normal to the plane. If the dot products have the same sign, the points are on the same side of the plane.

For line segments in space, an algorithm for determining whether two line segments intersect can proceed by first determining whether the two segments lie in the same plane: that is, whether the four end points all lie in the same plane. Three points determine a plane, so with three of the four end points, we find a normal to the plane. Now find the vector from one of the three points to the fourth point. If the dot product of this vector with the normal is zero, all four points lie in a plane. If not, then the segments cannot intersect.

If the two line segments do lie in the same plane, then the algorithm could continue as we did in two dimensions if we could find normals to each line segment that are parallel to the plane. The cross product of a line's direction vector and the plane's normal will give such a normal to the line. This reduces the problem to the two-dimensional case.

Example 3.18 (Intersection of Two Line Segments (3D)). Consider two line segments in space with the following end points and direction vectors:

$$P_0 = (-1, 5, 0) \qquad P_1 = (2, 0, 1) \qquad \vec{v}_1 = (3, -5, 1)$$
$$Q_0 = (-1, -1, 3) \qquad Q_1 = (3, 3, -1) \qquad \vec{v}_2 = (4, 4, -4)$$

To find the normal to the plane containing P_0, P_1, and Q_0, we find the cross product of $\vec{v}_1$ with the vector $\vec{w} = (Q_0 - P_0) = (0, -6, 3)$. The result is $\vec{v}_1 \times \vec{w} = (-9, -9, -18)$, so for simplicity we pick the normal $\vec{n} = (1, 1, 2)$.

To check whether Q_1 is in the plane of the other three, we find the dot product of $(Q_1 - P_0) = (4, -2, -1)$ and $\vec{n}$. The result is 0, implying that all four points lie in a plane.

Normals to the two line segments are calculated with cross products:

$$\vec{n}_1 = \vec{v}_1 \times \vec{n} = (-11, -5, 8)$$
$$\vec{n}_2 = \vec{v}_2 \times \vec{n} = (12, -12, 0)$$

First, test P_0 and P_1 against the second line:

$$(P_0 - Q_0) \cdot \vec{n}_2 = (0, 6, -3) \cdot (12, -12, 0) = -72 < 0$$
$$(P_1 - Q_0) \cdot \vec{n}_2 = (3, 1, -2) \cdot (12, -12, 0) = 24 > 0$$

P_0 and P_1 are on opposite sides of the second line. Similarly, we check Q_0 and Q_1.

$$(Q_0 - P_0) \cdot \vec{n}_1 = (0, -6, 3) \cdot (-11, -5, 8) = 54 > 0$$
$$(Q_1 - P_0) \cdot \vec{n}_1 = (4, -2, -1) \cdot (-11, -5, 8) = -42 < 0$$

Q_0 and Q_1 are on opposite sides of the first line. We conclude that the two line segments intersect. $\qquad\square$

The ability to determine whether two points are on the same side of a line is quite useful. It leads nicely to an algorithm for determining whether a point falls inside a triangle. Each side of the triangle determines a line, and the third vertex is on one side of this line. If the point in question is on the opposite side of the line, then it cannot be inside the triangle. The algorithm, then, is to test each side against the extra vertex and the given point.

Example 3.19 (Inside a Triangle). Suppose we have a triangle in two dimensions with vertices $P_0 = (4, 9)$, $P_1 = (8, 15)$, and $P_2 = (10, 13)$. We wish to check if $Q = (6, 13)$ is inside the triangle. Of course, a little algebra and the point-slope equation for each line can usually answer the question, but for an algorithm that tries to minimize calculations, we test each side against the point $(6, 13)$.

The side with vertices P_0 and P_1 is on a line with direction vector $(4, 6)$. The vector $(-6, 4)$ is normal. Comparing Q with P_2 gives

$$(Q - P_0) \cdot (-6, 4) = (2, 4) \cdot (-6, 4) = 4 > 0$$
$$(P_2 - P_0) \cdot (-6, 4) = (6, 4) \cdot (-6, 4) = -20 < 0$$

The two points are on opposite sides of $P_0 P_1$, so Q cannot be inside the triangle. We can stop here; there is no need to check the other sides. $\qquad\square$

We can actually expand this algorithm to three-dimensional triangles. We simply need to find normals that lie in the plane of the triangle. This requires cross products which can be a little expensive computationally. There are several other algorithms that can detect whether a point is inside a triangle or outside it. One approach projects the three dimensional triangle onto one of the coordinate planes. This turns the three-dimensional problem into a two-dimensional problem. Another approach, which we examine in detail when we study triangles in depth, uses barycentric coordinates which are particularly important in graphics applications.

3.5.2 Intersection of Line and Sphere

Another useful graphics object is the sphere and, although perfect spheres may not be in a scene, they can serve as convenient boundaries for regions of the scene. If a light ray does not intersect the boundary of the sphere, then it certainly does not intersect any object inside.

If C is the center of a sphere and P is an arbitrary point on the sphere, then the expression $|(P - C)| = r$ describes the sphere. In terms of dot products, we have the equivalent description $(P - C) \cdot (P - C) = r^2$. To find the intersection of a line with a sphere, we first visualize a cross section of the sphere and line as in Figure 3.16. Single out the point E (for eye) on the line where we might imagine an observer is standing, the point P where the line intersects the sphere, and the point C at the center of the sphere. It may be that the line actually misses the sphere, but if it does intersect, it could just touch the sphere in a single point (i.e., it is tangent to the sphere) or it could pass through the sphere intersecting at two distinct points.

A point of intersection is simultaneously on the line and the sphere. Plugging the line description $P = E + t\vec{v}$ into the description of a sphere gives

$$(P - C) \cdot (P - C) = (E + t\vec{v} - C) \cdot (E + t\vec{v} - C) = r^2$$

The dot product simplifies to give the following quadratic equation in t:

$$t^2|\vec{v}|^2 + 2((E - C) \cdot \vec{v})t + |(E - C)|^2 = r^2 \qquad (3.9)$$

The well-known quadratic formula will give us 0, 1, or 2 solutions.

There is another approach that saves a few computations and still finds the intersection closest to E. In the figure, the triangle ΔEQC is a right triangle; Q is the vertex of the right angle. Let vector $\vec{w} = C - E$ be the hypotenuse of the triangle and let $\vec{v}$ be a direction vector of length 1 for the line from E through P. (If the line does not intersect the sphere, then there is no P.)

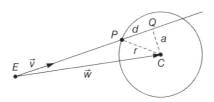

Figure 3.16 Line and sphere

By projecting $\vec{w}$ onto the vector $\vec{v}$, we can find the side EQ of the right triangle ΔEQC. The length of EQ is $L = \vec{w} \cdot \vec{v}$, since the length of $\vec{v}$ is 1. The Pythagorean theorem gives the final side, $a = |\vec{w}|^2 - L^2$.

If the line does not intersect the sphere, then $a > r$ and we can stop the algorithm. Otherwise, the smaller right triangle ΔCQP has sides a and d with hypotenuse r, so $d^2 = r^2 - a^2$. We take the square root to get d and then $P = E + (L - d)\vec{v}$.

Example 3.20 (Intersection of Line and Sphere). Suppose there is a sphere of radius 4 centered at the point $(5, 8, -4)$. We are standing with our eye at the point $(-3, 2, 1)$ looking in the direction $(4, 4, -3)$.

$$\vec{v} = \frac{1}{\sqrt{41}}(4, 4, -3) \approx (0.625, 0.625, -0.469)$$

$$\vec{w} = (8, 6, -5)$$

$$L = (8, 6, -5) \cdot (0.625, 0.625, -0.469) \approx 11.1$$

Continuing, we have

$$a^2 = |\vec{w}|^2 - L^2 \approx 1.79$$

$$d^2 = r^2 - a^2 \approx 14.21$$

Since $a < r$, we know there is an intersection.

$$P = (-3, 2, 1) + (11.1 - 3.77)(0.625, 0.625, -0.469) \approx (1.58, 6.58, -2.44)$$

Using the quadratic equation (3.9) (note that $(E - C) = -\vec{w}$), we get

$$t^2 - 2(11.1)t + (125 - 16) = 0$$

One of the solutions to this ($t = 7.33$) matches the intersection found above. Notice that using the quadratic equation requires figuring out which of two solutions is closest to the eye. If the sphere is opaque, we cannot see the other point.   □

3.5.3   Areas and Volumes

The definition of the cross product led naturally to the area of a parallelogram. Theorem 2.2 showed that the length of $\vec{v}_1 \times \vec{v}_2$ is the area of the parallelogram formed by the two vectors; we have $\vec{v}_1 \times \vec{v}_2 = |\vec{v}_1||\vec{v}_2| \sin \alpha$, where α is the angle between the vectors.

For a triangle with vertices A, B, and C, taking the cross product of any two vectors representing sides of the triangle will give us the area of a parallelogram that has

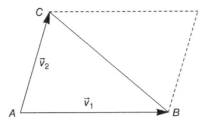

Figure 3.17 Triangle area

twice the area of the triangle. (The diagonal of the parallelogram divides it into two congruent triangles.) So setting $\vec{v}_1 = B - A$ and $\vec{v}_2 = C - A$, we have

$$\text{Area of } \triangle ABC = \frac{1}{2}|\vec{v}_1 \times \vec{v}_2| \tag{3.10}$$

This works fine for triangles in three dimensions where we have defined the cross product, but interestingly, it also works for two-dimensional triangles. The key is to treat the triangle as a three-dimensional triangle lying in the xy plane. That is, the z coordinate is zero (Figure 3.17).

Example 3.21 (Area of 2D Triangle). Suppose a triangle has vertices $A = (2, 6)$, $B = (7, 5)$, and $C = (8, 10)$. Then take $\vec{v}_1 = (B - A) = (5, -1)$ and $\vec{v}_2 = (C - A) = (6, 4)$. Now boost the coordinates to three dimensions and take the vectors as $\vec{v}_1 = (5, -1, 0)$ and $\vec{v}_2 = (6, 4, 0)$.

$$\vec{v}_1 \times \vec{v}_2 = \begin{vmatrix} -1 & 0 \\ 4 & 0 \end{vmatrix}\vec{i} - \begin{vmatrix} 5 & 0 \\ 6 & 0 \end{vmatrix}\vec{j} + \begin{vmatrix} 5 & -1 \\ 6 & 4 \end{vmatrix}\vec{k} = (0, 0, 26)$$

$$\text{Area of } \triangle ABC = \frac{1}{2}|\vec{v}_1 \times \vec{v}_2| = 13$$

The example makes it clear that the cross product is always going to have zero components for x and y. Consequently, the area is simply one-half of the determinant of a 2×2 matrix with the two-dimensional vectors in each row. Also in this example, the vertices were given in counterclockwise order which guaranteed that the cross product had a positive z coordinate. If the vertices appear in clockwise order, the cross product will be negative. $\qquad\square$

Two vectors determine a parallelogram and three vectors (not in the same plane) determine a solid figure called a *parallelepiped*. Multiplying the area of the parallelogram by the height of the parallelepiped will give the volume.

From Figure 3.18, the vectors $\vec{a}$ and $\vec{b}$ are edges of the parallelogram and $\vec{c}$ determines the height of the solid. To find the height, let θ be the angle between the cross product $\vec{a} \times \vec{b}$ and the vector $\vec{c}$. Since the cross product is perpendicular to the plane

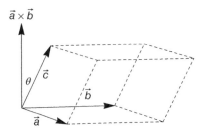

Figure 3.18   Parallelepiped

of the parallelogram, $|\vec{c}| \cos \theta$ is the height of the parallelepiped, assuming θ is less than $\pi/2$ radians.

$$\text{Volume} = \text{Height} \times \text{Area} = |\vec{c}| \cos \theta |\vec{a} \times \vec{b}| = \vec{c} \cdot (\vec{a} \times \vec{b}) \qquad (3.11)$$

The expression on the right is called the *triple scalar product*. If θ is greater than $\pi/2$, we will have to take the absolute value.

Example 3.22 (Volume of Parallelepiped). The four points $P_0 = (1, 1, 2)$, $P_1 = (5, -1, -3)$, $P_2 = (6, 0, 4)$ and $P_3 = (3, 8, 2)$ determine the corner edges P_0P_1, P_0P_2, P_0P_3 of a parallelepiped. To find the volume, set up the appropriate vectors and find the triple scalar product.

$$\vec{a} = (P_1 - P_0) = (4, -2, -5)$$
$$\vec{b} = (P_2 - P_0) = (5, -1, 2)$$
$$\vec{c} = (P_3 - P_0) = (2, 7, 0)$$
$$|\vec{c} \cdot (\vec{a} \times \vec{b})| = |(2, 7, 0) \cdot (-9, -33, 6)| = |(-249)| = 249$$

In this example, the angle between the cross product $\vec{a} \times \vec{b}$ and $\vec{c}$ is greater than $\pi/2$, so we took the absolute value of the scalar triple product.   □

3.5.4   Triangle Geometry

Many of the classical results in geometry take on a slightly different cast when reformulated in terms of vectors. For example, the classical result that the medians of a triangle meet in a point two-thirds of the way from any vertex to the opposite side is easy to verify with vectors.

Example 3.23 (Intersection of Three Medians). Start with a triangle formed by the points A, B, and C. The line between A and B is represented by the vector equation

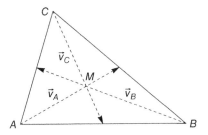

Figure 3.19   Medians

$P = A + t(B - A)$. The midpoint M_{AB} of the side AB is

$$M_{AB} = A + \frac{1}{2}(B - A) = \frac{1}{2}A + \frac{1}{2}B$$

So the vector representing the median from vertex C to the midpoint of AB is given by

$$\vec{v}_C = \frac{1}{2}A + \frac{1}{2}B - C$$

The right-hand side looks like a sum of points, and we know that adding points is in general not a legitimate operation. Yet, the expression here is really the difference of two points so it does make sense.

To get a point M two-thirds of the way along a median, we add two-thirds of the vector to the point C.

$$M = C + \frac{2}{3}\vec{v}_C = C + \frac{2}{3}\left(\frac{1}{2}A + \frac{1}{2}B - C\right) = \frac{1}{3}(A + B + C)$$

It should be easy to see that if we take any of the other two medians of the triangle and find the point two-thirds of the way along, we get exactly the same point M. All three medians must intersect at M (Figure 3.19).   □

3.5.5   Tetrahedron

Example 3.24 (Coordinates of Tetrahedron). A tetrahedron is an object with four identical faces each of which is an equilateral triangle. To use a tetrahedron in a graphics scene, we need the coordinates of the four vertices, and vector geometry can move the process along a little faster than using trigonometry alone.

To fix the position and size of the tetrahedron, let us center it at the origin and make the edge lengths 1. We will start by constructing a tetrahedron sitting on the xz plane and then drop it to put the origin in the center.

Since each face is an equilateral triangle, center a face at the origin with one vertex on the x-axis. Then the coordinates of the three vertices are $A = (x_1, 0, -z)$, $B = (x_1, 0, z)$, and $C = (x_2, 0, 0)$.

The length of side AB must be 1, so $4z^2 = 1$, which gives $z = \frac{1}{2}$. The angle between the vectors from the origin to A and B is $2\pi/3$ radians, so the cosine is $-\frac{1}{2}$. The dot product gives $(x_1, 0, -z) \cdot (x_1, 0, z) = x_1^2 - z^2$. Dividing the dot product by the length of the two vectors gives the cosine.

$$\frac{x_1^2 - z^2}{x_1^2 + z^2} = -\frac{1}{2} \implies x_1 = -\frac{\sqrt{3}}{6}$$

We take the negative square root because the vertices A and B are below the x-axis (Figure 3.20).

The vector from the origin to C must be the same length as the one from the origin to B.

$$x_2^2 = x_1^2 + z^2 = \frac{1}{3} \implies x_2 = \frac{\sqrt{3}}{3}$$

We have $A = (-\frac{\sqrt{3}}{6}, 0, -\frac{1}{2})$, $B = (-\frac{\sqrt{3}}{6}, 0, \frac{1}{2})$, and $C = (\frac{\sqrt{3}}{3}, 0, 0)$.

The vertex D has coordinates $(0, y, 0)$. The coordinate y must be positioned so that the edges AD, BD, and CD all have length 1. In particular, $|CD|^2 = (\frac{\sqrt{3}}{3})^2 + y^2 + 0^2 = 1$ and this implies that $y = \frac{\sqrt{2}}{\sqrt{3}}$ (Figure 3.21).

All that is left now is to center the tetrahedron at the origin. If we mimic the analysis for the medians of a triangle, we can determine where all the altitudes of a tetrahedron intersect. To form an altitude, we take a vector from D to P, the middle of the opposite face. Since P is the point where the medians of each face meet, it has coordinates $\frac{1}{3}(A + B + C)$. A vector from one vertex to the midpoint of the opposite face is an

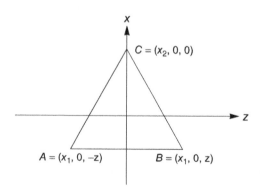

Figure 3.20   Equilateral triangle

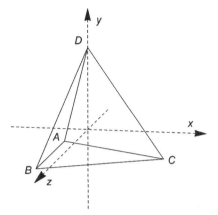

Figure 3.21 Tetrahedron

altitude for the tetrahedron and we have

$$\vec{v} = \frac{1}{3}(A + B + C) - D$$

By observation, it appears that if we go three-quarters of the way along the altitude, we get a point P^*, which will be the same regardless of which altitude we take. It is the intersection of all four altitudes and is the center of the tetrahedron.

$$P^* = D + \frac{3}{4}\vec{v} = \frac{1}{4}(A + B + C + D)$$

Substituting the coordinates as we currently have them gives $P^* = (0, \frac{1}{4}\frac{\sqrt{2}}{\sqrt{3}}, 0)$. We have to drop the tetrahedron along the y-axis $\frac{1}{4}\frac{\sqrt{2}}{\sqrt{3}}$ units.

The coordinates are now as follows:

$$A = \left(-\frac{\sqrt{3}}{6}, -\frac{\sqrt{2}}{4\sqrt{3}}, -\frac{1}{2}\right) \quad B = \left(-\frac{\sqrt{3}}{6}, -\frac{\sqrt{2}}{4\sqrt{3}}, \frac{1}{2}\right)$$

$$C = \left(\frac{\sqrt{3}}{3}, -\frac{\sqrt{2}}{4\sqrt{3}}, 0\right) \quad D = \left(0, \frac{\sqrt{6}}{4}, 0\right)$$

Since this tetrahedron is centered at the origin, we can make it larger by multiplying each coordinate by the same constant scalar. □

3.6 HOMOGENEOUS COORDINATES

The whole idea of the vector approach to geometry is to find descriptions of objects that are intuitive, simple, and as efficient as possible. So far, our vector descriptions of lines and planes are rather simple, but there is a little asymmetry especially with the constant term. A line is described as $P = P_0 + t\vec{v}$, where $\vec{v}$ is the direction vector. The point P_0 has to be treated differently than the vector $\vec{v}$. In an attempt to restore some symmetry, it helps to introduce a new coordinate system called *homogeneous coordinates*.

3.6.1   Two Dimensions

In two dimensions, instead of two coordinates representing a point in the plane, we add a third coordinate. Hence, instead of (x_c, y_c), we use (x_h, y_h, w_h) to represent a point where we have added subscripts to denote either Cartesian or homogeneous coordinates. To convert from homogeneous coordinates to our conventional Cartesian coordinates, we divide by the third coordinate.

$$\text{Homogeneous: } P = (x_h, y_h, w_h) \implies \text{Cartesian: } P = \left(\frac{x_h}{w_h}, \frac{y_h}{w_h} \right)$$

There are two things to notice here. First, it looks like there is trouble if w_h is zero. We will sort this out in Section 3.7. Second, homogeneous coordinates are not unique. For example, using homogeneous coordinates, the point $P = (1, 2, 1)$ is the same as the point $P = (2, 4, 2)$. Unlike Cartesian coordinates which are unique, there are an infinite number of homogeneous coordinates for each point. This may seem like a major disadvantage, but it is overcome by the ease with which we can calculate using homogeneous coordinates.

Recall that, in two dimensions, a line can be described by the vector description $\vec{n} \cdot (P - P_0) = 0$. Converting this to an expression with Cartesian coordinates gives $ax + by = c$, where a and b are the coordinates of the normal, $\vec{n}$, and $c = ap_x + bp_y$, where $P_0 = (p_x, p_y)$. If we replace the Cartesian coordinates with the homogeneous ones, we have

$$ax + by = c \implies a\left(\frac{x_h}{w_h}\right) + b\left(\frac{y_h}{w_h}\right) = c \implies ax_h + by_h - cw_h = 0$$

The last equation is the homogeneous equation for a line. If we think of the homogeneous coordinates of a two-dimensional point as a three-dimensional vector and also set $\vec{n} = (a, b, c)$, then our description of the line becomes a little simpler:

$$\boxed{\text{Two-dimensional Homogeneous Line equation: } \vec{n} \cdot P = 0} \qquad (3.12)$$

In fact, since $P = (x_h, y_h, w_h)$ is just an arbitrary point, it is the normal vector $\vec{n}$ that really describes the line. (To be entirely consistent with the notation, we should probably write $\vec{P}$ because it is considered a vector. However, leaving the arrow off keeps it clear that it is a geometric point.)

Example 3.25 (A Line Through Two Points). Two points determine a line and, using homogeneous coordinates, the points $(3, 2, 1)$ and $(5, 7, 3)$ determine a two-dimensional line. Using the homogeneous equation for a line, we have $\vec{n} \cdot (3, 2, 1) = 0$ and $\vec{n} \cdot (5, 7, 3) = 0$. Following the interpretation of homogeneous coordinates as vectors, the two equations say that $\vec{n}$ is perpendicular to the two vectors $(3, 2, 1)$ and $(5, 7, 3)$. Vector $\vec{n}$ must be parallel to the cross product.

$$\vec{n} = (3, 2, 1) \times (5, 7, 3) = (-1, -4, 11)$$

Any multiple of this vector would also work, but since we are thinking of the coordinates as homogeneous, all such multiples represent the same object and, in our case, that object is a normal to our line. Actually, we can think of the triple $(-1, -4, 11)$ not just as a normal but as the line itself. With homogeneous coordinates, we are blurring the distinction between points and lines. Vectors represent both objects, and now there is a nice duality between them.

The equation of the line is

$$\vec{n} \cdot P = 0 \implies -x_h - 4y_h + 11w_h = 0$$

This is the line $x + 4y = 11$ in Cartesian coordinates. □

Example 3.26 (Intersection of Two Lines). Now, consider two vectors $(2, 2, -1)$ and $(6, -5, 2)$ not as points as we just did, but now as lines. They then represent the lines $2x + 2y - 1 = 0$ and $6x - 5y + 2 = 0$. An intersection point P is on both lines, so we have $(2, 2, -1) \cdot P = 0$ and $(6, -5, 2) \cdot P = 0$. So P must be a vector perpendicular to the two homogeneous line vectors. This vector is the cross product $(-1, -10, -22)$ which represents the Cartesian point $(\frac{1}{22}, \frac{10}{22})$ and is easily verified as the point of intersection for the two lines.

In homogeneous coordinates, the same approach gives us the line through two points and the intersection of two lines. The symmetry is appealing even though the approach may not be more computationally efficient. □

3.6.2 Three Dimensions

Stepping up to three dimensions is easy. Every point has homogeneous coordinates of the form (x_h, y_h, z_h, w_h), and the conversion to conventional Cartesian coordinates just requires dividing by w_h. If we think of a homogeneous normal vector as having four coordinates in three dimensions, our vector equation for a plane in space is

Three-dimensional Homogeneous Plane equation: $\vec{n} \cdot P = 0$ (3.13)

Again, it is really the single vector $\vec{n}$ that describes the plane. The plane in three dimensions is analogous to the line in two dimensions. The plane is a two-dimensional object in three-dimensional space and the line is a one-dimensional object in two-dimensional space.

Two planes do not intersect in a single point, but three may determine a unique intersection point. In this case, we have three equations

$$\vec{n}_1 \cdot P = 0$$
$$\vec{n}_2 \cdot P = 0$$
$$\vec{n}_3 \cdot P = 0$$

There are four unknown components for the homogeneous coordinates of P and we have only three equations. However, since we are using homogeneous coordinates, we may still be in business. The three equations say that P is perpendicular to all three normals. We need some generalization of cross product in order to pin down P. This is not too hard because we can use our standard cross product as a template. There, the cross product was formally the determinant of a 3×3 matrix with the first row just the three vectors $\vec{i} = (1, 0, 0), \vec{j} = (0, 1, 0), \vec{k} = (0, 0, 1)$. The coefficients of the resulting vector were just 2×2 determinants. Now that we are considering homogeneous coordinates in 3D space, we have four components so the natural generalization of cross product is to find the determinant of a 4×4 matrix with the first row filled with basis vectors $\vec{e}_1 = (1, 0, 0, 0), \vec{e}_2 = (0, 1, 0, 0), \vec{e}_3 = (0, 0, 1, 0)$, and $\vec{e}_4 = (0, 0, 0, 1)$.

Example 3.27 (Three Intersecting Planes). Consider three planes given by $(-4, 2, 0, 2)$, $(1, 1, 1, 5)$, and $(-8, 2, 1, 1)$. Their intersection is then the point vector that is perpendicular to all three planes and is given by the determinant. (See Appendix B for details on finding the determinant of a 3×3 matrix.)

$$P = \begin{vmatrix} \vec{e}_1 & \vec{e}_2 & \vec{e}_3 & \vec{e}_4 \\ -4 & 2 & 0 & 2 \\ 1 & 1 & 1 & 5 \\ -8 & 2 & 1 & 1 \end{vmatrix} = \begin{vmatrix} 2 & 0 & 2 \\ 1 & 1 & 5 \\ 2 & 1 & 1 \end{vmatrix}\vec{e}_1 - \begin{vmatrix} -4 & 0 & 2 \\ 1 & 1 & 5 \\ -8 & 1 & 1 \end{vmatrix}\vec{e}_2$$

$$+ \begin{vmatrix} -4 & 2 & 2 \\ 1 & 1 & 5 \\ -8 & 2 & 1 \end{vmatrix}\vec{e}_3 - \begin{vmatrix} -4 & 2 & 0 \\ 1 & 1 & 1 \\ -8 & 2 & 1 \end{vmatrix}\vec{e}_4$$

$$= (-10, -34, -26, 14)$$

Checking the first equation, we get

$$\vec{n}_1 \cdot P = (-4, 2, 0, 2) \cdot (-10, -34, -26, 14) = 0$$

In Cartesian coordinates, the plane $(-4, 2, 0, 2)$ is $-2x + y + 1 = 0$ and $P = \frac{1}{14}(-10, -34, -26)$. It is easy to verify that P is indeed on the plane. We can similarly verify that P is on the other two planes.   □

Example 3.28 (A Plane Through Three Points). Just as in the two-dimensional case, there is a duality between points and lines in three dimensions. In the last example, three planes intersected in a point. Now, focus on three points determining a plane. Suppose $P_1 = (2, 5, -3, 2)$, $P_2 = (-8, 2, 1, 4)$, and $P_3 = (4, -2, 2, 6)$.

$$\vec{n} \cdot P_1 = 0$$
$$\vec{n} \cdot P_2 = 0$$
$$\vec{n} \cdot P_3 = 0$$

This time, $\vec{n}$ is the vector perpendicular to the three vectors representing the homogeneous points. The generalized cross product again gives the perpendicular vector.

$$P = \begin{vmatrix} \vec{e}_1 & \vec{e}_2 & \vec{e}_3 & \vec{e}_4 \\ 2 & 5 & -3 & 2 \\ -8 & 2 & 1 & 4 \\ 4 & -2 & 2 & 6 \end{vmatrix} = (62, 236, 376, -88)$$

A quick check shows the first of the three equations holds, and the others follow similarly.

$$\vec{n} \cdot P_1 = (62, 236, 376, -88) \cdot (2, 5, -3, 2) = 0$$

The vector $\vec{n}$ describes the plane. In Cartesian coordinates, it is

$$31x + 118y + 188z - 44 = 0$$

and the point $\frac{1}{2}(2, 5, -3)$ is on the plane.   □

At this stage of the game, homogeneous coordinates seem to have something to offer if only by adding a little symmetry to our descriptions of points, lines, and planes. We have skipped over three-dimensional lines; it is a little awkward to describe them, but they can be specified with line coordinates which are combinations of the homogeneous coordinates. One of the prime advantages of homogeneous coordinates will become clear later when we will see that they add significantly to our ability to describe transformations of geometric objects.

3.7   COMPLEMENTS AND DETAILS

3.7.1   Intersection of Three Planes Continued

Equation 3.8 gave a formula for the intersection point of three planes. To see where it came from, recall that P is the point of intersection and each normal is perpendicular to a vector formed by P and a point in the corresponding plane.

$$\vec{n}_1 \cdot (P - P_1) = 0$$
$$\vec{n}_2 \cdot (P - P_2) = 0$$
$$\vec{n}_3 \cdot (P - P_3) = 0$$

To see how to systematically solve these equations, we look at the associated matrix equation.

$$M = \begin{bmatrix} \cdots \vec{n}_1 \cdots \\ \cdots \vec{n}_2 \cdots \\ \cdots \vec{n}_3 \cdots \end{bmatrix} \text{ and } P = \begin{bmatrix} x \\ y \\ z \end{bmatrix} \implies MP = \begin{bmatrix} \vec{n}_1 \cdot P_1 \\ \vec{n}_2 \cdot P_2 \\ \vec{n}_3 \cdot P_3 \end{bmatrix}$$

Matrix M has rows that are the coordinates of the various normal vectors. The dot products on the right side of the matrix equation include points P_1, P_2, and P_3. They are not vectors, but if we think of them as vectors from the origin to the points, then our definition of dot product as an operation between vectors stays consistent.

With the matrix equation, the appropriate linear algebra gives us a solution by multiplying both sides by the inverse of M. If the normals are actually unit normals, then M^{-1} is easy to form (using the adjugate matrix; see Appendix B).

$$M^{-1} = \frac{1}{\det M} \begin{bmatrix} \vdots & \vdots & \vdots \\ \vec{n}_2 \times \vec{n}_3) & (\vec{n}_3 \times \vec{n}_1) & (\vec{n}_1 \times \vec{n}_2) \\ \vdots & \vdots & \vdots \end{bmatrix}$$

The solution becomes

$$P = M^{-1} \begin{bmatrix} \vec{n}_1 \cdot P_1 \\ \vec{n}_2 \cdot P_2 \\ \vec{n}_3 \cdot P_3 \end{bmatrix}$$

$$= \frac{1}{\det M}[(\vec{n}_1 \cdot P_1)(\vec{n}_2 \times \vec{n}_3) + (\vec{n}_2 \cdot P_2)(\vec{n}_3 \times \vec{n}_1) + (\vec{n}_3 \cdot P_3)(\vec{n}_1 \times \vec{n}_2)]$$

When we approach this same problem with homogeneous coordinates (Example 3.27), P now has four coordinates, and the three equations are simpler.

$$\vec{n}_1 \cdot P = 0, \qquad \vec{n}_2 \cdot P = 0, \qquad \vec{n}_3 \cdot P = 0$$
$$\implies MP = 0$$

Here, the matrix M is now a 3×4 matrix and P is 4×1. As noted earlier, P is perpendicular (in four-dimensional space) to the three vectors $\vec{n}_1$, $\vec{n}_2$, and $\vec{n}_3$. We determined P earlier by using a generalization of the cross product which in three dimensions is represented by the determinant of a 3×3 matrix. To understand how the generalization is derived, start with the following matrix:

$$M^* = \begin{bmatrix} a & b & c & d \\ \cdots & \vec{n}_1 & \cdots & \cdots \\ \cdots & \vec{n}_2 & \cdots & \cdots \\ \cdots & \vec{n}_3 & \cdots & \cdots \end{bmatrix}$$

Let M_{ij} be the submatrix obtained from M^* by deleting the ith row and jth column. One way to calculate the determinant of M^* is to use the first row as follows:

$$\det M^* = a \det M_{11} - b \det M_{12} + c \det M_{13} - d \det M_{14}$$
$$= (a, b, c, d) \cdot (\det M_{11}, - \det M_{12}, \det M_{13}, - \det M_{14})$$

The determinant is expressed here as a dot product between the vector (a, b, c, d) and a vector of determinants of submatrices. Look at the matrix M^* again and notice that, if the first row was any of the normal vectors $\vec{n}_i$, there would be two rows that were identical, and this means the matrix would have determinant zero. In other words, when (a, b, c, d) is one of the normal vectors, the dot product with the vector of determinants is zero. If we define P to be the vector of determinants, it is perpendicular to each $\vec{n}_i$. A convenient way to express P is by the following determinant:

$$P = \begin{vmatrix} \vec{e}_1 & \vec{e}_2 & \vec{e}_3 & \vec{e}_4 \\ \cdots & \vec{n}_1 & \cdots & \cdots \\ \cdots & \vec{n}_2 & \cdots & \cdots \\ \cdots & \vec{n}_3 & \cdots & \cdots \end{vmatrix}$$

This is the natural generalization of the cross product developed in three dimensions and is the source of the formulas for P that we developed earlier.

3.7.2 Homogeneous Coordinates Continued

To become comfortable with homogeneous coordinates, it helps to construct a more visual model of the system. In two dimensions, the homogeneous coordinates have three components (x, y, w) and hence can be thought of as vectors in three dimensions. The point in two dimensions represented in Cartesian coordinates as $P = (x, y)$ is represented in homogeneous coordinates as $P = (x, y, 1)$ or indeed as $P = (sx, sy, s)$ for any value of s. This is just $P = s(x, y, 1) = (0, 0, 0) + s(x, y, 1)$, which is the expression for a line in three dimensions that goes through the origin in the direction $(x, y, 1)$. In other words, a point in two dimensions corresponds to a line through the origin in three dimensions.

The homogeneous equation for a line in two dimensions is $\vec{n} \cdot P = 0$, where $\vec{n}$ and P are seen as vectors in three dimensions. The set of all vectors P that are perpendicular to $\vec{n}$ (the dot product is zero) are the vectors forming a plane through the origin in three dimensions. Consequently, a line in two dimensions corresponds to a plane in three dimensions (Figure 3.22).

Converting homogeneous coordinates (x_h, y_h, w_h) to Cartesian coordinates is simply a matter of dividing by w_h unless, of course, $w_h = 0$. Homogeneous points with $w_h = 0$ are called *points at infinity* and they do have some geometric significance.

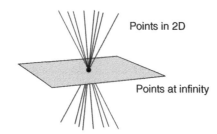

Figure 3.22   Visual model of homogeneous points

Consider two parallel lines given with an implicit description using Cartesian coordinates.

$$3x - 4y = 7$$

$$3x - 4y = 10$$

Trying to solve these two equations in two unknowns gives no solutions, reflecting the fact that the lines do not intersect. Now use homogeneous coordinates to express the same two lines.

$$3x_h - 4y_h = 7w_h$$

$$3x_h - 4y_h = 10w_h$$

With two equations and three unknowns, we do have a solution. For any value s, the values $x_h = 4s$, $y_h = 3s$, and $w_h = 0$ solves the two equations. The homogeneous point $(4s, 3s, 0)$ is a point at infinity. As usual, the coordinates are not unique because any value of s here gives the same point, but the distinguishing factor is that the third component is zero. Notice that the point $(2s, 3s, 0)$ is also a point at infinity, but it is different from $(4s, 3s, 0)$. There are indeed an infinite number of points at infinity. With $w_h = 0$, points at infinity correspond to three-dimensional lines through the origin lying in the xy plane.

One of the axioms of Euclidean geometry is that parallel lines do not intersect. However, when we look down a long straight road, it certainly looks like the straight lines forming the two sides of the road get closer and closer together in the distance. If we think of geometry the way we actually see objects, parallel lines do intersect eventually. If we replace the Euclidean axiom for parallel lines with one that claims all lines intersect, we are on our way to defining a new geometry called *projective geometry*. The set of homogeneous coordinates along with a few axioms produces a new mathematical object called a *projective space* which comes with its own geometry. Aspects of this geometry are relevant for computer graphics mainly because graphics scenes must be eventually projected onto a display screen. The nature of that transformation can be understood in terms of projective geometry.

We can reason by analogy to build projective spaces of higher dimensions. Points in three dimensions have four homogeneous coordinates and correspond to lines through the origin in four dimensions. The theoretical study of projective spaces is well developed in mathematics (starting in the seventeenth century with the applied mathematician Desargues) and does offer key approaches to graphics problems. Practically, the use of homogeneous coordinates gives us efficient ways to manipulate lines, planes, and, as we will see, transformations.

3.8 EXERCISES

In the following exercises, use vector techniques to find solutions.

1. Find the fourth vertex P_3 of the rectangle in Example 3.1.

2. A line goes through $P_0 = (10, 8)$ and $P_1 = (7, -3)$. Find an equation for the line perpendicular to this line through a point two-thirds of the way from P_0 to P_1.

3. The vertices $A = (30, 6)$ and $B = (52, 10)$ form the base of an isosceles triangle (two sides equal). Find vertex C so that the height of the triangle is 40.

4. Find the equation of the line through $(-8, 12, 7)$ and the midpoint of the segment from $(0, 2, 5)$ to $(-4, -4, 2)$.

5. Find the implicit coordinate equation of the plane through $(1, -4, 1)$, $(3, 6, 5)$, and $(-2, 2, 6)$.

6. How close is the point $(10, 15)$ to the line through $(11, 6)$ and $(24, 30)$?

7. Two planes have the same normal $(13, -2, 6)$. One contains the point $P_1 = (3, 3, 9)$ and the other contains $P_2 = (-7, 0, 6)$. How far apart are the planes?

8. Two planes have the same normal $(10, 12, -5)$. One contains the origin. Find the vector equation of the second plane so that it is 32 units from the first one. (Two possible answers.)

9. One face of a rectangular box in space is a plane with normal $(2, -1, -1)$. The face contains the vertex $A = (8, 3, 6)$ and the adjacent vertex $B = (5, 12, -9)$. Find the equation of all three planes meeting at vertex A.

10. In each of the following cases, A and B are the end points of one line segment and C and D form a second segment. Determine if the two segments intersect, and if they do, find the point of intersection.
    i. $A = (50, 240)$, $B = (500, 115)$, $C = (80, 100)$, $D = (400, 130)$
    ii. $A = (-10, 8)$, $B = (110, -17)$, $C = (200, 6)$, $D = (16, -50)$
    iii. $A = (100, 24, 19)$, $B = (-8, -3, -8)$, $C = (-11, -18, 21)$, $D = (17, 2, 1))$
    iv. $A = (-20, 31, 6)$, $B = (15, -12, 18)$, $C = (-34, -10, 12)$, $D = (10, 17, -1)$.

11. The vertices $(4, 5)$, $(30, 8)$, and $(25, 18)$ form a triangle. Determine if the point $(15, 16)$ is inside or outside the triangle.

12. Suppose you have a quadrilateral where only adjacent edges intersect (i.e., it is not twisted). Sketch an algorithm for finding a point guaranteed to be inside the quadrilateral.

13. Determine whether the line through the points $(1, 3, 3)$ and $(-2, 4, 8)$ intersects the plane with the implicit equation $3x + 6y - 2z = 8$. If it does intersect, find the point of intersection.

14. A triangle has vertices $(5, 1, 2)$, $(8, 4, 4)$, and $(2, 3, 6)$. Find where the medians meet and determine the distance from this point to each of the sides.

15. A sphere of radius 8 is centered at $(1, 2, 5)$. Determine if the line through the points $(-6, -4, 1)$ and $(9, 1, 1)$ intersects the sphere and if so, where.

16. With your eye at position $(2, 5, -1)$ looking in direction $(1, 1, 3)$, determine if the ray intersects the sphere with radius 3 centered at $(9,8,12)$. (Use both techniques given in the example to find the closest point to the eye.)

17. Your eye is at position $(2, 5, -1)$ looking in direction $(1, 1, 3)$. A sphere with radius 3 is currently centered at $(9,8,12)$. We move the sphere perpendicular to the ray from your eye until the ray just touches the sphere. Determine the new center of the sphere.

18. Suppose the plane with normal $(1, -3, 1)$ passes through $(10, 1, -1)$. Find the distance between $P = (4, -1, 5)$ and the plane. Then find a point Q on the plane such that the line through P and Q is perpendicular to the plane. (We might think of Q as the shadow of P when the light source is directly "overhead.")

19. The plane with equation $(4, -2, 1) \cdot (P - (0, 1, 7)) = 0$ contains the vertices of a triangle: $(0, 1, 7)$, $(1, 2, 5)$, and $(2, 5, 7)$. A light ray from position $(3, 2, 4)$ traveling in direction $(-2, -1, -1)$ strikes the plane. Determine the point of intersection and whether it falls inside or outside the triangle.

20. For the tetrahedron constructed in Example 3.24, calculate the volume by using the formula for the volume of a pyramid, $V = \frac{1}{3}bh$, where b is the area of the base and h is the height. Then calculate the volume of the parallelepiped containing the tetrahedron using the scalar triple product. What fraction of the parallelepiped's volume is the tetrahedron?

21. For the tetrahedron in Example 3.24, calculate the following:

i. The angle between two faces.

ii. The distance between edges AB and CD.

iii. The length of an altitude. (This is the distance from a vertex to the opposite face.)

iv. The angle between edge AB and the face ACD.

22. The two points $P_0 = (3, 8)$ and $P_1 = (5, -2)$ determine a line. Using homogeneous coordinates find the vector describing the line. Now let $3x - 5y = 8$ and

$4x + 2y = 7$ be two lines and use homogeneous coordinates to find the point of intersection.

23. The three points $P_0 = (1, 4, 8)$, $P_1 = (2, 2, -1)$, and $P_2 = (5, 4, 0)$ are three lines determining a plane. Using homogeneous coordinates, find the vector describing the plane. In terms of Cartesian coordinates, give the normal to the plane. Now, consider three planes with implicit equations $2x + 3y - 6z = 2$, $-x + 4y + z = 7$, and $-8x + y - z = 10$. Using homogeneous coordinates, find the point of intersection. Convert the result to Cartesian coordinates.

24. Determine if the two planes $x - 3y + 5z = -4$ and $2x - 2y + z = 8$ intersect and if so, find the vector equation of the line of intersection.

25. Three planes with normals $(1, 0, -3)$, $(2, 8, 3)$, and $(4, -4, 7)$ contain the points $P_1 = (-6, 2, 2)$, $P_2 = (1, 1, 0)$, and $P_3 = (5, -1, 1)$ respectively. Determine if the planes intersect in a single point and if so, find it.

26. One line goes through $(10, 7, 6)$ and $(-6, 4, 1)$. A second line goes through $(0, 2, 7)$ and $(9, 2, 14)$. How close do they get to each other? If we take the two line segments bounded by the points, how close do they get to each other?

27. A light ray leaves the source at position $(30, 12, 23)$, travels through $(25, 10, 15)$, and hits the plane $2x + 3y + 14z = 22$. What angle does it make with the plane?

28. One plane contains the points $(0, 2, 1)$, $(5, 1, 1)$, and $(-10, -4, -1)$ and another contains $(5, 11, 16)$ with normal $(1, 2, 1)$. Find a line parallel to both planes and one unit from each.

29. Find the area of the triangle in two dimensions with vertices $(10, 24)$, $(22, 38)$, and $(15, 4)$. If the vertices of a triangle have integer coordinates, what must be true about the area?

30. Find a vector parallel to the plane $6x - 2y + z = 15$ and perpendicular to the line $P = (2, 0, 4) + t(2, 7, -3)$.

31. For the following calculations, count how many additions (or subtractions), multiplications (or divisions), and square roots are necessary.

    i. Finding the distance from a point to a line.

    ii. Finding the intersection of two lines in space.

32. A line in space passes through $(3, 1, -9)$ with direction $(2, -6, 2)$ and a second line passes through $(7, 2, 1)$ with direction $(1, 0, -2)$. Find the points on the two lines that are closest together.

33. Determine if the four points $(13, -2, 7)$, $(-8, 20, 1)$, $(-22, 17, 9)$, and $(5, -30, 2$ are coplanar or not.

34. Given the implicit equation for either a line or a plane, how do we tell which side a point is on? For example, determine if $(2, 5, 1)$ and $(6, -2, 3)$ are on the same or opposite sides of the plane $4x + 11y - 4z = 13$ by using the equation itself.

3.8.1   Programming Exercises

1. Write a method (function) that takes the four end points of two line segments (two dimensions) as input and outputs whether or not the segments intersect.

2. Write a method (function) that takes the eight vertices of a box (not necessarily a parallelepiped) plus a point as input and outputs whether the point is inside the box. You may either assume the box is well formed or include a code to determine if it is indeed a box.

3. Write a method (function) that takes the vertices of two triangles (two dimensions) and outputs the vertices of the region of overlap between the two triangles. (Assume the input vertices are in counterclockwise order.)

4

TRANSFORMATIONS

Suppose you are in the modeling stage of the graphics pipeline and the task is to build a car for display on the computer screen. Building an object means that we need to find coordinates for points that delineate various features such as the windshield, the hood, the tires, and so on. Many of these features are curves, so we end up approximating them with very small line segments. Surfaces like the car body are three dimensional, and a mesh of small triangles does the job of approximating their shapes. To specify the line segments and the vertices of triangles, we can use the techniques of vector geometry to make the job considerably easier. However, if the right side of the car looks the same (or almost the same) as the left side of the car, it make sense to simply reflect one side of the car in a plane passing lengthwise down the car's middle. This process of reflection is a type of *transformation*. When we reach the tires for the car, we can model one tire finding appropriate vertices, but then just apply another transformation, a translation, to copy it from the front to the back of the car. Finally, another reflection transformation will then copy the tire from one side of the car to the other.

Once we have the list of triangles and associated vertices representing the car, we still need to position it in any broader scene; there may well be many other objects. This requires another transformation which will alter all the car's vertex coordinates once again. Finally, when we view the scene, we need to decide where the camera (or our eye) is and in which direction we are looking. This, too, requires another transformation plus a special one to convert our three-dimensional scene into a two-dimensional display. There is no escaping being adept at choosing and applying transformations.

Mathematical Structures for Computer Graphics, First Edition. Steven J. Janke.
© 2015 John Wiley & Sons, Inc. Published 2015 by John Wiley & Sons, Inc.

Technically, a transformation T is just a function that sends each point (or vertex), A, to another point called $T(A)$. The result is to transform an object into a new object. The new object may have the same shape as the old and just a new position, or it may have an altered shape. Before we can talk about the mechanics of actually performing a transformation, we need to once again consider the differences between vectors and points in order to be careful about how we deal with each. Recall that we decided to represent both vectors and points as a column of numbers, so

$$\text{Vector } \vec{v} = \begin{bmatrix} 3 \\ 5 \end{bmatrix} \quad \text{Point } P = \begin{bmatrix} 3 \\ 5 \end{bmatrix}$$

The vector, however, is a displacement and the point is a position in the plane. We know there is a connection between the two because we determine a vector by subtracting two points. We are most interested in thinking of transformations as moving points to points, but we can also think of them as acting on vectors. By singling out a point, say the origin O, every point P can be thought of as a vector from O to P. Then, if the transformation T is reasonably behaved, moving point P to $T(P)$ is analogous to moving the vector $\vec{OP}$ to a vector from O to $T(P)$.

To transform vectors, we can change their direction and length in various ways. It does not, however, make sense to translate them (move to a new position) because vectors are independent of position. In contrast, it does make sense to translate points by moving them to new positions. It also makes sense to transform points in a way that changes their direction or distance from the origin. To differentiate further between these cases, we call our complete collection of points an *affine space* and any associated transformations *affine transformations*. Then the collection of vectors formed by taking the difference of any two points is called the associated *vector space*. As we have seen, unlike the affine space, the vector space comes with a complete algebra allowing us, for example, to add vectors and multiply by scalars.

4.1 TYPES OF TRANSFORMATIONS

Transformations are functions that send points to points, and there are many such functions in the world. To focus our study, it is useful to categorize them based on some characterization of their properties. For example, one transformation that is admittedly not very interesting sends all points to the origin (or all vectors to the zero vector). This is an example of a type of transformation that takes many points to the same point, and, while there are some interesting examples of such transformations, we sometimes wish to restrict ourselves to transformations that are one to one. That is, each point comes from exactly one other point. In this case, we can imagine a transformation that goes backwards and undoes what the original transformation does. This class of transformations contains what we call *invertible* transformations.

For a second example, suppose the transformation keeps lengths fixed. That is, it does not change the length of vectors and therefore it does not change the distance between two points. Then it is referred to as an *isometry*; in two dimensions, a rotation around a given point is an isometric transformation of both vectors and points. Imagine a transformation that doubles the length of a vector or doubles the distance a point is from the origin. These are not isometries, but they form another class of transformations that are called *scaling transformations*; they serve to enlarge (or reduce) an object's size.

In computer graphics, it makes sense to focus on transformations that preserve lines taking any collinear points and sending them to new collinear points. Most of our objects are built from line segments, so preserving the line segments means we do not alter the shape of the object. To investigate these transformations, we start with what are called *linear transformations*.

4.2   LINEAR TRANSFORMATIONS

Since we generally do have a vector space associated with the affine space of points, it seems natural to consider transformations that preserve the algebra of vectors. This means that the transformation preserves the sum and the scalar multiplication of vectors. That is, it satisfies

$$T(\vec{v} + \vec{w}) = T(\vec{v}) + T(\vec{w}) \tag{4.1}$$

To preserve scalar multiplication, we must have

$$T(a\vec{v}) = aT(\vec{v}) \tag{4.2}$$

These two properties together define the class of linear transformations and give us considerable information about how the transformations behaves (Figure 4.1). In two dimensions, if we want to know where a linear transformation sends the vector $\vec{v} = (3, 5)$, we can begin by writing $\vec{v}$ as a linear combination of two other vectors, $(1, 0)$ and $(0, 1)$.

$$\vec{v} = \begin{bmatrix} 3 \\ 5 \end{bmatrix} = 3 \begin{bmatrix} 1 \\ 0 \end{bmatrix} + 5 \begin{bmatrix} 0 \\ 1 \end{bmatrix}$$

Actually, any vector can be decomposed into a similar linear combination because the vectors $(1, 0)$ and $(0, 1)$ form a basis for the vector space.

Figure 4.1   Linear transformations preserve addition

Now, applying the properties of linear transformations gives

$$T(\vec{v}) = 3T\left(\begin{bmatrix} 1 \\ 0 \end{bmatrix}\right) + 5T\left(\begin{bmatrix} 0 \\ 1 \end{bmatrix}\right)$$

In other words, in order to know where $\vec{v}$ is sent under the transformation, we need only to know where the vectors $(1, 0)$ and $(0, 1)$ are sent. In fact, once we know where these two are sent, we can calculate where any two-dimensional vector is sent because any vector can be written as a linear combination of these two. If $T((1, 0)) = (-1, 4)$ and $T((0, 1)) = (3, 2)$, then

$$T(\vec{v}) = 3T\left(\begin{bmatrix} 1 \\ 0 \end{bmatrix}\right) + 5T\left(\begin{bmatrix} 0 \\ 1 \end{bmatrix}\right) = 3\begin{bmatrix} -1 \\ 4 \end{bmatrix} + 5\begin{bmatrix} 3 \\ 2 \end{bmatrix} = \begin{bmatrix} 12 \\ 22 \end{bmatrix}$$

Under the transformation T, the vector $(3, 4)$ is sent to the vector $(12, 22)$.

Looking again at the last calculation, the pattern of arithmetic reminds us of matrix multiplication (see Appendix B). In fact, define the matrix M as follows:

$$M = \begin{bmatrix} -1 & 3 \\ 4 & 2 \end{bmatrix}$$

Now calculating the effect of transformation T is simply a matter of multiplying by M.

$$T(\vec{v}) = M \cdot \begin{bmatrix} 3 \\ 5 \end{bmatrix} = \begin{bmatrix} -1 & 3 \\ 4 & 2 \end{bmatrix}\begin{bmatrix} 3 \\ 5 \end{bmatrix} = \begin{bmatrix} 12 \\ 22 \end{bmatrix}$$

(One word of caution: when reading the graphics literature, you will notice that some like to write vectors and points as row vectors and put the matrix on the right of a multiplication rather than on the left as is done here. There are sound reasons for each approach. We will stick with column vectors and multiply with matrices on the left.)

It should be clear that we now have a general procedure for applying transformation T. In short, $T(\vec{v}) = M\vec{v}$. So with a new vector, say $\vec{v} = (-2, 6)$, we have $T(\vec{v}) = M\vec{v} = (20, 4)$. Generalizing to let T act on points is equally easy. We again just multiply the coordinates of our point by the matrix M. Since we can consider points as vectors from the origin, it is worth noting where T sends the zero vector and the zero point (origin): $T((0, 0)) = (0, 0)$. The origin remains fixed. This is true of all linear transformations because they preserve the vector addition and scalar multiplication.

$$T\left(\begin{bmatrix} 0 \\ 0 \end{bmatrix}\right) = 0T\left(\begin{bmatrix} 1 \\ 0 \end{bmatrix}\right) + 0T\left(\begin{bmatrix} 0 \\ 1 \end{bmatrix}\right) = \begin{bmatrix} 0 \\ 0 \end{bmatrix}$$

We were able to characterize T by noting where it sent the vectors $(1, 0)$ and $(0, 1)$. These are called *basis vectors* in linear algebra and we recognize them here as the vectors $\vec{i}$ and $\vec{j}$ from the Cartesian coordinate system. As we will see in a later chapter, changing the coordinate system will change these basis vectors and hence our characterization of T. The resulting new matrix just means we are using a new coordinate system.

Example 4.1 (Finding a Linear Transformation). Suppose we know that T sends the point $(1, 2)$ to $(5, -2)$ and the point $(3, 7)$ to $(-1, 4)$. If we know that T is a linear transformation, we have lots of additional information. In particular, the transformation is really multiplication by a matrix. So we know

$$T\left(\begin{bmatrix} 1 \\ 2 \end{bmatrix}\right) = M \begin{bmatrix} 1 \\ 2 \end{bmatrix} = \begin{bmatrix} 5 \\ -2 \end{bmatrix}$$

$$T\left(\begin{bmatrix} 3 \\ 7 \end{bmatrix}\right) = M \begin{bmatrix} 3 \\ 7 \end{bmatrix} = \begin{bmatrix} -1 \\ 4 \end{bmatrix}$$

The matrix M is currently unknown, so the four entries in M are the unknowns. Each of the above matrix equations gives us two linear equations once we do the multiplication. So we have four equations and four unknowns. Let $M = \begin{bmatrix} a & b \\ c & d \end{bmatrix}$. Then the previous equations give us

$$a + 2b = 5 \qquad c + 2d = -2$$

$$3a + 7b = -13 \quad 3c + 7d = 4$$

We can solve these any way we wish, but linear algebra gives us the more ordered way. First we combine the two transformation equations into a single matrix equation by combining the two points into a single matrix A and the two images of these points into a single matrix B. Then,

$$MA = M \begin{bmatrix} 1 & 3 \\ 2 & 7 \end{bmatrix} = \begin{bmatrix} 5 & -1 \\ -2 & 4 \end{bmatrix} = B \implies M = BA^{-1}$$

We can find M by taking the inverse of A (easy since it is a 2×2 matrix; see Appendix B) and multiplying to find BA^{-1}. Notice here that A has to have an inverse in order to proceed. If not, we do not have enough information from the original two points.

$$A^{-1} = \begin{bmatrix} 7 & -3 \\ -2 & 1 \end{bmatrix} \implies M = \begin{bmatrix} 5 & -1 \\ -2 & 4 \end{bmatrix} \begin{bmatrix} 7 & -3 \\ -2 & 1 \end{bmatrix} = \begin{bmatrix} 37 & -16 \\ -22 & 10 \end{bmatrix}$$

With M in hand, it is now simple to see where any other point is sent. For example, the midpoint of the line segment between the two original points is $(1/2)(1, 2) + (1/2)(3, 7) = (2, 4.5)$. To determine where T sends this point, multiply by M.

$$T\left(\begin{bmatrix} 2 \\ 4.5 \end{bmatrix}\right) = \begin{bmatrix} 37 & -16 \\ -22 & 10 \end{bmatrix} \begin{bmatrix} 2 \\ 4.5 \end{bmatrix} = \begin{bmatrix} 2 \\ 1 \end{bmatrix}$$

The midpoint of the original two points is sent to the midpoint of the two image points.   □

The fact that T sent a midpoint to a midpoint is not an accident. Indeed, we know that for any two points P_1 and P_2, the linear combination $(1 - t)P_1 + tP_2$ is a point

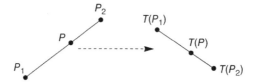

Figure 4.2   Preserving lines

on the line through the points. Since T is a linear transformation, we can apply the properties of linear transformations to discover

$$T((1 - t)P_1 + tP_2) = (1 - t)T(P_1) + tT(P_2) \tag{4.3}$$

The expression on the right is a point on the line between $T(P_1)$ and $T(P_2)$. That is, T sends points on a line to new points that are on a new line. The transformation preserves lines. This is the reason why it is called a *linear transformation* (Figure 4.2).

There is clearly an intimate connection between linear transformations and matrices. The algebra of matrices is indeed called *linear algebra*. The more we know about how matrices behave, the more we will know about how linear transformations work. Since in computer graphics these transformations help in designing and positioning objects, the details of manipulating matrices are particularly useful.

4.2.1   Rotation in Two Dimensions

Staying in two dimensions, our intuitive notion of a rotation suggests that this type of transformation just moves objects rigidly around a central point and sends lines to lines. Since it is not hard to convince ourselves that vector addition and scalar multiplication are preserved, it seems that rotation is a linear transformation and, at least for the time being, we will set the center of rotation to be the origin $(0, 0)$. Figure 4.3 shows the action of the transformation. Point P is rotated by an angle θ around the origin in a counterclockwise direction ending up at $T(P)$. (Recall that conventionally positive angles indicate a counterclockwise direction.)

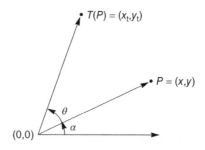

Figure 4.3   2D rotation

In the standard Cartesian coordinate system, let the coordinates of P be (x, y). To specify how the rotation works, we need to find the coordinates of $T(P)$, which we designate as (x_t, y_t). P is at distance r from the origin and, using the angle α shown in the figure, we know that the coordinates (x, y) can be written as $(r \cos \alpha, r \sin \alpha)$. Similarly, since the distance to the origin does not change as we rotate around the origin, we can also write the transformed coordinates (x_t, y_t) as $(r \cos(\alpha + \theta), r \sin(\alpha + \theta))$. Now we use the addition formulas for cosine and sine (see Appendix A) to get

$$x_t = r \cos(\alpha + \theta) = r(\cos \alpha \cos \theta - \sin \alpha \sin \theta) = x \cos \theta - y \sin \theta$$

$$y_t = r \sin(\alpha + \theta) = r(\sin \theta \cos \alpha + \sin \alpha \cos \theta) = x \sin \theta + y \cos \theta$$

From these expressions, we can readily deduce the matrix M_{rot} that gives us a rotation transformation.

$$T(P) = \begin{bmatrix} x_t \\ y_t \end{bmatrix} = M_{rot} \begin{bmatrix} x \\ y \end{bmatrix} = \begin{bmatrix} \cos \theta & -\sin \theta \\ \sin \theta & \cos \theta \end{bmatrix} \begin{bmatrix} x \\ y \end{bmatrix}$$

Example 4.2 (Rotating a Triangle). Start with a triangle having vertices $(0, 0)$, $(3, 0)$, and $(3, 2)$. To rotate this triangle by $\pi/6$ radians counterclockwise around the origin, we first find the correct transformation matrix:

$$M_{rot} = \begin{bmatrix} \cos \theta & -\sin \theta \\ \sin \theta & \cos \theta \end{bmatrix} = \begin{bmatrix} \cos \frac{\pi}{6} & -\sin \frac{\pi}{6} \\ \sin \frac{\pi}{6} & \cos \frac{\pi}{6} \end{bmatrix} = \begin{bmatrix} \frac{\sqrt{3}}{2} & -\frac{1}{2} \\ \frac{1}{2} & \frac{\sqrt{3}}{2} \end{bmatrix}$$

Then we multiply times each point to get

$$T\left(\begin{bmatrix} 0 \\ 0 \end{bmatrix}\right) = M_{rot} \begin{bmatrix} 0 \\ 0 \end{bmatrix} = \begin{bmatrix} 0 \\ 0 \end{bmatrix}$$

$$T\left(\begin{bmatrix} 3 \\ 0 \end{bmatrix}\right) = M_{rot} \begin{bmatrix} 3 \\ 0 \end{bmatrix} \approx \begin{bmatrix} 2.6 \\ 1.5 \end{bmatrix}$$

$$T\left(\begin{bmatrix} 3 \\ 2 \end{bmatrix}\right) = M_{rot} \begin{bmatrix} 3 \\ 2 \end{bmatrix} \approx \begin{bmatrix} 1.6 \\ 3.2 \end{bmatrix}$$

Since we are rotating around the origin, the origin does not move and is called a *fixed point* for the transformation. □

Applying a rotation transformation with angle α and then applying one with angle β should yield a composite rotation of angle $\alpha + \beta$. Using T_α and T_β to designate the individual rotations, the composition of the two transformations is

$$T_\beta(T_\alpha(P)) = T_\beta(M_\alpha P) = (M_\beta M_\alpha)P$$

The appropriate matrix for the composite rotation is the product of the individual matrices.

$$M_\beta M_\alpha = \begin{bmatrix} \cos\beta & -\sin\beta \\ \sin\beta & \cos\beta \end{bmatrix} \begin{bmatrix} \cos\alpha & -\sin\alpha \\ \sin\alpha & \cos\alpha \end{bmatrix}$$

$$= \begin{bmatrix} (\cos\beta\cos\alpha - \sin\beta\sin\alpha) & (-\cos\beta\sin\alpha - \sin\beta\cos\alpha) \\ (\sin\beta\cos\alpha + \cos\beta\sin\alpha) & (-\sin\beta\sin\alpha + \cos\beta\cos\alpha) \end{bmatrix}$$

Looking carefully at the product matrix and recalling the addition formulas for sine and cosine, we notice that this is just the matrix for a rotation of $\alpha + \beta$. As we would expect, applying the two rotations in the reverse order (β first then α) gives the same product matrix. The fact that we can commute the two transformations here is not true in general. Matrices do not always commute, so we will have to be careful about the order in which we apply transformations.

Finally, suppose that the second applied rotation was $\beta = -\alpha$. Then the product matrix is

$$M_{-\alpha} M_\alpha = \begin{bmatrix} \cos(-\alpha) & -\sin(-\alpha) \\ \sin(-\alpha) & \cos(-\alpha) \end{bmatrix} \begin{bmatrix} \cos\alpha & -\sin\alpha \\ \sin\alpha & \cos\alpha \end{bmatrix}$$

$$= \begin{bmatrix} \cos^2\alpha + \sin^2\alpha & -\cos\alpha\sin\alpha + \sin\alpha\cos\alpha \\ -\sin\alpha\cos\alpha + \cos\alpha\sin\alpha & \sin^2\alpha + \cos^2\alpha \end{bmatrix}$$

$$= \begin{bmatrix} 1 & 0 \\ 0 & 1 \end{bmatrix}$$

The composite matrix is the identity matrix, and consequently the composite transformation leaves everything fixed. The matrix $M_{-\alpha}$ is the inverse of the matrix M_α, and the corresponding rotation transformations are also inverses of each other. If α is a positive angle, then it represents a counterclockwise rotation and $-\alpha$ is the clockwise rotation of the same measure.

In general, the inverse of a transformation's matrix is the correct matrix for the inverse transformation. This will come in handy when making more complicated transformations of objects.

4.2.2 Reflection in Two dimensions

In the plane, we can consider reflections in lines. Such a transformation will take points from one side of the line to the other and will fix any points on the reflection line. Again, it seems clear that the reflection transformation takes lines and moves them to other lines; there is no warping because we are reflecting in a straight line. Reflection is a linear transformation. There is, however, one detail we have to address: linear transformations always fix the origin. Since the only points remaining fixed under a reflection are those on the reflection line, we must pick only those reflection lines going through the origin. Later we will deal with arbitrary lines.

Start with the line representing the x-axis. To reflect a point in this line, we simply send (x, y) to $(x, -y)$. This transformation is easily represented with a matrix.

$$T_x(P) = \begin{bmatrix} 1 & 0 \\ 0 & -1 \end{bmatrix} P$$

Correspondingly, we can use the matrix $M = \begin{bmatrix} -1 & 0 \\ 0 & 1 \end{bmatrix}$ to reflect the line representing the y-axis. The question is, how do we reflect in an arbitrary line through the origin?

One answer is that we could apply a series of transformations that effectively carry out the arbitrary reflection in small steps. For the first step, apply a rotation transformation which moves our reflection line until it coincides with the x-axis. This will rotate the original point P to a new position. Then we can reflect in the x-axis because we already have the appropriate matrix for this transformation. Finally, we can rotate back (or undo the rotation) to put the arbitrary line back where it was. The end result is to reflect P in the arbitrary line.

Example 4.3 (Reflection in an Arbitrary Line).   Suppose we are interested in reflecting points in the line through the origin and the point $(6, 2)$. In particular, take $P = (1, 7)$ and determine where it goes under the reflection. Our algorithm begins by rotating so that the line coincides with the x-axis. This is a clockwise rotation of angle α (Figure 4.4). Considering the right triangle formed by the origin and the point $(6, 2)$, we have that $\cos \alpha = \frac{6}{\sqrt{40}}$ and $\sin \alpha = \frac{2}{\sqrt{40}}$.

Using these values for the sine and cosine, we have the rotation matrix corresponding to a counterclockwise (ccw) rotation of angle α. Replacing α by $-\alpha$ gives the clockwise (cw) rotation.

$$M_{ccw} = \begin{bmatrix} \frac{6}{\sqrt{40}} & \frac{-2}{\sqrt{40}} \\ \frac{2}{\sqrt{40}} & \frac{6}{\sqrt{40}} \end{bmatrix} \quad M_{cw} = \begin{bmatrix} \frac{6}{\sqrt{40}} & \frac{2}{\sqrt{40}} \\ \frac{-2}{\sqrt{40}} & \frac{6}{\sqrt{40}} \end{bmatrix}$$

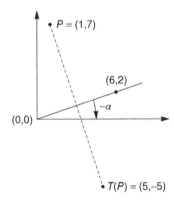

Figure 4.4   Arbitrary reflection

Following our algorithm, we want to apply the clockwise rotation first, then the reflection in the x-axis, and finally the counterclockwise rotation. We need to take care that we have the order of the matrices correct. Our point P must first be multiplied by the clockwise matrix, then the reflection matrix, then the counterclockwise matrix. We multiply $M_{ccw}M_{ref}M_{cw}$ to get a matrix for the composite transformation.

$$T(P) = \begin{bmatrix} \frac{6}{\sqrt{40}} & \frac{-2}{\sqrt{40}} \\ \frac{2}{\sqrt{40}} & \frac{6}{\sqrt{40}} \end{bmatrix} \begin{bmatrix} 1 & 0 \\ 0 & -1 \end{bmatrix} \begin{bmatrix} \frac{6}{\sqrt{40}} & \frac{2}{\sqrt{40}} \\ \frac{-2}{\sqrt{40}} & \frac{6}{\sqrt{40}} \end{bmatrix} P$$

$$= \begin{bmatrix} 0.8 & 0.6 \\ 0.6 & -0.8 \end{bmatrix} P$$

In calculating the composite matrix here, it was important to get the order of the matrix multiplications correct. If we multiplied the three matrices in the reverse order, we get a different composite matrix. Multiplying the point $P = (1, 7)$ by our final matrix gives the reflected point $T(P) = (5, -5)$.   □

In the previous example, we rotated in order to reflect around the x-axis. Clearly, we could have rotated appropriately to reflect around the y-axis instead. In fact, notice that a counterclockwise rotation of $\pi/2$ (radians) followed by a reflection in the x-axis and then followed by a clockwise rotation of $\pi/2$ gives us a reflection in the y-axis. Let M_x and M_y denote the matrices giving reflections in the x- and y-axis, respectively. Then using the correct $\pi/2$ rotation matrices gives

$$M_y = M_{cw}M_xM_{ccw} = \begin{bmatrix} 0 & 1 \\ -1 & 0 \end{bmatrix} \begin{bmatrix} 1 & 0 \\ 0 & -1 \end{bmatrix} \begin{bmatrix} 0 & -1 \\ 1 & 0 \end{bmatrix} = \begin{bmatrix} -1 & 0 \\ 0 & 1 \end{bmatrix}$$

Curiously, this time the multiplication order of the three matrices does not seem to make a difference. Either order gives the same product M_y. Yet, once we consider the geometry, it makes sense because applying either a counterclockwise or clockwise $\pi/2$ rotation first results in the same reflection in the y-axis.

4.2.3 Scaling in Two Dimensions

To change the size of an object (enlarge or reduce), the general idea is to move all the object's points further from (or closer to) the object's center. We can actually pick any point as the center and make all the adjustments relative to this key point, but it is most convenient to start by using the origin as the center. Then, to scale an object by a factor k, we simply multiply all the coordinates by k. A simple matrix does the trick:

$$T(P) = M_kP = \begin{bmatrix} k & 0 \\ 0 & k \end{bmatrix} \begin{bmatrix} x \\ y \end{bmatrix} = \begin{bmatrix} kx \\ ky \end{bmatrix}$$

The transformation $T(P) = M_k P$ is a linear transformation that scales the object by a factor k. It should be fairly clear that scaling by a factor k followed by scaling by a factor k^{-1} brings the object back to its original size. This follows because the product of the two scaling matrices is the identity matrix. If the origin is not at the center of the object, then the scaling transformation may not exactly do what we wish. In particular, if the origin is outside the object, then the scaling moves the entire object either further from or closer to the origin.

Occasionally, it is useful to scale in one direction differently than in the other. To scale in the x direction by k_1 and in the y direction by k_2, the appropriate matrix would be

$$M_k = \begin{bmatrix} k_1 & 0 \\ 0 & k_2 \end{bmatrix}$$

This differential scaling transformation is appropriate for adjusting an image to fit a display screen when the aspect ratios of the image and screen differ.

4.2.4 Matrix Properties

Every 2×2 matrix corresponds to a linear transformation because matrix multiplication preserves vector addition and scalar multiplication.

$$M(\vec{v} + \vec{w}) = M\vec{v} + M\vec{w}$$

$$M(a\vec{v}) = aM\vec{v} \tag{4.4}$$

So any transformation $T(P) = MP$ is a linear transformation and it is useful to look at the matrix and have some idea of how the transformation behaves. The determinant of the matrix M turns out to give some key information about the transformation:

1. $det(M) \neq 0$. In this case, we know the matrix has an inverse M^{-1} and the transformation $T(P) = M^{-1}P$ undoes whatever T does. The transformation is therefore one to one, so each vector has a unique image. The transformation may distort the object, but it does not collapse portions of it. Both the rotation and reflection transformations have matrices with nonzero determinant.

2. $det(M) = 0$. Here we know that the transformation does not have an inverse. In fact, the zero matrix has determinant zero and it sends everything to 0; an entire object will be squashed to a single point. Suppose the upper left entry in M is 1 and all the rest are 0. Then $T(P) = T((x, y)) = (x, 0)$. This squashes everything in the object to the x-axis; it is really a projection onto the x-axis.

3. $det(M) = 1$. From our work with vector geometry, we know that the determinant gives us the area of a parallelogram. If $det(M) = 1$, then the image of the unit square is a parallelogram with area 1. Using some linear algebra and properties of determinants (see Exercises), we can verify that areas are invariant under this transformation. In particular, any triangle is sent to another triangle with the same area.

4. $det(M) < 0$. The reflection matrices have determinants equal to -1. Reflection in the x-axis, for example, takes triangles to other triangles with the same shape and area. However, if we had listed the three vertices of the original triangle in clockwise order, then the vertices in the image triangle will be listed in counterclockwise order. Reflection switches the orientation and the negative determinant is indicative of this switch. In the case of reflection, the absolute value of the determinant is 1, so areas are still preserved.

The determinant is only one of several characteristics of transformation matrices. Much of linear algebra is involved with categorizing matrices and analyzing their properties. For 2×2 matrices, we can write out the general matrix as

$$M = \begin{bmatrix} a & b \\ c & d \end{bmatrix}$$

Then, we could exhaustively consider the various assumptions we could make about the entries a, b, c, d. We will look at one of the many possible assumptions and leave others as exercises.

Example 4.4 (Shear Matrices).   Consider all the matrices where $a = 1, b \neq 0, c = 0, d = 1$. The diagonal elements are both 1 and the lower left element is zero. One example is the matrix

$$M = \begin{bmatrix} 1 & 1 \\ 0 & 1 \end{bmatrix}$$

To visualize what the transformation $T(P) = MP$ does, track what it does to each vertex of the unit square. It fixes $(0,0)$ as do all linear transformations, and it sends $(1,0)$ to itself. However, $(0,1)$ goes to $(1,1)$ and $(1,1)$ goes to $(2,1)$. Keeping in mind that straight lines go to straight lines, the image of the unit square ends up pushed over (Figure 4.5). Such a transformation is called a *shear*.

Once we see how this shear behaves, it is a little easier to see what happens if the diagonal elements in the matrix are 2 instead of 1. Then we have another shear that enlarges the square at the same time it pushes it over again. It is a small step from shears with $c = 0$ to those with $b = 0$.   □

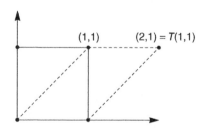

Figure 4.5   2D shear

4.3 THREE DIMENSIONS

If we remain focused on linear transformations, moving from two dimensions to three dimensions requires using 3×3 matrices instead of 2×2 matrices. The approach is the same as we took in two dimensions except that now there are three axes spanning our space of points with the associated three coordinates. Linear transformations are still equivalent to multiplication by matrices, and rotations, reflections, and scalings are still key transformations. We only have to tend to a few details in order to generalize to three dimensions.

4.3.1 Rotations in Three Dimensions

Compared to two dimensions where we rotate around a point, in three dimensions we rotate around an axis. Rotating around a point is not well defined until we pick an axis by selecting a direction (i.e., a vector). The three obvious axes (x, y, and z) corresponding to the vectors $\vec{i}, \vec{j}, \vec{k}$, still are key axes to choose, but there are also axes (through the origin) corresponding to any vector we want.

Rotation around the z-Axis   Rotation around the z-axis means we pick $\vec{k}$ as the vector indicating direction. Vector k points in the direction of increasing z coordinates, so when we rotate, we imagine looking down the z-axis in the direction $-\vec{k}$ toward the origin. From this vantage point, we see the x- and y-axis as they appear in a two-dimensional analysis. Positive rotations are again counterclockwise, and negative rotations are clockwise. If we take a point P with coordinates (x, y, z), then under a rotation around the z-axis, the z coordinate does not change, and the x and y coordinates change just as they did under a two-dimensional rotation (Figure 4.6).

Consequently, for a positive (counterclockwise) rotation through angle θ, we use the following matrix:

$$M_z = \begin{bmatrix} \cos\theta & -\sin\theta & 0 \\ \sin\theta & \cos\theta & 0 \\ 0 & 0 & 1 \end{bmatrix} \tag{4.5}$$

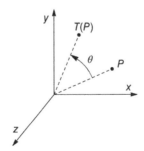

Figure 4.6   Rotation around z-axis

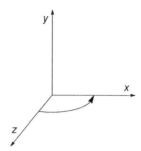

Figure 4.7   Rotation around y-axis

The third row of the matrix with two zeroes and a 1 indicates that the z coordinate remains fixed under the transformation.

Rotation around the y-Axis   Rotation around the y-axis means we pick $\vec{j}$ as the vector indicating direction. Looking down the y-axis, we see the xz plane. If necessary, we can rotate our eye around the y-axis until the z-axis points to the right and the x-axis points up. The situation looks closer to the two-dimensional case except that the z-axis now plays the role of the x-axis and the x-axis plays the role of the y-axis. Recall that under a two-dimensional rotation, the x coordinate of the rotated point becomes $x \cos\theta - y \sin\theta$. This is the result of our trigonometric analysis and is incorporated in the design of the rotation matrix. In our current case, z plays the role of x, and x plays the role of y, so the new z coordinate is $z \cos\theta - x \sin\theta$. Similarly, the new x is $z \sin\theta + x \cos\theta$. With the rotation around the y-axis, the y coordinate does not change, and the second row of our matrix is $0, 1, 0$.

$$M_y = \begin{bmatrix} \cos\theta & 0 & \sin\theta \\ 0 & 1 & 0 \\ -\sin\theta & 0 & \cos\theta \end{bmatrix} \tag{4.6}$$

The second row in this matrix indicates that the y coordinate is fixed, and the second column indicates that the y coordinate is not used in calculating the new x and z coordinates (Figure 4.7).

Rotation around the x-Axis   Looking down the x-axis, we see the yz plane, and we can adjust our eye until the y-axis is pointing to the right and the z-axis is pointing up. Now y plays the role of x in our two-dimensional analysis and z plays the role of x. Making the appropriate adjustments gives the rotation matrix

$$M_x = \begin{bmatrix} 1 & 0 & 0 \\ 0 & \cos\theta & -\sin\theta \\ 0 & \sin\theta & \cos\theta \end{bmatrix} \tag{4.7}$$

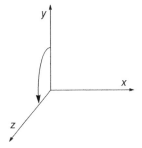

Figure 4.8 Rotation around x-axis

All three rotation matrices M_z, M_y, and M_x have the same determinant, but in this last case it is perhaps easiest to calculate. For M_x, the determinate is one times the determinate of the lower 2×2 corner, which is $\cos^2\theta + \sin^2\theta = 1$. This gels with our intuition because rotations should not change volumes in three dimensions just like they did not change areas in two dimensions (Figure 4.8).

Order of Rotations In two dimensions, two rotations centered at the origin can follow each other giving a composite rotation, for example, of $\alpha + \theta$. If we reverse the order of the transformations, we get a composite rotation of $\theta + \alpha$. Of course, these two composite rotations are exactly the same and the corresponding matrices are identical. This all means that two-dimensional rotation matrices commute.

$$M_\alpha M_\theta = M_\theta M_\alpha$$

This does not mean that all 2×2 matrices commute, but it does mean that, geometrically, rotations around zero do commute. In three dimensions, the situation is not so simple. With rotations around each of the three coordinate axes, it is harder to call on our intuition to predict what a composite rotation will look like. Moreover, these rotations do not commute.

Consider a $\pi/2$ counterclockwise rotation around the z-axis and a $\pi/2$ counterclockwise rotation around the y-axis. Calling the two associated rotation matrices M_z and M_y, we can multiply them in an order, indicating the z rotation followed by the y rotation.

$$M_y M_z = \begin{bmatrix} 0 & 0 & 1 \\ 0 & 1 & 0 \\ -1 & 0 & 0 \end{bmatrix} \begin{bmatrix} 0 & -1 & 0 \\ 1 & 0 & 0 \\ 0 & 0 & 1 \end{bmatrix} = \begin{bmatrix} 0 & 0 & 1 \\ 1 & 0 & 0 \\ 0 & 1 & 0 \end{bmatrix}$$

Just to help our intuition here, follow the point $(1, 0, 0)$. This point sits on the x-axis and is rotated by the $\pi/2$ counterclockwise z rotation to the point $(0, 1, 0)$ on the y-axis. The $\pi/2$ counterclockwise y rotation now fixes the point because it leaves all points on the y-axis alone. Multiplying the point $(1, 0, 0)$ by the product matrix gives $(0, 1, 0)$.

Now multiply the two rotation matrices in the reverse order corresponding to the y rotation followed by the z rotation.

$$M_z M_y = \begin{bmatrix} 0 & -1 & 0 \\ 1 & 0 & 0 \\ 0 & 0 & 1 \end{bmatrix} \begin{bmatrix} 0 & 0 & 1 \\ 0 & 1 & 0 \\ -1 & 0 & 0 \end{bmatrix} = \begin{bmatrix} 0 & -1 & 0 \\ 0 & 0 & 1 \\ -1 & 0 & 0 \end{bmatrix}$$

Our analysis now shows that the y rotation takes the point $(1, 0, 0)$ to $(0, 0, -1)$, and this last point is fixed by the z rotation. Multiplying the point $(1, 0, 0)$ by the product matrix indeed gives $(0, 0, -1)$. These two particular $\pi/2$ counterclockwise rotations give different results depending on the order in which they are applied.

It is not particularly surprising that order makes a difference because we do know that, in general, matrix multiplication is not commutative. However, it is also important to draw the connection between matrix multiplication and the underlying geometry of rotation transformations.

Rotation around an Arbitrary Axis   Rotations around the coordinate axes are really special cases because, when we look down one of these axes, we effectively see the rotation acting in the xy, yz, or xz planes. Then we recall rotations in two dimensions and the appropriate trigonometric addition formulas to produce the associated rotation matrix. If we are interested in a rotation around an arbitrary axis (through the origin), we have to work a little harder. There are two main methods we can take. The first takes advantage of the three rotations around coordinate axes to build a composite transformation that rotates around a given axis. The second, which we will cover later in this chapter, takes a more vector geometry approach that is independent of the coordinate system. Both are useful in designing graphics programs, but the first has the advantage of cementing some of the ideas we have developed so far.

Let the vector $\vec{a}$ represent the arbitrary axis of a rotation. Since we know the correct matrices for rotating around the coordinate axes, a good strategy is to first transform our space so that vector $\vec{a}$ coincides with one of the coordinate axes. The plan is to make this first transformation, then rotate using one of the known rotation matrices, and finally undo the first transformation so $\vec{a}$ is back in its original position. Suppose $\vec{a} = (a_x, a_y, a_z)$ and that $|\vec{a}|^2 = a_x^2 + a_y^2 + a_z^2 = 1$. That is, $\vec{a}$ is a unit vector. Just for illustration, imagine $\vec{a}$ is in the first quadrant as shown in Figure 4.9. Later we will let it point in any direction.

For the first step, refer to Figure 4.9 and notice that we can rotate $\vec{a}$ counterclockwise around the x-axis until it falls into the xz plane where we will call the vector $\vec{b}$. The shadow of $\vec{a}$ in the yz plane is called $\vec{s}$, and it moves onto the (positive) z axis as $\vec{a}$ transforms into $\vec{b}$. Now, a clockwise rotation around y moves $\vec{b}$ onto the z-axis, where we call the result $\vec{c}$. These two rotations together form our first composite transformation that moves $\vec{a}$ to $\vec{c}$. We need the corresponding matrices so we can multiply them together to get the composite transformation.

To determine the angle for the rotation sending $\vec{a}$ to $\vec{b}$, check the coordinates for the shadow $\vec{s}$, which are $(0, a_y, a_z)$. The length of $\vec{s}$ is then $g = \sqrt{a_y^2 + a_z^2}$. The shadow

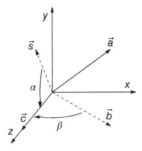

Figure 4.9   Arbitrary rotation

rotates through angle α shown in the figure, and this angle is found by taking the dot product of $\vec{s}$ and the unit vector along the z-axis, $(0, 0, 1)$.

$$\cos \alpha = \frac{\vec{s} \cdot (0, 0, 1)}{|\vec{s}||(0, 0, 1)|} = \frac{a_z}{g}$$

From trigonometry, we have $\sin \alpha = \sqrt{1 - (a_z/g)^2} = a_y/g$. The matrix $M_x(\alpha)$ for this rotation is

$$M_x(\alpha) = \begin{bmatrix} 1 & 0 & 0 \\ 0 & a_z/g & -a_y/g \\ 0 & a_y/g & a_z/g \end{bmatrix}$$

When $\vec{a}$ undergoes this rotation transformation, it ends up as vector $\vec{b}$ in the xz plane. The coordinates for $\vec{b}$ are $(v_x, 0, g)$ because the z coordinate is just the length of the shadow vector $\vec{s}$. The rotation does not change the length of vectors, so $|\vec{a}| = |\vec{b}|$ and $|\vec{b}| = \sqrt{a_x^2 + g^2} = 1$.

Now the task is to rotate clockwise around the y-axis until $\vec{b}$ becomes $\vec{c}$ on the z-axis. This angle is designated as β in the figure, and to find the cosine we again use the dot product.

$$\cos \beta = \frac{\vec{b} \cdot (0, 0, 1)}{|\vec{b}||(0, 0, 1)|} = g$$

To find the sine, we first use the trigonometric identity to get $\sin \beta = \pm\sqrt{1 - g^2} = \pm a_x$. This rotation is clockwise, so the angle is negative and we take $\sin \beta = -a_x$. Now we have the rotation matrix $M_y(\beta)$.

$$M_y(\beta) = \begin{bmatrix} g & 0 & -a_x \\ 0 & 1 & 0 \\ a_x & 0 & g \end{bmatrix}$$

The composite rotation given by $T(P) = M_y(\beta)M_x(\alpha)P$ takes the axis vector $\vec{a}$ to the vector $\vec{c}$ on the z-axis. Now, if we wish to rotate around the axis $\vec{a}$ by θ, we need to rotate around the z-axis by θ. So we call on the matrix $M_z(\theta)$ derived earlier. Finally, to undo a rotation, we just rotate by minus the particular angle. In rotation matrices, this just changes the sign of the sine entries, leaving the cosine entries alone. So we can find $M_x^{-1}(\alpha)$ and $M_y^{-1}(\beta)$ easily.

$$M_x^{-1}(\alpha) = \begin{bmatrix} 1 & 0 & 0 \\ 0 & a_z/g & a_y/g \\ 0 & -a_y/g & a_z/g \end{bmatrix} M_y^{-1}(\beta) = \begin{bmatrix} g & 0 & a_x \\ 0 & 1 & 0 \\ -a_x & 0 & g \end{bmatrix}$$

After this long derivation, we are ready to write down the complete transformation for rotating about the arbitrary axis. The transformation matrix M_{arb} is a product of matrices each of which corresponds to a transformation, and the order in which they are applied goes from right to left.

$$M_{arb} = M_x^{-1}(\alpha)M_y^{-1}(\beta)M_z(\theta)M_y(\beta)M_x(\alpha)$$

If we are going to rotate an object around an arbitrary axis in three dimensions, we first make sure we have a unit vector in the direction of the axis and then multiply all the individual matrices together to get M_{arb}. Then we simply multiply M_{arb} times each of the vertices in the object. Just for reference, we can multiply all five matrices together (using plenty of algebra to simplify) to find the single matrix that rotates around the arbitrary axis. (To compress the expressions, let $c = \cos\theta$ and $s = \sin\theta$.)

$$M_{arb} = \begin{bmatrix} c + (1-c)a_x^2 & (1-c)a_xa_y - sa_z & (1-c)a_xa_z + sa_y \\ (1-c)a_xa_y + sa_z & c + (1-c)a_y^2 & (1-c)a_ya_z - sa_x \\ (1-c)a_xa_z - sa_y & (1-c)a_ya_z + sa_x & c + (1-c)a_z^2 \end{bmatrix} \qquad (4.8)$$

One detail is still left. In our derivation, we were assuming that $\vec{a}$ was pointing to the first quadrant. In other words, the coordinates a_x, a_y, a_z were all positive. Do our calculations still work if the vector points to some other quadrant? The problem comes from the size and direction of the angles θ and β. If they are clockwise instead of counterclockwise or if they are greater than $\pi/2$ rather than less, then the sign of the cosine and sine functions might change.

For the matrix $M_x(\theta)$, the sign of a_x has no effect. Yet, the cosine and sine in the matrix have the same sign as the coordinates a_z and a_y, respectively. A quick check to see where the resulting vector $\vec{a}$ is pointing verifies that the matrix we derived is still correct.

Similarly, when considering the matrix $M_y(\beta)$, the entries equal to g are always positive but the value a_x can be negative. If it is negative, then $\vec{a}$ is pointing toward the negative x-axis and the vector $\vec{b}$ needs to be rotated counterclockwise around the y-axis instead of clockwise. This should change the sign of the sine function, and, indeed, the matrix changes appropriately because a_x is negative. Our derivation, then, is general and does not depend on where $\vec{a}$ points.

4.3.2 Reflections in Three Dimensions

Any plane through the origin can be thought of as a mirror reflecting objects in a scene. If it happens to be the xy plane, for example, then the reflection takes the point (x, y, z) to the point $(x, y, -z)$ and the corresponding matrix that implements the transformation is $M_{ref}(\vec{k})$, where $\vec{k}$ is the unit normal to the xy plane.

$$M_{ref}(\vec{k}) = \begin{bmatrix} 1 & 0 & 0 \\ 0 & 1 & 0 \\ 0 & 0 & -1 \end{bmatrix} \tag{4.9}$$

Matrices with -1 placed appropriately on the diagonal will correspond to reflections in the yz and xz planes as well. Reflection in an arbitrary plane (through the origin) is more interesting, but now that we know how to find arbitrary rotations, arbitrary reflections are easy. Basically, we first transform the space until the normal to the reflection plane is lined up with one of the coordinate axes. Then a reflection in the appropriate coordinate plane followed by the inverse of the first transformation completes the task.

Example 4.5 (Reflection in an Arbitrary Plane). To reflect the point $P = (3, -5, 8)$ in the plane through the origin with normal $(1, 2, 1)$, first normalize to find the unit normal $\vec{n} = \frac{1}{\sqrt{6}}(1, 2, 1)$. We can transform the space to line up $\vec{n}$ with any of the coordinate axes, but we have the matrices that will line it up with the z-axis. Referring to the rotation around an arbitrary axis, the vector $\vec{a}$ is now $\vec{n}$ and $g = \sqrt{a_y^2 + a_z^2} = \sqrt{(4/6) + (1/6)} = \sqrt{5/6}$. The composite matrix that transforms $\vec{n}$ to $\vec{k}$ on the z-axis is

$$M = \begin{bmatrix} \sqrt{5/6} & 0 & -(1/\sqrt{6}) \\ 0 & 1 & 0 \\ 1/\sqrt{6} & 0 & \sqrt{5/6} \end{bmatrix} \begin{bmatrix} 1 & 0 & 0 \\ 0 & 1/\sqrt{5} & -2/\sqrt{5} \\ 0 & 2/\sqrt{5} & 1/\sqrt{5} \end{bmatrix}$$

$$= \begin{bmatrix} \sqrt{5/6} & -2/\sqrt{30} & -1/\sqrt{30} \\ 0 & 1/\sqrt{5} & -2/\sqrt{5} \\ 1/\sqrt{6} & 2/\sqrt{6} & 1/\sqrt{6} \end{bmatrix}$$

By changing the sign of the angles and reversing the order, we can calculate the inverse M^{-1}.

$$M^{-1} = \begin{bmatrix} \sqrt{5/6} & 0 & 1/\sqrt{6} \\ -2/\sqrt{30} & 1/\sqrt{5} & 2/\sqrt{6} \\ -1/\sqrt{30} & -2/\sqrt{5} & 1/\sqrt{6} \end{bmatrix}$$

With these matrices, the arbitrary reflection is then

$$M_{ref}(\vec{n}) = M^{-1} \begin{bmatrix} 1 & 0 & 0 \\ 0 & 1 & 0 \\ 0 & 0 & -1 \end{bmatrix} M = \frac{1}{3} \begin{bmatrix} 2 & -2 & -1 \\ -2 & -1 & -2 \\ -1 & -2 & 2 \end{bmatrix}$$

Multiplying the point P by this matrix gives the reflected point $\frac{1}{3}(8, -17, 23)$. Finally, notice that multiplying the matrix times the vector $\vec{n}$ gives $-\vec{n}$ just as expected.   □

4.3.3 Scaling and Shear in Three Dimensions

With three dimensions, we can scale in the x, y, or z directions. The general scaling transformation has the matrix

$$M_s = \begin{bmatrix} s_x & 0 & 0 \\ 0 & s_y & 0 \\ 0 & 0 & s_z \end{bmatrix} \tag{4.10}$$

The constants (s_x, s_y, s_z) can all be equal, giving us the simple transformation that enlarges or reduces the size of our objects, or the constants can be unequal giving a transformation that distorts the object by stretching or shrinking in some directions differently than in others. Notice that making one of the constants negative introduces a reflection into the mix.

Just as in the two-dimensional case, an additional nonzero entry off the diagonal gives a shear transformation, which can be useful in modeling various objects. For example, the following matrix gives a transformation that pushes the unit cube in the x direction as though it were a stack of cards:

$$M_s = \begin{bmatrix} 1 & 1 & 0 \\ 0 & 1 & 0 \\ 0 & 0 & 1 \end{bmatrix}$$

When multiplied times a point (x, y, z), we get the point $(x + y, y, z)$. The only change is that x becomes $x + y$, so the x coordinates are increased for positive values of y. If the unit cube is sitting on the xz plane, the top will be pushed over and the bottom will stay put (Figure 4.10).

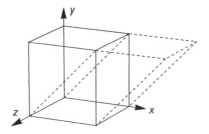

Figure 4.10   3D shear

Single nonzero entries in any of the off-diagonal positions produce shear-like transformations. The exercises ask for further details on the effects of these types of transformations.

4.4   AFFINE TRANSFORMATIONS

There is one glaring omission among all the transformations we have visited so far. We have not considered the simple translation that just moves all points in the same direction. A translation just adds a vector $\vec{Q} = (h, k)$ to every point: $T(P) = P + \vec{Q}$. This is certainly a useful, in fact essential, transformation for graphics work; objects are moved around all the time. Unfortunately, it is not technically a linear transformation because it does not preserve vector addition and scalar multiplication. (In particular, it does not fix the origin and $T(aP)$ is not, in general, equal to $aT(P)$ for constant a.) This does not cripple its use in manipulating graphics objects because it certainly still preserves lines. Yet, since translation is not a linear transformation, it apparently cannot be represented by standard matrix multiplication, putting it outside the system we have developed for all the other linear transformations.

Nevertheless, the essential nature of translations means we immediately add them to our transformation toolbox and define a larger class of transformations, called *affine transformations*, which are combinations of linear transformations and translations.

Definition 4.1 (Affine Transformation).   *For a square matrix M and a fixed vector $\vec{Q}$, an affine transformation is of the form $T(P) = MP + \vec{Q}$.*

This definition works in both two and three dimensions just by adjusting the matrix size (2×2 or 3×3) as well as the size of the vectors and points (2×1 or 3×1). If the matrix M has an inverse, then the affine transformation T is a one-to-one function and has inverse T^{-1}.

$$T^{-1}(P) = M^{-1}(P - \vec{Q}) \tag{4.11}$$

Affine transformations form a class that contains linear transformations and still captures the property that lines get sent to lines. Thinking of a general line

$P = P_0 + t\vec{v}$, the affine transformation sends it to

$$T(P) = T(P_0 + t\vec{v}) = M(P_0 + t\vec{v}) + \vec{Q}$$
$$= (MP_0 + \vec{Q}) + tM\vec{v}$$
$$= P_1 + t\vec{w}$$

Points on the original line are sent to points on a new line. In fact, if we restrict t (e.g., take $t \in ([0, 1])$, we see that line segments are sent to line segments.

One more important property of these transformations is that, along with preserving straight lines, they also preserve parallel lines. If we have two parallel lines, then the direction vectors for the lines are parallel and hence multiples of each other, say $\vec{v}$ and $a\vec{v}$. Hence the two lines are $P = P_0 + t\vec{v}$ and $P = P_1 + ta\vec{v}$. The affine transformation $T(P) = MP + \vec{Q}$ transforms the lines as follows:

$$T(P_0 + t\vec{v}) = M(P_0 + t\vec{v}) + \vec{Q} = (MP_0 + \vec{Q}) + t(M\vec{v})$$
$$T(P_1 + ta\vec{v}) = M(P_1 + ta\vec{v}) + \vec{Q} = (MP_1 + \vec{Q}) + ta(M\vec{v})$$

These transformed lines are parallel because their direction vectors are multiples of each other.

For computer graphics, perhaps the most important property of affine transformations is the ability to send triangles to triangles in two dimensions and tetrahedrons (pyramids with four vertices) to tetrahedrons in three dimensions. More specifically, we can single out two triangles and find an affine transformation that sends one to the other. (We are interested here in nondegenerate triangles and tetrahedrons; the triangle vertices should not be collinear.)

Theorem 4.1 *In two dimensions, there is a unique affine transformation that sends a given triangle to another specified triangle and maintains the order of their vertices. Similarly, in three dimensions, any given tetrahedron can be sent to any other tetrahedron using an affine transform.*

Example 4.6 (Transforming a Triangle to a Specified Triangle). The three vertices $A = (2, 5)$, $B = (4, -1)$, and $C = (5, 3)$ specify a triangle with the vertices in counterclockwise order. A second triangle has the vertices $D = (-8, 2)$, $E = (-5, -3)$, and $F = (1, 6)$, also in counterclockwise order. We would like an affine transformation sending $\triangle ABC$ to $\triangle DEF$. To do this, our plan will be to consider a third simpler triangle with vertices $(0, 0)$, $(1, 0)$, and $(0, 1)$. Call this the base triangle.

The complete plan is to find affine transformations T_1 and T_2 that send the base triangle to $\triangle ABC$ and $\triangle DEF$, respectively. Assuming T^{-1} exists, the affine transformation we seek is then the composition $T_2 T_1^{-1}$.

Translating by the vector $\vec{Q}_1 = (-2, -5)$ moves triangle $\triangle ABC$ to a triangle $\triangle A'B'C'$ with vertices $A' = (0, 0)$, $B' = (2, -6)$, and $C' = (3, -2)$. The trick is then to form a (2×2) matrix M by using the vertices B' and C' as columns. Multiplication by M gives us a transformation that moves the base triangle to $\triangle A'B'C'$. Translating back by $-\vec{Q}_1 = (2, 5)$ then gives us the transformation T_1.

$$T_1(P) = MP + (-\vec{Q}_1) = \begin{bmatrix} 2 & 3 \\ -6 & -2 \end{bmatrix} P + \begin{bmatrix} 2 \\ 5 \end{bmatrix}$$

Notice that $T_1((0,0)) = A$, $T_1((1,0)) = B$, and $T_1((0,1)) = C$.

Since the vertices of triangle $\triangle ABC$ are not collinear, the vectors forming the columns of M are not multiples of each other. The determinant of M is therefore nonzero, and M^{-1} exists as does T_1^{-1}. This inverse transformation maps $\triangle ABC$ to the base triangle. More explicitly

$$T_1^{-1}(P) = M^{-1}\left(P - \begin{bmatrix} 2 \\ 5 \end{bmatrix}\right) = \frac{1}{14}\begin{bmatrix} -2 & -3 \\ 6 & 2 \end{bmatrix} P - \frac{1}{14}\begin{bmatrix} -19 \\ 22 \end{bmatrix}$$

T_2 is constructed similar to T_1 using the translation vector $\vec{Q}_2 = (8, -2)$.

$$T_2(P) = MP + (-\vec{Q}_2) = \begin{bmatrix} 3 & 9 \\ -5 & 4 \end{bmatrix} P + \begin{bmatrix} -8 \\ 2 \end{bmatrix}$$

The final transformation is a composition.

$$T(P) = T_2(T_1^{-1}(P)) = \begin{bmatrix} 3 & 9 \\ -5 & 4 \end{bmatrix} (T_1^{-1}(P)) + \begin{bmatrix} -8 \\ 2 \end{bmatrix}$$

$$= \frac{1}{14}\begin{bmatrix} 3 & 9 \\ -5 & 4 \end{bmatrix}\begin{bmatrix} -2 & -3 \\ 6 & 2 \end{bmatrix} P - \frac{1}{14}\begin{bmatrix} 3 & 9 \\ -5 & 4 \end{bmatrix}\begin{bmatrix} -19 \\ 22 \end{bmatrix} + \begin{bmatrix} -8 \\ 2 \end{bmatrix}$$

$$\approx \begin{bmatrix} 3.43 & 0.64 \\ 2.43 & 1.64 \end{bmatrix} P + \begin{bmatrix} -18.07 \\ -11.07 \end{bmatrix}$$

We find that $T(A) = D$, $T(B) = E$, and $T(C) = F$, which keeps the counterclockwise order. □

4.4.1   Transforming Homogeneous Coordinates

The fact that translations are different from rotations, reflections, and scalings is conceptually awkward. It can also give the graphics programmer pause because it appears that translations are not easily included in a general transformation method. It would be nice if all transformations could be unified in one approach, and once again, homogeneous coordinates come to the rescue.

Start with the two-dimensional case, and first notice again that there is no appropriate way to use 2×2 matrices to perform a two-dimensional translation. However, shifting to homogeneous coordinates means we will use three coordinates (x, y, w) for each point, converting, when necessary, to the Cartesian representation $(x/w, y/w)$. Corresponding to the three homogeneous coordinates, the transformation matrices are now 3×3 matrices. In fact, translation is represented by an appropriate choice of these 3×3 matrices.

$$\text{Translation: } T(P) = \begin{bmatrix} 1 & 0 & h \\ 0 & 1 & k \\ 0 & 0 & 1 \end{bmatrix} \begin{bmatrix} x \\ y \\ w \end{bmatrix} = \begin{bmatrix} x + hw \\ y + kw \\ w \end{bmatrix} \tag{4.12}$$

The resulting point $(x + hw, y + kw, w)$ has Cartesian coordinates $((x/w) + h, (y/w) + k)$, which is just the original point translated by the vector (h, k). In the event we chose the homogeneous coordinates $(x, y, 1)$ for the original point $(w = 1)$, then the result $(x + h, y + k, 1)$ is immediately recognizable as a translation.

We have not lost anything by moving up to homogeneous coordinates (and 3×3 matrices) because all of our 2×2 matrices conveniently fit in the upper left corner of our larger matrices. For example, the rotation transformation in two dimensions can be expressed as the following matrix using homogeneous coordinates:

$$\text{Rotation: } T(P) = \begin{bmatrix} \cos\theta & -\sin\theta & 0 \\ \sin\theta & \cos\theta & 0 \\ 0 & 0 & 1 \end{bmatrix} \begin{bmatrix} x \\ y \\ w \end{bmatrix} = \begin{bmatrix} x\cos\theta - y\sin\theta \\ x\sin\theta + y\cos\theta \\ w \end{bmatrix} \tag{4.13}$$

A rotation followed by a translation is represented by the product of a translation matrix times a rotation matrix:

$$\begin{bmatrix} 1 & 0 & h \\ 0 & 1 & k \\ 0 & 0 & 1 \end{bmatrix} \begin{bmatrix} \cos\theta & -\sin\theta & 0 \\ \sin\theta & \cos\theta & 0 \\ 0 & 0 & 1 \end{bmatrix} = \begin{bmatrix} \cos\theta & -\sin\theta & h \\ \sin\theta & \cos\theta & k \\ 0 & 0 & 1 \end{bmatrix}$$

Notice that the order makes a difference here; a translation followed by a rotation gives a different product matrix.

We are in a position now to expand the use of our transformations. Previously, in two dimensions we rotated only around the origin. It is much more practically useful to rotate around an arbitrary point like the center of an object.

Example 4.7 (Rotating Around an Arbitrary Point in Two Dimensions). A triangle has vertices $A = (3, 2)$, $B = (4, 7)$, and $C = (6, 1)$. To rotate it $25°$ counterclockwise around vertex A, we first translate it so that vertex A is moved to the origin. Then we rotate around the origin and finally undo the original translation by translating back. The first translation vector should be $\vec{Q} = (-3, -2)$, and when we translate back we use $-\vec{Q} = (3, 2)$. If we let T_t be the translation and T_r be the rotation, our plan is to build the composite transformation $T_t^{-1} T_r T_t$.

$$T_t^{-1} T_r T_t = \begin{bmatrix} 1 & 0 & 3 \\ 0 & 1 & 2 \\ 0 & 0 & 1 \end{bmatrix} \begin{bmatrix} 0.91 & -0.42 & 0 \\ 0.42 & 0.91 & 0 \\ 0 & 0 & 1 \end{bmatrix} \begin{bmatrix} 1 & 0 & -3 \\ 0 & 1 & -2 \\ 0 & 0 & 1 \end{bmatrix}$$

$$= \begin{bmatrix} 0.91 & -0.42 & 1.11 \\ 0.42 & 0.91 & -1.08 \\ 0 & 0 & 1 \end{bmatrix}$$

Taking $(3, 2, 1)$, $(4, 7, 1)$, and $(6, 1, 1)$ as the homogeneous coordinates for the vertices, we multiply by the transformation matrix to get $(3, 2, 1)$, $(1.81, 6.97, 1)$, and $(6.15, 2.35, 1)$. These form the vertices for the rotated triangle. The key in this example was to position the center of rotation at the origin by applying the correct translation. Then a rotation is easy to apply, and we end by moving the center of rotation back to its original position. □

In designing reflection matrices in two dimensions, we took lines through the origin, but now we can take any line and first translate it so it goes through the origin, then reflect, and finally translate back. The same holds for scaling transformations; we can scale around the center of an object or around any other appropriate point.

There is nothing sacred here about two dimensions. We can use homogeneous coordinates in three dimensions as well, and build 4×4 matrices to incorporate three-dimensional translations. The nice theoretical breakthrough is that all our affine transformations are multiplications by matrices and we can therefore easily compose many transformations together. When it comes to designing code, homogeneous coordinates give us a unifying principle that helps incorporate more general methods to simplify design. It is not always the case, however, that this leads to the optimal efficiency.

4.4.2 Perspective Transformations

Near the end of the graphics pipeline, three-dimensional scenes have to finally be converted to two dimensions in order to be displayed on the screen. The way they are projected determines how realistic they will look. This is not unlike the problem facing Renaissance painters, as some trends in art led to more and more realism. Painters gradually realized that portraying distant and near objects in the same scene required adjusting their size in a rather mathematical way. Their task was actually a little harder than ours is today given that we have considerable computational power. Painters needed a constructive way of projecting a scene onto the canvas that did not require much algebraic computation and they succeeded with geometric algorithms introduced by Brunelleschi, Alberti, and Piero Della Francesca, to name a few. It was all based on a geometric view of vision that had been evolving over the centuries. In this view, light is composed of rays traveling in straight lines, so the process of putting a scene onto a canvas or a computer screen is analogous to physically tracing straight lines as we look at the scene as though the canvas was a window.

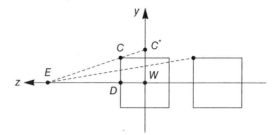

Figure 4.11   Perspective

In Figure 4.11, we have a side view of the situation with our eye positioned at point E, the window centered at point W, and two equal sized cubes in the scene one further away than the other. Point C is one vertex on the nearer cube. The straight line from C to E represents light traveling from the cube to make an impression on the retina of the eye. The point C^* is on the window (or canvas) and is exactly where we see the cube vertex. Actually, we now have a simple algorithm to determine where any point in the scene appears on the window. Just draw a straight line from the point in the scene to the eye at point E and determine the intersection with the window. This technique was generally impractical for Renaissance painters, although there were various attempts to build helpful apparatuses. There are just too many points in the scene to laboriously transfer to the window. With a computer, however, we simply implement an appropriate transformation.

As we transfer points from the scene to the window, notice that the front edge of the near cube gets transferred to a line segment on the window. Similarly, the front edge of the distant cube gets transferred, but the line segment will be smaller than for the first cube. This is the result of what we call a *perspective transformation*. Distant line segments are smaller than nearer line segments. Figure 4.11 shows an ideal situation where the line EW is perpendicular to the window. Therefore, triangle $\triangle EWC^*$ is a right triangle. Pick the point D so that $\triangle EDC$ is also a right triangle. In fact it is similar to the first triangle and consequently

$$\frac{CD}{C^*W} = \frac{ED}{EW} \implies C^*W = \frac{CD \cdot EW}{ED}$$

This helps us position C^* in the window because we know how far it is from the window's center. Yet we need an explicit transformation for converting coordinates for C into coordinates for C^*. To do this, we need to agree on the orientation of the coordinate system. We can make any arbitrary set up work, but to make things easy to start with, position the three dimensional coordinate system so that the origin coincides with W. Further, we often position the eye point E on the positive z-axis looking toward the origin. So the coordinates of E are $(0, 0, e)$. Orient the axes so that the x-axis is coming out of the figure and the y-axis is pointing up. Take the coordinates of C to be (x, y, z).

Distances in the figure now translate as follows: $EW = e, CD = y, ED = e - z$. Finally, we are trying to specify the point C^* on the screen, and the distance C^*W is actually the screen's y coordinate for C^*, so we call it y_s.

$$y_s = \frac{y \cdot e}{e - z} = \frac{y}{1 - \frac{z}{e}}$$

If we reoriented the coordinate system so that the x-axis was pointing up in the figure, then the same analysis would give the screen x coordinate for C^*.

$$x_s = \frac{x}{1 - \frac{z}{e}}$$

The perspective transformation simply divides the original x and y coordinates by the factor $(1 - \frac{z}{e})$. If $z = 0$, then C is already on the screen and the transformation leaves the coordinates alone. If C is on the other side of the screen, the transformation still works, because now $z < 0$ and $ED = e - z$ just as before. The triangles are still similar and we get exactly the same formulas for the screen coordinates.

On the surface, the perspective transformation does not look like it can be implemented by matrix multiplication but, again, considering homogeneous coordinates is the way to go.

$$T(P) = MP = \begin{bmatrix} 1 & 0 & 0 & 0 \\ 0 & 1 & 0 & 0 \\ 0 & 0 & 1 & 0 \\ 0 & 0 & -\frac{1}{e} & 1 \end{bmatrix} \begin{bmatrix} x \\ y \\ z \\ 1 \end{bmatrix} = \begin{bmatrix} x \\ y \\ z \\ 1 - \frac{z}{e} \end{bmatrix} \qquad (4.14)$$

T is a perspective transformation and the transformed point has Cartesian coordinates $(x/(1 - \frac{z}{e}), y/(1 - \frac{z}{e}), z/(1 - \frac{z}{e}))$. Since the screen is perpendicular to the line of sight, we can simply disregard the z coordinate of the transformed point (projecting onto the xy plane) to get the appropriate screen coordinates (Figure 4.12).

Putting the perspective transformation into a matrix keeps it in the same form as all our other transformations. However, the perspective transformation is a little different inasmuch as we really are transforming from three dimensions to two dimensions. Consequently, it is rare that we want to apply another three-dimensional transformation after the perspective transformation. Theoretically, the perspective

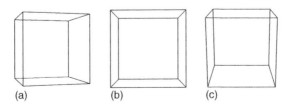

(a)   (b)   (c)

Figure 4.12   (a–c) Cube views in perspective

transformation is a transformation from a projective space to itself, but practically in graphics work its key role is to move three-dimensional scenes to the two-dimensional screen.

4.4.3 Transforming Normals

As an object is repositioned via a rotation or other transformation, normals to the object's faces (or edges in two dimensions) also change. Since normals are key in many graphics calculations including viewing positions and lighting determinations, it often makes sense to transform the normals with the object rather than recalculating normals (using the cross product) each time the object is moved. The question then is whether the normals move in the same way as the object itself.

Picture a cube in three dimensions with normal vectors perpendicular to each face. Certainly, a rigid motion like rotation or translation moves the normals just like it moves the cube. If we apply the rigid transformation to the cube, we can apply it to each normal as well. However, if the transformation is a shear transformation, for example, and pushes the cube over a little, then the normals on the slanted faces do not transform the same way as the cube itself.

Let $\vec{n}$ be a normal to a face, and let $\vec{v} = (P_1 - P_0)$ be a vector between two points on the face. Then $\vec{n} \cdot \vec{v} = 0$ because $\vec{n}$ is perpendicular to any vector on the face. Writing the dot product as a matrix multiplication gives

$$\vec{n} \cdot \vec{v} = \vec{n}^T \vec{v} = \begin{bmatrix} n_1 & n_2 & n_3 \end{bmatrix} \begin{bmatrix} v_1 \\ v_2 \\ v_3 \end{bmatrix} = 0$$

We use the transpose of the normal vector $(\vec{n}^T)$ to make the multiplication possible.

If we transform the object vertices through multiplication by M, then vector $\vec{v}$ is transformed into $M\vec{v}$. To find the transformation matrix L that properly transforms the normal vector $\vec{n}$, we need

$$L\vec{n} \cdot M\vec{v} = 0$$

That is, the transformed normal must be perpendicular to the transformed face vector. Again, write the dot product as a matrix multiplication and use the algebra of transposes.

$$(L\vec{n})^T M\vec{v} = \vec{n}^T L^T M\vec{v} = 0 \tag{4.15}$$

One choice for L makes this equation true: $L = (M^{-1})^T$.

$$(L\vec{n})^T M\vec{v} = ((M^{-1})^T \vec{n})^T M\vec{v} = \vec{n}^T (M^{-1} M)\vec{v} = \vec{n}^T \vec{v} = 0$$

Equation 4.15 must be true for any vector $M\vec{v}$ in the plane of the transformed face. There is only one normal to a plane (up to multiples), so the choice we found for L

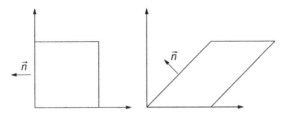

Figure 4.13   Shear with normals

must be the correct normal. Consequently, $L = (M^{-1})^T$ is the correct transformation matrix.

When does the same transformation matrix work on both the vertices and the normals? For that to be true, $L = M$ and, therefore, $M = (M^{-1})^T$. This is the definition of an *orthogonal* matrix. The columns of M are unit vectors that are perpendicular to each other. Rotation matrices are orthogonal matrices and, since they are rigid motions, the normals transform just like the vertices.

Example 4.8 (Transforming Normal Vectors).   An example in two dimensions makes it visually clear how the normals change (Figure 4.13). Imagine that we transform a unit square $((0,0), (1,0), (1,1), (0,1))$ in two dimensions with a shear transformation. The shear matrix is

$$M = \begin{bmatrix} 1 & 2 \\ 0 & 1 \end{bmatrix}$$

Then the appropriate matrix for transforming the normal is

$$(M^{-1})^T = \begin{bmatrix} 1 & -2 \\ 0 & 1 \end{bmatrix}^T = \begin{bmatrix} 1 & 0 \\ -2 & 1 \end{bmatrix}$$

The normal (pointing out of the square) to the left edge of the original square is $(-1,0)$. Compare the transformed normal under the shear transformation and under the correct transformation.

$$\begin{bmatrix} 1 & 2 \\ 0 & 1 \end{bmatrix} \begin{bmatrix} -1 \\ 0 \end{bmatrix} = \begin{bmatrix} -1 \\ 0 \end{bmatrix} \text{ and } \begin{bmatrix} 1 & 0 \\ -2 & 1 \end{bmatrix} \begin{bmatrix} -1 \\ 0 \end{bmatrix} = \begin{bmatrix} -1 \\ 2 \end{bmatrix}$$

The second transformed normal is correct because the square is pushed over by the shear transformation.   □

4.4.4   Summary

A large part of putting a graphics scene together is tied to applying the correct transformations. Our study has touched on several key ideas and attributes that should be enumerated once more.

1. Linear transformations together with translations form the class of affine transformations. Moreover, if we do include homogeneous coordinates, we can represent transformations in this class by matrix multiplication. Affine transformations preserve straight lines and parallel lines.

2. Some affine transformations, $T(P) = MP + \vec{Q}$, have inverses. We can determine this by checking the determinant of M. Nonzero determinant means the inverse exits and then $T^{-1}(R) = M^{-1}(R - \vec{Q})$.

3. In general, the order in which we apply affine transformations is critical. Since matrix multiplication is not commutative, the effect of transformations applied in one order can differ from the effect when applied in another order. It is true that some transformations do commute, but generally order matters.

4. Perspective projections are really transformations of projective space, but in practice we use them to project three-dimensional objects into two dimensions. They are not affine transformations because they do not preserve all parallel lines. In fact, the projection of a cube will turn at least some of the parallel edges into nonparallel lines.

5. Homogeneous coordinates lead to 4×4 matrices for three-dimensional transformations and unify the way they are represented. Several graphics systems (e.g., JAVA, OpenGL) assume this matrix representation and often automatically generate appropriate matrices for the standard transformations. Both translation and perspective projection can be represented with these matrices. Representing all transforms as matrices of a given size brings uniformity to the code, but is not always efficient. If all we are going to do is translate, for example, a simpler routine that adds to each coordinate is more efficient than full-blown matrix multiplication.

6. As we move further down the graphics pipeline, it will be more apparent that some transformations are used to construct the scene and some are used to position the camera in the scene. We might refer to transformations in the first case as *modeling* transformations and those in the second case as *viewing* transformations. In general, a transformation is a transformation, but cataloging them by use can help in understanding what it is we are actually transforming.

7. We have concentrated on transformations that preserve straight lines thinking that most tasks in graphics do not distort lines. However, especially when modeling, there may be a need to transform flat surfaces into curved ones, for example. There are clearly a lot of other types of transformations in the world that can be of use in the graphics setting.

4.5 COMPLEMENTS AND DETAILS

As we developed the various transformations we have seen so far, we always began by establishing a Cartesian coordinate system. Our analytical approach relied on considering the x, y, and z coordinates somewhat separately. Rotation around an arbitrary axis involved performing rotations around each of the three coordinate axes in turn.

The transformation matrices we finally constructed assumed that we would be multiplying times a coordinate vector with x, y, and z coordinates (or homogeneous coordinates).

All of this is fine, especially since we eventually have to convert our images to the two-dimensional Cartesian coordinates on the computer screen. However, it does have a tendency to constrain our modeling efforts when we are constantly thinking in terms of a coordinate system with perpendicular axes. The more we can free ourselves from a particular coordinate system, the more we can use whatever representation seems most efficient for a particular object and scene. In that vein, it is worthwhile to revisit a few transformations with the goal of representing them in ways that do not rely on a particular coordinate system.

It is not entirely clear how we can do this because it seems as though the Cartesian coordinate system is embedded in most of our work. Yet, when we think of the dot product, for example, we may recall that $\vec{A} \cdot \vec{B} = a_x b_x + a_y b_y + a_z b_z$ or, equivalently, $\vec{A} \cdot \vec{B} = |A||B| \cos \theta$. The first identity relies on the Cartesian coordinates and the second does not. Thinking of the dot product as proportional to the cosine of the angle between vectors gives us a more geometric description of the operation and is more independent of any particular coordinate system. With this sort of idea in mind, we revisit some transformations trying to represent them as geometrically as possible. In each case, to finally apply the transformation, we have to convert the vector expression to a coordinate-based matrix.

4.5.1 Vector Approach to Reflection in an Arbitrary Plane

Previously we developed an arbitrary reflection in a plane through the origin by applying rotations until the reflection plane coincided with one of the coordinate planes. Then we reflected a point or vector in the coordinate plane by adjusting the appropriate coordinates (replacing z with $-z$, for example). Finally, we applied the inverse of the rotations to restore the original orientation of the reflection plane. If we want to reflect in a plane that does not go through the origin, an initial translation can remedy the situation by moving any given point on the plane to the origin. After the reflection, we apply the inverse translation to restore the plane.

This time, let $\vec{n}$ be a unit normal to the arbitrary reflection plane, and let P_0 be a point on this plane. The task is to reflect some point P in the plane. If we set $\vec{v} = P - P_0$, then $\vec{v}$ is a vector that we could reflect in the plane. To find the reflection of P, we simply add the reflection of $\vec{v}$ to P_0 (Figure 4.14).

First we decompose $\vec{v}$ into the sum of two vectors, one of them parallel to $\vec{n}$ and the other perpendicular. That is, $\vec{v} = \vec{v}_{\parallel} + \vec{v}_{\perp}$. Now, the reflection transformation T_{ref} reverses the parallel component of $\vec{v}$, while it leaves the perpendicular component untouched.

$$T_{ref}(\vec{v}) = T_{ref}(\vec{v}_{\parallel} + \vec{v}_{\perp}) = T_{ref}(\vec{v}_{\parallel}) + T_{ref}(\vec{v}_{\perp}) = -\vec{v}_{\parallel} + \vec{v}_{\perp}$$

To calculate the parallel component, we look at the right triangle formed by the normal $\vec{n}$ and the vector $\vec{v}$. If the angle between the two vectors is θ, then the length

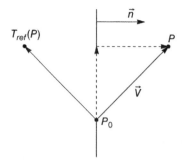

Figure 4.14   Parallel and perpendicular

of the component in the direction of $\vec{n}$ is $|\vec{v}| \cos \theta$. Since $\vec{n}$ is a unit normal, the component length is just $\vec{v} \cdot \vec{n}$. The vector $(\vec{v} \cdot \vec{n})\vec{n}$ is parallel to the normal, and therefore the perpendicular component is the difference between $\vec{v}$ and the parallel component.

$$\vec{v}_{\parallel} = (\vec{v} \cdot \vec{n})\vec{n}$$
$$\vec{v}_{\perp} = \vec{v} - (\vec{v} \cdot \vec{n})\vec{n}$$

Now we have a coordinate-free representation of the reflection transform.

$$T_{ref}(\vec{v}) = -\vec{v}_{\parallel} + \vec{v}_{\perp} = \vec{v} - 2(\vec{v} \cdot \vec{n})\vec{n} \tag{4.16}$$

The advantage of this representation is that it gives an algorithm for finding the reflection using vector operations rather than Cartesian coordinates. Of course, once we settle on a coordinate system, we can continue from here to actually get a transformation matrix using coordinates. The key idea is to look at the vector $(\vec{v} \cdot \vec{n})\vec{n}$ and write it as $M\vec{v}$ where M is some matrix. By keeping in mind what M must do, we can deduce its contents. In fact, $M = \vec{n}\vec{n}^T$, where $\vec{n}^T$ is the transpose of $\vec{n}$ and is therefore a (1×3) row matrix; the product is a 3×3 matrix.

Suppose the coordinates of $\vec{n}$ are (n_x, n_y, n_z).

$$M = \begin{bmatrix} n_x \\ n_y \\ n_z \end{bmatrix} \begin{bmatrix} n_x & n_y & n_z \end{bmatrix} = \begin{bmatrix} n_x^2 & n_x n_y & n_x n_z \\ n_y n_x & n_y^2 & n_y n_z \\ n_z n_x & n_z n_y & n_z^2 \end{bmatrix}$$

If you need a name for the matrix M, it is often written as $\vec{n} \otimes \vec{n}$ and is an example of a *tensor product*. Now, we can rewrite the transformation using I to indicate the identity matrix.

$$T_{ref}(\vec{v}) = \vec{v} - 2(\vec{v} \cdot \vec{n})\vec{n} = I\vec{v} - 2M\vec{v} = (I - 2M)\vec{v} \tag{4.17}$$

This derivation gives us the correct transformation matrix a little more quickly than our previous effort to rotate appropriately around each coordinate axis. Notice that, if $\vec{n} = (0, 1, 0)$, then we are reflecting in the xz plane and consequently we should replace y with $-y$. Calculating the matrix $(I - 2M)$ gives

$$I - 2M = \begin{bmatrix} 1 - 2n_x^2 & -2n_x n_y & -2n_x n_z \\ -2n_y n_x & 1 - 2n_y^2 & -2n_y n_z \\ -2n_z n_x & 2n_z n_y & 1 - 2n_z^2 \end{bmatrix} = \begin{bmatrix} 1 & 0 & 0 \\ 0 & -1 & 0 \\ 0 & 0 & 1 \end{bmatrix}$$

This is precisely the matrix that replaces y by $-y$.

Example 4.9 (Vector Approach to Reflection in an Arbitrary Plane). Referring back to Example 4.5, there we reflected the point $P = (3, -5, 8)$ in the plane through the origin with unit normal $\vec{n} = \frac{1}{\sqrt{6}}(1, 2, 1)$. We are assuming the origin is on the reflection plane, so in our new representation $\vec{v} = P - (0, 0, 0) = (3, -5, 8)$, and we find the correct matrix by calculating $(I - 2M)$

$$I - 2M = \begin{bmatrix} 1 & 0 & 0 \\ 0 & 1 & 0 \\ 0 & 0 & 1 \end{bmatrix} - 2 \cdot \frac{1}{6} \cdot \begin{bmatrix} 1 & 2 & 1 \\ 2 & 4 & 2 \\ 1 & 2 & 1 \end{bmatrix}$$

$$= \frac{1}{6} \begin{bmatrix} 4 & -4 & -2 \\ -4 & -2 & -4 \\ -2 & -4 & 4 \end{bmatrix}$$

Multiplying this matrix times $\vec{v}$ gives the reflected vector $\frac{1}{3}(8, -17, 23)$ and consequently this is the reflected point, the same reflection as in Example 4.5. We have verified that our new representation for an arbitrary reflection coincides with our earlier version. Notice that, if the reflection plane did not go through the origin, we would have replaced the origin in our calculations with a point on the plane. Forming the vector $\vec{v}$ really frees us from having to assume that the reflection plane goes through the origin. □

4.5.2 Vector Approach to Arbitrary Rotations

To accomplish rotation around an arbitrary axis in three dimensions, we carefully rotated around each of the coordinate axes in turn. Now we want to solve the problem with a vector-based approach rather than a coordinate-based approach. Suppose $\vec{a}$ is a unit vector along the arbitrary axis and that we wish to rotate the point P counterclockwise around the axis through angle θ. With a point P_0 on the axis, we can form vector $\vec{w} = P - P_0$. The problem then is to rotate $\vec{w}$ around $\vec{a}$ (Figure 4.15).

The key is to decompose $\vec{w}$ as the sum of a vector parallel to $\vec{a}$ and one perpendicular to $\vec{a}$. So we want $\vec{w} = \vec{w}_{\parallel} + \vec{w}_{\perp}$. The parallel vector $\vec{w}_{\parallel}$ is the projection of

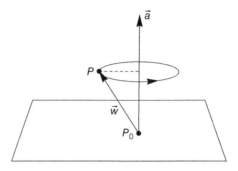

Figure 4.15   Vector rotation

$\vec{w}$ onto $\vec{a}$, and the perpendicular component $\vec{w}_\perp$ is the difference between $\vec{w}$ and the parallel component.

$$\vec{w}_\parallel = (\vec{a} \cdot \vec{w})\vec{a}$$

$$\vec{w}_\perp = \vec{w} - (\vec{a} \cdot \vec{w})\vec{a}$$

Under the rotation, the parallel component $\vec{w}_\parallel$ does not change. The perpendicular component $\vec{w}_\perp$ does rotate in a plane perpendicular to the axis $\vec{a}$. This plane is determined by $\vec{w}_\perp$ and the vector $\vec{a} \times \vec{w}_\perp$ which is perpendicular to both $\vec{a}$ and $\vec{w}_\perp$. The rotated component, which we call $\vec{w}_r$, can be expressed as a linear combination of both $\vec{w}_\perp$ and $\vec{a} \times \vec{w}_\perp$ because these two vectors span the plane; they form a coordinate system in the plane. Keeping in mind the length of the vectors, a rotation of θ gives

$$\vec{w}_r = (\vec{w} - (\vec{a} \cdot \vec{w})\vec{a}) \cos \theta + (\vec{a} \times \vec{w}_\perp) \sin \theta$$

Vector algebra verifies that $\vec{a} \times \vec{w}_\perp = \vec{a} \times \vec{w}$ because the cross products have the same direction and the same length. Making this substitution and then adding the rotated component to the parallel component defines the complete transformation.

$$T_{rot}(\vec{w}) = \vec{w}_r + \vec{w}_\parallel$$
$$= (\vec{w} - (\vec{a} \cdot \vec{w})\vec{a}) \cos \theta + (\vec{a} \times \vec{w}) \sin \theta + (\vec{a} \cdot \vec{w})\vec{a} \qquad (4.18)$$

This coordinate-free representation gives us a vector-geometric algorithm for finding the rotation. To find the associated (but coordinate-based) matrix, we need to draw on two identities.

$$(\vec{a} \cdot \vec{w})\vec{a} = (\vec{a} \otimes \vec{a})\vec{w} = \begin{bmatrix} a_x^2 & a_x a_y & a_x a_z \\ a_y a_x & a_y^2 & a_y a_z \\ a_z a_x & a_z a_y & a_z^2 \end{bmatrix} \vec{w}$$

$$\vec{a} \times \vec{w} = \begin{bmatrix} 0 & -a_z & a_y \\ a_z & 0 & -a_x \\ -a_y & a_x & 0 \end{bmatrix} \vec{w} = C_a \vec{w}$$

The first identity we saw earlier and uses the tensor notation. The second identity comes from the definition of cross product, and we call the resulting matrix C_a. With these expressions, we can rewrite the transformation as a matrix times a vector. (I is the identity matrix.)

$$
\begin{aligned}
T_{rot}(\vec{w}) &= (\vec{w} - (\vec{a} \cdot \vec{w})\vec{a})\cos\theta + (\vec{a} \times \vec{w})\sin\theta + (\vec{a} \cdot \vec{w})\vec{a} \\
&= (I\cos\theta + (\vec{a} \otimes \vec{a})(1 - \cos\theta) + C_a \sin\theta)\vec{w} \\
&= M_{rot}\vec{w}
\end{aligned}
\tag{4.19}
$$

Example 4.10 (Vector Approach to Arbitrary Rotation). To see this vector approach in action, we can rotate the point $P = (4, 1, 3)$ around the line going through $P_0 = (1, 1, 1)$ in the direction of the vector $(1, -1, 2)$. Take the angle of rotation to be $\pi/3$ counterclockwise. Normalizing, we get the unit vector $\vec{a} = (1/\sqrt{6})(1, -1, 2)$. The vector we should rotate is $\vec{w} = P - P_0 = (3, 0, 2)$. Further, we have $\cos\theta = 1/2$ and $\sin\theta = \sqrt{3}/2$.

Following the construction above, we find the rotation matrix M_{rot}. (We do not need homogeneous coordinates here so we stick with the 3×3 matrices.)

$$
M_{rot} = \begin{bmatrix} \frac{1}{2} & 0 & 0 \\ 0 & \frac{1}{2} & 0 \\ 0 & 0 & \frac{1}{2} \end{bmatrix} + \frac{1}{6}\begin{bmatrix} 1 & -1 & 2 \\ -1 & 1 & -2 \\ 2 & -2 & 4 \end{bmatrix}\left(1 - \frac{1}{2}\right)
$$

$$
+ \frac{1}{\sqrt{6}}\begin{bmatrix} 0 & -2 & -1 \\ 2 & 0 & -1 \\ 1 & 1 & 0 \end{bmatrix}\left(\frac{\sqrt{3}}{2}\right)
$$

$$
\approx \begin{bmatrix} 0.583 & -0.790 & -0.187 \\ 0.624 & 0.583 & -0.520 \\ 0.520 & 0.187 & 0.833 \end{bmatrix}
$$

Applying the rotation matrix to the vector $\vec{w} = (3, 0, 2)$ gives $(1.38, 0.83, 3.23)$, and adding this vector to P_0 gives the rotated point $(2.38, 1.83, 4.23)$. As a check, if we multiply the rotation matrix times the vector $\vec{a}$, it leaves it fixed (within round-off error) as we expect. The arbitrary rotation matrix given in Equation 4.8 was derived with the coordinate-based approach, and it can be verified that it gives the same matrix as M_{rot} in this example. □

Vector Approach to Perspective Transformation The perspective transformation sends three-dimensional objects to a two-dimensional display screen. It is actually an example of a broader class of transformations called *projections*. A very simple projection is one that squashes an object onto the screen by ignoring the z coordinate;

this is more specifically a parallel projection, as it imagines parallel lines perpendicular to the screen passing through each of the vertices in an object. A perspective projection takes lines passing through the eye point and then through each vertex in the object. The lines intersect a plane representing the screen, and the intersection points are the transformed vertices of the object.

Projective transformations are both useful and key in normal Euclidean spaces with Cartesian coordinates, but they can be more efficiently studied in projective spaces where homogeneous coordinates are the representations of choice. We saw earlier that three homogeneous coordinates represent both points and lines in the plane. That is, vectors with three components represent both these geometric entities. We will distinguish them by using vector notation $\vec{L}$ for lines and standard capital letters for points P. The expression $\vec{L} \cdot P = 0$ means the point is on the line. If two points P_1 and P_2 are on a line $\vec{L}$, then $\vec{L} \cdot P_1 = 0$ and $\vec{L} \cdot P_2 = 0$. But this says that vector $\vec{L}$ is perpendicular to both point vectors P_1 and P_2. Consequently, $\vec{L} = P_1 \times P_2$, the cross product of P_1 and P_2. Similarly, if a point P is on two lines, $\vec{L}_1$ and $\vec{L}_2$, then $P = \vec{L}_1 \times \vec{L}_2$.

Begin with the perspective projection in two dimensions. We have a point E, which is where we imagine our eye is sitting if we were in the plane, and a line $\vec{L}$, which acts as the screen in this two-dimensional scenario. To project a single point P onto the line, we draw a line through E and P noting that it intersects $\vec{L}$ in the projected image point P'. If we were projecting a two-dimensional object like a triangle onto the line $\vec{L}$, we would project each vertex in turn (Figure 4.16).

In the algebra of homogeneous coordinates, the line through E and P is the vector $E \times P$. Therefore the point of intersection P' is $\vec{L} \times (E \times P)$; this is the *vector triple product* and there is a nice identity that helps us simplify.

$$\vec{A} \times (\vec{B} \times \vec{C}) = (\vec{A} \cdot \vec{C})\vec{B} - (\vec{A} \cdot \vec{B})\vec{C} \qquad (4.20)$$

It is straightforward to establish the identity by calculating both sides using the definition of vector operations (see Exercises). Now we have a coordinate-free expression for the perspective projection.

$$T(P) = \vec{L} \times (E \times P) = (\vec{L} \cdot P)E - (\vec{L} \cdot E)P$$

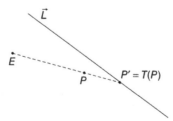

Figure 4.16   2D projection

To take another step and find the transformation matrix, recall the tensor notation that gives $(\vec{L} \cdot P)E = (E \otimes \vec{L})P$. Letting I denote the (3×3) identity matrix, we have

$$T(P) = (\vec{L} \cdot P)E - (\vec{L} \cdot E)P = ((E \otimes \vec{L}) - (\vec{L} \cdot E)I)P = MP \qquad (4.21)$$

This matrix M is a 3×3 matrix and sends points in two-dimensional projective space into points in two-dimensional projective space. However, the image points all lie on the same line, so we have effectively dropped a dimension.

Example 4.11 (Two-Dimensional Perspective Projection).   Suppose we wish to project the point $P = (3, 1)$ onto the line $6x + y - 5 = 0$ from the eye point $E = (8, 2)$. First, note that this is really a simple high school algebra problem. We need to find the intersection of two lines and it will take a few steps. However, our current approach using the coordinate-free representation can prove more efficient when projecting several points and easily generalizes to higher dimensions.

Setting up homogeneous coordinates, we have $\vec{L} = (6, 1, -5)$, $E = (8, 2, 1)$, and $P = (3, 1, 1)$. Next, calculate the matrix M.

$$M = (E \otimes \vec{L}) - (\vec{L} \cdot E)I$$

$$= \begin{bmatrix} 48 & 8 & -40 \\ 12 & 2 & -10 \\ 6 & 1 & -5 \end{bmatrix} - \begin{bmatrix} 45 & 0 & 0 \\ 0 & 45 & 0 \\ 0 & 0 & 45 \end{bmatrix}$$

$$= \begin{bmatrix} 3 & 8 & -40 \\ 12 & -43 & -10 \\ 6 & 1 & -50 \end{bmatrix}$$

Now we apply the transformation.

$$T(P) = MP = \begin{bmatrix} 3 & 8 & -40 \\ 12 & -43 & -10 \\ 6 & 1 & -50 \end{bmatrix} \begin{bmatrix} 3 \\ 1 \\ 1 \end{bmatrix} = \begin{bmatrix} -23 \\ -17 \\ -31 \end{bmatrix}$$

The corresponding Cartesian coordinates for the image of P are $(23/31, 17/31)$.   □

A perspective projection in three dimensions is analogous to the two-dimensional case. From an eye point, we now wish to project points onto a plane. We use the homogeneous coordinates in three-dimensional projective space where planes and points are represented by vectors with four components.

If $\vec{n}$ is a plane and P is a point, then P is on the plane if $\vec{n} \cdot P = 0$. The only hitch in mimicking the development for two dimensions is that in three dimensions we do not have a simple homogeneous representation of a line. In ordinary Cartesian

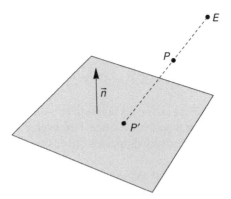

Figure 4.17   3D projection

coordinates, an affine combination of the points P and E is a point on the line through P and E. Moving to homogeneous coordinates, those Cartesian coordinates can be multiplied by any scalar and therefore a point on the line has the form $\alpha P + \beta E$, a linear combination (Figure 4.17).

In particular, the projected image point $P' = \alpha P + \beta E$. This point is on the plane and therefore

$$\vec{n} \cdot (\alpha P + \beta E) = 0 \implies \alpha = \frac{-\beta(\vec{n} \cdot E)}{(\vec{n} \cdot P)}$$

We now have an expression for P'.

$$P' = \frac{-\beta(\vec{n} \cdot E)}{\vec{n} \cdot P} P + \beta E$$

Since we are using homogeneous coordinates, we can multiply through by any constant and still have the same point. Multiplying by $\vec{n} \cdot \vec{P}$ divided by β gives a simplified formula for the transformation.

$$P' = T(P) = (\vec{n} \cdot P)E - (\vec{n} \cdot E)P \tag{4.22}$$

This is analogous to the representation in two dimensions, and remember once more that we are thinking of the points as vectors. As before, we can use the tensor product to find the transformation matrix $M = (E \otimes \vec{n}) - (\vec{n} \cdot E)I$.

Example 4.12 (Three-Dimensional Perspective Projection).   From the eye point $E = (7, 2, 6)$, we want to project the point $P = (4, 5, 0)$ onto the plane $2x - y + 2z = -4$. The plane's normal vector is $\vec{n} = (2, -1, 2, 4)$ and, using homogeneous coordinates, we have $E = (7, 2, 6, 1)$ and $P = (4, 5, 0, 1)$.

$$M = (E \otimes \vec{n}) - (\vec{n} \cdot E)I$$

$$= \begin{bmatrix} 14 & -7 & 14 & 28 \\ 4 & -2 & 4 & 8 \\ 12 & -6 & 12 & 24 \\ 2 & -1 & 2 & 4 \end{bmatrix} - \begin{bmatrix} 28 & 0 & 0 & 0 \\ 0 & 28 & 0 & 0 \\ 0 & 0 & 28 & 0 \\ 0 & 0 & 0 & 28 \end{bmatrix}$$

$$= \begin{bmatrix} -14 & -7 & 14 & 28 \\ 4 & -30 & 4 & 8 \\ 12 & -6 & -16 & 24 \\ 2 & -1 & 2 & -24 \end{bmatrix}$$

Multiplying times the point P gives $P' = (-63, -126, 42, -21)$ and converting to Cartesian coordinates gives $(3, 6, -2)$.   □

In our earlier development of the perspective projection in three dimensions, we took the plane representing the screen to be the xy plane which has homogeneous vector representation $\vec{n} = (0, 0, 1, 0)$. The eye point was $E = (0, 0, e, 1)$, and we were projecting $P = (x, y, z, 1)$. This gives the following transformation matrix:

$$M = \begin{bmatrix} -e & 0 & 0 & 0 \\ 0 & -e & 0 & 0 \\ 0 & 0 & 0 & 0 \\ 0 & 0 & 1 & -e \end{bmatrix}$$

When we use this matrix to project $P = (x, y, z, 1)$, we get the point P'.

$$P' = (-ex, -ey, 0, z - e) \implies P' = \left(\frac{x}{1 - \frac{z}{e}}, \frac{y}{1 - \frac{z}{e}}, 0 \right)$$

The $z = 0$ coordinate indicates that this point is on the xy plane.

The matrix M differs from the one we previously constructed, showing that there are several ways to represent the perspective projection transformation with matrices. One of the differences is in how the z coordinate is treated. Practically, we can ignore the z coordinate when displaying on the screen, but the z coordinate can hold useful information about the visibility of points. (Visibility is discussed in a later chapter.)

4.6 EXERCISES

1. Find the transformation matrix for the linear transformation that sends $(3, -1)$ to $(2, 4)$ and $(5, 1)$ to $(3, 8)$.

2. Let a triangle have vertices $A = (-2, -3)$, $B = (4, 1)$, and $C = (2, 5)$. Find the transformed vertices when the triangle is rotated by $\pi/4$ clockwise around vertex A.

3. Start with vertices $A = (30, 6)$ and $B = (52, 10)$. Find vertex C so that the three points form an equilateral triangle.

4. Let a triangle have one vertex at the origin. Show that, if the determinant of a 2×2 matrix is 1, then the associated linear transform preserves the area of this triangle. Expand this to verify that the area of any triangle is preserved under the transformation.

5. Reflect the point $(8, -2)$ in the line through the origin and the point $(4, 5)$.

6. Reflect the point $(6, -1, 3)$ in the plane through the origin with normal $(-1, 5, 2)$.

7. Give the transformation matrix for the two-dimensional linear transformation that projects everything on the x-axis. Use this matrix and a rotation to find the transformation matrix that projects everything onto the line $y = x$.

8. Find the two-dimensional linear transformation that reflects points in the line $y = 3x + 7$.

9. The 2×2 matrix M can be thought of as having two vectors $((a, b)$ and $(c, d))$ forming the rows. If the vectors are unit vectors and they are perpendicular, then the matrix is called *orthogonal*. Show that we can set $a = \pm \cos \theta$ and $b = \pm \sin \theta$. Show further that $d = a$ or $d = -a$, which implies $c = -b$ or $c = b$. Explain why rotation and reflection matrices are examples of orthogonal matrices and that products of these two types are also orthogonal. Intuitively, we know that rotations and reflections should not change the area of triangles and, indeed, the determinant of an orthogonal matrix is ± 1.

10. The reflection of the point (x, y, z) in the origin is $(-x, -y, -z)$. Find the 4×4 matrix for homogeneous coordinates that will reflect a point in the point $(2, 5, -1)$.

11. The unit cube with vertices (a, b, c), where each component is 0 or 1, is rotated by $\pi/6$ counterclockwise around the diagonal through $(0, 0, 0)$ and $(1, 1, 1)$. Find the transformation matrix and the coordinates of the transformed cube.

12. Show that a rotation of $2\pi/3$ clockwise around the line from $(0, 0, 0)$ to $(1, 1, 1)$ is the product of two rotations around coordinate axes.

13. The vertices $(1, 1, 1)$, $(1, -1, -1)$, $(-1, 1, -1)$, and $(-1, -1, 1)$ form a tetrahedron with equal sides. In Example 3.24 from Chapter 3, there is another set of vertices for a tetrahedron with equal sides. Find the transformation matrix that takes the first tetrahedron to the second.

14. Prove Equation 4.20.

15. A two-dimensional transformation reflects in the x-axis and then reflects in the line through the origin and $(3, 4)$. Show that the resulting transformation is a rotation, and give the angle of rotation.

16. Show that the three-dimensional shear transformation given by

$$M = \begin{bmatrix} 1 & 1 & 1 \\ 0 & 1 & 0 \\ 0 & 0 & 1 \end{bmatrix}$$

preserves volume by explaining what it does to a unit cube.

17. With the eye point (E) at $(0, 0, 20)$, project the line segment from $(2, -1, 7)$ to $(3, 6, -4)$ onto the xy plane.

18. With the eye point (E) at $(0, 0, 20)$, project the line segment from $(2, -1, 7)$ to $(3, 6, -4)$ onto the plane $2x + y + z = 0$.

19. Show that the perspective transformation does not preserve parallel lines by projecting two line segments with the same direction vectors onto the xy plane. When will parallel lines project to parallel lines?

20. The shear transformation $M = \begin{bmatrix} 1 & 0 \\ -2 & 1 \end{bmatrix}$ transforms an object; find the transformation that appropriately transforms the normals.

21. For the derivation in Section 4.5.2, verify that $\vec{a} \times \vec{w}_\perp = \vec{a} \times \vec{w}$.

22. A 3×3 identity matrix has the last row replaced with $(1, 1, 1)$. Explain what the resulting transformation does to the unit cube.

4.6.1 Programming Exercises

1. Write a program to present a cube on the screen. Controls allow rotation around any coordinate axis and around an arbitrary axis specified by the user. The cube should have colored faces and be rendered with perspective.

5

ORIENTATION

The quintessential setup in three-dimensional graphics is a scene composed of objects with a camera positioned somewhere looking in a particular direction. As a simple example, imagine a single cube sitting on the ground. This is our scene and we look at it from some point in space. We imagine either our eye or perhaps a camera at this point oriented in such a way that it is looking at the scene and probably focused on the cube in particular. There is much that we have to keep track of here. The cube has a given shape, it is positioned on the ground at a particular location with a particular orientation, the camera is centered at a given point, it is looking at some point in the scene, and it is positioned so the up direction is aligned in a way the user or programmer prefers. Our task now is to determine how to specify all of these orientations and how to keep them appropriately aligned with each other as we move the camera or move objects in the scene.

Start with the cube in our example, and note that most of the vector geometry developed so far was focused on determining the vertices for various objects like the cube. We actually want coordinates for these vertices, so we specified a Cartesian coordinate system which we now call the *local* coordinate system. It is local for the object at hand and usually we find it convenient to place the origin at the center of the object (assuming this center is convenient to find.) When we place the cube on the ground, we are really constructing yet another coordinate system called the *world* coordinate system where the ground is just a particular plane with a description in the world system and the center of the cube has a set of world coordinates (c_x, c_y, c_z) as well as a set of local coordinates $(0, 0, 0)$. The camera, too, has a set of world

Mathematical Structures for Computer Graphics, First Edition. Steven J. Janke.
© 2015 John Wiley & Sons, Inc. Published 2015 by John Wiley & Sons, Inc.

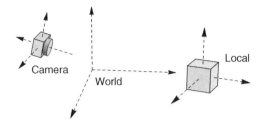

Figure 5.1 Coordinate systems in a scene

coordinates indicating where it is positioned in our scene, but in addition it has its own orientation. What we display on the computer screen is relative to the camera's orientation, so it is once again convenient to select another coordinate system called the *camera* coordinate system. (It is equally reasonable to call this last system either the *eye* coordinate system or the *view* coordinate system.) The origin of the camera coordinate system is at the center of the camera (Figure 5.1).

Using a local coordinate system, it is easy to find the vertices of our cube because we are free to first center it at the origin and orient it so that faces are parallel to the coordinate planes. We could take one vertex to be $(1, 1, 1)$ and then another is just $(-1, -1, -1)$, the reflection in the origin. In fact, all eight vertices have coordinates that are either 1 or -1. This is an easy representation to begin with in the local coordinate system and, if we need, we can apply rotation or scaling transformations to get the cube to any given size and orientation.

Positioning the cube in the scene requires finding world coordinates for the vertices, but this could be as simple as applying a translation to move the center of the cube to the required location. It could also be more complicated requiring some scaling and rotation to properly place the cube relative to other objects in the scene. Placing the camera is similar to placing objects, but once it is placed we need to point it towards the scene. This means we are picking the camera coordinate system appropriately, and consequently we are specifying the three coordinate axes for a Cartesian coordinate system. One axis should lie along a line from the camera to the center of the scene, one should point up, and the third should be perpendicular to the other two in such a way that we have a right-handed coordinate system.

Clearly, the orientation involved in viewing a scene depends on understanding the construction of coordinate systems (Cartesian systems in particular) and the transformation of one to another. It might seem that having one global coordinate system would simplify things, but as we saw previously, a local coordinate system, for example, can make designing an object much easier. The flexibility of several coordinate systems usually outweighs the simplicity of a single system.

5.1 CARTESIAN COORDINATE SYSTEMS

Throughout the development of vector geometry, whenever we give the coordinates of a vector such as $\vec{v} = (x, y, z)$, what we really mean is that $\vec{v} = x\vec{i} + y\vec{j} + z\vec{k}$. We say that $\vec{v}$ is a *linear combination* of the common vectors $\vec{i}, \vec{j}$, and $\vec{k}$. Since we selected the common vectors so that they did not lie in a single plane, every three-dimensional vector is a linear combination of these three common vectors, so we say they form a *basis*. Moreover, we actually selected the basis vectors so that they all had unit length and were perpendicular to each other. That is, their dot products with each other are zero and $\vec{i} \cdot \vec{i} = \vec{j} \cdot \vec{j} = \vec{k} \cdot \vec{k} = 1$. We say they form an *orthonormal* basis. One key feature of an orthonormal basis is the ease with which we can calculate dot products. For two vectors $\vec{w}_1 = x_1\vec{i} + y_1\vec{j} + z_1\vec{k}$ and $\vec{w}_2 = x_2\vec{i} + y_2\vec{j} + z_2\vec{k}$, the dot product is $\vec{w}_1 \cdot \vec{w}_2 = x_1x_2 + y_1y_2 + z_1z_2$. This is how we defined the dot product early on, but it really is a result of using an orthonormal basis.

A basis allows us to specify arbitrary vectors nicely, but we need an origin as well in order to specify points. An origin O is a point that we intuitively think of as the center of what we call a *coordinate system*. For an arbitrary point P in space, we first write P as a sum, $P = O + (P - O)$. This is the sum of a point and a vector, and earlier we understood that this type of sum gives us a point. The coordinates of P in the coordinate system are just the coordinates of the vector $(P - O)$ using the given basis.

Definition 5.1 (Coordinate System). *A coordinate system in three (or two) dimensions is a set of three (or two) basis vectors along with a designated point called the origin. If the basis vectors are perpendicular to each other and have unit length, the basis and the coordinate system are called orthonormal.*

In our graphics scenario with a cube sitting on the ground, we have three coordinate systems: the world coordinate system ($\mathscr{W}$), the local coordinate system ($\mathscr{L}$), and the camera coordinate system ($\mathscr{C}$). Their corresponding origins are O_w, O_l, and O_c. Since we imagine the world coordinate system as a global system, we will let our usual vectors $\{\vec{i}, \vec{j}, \vec{k}\}$ to be an orthonormal basis for $\mathscr{W}$. Then let $\{\vec{u}, \vec{v}, \vec{w}\}$ be an orthonormal basis for $\mathscr{L}$. We will hold off on specifying $\mathscr{C}$ until later because we want to let the user have some input into how the camera is oriented. Now consider one of the cube vertices which we have represented in local coordinates [e.g., $(1, 1, 1)$]. We would like to find the corresponding world coordinates for this vertex, and, more generally, what we need is an algorithm for moving from one coordinate system to another.

Suppose we have the coordinates of point P with respect to coordinate system $\mathscr{S}_1$ and we want the coordinates of P with respect to the system $\mathscr{S}_2$. We might guess that the change from one set of coordinates to the other requires an affine transformation because we once again want to preserve lines in the process. In fact, there are two parts to the transformation. First, since the origins of $\mathscr{S}_1$ and $\mathscr{S}_2$ may be different, a translation of the coordinates will be necessary. Second, we need to account for different sets of basis vectors in the two systems. It is possible that a rotation will account for the difference, but it is also possible that we may need some more complicated combination of scaling, shear, and rotation to account for the different orientation of basis vectors.

The first part of the transformation involving translation is relatively easy to describe. In $\mathscr{S}_1$, we represent the point P as $P = O_1 + (P - O_1) = O_1 + \vec{v}_1$. The $\mathscr{S}_1$ coordinates of P are the coordinates of $\vec{v}_1$. To move the origin from O_1 to O_2, we need to add the vector $\vec{t} = (O_2 - O_1)$. Rewriting the expression for P shows how to find the $\mathcal{S}_2$ coordinates for P.

$$P = O_1 + (P - O_1) = O_1 + \vec{v}_1 = O_2 - \vec{t} + \vec{v}_1 = O_2 + \vec{v}_2$$

The $\mathcal{S}_2$ coordinates are the coordinates of $\vec{v}_2$, which are the coordinates of $\vec{v}_1$ minus the shift vector $\vec{t}$. Intuitively, this all makes sense because coordinates are relative to the origin; they should change by the amount of any translation. When moving from $\mathcal{S}_1$ to $\mathcal{S}_2$, we subtract the vector $\vec{t}$.

We still need to account for a different set of basis vectors in $\mathcal{S}_2$, but as a first guess at how to quantify this difference, it seems that some linear transformation will do the trick. Once we have applied the translation, then both origins coincide so the problem is reduced to applying a linear transformation to align the axes. We can express the total transformation from one set of coordinates to another in terms of matrix multiplication. Let the 4×4 matrix M_T (with homogeneous coordinates) represent the translation, and let the matrix M_B represent the linear transformation necessary to adjust for a different basis. Then multiplication by $M_B M_T$ transforms $\mathcal{S}_1$ coordinates into $\mathcal{S}_2$ coordinates.

Example 5.1 (A Simple Coordinate System Change). Take $\mathcal{S}_1$ to be a system with orthonormal basis vectors $\{\vec{i}, \vec{j}, \vec{k}\}$. Let P have coordinates $(2, -1, 1)$ in this system. Now suppose that $\mathcal{S}_2$ is a second coordinate system with an origin that has $\mathcal{S}_1$ coordinates $(4, -2, 5)$; that is, its origin is displaced relative to the first coordinate system. Then, vector $(O_2 - O_1) = (4, -2, 5)$ and we need to subtract this shift.

$$M_T = \begin{bmatrix} 1 & 0 & 0 & -4 \\ 0 & 1 & 0 & 2 \\ 0 & 0 & 1 & -5 \\ 0 & 0 & 0 & 1 \end{bmatrix}$$

If coordinate system $\mathcal{S}_2$ has the same basis vectors as $\mathcal{S}_1$, then all we have to do in order to change from the first coordinate system to the second is to multiply by M_T. (M_B is then the identity.) Expressing P in homogeneous coordinates gives $(2, -1, 1, 1)$, and multiplying by M_T results in $(-2, 1, -4, 1)$. The $\mathcal{S}_2$ coordinates for P would be $(-2, 1, -4)$.

If coordinate system $\mathcal{S}_2$ does not have the same basis vectors as $\mathcal{S}_1$, we need another transformation. Suppose that system $\mathcal{S}_2$ has basis vectors $\{\vec{i}, \vec{k}, -\vec{j}\}$, which means that this system is just the $\mathcal{S}_1$ system rotated $\pi/2$ radians counterclockwise around the x-axis. Considering the effect on coordinates, rotating the basis vectors counterclockwise is equivalent to rotating the vector $(P - O_2)$ clockwise. We choose M_B to rotate clockwise around the x-axis (Figure 5.2).

$$M_B = \begin{bmatrix} 1 & 0 & 0 & 0 \\ 0 & 0 & 1 & 0 \\ 0 & -1 & 0 & 0 \\ 0 & 0 & 0 & 1 \end{bmatrix}$$

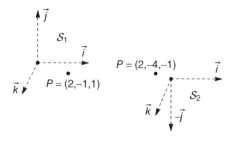

Figure 5.2   Changing coordinate systems

The complete coordinate change combines both the translation and the rotation. The order of the two is, of course, important. The translation vector was given with respect to the $\mathcal{S}_1$ system, so we apply it first to align the origins. Then we apply the rotation to align the axes. (If we apply a rotation first, then we have to adjust how we represent the translation. This can be done, but it is easier and more intuitive to apply the translation first.)

$$
M_B M_T = \begin{bmatrix} 1 & 0 & 0 & 0 \\ 0 & 0 & 1 & 0 \\ 0 & -1 & 0 & 0 \\ 0 & 0 & 0 & 1 \end{bmatrix} \begin{bmatrix} 1 & 0 & 0 & -4 \\ 0 & 1 & 0 & 2 \\ 0 & 0 & 1 & -5 \\ 0 & 0 & 0 & 1 \end{bmatrix} = \begin{bmatrix} 1 & 0 & 0 & -4 \\ 0 & 0 & 1 & -5 \\ 0 & -1 & 0 & -2 \\ 0 & 0 & 0 & 1 \end{bmatrix}
$$

Multiplying this matrix times the vector with homogeneous coordinates $(2, -1, 1, 1)$ gives $(-2, -4, -1, 1)$. The point P has $\mathcal{S}_1$ coordinates $(2, -1, 1)$ and $\mathcal{S}_2$ coordinates $(-2, -4, -1)$.   □

The M_B transformation matrix accounts for the differences in the basis vectors for the two systems. The simple example of a rotation around one axis is relatively easy to deal with, but we really need an approach that deals with more complicated situations. For example, if the systems are not orthonormal, then we have to adjust both for the length of the basis vectors and for the angle between them.

Assume that we have made an appropriate translation so that the origin of $\mathcal{S}_1$ coincides with the origin of $\mathcal{S}_2$. Imagine we have a vector $\vec{c}$ that we wish to express in both $\mathcal{S}_1$ coordinates and $\mathcal{S}_2$ coordinates. Let the basis vectors for system $\mathcal{S}_1$ be $\{\vec{q}, \vec{r}, \vec{s}\}$, and let the basis of $\mathcal{S}_2$ be $\{\vec{u}, \vec{v}, \vec{w}\}$. These are general bases, so although they are sets of independent vectors, they may not be orthonormal.

If in $\mathcal{S}_1$ the coordinates are $\vec{c} = (a_1, b_1, c_1)$, then this means that

$$\vec{c} = a_1 \vec{q} + b_1 \vec{r} + c_1 \vec{s} \tag{5.1}$$

In the $\mathcal{S}_2$ system, let the coordinates be $\vec{c} = (a_2, b_2, c_2)$, meaning that

$$\vec{c} = a_2 \vec{u} + b_2 \vec{v} + c_2 \vec{w} \tag{5.2}$$

Now suppose we have $\mathcal{S}_1$ coordinates for each of the basis vectors in the $\mathcal{S}_2$ system. That is, $\vec{u} = (u_q, u_r, u_s), \vec{v} = (v_q, v_r, v_s), \vec{w} = (w_q, w_r, w_s)$. Using these coordinates, we get equations for $\vec{u}, \vec{v},$ and $\vec{w}$ similar to Equation 5.1. For example, $\vec{u} = u_q\vec{q} + u_r\vec{r} + u_s\vec{s}$. Substituting these equations into Equation 5.2 and combining terms gives the following matrix equation:

$$\begin{bmatrix} a_1 \\ b_1 \\ c_1 \end{bmatrix} = \begin{bmatrix} u_q & v_q & w_q \\ u_r & v_r & w_r \\ u_s & v_s & w_s \end{bmatrix} \begin{bmatrix} a_2 \\ b_2 \\ c_2 \end{bmatrix} = M \begin{bmatrix} a_2 \\ b_2 \\ c_2 \end{bmatrix} \tag{5.3}$$

Here, M is a 3×3 matrix because temporarily we do not need to consider translation and therefore we do not need the larger 4×4 matrix operating on homogeneous coordinates. Multiplication by the matrix M converts $\mathcal{S}_2$ coordinates to $\mathcal{S}_1$ coordinates. Of course, if M has an inverse, then multiplication by M^{-1} converts $\mathcal{S}_1$ coordinates to $\mathcal{S}_2$ coordinates.

A closer look at the matrix M reveals that the columns are just the $\mathcal{S}_1$ coordinates for each of the basis vectors in $\mathcal{S}_2$. Since these columns come from a basis, they are independent and M has a nonzero determinant. This ensures that M has an inverse and consequently M_B is a 4×4 matrix with M^{-1} in the upper left-hand corner. We have found the matrix for the second part of the general coordinate transformation.

Result 5.1 (Coordinate Transformation). *Let $\mathcal{S}_1$ and $\mathcal{S}_2$ be two coordinate systems with origins O_1 and O_2 and basis vectors $\{\vec{q}, \vec{r}, \vec{s}\}$ and $\{\vec{u}, \vec{v}, \vec{w}\}$, respectively. Suppose the $\mathcal{S}_1$ coordinates of the vector $\vec{t} = (O_2 - O_1)$ are (t_q, t_r, t_s) and that the $\mathcal{S}_1$ coordinates for the basis vectors of $\mathcal{S}_2$ are $u = (u_q, u_r, u_s), v = (v_q, v_r, v_s),$ and $w = (w_q, w_r, w_s)$. Form the matrix M (defined in Equation 5.3) by using these $\mathcal{S}_1$ coordinates as columns.*

The coordinate transformation from $\mathcal{S}_1$ to $\mathcal{S}_2$ is an affine transformation represented by the matrix $M_{\mathcal{S}_1 \to \mathcal{S}_2}$, where

$$M_{\mathcal{S}_1 \to \mathcal{S}_2} = M_B M_T = \left[\begin{array}{ccc|c} & & & 0 \\ & M^{-1} & & 0 \\ & & & 0 \\ \hline 0 & 0 & 0 & 1 \end{array} \right] \begin{bmatrix} 1 & 0 & 0 & -t_q \\ 0 & 1 & 0 & -t_r \\ 0 & 0 & 1 & -t_s \\ 0 & 0 & 0 & 1 \end{bmatrix}$$

For the other direction from $\mathcal{S}_2$ to $\mathcal{S}_1$, the transformation matrix $M_{\mathcal{S}_2 \to \mathcal{S}_1}$ is the inverse of $M_{\mathcal{S}_1 \to \mathcal{S}_2}$.

If we are lucky enough to have orthonormal bases, then the inverse of M is actually the transpose of M, $M^{-1} = M^T$. In this case, the matrix $M_{\mathcal{S}_1 \to \mathcal{S}_2}$ has a convenient form:

$$M_{\mathcal{S}_1 \to \mathcal{S}_2} = \begin{bmatrix} u_q & u_r & u_s & -\vec{u} \cdot \vec{t} \\ v_q & v_r & v_s & -\vec{v} \cdot \vec{t} \\ w_q & w_r & w_s & -\vec{w} \cdot \vec{t} \\ 0 & 0 & 0 & 1 \end{bmatrix} \tag{5.4}$$

In the last column, we have dot products of basis vectors with the translation vector $\vec{t}$.

Example 5.2 (Local and World Coordinates). Return to the scenario where the graphics scene has a cube sitting on the ground in some orientation. We have both a world coordinate system, $\mathcal{W}$, and a local coordinate system, $\mathcal{L}$. We use the standard vectors $\{\vec{i}, \vec{j}, \vec{k}\}$ as an orthonormal basis for $\mathcal{W}$. Set the basis for $\mathcal{L}$ as $\{\vec{u}, \vec{v}, \vec{w}\}$, where temporarily $\vec{u} = \vec{i}$, $\vec{v} = \vec{j}$, and $\vec{w} = \vec{k}$. The bases of $\mathcal{L}$ and $\mathcal{W}$ are aligned. Recall that we set the cube vertices to have local coordinates $(1, 1, 1), (1, -1, 1), (1, 1, -1)$, and so on.

Since the coordinate systems use vectors $\{\vec{i}, \vec{j}, \vec{k}\}$, we will refer to the corresponding axes as x, y, and z. The origin O_w for the world system has, of course, world coordinates $(0, 0, 0)$, and the ground plane in our scene will be the xz plane leaving the y-axis pointing up. To position the cube so that it is sitting on the ground somewhere off-center in the scene, we set the world coordinates of the local system origin, O_l, to $(5, 1, 8)$. (The y coordinate equal to one moves the local system up a bit from the world system and pushes the cube up so that it is sitting on the ground plane.)

Rather than keeping the cube oriented with sides parallel to the coordinate axes, we may want it rotated around, say, the y-axis. We have two choices. We can rotate the cube vertices with respect to the local coordinate system, or we can rotate the local coordinate basis vectors with respect to world coordinates (keeping the local origin fixed). Rotating the basis vectors effectively rotates the cube as well, because we keep the same local coordinates for the cube vertices as before; the vertex $(1, 1, 1)$, for example, will be repositioned relative to the world coordinate system. The choice of approaches again depends on the context of the graphics application, but it may be useful to keep the cube aligned with the local axes so that rotating the entire local coordinate system seems like a decent choice.

Suppose we rotate the local coordinate system $\pi/4$ radians counterclockwise around the y-axis. Then vector $\vec{u}$ which was originally the same as $\vec{i} = (1, 0, 0)$ gets new world coordinates. The local coordinates of $\vec{u}$ are still $(1, 0, 0)$. We already know the appropriate transformation matrix for a rotation around the y-axis, so applying it gives the new world coordinates.

$$\vec{u}_{new} = M\vec{u} = \begin{bmatrix} \frac{1}{\sqrt{2}} & 0 & \frac{1}{\sqrt{2}} \\ 0 & 1 & 0 \\ \frac{-1}{\sqrt{2}} & 0 & \frac{1}{\sqrt{2}} \end{bmatrix} \begin{bmatrix} 1 \\ 0 \\ 0 \end{bmatrix} = \begin{bmatrix} \frac{1}{\sqrt{2}} \\ 0 \\ \frac{-1}{\sqrt{2}} \end{bmatrix}$$

Similar multiplications give the new basis vectors $\vec{v}_{new} = (0, 1, 0)$ and $\vec{w}_{new} = (\frac{1}{\sqrt{2}}, 0, \frac{1}{\sqrt{2}})$. These are all world coordinates for the new local coordinate basis. We did not change the local origin, so we have simply rotated the local coordinate system and, since the local coordinates for the cube vertices stayed the same, the cube was rotated as well.

The original task was to convert local coordinates to world coordinates. In the notation of Result 5.1, we are set to use the world system as $\mathcal{S}_1$ and the local system as $\mathcal{S}_2$. First, construct $M_{\mathcal{S}_1 \to \mathcal{S}_2}$, and then find the inverse to get $M_{\mathcal{S}_2 \to \mathcal{S}_1}$. We have $\mathcal{S}_1$ (world) coordinates for $\vec{t} = (O_l - O_w) = (5, 1, 8)$ and for the basis vectors of $\mathcal{S}_2$ (local coordinate system). The columns of M are the basis vectors of $\mathcal{S}_2$ and, because the systems are orthonormal, $M^{-1} = M^T$.

$$M_{(\mathscr{W} \to \mathscr{L})} = M_B M_T = \begin{bmatrix} \frac{1}{\sqrt{2}} & 0 & \frac{-1}{\sqrt{2}} & 0 \\ 0 & 1 & 0 & 0 \\ \frac{1}{\sqrt{2}} & 0 & \frac{1}{\sqrt{2}} & 0 \\ 0 & 0 & 0 & 1 \end{bmatrix} \begin{bmatrix} 1 & 0 & 0 & -5 \\ 0 & 1 & 0 & -1 \\ 0 & 0 & 1 & -8 \\ 0 & 0 & 0 & 1 \end{bmatrix}$$

$$= \begin{bmatrix} \frac{1}{\sqrt{2}} & 0 & \frac{-1}{\sqrt{2}} & \frac{3}{\sqrt{2}} \\ 0 & 1 & 0 & -1 \\ \frac{1}{\sqrt{2}} & 0 & \frac{1}{\sqrt{2}} & \frac{-13}{\sqrt{2}} \\ 0 & 0 & 0 & 1 \end{bmatrix}$$

The inverse matrix converts local coordinates to world coordinates:

$$M_{(\mathscr{L} \to \mathscr{W})} = (M_B M_T)^{-1} = M_T^{-1} M_B^{-1}$$

$$= \begin{bmatrix} 1 & 0 & 0 & 5 \\ 0 & 1 & 0 & 1 \\ 0 & 0 & 1 & 8 \\ 0 & 0 & 0 & 1 \end{bmatrix} \begin{bmatrix} \frac{1}{\sqrt{2}} & 0 & \frac{1}{\sqrt{2}} & 0 \\ 0 & 1 & 0 & 0 \\ \frac{-1}{\sqrt{2}} & 0 & \frac{1}{\sqrt{2}} & 0 \\ 0 & 0 & 0 & 1 \end{bmatrix}$$

$$= \begin{bmatrix} \frac{1}{\sqrt{2}} & 0 & \frac{1}{\sqrt{2}} & 5 \\ 0 & 1 & 0 & 1 \\ \frac{-1}{\sqrt{2}} & 0 & \frac{1}{\sqrt{2}} & 8 \\ 0 & 0 & 0 & 1 \end{bmatrix}$$

Multiplying $M_{(\mathscr{L} \to \mathscr{W})}$ times the local coordinates $(1, 1, 1)$ [homogeneous coordinates are $(1, 1, 1, 1)$] gives the world coordinates for one of the cube's vertices, $(5, 2, 9.41)$ (Figure 5.3). □

This example is somewhat simple in that rotation was around a coordinate axis. Later we will use the conversion technique to move to camera coordinates where the orientation of the basis vectors is not readily seen as a rotation.

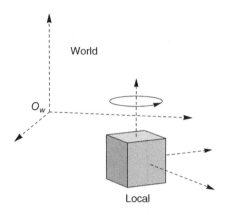

Figure 5.3 $\mathscr{L}$ and $\mathscr{W}$

5.2 CAMERAS

Usually, the selection of the world ($\mathscr{W}$) and local ($\mathscr{L}$) coordinate systems is a sim-plifying convenience. The graphics designer or graphics programmer picks the world system from a global perspective, and often the center of the world is the origin. The ground is possibly the xz plane formed by two basis vectors with the y-axis pointing up; in this case, the first and third basis vectors determine the ground plane, and the second basis vector is normal to the plane. Various attributes of the scene (mountain ranges, roads, buildings, etc.) may make one orientation of the axes more intuitive than another. For the local system, there may only be one object described by the system and therefore the symmetry of the object calls the shots in determining axis orientation. If there is more than one object, then maybe a subsystem inside the local coordinate system is an appropriate design choice.

When it comes to the camera coordinate system ($\mathscr{C}$), we need to know where we are looking and which way is up. It also is important to decide whether the system is a right-handed or left-handed coordinate system. Most graphics systems rely on right-handed systems, although in particular instances a left-handed system may be useful.

Suppose then that we first pick the camera's center position, P_c, and decide where in the scene we are looking, say at the point P_s. The vector $\vec{n} = P_c - P_s$ is normal to a plane (called the *view plane*) which we imagine holds the window into our scene. We see the scene through this window and our perspective transformation will map the scene onto this window. Just as a convention, the view plane normal $\vec{n}$ points in the positive z direction and we are looking in the negative z direction (Figure 5.4).

Let the vector $\vec{v}$ point in the up direction. This vector may be user-supplied and, although we know it should be perpendicular to $\vec{n}$, it may not be described that pre-cisely, so we intend to adjust $\vec{v}$ if necessary. To set up an orthonormal basis for the

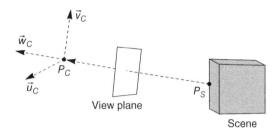

Figure 5.4 Camera orientation

camera system $\mathscr{C}$, we define the following basis vectors:

$$\vec{w}_c = \frac{\vec{n}}{|\vec{n}|}$$

$$\vec{u}_c = \frac{\vec{v} \times \vec{w}_c}{|\vec{v} \times \vec{w}_c|} \tag{5.5}$$

$$\vec{v}_c = \vec{w}_c \times \vec{u}_c$$

This set of vectors $\{\vec{u}_c, \vec{v}_c, \vec{w}_c\}$ forms an orthonormal basis for the coordinate system $\mathscr{C}$ and the point P_c is the designated origin. It is a right-handed coordinate system with $\vec{u}_c$ analogous to the x direction, $\vec{v}_c$ (the up vector) analogous to the y direction, and $\vec{w}_c$ (pointing at the camera) analogous to the z direction.

We started with the normal $\vec{n}$ and the up vector $\vec{v}$. Assuming the coordinates of these vectors are given in world coordinates, we have the world coordinates for the basis vectors in $\mathscr{C}$. To view the scene from the camera position, we need to convert the world coordinates for points in the scene to camera coordinates. Using the notation $\vec{u}_c = (u_x, u_y, u_z)$ for the world coordinates and letting $\vec{t} = (P_c - O_w)$, the appropriate matrix that performs the coordinate transformation is

$$M_{\mathscr{W} \to \mathscr{C}} = \begin{bmatrix} u_x & u_y & u_z & -\vec{u} \cdot \vec{t} \\ v_x & v_y & v_z & -\vec{v} \cdot \vec{t} \\ w_x & w_y & w_z & -\vec{w} \cdot \vec{t} \\ 0 & 0 & 0 & 1 \end{bmatrix} \tag{5.6}$$

Example 5.3 (Converting to Camera Coordinates).   In Example 5.2, the cube vertex $(1, 1, 1)$ in local coordinates became $(5, 2, 9.41)$ in world coordinates. Now, center the camera at the point $(10, 12, 18)$ and suppose we are looking at the origin of the world system. The view plane normal is $\vec{n} = (10, 12, 18)$. If we select an up vector of

$\vec{v} = (1, 1, 0)$, then

$$\vec{w}_c = \frac{(10, 12, 18)}{\sqrt{10^2 + 12^2 + 18^2}} \approx (0.42, 0.50, 0.76)$$

$$\vec{u}_c = \frac{\vec{v} \times \vec{w}_c}{|\vec{v} \times \vec{w}_c|} \approx (0.71, -.71, 0.08)$$

$$\vec{v}_c = \vec{w}_c \times \vec{u}_c \approx (0.57, 0.50, -0.65)$$

To transform $(1, 1, 1)$ to camera coordinates, we multiply by the transformation matrix using $\vec{t} = (10, 12, 18)$.

$$M_{\mathscr{W} \to \mathscr{C}} \begin{bmatrix} 5 \\ 2 \\ 9.41 \\ 1 \end{bmatrix} = \begin{bmatrix} 0.71 & -0.71 & 0.08 & -0.02 \\ 0.57 & 0.50 & -0.65 & 0 \\ 0.42 & 0.50 & 0.76 & -23.88 \\ 0 & 0 & 0 & 1 \end{bmatrix} \begin{bmatrix} 5 \\ 2 \\ 9.41 \\ 1 \end{bmatrix} = \begin{bmatrix} 2.95 \\ -2.42 \\ -13.63 \\ 1 \end{bmatrix}$$

The z coordinate of our vertex $(2.86, -2.27, -13.63)$ is negative because the camera position is far along the world system's positive z-axis. Also, the camera is relatively high with respect to the world system's origin, so the y coordinate of the vertex is also negative. (Note: The matrix M was calculated using the approximate values for the basis vectors in $\mathscr{C}$. The value -0.02 in the matrix should theoretically be 0. See Exercises for more detail.) $\qquad\qquad\qquad\qquad\qquad\qquad\qquad\qquad\qquad\qquad\qquad\qquad\qquad\square$

5.2.1 Moving the Camera or Objects

Now that we have analyzed the mechanics of coordinate transformations, we can combine the transformation matrix with the standard transformations we studied earlier for changing the position or shape of an object, perhaps a cube. The task is to start with a view of the scene from the camera-oriented position and to transform the cube in some way. Suppose, first, that the cube is centered at the origin and we would like to rotate it around an axis through its center. Multiplication by a rotation matrix will alter the cube's original vertex coordinates appropriately. The following transformation matrix A will accomplish the conversion of local coordinates to rotated coordinates and then to world coordinates.

$$A = M_{\mathscr{L} \to \mathscr{W}} R$$

As we saw in Example 5.2, an alternate way of thinking about this transformation is as a rotation of the local coordinate system itself rather than just the vertices of the cube. That is, we rotate the basis vectors into new positions. Call the new rotated coordinate system $\mathscr{L}^*$. Now we interpret the matrix R as transforming $\mathscr{L}^*$ coordinates into $\mathscr{L}$ coordinates. So the matrix A is really the matrix converting $\mathscr{L}^*$ coordinates to $\mathscr{W}$ coordinates.

$$A = M_{\mathscr{L}^* \to \mathscr{W}} = M_{\mathscr{L} \to \mathscr{W}} \cdot R$$

As an example, take the R matrix to be a rotation around the z-axis.

$$R = \begin{bmatrix} \cos\theta & -\sin\theta & 0 & 0 \\ \sin\theta & \cos\theta & 0 & 0 \\ 0 & 0 & 1 & 0 \\ 0 & 0 & 0 & 1 \end{bmatrix}$$

Referring to our general coordinate transformation, let $\mathcal{S}_1 = \mathscr{L}$ and $\mathcal{S}_2 = \mathscr{L}^*$. Then R is the matrix M because the columns of R are just the rotated coordinates of the basis vectors $\{(1,0,0),(0,1,0),(0,0,1)\}$. The first column of R is the vector $(\cos\theta, \sin\theta, 0)$, which is just the rotation of vector $(1,0,0)$. These are coordinates in the local coordinate system $\mathscr{L}$. So R is indeed a coordinate transformation matrix which converts $\mathscr{L}^*$ coordinates to $\mathscr{L}$ coordinates. Multiplying by $M_{\mathscr{L} \to \mathscr{W}}$ then converts the $\mathscr{L}$ coordinates to $\mathscr{W}$ coordinates.

Focus on the cube vertex $(1,1,1)$. These are local coordinates (system $\mathscr{L}$). Multiplying by R either changes the local coordinates to $(\cos\theta - \sin\theta, \sin\theta + \cos\theta, 1)$ or it changes the basis vectors of $\mathscr{L}$ giving a new system $\mathscr{L}^*$. In the $\mathscr{L}^*$ system, the vertex of the cube has coordinates $(1,1,1)$. The advantage of the second interpretation is that the coordinates of the cube vertices stay unchanged.

Transformations other than rotations work just as well here and the lesson is that transforming coordinates can be thought of as transforming coordinate systems. Yet, coordinate systems are all relative to each other, and usually there is some system, often the world coordinate system $\mathscr{W}$, that is absolute and unchanging. It is important to realize that we transformed the cube by thinking of it locally; we rotated around an axis through the center of the cube. Applying the rotation first accomplished this. If we wanted to rotate with respect to the world coordinate system and swing the cube around the world origin, we multiply by R after converting to world coordinates. In this case, it makes most sense to think of R as rotating coordinates because the world coordinate system is most likely fixed.

We view the scene from the camera position, so any movement or repositioning in the scene must ultimately take into account the camera coordinate system. The following five orientation tasks offer an overview of the order of operations in developing appropriate coordinate transformations:

1. *Object Rotation.* To rotate around an axis through the object's center, the rotation matrix R is applied to local coordinates first and then the sequence of coordinate transformations ends with the camera coordinate system.

$$M_{\mathscr{L} \to \mathscr{C}} = M_{\mathscr{W} \to \mathscr{C}} \cdot M_{\mathscr{L} \to \mathscr{W}} \cdot R$$

This matrix is applied to local coordinates of the cube vertices to generate the resulting camera coordinates showing the cube in a rotated position. To rotate around the world origin, we move the rotation matrix to act on world coordinates.

$$M_{\mathcal{L} \to \mathcal{C}} = M_{\mathcal{W} \to \mathcal{C}} \cdot R \cdot M_{\mathcal{L} \to \mathcal{W}}$$

2. *Eye Position.* The viewer's eye sees the scene through the camera and, if the viewer pivots his or her head left or right, the camera pivots left or right. When we have camera coordinates, we apply a rotation matrix. In this case, the rotation is around the up vector, which is the vector $\vec{v}_c$ in our notation.

$$M_{\mathcal{L} \to \mathcal{C}} = R \cdot M_{\mathcal{W} \to \mathcal{C}} . M_{\mathcal{L} \to \mathcal{W}}$$

Again, we imagine applying this matrix to local coordinates for an object.

3. *User Control.* As the viewer watches the scene, he or she may wish to move to the right or left via some sort of input (perhaps the mouse) as in a computer game. The resulting translation is a multiplication by a translation matrix T_n once we have camera coordinates.

$$M_{\mathcal{L} \to \mathcal{C}} = T_n \cdot M_{\mathcal{W} \to \mathcal{C}} \cdot M_{\mathcal{L} \to \mathcal{W}}$$

4. *Auxiliary Coordinate System.* We may want objects in our scene to move with respect to some temporary point. For example, to simulate the solar system with moons revolving around planets which revolve around the sun, we may want the position of Jupiter to perturb the orbit of some other body. To implement this type of movement, we need an auxiliary coordinate system $\mathcal{A}$ centered on Jupiter and we then convert to $\mathcal{A}$, transform perhaps through rotation, convert back to local coordinates, and continue the conversion to camera coordinates.

$$M_{\mathcal{L} \to \mathcal{C}} = M_{\mathcal{W} \to \mathcal{C}} \cdot M_{\mathcal{L} \to \mathcal{W}} M_{\mathcal{A} \to \mathcal{L}} \cdot R \cdot M_{\mathcal{L} \to \mathcal{A}}$$

Recall here that $M_{\mathcal{A} \to \mathcal{L}} = M_{\mathcal{L} \to \mathcal{A}}^{-1}$.

5. *Hierarchical Control.* Each of two cubes may have their own coordinate systems, but they may then be placed into a group coordinate system. This allows positioning of the cubes relative to each other and allows rotation of either cube around its center. By building scenes in this hierarchical way, quick changes can be made by transforming the coordinate systems.

In each of these listed cases, the sequence of transformation matrices can all be multiplied together, producing one matrix for the overall transformation. Graphics systems often use a stack data structure to keep track of the various matrices.

5.2.2 Euler Angles

Rotations and translations serve mostly to orient objects in a scene. Specifying translations is fairly straightforward, requiring the coordinates of a single vector showing
the displacement, but specifying the rotations can be more of a problem.

The three-dimensional rotations we developed were all relative to some axis. We
rotated around the coordinate axes x, y, and z, and then we derived the rotation around
an arbitrary axis (a_x, a_y, a_z), finding its transform matrix M_{arb}. From the derivation in
Chapter 4, recall the expression for M_{arb} where $c = \cos \theta$ and $s = \sin \theta$.

$$M_{arb} = \begin{bmatrix} c + (1-c)a_x^2 & (1-c)a_x a_y - sa_z & (1-c)a_x a_y + sa_y \\ (1-c)a_x a_y + sa_z & c + (1-c)a_y^2 & (1-c)a_y a_z - sa_x \\ (1-c)a_x a_z - sa_y & (1-c)a_y a_z + sa_x & c + (1-c)a_z^2 \end{bmatrix} \quad (5.7)$$

What happens when we have a sequence of several rotations one after the other?
We saw this earlier in the derivation of the rotation around an arbitrary axis; there,
we multiplied five individual rotations together to get the single matrix result in
Equation 5.7. Surprisingly, no matter how many rotations we apply, one after the
other, the result is always the same as a single rotation around some axis. The eighteenth century mathematician Leonard Euler showed that no matter what way a sphere
is rotated around its center, there always is an axis that remains fixed. For our purpose,
the theorem is clearer when stated for two rotations.

Theorem 5.1 (Euler on Rotations).   *In three dimensions, the composition of two
rotations is equivalent to a single rotation around some axis.*

Applying this theorem several times to a long string of rotations shows that any
composition of rotations is equivalent to a single rotation. We certainly know that
multiplying all the rotation matrices together gives a single matrix, but the theorem
claims this single matrix is actually the matrix for a rotation around some axis. There
are proofs of Euler's theorem using linear algebra or using the geometry on a sphere,
but here a simple example helps build some intuition about this result.

Example 5.4 (Two Rotations Equivalent to One).   Consider a rotation around the
x-axis (basis vector $\vec{i}$) followed by a rotation around the z-axis (basis vector $\vec{k}$.) In
both cases, the angle of rotation is $\pi/2$ counterclockwise. Then, the two rotation
matrices are R_x and R_z.

$$R_x = \begin{bmatrix} 1 & 0 & 0 \\ 0 & 0 & -1 \\ 0 & 1 & 0 \end{bmatrix} \quad R_z = \begin{bmatrix} 0 & -1 & 0 \\ 1 & 0 & 0 \\ 0 & 0 & 1 \end{bmatrix}$$

Respecting the order of the rotations, the product matrix is

$$R = R_z R_x = \begin{bmatrix} 0 & 0 & 1 \\ 1 & 0 & 0 \\ 0 & 1 & 0 \end{bmatrix}$$

Now notice that R fixes the vector $(1, 1, 1)$. If we normalize this vector, we get $\frac{1}{\sqrt{3}}(1, 1, 1)$ and, when we look at M_{arb} in Equation 5.7 using $a_x = a_y = a_z = \frac{1}{\sqrt{3}}$ and $\theta = 2\pi/3$, we see that $R = M_{arb}$. This composition of two rotations is equivalent to a single rotation of $\theta = 2\pi/3$ radians around the axis $(1, 1, 1)$. The point $(1, 1, 0)$ is sent to $(0, 1, 1)$ as expected (after checking a sketch of the coordinate system). $\quad\square$

There are various perspectives we can take on the transformation $R = R_z R_x$ from the last example. The easiest is to recall how the rotation matrices were derived by finding the new coordinates for a rotated point. Then the combination of two rotations, or many rotations, is seen as moving a point within a fixed (local) coordinate system. Points (hence, vertices) move and the coordinate system is fixed.

We can also imagine the coordinates of points staying fixed while the coordinate basis vectors change. In this case, the matrices are coordinate transformations and the coordinates for a vertex change because there is a new rotated coordinate system. Look at R_x in terms of the rotation angle.

$$R_x = \begin{bmatrix} 1 & 0 & 0 \\ 0 & \cos\theta & -\sin\theta \\ 0 & \sin\theta & \cos\theta \end{bmatrix}$$

The columns of R_x are the coordinates of the transformed basis vectors $(1, 0, 0)$, $(0, 1, 0)$, $(0, 0, 1)$ under a counterclockwise rotation around the x-axis. This means that, if M in Result 5.1 were a clockwise rotation, then $R_x = M^{-1}$ is the matrix that converts the original coordinates ($\mathcal{S}_1$) into coordinates in the transformed system ($\mathcal{S}_2$). The system $\mathcal{S}_2$ is the result of rotating the original system ($\mathcal{S}_1$) clockwise around the x-axis.

A similar interpretation of R_z as the inverse of a clockwise rotation around z allows us to give the composite conversion.

$$R_z R_x = M_{\mathcal{S}_2 \to \mathcal{S}_3} M_{\mathcal{S}_1 \to \mathcal{S}_2} = M_{\mathcal{S}_1 \to \mathcal{S}_3}$$

Coordinate system $\mathcal{S}_3$ is system $\mathcal{S}_2$ transformed by a clockwise rotation around its (new) z-axis. When thinking of coordinates, the vector $(0, 0, 1)$ in $\mathcal{S}_3$ is the z-axis and this is fixed by R_z. Figure 5.5 shows the three coordinate systems using the rotations from Example 5.4.

The point $P = (1, 1, 0)$ in system $\mathcal{S}_1$ has coordinates $(1, 0, 1)$ in transformed system $\mathcal{S}_2$ and coordinates $(0, 1, 1)$ in the system $\mathcal{S}_3$. These last coordinates are the same coordinates that the rotated point has in system $\mathcal{S}_1$.

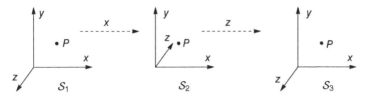

Figure 5.5 Two rotations

The rotation $R = R_z R_x$ from the example can be interpreted as rotating the basis vectors into a new coordinate system. These rotations are counterclockwise and the basis vector $(1, 0, 0)$ ends up as $(0, 1, 0)$. Looking at the final transformed coordinate system, multiplying R times the point with local coordinates $(1, 1, 0)$ gives original coordinates $(0, 1, 1)$. So the transformation R converts the local coordinates in the transformed coordinate system into original coordinates. This is exactly what we want. To rotate an object, we apply a rotation matrix to the basis vectors. Then, relative to the original coordinate system, to find the coordinates for any vertex in the rotated object, we multiply by the same rotation matrix.

In the previous analysis of two rotations, the fact that R_x, for example, has columns that are the transformed basis vectors is not unique. Actually, all rotation matrices have columns that are unit vectors perpendicular to each other. The same is true of the rows. This characterization is summarized in the following result.

Result 5.2 (Rotation Matrices). *Every rotation matrix is an orthogonal matrix, which means that the columns considered as vectors all have length 1 and are perpendicular to each other. The rows are also unit vectors that are perpendicular to each other. This implies that $R^{-1} = R^T$. Consequently, $(R_1 R_2)^{-1} = R_2^T R_1^T$.*

A combination of rotations is a single rotation, but since we are very comfortable with rotations around the x-, y-, and z-axis, it is has traditionally been practical to express any single rotation in terms of rotations around these axes. As an example, the orientations of spacecraft are given in terms of three angles of rotation around perpendicular axes. Unfortunately, there are various ways to order the three angles. We could, for example, rotate around the x-axis, then around the new z-axis, and finally around the new x-axis, or we could fix the three axes and rotate around each in some order. In both cases, we can achieve all possible rotations.

There are several (12) possibilities for the order of rotations around axes that can express all rotations. One common ordering is the one just given: rotate around the x-axis, then the new z-axis, and finally around the new x-axis. We will settle on rotating first around the x-axis through angle θ, then around the new y-axis through angle α, and finally around the newest z-axis through angle β. Form the product of the three matrices:

$$R_z R_y R_x = \begin{bmatrix} r_{11} & r_{12} & r_{13} \\ r_{21} & r_{22} & r_{23} \\ r_{31} & r_{32} & r_{33} \end{bmatrix}$$

The entries in the above matrix are

$$r_{11} = \cos \beta \cos \alpha$$
$$r_{12} = \cos \beta \sin \alpha \sin \theta - \sin \beta \cos \theta$$
$$r_{13} = \cos \beta \sin \alpha \cos \theta + \sin \beta \sin \theta$$
$$r_{21} = \sin \beta \cos \alpha$$
$$r_{22} = \sin \beta \sin \alpha \sin \theta + \cos \beta \cos \theta$$
$$r_{23} = \sin \beta \sin \alpha \cos \theta - \cos \beta \sin \theta$$
$$r_{31} = -\sin \alpha$$
$$r_{32} = \cos \alpha \sin \theta$$
$$r_{33} = \cos \alpha \cos \theta \tag{5.8}$$

If we are given a rotation matrix (around some axis), then we know the entries r_{ij} and, using the above equalities, we can solve for the angles θ, α, β. In particular, we get the following formulas for the three angles:

$$\theta = \tan^{-1} \left(\frac{r_{32}}{r_{33}} \right)$$
$$\alpha = -\sin^{-1}(r_{31})$$
$$\beta = \tan^{-1} \left(\frac{r_{21}}{r_{11}} \right)$$

The three angles θ, α, β are called the *Euler angles*, but there are a few subtleties in the formulas. For example, the second formula has more than one solution; we might try to fix this by restricting the range of each angle appropriately. However, there is still a problem with both the first and third formulas if $\cos \alpha = 0$. This is more significant and we can assess the difficulty by temporarily taking $\alpha = \pi/2$. Then the rotation matrix looks as follows:

$$\begin{bmatrix} 0 & \sin(\theta - \beta) & \cos(\theta - \beta) \\ 0 & \cos(\theta - \beta) & -\sin(\theta - \beta) \\ 1 & 0 & 0 \end{bmatrix}$$

Since the entries in this matrix are constant or depend on $\theta - \beta$, there are an infinite number of solutions for the three Euler angles that give this rotation matrix. All values that result, for example, in $\theta - \beta = \pi/3$, give the same rotation matrix. No amount of restricting the range of angles will help here. This situation is referred to as the *gimbal lock*, where the name comes from the mechanical design of gyroscopes. In orienting space craft, gimbal lock is a situation where the gyroscopic system cannot rotate appropriately to compensate for all perturbations. Mathematically, it means that changing angles θ and β changes the rotation only in a certain way. Changes in θ and β do not give us enough degrees of freedom to reach all orientations close to the current one.

Gimbal lock is indicative of a larger problem for computer graphics. In animation, we need to move smoothly from one orientation to another. Some method of interpolation is necessary to generate the intermediate orientations for the transition. One method is to take a linear combination of the initial and final orientations so that an intermediate angle could be generated by $(1 - t)\theta_1 + t\theta_2$. If we generate intermediate orientations by interpolating the three Euler angles in this way, the results are not always satisfactory. For initial positions that are near the gimbal lock, the trajectory for the animation can look odd. Many times the interpolations do look fine, but the odd cases can occur somewhat unexpectedly. Theoretically, there are fixes for these problems, but the resulting algorithms begin to become unwieldy. A better solution is to turn to quaternions to represent orientations.

Euler angles often prove useful in orienting the camera for a scene. We imagine our head positioned at the center of the camera looking toward the scene (down the z-axis). Then, we can turn our head side to side (called *yaw* in aeronautic terminology), or we can nod up and down (called *pitch*), or we can tilt our head side to side (called *roll*). All these orientations can be described by one of the Euler angles, and putting them together we get a single rotation matrix.

5.2.3 Quaternions

One of the predominant themes in the mathematics of computer graphics is the connection between algebra and geometry. Adding vectors and multiplying matrices both have relevant geometrical meaning when we consider the vertices of some object. Even the algebra of the real numbers can be connected to the geometry of points on the one-dimensional number line.

Moving up to the complex numbers is yet another story. Complex numbers have the form $a + bi$, where a and b are real numbers, and we then introduce i (not as a vector here) which is a new *imaginary* quantity such that when we square it we get -1. That is, $i^2 = -1$. We are not expected to immediately visualize this quantity or to have developed intuition about it. All we need to know is that its square is -1. The number $z = 2 + 3i$ is an example of a complex number, and we say it has real part equal to 2 and imaginary part equal to 3. There is an algebra for these numbers, which means we can add and multiply them.

$$(x_1 + y_1 i) + (x_2 + y_2 i) = (x_1 + x_2) + (y_1 + y_2)i$$

$$(x_1 + y_1 i)(x_2 + y_2 i) = (x_1 y_1 - y_1 y_2) + (x_1 y_2 + y_1 x_2)i \tag{5.9}$$

Notice that when multiplying two complex numbers we get a minus sign in the first term of the product because we replaced i^2 with -1. The theory of complex numbers was developed to help solve equations like $x^2 + 2 = 0$ where real numbers were simply insufficient. They now play a pivotal role in mathematics, both theoretical and applied, but our current interest is limited to their connections to the geometry that might benefit computer graphics. To that end, we need to go a little further in the algebra.

For real numbers, we talk about the absolute value as a way of measuring their size. The absolute value of a product is the product of absolute values. Similarly, we introduce an absolute value for complex numbers which is more accurately called a *norm*. We first define a conjugate and use the notation $\bar{z}$ for the conjugate of z. If $z = a + bi$ then $\bar{z} = a - bi$. The norm of z, denoted $|z|$ is defined by setting $|z|^2 = z\bar{z}$; the square of the norm is z times its conjugate.

$$|z|^2 = z\bar{z} = (a + bi)(a - bi) = a^2 + b^2 \implies |z| = \sqrt{a^2 + b^2} \qquad (5.10)$$

It looks like the norm of z is exactly the same as the length of the vector (a, b).

In fact, there is an intimate connection between complex numbers and vectors because we can represent both with two coordinates. The point $z = a + bi$ is the point in the regular Cartesian coordinate system with coordinates (a, b). We can also think of z as analogous to the vector from $(0, 0)$ to (a, b). Finally, it is important to note that in the algebra of complex numbers, $|z_1 z_2| = |z_1||z_2|$. The norm of a product is the product of the norms. One nice use of the norm is in producing a standard form for nonzero complex numbers.

$$z = a + bi = |z| \left(\frac{a}{|z|} + \frac{b}{|z|}i \right) = |z|(\cos \theta + i \sin \theta) \qquad (5.11)$$

The idea here is that the numbers $a/|z|$ and $b/|z|$ are numbers between -1 and 1 such that the sum of their squares is 1. This means we can find a θ so that one of the numbers is $\cos \theta$ and the other is $\sin \theta$. We have written the complex number z as its length times a complex number with length 1. This canonical form is often useful in calculations.

We are now in a position to focus on one of the key attributes of the connection between complex numbers and geometry. Let $w = \cos \theta + i \sin \theta$. (We have written the i before the $\sin \theta$ just for clarity.) Since $|w| = 1$, multiplying any $z = a + bi$ by w preserves the length of z.

$$wz = (\cos \theta + i \sin \theta)(a + bi) = (a \cos \theta - b \sin \theta) + (a \sin \theta + b \cos \theta)i$$

If we think of points and vectors, the vector (a, b) which represents z has been transformed through the multiplication by w to another vector $((a \cos \theta - b \sin \theta), (a \sin \theta + b \cos \theta))$. If we look closer and remember the two-dimensional rotation matrix, notice the result of multiplying by the rotation matrix:

$$\begin{bmatrix} \cos \theta & -\sin \theta \\ \sin \theta & \cos \theta \end{bmatrix} \begin{bmatrix} a \\ b \end{bmatrix} = \begin{bmatrix} a \cos \theta - b \sin \theta \\ b \cos \theta + a \sin \theta \end{bmatrix}$$

Complex multiplication by w and multiplication by the rotation matrix give the same resulting vector.

We have discovered that complex multiplication is really rotation. What if we multiplied by a w that was not of unit length? Then, we would use the canonical form $w = |w|(\cos\theta + i\sin\theta)$ and the product wz will be a scalar $|w|$ times the previous result. This means that we rotated z and multiplied its length by $|w|$. So geometrically multiplication is a counterclockwise rotation through angle θ where the length of the rotated vector is $|wz| = |w||z|$. This is the key observation, and the more we look at the algebra involved, the more we see how the addition of i to the number system allowed us to introduce a minus sign at just the right place to form a geometrical rotation. The natural next step is to see if we can generalize this to three dimensions in the hope that a new algebra will lead to a more efficient way to manipulate three-dimensional geometric objects.

5.2.4 Quaternion Algebra

In the middle of the nineteenth century, the Irish mathematician William Hamilton invented a new algebraic system by starting with a collection of imaginary quantities called *quaternions*. Although it might seem reasonable to start with complex numbers and add another imaginary quantity, quaternions require two new imaginary quantities giving a set of three denoted by $\{i, j, k\}$. (Again, these are not vectors although the letters conventionally used are also used for orthonormal basis vectors.) The square of each of these quantities is -1, that is, $i^2 = j^2 = k^2 = -1$. A quaternion is a generalized complex number: $\hat{q} = a + bi + cj + dk$. Historically, the tricky part was to define the algebra properly so that we get all the appropriate properties associated with addition, multiplication, and a norm. Hamilton hit on a set of rules for the imaginary quantities that led to a useful algebraic system.

Definition 5.2 (Quaternions). *A quaternion is a mathematical object of the form $\hat{q} = a + bi + cj + dk$, where the imaginary quantities $\{i, j, k\}$ satisfy the following rules:*

$$i^2 = j^2 = k^2 = -1$$

$$ij = -ji = k$$

$$jk = -kj = i$$

$$ki = -ik = j$$

It is not an accident that the rules for the imaginary quantities look similar to the rules we adopted for cross products of the basis vectors in an orthonormal coordinate system. (In fact, quaternions came first and led to the definitions of dot product and cross product.) Just as in complex numbers, addition of two quaternions and scalar multiplication takes place component-wise. If $\hat{q}_1 = a_1 + b_1 i + c_1 j + d_1 k$ and $\hat{q}_2 = a_2 + b_2 i + c_2 j + d_2 k$ with scalar s, then

$$\hat{q}_1 + \hat{q}_2 = (a_1 + a_2) + (b_1 + b_2)i + (c_1 + c_2)j + (d_1 + d_2)k$$
$$s\hat{q}_1 = sa_1 + sb_1 i + sc_1 j + sd_1 k \tag{5.12}$$

Multiplication of two quaternions happens just as we might expect by using the distributive property to find $4 \times 4 = 16$. Using the rules for the imaginary quantities, the result simplifies to

$$\hat{q}_1 \hat{q}_2 = (a_1 a_2 - b_1 b_2 - c_1 c_2 - d_1 d_2)$$
$$+ (a_1 b_2 + b_1 a_2 + c_1 d_2 - c_2 d_1)i$$
$$+ (a_1 c_2 + a_2 c_1 + d_1 b_2 - b_1 d_2)j$$
$$+ (a_1 d_2 + d_1 a_2 + b_1 c_2 - b_2 c_1)k \qquad (5.13)$$

It is a little easier to present calculations if we refer to the quaternion $\hat{q}$ by $(a, \vec{w})$ where $\vec{w} = (b, c, d)$. So a quaternion has a scalar part (a) and a vector part $(\vec{w})$. Using the dot product and cross product, we can express the product of two quaternions in vector form:

$$\hat{q}_1 \hat{q}_2 = (a_1, \vec{w}_1)(a_2, \vec{w}_2)$$
$$= ((a_1 a_2 - \vec{w}_1 \cdot \vec{w}_2), (a_1 \vec{w}_2 + a_2 \vec{w}_1 + \vec{w}_1 \times \vec{w}_2)) \qquad (5.14)$$

By looking at the rules for the imaginary quantities, or by noticing the cross product in the expression for the quaternion product, it is clear that quaternion multiplication is not commutative. The product $\hat{q}_1 \hat{q}_2$ does not always equal $\hat{q}_2 \hat{q}_1$. To finish describing the algebra, we need to define the conjugate for $\hat{q}$.

Definition 5.3 (Conjugate). *The conjugate for the quaternion $\hat{q} = (a, \vec{w})$ is $\hat{q}^* = (a, -\vec{w})$.*

Just as in the complex numbers, a quaternion times its conjugate gives the norm squared.

$$|\hat{q}|^2 = \hat{q}\hat{q}^* = ((a^2 + |\vec{w}|^2), (a\vec{w} - a\vec{w} - \vec{w} \times \vec{w}))$$
$$= a^2 + b^2 + c^2 + d^2 \qquad (5.15)$$

If a quaternion has norm equal to 1, we say it is a *unit* quaternion. In the case of conjugates, a quick check shows $\hat{q}\hat{q}^* = \hat{q}^*\hat{q}$. Using the conjugate again, we can define another useful quaternion, the inverse $\hat{q}^{-1}$.

$$\hat{q}^{-1} = \frac{\hat{q}^*}{|\hat{q}|^2} \implies (\hat{q}^{-1})\hat{q} = \hat{q}(\hat{q}^{-1}) = \frac{\hat{q}\hat{q}^*}{|q|^2} = 1 \qquad (5.16)$$

Finally, one more standard form helps us with calculations. For complex numbers, we were able to write any number in the canonical form $z = |z|(\cos \theta + i \sin \theta)$. For quaternions, there is a similar canonical form.

$$\hat{q} = (a, \vec{w}) = |\hat{q}| \left(\frac{a}{|\hat{q}|}, \frac{|\vec{w}|}{|\hat{q}|} \frac{\vec{w}}{|\vec{w}|} \right) = |\hat{q}|(\cos \theta, \vec{u} \sin \theta) \qquad (5.17)$$

The vector $\vec{u} = \vec{w}/|\vec{w}|$ has length 1, and since $a^2 + |\vec{w}|^2 = |\hat{q}|^2$, we can set $|\vec{w}|/|\hat{q}| = \sin\theta$. In fact, the quaternion $\hat{u} = (0, \vec{u})$ acts like i does in complex numbers; they are both square roots of -1. For any unit quaternion with zero scalar ($\hat{u}$), we have $\hat{u}^2 = -1$.

5.2.5 Rotations

We are interested in rotations of three-dimensional vectors, but quaternions are really four-dimensional objects. When we use the form $\hat{q} = a + bi + cj + dk$, the four parameters (a, b, c, d) suggest the connection with four-dimensional vectors. The alternative form $\hat{q} = (a, \vec{w})$ simply partitions the four parameters so that we have one scalar a and one three-dimensional vector $\vec{w} = (b, c, d)$. If we restrict our attention to quaternions with zero scalar, then we can draw a one-to-one relationship with vectors in three space. Interestingly, a relatively simple quaternion transformation results in rotating quaternions with zero scalar.

Theorem 5.2 (Quaternion Rotations). *If $\hat{v}$ is a quaternion with zero scalar and $\hat{q} = (a, \vec{w})$ is any unit quaternion, then the transformation $T(\hat{v}) = \hat{q}\hat{v}\hat{q}^{-1}$ rotates $\hat{v}$ around the axis $\vec{w}$.*

Along with establishing why the transformation T is a rotation, we will need to determine what the angle of rotation actually is. More practically, once we have an axis and angle, we need to find the quaternion $\hat{q}$ that defines a transformation giving the desired rotation.

Example 5.5 (Quaternion Rotation around x Axis). We have called the unit vector that defines the x-axis $\vec{i} = (1, 0, 0)$. So consider the unit quaternion $\hat{q} = \frac{1}{\sqrt{2}}(1, \vec{i}) = \frac{1}{\sqrt{2}} + \frac{1}{\sqrt{2}}i$. Note here that we have used both the vector $\vec{i}$ which is actually $(1, 0, 0)$ and the imaginary quantity i, a square root of -1, to define the quaternion. The standard basis vectors $\{\vec{j}, \vec{k}\}$ correspond to the imaginary quantities j and k in exactly the same way.

To see what the transformation $T(\hat{v}) = \hat{q}\hat{v}\hat{q}^{-1}$ does, we check its effect on the vectors $(3, 0, 0)$ and $(1, 0, 1)$, which correspond to quaternions $\hat{v}_1 = (0, 3\vec{i}) = 0 + 3i + 0j + 0k$, and on $\hat{v}_2 = (0, \vec{i} + \vec{k}) = 0 + i + 0j + k$.

First we find $\hat{q}^{-1} = \frac{1}{\sqrt{2}} - \frac{1}{\sqrt{2}}i$, and then we can calculate the effect of the transformation on $\hat{v}_1$.

$$T(\hat{v}_1) = \hat{q}\hat{v}_1\hat{q}^{-1} = \left(\frac{1}{\sqrt{2}} + \frac{1}{\sqrt{2}}i\right)(3i)\left(\frac{1}{\sqrt{2}} - \frac{1}{\sqrt{2}}i\right) = 3i = \hat{v}_1$$

The quaternion, and hence the vector $(3, 0, 0)$, remains fixed under the transformation T. This is consistent with the theorem, which claims the axis of rotation is $\vec{i}$.

For $\hat{v}_2$, the calculation is a touch trickier because we do need to keep track of the order of multiplication between imaginary quantities.

$$
\begin{aligned}
T(\hat{v}_2) = \hat{q}\hat{v}_2\hat{q}^{-1} &= \left(\frac{1}{\sqrt{2}} + \frac{1}{\sqrt{2}}i\right)(i+k)\left(\frac{1}{\sqrt{2}} - \frac{1}{\sqrt{2}}i\right) \\
&= \left(\frac{1}{\sqrt{2}}\right)^2 (1+i)(i+k)(1-i) \\
&= \frac{1}{2}(i+k+i^2+ik)(1-i) = \frac{1}{2}(i+k-1-j)(1-i) \\
&= \frac{1}{2}(i+k-1-j-i^2-ki+i+ji) = \frac{1}{2}(i+k-1-j+1-j+i-k) \\
&= (i-j)
\end{aligned}
$$

The transformation expectedly fixed the i component, but rotated the k component counterclockwise around $\vec{i}$ (x axis) through $\pi/2$. This is exactly the result of rotating the original vector $(1, 0, 1)$ around the x-axis. Just for practice, we can recalculate the transform using the vector form (Equation 5.14) of quaternion multiplication.

$$
\begin{aligned}
T(\hat{v}_2) = \hat{q}\hat{v}_1\hat{q}^{-1} &= \frac{1}{\sqrt{2}}(1, \vec{i})(0, (\vec{i}+\vec{k}))\frac{1}{\sqrt{2}}(1, -\vec{i}) \\
&= \left(\frac{1}{\sqrt{2}}\right)^2 ((0-1), (\vec{i}+\vec{k}-\vec{j}))(1, -\vec{i}) = \frac{1}{2}(-1, (\vec{i}-\vec{j}+\vec{k}))(1, -\vec{i}) \\
&= \frac{1}{2}((-1-(-1)), (\vec{i}+\vec{i}+\vec{k}-\vec{j}-(\vec{j}+\vec{k})) \\
&= (0, (\vec{i}-\vec{j}) \\
&= (i-j)
\end{aligned}
$$

As expected, we get the same result. Just to keep clear on the meaning of these quantities, the result of the transformation is $i - j$, which is the quaternion $i + (-1)j + 0k = (0, (1, -1, 0))$. The original vector $(1, 0, 1)$ was transformed to the vector $(1, -1, 0)$. It was rotated counterclockwise by $\pi/2$ around the x-axis (Figure 5.6).   □

The previous example gives a little intuition about how quaternion transformations can be used to rotate vectors, but we still need to establish carefully that the transformation $T(\hat{v}) = \hat{q}\hat{v}\hat{q}^{-1}$ is a rotation where $\hat{q}$ is a unit quaternion and $\hat{v}$ is a quaternion with zero scalar. The details are given in Section 5.4, but the idea is first to notice that T is a linear transformation. To show that it is a rotation, we need to establish that T transforms the basis vectors in a coordinate system the same way that a rotation

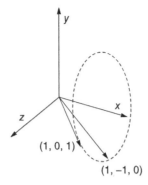

Figure 5.6   Quaternion rotation

does. The linear transformation property then implies that T transforms any vector the same way a rotation does.

Result 5.3 (Selecting $\hat{q}$). *If $\hat{q} = (\cos\theta, \vec{u}\sin\theta)$ and $\hat{v} = (0, \vec{v})$, then the transformation T defined by $T(\hat{v}) = \hat{q}\hat{v}\hat{q}^{-1}$ rotates $\vec{v}$ around the axis $\vec{u}$ through an angle 2θ.*

This result highlights the connection between the quaternion $\hat{q}$ and the angle of rotation. It is then easy to construct T.

Example 5.6 (Rotating with Quaternions). To rotate the vector $(2, -1, 5)$ counterclockwise around the axis $(1, 1, 2)$ through angle $\pi/3$, we begin by setting up the quaternion $\hat{v} = (0, (2, -1, 5))$. We need a unit vector in the direction of the rotation axis, so $\vec{u} = \frac{1}{\sqrt{6}}(1, 1, 2)$. Since the rotation angle is $2\theta = \pi/3$, we have $\theta = \pi/6$ and $\hat{q} = \left(\frac{\sqrt{3}}{2}, \frac{1}{\sqrt{6}}(1, 1, 2)\frac{1}{2}\right)$. Applying the transformation, we get

$$T(\hat{v}) = \left(\frac{\sqrt{3}}{2}, \frac{1}{\sqrt{6}}(1, 1, 2)\frac{1}{2}\right)(0, (2, -1, 5))\left(\frac{\sqrt{3}}{2}, -\frac{1}{\sqrt{6}}(1, 1, 2)\frac{1}{2}\right)$$

$$\approx (-2.25, (3.16, -1.07, 3.72))(0.87, (-0.2, -0.2, -0.41))$$

$$\approx (0, (4.38, 0.07, 3.31))$$

Within round-off error, the length of the rotated vector $(4.38, 0.07, 3.31)$ is equal to the length of the original vector $(2, -1, 5)$. This, of course, is expected of a rotation.   □

Composing two rotations is relatively easy. If the two corresponding unit quaternions are $\hat{q}_1$ and $\hat{q}_2$, then applying the first and then the second gives a new transformation T^*.

$$T^*(\hat{v}) = \hat{q}_2\hat{q}_1\hat{v}\hat{q}_1^{-1}\hat{q}_2^{-1} = (\hat{q}_2\hat{q}_1)\hat{v}(\hat{q}_2\hat{q}_1)^{-1}$$

Again, since quaternion multiplication is not commutative, we have to be careful which rotation we want to do first and which second. We can produce a single unit quaternion to do the combined rotations by simply multiplying $\hat{q}_2$ and $\hat{q}_1$ in that order. Finding the inverse is easy once we have the conjugate and the norm of the product. We have actually established a result we discovered earlier: the composition of two three-dimensional rotations is equivalent to a single three-dimensional rotation around the appropriate axis.

Using quaternions to rotate vectors is theoretically pleasing, but is it actually practical? We can compare elementary operations to give some indication of efficiency. To multiply two quaternions, think about the basic form of the quaternion as a sum $a + bi + cj + dk$ and count the number of multiplication and additions of numbers. It takes 16 multiplications and 12 additions. (Interestingly, multiplying using the vector form of quaternions takes the same number of multiplications and additions.) Consequently, to apply the transformation T for rotation, it takes 2 quaternion multiplications or 32 multiplications and 14 additions. On the other hand, multiplying by a single 3×3 rotation matrix takes only nine multiplications and six additions. The comparison is lopsided in favor of the matrix multiplication.

However, manipulation of a graphics scene requires rotation after rotation, so comparing the composition of two rotations is also key. To compose two quaternion rotations, we multiply two quaternions taking 16 multiplications and 12 additions. For matrices, we need to multiply two 3×3 matrices taking 27 multiplications and 18 additions. Now, it seems there is an advantage for quaternions. Often, primitive operations are implemented in hardware, so our comparisons are only indicative of how speeds might compare.

Regardless of the efficiency gains or losses, another key reason to use quaternions is to interpolate between two orientations of an object and this is what we turn to next.

5.2.6 Interpolation: Slerp

Summarizing what we have done, a unit quaternion $\hat{q}$ determines a rotation in three-space, with the vector part indicating the rotation axis and the scalar part determining the rotation angle. A quaternion $\hat{v}$ with zero scalar can be thought of as a three dimensional vector, and the transformation $T(\hat{v}) = \hat{q}\hat{v}\hat{q}^{-1}$ produces the rotated vector. (The presence of $\hat{q}^{-1}$ in the definition of the transformation means that, even if the quaternion $\hat{q}$ does not have unit norm, we still get the same rotation because $|\hat{q}|$ cancels out.) We now want to expand our concept of quaternions from rotations to orientations.

If we start with the standard orthonormal Cartesian coordinate system with origin O and unit basis vectors $\{\vec{i}, \vec{j}, \vec{k}\}$, then a unit quaternion represents a rotation which transforms each of the basis vectors to form a new orthonormal coordinate system. As an animated cube rotates while it moves from one position to another in the scene, its local coordinate system is changing orientation from step to step of the animation. So, in fact, a starting orientation represented by a unit quaternion $\hat{q}_1$ changes into a final orientation represented by quaternion $\hat{q}_2$. Along the way, there is an entire sequence of quaternions representing intermediate orientations. The center of the cube may also move through space, but this change is represented by translations and we can consider the change separately from the orientation.

The interpolation problem is simply to construct a sequence of orientation quaternions beginning with $\hat{q}_1$ and ending with $\hat{q}_2$. It is desirable that the change from quaternion to quaternion is smooth and that the rate of change is constant. A good first guess at a scheme for doing this is to compute quaternions $\hat{q}(t) = (1 - t)\hat{q}_1 + t\hat{q}_2$ as t goes from zero to 1. This is the affine combination we saw when finding points on a line segment, and we say it *interpolates* the end points $\hat{q}_1$ and $\hat{q}_2$.

This linear approach to interpolation changes the orientation smoothly, but it does not have a constant rate of change. To see this, it helps to envision the interpolation more geometrically. A quaternion is a four-dimensional vector, so when we consider unit quaternions, we are looking at points on a four-dimensional sphere. Visualizing such spheres is tough, but thinking by analogy with three-dimensional spheres is easier. Restricting ourselves to unit quaternions, we have two points indicated by $\hat{q}_1$ and $\hat{q}_2$ on the sphere in four dimensions. We want a path on the sphere between the two points and it makes some sense to find the shortest path. (Think analogously to the three-dimensional sphere where the shortest path between two points is the intersection of the sphere with a plane containing the two points and the center of the sphere.) The linear interpolation procedure draws a straight line between the points, but it is not on the sphere; the length of $\hat{q}(t)$ is not necessarily 1. Normalizing $\hat{q}(t)$ by dividing by its length gives a (shortest) path of quaternions that are on the sphere.

Figure 5.7 shows a cross section of the situation. The key observation is that, since linear interpolation takes uniform steps along the straight line, the angle θ in the figure changes faster in the middle of the line and slower near the two end points. Instead, we would like the angular change to be constant. To obtain this uniform change, the angle between $\hat{q}_1$ and $\hat{q}(t)$ should be $t\theta$. This sort of interpolation is called *spherical linear interpolation* (or *slerp*, for short).

To develop a convenient formula for slerp, look at $\hat{v}$ in the figure. The quaternions are four-dimensional vectors and we want to choose quaternion $\hat{v}$ so that it

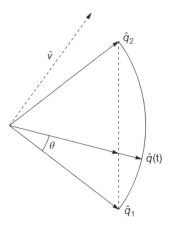

Figure 5.7   Slerp

is perpendicular to $\hat{q}_1$ with length 1; that is, $\hat{v} \cdot \hat{q}_1 = 0$. Define $\hat{q}(t)$ to be an affine combination of $\hat{q}_1$ and $\hat{v}$.

$$\hat{q}(t) = \cos(t\theta)\hat{q}_1 + \sin(t\theta)\hat{v}$$

Assuming we can find an appropriate $\hat{v}$, this definition has some nice properties. For $t = 0$, $\hat{q}(0) = \hat{q}_1$ and $\hat{q}(t)$ has unit length (see Exercises). By construction, the angle between $\hat{q}_1$ and $\hat{q}(t)$ changes uniformly. For $t = 1$, the definition should give $\hat{q}_2$, and we can use this constraint to solve for $\hat{v}$.

$$\hat{q}_2 = (\cos\theta)\hat{q}_1 + (\sin\theta)\hat{v}$$

$$\implies \hat{v} = \frac{\hat{q}_2 - (\cos\theta)\hat{q}_1}{\sin\theta} \tag{5.18}$$

A quick check shows that, assuming $\hat{q}_1$ and $\hat{q}_2$ have length 1, $\hat{v}$ does as well. Remember that the trigonometric addition formulas simplifies the expression for $\hat{q}(t)$.

$$\begin{aligned}
\hat{q}(t) &= \cos(t\theta)\hat{q}_1 + \sin(t\theta)\vec{v} \\
&= \cos(t\theta)\hat{q}_1 + \sin(t\theta)\frac{\hat{q}_2 - (\cos\theta)\hat{q}_1}{\sin\theta} \\
&= \frac{1}{\sin\theta}((\sin\theta\cos t\theta - \sin t\theta\cos\theta)\hat{q}_1 + (\sin t\theta)\hat{q}_2) \\
&= \frac{\sin(1-t)\theta}{\sin\theta}\hat{q}_1 + \frac{\sin t\theta}{\sin\theta}\hat{q}_2
\end{aligned}$$

This gives $\hat{q}(t)$ as a combination of $\hat{q}_1$ and $\hat{q}_2$. It smoothly changes the orientation and does so at a constant rate.

There is one ambiguity left. On the sphere, there are two paths between $\hat{q}_1$ and $\hat{q}_2$, one is on the "front" side of the sphere and the other is on the "back." We probably want the shortest one, and to determine that we calculate the dot product of $\hat{q}_1$ and $\hat{q}_2$ as four dimensional vectors. If the result is positive, we know the angle between them is less than $\pi/2$ and the slerp procedure will be mapping the shortest path on the sphere. Otherwise, changing $\hat{q}_2$ to $-\hat{q}_2$ will give a positive dot product. Since $-\hat{q}_2$ represents the same rotation as $\hat{q}_2$, using $-\hat{q}_2$ in this second case will give the shortest path.

Result 5.4 (Slerp Procedure). *Given two unit quaternions $\hat{q}_1$ and $\hat{q}_2$, spherical linear interpolation produces the quaternions*

$$\hat{q}(t) = \frac{\sin(1-t)\theta}{\sin\theta}\hat{q}_1 + \frac{\sin t\theta}{\sin\theta}\hat{q}_2$$

If $\hat{q}_1 \cdot \hat{q}_2 < 0$, use $-\hat{q}_2$ instead of $\hat{q}_2$.

We can use slerp to move objects or to move the camera position. However, when moving the camera position, there is no guarantee that the up vector will stay positioned up (i.e., parallel to its initial position) throughout the interpolation. This may be fine, but it may be necessary to adjust the orientations.

5.2.7 From Euler Angles and Quaternions to Rotation Matrices

To orient an object in space, we position its center using a translation and then rotate it into the desired orientation. The rotation can be described by a rotation matrix, by the three Euler angles, or by an corresponding quaternion. Sometimes, in the midst of coding a graphics application, it is necessary to move between these three descriptions. We have seen how to go from a rotation matrix to Euler angles, and the reverse direction simply requires multiplying the three individual rotation matrices together. Now we need an algorithm for converting quaternions to matrices.

Since rotation is a linear transformation, we only need to know what the transformation does to the basis vectors in order to determine what it does to any vector. So we will calculate the effect of a quaternion on the standard orthonormal basis vectors $\{\vec{i}, \vec{j}, \vec{k}\}$. Let $\hat{q} = (a, \vec{w}) = (a, b, c, d)$. Assume $\hat{q}$ is a unit quaternion, so $a^2 + b^2 + c^2 + d^2 = 1$.

$$\vec{v}_1 = \hat{q}\vec{i}\hat{q}^{-1} = (a, b, c, d)(0, 1, 0, 0)(a, -b, -c, -d)$$
$$= (-b, a, d, -c)(a, -b, -c, -d) = (0, a^2 + b^2 - c^2 - d^2, 2ad + 2bc, 2bd - 2ac)$$
$$\vec{v}_2 = \hat{q}\vec{j}\hat{q}^{-1} = (a, b, c, d)(0, 0, 1, 0)(a, -b, -c, -d)$$
$$= (-c, -d, a, b)(a, -b, -c, -d) = (0, -2ad + 2bc, a^2 - b^2 + c^2 - d^2, 2cd - 2ab)$$
$$\vec{v}_3 = \hat{q}\vec{k}\hat{q}^{-1} = (a, b, c, d)(0, 0, 0, 1)(a, -b, -c, -d)$$
$$= (-d, c, -b, a)(a, -b, -c, -d) = (0, 2bd + 2ac, 2cd - 2ab, a^2 - b^2 - c^2 + d^2)$$

Using these transformed vectors as columns gives us the correct rotation matrix.

$$R(\hat{q}) = \begin{bmatrix} a^2 + b^2 - c^2 - d^2 & 2bc - 2ad & 2bd + 2ac \\ 2bc + 2ad & a^2 - b^2 + c^2 - d^2 & 2cd - 2ab \\ 2bd - 2ac & 2cd + 2ab & a^2 - b^2 - c^2 + d^2 \end{bmatrix}$$

Going backwards to find the quaternion corresponding to a rotation matrix relies on the algebraic relations between entries in this rotation matrix. There are several algorithms for doing this, and one in particular starts by calculating the sum of the diagonal elements, $S = 3a^2 - b^2 - c^2 - d^2$. If the quaternion is a unit quaternion, then we can conclude that $S + 1 = 4a^2$. In a similar vein, we find formulas for the other parameters (r_{ii} is a diagonal entry in the rotation matrix).

$$2r_{11} - S + 1 = -a^2 + 3b^2 - c^2 - d^2 + 1 = 4b^2$$
$$2r_{22} - S + 1 = -a^2 - b^2 + 3c^2 - d^2 + 1 = 4c^2$$
$$2r_{33} - S + 1 = -a^2 - b^2 - c^2 + 3d^2 + 1 = 4d^2$$

We have an equation for each parameter, but solving them requires deciding whether to take the positive or negative square root. One of these decisions is fine, because we know that a quaternion and its negative represent the same orientation. However, once we solve for one parameter this way, we need other equations to guarantee the correct values of the remaining parameters. Notice that $r_{12} + r_{21} = 4bc$ and $r_{21} - r_{12} = 4ad$. Two other pairs of off-diagonal entries give similar equations, and no matter which parameter we solve for first, we can find all the others using these off-diagonal equations.

Since we can convert between Euler angles and rotation matrices in both directions and between quaternions and matrices in both directions, we can pass between all three of these representations.

5.3   OTHER COORDINATE SYSTEMS

Assigning numbers to points was a historical breakthrough that changed the way geometry was done. This led to a wide variety of coordinate systems with the venerable Cartesian coordinate system usually in the front and center. An orthonormal basis for the system adds considerably to the ease of calculation and fits reasonably with most geometric situations. Yet, although many geometric objects have nice descriptions in Cartesian coordinates, most objects in the natural world do not. We can try to approximate them with simpler objects and fancier mathematical techniques, but usually compact descriptions escape us. This argues for at least exploring the other options for coordinate systems.

Keep in mind some of the attributes of a coordinate system that make it particularly useful in graphics applications. First, it should be relatively easy to calculate with the coordinates. Note how dot products are easy to compute in orthonormal Cartesian systems. Second, although it is not necessary, it does help if there is a one-to-one relationship between coordinates and points. Cartesian coordinates have this property, but homogeneous coordinates do not. Without unique coordinates, algorithms often have to deal with several cases. Third, the coordinate system should allow simple or otherwise efficient descriptions of some common objects. Lines, planes, and therefore cubes are easy to describe in Cartesian systems and are even more unified when using homogeneous coordinates.

5.3.1   Non-orthogonal Axes

Rather than choosing basis vectors for a Cartesian coordinate system that are mutually perpendicular (i.e., orthogonal), we may decide that non-perpendicular axes match

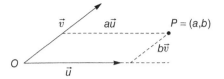

Figure 5.8   Non-perpendicular axes

the shape of our object better. As we will see later, sometimes a pattern we wish to superimpose on some flat face has a shape more conducive to skew axes. Much of our analysis of coordinate systems including converting from one set of coordinates to another allowed for non-perpendicular axes. In two dimensions, the situation is easy to assess, and Figure 5.8 shows two non-perpendicular axes $\vec{u}$ and $\vec{v}$ along with the origin O and the coordinates (a, b) of a point P. The point P is then expressed as $O + a\vec{u} + b\vec{v}$. A useful simplification is to require that $\vec{u}$ and $\vec{v}$ are unit vectors.

We can no longer use the standard formula for dot product in this system because $\vec{u} \cdot \vec{v} \neq 0$. If we do have two vectors described in this system $\vec{w}_1 = (a_1, b_1)$ and $\vec{w}_2 = (a_2, b_2)$, then the dot product requires a little more algebra.

$$\vec{w}_1 \cdot \vec{w}_2 = (a_1\vec{u} + b_1\vec{v}) \cdot (a_2\vec{u} + b_2\vec{v}) = (a_1a_2 + b_1b_2) + (a_1b_2 + a_2b_1)(\vec{u} \cdot \vec{v})$$

Here we assumed that $\vec{u}$ and $\vec{v}$ are unit vectors. The same approach gives a formula for the dot product of three-dimensional vectors described in a non-orthonormal coordinate system.

It is often convenient to convert from a set of non-orthogonal basis vectors into a set of orthogonal ones. The point is to find orthogonal vectors that in some sense match the original set reasonably well. In two dimensions, we simply keep one basis vector and write the other as a sum of a component projected on the first plus a component that is perpendicular to the first.

Example 5.7 (Two Dimensions: Finding Orthogonal Basis Vectors).   If the object or pattern we are working with suggests we use the basis vectors $\vec{u} = (1, 2)$ and $\vec{v} = (-1, 3)$, we can first normalize them to get $\vec{u} = \frac{1}{\sqrt{5}}(1, 2)$ and $\vec{v} = \frac{1}{\sqrt{10}}(-1, 3)$. Then decide which vector fits the object or pattern best and take it as the first vector in our new basis. Say $\vec{u}$ is the key vector, so set $\vec{u}_* = \vec{u}$. Now project $\vec{v}$ onto $\vec{u}_*$ to get $(\vec{u}_* \cdot \vec{v})\vec{u}_*$. This projection is in the direction of $\vec{u}_*$, so subtracting this from $\vec{v}$ gives a vector $\vec{v}^*$ that is perpendicular to $\vec{u}_*$

$$\vec{v}_* = \vec{v} - (\vec{u}_* \cdot \vec{v})\vec{u}_* = \frac{1}{\sqrt{10}}(-1, 3) - \frac{1}{\sqrt{10}}(1, 2) = \frac{1}{\sqrt{10}}(-2, 1)$$

We could have found a vector perpendicular to $\vec{u}_*$ in our sleep, but using the projection helps us to ensure that we find the one in the direction that matches $\vec{v}$. After renormalizing $\vec{v}^*$, the two vectors form an orthonormal basis.   □

The situation in three dimensions is not much harder and we have already dealt with the problem when looking for a suitable camera coordinate system. There we started with the vector pointing at the scene plus an approximation to the vector pointing up. Then using cross products, we produced a perpendicular up-vector and a third forming a right-hand coordinate system. In the current situation, we might have three vectors to start with, $\{\vec{u}, \vec{v}, \vec{w}\}$. Take $\vec{u}_* = \vec{u}$. Then either $\vec{u}_* \times \vec{v}$ or $\vec{v} \times \vec{u}_*$ gives a perpendicular vector that could serve as $\vec{w}_*$. We decide which based on the dot product with $\vec{w}$. Then again, either $\vec{u}_* \times \vec{w}_*$ or $\vec{w}_* \times \vec{u}_*$ gives $\vec{v}_*$.

Example 5.8 (Three Dimensions: Finding Orthogonal Basis Vectors). Take the vectors $\vec{u} = (1, 1, 1)$, $\vec{v} = (0, -2, 1)$, and $\vec{w} = (-2, 0, 3)$ as the initial basis vectors. Then, $\vec{u}_* = \vec{u} = (1, 1, 1)$. Finding the cross product gives $\vec{u}_* \times \vec{v} = (3, -1, -2)$ or $\vec{v} \times \vec{u}^* = (-3, 1, 2)$.

If it is in the same direction as $\vec{w}$, then the angle between them should be less than $\pi/2$ and the dot product will be positive.

$$\vec{w} \cdot (-3, 1, 2) = 12 > 0 \implies \vec{w}_* = (-3, 1, 2)$$

Now, $\vec{w}_* \times \vec{u}_* = (-1, 5, -4)$ and the dot product with $\vec{v}$ is negative, so we take the opposite direction, $\vec{v}_* = (1, -5, 4)$.

The three vectors $\{(1, 1, 1), (1, -5, 4), (-3, 1, 2)\}$ form an orthogonal system, and once we normalize, they form an orthonormal system. Checking the cross products, we find that the system is right-handed.

Instead of using cross products as we did in this example, we could proceed as we did in Example 5.7 by projecting $\vec{v}$ onto $\vec{u}_*$ and then projecting $\vec{w}$ onto the plane determined by $\vec{u}_*$ and $\vec{v}_*$. In linear algebra, this approach is called the *Gram–Schmidt process*.   □

5.3.2 Polar, Cylindrical, and Spherical Coordinates

We have already used angles for designating orientations, and if we push further, we can use them for identifying points. In two dimensions, the origin plus the distance to a particular point gets us started and the angle then indicates direction. The coordinates called *polar coordinates* are (r, θ); r is the distance and θ is the direction given in radians. The direction angle is relative to a fixed direction, so this coordinate system requires both a point designated as the origin and a direction designated as the fixed direction. If there is a Cartesian coordinate system already established, then the fixed direction is usually along the positive x-axis (Figure 5.9). If $\theta = 0$, then the point is somewhere on the positive x-axis. Angles are measured in a counterclockwise manner, so $\theta = \pi/2$ radians means the point is on the positive y-axis. A negative angle would then be a clockwise direction, so $\theta = -\pi/2$ indicates a point on the negative half of the y-axis.

Polar coordinates are not unique. The point P with Cartesian coordinates $(1, 1)$ has polar coordinates $(\sqrt{2}, \pi/4)$, where the polar coordinate system is arranged so $\theta = 0$ indicates the positive x-axis. Clearly, adding a multiple of 2π to θ gives the

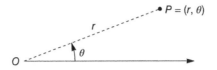

Figure 5.9   Polar coordinate system

same point, so, for example, $P = (\sqrt{2}, 9\pi/2)$. This minor annoyance can be partially patched up by insisting that the direction angle θ be constrained by $0 \le \theta < 2\pi$. The possibility of r being negative means that the polar coordinates $(-\sqrt{2}, -3\pi/4)$ also denotes P. Again, nonuniqueness rears its head, forcing us to restrict the distance to be nonnegative if we want unique coordinates. However, even with constraints, the origin still has multiple polar coordinates since $r = 0$ and θ can be anything. It is probably not worth obsessing over this uniqueness problem and instead design algorithms to deal with it appropriately.

Polar coordinates are particularly nice for planar objects that have circular symmetry. A circle, for example, has the property that all points are at a fixed distance from the center. So in a local polar coordinate system with the origin at the center, a circle of radius 4 can be described with the simple equation $r = 4$; all points with $r = 4$ and with θ equal to anything are on the circle. A spiral becomes $r = \theta$, where we take only nonnegative values for θ, and one flower-like object is $r = \cos 2\theta$. See the Exercises for relatively simple polar equations that produce aesthetically pleasing (if not practical) patterns (Figure 5.10).

Of course, points have both polar and Cartesian coordinates, and to move between them a little trigonometry finds the relationships.

$$x = r \cos \theta$$
$$y = r \sin \theta$$
$$r = \sqrt{x^2 + y^2}$$
$$\theta = \tan^{-1} y/x \tag{5.19}$$

Adding an axis perpendicular to the polar plane boosts polar coordinates into three dimensions. The new axis, which we might call z, gives a third coordinate, and (r, θ, z)

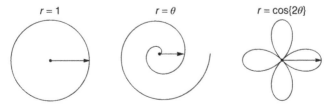

Figure 5.10   Polar curves

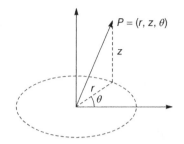

Figure 5.11   Cylindrical coordinate system

now describes points in space. This *cylindrical* coordinate system easily describes a cylinder because $r = 4$ now says that both θ and z can be anything. By using a set of equations, we can extend our descriptive capabilities as, for example, when we use $r = 4$ and $z = 5$ to describe a circle in space. The set of equations $r = 4$ and $z = \theta$ gives a spring (or helix) (Figure 5.11).

Thinking in terms of cylindrical coordinates can make some objects easier to describe and then, if we need, we can convert to Cartesian coordinates for the standard transformations like rotation, scaling, and translation. The conversion proceeds easily because x and y coordinates obey the polar coordinate conversion and z is the same in both cylindrical and Cartesian coordinates.

Instead of just circular symmetry, many objects have close to spherical symmetry. To design a coordinate system which better fits these objects, we start with polar coordinates and add another angular direction rather than a standard axis. Imagine that we have an established three-dimensional Cartesian right-handed coordinate system. Then once again $\theta = 0$ indicates points along the positive x-axis. Now we introduce a new direction designated with the angle ϕ where $0 \leq \phi \leq \pi$ and $\phi = 0$ indicates points along the positive z-axis (Figure 5.12). The distance coordinate is now a distance in three dimensions rather than just two, so we give it a new designation, ρ. The coordinates (ρ, θ, ϕ) are called *spherical coordinates*. (Unfortunately, presentations of spherical coordinates are not all consistent; the two directions θ and ϕ can appear reversed from this presentation and sometimes just the names are reversed.)

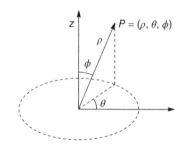

Figure 5.12   Spherical coordinate system

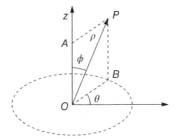

Figure 5.13 Conversion between spherical and Cartesian coordinates

The point with spherical coordinates $(\sqrt{2}, \frac{\pi}{2}, \frac{\pi}{4})$ is the point $(0, 1, 1)$ in the Cartesian system. Again, you can construct several sets of coordinates that denote the same point in space. For example, any point on the z-axis has $\phi = 0$, so the value of θ is irrelevant; both $(1, 0, 0)$ and $(1, \pi, 0)$ are the same point.

In the spherical coordinate system, the equation $\rho = 4$ now describes a sphere of radius 4, and, together, the two equations $\rho = \theta$ and $\phi = \pi/6$ (for nonnegative θ) describe a conical spiral.

To convert from spherical coordinates to Cartesian coordinates and back, take a point P and drop perpendiculars to the z-axis and the xy plane. Then, consider the triangles $\triangle POA$ and $\triangle POB$ in Figure 5.13. The segment PA has length $\rho \sin \phi$ and segment PB is $\rho \cos \phi$ which is just the z coordinate. The equations to convert from spherical to Cartesian coordinates become

$$x = \rho \sin \phi \cos \theta$$
$$y = \rho \sin \phi \sin \theta$$
$$z = \rho \cos \phi \tag{5.20}$$

Going from Cartesian to spherical coordinates requires the following formulas:

$$\rho = \sqrt{x^2 + y^2 + z^2}$$
$$\theta = \tan^{-1} \frac{y}{x}$$
$$\phi = \cos^{-1} \frac{z}{\rho} \tag{5.21}$$

5.3.3 Barycentric Coordinates

Cartesian, polar, cylindrical, and spherical coordinates all require reference objects; they need an origin and either axes or specified directions. What we are doing in most coordinate systems is selecting references that match particular geometric situations. When we are focused on line segments, for example, picking the two end points as references leads to a convenient way for identifying points on the segment.

With A and B as end points, a point P on the segment can be described by noting that
$P = A + t(B - A) = (1 - t)A + tB$.

This expresses P as an affine combination of the two end points A and B. It is a weighted average of the two points, and the coordinates $1 - t$ and t are called *barycentric coordinates*. (The prefix "bary" refers to the Greek word for weight.) These coordinates uniquely determine P. When $t = 0$, then $P = A$, and when $t = 1$, $P = B$. The barycentric coordinates are weights and they always sum to 1. (Technically, we could just give the coordinate t knowing that the second one $(1 - t)$ can be readily calculated.)

Without constraining t to the interval $0 \leq t \leq 1$, we can describe any point on the line. If $t > 1$, then we are reaching a point P on the line extending past end point B. Similarly, negative values of t give points on the line extending past end point A. In both these situations, one of the barycentric coordinates is negative and the other positive; the sum is always 1. If we have Cartesian coordinates for the end points, then the weighted average produces Cartesian coordinates for P.

By specifying three reference points instead of two, we can use the same technique to locate points in the plane. Consider points A, B, and C that are not collinear and set them as reference points. Then, an arbitrary point P in the plane can be described by $P = \alpha_0 A + \alpha_1 B + \alpha_2 C$. The three barycentric coordinates $(\alpha_0, \alpha_1, \alpha_2)$ sum to 1, and if they are all nonnegative, then the point is inside the triangle. This coordinate system turns out to be very useful in computer graphics and will be explored in more detail in the Chapter 6.

Generalizing to more reference points unfortunately proves difficult, but various schemes have proved useful in specific situations. If the points are vertices of a polygon with equal sides and angles, the generalization is almost straightforward.

5.4 COMPLEMENTS AND DETAILS

5.4.1 Historical Note: Descartes

The Cartesian coordinate system is named after René Descartes, a French philosopher who wrote a book called *Discourse on Method* published in 1637. The book is really the beginning of modern philosophy and contained three appendices which were more scientific treatises. One of those treatises discussed geometry and suggested the connections between algebra and geometry. There is no mention of perpendicular axes or coordinates, so placing his name on a coordinate system is more the result of good publicity than inventive mathematics. As with most results that bear someone's name, the true history is most likely more convoluted involving the contributions of many along the way.

5.4.2 Historical Note: Hamilton

Sir William Rowan Hamilton was born in Dublin in 1843. As a student at Trinity College, he proved to have exceptional ability in mathematics and went on to make major discoveries in optics and dynamics. He effectively unified dynamics with his equations and brought the same level of analysis to optics. The worldwide recognition that followed made him one of the most influential mathematicians of the time.

In the middle of the nineteenth century, complex numbers were proving their worth and many were drawing connections between complex numbers and two-dimensional geometry. The desire to generalize the ideas to three dimensions piqued Hamilton's interest and he worked steadily trying to devise an algebra that mimicked the complex number system where one imaginary quantity (i) plus the real numbers formed a coherent system of numbers. For three dimensions, the natural generalization was to add a second imaginary quantity. Yet, no one could define multiplication and addition in order to produce an algebra with useful properties like associativity, commutativity, and distributivity.

It turns out that there is no way to define an appropriate algebra for two imaginary quantities, but there is for three imaginary quantities (i, j, k) if the insistence on commutativity is abandoned. After years of work, the solution came to Hamilton one night while walking over the Brougham Bridge in Dublin. The idea was so exciting to him that he reportedly scratched the equations $(i^2 = j^2 = k^2 = ijk = -1)$ in one of the bridge stones. Hamilton spent the next 22 years of his life developing techniques for using quaternions in physics and mathematics. Others joined the cause, but possibly due to the ponderous nature of the book Hamilton produced, not many reached the inner circle and quaternions were somewhat slow to catch on. Later in the century, the American physicist Josiah Gibbs (among others like Oliver Heaviside) drew from Hamilton's work to establish the foundations of modern vector analysis; in particular, the cross product operation grew out of quaternion algebra and became the key in many analytical calculations.

Quaternions themselves never quite caught on although Hamilton was convinced of their central position in mathematics. (Arguably, it was Hamilton's work on quaternions that introduced the words "vector" and "scalar" into the mathematical lexicon). In the twentieth century, their connection with rotations pulled them from curious examples to key analytical tools, and the development of computer graphics, no doubt, helped assure quaternions a permanent position among important mathematical objects.

5.4.3 Proof of Quaternion Rotation

To establish carefully that the transformation $T(\hat{v}) = \hat{q}\hat{v}\hat{q}^{-1}$ is a rotation where $\hat{q}$ is a unit quaternion and $\hat{v}$ is a quaternion with zero scalar, we can start by simplifying the problem.

First, write $\hat{q}$ in its canonical form $|\hat{q}|(\cos\theta, \vec{u}\sin\theta)$. This means the conjugate is $\hat{q}^* = |\hat{q}|(\cos\theta, -\vec{u}\sin\theta)$ and the inverse is $\hat{q}^{-1} = \frac{1}{|\hat{q}|}(\cos\theta, -\vec{u}\sin\theta)$. Then the transform T simplifies to

$$T(\hat{v}) = \hat{q}\hat{v}\hat{q}^{-1} = |\hat{q}|(\cos\theta, \vec{u}\sin\theta)(\hat{v})\frac{1}{|\hat{q}|}(\cos\theta, -\vec{u}\sin\theta)$$

$$= (\cos\theta, \vec{u}\sin\theta)(\hat{v})(\cos\theta, -\vec{u}\sin\theta) \tag{5.22}$$

In the transformation T, the length of $\hat{q}$ cancels out, implying that any scalar multiple of $\hat{q}$ will give the same transformation. Specifically, $\hat{q}$ and $-\hat{q}$ correspond to the same transformation.

Second, T is in fact a linear transformation. Using the definition of quaternion multiplication, we can show that $T(\hat{v}_1 + \hat{v}_2) = T(\hat{v}_1) + T(\hat{v}_2)$ and that $T(a\hat{v}) = aT(\hat{v})$ (see Exercises). Rotation of three-dimensional vectors is also a linear transformation (it is multiplication by a matrix). To show that these two linear transformations are the same, we only need to show that they act the same on the orthonormal basis vectors for a coordinate system. Then the linear transformation property implies that they act the same on all vectors.

We will pick a coordinate system by starting with the quaternion $\hat{u}$ that appears in the expression for $\hat{q}$. This is a unit quaternion with zero scalar, so it corresponds to a unit vector $\vec{u}$. For the second basis vector, any vector $\vec{r}$ perpendicular to $\vec{u}$ will do, and for the third basis vector we can use $\vec{u} \times \vec{r}$ (Figure 5.14). We will show that T fixes $\vec{u}$ and rotates the other two basis vectors through the same angle. Start with vector $\vec{u}$ and the canonical form $\hat{q} = (\cos\theta, \vec{u}\sin\theta)$. We calculate how T transforms $\hat{u} = (0, \vec{u})$.

$$
\begin{aligned}
T(\hat{u}) = \hat{q}\hat{u}\hat{q}^{-1} &= (\cos\theta, \vec{u}\sin\theta)(\hat{u})(\cos\theta, -\vec{u}\sin\theta) \\
&= (-(\vec{u}\cdot\vec{u})(\sin\theta), \vec{u}\cos\theta + \vec{u}\sin\theta\times\vec{u})(\cos\theta, -\vec{u}\sin\theta) \\
&= (-\sin\theta, \vec{u}\cos\theta)(\cos\theta, -\vec{u}\sin\theta) \\
&= (-\sin\theta\cos\theta + (\cos\theta\sin\theta)(\vec{u}\cdot\vec{u}), (\sin\theta)^2\vec{u} + (\cos\theta)^2\vec{u} \\
&\quad - (\cos\theta\sin\theta)(\vec{u}\times\vec{u}) \\
&= (0, (\sin\theta)^2\vec{u} + (\cos\theta)^2\vec{u})) \\
&= (0, \vec{u}) = \hat{u}
\end{aligned}
$$

T fixes $\hat{u}$ and therefore fixes the vector $\vec{u}$. It follows that it fixes any multiple of $\vec{u}$ as well. This is exactly what a three-dimensional rotation around the axes $\vec{u}$ does, so T and the rotation agree on multiples of $\vec{u}$.

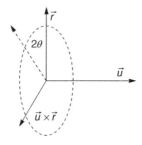

Figure 5.14   Quaternion rotation

Now, take a vector $\vec{r}$ perpendicular to $\vec{u}$ and consider the quaternion $\hat{r} = (0, \vec{r})$.

$$
\begin{aligned}
T(\hat{r}) = \hat{q}\hat{r}\hat{q}^{-1} &= (\cos\theta, \vec{u}\sin\theta)(\hat{r})(\cos\theta, -\vec{u}\sin\theta) \\
&= (-(\vec{u}\cdot\vec{r})(\sin\theta), \vec{r}\cos\theta + \vec{u}\sin\theta \times \vec{r})(\cos\theta, -\vec{u}\sin\theta) \\
&= (0, \vec{r}\cos\theta + (\sin\theta)(\vec{u}\times\vec{r}))(\cos\theta, -\vec{u}\sin\theta) \\
&= (0 - (-\sin^2\theta)((\vec{u}\times\vec{r})\cdot\vec{u}), (\cos^2\theta)\vec{r} + (\cos\theta\sin\theta)(\vec{u}\times\vec{r}) \\
&\quad - (\cos\theta\sin\theta)(\vec{r}\times\vec{u}) - (\sin^2\theta)(\vec{u}\times\vec{r})\times\vec{u}) \\
&= (0, (\cos^2\theta)\vec{r} + 2\cos\theta\sin\theta(\vec{u}\times\vec{r}) - (\sin^2\theta)\vec{r}) \\
&= (0, \cos(2\theta)\vec{r} + \sin(2\theta)(\vec{u}\times\vec{r}))
\end{aligned}
$$

T sends $\hat{r}$ to the quaternion $(0, \vec{w})$, where $\vec{w}$ is a linear combination of $\vec{r}$ and $\vec{u}\times\vec{r}$. In the plane of these last two vectors, $\vec{r}$ has been rotated counterclockwise through an angle of 2θ. In other words, vectors perpendicular to $\vec{u}$ are rotated around the axis formed by $\vec{u}$. This is precisely what the rotation would do.

For vectors along the axis $\vec{u}$ and for those perpendicular to it, the transformation T and the three-dimensional rotation around $\vec{u}$ agree. For any vector, we can write it as a sum of a vector parallel to $\vec{u}$ and one that is perpendicular. Consequently, T and the rotation agree on every vector. We have shown that T is indeed a three-dimensional rotation. Moreover, we have discovered the appropriate unit quaternion q for accomplishing a given rotation.

5.5 EXERCISES

1. Let the coordinate system $\mathscr{S}_1$ have basis vectors $\{\vec{i}, \vec{j}, \vec{k}\}$. Relative to system $\mathscr{S}_1$, the system $\mathscr{S}_2$ has origin $(2, -1, 5)$ and basis vectors $\vec{k}, \vec{j}, -\vec{i}$. Find the matrices $M_{\mathscr{S}_1 \to \mathscr{S}_2}$ and $M_{\mathscr{S}_2 \to \mathscr{S}_1}$. Use the matrices to find the $\mathscr{S}_2$ coordinates of $P = (-3, 6, 2)$ where these coordinates are in $\mathscr{S}_1$.

2. In Example 5.1, find the $\mathscr{S}_1$ coordinates for the basis vectors in $\mathscr{S}_2$ and use them to verify the $\mathscr{S}_2$ coordinates found for P.

3. Let the coordinate system $\mathscr{S}_1$ have basis vectors $\{\vec{i}, \vec{j}, \vec{k}\}$. Relative to system $\mathscr{S}_1$, the system $\mathscr{S}_2$ has origin $(0, 0, 0)$ and basis vectors $-\vec{k}, \vec{i}, -\vec{j}$. Find the matrices $M_{\mathscr{S}_1 \to \mathscr{S}_2}$ and $M_{\mathscr{S}_2 \to \mathscr{S}_1}$. Use the matrices to find the $\mathscr{S}_2$ coordinates of $P = (1, 2, 3)$ where these coordinates are in $\mathscr{S}_1$.

4. Let the coordinate system $\mathscr{S}_1$ have basis vectors $\{\vec{i}, \vec{j}, \vec{k}\}$. Relative to system $\mathscr{S}_1$, the system $\mathscr{S}_2$ has origin $(0, 0, 0)$ and basis vectors $\{(0, 1, 1), (1, 0, 2), (1, -1, 0)\}$. Find the matrices $M_{\mathscr{S}_1 \to \mathscr{S}_2}$ and $M_{\mathscr{S}_2 \to \mathscr{S}_1}$. Use the matrices to find the $\mathscr{S}_2$ coordinates of $P = (1, 1, 1)$ where these coordinates are in $\mathscr{S}_1$.

5. Assume the world coordinate system has basis vectors $\{\vec{i}, \vec{j}, \vec{k}\}$. There is a cube with vertices $(\pm 1, \pm 1, \pm 1)$ sitting in the world. A camera is centered at location

(20, 10, 5) looking at the point (1, 2, 2). The up vector is approximately (0, 1, 1). Find the matrix $M_{\mathcal{W} \to \mathcal{C}}$ and use it to find the camera coordinates of the cube's vertices.

6. In the previous problem, suppose the cube is in its own local coordinate system which coincides with the world coordinate system. Rotate the local system $\pi/4$ around the y-axis. Now determine the camera coordinates for the cubes vertices.

7. By using the properties of linear transformations, show that once we know where a linear transformation sends the basis vectors in a coordinate system, we can determine where any vector is sent.

8. If system $\mathcal{S}_1$ is right-handed and system $\mathcal{S}_2$ is left-handed, what can we say about the matrix $M_{\mathcal{S}_1 \to \mathcal{S}_2}$?

9. In Example 5.3, the matrix $M_{\mathcal{W} \to \mathcal{C}}$ has -0.02 in the upper right corner. Show that, theoretically, this should be zero and, therefore, round-off error must explain the difference.

10. An *orthogonal* matrix is square with orthonormal columns. Show that if M is orthogonal, then $M^T M = I$ and hence $M^{-1} = M^T$.

11. Reasoning by analogy with the three-dimensional case, give the 3 matrix that transforms coordinates from one system to another. In particular, find $M_{\mathcal{S}_1 \to \mathcal{S}_2}$ where $\mathcal{S}_1$ has basis vectors $\{\vec{i}, \vec{j}\}$ (two dimensions) and $\mathcal{S}_2$ has origin $(2, 6)$ and basis vectors $\{(2, 2), (1, 3)\}$. Verify the matrix by converting $(4, 5)$ from $\mathcal{S}_1$ coordinates to $\mathcal{S}_2$ coordinates.

12. Start with the standard orthonormal coordinate system in three dimensions and rotate counterclockwise through $\pi/2$ around the x-axis. Now, rotate $\pi/2$ clockwise around the z-axis. This produces coordinate systems $\mathcal{S}_1$, $\mathcal{S}_2$, and $\mathcal{S}_3$. Find the $\mathcal{S}_1$ coordinates for a point given in $\mathcal{S}_3$ coordinates. Determine which matrices transform coordinates from each of these systems to the others.

13. Let $R = \begin{bmatrix} 0.577 & 0.408 & 0.707 \\ 0.577 & -0.816 & 0 \\ 0.577 & 0.408 & -0.707 \end{bmatrix}$. Verify that R is a rotation matrix and find the Euler angles appropriate for rotations around x, y, and z in that order.

14. Let z_1 and z_2 be complex numbers. Note that dividing z_1 by z_2 gives $z_1 \bar{z}_2 / |z_2|^2$. Now take four points in the plane A, B, C, and D. Consider their coordinates as complex numbers. Show that the line through A and B is parallel to the one through C and D if and only if $(A - B)/(C - D)$ is a real (not complex) number. Similarly, show that the lines are perpendicular if and only if $(A - B)/(C - D)$ is a purely imaginary number (no real part).

15. If $\hat{q}$, $\hat{r}$, and $\hat{s}$ are quaternions, show that $\hat{q}(\hat{r} + \hat{s}) = \hat{q}\hat{r} + \hat{q}\hat{r}$.

16. Use quaternions to rotate the vector $(1, 1, 2)$ around the axis $(-1, 2, 6)$ by $\pi/6$ radians.

17. Find the quaternions for a rotation of $\pi/3$ around the axes $(2, 0, -2)$ and $(-3, 1, 1)$. Determine the quaternion representing the composition of these two in order. Find the axis of the resulting rotation.

18. In the slerp derivation, we assumed $\hat{q}_1$ and $\hat{v}$ had unit length. Show that this implies $\hat{q}(t)$ has unit length. Verify that the expression for $\hat{v}$ in Equation 5.18 has unit length.

19. Sketch the graph of the polar equations $r = 1 + \sin\theta$ and $r = \cos(2\theta)$.

20. Find the polar equation of a unit circle.

21. In cylindrical coordinates, describe the shapes $z = 5$, $r = 5$, $z = r$.

22. Using spherical coordinates, describe a unit sphere with a cylindrical hole of diameter 0.25 through the north pole and the south pole of the sphere.

23. An implicit or explicit equation for a two-dimensional line can be put in the form $mx + ny = 1$. Then, the coordinates (m, n) uniquely describe the line since the intercepts on the x- and y-axis are $\left(\frac{1}{m}, 0\right)$ and $\left(0, \frac{1}{n}\right)$. The line can easily be drawn between these intercepts (allowing for m or n to be zero). Show that the equation $m^2 + n^2 = 1$ represents all lines tangent to the unit circle. (Other interesting patterns of lines can be described by various equations using the line coordinates.)

24. Show that $T(\hat{v}) = \hat{q}\hat{v}\hat{q}^{-1}$ is a linear transformation by showing that it satisfies the addition and scalar multiplication properties.

5.5.1 Programming Exercises

1. Write a program to keeping track of a cube of edge length 2 centered at $(0, 0, 1)$. Use a world coordinate system, a local coordinate system, and a camera coordinate system. Draw the cube on the screen and allow the user to rotate around the cube's center or around the world origin. (If possible, draw the cube in perspective.)

2. Write a program for graphing a polar equation. Use it to graph $r = e^{\sin\theta} - 2\cos(4\theta) + \sin^5(\theta/12)$.

6

POLYGONS AND POLYHEDRA

Since lines and planes are fundamental to geometry, shapes bounded by lines and planes at least have access to the center stage in computer graphics. Most modeling efforts, no matter how they begin, usually end up with a vast assortment of triangles because this shape is guaranteed to be planar even when the vertices are points in space. There are online repositories of models composed entirely of very large sets (thousands) of triangles. Understanding the geometry of triangles and how to efficiently use them in computation is particularly important in graphics. More general polygons arise when constructing complex objects (polyhedra) and when projecting those objects to find shadows. The geometry of both polygons and polyhedra is the key to much of graphics and gives rise to a wide range of mathematical tools.

6.1 TRIANGLES

Triangles are well studied in elementary geometry, and with vector geometry we have the tools to calculate most of what we need in graphics: side lengths, angles, and areas. One key problem is to determine whether a point of intersection is inside a triangle in space. Although elementary tools can suffice, there is always a quest to find better ways to express the problem in the hope of improving computational efficiency. Barycentric coordinates offer a different view of triangle geometry and thereby lead to some nice algorithms.

Mathematical Structures for Computer Graphics, First Edition. Steven J. Janke.
© 2015 John Wiley & Sons, Inc. Published 2015 by John Wiley & Sons, Inc.

6.1.1   Barycentric Coordinates

Recall from Chapter 2 (Section 2.1.1) that addition of points cannot be defined uniquely. However, if we take an affine combination $\sum_{i=0}^{n} \alpha_i P_i$, where $\sum_{i=0}^{n} \alpha_i = 1$, then we do get a well-defined point. This is why we can represent points on a line as $P = (1 - t)P_0 + tP_1$. The numbers $(1 - t)$ and t are called *barycentric coordinates* and determine the location of a point relative to the reference points P_0 and P_1. For a triangle, the three vertices become reference points.

Start with an arbitrary point P somewhere inside $\triangle P_0 P_1 P_2$ and let the line through P_0 and P intersect the side $P_1 P_2$ at point Q (Figure 6.1). Drawing on our experience with line segments, $Q = (1 - t)P_1 + tP_2$ for $0 \leq t \leq 1$. Now let P_0 and Q be the two end points so $P = (1 - s)P_0 + sQ$, where $0 \leq s \leq 1$. Algebraic simplification gives P as a weighted average of the three reference points.

$$
\begin{aligned}
P &= (1 - s)P_0 + sQ \\
&= (1 - s)P_0 + s(1 - t)P_1 + stP_2 \\
&= \alpha_0 P_0 + \alpha_1 P_1 + \alpha_2 P_2
\end{aligned}
\tag{6.1}
$$

A quick check shows that $\alpha_0 + \alpha_1 + \alpha_2 = 1$ and $0 \leq \alpha_i \leq 1$ for $i = 0, 1, 2$. The three coefficients $(\alpha_0, \alpha_1, \alpha_2)$ are the barycentric coordinates of P relative to the triangle $\triangle P_0 P_1 P_2$.

If P is outside the triangle as shown on the right in Figure 6.1, then the line from P_0 to P still intersects $P_1 P_2$ at Q, but now $P = (1 - s)P_0 + sQ$ with $s > 1$. The sum of the α_i's is still 1, but now one of them is negative. In the figure, the geometric construction takes a line from P_0 through P. Yet, the same sort of construction could have taken a line starting at P_1 through P. (In fact, when P is outside the triangle, it may be necessary to take a line starting at some vertex other than P_0 in order to ensure intersection with the opposite side.) If we use one of these other lines to find the barycentric coordinates, will we get the same answer as before?

To answer this question, revisit Equation 6.1 and notice that, since the sum of the barycentric coefficients is 1 ($\alpha_0 = 1 - \alpha_1 - \alpha_2$), we can rearrange the equation to get

$$
P - P_0 = \alpha_1(P_1 - P_0) + \alpha_2(P_2 - P_0)
\tag{6.2}
$$

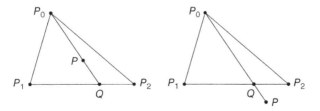

Figure 6.1   Determining barycentric coordinates

This is an equation about vectors because the subtraction of one point from another gives a vector. A linear combination of the two vectors $(P_1 - P_0)$ and $(P_2 - P_0)$ gives the vector $(P - P_0)$. We can actually think of the two vectors on the right as designating the axes of a coordinate system (possibly non-orthogonal axes) and the coefficients are coordinates in that coordinate system. If there were another possible set of barycentric coordinates, then there would be different values for either α_1 or α_2 (or both) that satisfy the equation. That is

$$P - P_0 = \alpha_1^*(P_1 - P_0) + \alpha_2^*(P_2 - P_0) \tag{6.3}$$

Subtracting Equation 6.3 from Equation 6.2 gives

$$(\alpha_1 - \alpha_1^*)(P_1 - P_0) + (\alpha_2 - \alpha_2^*)(P_2 - P_0) = 0$$

$$\implies (P_1 - P_0) = \frac{(\alpha_2 - \alpha_2^*)}{(\alpha_1 - \alpha_1^*)}(P_2 - P_0)$$

If there were another set of barycentric coordinates, then $(P_1 - P_0)$ is a multiple of $(P_2 - P_0)$, but this could only be true if the triangle were really just a line. If the vertices are noncollinear, then the barycentric coordinates must be unique.

Definition 6.1 (Barycentric Coordinates). *Given three noncollinear points P_0, P_1, and P_2 forming the vertices of a triangle, if an arbitrary point P can be expressed as $P = \alpha_0 P_0 + \alpha_1 P_1 + \alpha_2 P_2$ with $\alpha_0 + \alpha_1 + \alpha_2 = 1$, then the coefficients $(\alpha_0, \alpha_1, \alpha_2)$ are called barycentric coordinates relative to the triangle $\triangle P_0 P_1 P_2$.*

Result 6.1 (Barycentric Coordinates). *Every point in the plane of a triangle has unique barycentric coordinates with respect to that triangle. The point P is inside or on the triangle if and only if its barycentric coordinates satisfy $\alpha_i \geq 0$ for $i = 1, 2, 3$.*

The definition of barycentric coordinates only requires that we have the vertices of a triangle. That triangle can be positioned in two or three dimensional space. If we have the barycentric coordinates of a point and the Cartesian coordinates (ordered pairs or ordered triples) for the vertices of the reference triangle, then we can calculate the Cartesian coordinates of the given point. For example, to find $P(x)$, the x coordinate of the point P, calculate $P(x) = \alpha_0 P_0(x) + \alpha_1 P_1(x) + \alpha_2 P_2(x)$.

Notice that the barycentric coordinates of the reference points P_0, P_1, and P_2 are, respectively, $(1, 0, 0)$, $(0, 1, 0)$, and $(0, 0, 1)$. For any point on the line through P_1 and P_2, we have $\alpha_0 = 0$. Similarly, $\alpha_1 = 0$ and $\alpha_2 = 0$ indicate points on lines containing the sides opposite the reference points P_1 and P_2, respectively.

6.1.2   Areas and Barycentric Coordinates

Somewhat surprisingly, barycentric coordinates are related to areas in the triangle. In Figure 6.2, $\triangle P_0 P_1 P_2$ is drawn with dotted lines $P_0 E$ and PF indicating the altitudes

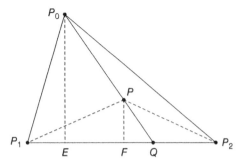

Figure 6.2 Barycentric coordinates and areas

of the larger triangle and the smaller ΔPP_1P_2, respectively. Both triangles have the same base P_1P_2, so the ratio of the smaller triangle's area to the larger triangle's area is the same as the ratio of the lengths of PF to P_0E.

ΔPFQ and ΔP_0EQ are similar (right) triangles, so PF/P_0E equals PQ/P_0Q. This ratio is $\alpha_0 = (1 - s)$ because in our derivation $P = (1 - s)P_0 + sQ$. So the barycentric coordinate α_0 is the ratio of the area of a triangle formed by P to the area of the entire reference triangle.

Barycentric coordinates are unique, so drawing a similar diagram with a line through P_1 and P shows that the barycentric coordinate for P_1 is also a ratio of areas. One more application of the argument shows that it is true for P_2 as well. Let T be the area of the reference triangle $\Delta P_0P_1P_2$.

$$\alpha_0 = \frac{\text{Area of } \Delta PP_1P_2}{T}$$

$$\alpha_1 = \frac{\text{Area of } \Delta PP_2P_0}{T}$$

$$\alpha_2 = \frac{\text{Area of } \Delta PP_0P_1}{T} \tag{6.4}$$

Figure 6.2 places the point P inside the triangle. If it is outside the triangle, then at least one of the barycentric coordinates must be negative. In particular, suppose P is underneath the bottom edge P_1P_2 in the figure. Then ΔPP_1P_2 has a negative altitude and the vertices given in the order P, P_1, P_2 are traced in a clockwise order rather than in the counterclockwise order when P is above the bottom edge. Both these characteristics indicate that we should assign a negative area to the triangle. Now the ratio of this area to the area of the reference triangle is negative, indicating that α_0 will be negative.

The point P could be outside the triangle but still above the bottom edge P_1P_2, indicating that the area is still positive. Yet, the other two coordinates, α_1 and α_2, are determined by the triangles P forms with the other two sides of the triangle. If P is outside the reference triangle, at least one of these smaller triangles will have negative area.

We know how to find the areas of triangles by using cross products, and using the order of the vertices to determine the order of the cross product will guarantee that we keep track of positive and negative areas. However, another slightly more straightforward method offers an approach that can be more computationally efficient.

Figure 6.3 again shows the reference triangle, but we set up vectors for two of the sides plus one vector locating the point P.

$$\vec{v}_1 = P_0 - P_1 \qquad \vec{v}_2 = P_2 - P_1 \qquad \vec{w} = P - P_1$$

The vector $\vec{n}$ in the figure is a unit vector perpendicular to P_1P_2 and pointing to the inside of the triangle. Projecting $\vec{v}_1$ onto $\vec{n}$ gives the altitude of the reference triangle, and by keeping track of the direction of the altitude we can tell whether the area should be positive or negative.

First we need an expression for $\vec{n}$. The plan is to break $\vec{v}_1$ into two components: one called $\vec{u}_\parallel$, which is parallel to $\vec{v}_2$, and one called $\vec{u}_\perp$, which is perpendicular to $\vec{v}_2$. To start, normalize $\vec{v}_2$ and then project $\vec{v}_1$ onto it. The projection is $\vec{u}_\parallel$. Subtracting this from $\vec{v}_1$ gives $\vec{u}_\perp$, and normalizing gives $\vec{n}$.

$$\vec{u}_\perp = \vec{v}_1 - \vec{u}_\parallel = \vec{v}_1 - (\vec{v}_1 \cdot \vec{v}_2)\frac{\vec{v}_2}{|\vec{v}_2|^2}$$

$$\vec{n} = \frac{\vec{u}_\perp}{|\vec{u}_\perp|}$$

Referring back to the figure, the altitude of $\Delta P_0 P_1 P_2$ is the projection of $\vec{v}_1$ onto $\vec{n}$, and the altitude of $\Delta P P_1 P_2$ is the projection of $\vec{w}$ onto $\vec{n}$. They both have the same base, which is the length of $\vec{v}_2$. The areas are now simple to compute.

$$\text{Area of } \Delta P_0 P_1 P_2 = \frac{1}{2}(\vec{v}_1 \cdot \vec{n})|\vec{v}_2|$$

$$\text{Area of } \Delta P P_1 P_2 = \frac{1}{2}(\vec{w} \cdot \vec{n})|\vec{v}_2|$$

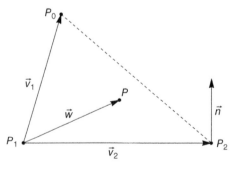

Figure 6.3   Using vectors to find barycentric coordinates

The ratio of the two areas is α_0.

$$\alpha_0 = \frac{(\vec{w} \cdot \vec{n})|\vec{v}_2|}{(\vec{v}_1 \cdot \vec{n})|\vec{v}_2|} = \frac{\vec{w} \cdot \vec{u}_\perp}{\vec{v}_1 \cdot \vec{u}_\perp}$$

$$= \vec{w} \cdot \frac{\vec{u}_\perp}{\vec{v}_1 \cdot \vec{u}_\perp} = \vec{w} \cdot \frac{|\vec{v}_2|^2 \vec{v}_1 - (\vec{v}_1 \cdot \vec{v}_2)\vec{v}_2}{|\vec{v}_2|^2|\vec{v}_1|^2 - (\vec{v}_1 \cdot \vec{v}_2)^2} = \vec{w} \cdot \vec{k}_0 \qquad (6.5)$$

The barycentric coordinate α_0 is the dot product of $\vec{w}$ with a vector called $\vec{k}_0$ which depends on $\vec{v}_1$ and $\vec{v}_2$. This vector can be precomputed and then used to find α_0 for any point P. Moreover, returning to Figure 6.3, the coordinate α_2 can be derived in a manner similar to what we did for α_0. This time, vector $\vec{w}$ and $\vec{v}_2$ are projected onto a vector perpendicular to $\vec{v}_1$. The result is simply the expression we have for α_0 with $\vec{v}_1$ and $\vec{v}_2$ interchanged. The vector $\vec{k}_0$ becomes $\vec{k}_2$, and $\alpha_2 = \vec{w} \cdot \vec{k}_2$. Finally, $\alpha_1 = 1 - \alpha_0 - \alpha_2$. Little changes if P is outside the triangle because the dot products can be negative and produce a negative coordinate.

Example 6.1 (Finding Barycentric Coordinates). Suppose the reference triangle has vertices with the following Cartesian coordinates:

$$P_0 = (1, 1, 1)$$
$$P_1 = (-5, -2, 13)$$
$$P_2 = (5, -7, 17)$$

To find the barycentric coordinates of the point $P = (0, -2, 9)$, first determine the vectors we designated in the derivation.

$$\vec{v}_1 = P_0 - P_1 = (6, 3, -12)$$
$$\vec{v}_2 = P_2 - P_1 = (10, -5, 4)$$
$$\vec{w} = P - P_1 = (5, 0, -4)$$

At this stage, we are assuming that P actually is in the plane of the triangle. We can check this quickly by taking the cross product $\vec{v}_1 \times \vec{v}_2$ to find a vector perpendicular to the plane of the triangle.

$$\vec{v}_1 \times \vec{v}_2 = \begin{vmatrix} 3 & -12 \\ -5 & 4 \end{vmatrix}\vec{i} - \begin{vmatrix} 6 & -12 \\ 10 & 4 \end{vmatrix}\vec{j} + \begin{vmatrix} 6 & 3 \\ 10 & -5 \end{vmatrix}\vec{k} = (-48, -144, -60)$$

Then we calculate $\vec{w} \cdot (-48, -144, -60) = 0$ and conclude that $\vec{w}$ is in the plane, which implies P is also in the plane.

The calculation of $\vec{k}_0$ proceeds as follows:

$$\vec{k}_0 = \frac{|\vec{v}_2|^2 \vec{v}_1 - (\vec{v}_1 \cdot \vec{v}_2)\vec{v}_2}{|\vec{v}_2|^2 |\vec{v}_1|^2 - (\vec{v}_1 \cdot \vec{v}_2)^2}$$

$$= \frac{141(6, 3, -12) - (-3)(10, -5, 4)}{141 \cdot 189 - (-3)^2}$$

$$\approx (0.033, 0.015, -0.063)$$

Now, $\alpha_0 = \vec{w} \cdot \vec{k}_0 \approx 0.417$. We need $\vec{k}_2$ in order to calculate α_2.

$$\vec{k}_2 = \frac{|\vec{v}_1|^2 \vec{v}_2 - (\vec{v}_1 \cdot \vec{v}_2)\vec{v}_1}{|\vec{v}_2|^2 |\vec{v}_1|^2 - (\vec{v}_1 \cdot \vec{v}_2)^2}$$

$$= \frac{189(10, -5, 4) - (-3)(6, 3, -12)}{141 \cdot 189 - (-3)^2}$$

$$\approx (0.072, -0.035, 0.027)$$

This gives $\alpha_2 = \vec{w} \cdot \vec{k}_2 \approx 0.252$, and, finally, $\alpha_1 = 1 - 0.417 - 0.252 \approx 0.331$ (The exact coordinates are $(\frac{5}{12}, \frac{1}{3}, \frac{1}{4})$. Round-off error explains our approximations.) We could have rearranged Figure 6.3 and defined vectors from P_2 to the other vertices. This would have given us an expression for $\vec{k}_1$ which we could use to find α_1. However, once we have α_0 and α_2, subtracting from 1 gives us the third coordinate immediately.

Before we leave this example, notice that the barycentric coordinates for P are all positive and less than 1. The point is actually inside the triangle. Since we have calculated k_0 and k_2, we can find the coordinates for any point in the plane. For example, take $P_0 = (1, 1, 1)$ with a new $\vec{w} = (1, 1, 1) - (-5, -2, 13) = (6, 3, -12)$. To find the barycentric coordinates, two dot products do the trick.

$$\alpha_0 = \vec{w} \cdot \vec{k}_0 = (6, 3, -12) \cdot (0.033, 0.015, -0.063) \approx 0.999$$

$$\alpha_2 = \vec{w} \cdot \vec{k}_2 = (6, 3, -12) \cdot (0.072, -0.035, 0.027) \approx 0.003$$

These are reasonable approximations to the exact coordinates $(1, 0, 0)$.   □

Example 6.2 (Intersection). Many of the calculations in graphics begin by considering a ray of light emanating from some point in space and traveling in a given direction. Imagine a ray emanating from the point with Cartesian coordinates $(5, 41, 18)$ and traveling in the direction of the vector $(-2, -5, -3)$.

To determine whether this ray intersects the triangle in Example 6.1, we first find the plane containing the triangle and then calculate where the ray intersects the plane.

As we calculated in the previous example, the vector $(-48, -144, -60)$ is perpendicular to the plane and we know that the point $P_0 = (1, 1, 1)$ is on the plane. To simplify a little, the vector $(4, 12, 5)$ is also perpendicular to the plane. The ray is just a line, and any point on the line is $P = (5, 41, 18) + t(-2, -5, -3)$. Recalling the vector solution for the intersection of a line and plane gives the value of t.

$$t = \frac{(4, 12, 5) \cdot ((5, 41, 18) - (1, 1, 1))}{(4, 12, 5) \cdot (-2, -5, -3)} = 7$$

We then find the point of intersection and the new vector $\vec{w}$.

$$P = (5, 41, 18) + 7(-2, -5, -3) = (-9, 6, -3)$$
$$\vec{w} = (-9, 6, -3) - (-5, -2, 13) = (-4, 8, -16)$$

Following Example 6.1, we calculate the barycentric coordinates using the vectors $\vec{k}_0$ and $\vec{k}_2$.

$$\alpha_0 = \vec{w} \cdot \vec{k}_0 = (-4, 8, -16) \cdot (0.033, 0.015, -0.063) \approx 0.996$$
$$\alpha_2 = \vec{w} \cdot \vec{k}_2 = (-4, 8, -16) \cdot (0.072, -0.035, 0.027) \approx -1.00$$

One coordinate is negative, indicating that the point of intersection is outside the triangle. (Again, the approximations are within round-off error of the exact barycentric coordinates $(1, 1, -1)$).   □

6.1.3 Interpolation

Barycentric coordinates in one dimension express points on a line as $P = (1 - t)P_0 + tP_1$ using P_0 and P_1 as reference points. In two dimensions, points in the plane of a triangle can be expressed as affine combinations of the triangle's vertices. We can, if we wish, move up another dimension and express a point P in space as an affine combination of four points. In each of these cases, the barycentric coordinates give us a convenient way to explore a particular geometry by tying everything to the reference points.

One very useful result is the ability to interpolate other quantities, like color, across a line segment or across the face of a triangle. Suppose that the line segment is part of an object sitting in a scene and that the color of the point P_0 is red with intensity 0.2 on a scale 0–1. Let the reference point P_1 also be red with intensity 0.8. What colors are the rest of the points on the line segment? This again is a standard graphics problem where we only know colors at a few points and need to fill in the rest.

To determine the color of the midpoint of the line segment, we could argue that the intensity of the red color increases linearly across the segment, so at the midpoint the intensity is $0.2 + \frac{1}{2}(0.8 - 0.2) = 0.5$. Of course, this is the same as using the barycentric coordinates to calculate $\frac{1}{2}0.2 + \frac{1}{2}0.8 = 0.5$. In general, if $c(P)$ is the color of a point, and if we assume that it changes linearly across a line segment, then $c(P) = (1 - t)c(P_0) + tc(P)$, where the barycentric coordinates of P are $((1 - t), t)$.

Looking just a little closer at the characteristics of the function c, notice that it is a linear function. That is, $c(x + y) = c(x) + c(y)$ and $c(kx) = kc(x)$ for constant k. The function could be a function of scalar quantities (like intensity of red), or it could be a vector quantity (like three color components red, green, blue). The technique we are describing is a way of assigning the values of a linear function to points on a line when we only know the values at the reference points. If f is a linear function and the values $f(P_0)$ and $f(P_1)$ are known, then $f(P) = (1 - t)f(P_0) + tf(P_1)$. This is called *linear interpolation*.

Barycentric coordinates relative to a triangle give us a convenient way to linearly interpolate colors across the entire triangle. If P_0 and P_1 are the intensity of red given before and P_2 has intensity 0.3, then the color of a point P (probably inside the triangle) with barycentric coordinates $(\alpha_0, \alpha_1, \alpha_2)$ is $c(P) = \alpha_0(0.2) + \alpha_1(0.8) + \alpha_2(0.3)$. In a later chapter when discussing lighting, we will associate vectors with each reference point. Then, the same linear interpolation technique applied to each vector coordinate could find vectors associated with any point in the triangle. There is one caveat with vector interpolation, however; that is, if we want unit vectors, there is no guarantee that the interpolated vectors will have unit length. We may have to normalize.

Interpolation plays a key role throughout graphics, and the current technique assumes that the function we are interpolating is linear. This is often a desirable assumption, but there are other techniques that do not make the linearity assumption. We saw this when interpolating quaternions for orientation purposes; linear interpolation applied directly to quaternions gave awkward orientation changes, so the better method was to try a spherical interpolation.

6.1.4 Key Points in a Triangle

Barycentric coordinates form a particularly useful tool when investigating the geometry of the triangle. The fact that a point is inside a triangle precisely when the barycentric coordinates are all positive (and sum to 1) is a key result, but there are other cases where the barycentric coordinates offer relatively simple algebraic interpretations of important geometric relationships. Ceva's theorem is somewhat central to the geometry of triangles and follows readily from the development of barycentric coordinates.

Figure 6.4 shows three line segments starting at vertices and intersecting at the point P. The line segments intersect the sides of the triangle at Q, R, and M. As before,

$$Q = (1 - t)P_1 + t(P_2) \implies \frac{P_1 Q}{Q P_2} = \frac{t}{1 - t}$$

Also, as before, $P = (1 - s)P_0 + sQ$, and this leads us to

$$P = (1 - s)P_0 + s(1 - t)P_1 + stP_2 = \alpha_0 P_0 + \alpha_1 P_1 + \alpha_2 P_2$$

$$\implies \frac{\alpha_2}{\alpha_1} = \frac{t}{1 - t} = \frac{P_1 Q}{Q P_2}$$

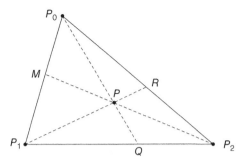

Figure 6.4 Ceva's theorem

Now move on to the line segment P_1R and suppose $R = (1-r)P_2 + rP_0$. Since barycentric coordinates are unique, the same reasoning as before leads us to

$$\frac{\alpha_0}{\alpha_2} = \frac{r}{1-r} = \frac{P_2R}{RP_0}$$

The third side of the triangle equates another two ratios and the following equations summarize the results:

$$\alpha_2 = \frac{t}{1-t}\alpha_1, \quad \alpha_0 = \frac{r}{1-r}\alpha_2, \quad \alpha_1 = \frac{m}{1-m}\alpha_0$$

$$\Longrightarrow \quad \frac{t}{(1-t)}\frac{r}{(1-r)}\frac{m}{(1-m)} = 1 \qquad (6.6)$$

Each of the three ratios in this last equation is equal to the ratio of line segments in the triangle. Substituting these segment ratios into the equation gives Ceva's theorem (named after the Italian mathematician who published it in 1678).

Theorem 6.1 (Ceva). *In $\triangle P_0P_1P_2$, if line segments from each vertex to the opposite side intersect in point P, then*

$$\frac{P_1Q}{QP_2} \cdot \frac{P_2R}{RP_0} \cdot \frac{P_0M}{MP_1} = 1.$$

The theorem assumes that the three line segments intersect at point P, but we can also argue in the other direction. Suppose three line segments produce three ratios (call them ρ_0, ρ_1, ρ_2) such that $\rho_0\rho_1\rho_2 = 1$. Then, if the third segment did not pass through P, there is another segment from the same vertex that does and it divides the opposite side into the ratio ρ_2^*. But then Ceva's theorem holds, and $\rho_0\rho_1\rho_2^* = 1$. This forces $\rho_2^* = \rho_2$, and the original third segment must have passed through the point P.

Figure 6.4 shows Q, R, and M on the three sides of the triangle. However, the theorem still holds if, for example, t or $(1-t)$ is negative. This puts Q outside the line segment P_1P_2 but still on the line containing it. The derivation of the theorem works just as before, although we have to think of line segment lengths as being signed. P_1Q has a positive length, but QP_1 is negative. Often, the line segments $P_0Q, P_1R,$ *and* P_2M, called *cevians*, intersect inside the triangle, yet they can intersect outside. In both cases, Ceva's theorem holds.

Example 6.3 (Medians). A median of a triangle connects a vertex to the midpoint of the opposite side. So it divides the side in two parts with a ratio of 1. Consequently, all three medians produce ratios whose product is 1 and they must meet at a point C (Figure 6.5).

This point is called the *centroid* of the triangle. Since all the ratios are 1, Equation 6.6 implies that all the barycentric coordinates for C are equal. Since they sum to 1 and C is inside the triangle, we can solve for the coordinates.

$$\boxed{\text{Centroid: } \frac{1}{3}P_0 + \frac{1}{3}P_1 + \frac{1}{3}P_2} \tag{6.7}$$

One result of the three coordinates being equal is that the centroid divides each median in the ratio of $2 : 1$ (see Exercises).   □

Example 6.4 (Angle Bisectors). Another set of three line segments bisect each vertex angle and intersect the opposite side. In Figure 6.6, segment P_0Q bisects the angle $\theta = \angle P_1 P_0 P_2$. There are two triangles formed by this angle bisector, $\Delta P_0 Q P_1$ and $\Delta P_0 Q P_2$.

Let $\beta_1 = \angle P_1 Q P_0$ and $\beta_2 = \angle P_2 Q P_0$. Then $\beta_1 + \beta_2 = \pi$, so $\sin \beta_1 = \sin \beta_2$. Applying the law of sines (Chapter 1) to two angles in each of the two triangles gives

$$\frac{\sin \frac{1}{2}\theta}{P_1 Q} = \frac{\sin \beta_1}{P_1 P_0} \quad \frac{\sin \frac{1}{2}\theta}{Q P_2} = \frac{\sin \beta_2}{P_2 P_1}$$

$$\implies \frac{P_1 Q}{Q P_2} = \frac{P_1 P_0}{P_2 P_0}$$

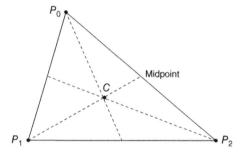

Figure 6.5 Triangle medians

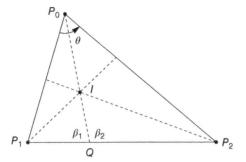

Figure 6.6 Triangle angle bisectors

The angle bisectors divide the opposite side in a ratio equal to the ratio of the length of two adjacent sides. For notational simplicity, label the side lengths, $l_0 = P_1P_2, l_1 = P_2P_0$, and $l_2 = P_0P_1$. The product of the ratios is now

$$\frac{P_1Q}{QP_2} \cdot \frac{P_2R}{RP_0} \cdot \frac{P_0M}{MP_1} = \frac{l_2}{l_1} \cdot \frac{l_0}{l_2} \cdot \frac{l_1}{l_0} = 1$$

This shows, again via Ceva's theorem, that the angle bisectors all meet at point I called the *incenter*. Since any point on a bisector is equidistant from the sides of the angle, the incenter is the center of a circle inscribed in the triangle just touching the sides.

Recalling Equation 6.6 , we have

$$\alpha_2 = \frac{l_2}{l_1}\alpha_1, \quad \alpha_0 = \frac{l_0}{l_2}\alpha_2, \quad \alpha_1 = \frac{l_1}{l_0}\alpha_0$$

From these equations, we can write α_1 and α_2 in terms of α_0. Then, since the sum of the three coordinates is 1, we get an equation in α_2.

$$\alpha_0 + \frac{l_1}{l_0}\alpha_0 + \frac{l_2 \cdot l_1}{l_1 \cdot l_0}\alpha_2 = 1 \implies \alpha_0 = \frac{l_0}{l_1 + l_2 + l_3}$$

Let the perimeter of the triangle be $L_p = l_0 + l_1 + l_2$.

$$\boxed{\text{Incenter:} \quad \frac{l_0}{L_p}P_0 + \frac{l_1}{L_p}P_1 + \frac{l_2}{L_p}P_2} \tag{6.8}$$

The radius r_I of the incircle is not difficult to find because it is the altitude, for example, of ΔP_1IP_2, which means the area of the triangle is $\frac{1}{2}r_Il_0$. Similarly, the radius is the altitude of ΔP_2IP_0 and ΔP_0IP_1. Adding the area of the three triangles together gives the area of the whole triangle.

$$\text{Area of } \Delta P_0P_1P_2 = \frac{1}{2}r_I(l_0 + l_1 + l_2)$$

The radius of the incircle is twice the area of the entire triangle divided by its perimeter. With the incenter and the radius, we can draw the incircle. Any time we need a circle tangent to three lines, we can use this technique.   □

Example 6.5 (Altitudes). If the cevians P_0Q, P_1R, and P_2M are perpendicular to the opposite sides, they are called the *altitudes*. Figure 6.7 shows the case where the altitudes all lie inside the triangle. Once more, for notational simplicity, denote the length of the sides by $l_0 = P_1P_2, l_1 = P_1P_0$, and $l_2 = P_0P_1$.

Both ΔP_1QP_0 and ΔP_2QP_0 are right triangles, so $\cos\beta_1 = \frac{P_1Q}{l_2}$ and $\cos\beta_2 = \frac{QP_2}{l_1}$. Dividing the two equations gives $\frac{P_1Q}{QP_2} = \frac{l_2\cos\beta_1}{l_1\cos\beta_2}$. This same analysis looking at the triangles formed by the other cevians establishes formulas for the three ratios in Ceva's theorem.

$$\frac{P_1Q}{QP_2} = \frac{l_2\cos\beta_1}{l_1\cos\beta_2}, \quad \frac{P_2R}{RP_0} = \frac{l_0\cos\beta_2}{l_2\cos\beta_0}, \quad \frac{P_0M}{MP_1} = \frac{l_1\cos\beta_0}{l_0\cos\beta_1}$$

Multiplying the three equations together shows that the product of the segment ratios is 1. It follows that the altitudes intersect in a point O called the *orthocenter* of the triangle. If the triangle has an angle larger than $\pi/2$, then the altitudes will intersect at a point outside the triangle and we need to keep track of the signed lengths of the appropriate segments.

Just as we did for the angle bisectors, we can use Equations 6.6 along with the ratios we have established for the altitudes to calculate the barycentric coordinates.

$$\alpha_2 = \frac{l_2\cos\beta_1}{l_1\cos\beta_2}\alpha_1, \quad \alpha_0 = \frac{l_0\cos\beta_2}{l_2\cos\beta_0}\alpha_2, \quad \alpha_1 = \frac{l_1\cos\beta_0}{l_0\cos\beta_1}\alpha_0$$

Since the sum of the barycentric coordinates is 1, the three equations above can be solved for α_0.

$$\alpha_0 = \frac{l_0\cos\beta_1\cos\beta_2}{l_0\cos\beta_1\cos\beta_2 + l_0\cos\beta_1\cos\beta_2 + l_0\cos\beta_1\cos\beta_2}$$

This expression is a little messy, so we write the cosines in terms of dot products.

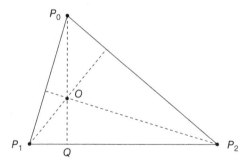

Figure 6.7   Triangle altitudes

$$b_0 = (P_2 - P_0) \cdot (P_1 - P_0) = l_1 l_2 \cos \beta_0$$

$$b_1 = (P_0 - P_1) \cdot (P_2 - P_1) = l_2 l_0 \cos \beta_1$$

$$b_2 = (P_1 - P_2) \cdot (P_0 - P_2) = l_0 l_1 \cos \beta_2$$

$$k_0 = b_1 b_2, \quad k_1 = b_0 b_2, \quad k_2 = b_0 b_1$$

$$K = k_0 + k_1 + k_2$$

$$\boxed{\text{Orthocenter:} \quad \frac{k_0}{K} P_0 + \frac{k_1}{K} P_1 + \frac{k_2}{K} P_2} \qquad (6.9)$$

If the altitudes intersect outside the triangle, some of the dot products will be negative, which is consistent with the barycentric coordinates for the points outside. □

Example 6.6 (Perpendicular Bisectors). For one more key point in the triangle, we look for the center of a circle that goes through the three vertices. The center must be equidistant from each of the vertices, so it is on the perpendicular bisectors for each of the triangle's sides. These bisectors are not cevians because they do not go through the vertices, but they are related to cevians in another triangle.

In Figure 6.8, the points Q_0, Q_1, and Q_2 are midpoints of the sides and the dotted lines are perpendicular bisectors for each side. Although the bisectors are not cevians for $\Delta P_0 P_1 P_2$, notice that they are cevians for0 $\Delta Q_0 Q_1 Q_2$. In addition, because each Q_i is a midpoint, the sides of $\Delta Q_0 Q_1 Q_2$ are each parallel to a side of $\Delta P_0 P_1 P_2$. This means that the perpendicular bisectors of $\Delta P_0 P_1 P_2$ are altitudes of $\Delta Q_0 Q_1 Q_2$. We know the altitudes intersect in a single point labeled CC in the figure and we have the barycentric coordinates relative to $\Delta Q_0 Q_1 Q_2$. The point CC is the *circumcenter* for $\Delta P_0 P_1 P_2$.

Since each Q_i is a midpoint, they can be expressed as affine combinations of the larger triangle's vertices; for example, $Q_0 = \frac{1}{2} P_1 + \frac{1}{2} P_2$. This allows computation of

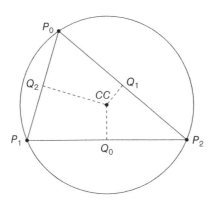

Figure 6.8 Perpendicular bisectors of triangle sides

barycentric coordinates relative to the larger triangle $\Delta P_0 P_1 P_2$. Using the notation from the previous example on altitudes, we have

$$CC = \frac{k_0}{K}Q_0 + \frac{k_1}{K}Q_1 + \frac{k_2}{K}Q_2$$

$$= \frac{k_0}{K}\left(\frac{1}{2}P_1 + \frac{1}{2}P_2\right) + \frac{k_1}{K}\left(\frac{1}{2}P_0 + \frac{1}{2}P_2\right) + \frac{k_2}{K}\left(\frac{1}{2}P_0 + \frac{1}{2}P_1\right)$$

$$= \frac{(k_1 + k_2)}{2K}P_0 + \frac{(k_0 + k_2)}{2K}P_1 + \frac{(k_0 + k_1)}{2K}P_2$$

$$\boxed{\text{Circumcenter: } \frac{(k_1 + k_2)}{2K}P_0 + \frac{(k_0 + k_2)}{2K}P_1 + \frac{(k_0 + k_1)}{2K}P_2} \qquad (6.10)$$

The quantity $2K$ is equal to the perimeter of $\Delta P_0 P_1 P_2$. The circumcenter is equidistant from each vertex and is the center of the circumcircle that encloses the triangle. Just as for altitudes, the circumcenter can be outside the triangle, and in that case some of the barycentric coordinates will be negative. □

6.2 POLYGONS

Triangles are the most primitive shape in graphics, but polygons show up so often that we have to be prepared to analyze and manipulate them. A polygon description includes a set of vertices and a set of edges; more precisely, we have the following definition:

Definition 6.2 (Polygon). *A polygon is an ordered set of distinct points $P_0, P_1, \ldots, P_{n-1}$, called* vertices *such that* $(P_0 P_1), (P_1 P_2), \ldots, (P_{n-1} P_0)$ *are the edges.*

With distinct points and edges that go from one vertex to the next, the definition does not allow polygons to have holes inside. Clearly, a triangle is a polygon and there can be all types of other polygons from those that appear nicely symmetric with equal sides to those that are twisted with edges that intersect each other. To categorize them, we start by defining *simple* polygons to be those such that only two edges intersect at each vertex, and no two edges intersect anywhere else. This eliminates twisted figures, so we will concentrate our investigation on simple polygons (Figure 6.9).

The edges of a simple polygon form an enclosed fence around the inside. However, the fence can be quite wiggly, so we further categorize polygons into those that are *convex* and those that are *concave*.

Definition 6.3 (Convex Polygon). *If for any two points inside or on an edge of a polygon the line segment bounded by those points is entirely inside (or on an edge) the polygon, the polygon is convex.*

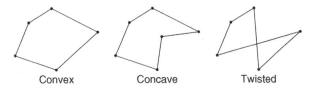

Convex   Concave   Twisted

Figure 6.9   Types of polygons

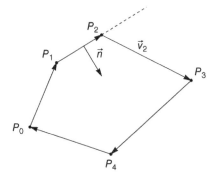

Figure 6.10   Traversing polygon edges

6.2.1   Convexity

A triangle is always a convex polygon. Convexity is a nice geometric property and constrains the position of the edges so that, as we follow the edges around the polygon, we always turn in the same direction at each vertex. We do not turn right at one vertex and left at the next. It is convenient to think of the edges as vectors, so we let $\vec{v}_i = P_{i+1} - P_i$ for $i = 0, 1, \dots, n-2$ and $\vec{v}_{n-1} = P_0 - P_{n-1}$. Following the edge vectors one after the other gives a direction to the perimeter of the polygon. The definition of vector addition shows that the sum of all the edge vectors is the zero vector, that is, $\sum_{i=0}^{n-1} \vec{v}_i = 0$.

Imagine rotating an edge vector $\pi/2$ radians clockwise to get a normal vector. The normal can help determine if the next edge vector in the sequence involves turning to the right or left. If the dot product of the normal with the next edge vector is positive, then it is a right turn. Otherwise, it is a left turn. The turns are not necessarily $\pi/2$ radians, but rather simply in the left or right direction. This leads to a method for deciding if the polygon is convex. If all the turns are in the same direction, the polygon is convex (Figure 6.10).

Example 6.7 (Determining Convexity). In order, the points $(1, 5)$, $(4, 8)$, $(5, 4)$, $(6, 2)$, $(2, -1)$ describe a polygon. The edge vectors are then

$$\vec{v}_0 = (3, 3) \qquad \vec{v}_1 = (1, -4) \quad \vec{v}_2 = (1, -2)$$
$$\vec{v}_3 = (-4, -3) \quad \vec{v}_4 = (-1, 6)$$

Rotating a vector by $\pi/2$ radians in the clockwise direction involves multiplying by the correct rotation matrix, and in this case the vector (x, y) becomes $(y, -x)$. So the normals are

$$\vec{n}_0 = (3, -3) \quad \vec{n}_1 = (-4, -1) \quad \vec{n}_2 = (-2, -1)$$
$$\vec{n}_3 = (-3, 4) \quad \vec{n}_4 = (6, 1)$$

To determine the turn moving from $\vec{v}_0$ to $\vec{v}_1$, calculate $\vec{n}_0 \cdot \vec{v}_1 = 15 > 0$. The positive dot product implies it is a right turn. The rest of the turns can be calculated similarly, but from $\vec{v}_1$ to $\vec{v}_2$, we get $\vec{n}_1 \cdot \vec{v}_2 = -2 < 0$. This is a left turn and indicates that the polygon is not convex.

Notice that, if the vertices are given in a clockwise order, then the normals point inside the polygon.   □

A problem that emerges often in graphics and is common in computational geometry is to enclose a set of points in a convex polygon. The smallest such polygon is called the *convex hull*. One simple algorithm for finding the convex hull proceeds by forming the set of all vectors between points (in both directions). Then select all vectors that do not have any of the other points sitting to the left of the vector. (We can calculate the appropriate normal and test the appropriate dot product.) Of all the selected vectors, pick one and find the next that starts where the first ends. Continue until there is an ordered set of vectors and hence an ordered set of points describing the convex polygon (Figure 6.11).

This straightforward algorithm checks all possible vectors (n^2 vectors) and is consequently a little slow. Faster algorithms exist that consider the coordinates of the points when selecting the next vector.

6.2.2   Angles and Area

An interior angle for a polygon is an angle at a vertex between the two adjacent edges measured on the inside of the polygon. An exterior angle is the angle of a right turn at a vertex as we travel around the polygon perimeter with the interior on the right. It should be easy to see that the sum of all the exterior angles is 2π.

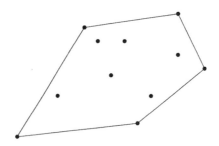

Figure 6.11   Convex hull

For convex polygons, select any vertex and draw new edges to each other vertex. (There are already edges to the adjacent vertices.) Each new edge lies entirely inside the polygon, so they divide the polygon into $n - 2$ triangles where n is the number of polygon edges. Each triangle has three angles summing to π radians and, consequently, all the interior angles of the polygon sum to $(n - 2)\pi$. In a convex hexagon, for example, the sum of the interior angles is $(6 - 2)\pi = 4\pi$. As long as the polygon (convex or not) can be divided into k triangles by drawing nonintersecting diagonals, the sum of the interior angles is $k\pi$.

If the angles in a convex polygon are all equal and the edges are also equal, then the polygon is called *regular*. The interior angles of a regular polygon are each equal to $(1 - \frac{2}{n})\pi$. For a regular hexagon, each of the angles is $\frac{2}{3}\pi$ (Figure 6.12).

For the area of a convex polygon, consider the previous division into triangles and simply sum the areas of each triangle. For polygons in two dimensions, we pick the vertex P_0 as the common vertex (any vertex will do) and take half the sum of the lengths of the cross products. However, in two dimensions the length of a cross product reduces to a determinant.

$$\text{Area of polygon (2D)} = \left| \frac{1}{2} \sum_{i=1}^{n-2} \left| \begin{matrix} (P_i - P_0) \\ (P_{i+1} - P_0) \end{matrix} \right| \right| \tag{6.11}$$

The vectors between vertices are rows in the 2×2 determinants. If the vertices of the polygon are listed in counterclockwise order, then the determinants are positive. If the order is clockwise, then each determinant is negative. In either case, an absolute value gives the area.

If the polygon is concave, then we may have the situation shown at the right in Figure 6.13. Here, the trouble is that the triangles $\Delta P_0 P_1 P_2$, $\Delta P_0 P_2 P_3$, and $\Delta P_0 P_3 P_4$ all contain some area outside the polygon. With the vertices listed in counterclockwise order, triangles $\Delta P_0 P_1 P_2$ and $\Delta P_0 P_2 P_3$ will both yield positive determinants, and $\Delta P_0 P_3 P_4$ will have a negative determinant. So if we consider signed areas, then the area of $\Delta P_0 P_3 P_4$ is both added and subtracted, leaving just the area of the polygon. When a triangle "folds back" over others, then it generates a negative determinant.

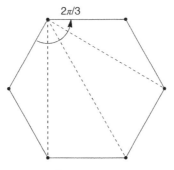

Figure 6.12 Angles in a hexagon

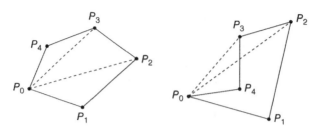

Figure 6.13 Area of a polygon

By counting the regions of fold-back, we can prove that the final sum is indeed the area of the polygon. If the vertices appear in clockwise order, the same argument works, but the final sum will be negative. In both cases, Equation 6.11 gives the correct area.

In three-dimensional polygons, the areas of the triangles do not reduce to one-half the determinants; rather, the cross products produce arbitrary vectors and do not generally simplify. To account for signed areas, we use the direction of the cross product which either points in the same direction as a normal to the polygon plane or in the opposite direction. Let $\vec{n}$ be a unit normal to the plane of the polygon. Then $\vec{n} \cdot ((P_1 - P_0) \times (P_2 - P_0))$, the scalar triple product, gives the volume of a parallelepiped, but since the height is 1 (because of the unit normal), the volume is just twice the signed area of the triangle $\triangle P_0 P_1 P_2$. Summing over triangles gives us a formula for the area.

$$\text{Area of Polygon (3D)} = \left| \frac{1}{2} \vec{n} \cdot \sum_{i=1}^{n-2} (P_i - P_0) \times (P_{i+1} - P_0) \right| \qquad (6.12)$$

We may need to check three-dimensional polygons to see if they are indeed planar. Two tests present themselves immediately. We can take any four vertices and use the scalar triple product to determine the volume of a parallelepiped; zero volume implies the points are coplanar. Unfortunately, we need to check several sets of four vertices to guarantee that all vertices are in the plane. For a more basic method, we can find the equation of the plane containing any three vertices and check to see if all other vertices are in that plane. (Computationally, all these calculations are looking to see if the dot products are within a small distance of zero.)

There is one last useful generalization. The common vertex P_0 we selected in the previous derivations could be any point in the plane of the polygon. For two-dimensional polygons, it could be the origin. This means we do not have to subtract to find vectors. Yet, it often means that the vectors have large lengths which could lead to computational errors.

Example 6.8 (Area of a Polygon). The vertices of a two-dimensional polygon are $P_0 = (4, 1), P_1 = (5, 3), P_2 = (3, 4), P_3 = (4, 7),$ and $P_4 = (1, 3)$. It is clear by sketching their positions that the vertices are in counterclockwise order. Using P_0 as the common vertex, the vectors are $(1, 2)$, $(-1, 3)$, $(0, 6)$, and $(-3, 2)$.

$$\text{Area} = \frac{1}{2}\left(\begin{vmatrix} 1 & 2 \\ -1 & 3 \end{vmatrix} + \begin{vmatrix} -1 & 3 \\ 0 & 6 \end{vmatrix} + \begin{vmatrix} 0 & 6 \\ -3 & -2 \end{vmatrix}\right) = 8.5$$

Notice that the second determinant is negative.

If we use the origin as the common vertex, then, for example, $v_0 = P_0 - 0 = (4, 1)$, so the vectors have the same components as the points.

$$\text{Area} = \frac{1}{2}\left(\begin{vmatrix} 4 & 1 \\ 5 & 3 \end{vmatrix} + \begin{vmatrix} 5 & 3 \\ 3 & 4 \end{vmatrix} + \begin{vmatrix} 3 & 4 \\ 4 & 7 \end{vmatrix} + \begin{vmatrix} 4 & 7 \\ 1 & 3 \end{vmatrix} + \begin{vmatrix} 1 & 3 \\ 4 & 1 \end{vmatrix}\right) = 8.5$$

With this second approach, there are as many determinant terms as there are vertices. However, we did not have to subtract vertices to find the vectors.

The two-dimensional polygon lies in the xy plane. Suppose we project it onto another plane (by following lines perpendicular to the first polygon) and get the following vertices:

$$Q_0 = (4, 1, 1) \qquad Q_1 = (5, 3, -1) \quad Q_2 = (3, 4, 0.5)$$
$$Q_3 = (4, 7, -2) \quad Q_4 = (1, 3, 3)$$

For a quick check to see if the vertices do lie on a plane, calculate the scalar triple products:

$$(Q_3 - Q_0) \cdot ((Q_1 - Q_0) \times (Q_2 - Q_0))$$
$$= (0, 6, -3) \cdot ((1, 2, -2) \times (-1, 3, -0.5))$$
$$= (0, 6, -3) \cdot (5, 2.5, 5) = 0$$
$$(Q_4 - Q_0) \cdot ((Q_1 - Q_0) \times (Q_2 - Q_0))$$
$$= (-3, 2, 2) \cdot ((1, 2, -2) \times (-1, 3, -0.5))$$
$$= (0, 6, -3) \cdot (5, 2.5, 5) = 0$$

The two scalar products are zero and they include all vertices, so the polygon is planar. To calculate its area, we need to find a normal to the polygon. The cross product just calculated will do, and we divide by its length to get a unit normal: $\vec{n} = \frac{1}{\sqrt{56.25}}(5, 2.5, 5)$. Now the area is a scalar triple product.

$$\text{Area} = \frac{1}{2}\vec{n} \cdot ((Q_1 - Q_0) \times (Q_2 - Q_0) + (Q_2 - Q_0) \times (Q_3 - Q_0)$$
$$+ (Q_3 - Q_0) \times (Q_4 - Q_0))$$
$$= \frac{1}{2\sqrt{56.2}}(5, 2.5, 5) \cdot (17, 8.5, 17) = 12.75$$

The fact that this area is larger than the area of the polygon in the xy plane makes intuitive sense because the second polygon is projected perpendicularly onto the xy plane to get the first polygon. The angle between the two planes is the angle between their normals, and the cosine of that angle is $\frac{2}{3}$. A little trigonometry shows that the ratio of the areas should be the same as the cosine of the angle between the planes. Consequently, the ratio of the two areas (8.5/12.75) is two to three.   □

6.2.3 Inside and Outside

As with triangles in particular, checking a point to see if it is inside or outside of a polygon is a common task in graphics. Barycentric coordinates formed a key tool in working with triangles, but, although generalizing these coordinates to arbitrary polygons can work for convex polygons, it is not practical for concave polygons. In the case of convex polygons, one approach defines the barycentric coordinates as ratios of areas much like the case for triangles. However, the areas used are more complicated than those used for triangles (See Section 6.4 for details).

Recall that the point $P = \frac{1}{3}(P_0 + P_1 + P_2)$ is the centroid of a triangle and is inside the triangle. It is natural to consider the point $P = \frac{1}{n}(P_0 + P_1 + \cdots + P_{n-1})$ for an arbitrary polygon with n vertices. Assume the polygon is convex. Then, the affine combination of two vertices P_0 and P_1 is on the edge of the polygon, and hence we consider it inside the polygon. Moving up one step to three vertices, the affine combination of three vertices is also inside the polygon because we can write it as an affine combination of a point on the edge and a vertex. This process can be continued until we reach an affine combination of all vertices.

$$Q_0 = \frac{1}{2}(P_0 + P_1)$$

$$Q_1 = \frac{1}{3}P_2 + \frac{2}{3}Q_0 = \frac{1}{3}(P_0 + P_1 + P_2)$$

$$\vdots$$

$$Q_{n-2} = \frac{1}{n}P_{n-1} + \frac{n-1}{n}Q_{n-3} = \frac{1}{n}(P_0 + P_1 + \cdots + P_{n-1}) \tag{6.13}$$

Each Q_i is a point inside the polygon because it is on the line segment between two points already in the polygon and the polygon is convex. Consequently, $P = \frac{1}{n}(P_0 + P_1 + \cdots + P_{n-1})$ is inside a convex polygon. (Note: This point is not the centroid of a polygon where a uniform polygonal plate would balance; it is, instead, the balance point if weights were only at the vertices.) The same type of argument can be used to find a variety of points inside the polygon. However, for concave polygons, the point may well be outside.

Convex polygons have some nice properties. One in particular is useful in answering the question about whether a point is inside or outside the polygon. Consider the line containing any edge of the polygon; it is determined by two adjacent vertices. All the other vertices in the polygon are on the same side of this line. This can be detected by taking the dot products with a normal to the edge. (There is a slight complication if a point falls on the line, but then it is inside only if it is on an edge.) Each edge of the polygon has this same property if the polygon is convex. Now, a given point P is inside a convex polygon if and only if it is on the same side of each edge (line) as the other vertices. For each edge, the algorithm for implementing this technique checks P and one vertex to see if they are on the same side.

A more general technique for deciding whether a point is inside or outside a polygon (convex or concave) starts by considering a ray emanating from the point in any direction. A ray here means that we take a line $P + t\vec{v}$ containing the point P in question and consider only positive values for t. The idea is to determine how many times the ray crosses the polygon's boundary. More precisely, the polygon's vertices are given in some order, so they form edge vectors following the boundary. If an edge crosses (intersects) our ray, then we note the direction it crosses. A crossing from left to right will be recorded as $+1$ and a crossing from right to left will be noted as -1. If the sum of all the crossing numbers (often called the *winding* number) is zero, then the point P is outside the polygon. Otherwise, it is inside (Figure 6.14).

To determine whether a crossing is left to right $(+1)$ or right to left (-1), one technique is to calculate a normal to the ray vector v by rotating the vector $\pi/2$ clockwise. Then take the dot product of this normal with an edge vector, and if it is positive, the crossing is left to right $(+1)$; negative means it is right to left (-1).

The algorithm then first determines which edge vectors cross the ray. This can be done by deciding whether the end points of the edge vector are on opposite sides of the ray's line or not. Then for each intersection, the direction of the crossing is recorded as $+1$ or -1. Checking the sum of these directions tells whether the point is inside or outside the polygon.

Example 6.9 (Inside or Outside of a Polygon). Assume a polygon has the following vertices:

$$P_0 = (1, -1) \quad P_1 = (8, 3) \quad P_2 = (2, 4)$$
$$P_3 = (6, 7) \quad P_4 = (-1, 8)$$

Note that the polygon is concave.

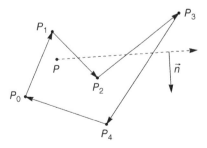

Figure 6.14   Inside or outside a polygon

To decide whether the point $P = (3, 6)$ is inside or outside the polygon, we pick a ray emanating from P. A simplifying choice is the ray $(3, 6) + t(0, -1)$; this is a vertical ray with a simple direction vector. The first task is to find the edges that intersect the ray. Pick $(-1, 0)$ as the normal to the ray because it results from rotating the direction vector $\pi/2$ clockwise. Now form vectors from P to each vertex and take the dot product with the normal:

$$P_0 - P = (-2, -7) \implies (-2, -7) \cdot (-1, 0) = 2 > 0$$
$$P_1 - P = (5, -3) \implies (5, -3) \cdot (-1, 0) = -5 < 0$$
$$P_2 - P = (-1, -2) \implies (-1, -2) \cdot (-1, 0) = 1 > 0$$
$$P_3 - P = (3, 1) \implies (3, 1) \cdot (-1, 0) = -3 < 0$$
$$P_4 - P = (-4, 2) \implies (-4, 2) \cdot (-1, 0) = 4 > 0$$

Because of the choice of the ray, the dot product is particularly easy to calculate. Systematically checking all five edges, if the two end points are on opposite sides of the ray (positive and negative dot products), there is an intersection. Edge P_0P_1 has end points on opposite sides, so there is an intersection, but edge P_4P_0 does not intersect. Four edges P_0P_1, P_1P_2, P_2P_3, and P_3P_4 intersect the line containing the ray. The corresponding edge vectors are

$$v_0 = (7, 4) \quad v_1 = (-6, 1)$$
$$v_3 = (4, 3) \quad v_4 = (-7, 1)$$

One edge, P_3P_4, is behind the ray. That is, the intersection with the line containing the ray has $t < 0$. The algorithm could actually calculate the intersection and get $t \approx -1.43$, or it could employ additional checks to eliminate this edge (see Exercises). In this particular example, the dot products between the direction vector for the ray $\vec{v}$ and the vectors to P_3 and P_4 are both negative, indicating that the intersection will occur for $t < 0$.

The three edges P_0P_1, P_1P_2, and P_2P_1 intersect the ray and need to be classified as left to right or right to left. Dot products between edge vectors and the normal $(-1, 0)$ determine the directions.

$$\vec{v}_0 \cdot (-1, 0) = -7 < 0 \implies \text{Direction: } -1$$
$$\vec{v}_1 \cdot (-1, 0) = 6 > 0 \implies \text{Direction: } +1$$
$$\vec{v}_2 \cdot (-1, 0) = -4 < 0 \implies \text{Direction: } -1$$

The directions are based on looking down the ray in the direction of $\vec{v}$, so the edge P_0P_1, for example, crosses from right to left which is denoted -1. The sum of the directions is -1, which is not zero, so we conclude that the point P is inside the polygon.

From this example, it appears that we could have just counted the number of intersections with the ray and noted whether the number was odd or even. An odd number indicates that the point is inside. This works for a simple polygon, but for twisted ones the directional approach can be more useful. □

6.2.4 Triangulation

Three-dimensional objects in computer graphics are usually built from triangular patches which match up at edges and vertices. Practically, points on the object can often be sampled and stored in preparation for some algorithm to turn the set of points into a coherent set of triangles (called a *mesh*). It is not a simple matter to decide how to do this or what division into triangles is the best. To get an idea of the analysis involved in producing a mesh of triangles, a more common two-dimensional example shows some of the key geometry. A terrain map results from sampling the altitudes of several points in a geographic area. If we position the points on a plane, draw triangles with the points as the vertices, and then raise the points according to their altitudes, we get a three-dimensional look at the terrain (Figure 6.15). The key in this construction is to find a triangulation of the points in the plane.

Definition 6.4 (Triangulation). *A triangulation of a set of points is a set of edges between the points such that no two edges cross (i.e., intersect other than at their end points) and any additional edge not in the set would cross some edge in the set.*

This definition implies that, starting with a set of points, the edges forming the convex hull of the points are always in the triangulation. It also implies that the interior of the convex hull is divided into triangles. So to study triangulations, we can begin with a convex polygon and analyze ways to divide the polygon into triangles (Figure 6.16).

There is a simple way to make the division. Start with the edges of the convex polygon and add diagonals from a selected vertex to all the others. This produces $N - 2$ triangles if the polygon has N edges.

There are several ways to divide a convex polygon into triangles, but any one will work to triangulate a set of points. Beginning with any set of M points, find the convex

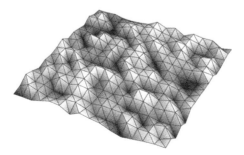

Figure 6.15 Terrain from a triangular mesh

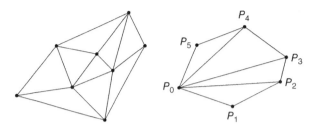

Figure 6.16   Triangulations

hull, and triangulate the resulting convex polygon. If we assume that no three points are collinear, then N points are on the convex hull, N edges are in the convex hull, $N - 2$ triangles partition the polygon, and $M - N$ points are left inside the polygon.

Each of these inside points falls inside one of the triangles. Pick one of the points and connect it to the vertices of its containing triangle. One triangle has been divided into three, so there is a net addition of two triangles. Again pick an inside point and locate its containing triangle. Connect it to the three vertices. Continue in this manner until there are edges to each point.

The assumption that no three points are collinear was convenient for presenting the method, but it is not critical. If some point is on the edge between two others, we can simply add additional edges, forming more triangles. The only difficulty with collinearity is the degenerate case where all the points lie on a line.

Result 6.2 (Number of Triangles).   *Let N_h be the number of vertices in the convex hull and let N_I be the number of points inside the hull. As long as not all the points are collinear, the number of triangles in a triangulation of the set of points is always $2N_I + N_h - 2$.*

The number of triangles in a partition of the convex hull is $N_h - 2$. Then each time we select an interior point, we add two triangles to this total (Figure 6.17). Consequently, the total is $2N_I + N_h - 2$. This verifies the result for the algorithm developed above, but the result is actually true for any triangulation. The proof depends on Euler's formula and is presented in Section 6.3.4.

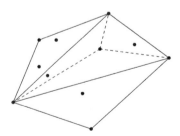

Figure 6.17   Triangulating a cluster of points

6.2.5 Delaunay Triangulation

Two triangulations of a set of points have the same number of triangles, but that does not guarantee that the two triangulations are equally desirable. There are many criteria we could bring to bear in measuring the optimality of a triangulation. For example, in producing a terrain map, we may have four points forming a quadrilateral, with high altitudes at two diagonally opposite vertices and low altitudes at the other two. Then, depending on how we triangulate, there could be an edge between the high vertices or between the low vertices. In the first case, the terrain map indicates a mountain range, and in the other there is a valley. This type of detail is a little difficult to resolve because one or the other may indicate the true topography but one choice of an edge often looks more natural than the other.

One situation that is often troublesome for graphics is the presence of "skinny" triangles in the triangulation. These are triangles with at least one small angle. Since the lighting characteristics of an object depend on treating the triangles individually, skinny triangles could complicate the lighting calculations and introduce artifacts into the resulting image. An awkward look to the object can often be traced to these skinny triangles.

The Delaunay triangulation, named after a twentieth century Russian mathematician, addresses this problem by ordering triangulations based on the presence of skinny triangles. If a triangulation for a set of points has k triangles, then there are $m = 3k$ angles and we can order these angles from the smallest to the largest. For two triangulations T_1 and T_2 of the same set of points, order them by comparing their associated list of increasing angles. Let $A_1 = (\theta_1, \theta_2, \ldots, \theta_m)$ be the angle list for T_1; similarly, $A_2 = (\beta_1, \beta_2, \ldots, \beta_m)$ is the list for T_2.

Definition 6.5 (Order of Triangulations). *By comparing θ_i to β_i (starting with $i = 1$), let j be the first index where the two angles differ. If $\theta_j < \beta_j$, then T_2 is said to be larger than T_1.*

For example, suppose there are only two triangles in each of T_1 and T_2 and suppose the angle lists are as follows:

$$A_1 = (10°, 10°, 20°, 80°, 80°, 160°)$$
$$A_2 = (10°, 10°, 80°, 80°, 90°, 90°)$$

Then the two sequences differ for the first time in the third position where $20° < 80°$. This means that T_2 is larger than T_1. Small angles have to be accompanied by larger angles because the sum of the angles in a triangle is π. To say that T_2 is larger than T_1 is to say that the triangulation T_2 tends to have fewer skinny triangles than T_1. This captures the essence of the problem we are trying to minimize.

Every interior edge (not on the convex hull) in a triangulation borders two triangles which together form a quadrilateral. The interior edge forms a diagonal in the quadrilateral (Figure 6.18). We could delete this diagonal and add the other diagonal. If it results in a larger triangulation based on the ordered angle lists, then we will call

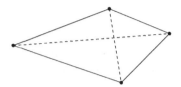

Figure 6.18 Two diagonals in a quadrilateral

this new edge *good* and the original edge *bad*. Otherwise, the original edge is *good* and new one is *bad*.

There is an awkward case that arises if the quadrilateral has vertices on a circle. Envision a square where each diagonal divides the square into triangles with the same angle list. The diagonals are both *good* edges. Usually, we assume that no four points in the original set of points lie on a common circle. Then an edge is either *good* or *bad*. It is not difficult to handle this awkward case when designing an algorithm.

Definition 6.6 (Delaunay Triangulation). *A triangulation that only includes good edges is a Delaunay triangulation.*

The Delaunay triangulation maximizes the minimum angle in all triangles. The definition of triangulation suggests that one algorithm is to simply consider all adjacent triangles and decide whether to flip the diagonal of the quadrilateral formed by the pair of triangles. In order to make the decision, we need to find a new angle list and again compare the two triangulations.

Actually, with two triangles, changing the diagonal means that we need to revise six angles in the original angle list. So if T_1 is revised into T_2, the two angle lists differ only in six positions. It still seems like a bit of work to decide whether a particular edge is good or bad, but further geometric analysis can clear things up.

Figure 6.19 shows the circumcircle for triangle $\triangle ABC$. The vertex D is inside the circumcircle and forms the triangle $\triangle ADC$. These two adjacent triangles share the edge AC. From basic geometry, $\angle ACB$ is one-half the angle extended by the arc AB.

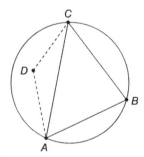

Figure 6.19 Triangle circumcircle

Since D is inside the circle, $\angle ADB > \angle ACB$. (This can be verified by considering $\triangle ADB$ and comparing it with the one where D is on the circle.) If D is on the circle, then $\angle ADB = \angle ACB$, and if D is outside the circle, $\angle ADB < \angle ACB$.

Viewing the two triangles ($\triangle ABC$ and $\triangle ADC$) as coming from a triangulation, they form a quadrilateral $ABCD$ with the edge AC. To see whether this edge is good or bad, we compare the angles in the current configuration with those we get by replacing AC with DB. Figure 6.20 labels the angles inside the two triangles. With D inside the circumcircle, $\beta_1 > \theta_1$. Similar reasoning shows that $\beta_2 > \theta_2$.

The angles $\angle ADC = \beta_1 + \beta_2$ and $\angle ABC = \beta_3 + \beta_4$ are opposite angles in the quadrilateral. If D were on the circle, then the sum of these two angles would be π radians because both angles are one-half the angle extended by the arcs bounded by A and C. Since D is inside the circle, $(\beta_1 + \beta_2) + (\beta_3 + \beta_4) > \pi$. Now, consider the circumcircle for $\triangle ADC$. If B were on or outside the circumcircle, then the sum of the β_i's would not be larger than π. This implies that B must be inside the circumcircle for $\triangle ADC$ (Figure 6.21).

Using this new circumcircle, the same arguments as before establishes that $\beta_3 > \theta_3$ and $\beta_4 > \theta_4$. Let T_1 be the triangulation which includes the edge AC, and let T_2 be the triangulation which includes the edge BD. The angle lists differ only in six angles.

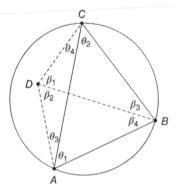

Figure 6.20   Quadrilateral angles

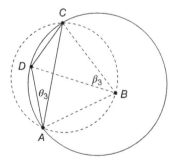

Figure 6.21   Circumcircle for $\triangle ADC$

The six angles for each triangulation (not given in any particular order) are

$$T_1 : (\theta_1, \theta_2, \theta_3, \theta_4, (\beta_1 + \beta_2), (\beta_3 + \beta_4))$$
$$T_2 : (\beta_1, \beta_2, \beta_3, \beta_4, (\theta_2 + \theta_4), (\theta_1 + \theta_3))$$

We do not have to put these angles in order to see the outcome. For every angle in T_2, there is an angle in T_1 that is smaller. This argues that T_2 is larger than T_1. Consequently, the edge AC should be replaced with BD. If we start again and assume that D is not in the original circumcircle, then our result will be reversed and we keep AC. This is the heart of a criterion for determining whether we do have a Delaunay triangulation.

Result 6.3 (Delaunay Criteria). *If in a triangulation each pair of adjacent triangles, $\triangle ABC$ and $\triangle ADC$, has vertex D outside the circumcircle of $\triangle ABC$, then the triangulation is a Delaunay triangulation.*

(Again, we are avoiding the awkward case where D is on the circumcircle by assuming that no four of our original points lie on the same circle.) With the barycentric coordinates for the circumcircle, the algorithm for implementing this result is more or less straightforward. To construct a Delaunay triangulation, one point after another can be added, ensuring each time that the Delaunay criterion is still true.

6.3   POLYHEDRA

Polygons can be taped together along an edge to form a solid called a *polyhedron* (derived from the Greek for "many bases"). Graphics objects are often custom polyhedra with large numbers of polygons; simpler polyhedra can form building blocks for the more complicated ones. Perhaps the most common polyhedron is the cube, which plays a significant role in computer graphics, but there are many others including those in Figure 6.22 called *Platonic* solids which are rather symmetric and uniform.

Of course, there are many other, less uniform, polyhedra with various polygonal faces, occasional stellations, and even holes (Figure 6.23).

Defining polyhedra is not a simple matter, mostly because there are odd solids like two tetrahedrons joined only at one vertex, two cubes joined along one edge, or self-intersecting solids that violate the spirit of what is means to be a solid. A core intuitive definition is the following:

Definition 6.7 (Polyhedron). *A polyhedron is a collection of polygons with the following properties:*

1. *Each edge of a polygon meets exactly one other polygon along a mutual edge.*
2. *Each corner of a polygon meets another polygon at a corner.*
3. *The subset of polygons meeting at a vertex are all connected to each other without passing through the vertex.*

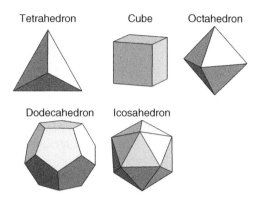

Figure 6.22 Regular (Platonic) polyhedra

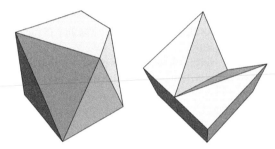

Figure 6.23 Asymmetric polyhedra

The third property in the definition ensures that we do not have, for example, two tetrahedra touching only at one vertex. (There are more awkward examples that are also avoided with this property.)

For polyhedra, we have vertices where polygons meet at corners, edges where two polygons meet along their mutual side, and faces (which are just the polygons). The faces are all planar, and the angle between the planes containing two adjacent faces is called the *dihedral angle*.

To bring some order to the study of polyhedra, there are a variety of ways to classify them. One of the most important categories relies on convexity and mimics the similar property for polygons.

Definition 6.8 (Convex Polyhedra). *If for any two points inside or on an edge of a polyhedron the line segment bounded by those points is entirely inside (or on an edge) the polyhedron, then the polyhedron is convex.*

Other classifications count the number of holes through the solid, so polyhedra like those in Figures 6.22 and 6.23 are said to have *genus* zero, and polyhedra shaped like doughnuts have genus 1. Mathematicians over the ages have settled on various classes of polyhedra and then set about counting how many there are in each class and what properties they share.

6.3.1   Regular Polyhedra

The Platonic solids in Figure 6.22 are convex, and each one has faces that are regular polygons (equal edges and equal interior angles). Moreover, all the faces are congruent (i.e., all equal polygons). Surprisingly, there are other polyhedra that share this property of having regular polygons as faces but are not quite as symmetric as the Platonic solids. Figure 6.24 shows two examples.

A key to regaining some symmetry is the configuration at a vertex. If a vertex is cut off uniformly across each face, it reveals a polygonal cross section called a *vertex figure*. For the Platonic solids, each vertex figure is a regular polygon; for example, the vertex figure in a cube is an equilateral triangle. In this class of polyhedra, the faces are congruent regular polygons and the vertex figures are all the same regular polygon. This class is referred to as *regular polyhedra* and it contains the Platonic solids. For example, the dodecahedron's faces are regular pentagons and its vertex figures are equilateral triangles.

Instead of requiring the vertex figures to be regular polygons, there are several other properties that would also define the regular polyhedra.

Result 6.4 (Regular Polyhedra). *A regular polyhedron is convex, has congruent regular polygons for faces, and displays the following equivalent properties:*

1. *The vertex figures are all the same regular polygon.*
2. *All the vertices lie on a sphere.*
3. *The same number of faces meet at each vertex.*
4. *All the dihedral angles are equal.*

In other words, once we have a convex polyhedron with congruent regular faces, then any one of the listed properties implies that all of the properties hold and the polyhedron is regular. Table 6.1 gives the vertex coordinates for the

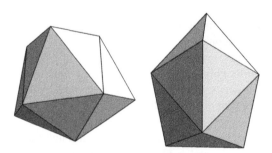

Figure 6.24   Deltahedra

TABLE 6.1   Coordinates for the Platonic Solids ($\phi = \frac{1+\sqrt{5}}{2}$)

Tetrahedron	$(1,1,1)$	$(1,-1,-1)$	$(-1,1,-1)$	$(-1,-1,1)$
Cube	$(\pm1,\pm1,\pm1)$			
Octahedron	$(\pm1,0,0)$	$(0,\pm1,0)$	$(0,0,\pm1)$	
Dodecahedron	$(0,\pm\phi^{-1},\pm\phi)$	$(\pm\phi,0,\pm\phi^{-1})$	$(\pm\phi^{-1},\pm\phi,0)$	$(\pm1,\pm1,\pm1)$
Icosahedron	$(0,\pm\phi,\pm1)$	$(\pm1,0,\pm\phi)$	$(\pm\phi,\pm1,0)$	

Platonic solids. (In the table, ϕ is the golden ratio, which is a root of the quadratic $\phi^2 - \phi - 1 = 0$.)

Are there more Platonic solids than those shown in Figure 6.22? Each of these polyhedra has faces that are regular polygons, so let p be the number of edges in each polygon, which means the interior angles are $(1 - \frac{2}{p})\pi$. At each vertex, the same number of faces meet, so let q be this number. Then, at each vertex the sum of the angles in all the faces meeting is q times the interior angle of a polygon. This sum must be less than 2π because this is the sum of the angles completely surrounding a point in the plane.

$$q\left(1 - \frac{2}{p}\right)\pi < 2\pi \implies \frac{1}{q} + \frac{1}{p} > \frac{1}{2}$$

The only positive integer solutions, (p,q), to the last inequality are $(3,3),(3,4),(4,3)$, $(5,3)$, $(3,5)$ and these correspond to the five polyhedra in Figure 6.22. There are only five convex regular polyhedra. An inventory of their vertices, edges, and faces is listed in Table 6.2. Yet another nice symmetry emerges from the five Platonic solids by forming new polyhedra from each of the five. Take the midpoint of each face and connect it to another midpoint if the two faces share an edge. This means, for example, that there are six midpoints for a cube and connecting them gives eight new faces, forming an octahedron. Similarly, the midpoints of the octahedron connected appropriately give a cube. These two polyhedra are *duals* as are the dodecahedron and the icosahedron. The dual of the tetrahedron is itself.

One way to enlarge the class of regular polyhedra is to loosen the restriction that the faces are all congruent regular polygons. Instead, drop the congruency requirement

TABLE 6.2   Shape of the Platonic Solids (Angles in radians)

	Faces	Vertices	Edges	Dihedral Angle
Tetrahedron	4	4	6	1.23
Cube	6	8	12	1.57
Octahedron	8	6	12	1.91
Dodecahedron	12	20	30	2.03
Icosahedron	20	12	30	2.41

Figure 6.25   Some of the 13 Archimedean solids

Figure 6.26   Nonconvex regular polyhedra

and focus on regular polygons of any number of edges. This adds 13 polyhedra to the 5 regular polyhedra. The discovery of these extra somewhat regular polyhedra is attributed to Archimedes and, consequently, they are called the *Archimedean solids*. A few are shown in Figure 6.25.

Finally, dropping the convexity requirement from regular polygons admits some stellated examples to the class. There are some subtleties involved in handling faces that intersect; Figure 6.26 shows three of these polyhedra.

6.3.2   Volume of Polyhedra

Finding the area of a polygon involves dividing it into triangles, and the area of a triangle is half the length of the cross product of vectors formed from the edges. The same type of approach works for the volume of a polyhedron; only here the primitive shape is a pyramid and we can divide the polyhedron into pyramids. The first step is then to find the volume of a pyramid (Figure 6.27).

Start with a pyramid that has a triangular base with one side s and the altitude a. Let h be the height of the pyramid. There are geometric dissections that divide easily calculated volumes (like that of a cube) into pyramids in order to deduce particular volumes, but a foolproof way to find a pyramid's volume is to turn to calculus. Think of the cross sections as we move down the pyramid from the apex to the base. Halfway down, the triangular cross section has a side that is half the side of the base and an altitude that is half the altitude of the base. At the apex the cross-sectional area is zero, and at the base the area is the area of the triangle. Anywhere in between, we

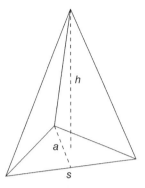

Figure 6.27 Volume of a triangular pyramid

have gone a fraction, $\frac{x}{h}$, of the distance to the base, and the area is

$$\text{Cross-sectional area} \ = \ \frac{1}{2}\left(\frac{x}{h} \cdot a\right)\left(\frac{x}{h} \cdot s\right) = \frac{x^2}{h^2}\left(\frac{1}{2}as\right)$$

Adding up all these cross sections gives the following integral:

$$\text{Volume of Pyramid} \ = \ \int_0^h \frac{x^2}{h^2}\left(\frac{1}{2}as\right)dx$$

$$= \ \frac{1}{2}as \cdot \frac{x^3}{3h^2}\Big|_{x=0}^{x=h} = \frac{1}{3}\left(\frac{1}{2}as\right)h$$

$$= \ \frac{1}{3} \times \text{Base} \times \text{Height}$$

Let P_0, P_1, and P_2 be the vertices of the base triangle and let P_3 be the apex. Then, form vectors $v_1 = (P_1 - P_0)$, $v_2 = (P_2 - P_0)$, and $v_3 = (P_3 - P_0)$. The area of the base is $\frac{1}{2}|\vec{v}_1 \times \vec{v}_2|$, and the volume is then one-sixth of the scalar triple product.

$$\boxed{\text{Volume of Triangular Pyramid} \ = \ \frac{1}{6}|\vec{v}_3 \cdot (\vec{v}_1 \times \vec{v}_2)|} \qquad (6.14)$$

Example 6.10 (Volume of Dodecahedron). Table 6.1 gives the vertex coordinates of a dodecahedron. The distance from any vertex to the origin is $\sqrt{3}$, and notice that the affine combination $\sum_{i=0}^{19} \frac{1}{20}P_i$ of the vertices gives $(0,0,0)$. We conclude that the dodecahedron is centered at the origin. It is a little hard to tell which vertices belong to a single pentagonal face, but by referring to the figure of a dodecahedron, we can settle on the following five vertices (in counterclockwise order looking from the outside of the dodecahedron):

$$\left(\frac{1}{\phi},\phi,0\right), (1,1,1), \left(\phi,0,\frac{1}{\phi}\right), \left(\phi,0,-\frac{1}{\phi}\right), (1,1,-1)$$

These are the vertices for one of the 12 faces of the dodecahedron. Together with the origin, they form one of 12 pyramids that comprise the volume of the dodecahedron.

Remember that $\phi = \frac{\sqrt{5}+1}{2}$ and that $\phi^2 - \phi - 1 = 0$. Some algebra also shows that $\phi^2 = \phi + 1$ and $\frac{1}{\phi} = \phi - 1$. We will keep ϕ in the picture as long as possible to minimize round-off. To find the center of the pentagonal face, take the affine combination of the vertices using coefficients $\frac{1}{5}$ to get

$$\text{Midpoint of face} = \frac{1}{5}(3\phi + 1, \phi + 2, 0)$$

Form vectors $\vec{v}_1$ and $\vec{v}_2$ from the midpoint of the face to two consecutive vertices.

$$\vec{v}_1 = \left(\frac{1}{\phi},\phi,0\right) - \frac{1}{5}(3\phi + 1, \phi + 2, 0) = \left(\frac{2\phi - 6}{5}, \frac{4\phi - 2}{5}, 0\right)$$

$$\vec{v}_2 = (1,1,1) - \frac{1}{5}(3\phi + 1, \phi + 2, 0) = \left(\frac{-3\phi + 4}{5}, \frac{-\phi + 3}{5}, 1\right)$$

The cross product of the two vectors gives a normal to the face:

$$\vec{v}_1 \times \vec{v}_2 = \left(\frac{4\phi - 2}{5}, -\frac{2\phi - 6}{5}, 0\right)$$

It may not look like it at first glance, but this vector is parallel to the vector, call it $\vec{v}_3$, from the origin to the midpoint of the face and again verifies that the dodecahedron's vertices are on a sphere centered at the origin.

The volume of the pyramid with apex at the origin and base formed by the two vectors $\vec{v}_1$ and $\vec{v}_2$ is given by

$$\text{Volume of pyramid} = \frac{1}{6}|\vec{v}_3 \cdot (\vec{v}_1 \times \vec{v}_2)|$$

$$= \frac{1}{6}\left|\frac{1}{5}(3\phi + 1, \phi + 2, 0) \cdot \left(\frac{4\phi - 2}{5}, -\frac{2\phi - 6}{5}, 0\right)\right|$$

$$= \frac{\phi + 2}{15}$$

There are five of these pyramids in a larger pyramid with one pentagonal face as the base. Twelve of these larger pyramids fill the dodecahedron.

$$\text{Volume of dodecahedron } = 12 \times 5 \times \frac{\phi + 2}{15} = 4(\phi + 2) \approx 14.47$$

Clearly, the volume depends on the edge size of the dodecahedron, so to uncover that connection, find the distance between two adjacent vertices to get the edge size for this particular dodecahedron.

$$\left| \left(\frac{1}{\phi}, \phi, 0 \right) - (1, 1, 1) \right| = \sqrt{\left(\frac{1}{\phi} - 1 \right)^2 + (\phi - 1)^2 + 1} = \frac{2}{\phi}$$

The volume is proportional to the cube of an edge, so to find the proportionality constant, divide the volume by the cube of the edge length.

$$4(\phi + 2) \cdot \frac{\phi^3}{8} = \frac{7\phi + 4}{2} = \frac{15 + 7\sqrt{5}}{4}$$

A formula for the volume as a function of the edge length s is

$$\text{Volume of dodecahedron } = \left(\frac{15 + 7\sqrt{5}}{4} \right) s^3$$

□

Generalizing to other pyramids is not difficult. The dodecahedron in the example was a regular polyhedron, so all the internal pyramids making up the volume were all congruent with equal volumes. Other regular polyhedra can be treated similarly, and for nonregular polyhedra the dissection into pyramids involves constructing a pyramid for each face where the apex of each pyramid can conveniently be some common center point for the polyhedron. The altitude for each pyramid may not be the vector from the apex to the center of a face, but by projecting this vector onto the normal to the face we do get the altitude. Let $\vec{A}_i$ be a normal vector to the ith face with length equal to the area of the face. (In the dodecahedron example, $\vec{A}_i$ was a cross product used to find the area of a triangular face.) If $\vec{w}_i$ is the vector from the apex to the face, then the volume of the polyhedron is

$$\text{Volume of polyhedron } = \sum_{i=1}^{n} \frac{1}{6} (\vec{w}_i \cdot \vec{A}_i) \tag{6.15}$$

The vector $\vec{A}_i$ is a normal to the face, and if it consistently points out of the polyhedra, then the volume of each pyramid is a signed volume. Consequently, the common apex point for the pyramids can be anywhere. Just as with polygons, some areas are negative and some positive, but the sum is exactly the area of the polygon. These signed volumes also allow generalization to nonconvex polyhedra. Volumes will cancel each other when lying outside the polyhedra.

6.3.3 Euler's Formula

The number of vertices, faces, and edges in a polyhedron is not arbitrary. As the mathematician Leonard Euler discovered, there is a simple formula that ties all these quantities together. Thinking first of polyhedra that do not have holes through them, imagine that the edges are all made of some elastic material. Looking at one face, stretch it until it encompasses the rest of the faces and then squash the entire network onto a plane. When this is done to a cube and the projection is straightened out, the result looks like the diagram in Figure 6.28(a). The planar network preserves the number of vertices and edges, but the stretched face is not apparent. All the other faces have become polygons in the network, so the total number of faces depicted is one less than the number of faces in the cube.

Letting V be the number of vertices, F the number of faces, and E the number of edges, the quantity key to Euler's formula is $V + F - E$. In the diagram for the cube, the faces are quadrilaterals, and by adding diagonals (Figure 6.28(b)) we create a network of triangles. Adding one diagonal increases the number of faces by 1 and increases the number of edges by 1. The number of vertices stays fixed, so the quantity $V + F - E$ remains the same. For the network of triangles, the quantity $V + F - E$ is the same as in the first diagram and it is one less than in the cube because one face is missing.

The idea is to now remove boundary triangles one after the other keeping track of how the quantity $V + F - E$ changes. Removing one triangle from the cube's network requires that we remove one outer edge. This decreases both F and E by 1, leaving $V + F = E$ the same. Boundary triangles are actually of two types: those that can be removed by deleting a single edge, and those that must have two edges and one vertex deleted to complete the removal. For the second sort, F and V are decreased by 1 and E is decreased by 2; the quantity $V + F - E$ again stays the same.

Continuing in this manner by removing boundary triangles of either type, the diagram reduces to a single triangle where $V = 3$, $F = 1$, and $E = 3$. Finally, $V + F - E = 1$. Since the quantity has not changed throughout the process, the original count must have given $V + F - E = 1$. There was one face missing in the planar diagram, so for the cube $V + F - E = 2$.

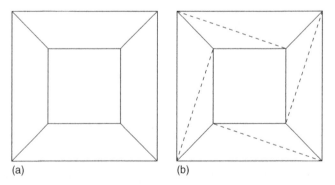

(a)   (b)

Figure 6.28   (a,b) Planar version of Euler's formula

Reviewing the procedure for reaching this final formula shows that any time we can stretch a face and squash the polyhedron onto the plane, we can deduce that $V + F - E = 2$. There are some subtleties. The planar diagram cannot have any edges that cross each other, and it is important to remove the boundary triangles in a way that does not leave degenerate cases, although even in these cases the verification can be patched up. It intuitively appears that for any convex polyhedra the procedure and hence the formula hold. In fact, it is even more general. As long as we can deform the polyhedron by stretching and shrinking (but not tearing) into a sphere, the formula holds.

Result 6.5 (Euler's Formula). *For any polyhedron that can be deformed smoothly into a sphere, $V + F - E = 2$.*

The formula applies to each of the regular polyhedra listed in Table 6.2. For example, the icosahedron has $V = 12$, $F = 20$, and $E = 30$, giving $12 + 20 - 30 = 2$.

To construct an example where the formula does not hold, start with a cube and cut a square hole from the middle of the front face to the middle of the back face. This is not technically a polyhedron because the front and back faces are no longer polygons, so by adding edges as in the figure, the front and back each has four quadrilateral faces. The altered cube has 16 vertices, 16 faces, and 32 edges, giving $V + F - E = 0$. The altered cube can no longer be smoothly deformed into a sphere, which is why it no longer satisfies Euler's formula as given above (Figure 6.29).

However, there is a generalization of Euler's formula that does work for the cube with a hole. The key is to classify polyhedra according to how many holes there are. A standard cube has zero holes, which is why we can deform it into a sphere, but with one hole it can be smoothly deformed into a doughnut (torus). By incorporating the number of holes, called the *genus* and denoted g, we get the general version of Euler's formula: $V + F - E = 2 - 2g$. For the cube with a hole, $16 + 16 - 32 = 2 - 2(1)$. (See [2] for a more thorough historical approach to Euler's formula.)

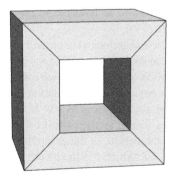

Figure 6.29   Cube with a hole

To count edges on a polyhedron, notice that each edge borders two faces, and if the faces are all triangles, then each face borders three edges. The quantity $2E$ counts each face as many times as there are edges on a face. This means $2E = 3F$ if all the faces are triangles. Triangles are the polygon with the least number of edges, so, in general, for any polyhedron, twice the number of edges is greater than or equal to three times the number of faces. Similar reasoning applied to the vertices leads to two inequalities:

$$2E \geq 3F \text{ and } 2E \geq 3V \qquad (6.16)$$

Combining these inequalities with Euler's formula $(V + F - E = 2)$ algebraically leads to the following inequalities:

$$V \leq 2F - 4 \text{ and } V \geq \frac{1}{2}F + 2 \qquad (6.17)$$

These four inequalities (6.16 and 6.17) taken together constrain the number of vertices, faces, and edges that can appear in a polyhedron (without holes).

For one curious application, suppose a polyhedron had no triangles, quadrilaterals, or pentagons as faces. Then, $2E \geq 6F$ and substituting into Euler's formula gives $V \geq 2F + 2$, which contradicts an inequality in 6.17 . Hence, every polyhedron must have at least one face with less than six edges.

6.3.4 Rotational Symmetries

Some polyhedra, particularly the regular ones, exhibit various degrees of symmetry under a rotation. To understand what is meant by symmetry, recall the coordinates for the cube given earlier. These coordinates position the cube centered at the origin with the centers of opposite faces along one of the three Cartesian axes. A rotation of $\pi/2$ counterclockwise around the x-axis brings the cube back to a position indistinguishable from the original one, but the vertices, edges, and faces have been moved. There are some fixed points: the centers of the two faces on the x-axis have not moved. The cube position, however, looks like its starting position. The counterclockwise rotation of $\pi/2$ is said to be a symmetry transformation. Each rotation has a representation as a matrix, so the current task is to account for all the matrices that are symmetry rotations for the cube (Figure 6.30).

Rotations of π and $3\pi/2$ counterclockwise around the x-axis are also symmetry rotations. Since the clockwise rotation of $\pi/2$ brings the cube to the same position as the counterclockwise rotation of $3\pi/2$, these two rotations are equivalent. Each of the three axes allows three counterclockwise rotations. These three rotations along with the identity rotation give four matrices $M_x(0)$, $M_x(\pi/2)$, $M_x(\pi)$, and $M_x(3\pi/2)$. Together, these four matrices form a mathematical entity called a *group*. Given any matrix in the group, there is another one in the group that is the inverse. For example, $M_x(\pi/2)M_x(3\pi/2) = M_x(0) = I$, where I is the identity matrix. These four matrices represent four symmetries for the cube. (The identity matrix is counted as a symmetry matrix because it leaves the cube in a position indistinguishable from the original.)

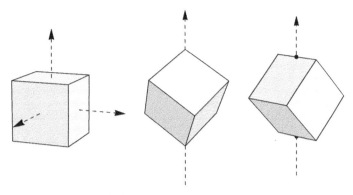

Figure 6.30 Rotations of a cube around axes

Focusing on counterclockwise rotations here is not a restriction. A rotation of $3\pi/2$ counterclockwise, for example, has the same effect as a clockwise rotation of $\pi/2$. In fact, the corresponding matrices are the same.

Of course, there are two other groups of matrices: one for rotations around the y-axis, and one for those around the z-axis. All three groups of four matrices share the identity matrix $M(0)$, so we have identified 10 symmetry matrices for the cube.

Yet, there are more rotational axes to explore. There are four diagonals in the cube running from one vertex to the opposite vertex. Around each of these axes, the cube can be rotated by $2\pi/3$ and $4\pi/3$ counterclockwise and these rotations leave the cube in a position indistinguishable from the original. Each set of two rotations plus the identity forms another group. Recall from earlier work on transformations that there is a matrix that corresponds to each rotation around the diagonal axes. We have introduced 8 new symmetry matrices and now have a total of 18.

Any symmetry axis for the cube must go through the center of the cube and be symmetrically positioned relative to other parts of the cube. The only axes not yet considered are those that go through the midpoints of opposite edges. With 12 edges, there are 6 of these axes. Around each axis, a rotation of π puts the cube back in position. This introduces 6 new symmetry matrices, bringing the final total to 24. Not surprisingly, this corresponds to all the ways we can position a cube. Imagine placing a cube on the table. Any of six faces can be placed down, and then any of four other faces can be rotated to the front position. The total is $6 \times 4 = 24$.

Taken all together, the 24 matrices form the *octahedral* symmetry group. Any matrix in the group has an inverse that is also in the group, and multiplying two of the matrices results in another matrix in the group. The earlier smaller sets of matrices, like the rotations around the x-axis, are subgroups of this larger one.

All of the regular polyhedra have corresponding symmetry groups. Interestingly, since the cube and the octahedron are dual polyhedra (the centers of each face of the cube form an octahedron), any symmetry transformation of the cube is a symmetry transformation of the octahedron, and vice versa; they share the same symmetry group. Similarly, the icosahedron and the dodecahedron share the symmetry

TABLE 6.3   Symmetry Groups for Regular Polyhedra

Axes	Tetrahedral		Octahedral		Icosahedral	
Opp. faces	0		3	(3)	10	(2)
Opp. vertices	0		4	(2)	6	(4)
Edges	3	(1)	6	(1)	15	(1)
Vertex/face	4	(2)	0		0	
Total		12		24		60

group called the *icosahedral* symmetry group, and the tetrahedron is left by itself with the *tetrahedral* symmetry group. The three symmetry groups are summarized in Table 6.3, with the number of each type of axis shown along with the number of rotations around those axes in parentheses. (The identity matrix is in each group.)

Regular polyhedra are not the only ones that can have rotational symmetries. The pyramid and prism shown in Figure 6.31 also can be rotated into a new position indistinguishable from the original position. For the pyramid, the axis of rotation must be from the apex through the center of the base. Then, a rotation of $2\pi/5$ is a symmetry rotation, and if we denote the corresponding rotation matrix as R, then $R^0 = I$, R^1, R^2, and R^3 are all symmetry rotations. Notice that $R^4 = I$. The pattern here is cyclic and the symmetry group is called *cyclic*.

The prism in the figure has equilateral triangles as the top and bottom faces. An axis running through the middle of these faces is a principal axis for the polyhedron, and three rotations (including the identity) around this axis are symmetry rotations for the prism. In addition, there are three other axes that are all perpendicular to the principal axis. They pass through the middle of one side edge and one rectangular face. The identity rotation and a rotation of π around these axes are symmetry rotations for the prism. One principal axis and several perpendicular secondary axes make this symmetry group the *dihedral* group.

Interestingly, the five symmetry groups profiled so far cover all the possible cases. If a polyhedron has any rotational symmetry at all (some do not), then the symmetry group must be one of these five.

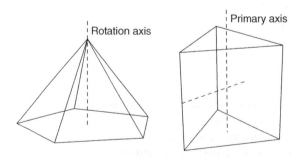

Figure 6.31   Cyclic and dihedral symmetry

Result 6.6 (Polyhedral Symmetry Groups). *If a polyhedron has rotational symmetry, then the symmetry group must be cyclic, dihedral, tetrahedral, octahedral, or icosahedral.*

A proof of this result involves enumerating the characteristics of rotation axes. (See [2] for a detailed exposition.)

6.4 COMPLEMENTS AND DETAILS

6.4.1 Generalized Barycentric Coordinates

Barycentric coordinates are convenient to use in modeling situations and especially for interpolation. It is natural to consider generalizations to more than three reference points. Instead of using a triangle as the basic reference, could the vertices of a polygon serve the same purpose? To examine the possibilities here, the following properties ensure that the coordinates are useful.

1. For point P inside the convex hull of $P_0, P_1, \ldots, P_n$,

$$P = \sum_{i=1}^{n} \alpha_i P_i \text{ with } 0 \le \alpha_i \le 1 \text{ and } \sum_{i=1}^{n} \alpha_i = 1$$

2. For points outside the convex hull, at least one α_i is negative.
3. For points on the edge between two adjacent vertices, only the coordinates associated with the two vertices should be nonzero.
4. Each α_i changes smoothly as any reference point changes.

The first two properties imply that examining the coordinates of a point determines whether it is inside the convex hull of the reference points. The third property just fits our intuition that the coordinates should reduce to those for a line segment. As the reference points are repositioned, the third property guarantees that sharp or sudden changes do not occur in the coordinates. In fact, a more mathematical translation of this property is that each α_i is an infinitely differentiable function of the reference points.

Generalizing barycentric coordinates to regular polygons is almost straightforward. Consider the regular pentagon in Figure 6.32 with point P inside. Mimicking the technique for a triangle, where the area opposite a vertex is used to calculate the barycentric coordinate, the areas of triangles opposite a vertex in the pentagon are used to determine coordinates.

This time, the product of areas is the key idea, and to find α_0, take the product of the areas of triangles ΔPP_1P_2, ΔPP_2P_3, and ΔPP_3P_4. That is, take all the triangles except the ones containing the vertex P_0. Call the product A_0. In general,

$$A_i = \prod_{\substack{j \ne i-1 \\ j \ne i}} Area(\Delta PP_jP_{j+1}) \implies \alpha_i = \frac{A_i}{\sum_{j=0}^{n} A_j} \tag{6.18}$$

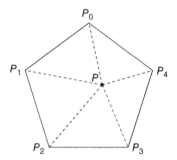

Figure 6.32   Barycentric coordinates in a regular pentagon

After calculating A_i, division by the sum of all A_j normalizes the coordinates, so that $\sum_{i=1}^{n} \alpha_i = 1$. The fact that the polygon is regular (edges are equal) ensures that the coordinates satisfy the listed properties.

To generalize further to irregular convex polygons, a little more work has to be done. A_i must be multiplied by the area of $\Delta P_{i-1} P_i P_{i+1}$. This compensates for the fact that the angles and edges are no longer equal. (See [3] and [4] for details.) Barycentric coordinates are unique for triangles, but there are several approaches available when using larger polygons as a reference. It is also possible to move up a dimension and locate points inside a polyhedron.

6.4.2   Data Structures

To incorporate polyhedra in graphics programs, information about vertices, faces, and edges has to be stored in a way that allows easy access during computation. The obvious approach is to build a table for the vertices and a table for the faces, that is, an ordered list of vertices giving the three coordinates for each one and an ordered list of faces specifying which vertices form each face. Table 6.4 shows the two tables for a cube.

The face table adds more information than is immediately apparent since the vertices listed for each face are given in counter-clockwise order looking from the outside

TABLE 6.4   Vertex and Face Tables

Vertex	x	y	z
0	1	1	1
1	1	1	− 1
2	1	− 1	− 1
3	1	− 1	1
4	− 1	1	1
5	− 1	− 1	1
6	− 1	− 1	− 1
7	− 1	1	− 1

Face	v_1	v_2	v_3	v_4
0	0	3	2	1
1	1	2	6	7
2	7	6	5	4
3	4	5	3	0
4	1	7	4	0
5	6	2	3	5

of the cube. This makes computing normals simpler in terms of keeping the direction correct; a vector from the first vertex to the second cross the first vertex to the fourth will always point out of the cube.

The two tables are sufficient to hold the basic information needed to produce the cube on the display screen. However, there is information that is not readily available. Which faces meet at vertex number 3? This type of information will be useful later when discussing lighting calculations. From the two tables, it is not hard to compute the answer by searching through the face table to find all faces that include vertex 3. Faces 0, 3, and 5 meet at vertex 3. Imagine, though, the work required to search through a face table with hundreds of thousands of entries.

There are often tradeoffs made in deciding what data structure to use in a particular case. The vertex and face tables minimize space used in memory, but some queries about the polyhedron might take a while to answer. Balancing speed and space is often the key task in designing data structures. In the case of polyhedra, there are several pieces of information that an algorithm might need. Which edges bound a face? What two faces meet at a given edge? What is the counterclockwise order of the faces meeting at a vertex? These and other questions can be answered by the simple vertex and face tables, but the computation might be considerable. Adding an edge table helps, but a sophisticated data structure is really needed to field the many possible queries.

One successful approach to storing information about polyhedra is the *winged edge* data structure introduced in the 1970s by Bruce Baumgart. This data structure adds an edge table to the vertex and face tables, but it includes additional information that further details the topology of the polyhedron. Figure 6.33 shows a schematic of edge information.

In addition to the vertices at the end points of an edge, the structure stores a direction by distinguishing the first and second end points. Then, while moving in the direction of the edge, the faces on the left and right are stored. Traversing the left face counterclockwise gives a previous edge and a successor edge to the main edge. Traversing the right face counterclockwise means switching the direction of the main edge, but it also gives a previous edge and a successor edge. The first entry in Table 6.5

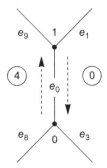

Figure 6.33   Winged edge data structure for a cube's edge

TABLE 6.5 Winged Edge Data Table for the Cube

Edge	V_1	V_2	F_L	F_R	Pr.L	Su.L	Pr.R	Su.R
e_0	0	1	4	0	e_8	e_9	e_1	e_3
e_1	1	2	1	0	e_9	e_{10}	e_2	e_0
e_2	2	3	5	0	e_{10}	e_{11}	e_3	e_1
e_3	3	0	3	0	e_{11}	e_8	e_0	e_2
e_4	4	5	3	2	e_8	e_{11}	e_5	e_7
e_5	5	6	5	2	e_{11}	e_{10}	e_6	e_4
e_6	6	7	1	2	e_{10}	e_9	e_7	e_5
e_7	7	4	4	2	e_9	e_8	e_4	e_6
e_8	0	4	3	4	e_3	e_4	e_7	e_0
e_9	1	7	4	1	e_0	e_7	e_6	e_1
e_{10}	2	6	1	5	e_1	e_6	e_5	e_2
e_{11}	3	5	5	3	e_2	e_5	e_4	e_3

for the cube is for edge e_0. When traversing this edge from vertex 0 to vertex 1, face 4 is on the left and face 0 is on the right. In a counterclockwise listing of edges bounding face 4, edge e_8 (Pr.L) comes before edge e_0 and edge e_9 (Su.L) comes after. Similarly, for face 0, the counterclockwise ordering gives e_1, e_0, and e_3. There are other edges bounding the faces, but the table immediately gives the order for three edges.

To find faces meeting at vertex 3, a search that discovers edge e_3 starts at vertex 3. Then the Pr.L (e_{11}) and Su.R (e_2) entries lead to the other edge entries that will complete the three faces meeting at 3. Various searches like this will answer the needed queries in, hopefully, reasonable amounts of time.

6.5 EXERCISES

1. A triangle has vertices $P_0 = (2, 8)$, $P_1 = (15, -1)$, $P_2 = (9, 16)$. Find the barycentric coordinates of $P = (8, 12)$ and $Q = (16, 6)$.

2. Extend the lines of a triangle to divide the plane into seven sections. Explain what the barycentric coordinates look like in each section.

3. Using the reference triangle with vertices $P_0 = (1, 1, 4)$, $P_1 = (-2, 8, -15)$, and $P_2 = (10, 4, 1)$. Find the barycentric coordinates for $P = (3, 1, 5)$.

4. Suppose point P is not in the plane of the triangle, but does project to the interior of the triangle. After calculating the barycentric coordinates using the standard area method, what is true of the coordinates?

5. In Example 6.1, find k_1 directly and use it to verify the value for α_1.

6. For the triangle with vertices $P_0 = (-5, 2)$, $P_1 = (-1, -6)$, and $P_2 = (3, 3)$, the color of vertex P_0 is $(50, 100, 80)$ where the three components represent the intensity of red, green, and blue light, respectively. The color of P_1 is $(60, 75, 90)$

and the color of P_2 is $(30, 58, 104)$. Using linear interpolation, what is the color of the origin $(0, 0, 0)$?

7. In Example 6.3, $\vec{w} = \alpha_0 \vec{v}_1 + \alpha_2 \vec{v}_2$. By taking the dot product of both sides of this equation with $\vec{v}_1$ and with $\vec{v}_2$, produce two equations in the unknowns α_0 and α_2. Solve for both, and verify they give the same barycentric coordinates as in the example.

8. Show that points on a line through P_0 in a triangle satisfy the equation $\alpha_1 = c\alpha_2$ for some constant c.

9. Let P be a point with barycentric coordinates $(\alpha_0, \alpha_1, \alpha_2)$ relative to triangle T. If the vertices of T are transformed by an affine transformation, show that the barycentric coordinates of P are unchanged.

10. A face of a polyhedron has vertices $A = (4, 0, 12)$, $B = (-3, -4, -1)$, and $C = (2, 36, -1)$. A light source is at $(16, 25, -4)$ and a ray travels in the direction $(-3, -1, 2)$. Doe is hit the face? (Use barycentric coordinates.)

11. Consider the triangle with vertices $P_0 = (-6, -3)$, $P_1 = (-1, 7)$, and $P_2 = (4, -1)$. Find a circle tangent to all three sides. (Note that there is more than one such circle.)

12. Show that the centroid of a triangle divides the medians in the ratio $2 : 1$.

13. Compare the tetrahedron's coordinates from Example 3.24 to those in Table 6.1. Find a transformation (matrix) that converts one set to the other.

14. Find the vertices of a regular pentagon with edge length 1. Show the connection between the pentagon and the golden ratio by finding the length of a diagonal.

15. The three vertices $(-8, 7)$, $(10, 2)$, and $(4, -6)$ form a triangle. Find the center and radius for both the incircle and the circumcircle.

16. Consider the points $(2, 1)$, $(12, -1)$, $(4, 8)$, $(6, 1)$, $(9, -8)$, and $(6, -9)$. Using determinants, find the area of the convex hull.

17. The following points are vertices of a polygon given in counterclockwise order: $(-2, 3)$, $(-5, 0)$, $(-4, -1)$, $(12, -3)$, $(1, 1)$, $(11, 2)$. Determine whether the point $(3, 0.4)$ is inside or outside the polygon by using a horizontal ray and the winding number. Repeat using a vertical ray.

18. Start with an arbitrary convex pentagon and count how many triangulations there are. Repeat the count for convex polygons with six and seven edges. (In general, if there are $m + 2$ vertices, there are $\frac{1}{m+1} \binom{2m}{m}$ triangulations.)

19. Determine the Delaunay triangulation for the four points $(1, 8)$, $(4, -3)$, $(5, 10)$, and $(7, 2)$.

20. For the regular polyhedra listed in Table 6.2, verify the dihedral angles by calculating the angles between faces.

21. Find the volume of the icosahedron whose coordinates are given in Table 6.1.

22. In Example 6.10, the volume of the dodecahedron was calculated by adding smaller pyramids together. Instead of using the origin as the apex for each pyramid, use $(2, 0, 0)$ which is outside the dodecahedron. Using signed volumes, find the volume of the dodecahedron and verify that it agrees with the calculation in the example.

23. The inequalities 6.17 are satisfied for $V = F$ as long as $V \geq 4$. Show that there actually exist such polyhedra for all $V \geq 4$. (Hint: Consider pyramids.)

24. Construct a winged edge table for the tetrahedron.

25. A right tetrahedron is one where three faces meet at right angles. Such a polyhedron can be positioned with a vertex at the origin and edges along each of the three axes. The face that does not contain the origin is analogous to the hypotenuse of a right triangle. In fact, there is a generalization of the Pythagorean formula that works for the right tetrahedron. Show that the square of the area of the "hypotenuse" face is equal to the sum of the squares of the areas of the other three faces.

26. Another, occasionally useful, formula for the area of a triangle is based on the lengths of the sides. For a triangle with sides a, b, and c, the area is $A = \sqrt{s(s-a)(s-b)(s-c)}$ where $s = \frac{1}{2}(a+b+c)$. This is known as *Heron's formula*. For the triangle with vertices $(-5, 7)$, $(4, 2)$, and $(1, -8)$, show that Heron's formula gives the correct area.

27. In the Example 6.9, the ray intersects some of the edges of the polygon. Edges that intersect the ray where $t < 0$ can be ignored. Develop an algorithm for determining if an edge intersects the ray with $t < 0$.

28. Suppose we color the cube with six different colors, one for each face. Two colorings are indistinguishable if there is a rotation symmetry that transforms a cube with the first coloring to a cube with the second coloring so that the colors on the faces match up. How many distinguishable colorings (using six colors) are there for the cube?

29. Three vectors determine a tetrahedron. Show that the volume of the tetrahedron is one-sixth the determinant of the 3×3 matrix formed by putting the three vectors in the three rows of the matrix.

30. For a triangulation (or any triangular mesh without holes), show that an altered Euler's formula, $V + F - E = 1$, holds.

31. To send one triangle face of an object to the graphics processor for rendering on the screen, three vertices must be sent. A triangle *strip* is a series of triangles. More specifically, a set of vertices $P_0, P_1, P_2, \ldots, P_n$ is a strip if each consecutive sequence of three vertices $(P_{i-1}P_iP_{i+1})$ forms a triangle in the strip. Show that the average number of vertices per triangle approaches 1 as the strip gets longer. This is a more efficient way to transfer triangle data.

6.5.1   Programming Exercises

1.   Implement the algorithm for determining whether a point is inside a polygon (given by an ordered set of vertices) by calculating the winding number.

2.   Code an algorithm for finding the convex hull for a set of points in the plane. Input a set of coordinates and output the points forming the vertices for the convex hull.

3.   Write a method (function) for taking a list of points and returning a list of edges in the Delaunay triangulation.

7

CURVES AND SURFACES

A straight line segment is a key primitive in computer graphics and, consequently, any flat triangular (or more generally, polygonal) surface is easy to draw on the screen. Yet, curves are indispensable when designing objects like cars, door knobs, archways, and any number of animated characters. Although we end up approximating these forms with many triangles with their straight edges, the problem is still how to find vertices that ultimately give a global look of curvature. If we add the animation stage where we let a car bounce along the dirt roadway or move the camera as though we are flying through the city, then the paths describing these motions rely on various curves.

There are several ways to describe curves, but in order to display them on a computer screen we eventually need coordinates for various points on the curve. Connecting the points with line segments then completes the approximation of the curve (Figure 7.1). An implicit algebraic description of a circle, such as $x^2 + y^2 = 4$, is familiar and compact, but to find point coordinates we have to solve for one coordinate in terms of another. An alternative description, $x = 2\cos(t)$ and $y = 2\sin(t)$, relies on computing trigonometric functions but, unlike the implicit description, it has the nice property of uniformly moving around the circle as the parameter t increases uniformly. Which sort of representation is best for graphics algorithms? How do we alter the description if we need a circle slightly flattened on one side? If we push a curve here and pull it there, how do we encode the changes? Can we put two or more pieces of curves together and guarantee that they look smooth? These are the issues that command the attention of the graphics designer and programmer.

Mathematical Structures for Computer Graphics, First Edition. Steven J. Janke.
© 2015 John Wiley & Sons, Inc. Published 2015 by John Wiley & Sons, Inc.

Figure 7.1 Curve composed of line segments

7.1 CURVE DESCRIPTIONS

Setting aside a straight line, which is indeed a curve, perhaps the most familiar two-dimensional curves are the circle and the parabola. The general circle with implicit algebraic description $(x - h)^2 + (y - k)^2 = r^2$ is centered at the point (h, k) and has radius r. Its symmetry certainly constrains which points are on the curve, but if the designer specifies three noncollinear points, P_0, P_1, and P_2, there is always a circle passing through them. (Pick the circumscribing circle for the triangle.) Mathematically, we say that the circle *interpolates* the points P_0, P_1, and P_2; the curve includes the given points and fills in points between them. Similarly, one form of the parabola has an explicit algebraic description $y = x^2$. (The description is explicit because it directly gives one coordinate in terms of the other.) Generalizing this gives $y = ax^2 + bx + c$, which describes parabolas with a central axis parallel to the y-axis. It still allows the designer to find a parabola passing through three specified points (no two on the same vertical line). The parabola is determined by the values of a, b, and c, and with three specified points, we have three equations in the three unknowns.

Another way to describe the circle is to introduce a new parameter, often denoted t, and let the coordinates change as t changes. Since the coordinates x and y are now functions of t, we should write $x(t)$ and $y(t)$, but the simpler notation, x and y, usually is not confusing. If we set $x = r\cos(t)$ and $y = r\sin(t)$, where r is fixed and t varies over all real numbers, then we generate points on a circle of radius r centered at the origin. To see that we still have a circle, calculate $x^2 + y^2$ and note that it equals r^2. This is a parametric description of the circle and we can make it more general by including an arbitrary center: $x = r\cos(t) + h$ and $y = r\sin(t) + k$.

One advantage of this description is that t is really the angle around the center and increasing the parameter t in equal amounts guarantees that we are taking equal steps around the circumference of the circle. This means that drawing line segments from one point to the next gives a regular polygon approximation to the circle.

In constructing parametric descriptions, flexibility in choosing the parameter (or parameters) means that these descriptions are not unique. A simple second example for the circle is $x = r\cos(2\pi - t) + h$ and $y = r\sin(2\pi - t) + k$. These coordinate expressions trace the circle in the opposite direction from before. For the parabola, $x = t$ and $y = at^2 + bt + c$ form a trivial parametric description, and replacing t with $2t$ gives another one that traces the parabola twice as fast (i.e., $\frac{dx}{dt}$ has doubled).

In fact, replacing t with other functions like $t^2 + 1$ produces yet other parametric descriptions.

Definition 7.1 (Curve Descriptions). *A two-dimensional curve is a collection of points described by any of the following expressions:*

1. *Explicit: $y = f(x)$ for some continuous function f.*
2. *Implicit: $F(x, y) = 0$ for some continuous function F.*
3. *Parametric: $x = f(t)$ and $y = g(t)$ for continuous functions f and g.*

Three-dimensional curves simply add a third coordinate to the points. For an explicit description, we need two equations expressing two of the coordinates in terms of the third [e.g., $x = f(z)$ and $y = f(z)$]. Implicit descriptions require two conditions: $F(x, y, z) = 0$ and $G(x, y, z) = 0$. The two equations allow us to pick one coordinate and solve for the other two. Finally, the parametric descriptions use one expression for each coordinate: $x = f(t)$, $y = g(t)$, $z = h(t)$.

Parametric descriptions are arguably the most useful descriptions for computer graphics. Actually, we have already been using these descriptions because our expression for a line segment (a curve) is $P(t) = tP_0 + (1 - t)P_1$ where $0 \le t \le 1$ and P_0 and P_1 are points. Here, instead of one equation for each coordinate, we have combined them into one using points. The individual coordinate functions for a line segment in two dimensions are $x = tx_0 + (1 - t)x_1$ and $y = ty_0 + (1 - t)y_1$. For a line segment in three dimensions, we add a third coordinate, $z = tz_0 + (1 - t)z_1$. If the coordinates are polynomial functions of the parameter, we say the curve is a *polynomial curve* and its degree is the highest power of the parameter in any of the coordinate functions. More generally, if the coordinate functions are quotients of polynomials $(f(t)/g(t))$, then the curve is a *rational curve*.

Example 7.1 (Conics).   Conics are the familiar two-dimensional curves obtained by intersecting a plane with a cone. They can be implicitly described by

$$Ax^2 + Bxy + Cy^2 + Dx + Ey + F = 0 \qquad (7.1)$$

Various restrictions on the coefficients classify the conics as a pair of straight lines, parabola, ellipse, or hyperbola (see Exercises). For example, the following expression factors nicely:

$$x^2 - 2xy - 3y^2 + 3x - 5y + 2 = (x - 3y + 1)(x + y + 2) = 0$$

This implies that the curve includes points such that $x = 3y - 1$ or $x = -y - 2$. Hence the curve is just a pair of straight lines, a degenerate conic. If we wish, we can easily give parametric equations for each of the lines.

If the coefficients are $A = 2, B = 0, C = 0, D = -4, E = -1, F = 5$, then the description becomes $2x^2 - 4x - y + 5 = 0$ and this easily rearranges to become $y = 2(x - 1)^2 + 3$, a parabola. Again, the parametric description is easy, $x = t$ and $y = 3(t - a)^2 + 3$ (Figure 7.2).

The familiar equation of an ellipse centered at the origin and oriented so its axes are parallel to the coordinate axes is

$$\frac{x^2}{a^2} + \frac{y^2}{b^2} = 1$$

It is easy to see that this equation comes from Equation 7.1 by setting $A = b^2$, $C = a^2$, $F = -a^2b^2$ and the rest equal to zero. One parametric description for the ellipse is $x = a\cos(t)$ and $y = b\sin(t)$. With $a = b = r$, we get the description of a circle which we saw earlier. The advantage of this parametric description is the fact that the parameter t does represent the angle around the center.

Another more curious parametric description for the ellipse is composed of these two functions:

$$x = \frac{a(1 - t^2)}{1 + t^2} \quad \text{and} \quad y = \frac{2bt}{1 + t^2}$$

(Check to see that these expressions for x and y do satisfy the familiar equation for the ellipse.) For $a = b$, this gives a circle where, for uniformly spaced t, the points are almost equally spaced around the circle and it only requires simple calculation rather than trigonometric functions.

Finally, the hyperbola with the familiar equation $\frac{x^2}{a^2} - \frac{y^2}{b^2} = 1$ can also be put into the implicit form of Equation 7.1. The equations $x = a\sec(t)$ and $y = b\tan(t)$ give a parametric description (for values of t where the functions are defined). There is also another interesting description for hyperbolas:

$$x = \frac{a(b^2 + a^2t)}{a^2t^2 - b^2} \quad \text{and} \quad y = \frac{2ab^2t}{a^2t^2 - b^2}$$

where $t \neq \frac{b}{a}$.   □

Example 7.2 (Conics Continued).   In graphics work, it is useful to be able to look at a description and determine if it is a conic. The key will be to compare the description to Equation 7.1 which is a general form for conics; all conics can be put in this implicit form.

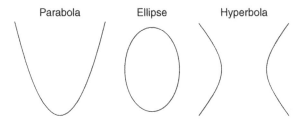

Parabola   Ellipse   Hyperbola

Figure 7.2   Conics

Consider the following parametric description:

$$x = \frac{t^2}{t+1} \quad \text{and} \quad y = \frac{2t^2 + 3}{t+1}$$

Multiplying through to clear denominators gives us two quadratic equations in t which must both be true for any point on the curve. We solve the two simultaneously to get an expression for t.

$$(t+1)x - t^2 = 0$$
$$(t+1)y - 2t^2 - 3 = 0$$
$$\implies (t+1)(y - 2x) - 3 = 0$$
$$\implies t = \frac{3}{y - 2x} - 1$$

Substituting this expression for t into either of the original parametric equations gives

$$10x^2 - 7xy + y^2 + 12 - 6y + 9 = 0$$

Consequently, the curve is a conic. In fact, it turns out that by checking the sign of $B^2 - 4AC \,(= (-7)^2 - 4 \cdot 10 \cdot 1 > 0)$ we can determine that this conic is a hyperbola. Or, we can actually plot it and see what it looks like. $\square$

The parametric description for our conic used rational functions and in such a description, as long as the denominators are the same and both the numerators and denominators are quadratic functions, we have a conic.

Result 7.1 (A Parametric Form for Conics). *The parametric description given by*

$$x = \frac{p_x(t)}{q(t)} \quad \text{and} \quad y = \frac{p_y(t)}{q(t)}$$

where p_x, p_y, and $q(t)$ are quadratic functions of t, describes a conic. Moreover, all nondegenerate conics can be described in this way.

This result does not claim that all parametric descriptions of conics have this rational form, but it does say that given a conic we can find such a rational parameterization. It also gives us a convenient way to quickly use the parametric form to determine whether the curve is a conic.

Example 7.3 (Change of Coordinates). Curves can have more or less convenient descriptions in different coordinate systems. Consider the curve with implicit description $xy - 1 = 0$. This is a conic because it fits our general form, but it may not be clear which conic it is. A change of coordinate system will change the description and perhaps put it in a form we recognize. Suppose we wish to describe the curve in a coordinate system where the x- and y-axis have been rotated counterclockwise by θ. The coordinates of a point on the curve will then be rotated clockwise by θ. Letting the new coordinates be (u, v), we convert with the following expressions:

$$x = u \cos \theta - v \sin \theta$$

$$y = u \sin \theta + v \cos \theta$$

Setting $\theta = 45°$, we can substitute into the original implicit description.

$$xy - 1 = \left(\frac{u}{\sqrt{2}} - \frac{v}{\sqrt{2}} \right) \left(\frac{u}{\sqrt{2}} + \frac{v}{\sqrt{2}} \right) - 1 = \frac{u^2}{2} - \frac{v^2}{2} - 1 = 0$$

The expression on the right is the implicit description of a hyperbola. If the coefficient for xy in the general implicit form for a conic is nonzero, it is a good indication that the conic is oriented with axes that are not parallel to the coordinate axes. □

Of course, not all curves are conics, and not all curves are described efficiently in Cartesian coordinates. In polar coordinates, a spiral is given by $r = \theta$; converting to Cartesian coordinates gives $x = t \cos(t)$ and $y = t \sin(t)$, a little less compact.

Example 7.4 (Three-Dimensional Curves). Adding a z coordinate gives us three-dimensional curves. For example, the helix (a spring-shaped spatial curve) can be described parametrically by $x = \cos(t)$, $y = \sin(t)$, and $z = t$.

Any of the two-dimensional curve can be made three dimensional by positioning it in space. The curve $x = 1$, $y = t$, and $z = t^2$ lies on the plane $x = 1$, and since $z = y^2$, it is a parabola in this plane. We can rotate the plane and the curve to get another spatial parabola. Suppose we rotate counterclockwise around the z-axis by $\theta = \pi/3$ radians. Then the transformed coordinates (x_r, y_r) of points on the curve satisfy

$$x_r = x \left(\frac{1}{2} \right) - y \left(\frac{\sqrt{3}}{2} \right)$$

$$y_r = x \left(-\frac{\sqrt{3}}{2} \right) + y \left(\frac{1}{2} \right)$$

Since $x = 1$ and $y = t$, we have a new parameterization:

$$x_r = \frac{1 - t\sqrt{3}}{2} \qquad y_r = \frac{\sqrt{3} + t}{2} \qquad z_r = t^2$$

The result is still a parabola in space. □

Example 7.5 (Tangents). Parametric descriptions give each coordinate as a function of t. Consider the two-dimensional curve given by $x = 2t + 1$ and $y = t^3$. The vector from the origin to a point on the curve is then

$$\vec{r}(t) = x\vec{i} + y\vec{j} = (2t+1)\vec{i} + t^3\vec{j}$$

From calculus, we can find the slope of a tangent to the curve by calculating the derivative dy/dx. The chain rule helps for parametric descriptions.

$$\frac{dy}{dx} = \frac{dy/dt}{dx/dt} = \frac{3t^2}{2}$$

The slope of the tangent line in terms of t is the quotient of dy/dt and dx/dt. If we use these individual derivatives as components of a vector, we get the tangent vector $\vec{r}'(t)$.

$$\vec{r}'(t) = \left(\frac{dx}{dt}\right)\vec{i} + \left(\frac{dy}{dt}\right)\vec{j} = 2\vec{i} + 3t^2\vec{j}$$

This vector is the direction vector for the tangent line and its length tells us how fast we are moving around the curve relative to the change in t. For this particular curve, the length is $|\vec{r}'(t)| = \sqrt{4 + 9t^4}$. At the point where $t = 1$, we are moving in the direction of the tangent vector at a rate which covers 13 units on the curve for every 1 unit of change in t (Figure 7.3).

Tangent vectors are handy when we are trying to match the end of one curve segment to the next. If the tangent vectors are parallel, then the tangents to the curve segments have the same direction and the transition will look smooth. For our curve, the slope of the tangent at the point where $t = 1$ is 1.5, and if a new curve segment starts with this slope, the transition will have what we call C^1 continuity. C^0 continuity simply means that one curve segment starts where the other ends and higher levels of continuity (C^2 and above) mean that several higher derivatives match.   □

7.1.1 Lagrange Interpolation

Curve descriptions whether they are explicit, implicit, or parametric give the recipe for putting a curve on the screen, but we need to know how to pick the right curve to

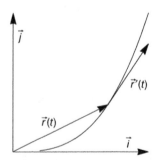

Figure 7.3 Tangent vector

achieve what we want graphically. Moving the camera, for instance, in an animation sequence most likely involves following a smooth custom curve that passes through key points along the way. If there are only two key points, then perhaps a straight line path will work and the curve is then $P(t) = (1 - t)P_0 + tP_1$.

Suppose, however, there are three key points and we need a curve to interpolate the key points P_0, P_1, and P_2. Then a compact parametric description might look like this:

$$P(t) = \alpha_0(t)P_0 + \alpha_1(t)P_1 + \alpha_2(t)P_2 \qquad (7.2)$$

The functions α_0, α_1, and α_2 are *blending functions* and serve to combine the influences of the three points as the parameter t changes. In particular, if $\alpha_0(0) = 1$ while $\alpha_1(0)$ and $\alpha_2(0)$ are both zero, then $P(0) = P_0$; the first point is on the curve when $t = 0$. Following this pattern, we could specify the blending function values at $t = 1$ and $t = 2$ in order to guarantee that $P(1) = P_1$ and $P(2) = P_2$.

An easy way to pick the function α_0 is to realize that it should be 1 for $t = 0$ and zero for $t = 1$ and $t = 2$. This suggests the form

$$\alpha_0(t) = c(t - 1)(t - 2)$$

for some constant c. Since $\alpha_0(0) = 1$, we have $c = 1/2$. Reasoning in this way gives the blending functions:

$$\alpha_0(t) = \frac{1}{2}(t - 1)(t - 2)$$

$$\alpha_1(t) = -t(t - 2)$$

$$\alpha_2(t) = \frac{1}{2}t(t - 1)$$

The final parametric description is

$$P(t) = \frac{1}{2}(t - 1)(t - 2)P_0 - t(t - 2)P_1 + \frac{1}{2}t(t - 1)P_2 \qquad (7.3)$$

In two dimensions, this compact form includes two parametric equations, one for each coordinate, each of which is a quadratic function of t.

Example 7.6 (Curve to Interpolate Three Points).   Take $P_0 = (-1, 3)$, $P_1 = (2, 5)$, and $P_2 = (4, 1)$. Then our interpolation procedure gives the following description:

$$P(t) = \frac{1}{2}(t - 1)(t - 2)\begin{bmatrix} -1 \\ 3 \end{bmatrix} - t(t - 2)\begin{bmatrix} 2 \\ 5 \end{bmatrix} + \frac{1}{2}t(t - 1)\begin{bmatrix} 4 \\ 1 \end{bmatrix}$$

$$\Rightarrow x = -\frac{1}{2}(t^2 - 7t + 2) \quad \text{and} \quad y = -3t^2 + 5t + 3$$

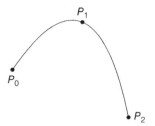

Figure 7.4   Lagrange interpolation

The coordinate parametric equations are both quadratic as our method predicts from the way we chose the blending functions. A quick check when $t = 0, 1, 2$ shows that the curve does pass through the three specified points (Figure 7.4).

From 7.1, we know this curve is a conic, and if we use the procedure we saw earlier for converting a parametric description to an implicit description, we can verify that this curve is a parabola (since $B^2 - 4AC = 0$). □

This interpolation procedure is named after the mathematician Lagrange (who published his investigations in 1795) although others including Edward Waring (1779) used the technique earlier. It can be generalized to interpolate $n + 1$ points by picking $n + 1$ blending functions so that the curve goes through the specified points when $t = 0, 1, \ldots, n$. The blending functions are defined as the product of terms, so we use the symbol $\prod$ to indicate product.

$$\alpha_i(t) = \prod_{\substack{k=0 \\ k \neq i}}^{n} \frac{(t - k)}{(i - k)} \tag{7.4}$$

The definition ensures that $\alpha_i(i) = 1$ and $\alpha_i(j) = 0$ for j an integer between 0 and n but not equal to i. Each blending function is a polynomial of degree n.

Result 7.2 (Lagrange Interpolation). *Given the $n + 1$ points $P_0, P_1, \ldots, P_n$, define the $n + 1$ blending functions $\alpha_0, \alpha_1, \ldots, \alpha_n$ by Equation 7.4. Then the curve with parametric description $P(t) = \sum_{i=0}^{n} \alpha_i(t)P_i$ interpolates the $n + 1$ given points.*

Since each blending function is a polynomial, the resulting coordinate parametric equations are also polynomials. For example, $x = \sum_{i=0}^{n} \alpha_i(t)x_i$ is a polynomial of degree at most n, and since the curve goes through each of the given $n + 1$ points, the value of the polynomial is x_i for $t = i$ $(0 \leq i \leq n)$.

If there were another polynomial that took the same values x_i when $t = i$ $(0 \leq i \leq n)$, then we could subtract one from the other to get a polynomial of degree at most n that was zero at $n + 1$ values of t. Although it is an advanced result, we know that a polynomial of degree n can have at most n zeroes unless it is identically zero. This implies that the difference of our two polynomials must be identically zero. In other words, the Lagrange polynomial we constructed is unique.

In addition to the uniqueness, there is one other property of the Lagrange method that is very important. Notice in Example 7.6 that the sum of the three blending functions is 1.

$$\alpha_0(t) + \alpha_1(t) + \alpha_2(t) = \frac{1}{2}(t-1)(t-2) - t(t-2) + \frac{1}{2}t(t-1) = 1$$

This is not accidental. Rather, using an argument similar to the one for uniqueness, if all x_i are 1, then the polynomial must be identically 1. However, when all $x_i = 1$, we just have the sum of the blending functions, so this sum must be 1.

Result 7.3 (Lagrange Interpolation Properties). *Using Lagrange interpolation on n points gives a parametric description with the following two properties:*

1. *The parametric coordinate functions are unique polynomials of degree at most* $n - 1$.
2. *The sum of the blending functions is 1:* $\sum_{i=0}^{n} \alpha_i(t) = 1$.

These two properties indicate both a drawback and an advantage to using the Lagrange interpolation method. Using the technique, the graphics designer can find the description of a curve passing through an arbitrarily finite set of points. However, our work is not done because with $n + 1$ specified points, the resulting coordinate parametric functions may have degree as high as n. From calculus, we know that such polynomials can have as many as $n - 1$ maxima and minima, indicating that the curve could be very wiggly (Figure 7.5). Adding points in an effort to further constrain the curve will generate higher degree polynomials for the parametric functions and possibly introduce more gyrations in the curve. Another approach is to reduce the number of points and try to patch several segments of curves together. This is a reasonable approach, but patching curves in a smooth way requires knowing their tangents, and for Lagrange curves these depend in complicated ways on the specified points.

The advantage to the method has to do with transforming the curve. In constructing graphics scenes, we apply many transformations and often change coordinate

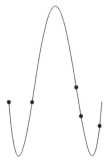

Figure 7.5   Rapidly changing Lagrange curve

systems. We would like any curves we design to hold their general shapes as we apply these transformations. That is, if we transform the specified points and then apply the blending functions, we would like a curve of the same type as before. Luckily, the Lagrange blending functions sum to 1, making the description an affine combination of the given points. This ensures that transformations of Lagrange curves end up being Lagrange curves.

Recalling that an affine transformation has the form $T(P) = MP + \vec{Q}$, where M is a matrix and $\vec{Q}$ is a vector, we have

$$T(P(t)) = M(\alpha_0(t)P_0 + \alpha_1(t)P_1 + \alpha_2(t)P_2) + \vec{Q}$$

$$= \alpha_0(t)(MP_0 + \vec{Q}) + \alpha_1(t)(MP_1 + \vec{Q}) + \alpha_2(MP_2 + \vec{Q})$$

$$= \alpha_0(t)T(P_0) + \alpha_1(t)T(P_1) + \alpha_2 T(P_2)$$

The result shows that the transformed curve is the same as we get by applying the Lagrange interpolation method to the transformed points $(T(P_0), T(P_1), T(P_2))$. We say the curve description has *affine invariance*.

7.1.2 Matrix Form for Curves

Expressing curves in terms of points and blending functions gives us an opportunity to write the description using matrices. Then we can often use the algebra of matrices when manipulating descriptions in various ways. If the blending functions are polynomials in t, then we can describe them as a product of two matrices where the second is formed from the elementary polynomials $1, t, t^2, \ldots, t^n$. For example, to describe the Lagrange blending functions for three points (see Example 7.4), we have the following matrix expression:

$$\begin{bmatrix} \alpha_0(t) \\ \alpha_1(t) \\ \alpha_2(t) \end{bmatrix} = \begin{bmatrix} 1 & -\frac{3}{2} & \frac{1}{2} \\ 0 & 2 & -1 \\ 0 & -\frac{1}{2} & \frac{1}{2} \end{bmatrix} \begin{bmatrix} 1 \\ t \\ t^2 \end{bmatrix} \tag{7.5}$$

Suppose we are using the points P_0, P_1, and P_2. If the coordinates of P_i are (x_i, y_i), then we can form a matrix with the coordinates of each point in a separate column. This matrix can be multiplied by the matrix of blending functions to give us the parametric coordinate functions:

$$\begin{bmatrix} x(t) \\ y(t) \end{bmatrix} = \begin{bmatrix} x_0 & x_1 & x_2 \\ y_0 & y_1 & y_2 \end{bmatrix} \begin{bmatrix} 1 & -\frac{3}{2} & \frac{1}{2} \\ 0 & 2 & -1 \\ 0 & -\frac{1}{2} & \frac{1}{2} \end{bmatrix} \begin{bmatrix} 1 \\ t \\ t^2 \end{bmatrix} \tag{7.6}$$

In general, if we think of $P(t)$ as a column matrix of coordinate functions and M as the matrix of coefficients for the blending functions, then we can write the curve description as

$$P(t) = \begin{bmatrix} P_0 & P_1 & \cdots & P_n \end{bmatrix} M \begin{bmatrix} 1 \\ t \\ \vdots \\ t^n \end{bmatrix} \tag{7.7}$$

The elementary polynomials $1, t, t^2, \ldots, t^n$ form a basis for all polynomials of degree n or less. This means that any other polynomial can be written as a combination of elementary polynomials. If the matrix M has an inverse, then the blending functions also form a basis for all polynomials of degree n or less. The matrix description of a curve becomes useful when moving between different sets of blending functions or different sets of points.

7.2 BÉZIER CURVES

Around 1960, two applied mathematicians working for French car manufacturers independently developed a flexible technique for designing curves. Paul de Casteljau working for Citroën and Pierre Bézier working for Renault took different approaches to fundamentally the same technique and since Bézier published his work, his name is attached to the methods. Yet, the geometric approach of de Casteljau is more visual and offers a good starting point.

Given three initial points P_0, P_1, and P_2 (call them *control points*), imagine the line segments P_0P_1 and P_1P_2. To find a point $P_B(t)$ on the Bézier curve, we proceed with the following steps.

Algorithm (de Casteljau):

1. Calculate P_3 on the first line segment: $P_3 = (1 - t)P_0 + tP_1$
2. Calculate P_4 on the second line segment: $P_4 = (1 - t)P_1 + tP_2$
3. Calculate $P_B(t)$ on the line segment P_3P_4: $P_B(t) = (1 - t)P_3 + tP_4$.

By stepping through values of t, we generate enough points to approximate the curve. With $t = 0$, the first pass through the steps produces $P_B(0) = P_0$, so the first control point is on the curve. Similarly, $t = 1$ produces $P_B(1) = P_2$ and the third control point is on the curve. Unless all three control points lie in a line, $0 < t < 1$ means the line segment P_3P_4 never includes P_1 and the result is that the second control point is not on the curve (Figure 7.6).

To get a more analytic description of the curve we generated, we can algebraically unfold the algorithm steps.

$$\begin{aligned} P_B(t) &= (1 - t)P_3 + tP_4 \\ &= (1 - t)((1 - t)P_0 + tP_1) + t((1 - t)P_1 + tP_2) \\ &= (1 - t)^2 P_0 + 2t(1 - t)P_1 + t^2 P_2 \end{aligned} \tag{7.8}$$

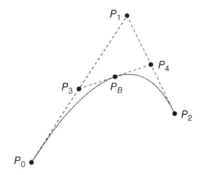

Figure 7.6   Bézier curve with three control points

This form reveals three blending functions $B_{(0,2)}(t) = (1 - t)^2$, $B_{(1,2)}(t) = 2t(1 - t)$, and $B_{(2,2)}(t) = t^2$, which in mathematical lore are called *Bernstein polynomials* after the Russian mathematician who studied them in 1912. An ordered pair serves as the subscript on the blending functions indicating which point they multiply and the degree of the polynomial (one less than the number of control points). The parametric description of the curve has quadratic functions of t for each of the coordinates indicating a parabola which interpolates the first and third point.

The parabola is not all that flexible when it comes to shape, so we can boost the technique up to four control points and try again. We will have to add one more step to the procedure because we have one more level of line segments to calculate before we reach the point $P_B(t)$ on the curve. The same algebraic manipulation unfolds the geometry to give the parametric description of the curve:

$$P_B(t) = (1 - t)^3 P_0 + 3t(1 - t)^2 P_1 + 3t^2(1 - t)P_2 + t^3 P_3$$

The blending functions are now cubic Bernstein polynomials and the curve still interpolates the first (P_0) and last (P_3) control points. The intermediate points P_1 and P_2 are not generally on the curve. Describing the curve in matrix form, we have

$$P(t) = \begin{bmatrix} P_0 & P_1 & P_2 & P_3 \end{bmatrix} \begin{bmatrix} 1 & -3 & 3 & 1 \\ 0 & 3 & -6 & 3 \\ 0 & 0 & 3 & -3 \\ 0 & 0 & 0 & 1 \end{bmatrix} \begin{bmatrix} 1 \\ t \\ t^2 \\ t^3 \end{bmatrix} \tag{7.9}$$

The middle matrix on the right (which we called M) is the matrix of coefficients for the Bernstein polynomials of degree 3.

All the control points influence the curve in the sense that, if any of them is moved, the curve changes shape. Clearly, the first and last points alter the curve because the latter passes through these points. The other two influence the curve by drawing it to them as they move further away. The blending functions are all nonzero for $0 < t < 1$, so if one control point is moved, it affects all other points on the curve except the two

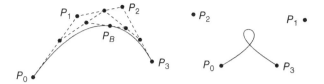

Figure 7.7 Bézier curves with four control points

endpoints. Some are affected more than others, but all of them move. The designer, then, has four points to move in various ways in order to achieve curves that look widely different, from those that are close to a straight line to those that include a loop. The cubic curve here has enough flexibility to be useful, but not quite so much that it is hard to work with (Figure 7.7).

The Bézier curve method is clearly generalizable to any number of control points. The resulting blending functions are polynomials of higher and higher degree, but their pattern stays recognizable. If we let $a = (1 - t)$ and $b = t$, then the terms in the expansion of $(a + b)^n$ give the blending functions for $n + 1$ control points. When $n = 3$, we have four control points.

$$(a + b)^3 = a^3 + 3a^2b + 3ab^2 + b^3$$

$$B_{(0,3)}(t) = a^3 = (1 - t)^3$$

$$B_{(1,3)}(t) = 3a^2b = 3(1 - t)^2t$$

$$B_{(2,3)}(t) = 3ab^2 = 3(1 - t)t^2$$

$$B_{(3,3)}(t) = a^3 = t^3$$

For an arbitrary n, we have $B_{(i,n)}(t) = \binom{n}{i}(1 - t)^{n-i}t^i$, where $0 \le i \le n$. Here, $\binom{n}{i}$ is the binomial coefficient which is most easily remembered from Pascal's triangle (partially given below) where a row is calculated from the row above. (Note that 6 in the fourth row is the sum of 3 plus 3 just above and left in the third row.)

$$\begin{array}{ccccc} 1 & 1 & & & \\ 1 & 2 & 1 & & \\ 1 & 3 & 3 & 1 & \\ 1 & 4 & 6 & 4 & 1 \end{array}$$

There is actually a formula for $\binom{n}{i}$ which derives from basic counting arguments:

$$\binom{n}{i} = \frac{n!}{i!(n-i)!} \implies \binom{n}{i} = \binom{n-1}{i} + \binom{n-1}{i-1}$$

The recursive formula on the right leads to a recursive relation among the Bernstein polynomials.

$$B_{(i,n)}(t) = (1 - t)B_{(i,n-1)}(t) + tB_{(i-1,n-1)}(t) \tag{7.10}$$

Finally, when we add up the blending functions, we get 1 because the sum is actually $(a + b)^n$.

$$\sum_{i=0}^{n} B_{(i,n)}(t) = \sum_{i=0}^{n} \binom{n}{i} (1 - t)^{n-i} t^i = ((1 - t) + t)^n = 1$$

This means that the general Bézier parametric description is an affine combination of the control points.

$$P_B(t) = \sum_{i=0}^{n} B_{(i,n)}(t)P_i \tag{7.11}$$

7.2.1   Properties for Two-Dimensional Bézier Curves

A set of useful properties makes Bézier curves relatively easy to use for design. We already saw that they interpolate the first and last control points because the only blending function that is nonzero when $t = 0$ is the first and the only nonzero one when $t = 1$ is the last. Otherwise, the blending functions are all nonzero for other values of t, and all points are combined for interior points on the curve segment. (This can be a little awkward if we desire to only change a small portion of the curve. This needs to be addressed later.) We should also note that, if we take the control points in reverse order, making the first the last and the last the first, we get exactly the same curve; the parametric description just traverses the curve in reverse order. This symmetry is a direct result of the symmetry in the blending functions between $(1 - t)$ and t.

Bézier curves are well controlled because we know approximately how they are positioned relative to the control points. The de Casteljau geometric construction continually takes points that are on line segments between previously calculated points. This implies that, if we form a polygon surrounding all the control points (in two dimensions), then the curve must stay inside the polygon. The smallest such polygon is the convex hull of the control points, so the curve stays inside the convex hull (Figure 7.8).

As we have noted above, the blending functions for Bézier curves sum to 1. The parametric description is an affine combination and consequently we have affine invariance. If we transform the control points and apply the parametric description, we get a curve that is the transform of the original curve. When designing, if we want the curve rotated, it suffices to rotate the control points.

$$T(P_B(t)) = \sum_{i=0}^{n} B_{(i,n)}(t)T(P_i)$$

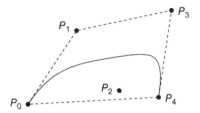

Figure 7.8 Convex hull for Bézier curve

To further control our curves, it would be helpful to know the tangent vectors at the endpoints of the curve segment. To do this, we need to take derivatives. Consider again the cubic Bézier curve

$$P_B(t) = (1-t)^3 P_0 + 3t(1-t)^2 P_1 + 3t^2(1-t)P_2 + t^3 P_3$$

This expression encapsulates equations for both x and y coordinates, so we can take the derivative directly.

$$P'_B(t) = -3(1-t)^2 P_0 + (3(1-t)^2 - 6t(1-t))P_1$$
$$+ (6t(1-t) - 3t^2)P_2 + 3t^2 P_3$$

Substituting in $t = 0$ and $t = 1$ gives us the derivative at the first and last control points.

$$P'_B(0) = -3P_0 + 3P_1 = 3(P_1 - P_0)$$
$$P'_B(1) = -3P_2 + 3P_3 = 3(P_3 - P_2) \tag{7.12}$$

The derivatives are vectors because each is a difference of points. Their slope gives us dy/dx, but geometrically they are vectors from P_0 to P_1 and from P_2 to P_3 (Figure 7.7). We can immediately see the tangents because they are line segments between two control points. (The length of the tangent is also meaningful, but here we are only interested in the shape of the curve and hence the direction of the tangents at the endpoints.) By moving the control points, we know exactly how the tangents will change.

We were concerned earlier about how wiggly a curve can be, and with Bézier curves we have eased the concern somewhat. Since the curve interpolates only the first and last points, we may not see the number of maxima and minima that make a wiggly curve. Actually, there is another property that further ensures some reasonable behavior for Bézier curves. If we connect the control points in order with line segments, we form what is called the *control polygon*. A straight line may cross this control polygon at a number of points. However, a straight line cannot cross the Bézier curve more times that it crosses the control polygon; this property is called *variation diminishing*. This gives some assurance that the curve is not too wiggly and it offers a

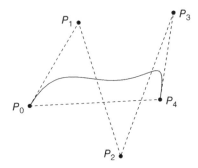

Figure 7.9 Bézier variation diminishing

way to reduce any wiggliness by moving the control points to smooth out the control polygon (Figure 7.9).

Result 7.4 (Properties of Bézier Curves). *The two-dimensional curve with control points $P_0, P_1, \ldots, P_n$ given by $P_B(t) = \sum_{i=0}^{n} B_{(i,n)}(t)P_i$ has the following properties:*

1. *The curve interpolates P_0 and P_n.*
2. *The curve is contained in the convex hull of the control points.*
3. *The tangent vector at P_0 is parallel to $(P_1 - P_0)$ and the tangent vector at P_n is parallel to $(P_n - P_{n-1})$.*
4. *The curve is affinely invariant.*
5. *A straight line does not cross the curve more times than it crosses the control polygon.*

7.2.2   Joining Bézier Curve Segments

To improve the flexibility of Bézier curves, there are two key adjustments we could make. First, we could add another control point, giving a little finer control over the curve. Optimally, we would want to add a new control point without disturbing the current curve, and then be able to move it to obtain some careful change in shape. (This addition procedure is covered in Section 7.6.)

The second way to improve flexibility is to concatenate two segments. If the last control point of one curve is the first control point of the next, then we are guaranteed the two segments will form a continuous curve; the curve is C^0 continuous (Figure 7.10).

If our curve has control points P_i, we know that the tangents at the first and last control point are parallel to the vectors $P_1 - P_0$ and $P_n - P_{n-1}$. We can easily adjust the joint between two segments so that the tangents match. If the control points of the second segment are R_i, then $R_0 = P_n$ and R_1 should be placed on the line through P_{n-1} and P_n. With matching tangent directions, the curve containing both segments is C^1

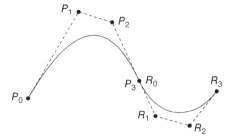

Figure 7.10   Joining two Bézier segments

continuous. Matching the length of the tangents is not strictly necessary because the length determines how fast the curve is being traversed with respect to the change in t. A change in speed will not be visually noticeable unless the increments in t used to approximate the curve are particularly large. Yet, if the curve is a path for animation, the speed is important and we should match speeds at the join.

In some cases, higher levels of smoothness are necessary, and to achieve this we need to match second derivatives at the joining points between segments. As we might guess, C^2 continuity and above depends on positioning more control points in the second segment correctly and this can be difficult. This is a bit of a drawback to Bézier curves and one that is addressed with the use of spline curves.

7.2.3   Three-Dimensional Bézier Curves

If the control points for a Bézier curve are actually points in three-dimensional space, then we have a three-dimensional curve. The de Casteljau algorithm for constructing the curve still works because the linear interpolation of two points ($P(t) = (1 - t)P_0 + tP_1$) works just fine in space. The algebra for describing the curve is still the same, and the matrix form of the curve differs only in that the matrix of points now has a third row corresponding to the third coordinate. Moving the control points shapes the curve similar to the two-dimensional case, although practically it is a little trickier to design curves with the extra degree of freedom in three dimensions.

If the control points happen to be all in the same plane (coplanar), then the curve, of course, satisfies all the properties we discovered earlier for two-dimensional curves. Actually, the properties still hold for nonplanar three-dimensional curves. The Bézier curve interpolates the first and last points and it stays within the convex hull of the control points. In three dimensions, however, the convex hull is generally a polyhedron rather than a polygon. Yet, following de Casteljau's algorithm, we note that construction of the curve stays within line segments that are always within the convex hull.

We are still taking affine combinations of the control points, so the curve displays affine invariance. However, three-dimensional curves have to be projected into two dimensions for display on the screen. Since this projective transformation is not an affine transformation, the three-dimensional Bézier curve is not necessarily projectively invariant. If we project the control points and construct the associated two-dimensional Bézier curve, we do not get the same curve as we would by projecting the three-dimensional one. This is a minor annoyance that can be avoided by using rational Bézier curves which we examine in the next section.

Finally, to patch two three-dimensional Bézier curves together, we take the same approach as before and match the tangent vector directions. Now, however, they are three-dimensional directions. As before, it is not necessary to match the length of the vectors unless we need continuity in the speed with which the curve is traversed.

7.2.4 Rational Bézier Curves

The parametric coordinate functions for Bézier curves are polynomials in t, and this means that we cannot represent an ellipse (including a circle) or a hyperbola, for example, as Bézier curves; their parametric descriptions are not polynomials. Despite its flexibility, the Bézier is just not able to cover all curves. With all curve schemes, there is a desire to increase flexibility, at the same time keeping the complexity in check, so a logical next step for Bézier curves is to use rational functions (i.e., quotients of polynomials) for the blending functions. In particular, we introduce weights w_i to help control the shape of the curve.

$$P(t) = \sum_{i=0}^{n} \frac{w_i B_{(i,n)}(t)}{\sum_{j=0}^{n} w_j B_{(j,n)}(t)} P_i \tag{7.13}$$

The blending functions are weighted and normalized versions of the standard Bézier blending functions. While useful, the weights sometimes lead to awkward situations, so we usually require both that the values are nonnegative and that they are not all zero. If $w_i = 1$ for all i, the rational curve becomes the regular Bézier curve.

Example 7.7 (Circles as Rational Bézier Curves). Just to verify that we actually get a little more out of these new rational curves than we do out of the standard Bézier curves, we can pick control points and weights to form a circle in the case where $n = 2$ and we have three control points. Let $P_0 = (1, 0), P_1 = (1, 1)$, and $P_2 = (0, 1)$. These are the points at the corners of a unit square. Now set the weights so $w_0 = 1, w_1 = 1$, and $w_2 = 2$.

$$\sum_{j=0}^{2} w_j B_{(j,2)}(t) = 1 \cdot (1-t)^2 + 1 \cdot 2t(1-t) + 2 \cdot t^2 = 1 + t^2$$

This gives the curve

$$P(t) = \frac{1}{(1+t^2)} [(1-t)^2 P_0 + 2t(1-t) P_1 + 2t^2 P_2]$$

The coordinate functions are now

$$x(t) = \frac{(1-t)^2 + 2t(1-t)}{1+t^2} = \frac{1-t^2}{1+t^2}$$

$$y(t) = \frac{2t(1-t) + 2t^2}{1+t^2} = \frac{2t}{1+t^2}$$

For $0 \leq t \leq 1$, this is a parameterization for a quarter circle (see Example 7.1).

With three control points, the coordinate functions are quadratic rational functions. Conics can be parameterized by quadratic rational functions and any such parameterization is a conic. It follows that the quadratic rational Bézier curves are all conics.   □

With rational Bézier curves, homogeneous coordinates simplify the description because the weights play the role of the last homogeneous coordinate. The control point P_i becomes the homogeneous point P_i^h with coordinates $(w_i x_i, w_i y_i, w_i)$ for two dimensional curves and $(w_i x_i, w_i y_i, w_i z_i, w_i)$ for three-dimensional curves. The point $P(t)$ on the rational curve corresponds to the homogeneous point $P^h(t)$ which has the following simpler form:

$$P^h(t) = \sum_{i=0}^{n} B_{(i,n)}(t) P_i^h \tag{7.14}$$

This expression makes it clear that we have the same form as a standard Bézier curve where we use homogeneous coordinates for the control points. Then it is also clear that the de Casteljau algorithm proceeds as before interpolating homogeneous coordinates this time. This implies that the convex hull property still holds for the rational Bézier curves. In fact, all the Bézier properties still hold. It takes a little more computation to find the tangents to the first and last points, but they are still parallel to $P_1 - P_0$ and $P_n - P_{n-1}$.

Affine invariance follows as before, but now we also have a projective invariance. Recall that a projective transformation (in particular, a perspective transformation) can be represented by matrix multiplication of homogeneous coordinates.

$$T(P^h(t)) = MP^h(t) = M\left(\sum_{i=0}^{n} B_{(i,n)}(t) P_i^h\right)$$

$$= \sum_{i=0}^{n} B_{(i,n)}(t) MP_i^h$$

$$= \sum_{i=0}^{n} B_{(i,n)}(t) TP_i^h$$

So when we project a three-dimensional rational Bézier curve into two dimensions, the resulting curve is the same as if we constructed a two-dimensional rational Bézier curve using the control points $T(P_i^h)$ that are projected from the original control points. Projecting the homogeneous points has the effect of adjusting both weights and points.

7.3   B-SPLINES

Designing a curve is not simple. The Bézier approach helps significantly, and the key idea is that the curve is not forced to go through all the control points. Still, moving a control point affects the shape of the entire curve and often we need to adjust only a small portion. The optimal balance between global and local control is hard to achieve in all situations. One good technique is to build curves in pieces hoping that the pieces can be put together in a reasonably smooth way.

Before the widespread use of computer techniques in design, those doing drafting for architectural drawings often used thin strips of wood or metal to shape a curve and then trace it onto paper. These *splines* have a natural smoothness and a minimum amount of fluctuations. It is not entirely easy to adjust only small regions of the spline, but if they are thin enough, the perturbations can be isolated to smaller lengths of the whole strip.

Attempts to mathematically model the flexibility of the spline by incorporating the relevant physics become complicated, and, instead, several approximations have been proposed emphasizing some aspects of the physical spline over others. Useful directions usually describe the curve as an affine combination of control points with polynomial or rational blending functions plus some extra constraints (like specified tangents). Curve segments are then put together piecewise to form a larger easy-to-alter curve. Several mathematicians in the past have studied curves using this general approach, but it appears that Isaac Schoenberg in 1946 was the first to call the curves "splines" and set the stage for modern development.

While there are many possible approaches here, one that has endured and incorporates several desirable properties involves curves called *B-splines*. The B stands for *basis* and refers to the fundamental nature of the blending functions which serve as building blocks for a very wide range of curves. B-splines approximate rather than interpolate points, and they use blending functions to form combinations of control points.

To be more specific, the B-spline is a curve determined by $n + 1$ control points denoted $P_0, P_1, \ldots, P_n$ and $n + 1$ blending functions conventionally denoted $N_{(0,k)}(t), N_{(1,k)}(t), \ldots, N_{(n,k)}(t)$, where k is the degree of the polynomials used in a piecewise construction of the blending functions. (The subscripts used here actually vary slightly from one treatment to the next.) For reasons that will be clearer soon, the *order* of this B-spline is $k + 1$; an order $k + 1$ curve has blending functions of degree k.

As the parameter t runs through its range, the following expression traces the complete B-spline:

$$P(t) = \sum_{i=0}^{n} N_{(i,k)}(t)P_i \qquad (7.15)$$

Defining the blending functions is really the key issue, and there are two main criteria:

1. *Local Control.* As the parameter t moves through its values, the jth blending function should reach its maximum at some parameter value t_j^* and therefore allow its associated control point to exert maximum influence over the developing curve. However, if t is far from t_j^*, the blending function should be zero, guaranteeing that the control point has no influence over distant parts of the curve. This is the essence of local control.

2. *Smoothness.* B-splines are piecewise curves built from a series of segments that fit together smoothly. If we use polynomials of degree k to form the blending functions, then we need $k + 1$ points to determine a segment. (This is one reason why the order of the curve is $k + 1$.) The first segment depends on the points $P_0, P_1, \ldots, P_k$, and the second segment depends on the overlapping set of points $P_1, P_2, \ldots, P_{k+1}$. The rest of the segments are defined similarly, allowing an arbitrary number of control points to define the B-spline. Adjacent segments should meet smoothly, in fact forming a curve with C^{k-1} continuity.

Even given these criteria, there is still some flexibility in defining the blending functions. They are defined in a piecewise manner using polynomials of degree k which fit together appropriately to guarantee the smoothness of the entire spline curve. The designer can delineate the blending function pieces by specifying key values of the parameter t called *knots*. These will be used to determine the beginning and ending points for each piece. While arbitrary knot choices are allowed, we start by using the knots $t_i = i$ where i is an integer with $0 \le i \le n + k$. (The range here is chosen only because of the way we will be defining blending functions; the notation for B-splines can become confusing, so starting with knot values that are integers considerably simplifies some expressions.) Using integer knot values means there is uniform spacing between knots and therefore we have an example of what are called *uniform B-splines*.

Unlike Bézier curves where the number of control points determined the degree of the polynomial curve, we can set the degree for B-splines regardless of how many control points there are. So to build our experience with B-splines, we start with degree 1 (linear polynomials) and work up to any arbitrary degree.

7.3.1 Linear Uniform B-Splines

For linear uniform B-splines, the degree is 1 (the order is 2) because we are using linear polynomials to form the blending functions. Imagine we have $n + 1$ control points, $P_0, P_1, \ldots, P_n$. The B-spline with blending functions that are piecewise linear polynomials simply interpolates between each pair of control points in a linear way. So points P_0 and P_1 determine the first straight segment, and in general P_{i-1} and P_i determine the ith segment. The endpoint of one segment is the beginning point of the next, so we have C^0 continuity. We cannot ask for higher levels of smoothness because linear segments are not very flexible. Now, constructing such a piecewise

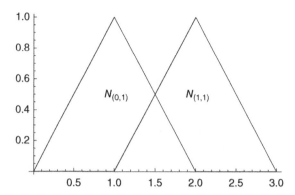

Figure 7.11 Linear B-Spline blending functions

linear curve is straightforward; the ith segment is given by $P(t) = (1 - t)P_{i-1} + tP_i$ for $0 \le t < 1$.

To view the construction of this linear B-spline in a more general light, we would like to put it in the form of Equation 7.15 where we have designated the blending functions and let t range from 1 to $n + 1$. (Either the notation $1 \le t < n + 1$ or $t \in [1, n + 1)$ will work to describe this range.) We use the uniform knot sequence described above, so that the first pieces of the blending function are defined between knots. Then, the first segment of the B-spline corresponds to the parameter values $1 \le t < 2$, and the ith segment corresponds to $i \le t < i + 1$.

Each blending function shown in Figure 7.11 has a tent shape made from two linear pieces which we refer to as *basis* pieces. The first function, $N_{(0,1)}(t)$, starts at zero when $t = 0$, rises to the maximum value 1 when $t = 1$, and falls back to zero when $t = 2$. Everywhere else, the function is zero. Since our B-spline will start with $t = 1$, we will not actually use the first piece of this blending function, but notice that every other blending function is a translate of the full function $N_{(0,1)}(t)$. In particular, $N_{(1,1)}(t) = N_{(0,1)}(t - 1)$. The blending function $N_{(0,1)}(t)$ is only nonzero in the interval $0 \le t \le 2$, so the point P_0 alone has influence over the curve when t is in that interval. Starting at $t = 1$, $N_{(0,1)}(1) = 1$ and $N_{(1,1)}(1) = 0$, hence our B-spline has $P(1) = P_0$. The first control point is on the curve. Similarly, $P(2) = P_1$, and the second control point is also on the curve. For any arbitrary spline, the control points may not be on the curve, but in the linear case they are.

In any interval between two successive knots, at most two blending functions are nonzero. This is a result of local control and implies that, on any knot interval, the global description of the linear B-spline reduces to a sum over just two terms. When $k \le t < k + 1$, we trace out one segment of the curve.

$$P(t) = \sum_{i=1}^{n} N_{(i,1)}(t)P_i = N_{(k,1)}(t)P_k + N_{(k+1,1)}(t)P_{k+1}$$

$$= (1 - (t - k))P_k + (t - k)P_{k+1} \qquad (7.16)$$

Since the blending functions are built from two basis pieces, Equation 7.16 is only correct when $k \leq t < k + 1$; it is only on that interval that the blending functions equal the pieces given in the equation.

Any particular control point P_i appears in only two of the spline segments, which agrees with the observation that each blending function is nonzero on only two successive knot intervals. It should also be clear that the end of each spline segment is the beginning of the next segment. As we let t go from 1 to $n + 1$, we trace out n segments of this linear uniform B-spline.

Finally, we can carefully define the first blending function $N_{(0,1)}(t)$.

$$N_{(0,1)}(t) = \begin{cases} 0 & \text{if } t < 0; \\ t & \text{if } t \in [0, 1); \\ (2 - t) & \text{if } t \in [1, 2); \\ 0 & \text{if } 2 \geq t; \end{cases} \tag{7.17}$$

All other blending functions are translates of this one, $N_{(i,1)}(t) = N_{(0,1)}(t - i)$. In the interval $1 \leq t < 2$, we have $N_{(0,1)}(t) = (2 - t)$ and $N_{(1,1)}(t) = N_{(0,1)}(t - 1) = t - 1$. The sum of the two blending functions is 1 and this is true for any value of t in the range $1 \leq t \leq n + 1$.

The matrix form of a B-spline segment emphasizes the local description in Equation 7.16. Since the blending functions are all translates of each other, we can effectively translate any interval $k \leq t < k + 1$ to the interval $0 \leq t < 1$. If we want the ith B-spline segment, we let $0 \leq t < 1$ and use the following matrix expression:

$$P(t) = \begin{bmatrix} P_i & P_{i+1} \end{bmatrix} \begin{bmatrix} 1 & -1 \\ 0 & 1 \end{bmatrix} \begin{bmatrix} 1 \\ t \end{bmatrix} \tag{7.18}$$

When $i = 0$, we get $P(t) = (1 - t)P_0 + tP_1$, and when $i = 1$, we get $P(t) = (1 - t)P_1 + tP_2$. The shape of this last segment is correct, but the t values have been translated from $1 \leq t < 2$ to $0 < let < 1$. This inconvenience is balanced by the simplicity of the matrix description.

The linear B-spline is rather simple, but it does incorporate local control because moving any control point affects only two adjacent linear segments of the curve. Although it is continuous, we do not really see smoothness beyond continuity in the curve. Also, the definition of the blending functions came rather intuitively in this linear case; we will really need a more systematic way of finding blending functions for higher degree splines.

7.3.2 Quadratic Uniform B-Splines

For quadratic uniform B-splines, the degree is 2 (order is 3) and the blending functions now contain three pieces. Consequently, any single blending function is nonzero

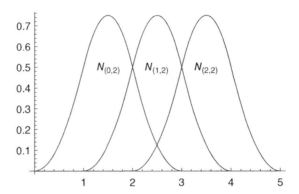

Figure 7.12   Quadratic B-Spline blending functions

on only three successive knot intervals. With quadratic polynomials, we can require C^1 continuity, which means that the spline segments have matching tangents at the joining points. Requiring local control together with more smoothness means that the resulting spline will not necessarily pass through the control points and this time we do not have a lot of intuition about the definition of the blending functions. We need to take a more measured approach to find their shape.

The quadratic B-spline is again a series of segments fitting together nicely. The blending functions are shown in Figure 7.12 and the first curve segment is traced as $2 \leq t < 3$.

$$P(t) = N_{(0,2)}(t)P_0 + N_{(1,2)}(t)P_1 + N_{(2,2)}(t)P_2 \qquad (7.19)$$

In the interval from 2 to 3, $N_{(0,2)}$ is waning (decreasing to zero), $N_{(1,2)}$ reaches its peak, and $N_{(2,2)}$ is rising. The influence of P_0 is therefore dropping off, while the influence of P_1 is at its peak and that of P_2 is increasing. Figure 7.13 shows the three pieces q_1, q_2, q_3 of a single blending function.

The shape of these three pieces is determined by several criteria.

1. The endpoint of one piece must match the beginning point of another piece. For example, the endpoint of piece q_1 must match the beginning point of piece q_2.
2. The derivative at the endpoint of one piece must match the derivative at the beginning of another piece. For example, the derivative at the endpoint of q_2 must match that of the beginning point of piece q_3.
3. The sum of the three pieces at any point t in the interval must be 1 to ensure an affine combination of the control points.

Assuming that the blending functions are quadratic, these criteria generate several algebraic equations that can be solved to specify the functions exactly (see Section 7.6

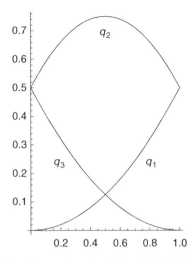

Figure 7.13   Pieces of quadratic B-spline blending function

for details). The end result is the following definition of $N_{(0,2)}(t)$:

$$N_{(0,2)}(t) = \begin{cases} 0 & \text{if } t < 0; \\ \frac{1}{2}t^2 & \text{if } t \in [0,1); \\ \frac{1}{2} + (t-1) - (t-1)^2 & \text{if } t \in [1,2); \\ \frac{1}{2} - (t-2) + \frac{1}{2}(t-2)^2 & \text{if } t \in [2,3); \\ 0 & \text{if } 3 \geq t; \end{cases} \qquad (7.20)$$

The other blending functions are all translates of this one.

$$N_{(i,2)}(t) = N_{(0,2)}(t-i)$$

With $i = 1$ and $t = 2$,

$$N_{(0,2)}(2) = 1/2$$
$$N_{(1,2)}(2) = N(0,2)(2-1) = 1/2$$
$$N_{(2,2)}(2) = N(0,2)(2-2) = 0$$

The first point on the spline is then

$$P(0) = \frac{1}{2}P_0 + \frac{1}{2}P_1 + 0 \cdot P_2$$

The spline begins midway between the first two control points. Similarly, at $t = 3$, the spline segment ends at the midpoint of P_1 and P_2.

With the definition of the blending functions, we can write down a global description of the quadratic B-spline by substituting into Equation 7.15. If we have $n + 1$ control points, then $2 \leq t < n + 2$.

The matrix description of one segment of the quadratic B-spline (using the interval $0 \leq t < 1$) is

$$P(t) = \begin{bmatrix} P_{i-1} & P_i & P_{i+1} \end{bmatrix} \frac{1}{2} \begin{bmatrix} 1 & -2 & 1 \\ 1 & 2 & -2 \\ 0 & 0 & 1 \end{bmatrix} \begin{bmatrix} 1 \\ t \\ t^2 \end{bmatrix} \qquad (7.21)$$

Example 7.8 (Uniform Quadratic Spline with Two Segments). With the control points $P_0 = (0, 2)$, $P_1 = (2, 5)$, $P_2 = (3, 4)$, and $P_3 = (4, 1)$, we can build a quadratic B-spline with two segments. The curve is

$$P(t) = N_{(0,2)}(t) \begin{bmatrix} 0 \\ 2 \end{bmatrix} + N_{(1,2)}(t) \begin{bmatrix} 2 \\ 5 \end{bmatrix} + N_{(2,2)}(t) \begin{bmatrix} 3 \\ 4 \end{bmatrix} + N_{(3,2)}(t) \begin{bmatrix} 4 \\ 1 \end{bmatrix}$$

Since $N_{(1,2)}$ is a translate of $N_{(0,2)}$, its definition is

$$N_{(1,2)}(t) = \begin{cases} 0 & \text{if } t < 1; \\ \frac{1}{2}(t-1)^2 & \text{if } t \in [1, 2); \\ \frac{1}{2} + (t-2) - (t-2)^2 & \text{if } t \in [2, 3); \\ \frac{1}{2} - (t-3) + \frac{1}{2}(t-3)^2 & \text{if } t \in [3, 4); \\ 0 & \text{if } 4 \geq t; \end{cases}$$

The blending functions $N_{(2,2)}(t)$ and $N_{(3,2)}(t)$ are similar translates. Carefully keeping track of the basis pieces of the blending functions, we have for $2 \leq t < 3$

$$P(t) = \left(\frac{1}{2} - (t-2) + \frac{1}{2}(t-2)^2 \right) \begin{bmatrix} 0 \\ 2 \end{bmatrix} + \left(\frac{1}{2} + (t-2) - (t-2)^2 \right) \begin{bmatrix} 2 \\ 5 \end{bmatrix}$$
$$+ \frac{1}{2}(t-2)^2 \begin{bmatrix} 3 \\ 4 \end{bmatrix} + 0 \cdot \begin{bmatrix} 4 \\ 1 \end{bmatrix}$$

The first segment of the B-spline begins at the point $(1, 3.5)$ and ends at $(2.5, 4.5)$. The second segment is traced as $3 \leq t < 4$ and

$$P(t) = 0 \cdot \begin{bmatrix} 0 \\ 2 \end{bmatrix} + \left(\frac{1}{2} - (t-3) + \frac{1}{2}(t-3)^2 \right) \begin{bmatrix} 2 \\ 5 \end{bmatrix}$$
$$+ \left(\frac{1}{2} + (t-3) - (t-3)^2 \right) \begin{bmatrix} 3 \\ 4 \end{bmatrix} + \frac{1}{2}(t-3)^2 \begin{bmatrix} 4 \\ 1 \end{bmatrix}$$

The second segment goes from $(2.5, 4.5)$ to $(3.5, 2.5)$ (Figure 7.14).

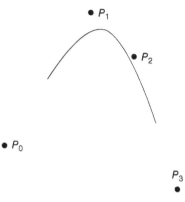

Figure 7.14   Quadratic B-spline

To find the value of the spline when $t = 2.5$, we first identify the knot interval containing the value and then notice that this is the first segment of the spline. Using the expression above for the first segment, we calculate with $t = 2.5$.

$$P(2.5) = \frac{1}{8} \begin{bmatrix} 0 \\ 2 \end{bmatrix} + \frac{3}{4} \begin{bmatrix} 2 \\ 5 \end{bmatrix} + \frac{1}{8} \begin{bmatrix} 3 \\ 4 \end{bmatrix} + 0 \cdot \begin{bmatrix} 4 \\ 1 \end{bmatrix} = \begin{bmatrix} 1.875 \\ 4.5 \end{bmatrix}$$

Notice that for each segment, the blending functions sum to 1 for all values of t in the appropriate interval. For the first segment on $2 \leq t < 3$,

$$\left(\frac{1}{2} - (t-2) + \frac{1}{2}(t-2)^2 \right) + \left(\frac{1}{2} + (t-2) - (t-2)^2 \right) + \frac{1}{2}(t-2)^2 = 1$$

Since the sum is 1, we have an affine combination of the control points, which ensures affine invariance of the spline. An affine transformation of the spline is the same as transforming the control points and then constructing a new spline.

The transition between the two segments in the spline is C^1 continuous. To see this, we can calculate and compare the derivatives of each segment. For the first segment on $2 \leq t < 3$, we get

$$P'(t) = (-3 + t) \begin{bmatrix} 0 \\ 2 \end{bmatrix} + (5 - 2t) \begin{bmatrix} 2 \\ 5 \end{bmatrix} + (t - 2) \begin{bmatrix} 3 \\ 4 \end{bmatrix} + 0 \cdot \begin{bmatrix} 4 \\ 1 \end{bmatrix}$$

Therefore, $P'(3) = -(2, 5) + (3, 4) = (1, -1)$. (Technically, we are taking the limit of $P'(t)$ as t goes to 3.) The tangent vector is in the direction of the vector $P_2 - P_1$. A similar calculation for the second spline segment gives

$$P'(t) = 0 \cdot \begin{bmatrix} 0 \\ 2 \end{bmatrix} + (-4 + t) \begin{bmatrix} 2 \\ 5 \end{bmatrix} + (-2t + 7) \begin{bmatrix} 3 \\ 4 \end{bmatrix} + (t - 3) \begin{bmatrix} 4 \\ 1 \end{bmatrix}$$

At $t = 3$, we again get $P'(3) = -(2, 5) + (3, 4) = (1, -1)$. The two tangents match. $\square$

7.3.3 Cubic Uniform B-Splines

Linear B-splines are not very smooth, and although quadratic B-splines are smoother, they are still a little constrained when it comes to design. The higher the degree of the polynomials used to build the blending functions, the more the flexibility and the more the smoothness we can guarantee. B-splines with polynomials of degree k (the order is $k + 1$) have $C^{(k-1)}$ continuity. Yet, large degree splines start to be cumbersome in their computation and control; practice suggests that cubic B-splines are a good compromise and offer both a satisfactorily smooth curve and plenty of design control.

Cubic B-splines have blending functions with four basis pieces and each piece is a cubic polynomial (degree 3). The constraints of C^0, C^1, and C^2 continuity along with the requirement that the blending functions sum to 1 give enough equations to completely specify the pieces. A single blending function is nonzero on four consecutive knot intervals and, again because of the uniform knot sequence, the functions are symmetric around their middle. The complete spline is traced over the parameter interval $3 \le t < n + 3$.

The blending functions are shown in Figure 7.15; in particular, the definition of $N_{(0,3)}(t)$ is

$$N_{(0,3)}(t) = \begin{cases} 0 & \text{if } t < 0; \\ \frac{1}{6}t^3 & \text{if } t \in [0,1); \\ \frac{1}{6}(-3(t-1)^3 + 3(t-1)^2 + 3(t-1) + 1 & \text{if } t \in [1,2); \\ \frac{1}{6}(3(t-2)^3 - 6(t-2)^2 + 4) & \text{if } t \in [2,3); \\ \frac{1}{6}(-(t-3)^3 + 3(t-3)^2 - 3(t-3) + 1) & \text{if } t \in [3,4); \\ 0 & \text{if } 4 \le t; \end{cases} \qquad (7.22)$$

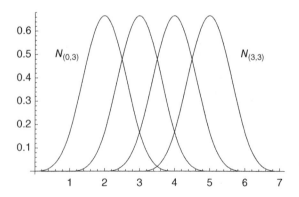

Figure 7.15   Cubic blending functions

The first segment of the cubic B-spline is traced as $3 \leq t < 4$.

$$P(t) = \frac{1}{6}(-(t-3)^3 + 3(t-3)^2 - 3(t-3) + 1)P_0$$

$$+ \frac{1}{6}(3(t-3)^3 - 6(t-3)^2 + 4)P_1$$

$$+ \frac{1}{6}(-3(t-3)^3 + 3(t-3)^2 + 3(t-3) + 1)P_2$$

$$+ \frac{1}{6}(t-3)^3 P_3 \tag{7.23}$$

Notice that the spline begins at the point $\frac{1}{6}P_0 + \frac{4}{6}P_1 + \frac{1}{6}P_2$, which is not on the control polygon. The spline only approximates the control points (Figure 7.16).

To check the C^2 continuity between two segments of the spline, we need the second derivatives. Consider the first segment (traced on $3 \leq t < 4$) and the second segment (traced on $4 \leq t < 5$). The second segment looks like this:

$$P(t) = \frac{1}{6}(-(t-4)^3 + 3(t-4)^2 - 3(t-4) + 1)P_1$$

$$+ \frac{1}{6}(3(t-4)^3 - 6(t-4)^2 + 4)P_2$$

$$+ \frac{1}{6}(-3(t-4)^3 + 3(t-4)^2 + 3(t-4) + 1)P_3$$

$$+ \frac{1}{6}(t-4)^3 P_4$$

Note how this expression for the second segment can be derived from the expression for the first segment by translation.

Taking the first and second derivatives of the first segment at $t = 4$ gives

$$P'(4) = \frac{1}{2}P_1 + \frac{1}{2}P_3 \quad \text{and} \quad P''(4) = P_1 - 2P_2 + P_3$$

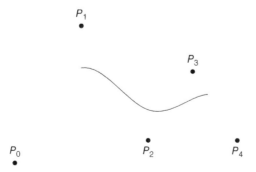

Figure 7.16   Cubic B-spline

There is enough similarity between the first and second segment expressions that calculating the second derivative comes quickly. The first and second derivatives match between the two segments, establishing the C^2 continuity.

Finally, the compact matrix description of a single segment (over the interval $0 \leq t < 1$) clearly displays the coefficients for the cubic polynomial pieces.

$$P(t) = \begin{bmatrix} P_{i-1} & P_i & P_{i+1} & P_{i+2} \end{bmatrix} \frac{1}{6} \begin{bmatrix} 1 & -3 & 3 & -1 \\ 4 & 0 & -6 & 3 \\ 1 & 3 & 3 & -3 \\ 0 & 0 & 0 & 1 \end{bmatrix} \begin{bmatrix} 1 \\ t \\ t^2 \\ t^3 \end{bmatrix} \tag{7.24}$$

7.3.4 B-Spline Properties

It is not immediately clear from the B-splines we have seen so far that there is a pattern emerging among the blending functions. If we stick with a uniform knot sequence where the knots are integers $t_i = i$, the following recursive formula will generate the blending functions starting from functions of degree zero, $N_{(i,0)}(t)$.

$$N_{(i,0)}(t) = \begin{cases} 1 & \text{if } t \in [i, i+1) \\ 0 & \text{otherwise} \end{cases}$$

$$N_{(i,k)}(t) = \frac{t-i}{k} N_{(i,k-1)}(t) + \frac{i+k+1-t}{k} N_{(i+1,k-1)}(t) \tag{7.25}$$

Example 7.9 (Calculating $N_{(0,2)}(t)$). Just to get a feeling for how this recursive formula works, we calculate $N_{(0,2)}(t)$ step by step.

$$N_{(0,1)} = \frac{(t-0)}{1} N_{(0,0)}(t) + \frac{(2-t)}{1} N_{(1,0)}(t)$$

$$= \begin{cases} 0 & \text{if } t < 0 \\ t & \text{if } t \in [0,1) \\ (2-t) & \text{if } t \in [1,2) \\ 0 & \text{if } 2 < t \end{cases}$$

$$N_{(1,1)} = \frac{(t-1)}{1} N_{(0,0)}(t) + \frac{(3-t)}{1} N_{(1,0)}(t)$$

$$= \begin{cases} 0 & \text{if } t < 1 \\ (t-1) & \text{if } t \in [1,2) \\ (3-t) & \text{if } t \in [2,3) \\ 0 & \text{if } 3 \leq t \end{cases}$$

$$N_{(0,2)} = \frac{(t-0)}{2}N_{(0,1)}(t) + \frac{(3-t)}{2}N_{(1,1)}(t)$$

$$= \begin{cases} 0 & \text{if } t < 0 \\ \frac{1}{2}t^2 & \text{if } t \in [0,1) \\ \frac{1}{2}t(2-t) + \frac{1}{2}(3-t)(t-1) & \text{if } t \in [1,2) \\ \frac{1}{2}(3-t)^2 & \text{if } t \in [2,3) \\ 0 & \text{if } 3 \le t \end{cases}$$

A little algebraic simplification and a quick check of the graphs show that these results match our previous descriptions of the blending functions. □

Since the global description of a B-spline, $P(t) = \sum_{i=0}^{n} N_{(i,k)}(t)P_i$, includes the blending functions, we can apply the recursive formula for blending functions to get a recursive formula for calculating any value $P(t)$. This leads to the de Boor algorithm which is reminiscent of the de Casteljau algorithm for Bézier curves. A point on the spline of degree k is represented as a linear combination of the points on splines of degree $k-1$. Degree zero points are the original control points. Let $P_i^j(t)$ be a point from a degree j spline. (The subscript i will keep the points in order.)

Result 7.5 (The de Boor Algorithm). *Let $P_i^0(t) = P_i$ for $i = 0, 1, \ldots, n$ be the $n+1$ control points for a B-spline of degree k. To calculate $P(t)$ where $t \in [a, a+1)$, define points with the following recursion:*

$$P_i^{(j)}(t) = \left(1 - \frac{t-i}{k-j+1}\right)P_{i-1}^{(j-1)} + \frac{t-i}{k-j+1}P_i^{(j-1)}$$

Then $P(t) = P_a^{(k)}$.

The algorithm allows us to start with the control points and build up intermediate points until we have the desired $P(t)$.

Example 7.10 (Calculating Points using the de Boor Algorithm). In Example 7.8, we calculated $P(2.5)$ for a uniform quadratic B-spline with four control points. The procedure was to actually find all the blending functions, construct the global description of the spline, plug in t, and finally calculate the affine combination of the control points. Now we try to reach the same result by using the de Boor algorithm.

The control points are

$$P_0^{(0)} = P_0 = \begin{bmatrix} 0 \\ 2 \end{bmatrix} \quad P_1^{(0)} = P_1 = \begin{bmatrix} 2 \\ 5 \end{bmatrix}$$

$$P_2^{(0)} = P_2 = \begin{bmatrix} 3 \\ 4 \end{bmatrix} \quad P_3^{(0)} = P_3 = \begin{bmatrix} 4 \\ 1 \end{bmatrix}$$

Since $t = 2.5$ is in the interval $2 \le t < 3$, only the first three control points are relevant, so we start with these. The intermediate points that we calculate are best given in the following array:

$$\begin{array}{ccc} P_0^{(0)} & P_1^{(0)} & P_2^{(0)} \\ P_1^{(1)} & P_2^{(1)} & \\ P_2^{(2)} & & \end{array}$$

Applying the de Boor algorithm gives the formula for $P_1^{(1)}$.

$$P_1^{(1)}(t) = \left(1 - \frac{t-1}{2-1+1} \right) P_0^{(0)} + \frac{t-1}{2-1+1} P_1^{(0)}$$

$$= \frac{1}{4} \begin{bmatrix} 0 \\ 2 \end{bmatrix} + \frac{3}{4} \begin{bmatrix} 2 \\ 5 \end{bmatrix} = \begin{bmatrix} 1.5 \\ 4.25 \end{bmatrix}$$

The rest of the intermediate points are calculated similarly.

$$P_2^{(1)}(t) \quad = \frac{3}{4} \begin{bmatrix} 2 \\ 5 \end{bmatrix} + \frac{1}{4} \begin{bmatrix} 3 \\ 4 \end{bmatrix} = \begin{bmatrix} 2.25 \\ 4.75 \end{bmatrix}$$

$$P_2^{(2)}(t) = \frac{1}{2} \begin{bmatrix} 1.5 \\ 4.25 \end{bmatrix} + \frac{1}{2} \begin{bmatrix} 2.25 \\ 4.75 \end{bmatrix} = \begin{bmatrix} 1.875 \\ 4.5 \end{bmatrix}$$

The result agrees with the answer in Example 7.8.   □

Example 7.11 (Multiple Control Points). The B-spline certainly depends on the control points, and moving one control point does indeed change the curve locally. In the definition of the B-spline, there is no constraint on where the control points are placed and, in fact, we could place several adjacent control points at the same location.

Suppose we have control points $P_0, P_1, \ldots, P_n$, where $P_2 = P_3 = P_4$. Then the third segment of a uniform quadratic spline will depend only on P_2, P_3, and P_4, and since they are all equal, if $4 \le t < 5$, we have

$$P(t) = N_{(2,2)} P_2 + N_{(3,2)} P_3 + N_{(4,2)} P_4 = P_2$$

The point P_2 is on the spline (for $4 \le t < 5$). Actually, at the endpoints of the interval, one of the blending functions is zero, which means we only need two adjacent control

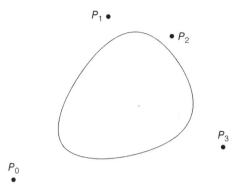

Figure 7.17   Closed B-spline

points to be equal to guarantee that it is on the B-spline. This gives an easy way to ensure that the spline begins and ends at specified points. If the first two control points are equal to, say P, and the last two are equal to Q, then the quadratic B-spline starts at P and ends at Q. In general, repeating a control point k times (we say the *multiplicity* is k) makes a degree k spline go through the point (Figure 7.17).

In a similar vein, repeating control points periodically can give us a closed curve. For example, take the control points $P_n, P_0, P_1, \ldots, P_{n-1}, P_n, P_0$. Both P_0 and P_n are repeated in a periodic (or cyclic) manner. If we put a quadratic B-spline through these points, the first segment depends on P_n, P_0, and P_1, and the last segment depends on P_{n-1}, P_n, and P_0. Looking back at the properties of the quadratic B-spline, we notice that the first point is midway between the first two control points and ends midway between the last two control points. So in the current case, it begins at $\frac{1}{2}P_n + \frac{1}{2}P_0$ and ends at $\frac{1}{2}P_n + \frac{1}{2}P_0$. Therefore, the spline is a closed curve.

For the cubic B-spline, adding P_n to the beginning of the control points and P_0 and P_1 to the end will do the trick. The spline begins at a combination of the first three points and ends at the same combination of the last three points. Here, the cubic spline begins at $\frac{1}{6}P_n + \frac{4}{6}P_0 + \frac{1}{6}P_1$ and ends at the same combination of points.   □

The following result summarizes the key properties of B-splines. (Remember that the splines developed so far were designed using a uniform knot sequence, ensuring that the blending functions were symmetric.)

Result 7.6 (B-Spline Properties).   *A B-spline curve of degree k (order $k + 1$), given by $n + 1$ control points, the knot vector $(0, 1, 2, \ldots, n + k)$, and the expression $P(t) = \sum_{i=0}^{n} N_{(i,k)}(t)P_i$ where $k \leq t < n + k$, satisfies the following properties:*

1. *The blending functions $N_{(i,k)}(t)$ are positive in the interval $i < t < i + k$ and zero elsewhere. This gives the spline local control.*

2. *For $j \leq t < j + 1$, the spline is contained in the convex hull of the control points $P_{(j-k)}, \ldots, P_j$. Hence, the entire spline is contained in the union of these convex hulls.*

3. *The spline has $C^{(k-1)}$ continuity.*

4. *The blending functions sum to 1, giving the spline affine invariance. That is, if T is an affine transformation, then $T(P(t)) = \sum_{i=0}^{n} N_{(i,k)}(t) T(P_i)$.*

5. *A straight line cannot intersect the spline at more points than it intersects the control polygon.*

The convex hull property is again a result of the blending functions summing to 1. Constructing the spline by using the de Boor algorithm shows that the spline points are the result of a sequence of affine combinations. This means that no point is outside the convex hull of an initial subset of control points. For the designer, this property simply gives a visual boundary for where the spline will go.

7.4 NURBS

In an almost never-ending search for more flexibility in curve design, graphics researchers realized that the uniform B-splines with their polynomial blending functions were not quite good enough to do everything a designer might want. Actually, just as with Bézier curves, there is one serious gap. B-splines cannot represent some of the basic conic curves (e.g., ellipses and hyperbolas). The transition to rational B-splines solves that problem and introduces more flexibility by allowing the specification of various weights. Moving beyond uniform knot sequences to arbitrary sequences, the designer now could specify control points, knot vectors, and weights in an effort to fully control the resulting curve. These *nonuniform rational B-splines* (or NURBS) possessed enough flexibility to be seriously considered for modeling systems, and the first such commercial system was introduced in 1983. Most current modeling systems now incorporate NURBS for curve design.

To develop some intuition about the advantage of NURBS over uniform B-splines, recall the recursive formulation of the blending functions given in Equation 7.25. There we assumed that we specified a uniform knot sequence $(0, 1, \ldots, n+k)$. Allowing an arbitrary knot sequence generalizes the recursion formulas and changes the shape of the blending functions. Assume that the knot sequence is now $(t_0, t_1, \ldots, t_{n+k})$.

$$N_{(i,0)}(t) = \begin{cases} 1 & \text{if } t \in [t_i, t_{i+1}) \\ 0 & \text{otherwise} \end{cases}$$

$$N_{(i,k)}(t) = \frac{t - t_i}{t_{i+k} - t_i} N_{(i,k-1)}(t) + \frac{t_{i+k+1} - t}{t_{i+k+1} - t_{i+1}} N_{(i+1,k-1)}(t) \qquad (7.26)$$

Though not immediately clear here, the sum of the blending functions over an interval is still 1.

Example 7.12 (Nonuniform Knot Sequence). As an example of how nonuniform knot sequences effect the shape of the blending functions, consider the knot sequence $(0, 1, 3, 4, 6, 7)$. Recall that this means $t_0 = 0, t_1 = 1, t_2 = 3$, and so on. Using the recursion formulas in Equation 7.26, we begin with the first three $N_{(i,0)}(t)$ functions. (The functions are zero outside the indicated range.)

$$N_{(0,0)}(t) = 1 \text{ if } t \in [0, 1)$$

$$N_{(1,0)}(t) = 1 \text{ if } t \in [1, 3)$$

$$N_{(2,0)}(t) = 1 \text{ if } t \in [3, 4)$$

Now the recursion gives the first two $N_{(i,1)}(t)$ functions.

$$N_{(0,1)}(t) = \frac{t-0}{1-0}N_{(0,0)}(t) + \frac{3-t}{3-1}N_{(1,0)}(t) = \begin{cases} t & \text{if } t \in [0, 1) \\ \dfrac{3-t}{2} & \text{if } t \in [1, 3) \end{cases}$$

$$N_{(1,1)}(t) = \frac{t-1}{2-1}N_{(1,0)}(t) + \frac{4-t}{4-3}N_{(1,1)}(t) = \begin{cases} \dfrac{t-1}{2} & \text{if } t \in [1, 3) \\ 4-t & \text{if } t \in [3, 4) \end{cases}$$

Finally, we calculate $N_{(0,2)}(t)$ to see what the first quadratic blending function looks like.

$$N_{(0,2)}(t) = \frac{t-0}{3-0}N_{(0,1)}(t) + \frac{4-t}{4-1}N_{(1,1)}(t) = \begin{cases} \dfrac{t^2}{3} & \text{if } t \in [0, 1) \\ \dfrac{3t-t^2}{6} + \dfrac{(4-t)(t-1)}{6} & \text{if } t \in [1, 3) \\ \dfrac{(4-t)^2}{3} & \text{if } t \in [3, 4) \end{cases}$$

Figure 7.18 shows that the first-degree blending functions are not symmetric, unlike when we chose the uniform knot sequence $(0, 1, \ldots, n + k)$. Although the second-degree functions are symmetric, adjacent functions are not translates of each other. It takes some experience to guess which knot sequences to try when designing a curve and, in fact, the better approach is to insert or delete a knot watching the incremental changes in the spline. There are algorithms for both these procedures.   □

Example 7.13 (Multiple Knots). Repeated knots (or knots with multiplicity >1) also have interesting effects on a spline. One particularly interesting sequence is $(0, 0, 0, 1, 1, 1)$. With this sequence, look carefully at the definitions to see that $N_{(2,0)}(t) = 1$ in the interval $0 \le t < 1$, but all other $N_{(i,0)}(t)$ functions are zero

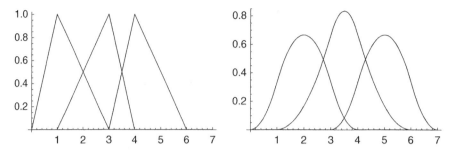

Figure 7.18   Blending functions (linear and quadratic) for a nonuniform knot sequence

everywhere. Then $N_{(1,1)}(t)$ and $N_{(2,1)}(t)$ are the only first-degree blending functions that are nonzero. (To apply the recursion formula, we need to adjust the terms, so division by zero is replaced by a zero coefficient.)

$$N_{(1,1)}(t) = \frac{t-0}{0-0}N_{(1,0)}(t) + \frac{1-t}{1-0}N_{(2,0)}(t) = (1-t) \text{ for } t \in [0,1)$$

$$N_{(2,1)}(t) = \frac{t-0}{1-0}N_{(2,0)}(t) + \frac{1-t}{1-0}N_{(3,0)}(t) = t \text{ for } t \in [0,1)$$

It should be clear that all the nonzero blending functions are nonzero only in the interval $0 \le t < 1$. In particular, all the second-degree blending functions are nonzero only in $0 \le t < 1$.

$$N_{(0,2)}(t) = \frac{t-0}{0-0}N_{(0,1)}(t) + \frac{1-t}{1-0}N_{(1,1)}(t) = (1-t)^2$$

$$N_{(1,2)}(t) = \frac{t-0}{1-0}N_{(1,1)}(t) + \frac{1-t}{1-0}N_{(2,1)}(t) = 2t(1-t)$$

$$N_{(2,2)}(t) = \frac{t-0}{1-0}N_{(2,1)}(t) + \frac{1-t}{1-1}N_{(3,1)}(t) = t^2$$

Surprisingly, these are exactly the blending functions for a Bézier curve of degree 2. It turns out that all knot sequence with zeroes followed by an equal number of 1's gives a Bézier curve. In the current case, we need three control points P_0, P_1, and P_2, and we trace only one segment of the spline as t goes from 0 to 1. The blending functions also ensure that P_0 and P_1 are on the curve. Although this example is a special case (since the Bézier curve shows up), the use of repeating knots at the beginning and end of a sequence can (depending on the rest of the sequence) guarantee that the spline interpolates the first and last control points. This is similar, but not precisely the same, as repeating the control points for the same effect.   □

To move from B-splines to rational B-splines, the blending functions become the quotient of two polynomials. Adding a weight coefficient (w_i) gives more flexibility.

Definition 7.2 (NURBS). *A nonuniform rational B-spline of degree k (order k + 1) is a spline with control points $P_0, P_1, \ldots, P_n$, a knot vector $(t_0, t_2, \ldots, t_{n+k})$, and a set of nonnegative weights $(w_0, w_1, \ldots, w_n)$. Points on the curve are given by*

$$P(t) = \frac{\sum_{i=0}^{n} w_i N_{(i,k)}(t) P_i}{\sum_{i=0}^{n} w_i N_{(i,k)}(t)}$$

One way to understand the definition of a NURBS is to jump up to homogeneous coordinates just as we did for rational Bézier curves. The three-dimensional point $P_i = (x_i, y_i, z_i)$ is the four-dimensional homogeneous point $P_i^h = (w_i x_i, w_i y_i, w_i z_i, w_i)$. The definition of the NURBS becomes

$$P^h(t) = \sum_{i=0}^{n} N_{(i,k)}(t) P_i^h \tag{7.27}$$

Converting the point $P^h(t)$ to Cartesian coordinates involves dividing by the same sum of blending functions as in Definition 7.2. The homogeneous form of the NURBS also implies that the curve is invariant under projective transformations.

It is a little unclear how to select the weights for a NURBS, but certainly if $w_i = 0$, then the point P_i has no effect on the spline. If all the weights are 1, then the spline reduces to the standard B-spline because the denominator in the definition is 1. Suppose now that we start increasing one of the weights, say w_j. By dividing the numerator and denominator of $P(t)$ by w_j, the denominator in Definition 7.2 becomes

$$\text{Denominator} = \sum_{i=0, i \neq j}^{n} \frac{w_i}{w_j} N_{(i,k)}(t) + N_{(j,k)}$$

As w_j increases, the denominator gets closer to $N_{(j,k)}$. For the numerator, the jth term is again singled out from the rest.

$$\text{Numerator} = \sum_{i=0, i \neq j}^{n} \frac{w_i}{w_j} N_{(i,k)}(t) P_i + N_{(j,k)} P_j$$

Here, as w_j increases, the coefficient in front of P_i approaches zero except when $i = j$. The conclusion is that any segment of the spline that depends on P_j will get closer to P_j as w_j grows. The B-spline will be drawn to the point P_j. This is a different type of control than moving the point P_j and thereby pulling the spline in that direction.

Example 7.14 (Producing a Circle with a NURBS). Example 7.7 showed that rational Bézier curves can be used to produce circles and this suggests a plan for using NURBS. Take the control points $P_0 = (1, 0), P_1 = (1, 1), P_2 = (0, 1)$ as three corners of a square. Use the knot sequence $(0, 0, 0, 1, 1, 1)$ and the weights (w_0, w_1, w_2). We know from Example 7.13 that this particular knot sequence produces the quadratic

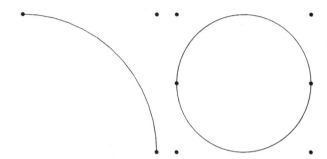

Figure 7.19   NURBS circle

Bézier blending functions, so our NURBS is defined in the interval $0 \leq t \leq 1$ and has the form

$$P(t) = \frac{w_0(1-t)^2 P_0 + w_1 2t(1-t)P_1 + w_2 t^2 P_2}{w_0(1-t)^2 + w_1 2t(1-t) + w_2 t^2}$$

If we set $w_0 = 1$ and $w_2 = 1$, then we are certain that the spline interpolates P_0 and P_2. Now, if we can pull the curve toward P_1 appropriately, it may become the arc of a circle. Plugging in the values of the control points and looking at the parametric expressions for the coordinates x and y, we can determine when $x^2 + y^2 = 1$. Taking $w_1 = \frac{\sqrt{2}}{2}$ works.

Actually, as long as the weights satisfy $c = \frac{w_1^2}{w_0 w_2} < 1$, the NURBS in this example is the arc of an ellipse. If $c = \frac{1}{2}$, then the conic is a circle. So the weights $w_0 = 1$, $w_1 = 1$, and $w_2 = 2$ also produce the arc of a circle.

To draw the complete circle using a NURBS, we can piece together arcs using the technique we just developed, or we can try the seven control points on the right in Figure 7.19 along with the knot sequence $\left(0, 0, 0, \frac{1}{4}, \frac{1}{2}, \frac{1}{2}, \frac{3}{4}, 1, 1, 1\right)$ and the weights $\left(1, \frac{1}{2}, \frac{1}{2}, 1, \frac{1}{2}, \frac{1}{2}, 1\right)$. This is a common representation for the circle, but notice that the storage requirements are considerably larger than when simply storing a center and radius.   □

There is a large theory behind NURBS design, and several references ([5] and [6]) give much of the detail.

7.5   SURFACES

The serious study of curves in computer graphics probably has many roots, but certainly Bézier curves began in automotive design where they served as silhouettes of the real goal, an aesthetically pleasing and aerodynamically efficient car body. Surfaces were the end result. Curves play several roles in computer graphics, and the two key uses are as paths for cameras and objects in animated sequences and as the skeletal elements in surface design. We can think of surfaces as some kind of mesh of curves.

Perhaps the most common surfaces expressed mathematically are the plane ($ax + by + cz + d = 0$) and the sphere ($x^2 + y^2 + z^2 = r^2$). These implicit descriptions hide almost all hints of a curve, but intuition can prompt us to view the plane as a straight line swept in a constant direction and similarly the sphere as a circle rotated around a diameter.

One of the advantages of this viewpoint is that it can make it easier to design a surface and to find an array of points on the surface. Ultimately, in order to present a surface on the computer screen, we need an array of points. If the points are vertices in a triangular mesh, then rendering the surface is a matter of drawing many triangles, suitably shaded, on the screen. Finding the appropriate points is not a trivial task, but if we can visualize a collection of curves on the surface, then incremental points on those curves or even the intersections of many curves may form an array of surface points that can be partitioned into triangles.

Implicit descriptions ($F(x, y, z) = 0$) and explicit descriptions ($z = f(x, y)$) are sufficient for standard surfaces like the plane, sphere, and paraboloid ($z = x^2 + y^2$). One way to draw these in Figure 7.20 is to resort to some behind-the-scene algorithm for finding an appropriate array of curves. For example, with the paraboloid, setting z to the value 4 results in $x^2 + y^2 = 4$, which is a circle of radius 2. Hence, the paraboloid is made up of a system of circles. The radius of the circles at height z is $\sqrt{z}$. Connecting points on the circles forms an array of points which then approximates the surface.

Analogous to the conic curves which are represented by quadratic expressions, a class of surfaces called *quadrics* is represented implicitly by the quadratic form

$$Q(x, y, z) = ax^2 + by^2 + cz^2 + 2dxy + 2exz$$
$$+ 2fyz + 2px + 2qy + 2rz + w = 0 \qquad (7.28)$$

This expression can be written a little more succinctly with matrices:

$$Q(x, y, z) = \begin{bmatrix} x & y & z & 1 \end{bmatrix} \begin{bmatrix} a & d & e & p \\ d & b & f & q \\ e & f & c & r \\ p & q & r & w \end{bmatrix} \begin{bmatrix} x \\ y \\ z \\ 1 \end{bmatrix} \qquad (7.29)$$

Figure 7.20   Sphere, plane, and paraboloid

If the determinant of the 4×4 matrix is not zero, then the surface is said to be *nonsingular* and the determinant of the 3×3 submatrix in the upper left corner determines the type of surface. If the determinant is less than zero, the surface is an ellipsoid, greater than zero indicates a hyperboloid, and equal to zero denotes a paraboloid.

We can identify other classes of surfaces using explicit and implicit descriptions, but just as with conics, a more flexible way to describe surfaces is parametrically. Of the many different parametric schemes, we choose to focus on the Cartesian coordinate system and view each of the coordinates as functions of two parameters, s and t.

$$x = x(s, t)$$

$$y = y(s, t)$$

$$z = z(s, t)$$

Definition 7.3 (Surface). *A parametric surface $S(s,t)$ is a function from a set of parameters (s, t) in the plane to a set of points (x, y, z) in space. Each of the coordinates is a function of the parameters*

$$S(s, t) = (x(s, t), y(s, t), z(s, t))$$

If $s = s^*$ is a fixed value, then $S(s^*, t)$ is a curve on the surface. Similarly, $S(s, t^*)$ is a curve on the surface.

Example 7.15 (Parametric Description of a Plane).   Consider the plane $x + y + z - 1 = 0$. The point $(1, 0, 0)$ is on the plane and the vector $\vec{n} = (1, 1, 1)$ is a normal. Vectors $\vec{v} = (1, -1, 0)$ and $\vec{w} = (1, 1, -2)$ are both perpendicular to the normal and therefore parallel to the plane. The perpendicular lines $(1, 0, 0) + t\vec{v}$ and $(1, 0, 0) + s\vec{w}$ are both on the plane.

One parametric description works like this. The two vectors along with the point $(1, 0, 0)$ effectively form a coordinate system on the plane. This means that $(1, 0, 0) + t\vec{v} + s\vec{w}$ is a general point on the surface. Pulling apart the x, y, and z coordinates gives the plane.

$$S(s, t) = (1 + t + s, -t + s, -2s)$$

If we set $t = t^*$, then

$$S(s, t^*) = (1 + t^* + s, -t^* + s, -2s) = (1 + t^*, -t^*, 0) + s(1, 1, -2)$$

which is a curve on the surface (a line in this case) traced as s varies. Similarly, setting $s = s^*$ gives the curve

$$S(s^*, t) = (1 + s^*, s^*, -2s^*) + t(1, -1, 0)$$

We get a system of intersecting lines by setting each parameter in turn to various fixed values.   □

In general, the curves $S(s, t^*)$ and $S(s^*, t)$ are on the surface, and their intersections $S(s^*, t^*)$ are also on the surface. This array of intersection points can be used for the vertices of triangles that approximate the surface. Assigning the vertices to the triangles is not a trivial task, and, often, when the surface has a sharp bend, we may want smaller triangles to better approximate the surface.

Tangents to the surface are found by taking derivatives, and since the surface is a function of two parameters, we have two partial derivatives. $S_s(s, t)$ is the derivative with respect to s, and $S_t(s, t)$ is the derivative with respect to t. These are both vectors and their cross product gives a normal to the surface; of course, the order in which we take the cross product determines whether the normal is pointing "out" or "in" and we have to keep track of what we want. The unit normal $N(s, t)$ is

$$N(s, t) = \frac{S_s(s, t) \times S_t(s, t)}{|S_s(s, t) \times S_t(s, t)|} \tag{7.30}$$

Example 7.16 (Surface Normal).   Suppose we have the following surface:

$$S(s, t) = (s + t, 3s^2, s - t)$$

If we constrain the parameters to the ranges $0 \le s \le 1$ and $0 \le t \le 1$, we actually have only a piece of a surface which is often called a *patch*. With $t = 0$, the curve $S(s, 0) = (s, 3s^2, s)$ forms one boundary of our patch. Similarly, setting each parameter in turn to one of its extreme values gives the other three boundary curves for the surface.

The partial derivatives are $S_s(s, t) = (1, 6s, 1)$ and $S_t(s, t) = (1, 0, -1)$. The unit normal to the surface at $S(s, t)$ is

$$N(s, t) = \frac{(1, 6s, 1) \times (1, 0, -1)}{|(1, 6s, 1) \times (1, 0, -1)|} = \frac{1}{\sqrt{19}}(-3s, 1, -3s)$$

The four corners of the patch are $S(0, 0) = (0, 0, 0)$, $S(0, 1) = (1, 0, -1)$, $S(1, 0) = (1, 3, 1)$, and $S(1, 1) = (2, 3, 0)$. The normal at each of the first two corners is $(0, \frac{1}{\sqrt{19}}, 0)$, and the normal at the each of the last two corners is $\frac{1}{\sqrt{19}}(-3, 1, -3)$ (Figure 7.21).   □

One effective way to design a surface is to build on the development of Bézier curves. Thinking of a surface as a net of curves in two different directions, the aim is to make the curves $S(s^*, t)$ and $S(s, t^*)$ Bézier curves, and to do this we combine two sets of Bézier curves using a Cartesian product.

Figure 7.21   Surface patch

Definition 7.4 (Cartesian Product Bézier Surface). *A Cartesian product Bézier surface* $S(s, t)$ *is formed from two sets of Bézier curves.*

$$S(s, t) = \sum_{i=0}^{n} \sum_{j=0}^{m} B_{(i,n)}(s)B_{(j,m)}(t)P_{(i,j)}$$

The $P_{(i,j)}$ *form an array of control points.* $B_{(i,n)}$ *and* $B_{(j,m)}$ *are the Bernstein polynomials of degrees n and m. The parameters s and t both range from 0 to 1.*

In the definition, the two blending functions represent two different sets of Bézier curves that are effectively weaved together to form the surface. A different view of this structure is shown by the equivalent matrix formulation.

$$S(s, t) = \begin{bmatrix} 1 & s & s^2 & \cdots & s^n \end{bmatrix} B(n) \begin{bmatrix} P_{(0,0)} & \cdots & P_{(0,m)} \\ P_{(1,0)} & \cdots & P_{(1,m)} \\ P_{(2,0)} & \cdots & P_{(2,m)} \\ \vdots & \vdots & \vdots \\ P_{(n,0)} & \cdots & P_{(n,m)} \end{bmatrix} B(m) \begin{bmatrix} 1 \\ t \\ t^2 \\ \vdots \\ t^n \end{bmatrix}$$

The matrices $B(n)$ and $B(m)$ are the matrices of coefficients for the Bernstein polynomials of degrees n and m, respectively. (These matrices are symmetric around their main diagonal.)

Example 7.17 (Bicubic Bézier Patch). It takes four control points to determine a cubic Bézier curve and therefore $n = m = 4$, leading to $4 \times 4 = 16$ control points to determine a Bézier patch. Curves in either direction are cubic curves. This is a bicubic patch.

$$S(s, t) = \sum_{i=0}^{3} \sum_{j=0}^{3} B_{(i,3)}(s)B_{(j,3)}(t)P_{(i,j)}$$

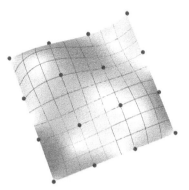

Figure 7.22 Bicubic Bézier patch

When $s = 0$, $B_{(0,3)}(0) = 1$ and $B_{(i,3)}(0) = 0$ otherwise. Similar equalities hold when $t = 0$. Therefore, when both s and t are zero, only one term in the double sum is positive, and $Q(0,0) = P_{(0,0)}$. The same reasoning shows that the surface goes through the four corner points on the patch. The eight other boundary points control the shape of the boundary curves and the four interior points determine the interior curvature of the surface. An example of a bicubic patch is shown in Figure 7.22.

The matrix description of the bicubic patch depends on the coefficient matrix $B(3)$.

$$B(3) = \begin{bmatrix} 1 & 0 & 0 & 0 \\ -3 & 3 & 0 & 0 \\ 3 & -6 & 3 & 0 \\ -1 & 3 & -3 & 1 \end{bmatrix}$$

Letting P be the matrix of 16 control points, we have the full matrix description:

$$S(s,t) = \begin{bmatrix} 1 & s & s^2 & s^3 \end{bmatrix} B(3)PB(3) \begin{bmatrix} 1 \\ t \\ t^2 \\ t^3 \end{bmatrix} \tag{7.31}$$

The four boundary curves for the patch are $S(0,t)$, $S(1,t)$, $S(s,0)$, and $S(s,1)$. The control points for the first boundary curve are in the first row of the control point matrix and the other boundary curves correspond to the last row, first column, and last column. Actually, all curves of the form $S(s^*,t)$ or $S(s,t^*)$ are Bézier curves; however, it is not immediately apparent what the control points are.

Both parameters s and t range from 0 to 1. Dividing this range up into equal increments will give a mesh of points on the surface and delineate an array of quadrilaterals. The quadrilaterals are not necessarily flat (all vertices coplanar), but a diagonal divides each quadrilateral into two flat triangles.

In order to fit two bicubic Bézier patches together, the two adjacent boundary curves must match. This simply involves matching the four control points on the edge. However, to get C^1 continuity, the surface normals on the edges must match, and this can be achieved by adjusting the control points adjacent to the joining edge so that the control polygon line segments that cross the boundary are collinear. This is the way we matched two Bézier curves for C^1 continuity.

The iconic Utah teapot, a model used in the earlier days of computer graphics to test rendering algorithms, was originally designed as a series of bicubic Bézier patches each with 16 control points.   □

The idea of constructing a surface as a Cartesian product of two sets of curves can be extended from Bézier curves to rational Bézier curves to B-splines to rational B-splines and finally to NURBS.

Definition 7.5 (NURBS Surface). *A Cartesian product NURBS surface, $S(s,t)$, is formed from two sets of NURBS curves.*

$$S(s,t) = \frac{\sum_{i=0}^{n} \sum_{j=0}^{m} w_{(i,j)} N_{(i,k)}(s) N_{(j,h)}(t) P_{(i,j)}}{\sum_{i=0}^{n} \sum_{j=0}^{m} w_{(i,j)} N_{(i,k)}(s) N_{(j,h)}(t)}$$

The $P_{(i,j)}$'s form an array of control points and $w_{(i,j)}$'s are the weights. $N_{(i,k)}$ and $N_{(j,h)}$ are the blending functions of degrees k and h based on knot vectors for the two sets of curves.

Notice that the two blending functions in the definition correspond to two sets of NURBS. They may have different degrees along with different knot sequences. However, their control points and weights are tied together to construct a surface. It is not surprising that the NURBS surface (and the Bézier surfaces) inherits properties from its (their) constituent curves. In particular, we have the following result:

Result 7.7 (NURBS Surface Properties). *Surfaces constructed using the Cartesian product of NURBS satisfy the following properties:*

1. *Local Control. Each of the blending functions is nonzero only in an interval leading to only local changes when a control point is moved.*
2. *Convex Hull. Assuming positive weights, then as in Result 7.6, the curves and hence the surface locally stay within the convex hull of a subset of control points and therefore within the union of all these convex hulls.*
3. *Affine Invariance. With affine combinations of control points, affine transformations of the surface gives the same result as transforming the control points and constructing the surface from the transformed points.*
4. *Projective Invariance. Transforming a surface using homogeneous coordinates and a projective transformation is equivalent to transforming the homogeneous points first and then constructing the surface.*

NURBS surfaces offer plenty of flexibility when designing complex objects. By choosing the control points, knot sequences, and weights, the designer has many degrees of freedom in crafting custom patches. However, building entire objects (or characters) by combining many patches is often nontrivial. There are a variety of techniques for constructing additional surfaces to join two patches together, and many details still can go wrong. Gaps between surfaces as well as awkward curvatures especially when objects are transformed can frustrate designers and offer new mathematical problems for researchers.

NURBS surfaces are fairly general, and in order to develop design techniques, it helps to categorize the surfaces. One useful category includes surfaces that can be constructed by continuously transforming a particular curve. Just as a plane can be thought of as a linear curve translated in a fixed direction, more complicated surfaces can be thought of as a NURBS curve transformed by rotations, translations, or scalings. Such surfaces are usually called *swept surfaces* because a curve sweeps in a particular way to form the surface.

To more carefully describe a swept surface, start with a particular curve parameterized by t, say $C(t) = (C_x(t), C_y(t), C_z(t))$. Then apply a transformation $T(s)$ to it. The transformation is parameterized by s, meaning that it possibly changes with s. If we use homogeneous coordinates for the points on the curve, then the affine transform $T(s)$ can be a 4×4 matrix. The swept surface is $S(s, t) = T(s)C(t)$.

Example 7.18 (Extruded Surfaces).   Take a three-dimensional curve $C(t)$ and a vector $\vec{v} = (v_1, v_2, v_3)$. Assuming we are using homogeneous coordinates, let transformation $T(s)$ be a translation represented by the following matrix:

$$T(s) = \begin{bmatrix} 1 & 0 & 0 & sv_1 \\ 0 & 1 & 0 & sv_2 \\ 0 & 0 & 1 & sv_3 \\ 0 & 0 & 0 & 1 \end{bmatrix}$$

As s ranges from 0 to 1, the surface $S(s, t) = T(s)C(t)$ translates the curve $C(t)$ in the direction $\vec{v}$. The result is an *extruded* surface. To avoid singularities in the surface, we pick $\vec{v}$ so that the curve does not intersect itself as it is translated (Figure 7.23).

We can describe this extruded surface as a NURBS surface by considering two curves: the curve $C(t)$ as above, and the curve $D(t)$ which is simply a line segment

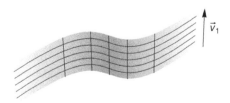

Figure 7.23   Extruded surface

in the direction of $\vec{v}$. The curve $C(t)$ is a NURBS of degree k with control points $C_0, C_1, \ldots, C_n$, with some knot vector and with weights w_i. Curve $D(t)$ is a degree 1 curve with knot vector $(0, 0, 1, 1)$ (ensuring that it interpolates its control points), and the weights all equal to 1. The control points depend on $C(t)$ and so are C_0 and $C_0 + \vec{v}$.

Define the surface control points by $P_{(i,0)} = C_i$ and $P_{(i,1)} = C_i + \vec{v}$. Set new weights $u_{(i,j)} = u_i$. Now the surface is

$$S(s,t) = \frac{\sum_{i=0}^{n} \sum_{j=0}^{1} u_{(i,j)} N_{(i,k)}(s) N_{(j,1)}(t) P_{(i,j)}}{\sum_{i=0}^{n} \sum_{j=0}^{1} u_{(i,j)} N_{(i,k)}(s) N_{(j,1)}(t)}$$

The blending functions are those $(N_{(i,k)})$ for degree k corresponding to the curve $C(t)$ and those $(N_{j,1})$ for degree 1 corresponding to the line segment we traverse as s goes from 0 to 1. The result is the same extruded surface as before. □

Example 7.19 (Surface of Revolution). Another subcategory of swept surfaces includes those surfaces constructed by rotating a profile curve around an axis. These are *surfaces of revolution*. The affine transform T(s) is now a rotation. Usually, we take a curve $C(t)$ lying in a plane, perhaps the xy plane. Pick an axis in the same plane (take the x-axis). Since our transformation does not include a translation, we can stick with regular Cartesian coordinates instead of homogeneous coordinates and use the following matrix:

$$T(s) = \begin{bmatrix} 1 & 0 & 0 \\ 0 & \cos(2\pi s) & \sin(2\pi s) \\ 0 & -\sin(2\pi s) & \cos(2\pi s) \end{bmatrix}$$

The surface $S(s,t) = T(s)C(t)$ is a surface of revolution (Figure 7.24).

Again, this type of surface can be expressed as a NURBS surface. The basic idea is straightforward, although the details require a little attention. The surface is formed using the Cartesian product of two curves. The first is a profile curve and the second is a circle.

Recall that one way to form a NURBS circle is to use control points (total of seven) forming a square. We construct an array of these squares corresponding to each control point from the profile curve. The squares have different sizes because the cross-sectional circles have different radii. The knot sequences are just those for the profile curve and the circle. The weights used in the definition of the surface are the products of the weights for the individual curves. □

Example 7.20 (Ruled Surfaces). For some surfaces, line segments lie entirely on the surface. A plane is one example, but so is a cylinder, where the line segments run along the length of the cylinder, and so is any extruded surface. Such surfaces can be generated by applying affine transformations to a line segment and are therefore called *ruled surfaces*. Another way to construct a ruled surface is to draw line

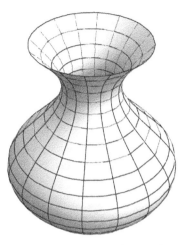

Figure 7.24   Surface of revolution

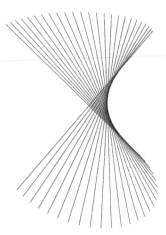

Figure 7.25   Ruled surface

segments between two boundary curves. If two curves, $C_1(s)$ and $C_2(s)$, both depend on the same parameter, then the following parametric description produces a ruled surface (Figure 7.25):

$$S(s, t) = (1 - t)C_1(s) + tC_2(s) \tag{7.32}$$

If the two boundary curves are both NURBS of the same degree with the same knot sequence, then using the these curves along a line segment produces the Cartesian product NURBS surface.

$$S(s, t) = \frac{\sum_{i=0}^{n} \sum_{j=0}^{1} u_{(i,j)} N_{(i,k)}(s) N_{(j,1)}(t) P_{(i,j)}}{\sum_{i=0}^{n} \sum_{j=0}^{1} u_{(i,j)} N_{(i,k)}(s) N_{(j,1)}(t)}$$

This expression is the same as for the extruded surface, but this time the control points are defined a little differently. If the control points for the first boundary curve are $Q_0, Q_1, \dots, Q_n$ and those for the second are $R_0, R_1, \dots, R_n$, then the surface points are $P_{(i,0)} = Q_i$ and $P_{(i,1)} = R_i$. We use the common knot sequence for the boundary curves along with the sequence $(0, 0, 1, 1)$ for the interpolating line segment. If the first boundary curve has weights q_i and the second has weights r_i, then the surface weights are $w_{(i,0)} = q_i$ and $w_{(i,1)} = r_i$.   □

From these examples of swept surfaces, it appears that we could generalize even further and sweep an arbitrary curve along another curve. The idea here is that we are translating one curve by an amount specified by the second curve: $S(s, t) = C_1(s) + C_2(t)$. If the two curves are NURBS, we can form a NURBS surface where the control points are $P_{(i,j)} = Q_i + R_j$, the sum of the control points from each curve, and the weights are the products, $w_{(i,j)} = q_i r_j$. It takes practice to design with such curves because it is easy to generate singularities including self-intersections.

7.6 COMPLEMENTS AND DETAILS

7.6.1 Adding Control Points to Bézier Curves

When designing with Bézier curves, there may be the need for even more control over the curve. It would be convenient to add a control point without disturbing the curve as it currently stands; in effect, we are raising the degree of the curve. Then, with one more control point, there is just a little more flexibility in tweaking the shape of the curve. To analyze the situation, let $P_0, P_1, \dots, P_n$ be the original $n + 1$ control points leading to the curve $P(t) = \sum_{i=0}^{n} B_{(i,n)}(t)P_i$. We want $n + 2$ control points $Q_0, Q_1, \dots, Q_{n+1}$ with the resulting curve $Q(t) = \sum_{i=0}^{n+1} B_{(i,n+1)}(t)Q_i$. The two curves should be identical, so $Q(t) = P(t)$ for $0 \leq t \leq 1$.

Substituting the correct blending functions into the equation gives

$$\sum_{i=0}^{n+1} \binom{n+1}{i} (1-t)^{(n+1-i)} t^i Q_i = \sum_{i=0}^{n} \binom{n}{i} (1-t)^{(n-i)} t^i P_i \qquad (7.33)$$

At this stage of the game, it looks as though we need a completely new set of control points Q_i, but since we know the curves interpolate the first and last points, we know $Q_0 = P_0$ and $Q_{n+1} = P_n$. Although some cleverly chosen algebraic manipulations can lead us directly to expressions for the other Q_i, it perhaps gives a little better picture of the situation to work backwards from the solution. Since we have the first and last points, there are n more points to find. There are also n line segments $P_0 P_1, P_1 P_2, \dots, P_{n-1} P_n$, so we might guess that each segment contains a new point Q_i. It turns out that the correct guess is the following:

$$Q_i = \frac{i}{n+1} P_{i-1} + \left(1 - \frac{i}{n+1}\right) P_i \quad \text{for } 1 \leq i \leq n \qquad (7.34)$$

Substitute this expression for the points Q_i into Equation 7.33. To verify that we indeed have the correct points, we need to show that the coefficient for P_i on the right in Equation 7.33 is the same as that for P_i on the left. Focusing on $1 \le i < n$, notice that only Q_i and Q_{i+1} will have P_i in their expressions. On the left of Equation 7.33, let C_i designate the coefficient of P_i in the Q_i term, and let C_{i+1} designate the coefficient of P_i in the Q_{i+1} term.

$$C_i = \left(1 - \frac{i}{n+1}\right)\binom{n+1}{i}(1-t)^{(n+1-i)}t^i$$

$$= \frac{n+1-i}{n+1}\frac{(n+1)!}{(n+1-i)!i!}(1-t)^{(n+1-i)}t^i = \binom{n+1}{i}(1-t)^{(n+1-i)}t^i$$

$$C_{i+1} = \frac{i+1}{n+1}\binom{n+1}{i+1}(1-t)^{(n+1-(i+1))}t^{(i+1)}$$

$$= \frac{i+1}{n+1}\frac{(n+1)!}{(n-i)!(i+1)!}(1-t)^{(n-i)}t^{(i+1)} = \binom{n+1}{i}(1-t)^{(n-i)}t^{(i+1)}$$

$$C_i + C_{i+1} = \binom{n+1}{i}((1-t)^{(n+1-i)}t^i + (1-t)^{(n-i)}t^{(i+1)})$$

$$= \binom{n+1}{i}(1-t)^{(n-i)}t^i((1-t)+t) = \binom{n+1}{i}(1-t)^{(n-i)}t^i$$

The coefficient $C_i + C_{i=1}$ is exactly the same as that for P_i on the right in Equation 7.33.

The points P_0 and P_n have to be treated just a little differently from the other points but the result is the same, and the verification is left as an exercise. For $1 \le i \le n$, the Q_i's are successive combinations of the P_i's, and together with the first and last points (Q_0 and Q_1) we have $n+2$ control points. The resulting Bézier curve has degree $n+1$ and matches the original curve of degree n. Now there is added flexibility because theere is one more control point to adjust if necessary.

Example 7.21 (Adding a Point to a Quadratic Bézier Curve). Let the control points for a Bézier curve be $P_0 = (1, 1)$, $P_1 = (3, 6)$, and $P_2 = (4, 2)$. The curve is then $P(t) = (1-t)^2 P_0 + 2t(1-t)P_1 + t^2 P_2$, and the two coordinate functions are

$$x(t) = (1-t)^2 + 6t(1-t) + 4t^2 = 1 + 4t - t^2$$
$$y(t) = (1-t)^2 + 12t(1-t) + 2t^2 = 1 + 10t - 9t^2$$

Suppose we need more flexibility, so we wish to add a control point; the new set of control points is Q_0, Q_1, Q_2, Q_3. These points have to produce exactly the curve we currently have. Since we are using Bézier curves, we know $Q_0 = P_0$ and $Q_3 = P_2$. Otherwise, we have

$$Q_1 = \frac{1}{3}P_0 + \left(1 - \frac{1}{3}\right)P_1 = \left(\frac{7}{3}, \frac{13}{3}\right)$$

$$Q_2 = \frac{2}{3}P_1 + \left(1 - \frac{2}{3}\right)P_2 = \left(\frac{10}{3}, \frac{14}{3}\right)$$

The new curve is $Q(t) = (1 - t)^3 Q_0 + 3(1 - t)^2 t Q_1 + 3(1 - t)t^2 Q_2 + t^3 Q_3$. The corresponding coordinate functions are

$$x(t) = (1 - t)^3 (1) + 3(1 - t)^2 t \left(\frac{7}{3}\right) + 3(1 - t)t^2 \left(\frac{10}{3}\right) + t^3(4)$$

$$= 1 + 4t - t^2$$

$$y(t) = (1 - t)^3 (1) + 3(1 - t)^2 t \left(\frac{13}{3}\right) + 3(1 - t)t^2 \left(\frac{14}{3}\right) + t^3(2)$$

$$= 1 + 10t - 9t^2$$

The coordinate functions are exactly equal to those for the original curve. These four new points define the original curve and give us one more control point to work with.   □

7.6.2 Quadratic B-Spline Blending Functions

In Section 7.3.2, a blending function for the quadratic B-spline was divided into three sections, namely q_1, q_2, and q_3. When put together in the order given, the pieces form one complete blending function which is then translated to form all the other blending functions. For convenience, we look at the three pieces in the interval $0 \le t < 1$ (Figure 7.13). Each piece is a quadratic function that satisfies the criteria given in the section. To specify each piece, start with the following descriptions:

$$q_1(t) = a_1 + b_1 t + c_1 t^2$$

$$q_2(t) = a_2 + b_2 t + c_2 t^2$$

$$q_3(t) = a_3 + b_3 t + c_3 t^2$$

There are nine unknown coefficients in these descriptions that we need to find. Call the first and second segments of the quadratic B-spline $S_1(t)$ and $S_2(t)$.

$$S_1(t) = q_3(t)P_0 + q_2(t)P_1 + q_1(t)P_2(t)$$

$$S_2(t) = q_3(t)P_1 + q_2(t)P_2 + q_1(t)P_3(t)$$

For both segments, we have translated the blending functions to the interval $0 \le t < 1$ to make the algebraic manipulations a little simpler and transparent. (For the actual spline, we use the interval $2 \le t \le n + 2$ when we have $n + 1$ control points.) Now we recall the criteria that govern how the segments should fit together.

1. Since the first spline segment ends (at $t = 1$) where the second segment begins $(t = 0)$, we have $S_1(1) = S_2(0)$.

$$(a_3 + b_3 + c_3)P_0 + (a_2 + b_2 + c_2)P_1 + (a_1 + b_1 + c_1)P_2$$
$$= a_3P_1 + a_2P_2 + a_1P_3$$

This equation must remain true for any choice of P_0, so it follows that $a_3 + b_3 + c_3 = 0$. Moreover, since the equation holds for all choices of P_3, it must also be true that $a_1 = 0$. Points P_1 and P_2 are also arbitrary, so similar arguments can be made about their coefficients. In summary, we have

$$a_3 + b_3 + c_3 = 0$$
$$a_2 + b_2 + c_2 = a_3$$
$$a_1 + b_1 + c_1 = a_2$$
$$a_1 = 0$$

2. For C^1 continuity, the derivatives where the segments meet must be equal, so $S_1'(1) = S_2'(0)$.

$$(b_3 + 2c_3)P_0 + (b_2 + 2c_2)P_1 + (b_1 + 2c_1)P_2 = b_3P_1 + b_2P_2 + b_1P_3$$

Again, since all points can be arbitrary, we conclude that

$$b_3 + 2c_3 = 0$$
$$b_2 + 2c_2 = b_3$$
$$b_1 + 2c_1 = b_2$$
$$b_1 = 0$$

3. We have eight equations so far, but since we must have an affine combination, the blending functions sum to 1, giving

$$(a_3 + b_3t + c_3t^2) + (a_2 + b_2t + c_2t^2) + (a_1 + b_1t + c_1t^2) = 1$$

This equation has a polynomial on both sides and is true for all t. This means we have three equations:

$$a_3 + a_2 + a_1 = 1$$
$$b_3 + b_2 + b_1 = 0$$
$$c_3 + c_2 + c_1 = 0$$

4. We now have 11 equations for the nine unknowns, but not all of the equations are independent. Solving algebraically gives the unique nine values.

$$q_1(t) = 0 + (0)t + \frac{1}{2}t^2$$

$$q_2(t) = \frac{1}{2} + (1)t + (-1)t^2$$

$$q_3(t) = \frac{1}{2} + (-1)t + \frac{1}{2}t^2$$

To describe $N_{(0,2)}(t)$, the piece $q_2(t)$ needs to be translated one interval to the left by replacing t with $t - 1$. The third piece $q_3(t)$ must be translated by replacing t with $t - 2$.

$$N_{(0,2)}(t) = \begin{cases} 0 & \text{if } t < 0; \\ \frac{1}{2}t^2 & \text{if } t \in [0, 1); \\ \frac{1}{2} + (t - 1) - (t - 1)^2 & \text{if } t \in [1, 2); \\ \frac{1}{2} - (t - 2) + \frac{1}{2}(t - 2)^2 & \text{if } t \in [2, 3); \\ 0 & \text{if } 3 \geq t; \end{cases}$$

The rest of the blending functions are translates of this one.

7.7 EXERCISES

1. Example 7.1 shows the general form of a conic. Suppose we translate the curve by making the substitution $x^* = x - h$ and $y^* = y - k$. Show that we can pick h and k appropriately so the general form of the new curve has $D^* = E^* = 0$. Also show that $A^* = A$, $B^* = B$, and $C^* = C$.

2. Assuming that the conic is not a pair of lines, the quantity $\delta = B^2 - 4AC$ determines whether it is a parabola ($\delta = 0$), ellipse ($\delta < 0$), or hyperbola ($\delta > 0$). Show that if the conic is a parabola, then $Ax^2 + Bxy + Cy^2$ is a perfect square.

3. Consider the ellipse $4x^2 + y^2 = 1$. Using the technique shown in Example 7.3, rotate the axes $\pi/6$ radians counterclockwise and give the new description of the ellipse.

4. Given a conic description $Ax^2 + Bxy + Cy^2 + Dx + Ey + F = 0$, show that an axis rotation of θ where $\cot(\frac{A-C}{B})$ will make $B = 0$.

5. The circle of radius a can be parameterized as $x = a\cos(t)$ and $y = a\sin(t)$. Find $r(t)$ and $r'(t)$. Determine the unit tangent $T(t)$ and find its value at various points on the circle including $t = 0$, $t = \pi/4$, and $t = \pi/2$.

6. Verify that the curve in Example 7.6 is a parabola by finding the implicit expression of the curve and then calculating $B^2 - 4AC$ (see Exercise 2).

7. Let $P_0 = (4, 2)$ and $P_1 = (8, -16)$. Consider the curve $P(t) = (1 - t)P_0 + t^2P_1$. This is not an affine combination, but it does interpolate the two points. By translating the points and curve two units to the right, show that this curve is not affine-invariant.

8. Using the Lagrange interpolation method, find a curve through the points $(0, 1)$, $(3, -1)$, $(4, 3)$, and $(6, 5)$. Verify that the blending functions sum to 1.

9. The construction of Bézier curves uses the Bernstein polynomials $B_{(i,n)}(t)$. Determine where these polynomials reach their maximum value.

10. Find the quadratic Bézier curve for the control points $(-2, 4)$, $(1, 3)$, and $(2, -1)$. Find the point on the curve when $t = 0.25$ and verify that the de Casteljau algorithm gives the same point.

11. Find the cubic Bézier curve for the control points $(-3, 0)$, $(-1, 4)$, $(2, 3)$, and $(4, 1)$. Find the slope of the tangents at the first and last control points by finding the derivative of the blending functions. Verify that the slopes match the slopes of the line segments P_0P_1 and P_2P_3.

12. The quadratic Bézier curve has control points $(-2, 4)$, $(1, 3)$, and $(2, -1)$. Consider this curve as the first segment in a combination curve and find two more control points so that the second segment is formed by a quadratic Bézier curve that joins the first one with C^1 continuity.

13. Give the complete description of the blending function $N_{(n,1)}(t)$.

14. Construct a uniform quadratic B-spline using the control points $(-1, 0)$, $(1, 4)$, $(3, -2)$, and $(4, 3)$. Find the point on the curve at $t = 3.5$.

15. Use the de Boor algorithm to verify the point on the curve at $t = 3.5$ in Exercise 14.

16. Construct a uniform cubic B-spline using the control points $(-1, 0)$, $(1, 4)$, $(3, -2)$, $(4, 3)$, and $(6, 1)$. Find the parametric expressions for the coordinates x and y. Verify by finding the derivatives that, at the joining point between the first and second segment, the first and second derivatives match.

17. Verify that the blending functions for the uniform cubic B-spline sum to 1.

18. In Example 7.14, a NURBS was used to produce one-quarter of a circle. Show that selecting the weights $w_0 = 1$, $w_1 = \sqrt{2}/2$, and $w_2 = 1$ does produce an arc of a circle.

19. In Example 7.15, use the vectors $\vec{v} = (1, 0, -1)$ and $\vec{w} = (3, -2, -1)$ to parameterize the plane. Show that both parameter descriptions do give all the points on the plane. Do any two vectors parallel to the plane work to parameterize the plane?

20. From the definition of a Cartesian product Bézier surface, show that the bicubic Bézier patch does interpolate the four corner control points. Also show that each of the four boundary curves is a (spatial) Bézier curve.

21. In the derivation for adding a control point to a Bézier curve, it was shown that the coefficients for P_i ($1 \leq i < 1$) match on both side of Equation 7.33. Now verify that the coefficients for both P_0 and P_n also match on both sides of the equation.

22. After finding the quadratic Bézier curve for the control points $(-2, 4)$, $(1, 3)$, and $(2, -1)$, add a fourth control point keeping the same curve. Verify that it is the same curve.

23. Solve the coefficient equations for the quadratic B-spline to verify the formulas for $q_1(t)$, $q_2(t)$, and $q_3(t)$.

7.7.1 Programming Exercises

1. Write a program to plot two-dimensional parametric curves. Use the program to verify the parametric descriptions of ellipses and hyperbolas given in Example 7.1.

2. Use the program from Exercise 1 to investigate curves generated by the following parametric description:

$$x = A_1 \sin(mt + d) \qquad y = A_2 \sin(nt)$$

The quantities A_1, A_2, m, n, and d are all constants. In particular, determine the curve's behavior as the ratio m/n changes. These figures arise in various harmonic motions (both mechanical and electrical) and are named after Jules Lissajous who studied them in 1857.

3. Write a program for designing standard Bézier curves. The program inputs the control points, draws the curve, and then updates the curve as the control points are moved.

8

VISIBILITY

Without light, we see nothing, and without turning our heads, we only see what is in a cone in front of us. Even if we have sufficient light, a scene with objects suitably arranged, lists of vertices for every triangle on every surface, and a camera peering from some interesting angle, there is still work to be done before we can have an image on the computer screen. Objects either outside the field of view or obscured by another object need to be temporarily culled from the scene, and objects partially in the field of view need to be trimmed (clipped) so that only the visible parts are considered. Then everything needs to be projected onto a two-dimensional window in preparation for transferring it to the actual display screen.

We start this work by mathematically determining what it is we can actually see so that we do not inadvertently draw triangles or edges hidden by other objects. Since there may well be thousands or millions of triangles in the scene, we always have to be attuned to the efficiency of our calculations; designing good, speedy algorithms is also key.

8.1 VIEWING

In an earlier chapter, we examined the camera position and determined how to transform coordinates for object vertices into the camera coordinate system. Recall that, in this system, the camera is sitting at the origin looking down the vector coming from a point in the scene toward the camera. Often the axis determined by this direction

Mathematical Structures for Computer Graphics, First Edition. Steven J. Janke.
© 2015 John Wiley & Sons, Inc. Published 2015 by John Wiley & Sons, Inc.

vector is called z, so the camera is looking down the z-axis toward the negative portion. The up-vector determines the y-axis and the third perpendicular axis forming a right-handed system is x. The camera analogy is slightly misleading inasmuch as we imagine looking through a window placed somewhere in front of the camera. (It is as though we have put the camera's film plane or digital sensors in front of the camera.) The plane holding the window where the scene image will be projected is called the *view plane* and it is perpendicular to the z-axis. The window is usually rectangular and centered on the z-axis.

The parts of the scene we actually see depend, of course, on the direction the camera is pointing, but also on the size of the window and the distance between the camera and the view plane. In keeping with the camera analogy, we might say the view depends on the type of lens we have; it is, for example, a wide-angle lens or a telephoto lens. For anything in front of the view plane, we assume it cannot be seen, and for anything beyond a specified *far plane* we also assume it cannot be seen. With the rectangular window plus a *near plane* (which here coincides with the view plane) and a far plane (which limits distant objects), the visible segment of the scene falls within a region shaped like a truncated pyramid. This is called the *view frustum*.

It is not strictly necessary that the view plane and the near plane coincide, but it is both convenient and commonly implemented in graphics systems. Each vertex in the scene that can be seen is projected onto the window in the view plane. The far plane limits the vertices we have to project, and the general idea is that any object beyond the far plane projects into a very small object on the screen and perhaps does not have to be rendered. If this is unacceptable, the far plane can be moved to infinity. The frustum displayed in Figure 8.1 is a symmetric one because the z-axis goes through the center of the window. Again, this symmetry is not necessary. In fact, to introduce just a little more flexibility, the window in the view plane is occasionally off center, which allows for a little more adjustment of the view. Deviation from the symmetric frustum can often be accommodated by transforming the scene or the camera coordinate system.

To carefully describe the shape of the frustum, notice that six planes form the boundary. We label the planes left, right, top, bottom, near, and far. The camera is at the origin, and the near plane crosses the z-axis at coordinate z_n. Because of the orientation of the z-axis, z_n is a negative number. The equation of the near plane is $z = z_n$, and if we select normal vectors pointing into the frustum, the unit normal vector for the near plane is $(0, 0, -1)$. Similarly, the far plane is positioned at z_f and has equation $z = z_f$ with unit normal vector $(0, 0, 1)$. The four side planes depend on whether we have a wide or narrow field of view. If the window on the view plane

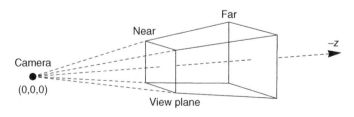

Figure 8.1 View frustum

(hence, on the near plane) has width w and height h, then the angle (α) formed at the camera position by the left and right planes satisfies

$$\tan\left(\frac{\alpha}{2}\right) = \frac{w}{2z_n} \implies \alpha = 2\tan^{-1}\left(\frac{w}{2z_n}\right)$$

This is the horizontal field of view angle. For the analogous vertical angle (β), we have

$$\tan\left(\frac{\beta}{2}\right) = \frac{h}{2z_n} \implies \beta = 2\tan^{-1}\left(\frac{h}{2z_n}\right)$$

The ratio of window width to height is called the *aspect ratio* which we denote by a_r. If we wish, we can express angle β in terms of the window width:

$$\beta = 2\tan^{-1}\left(\frac{w}{2a_r z_n}\right)$$

To calculate the normal vector for the left plane, take the vector $(-\frac{w}{2}, 0, z_n)$ which lies in the left plane and rotate it clockwise around the y-axis by $\pi/2$. The result is $(-z_n, 0, -\frac{w}{2})$, and when normalized it becomes

$$\vec{n}_l = \frac{1}{\sqrt{z_n^2 + \frac{w^2}{4}}}\left(-z_n, 0, -\frac{w}{2}\right)$$

The normals for the other planes can be calculated similarly.

8.2 PERSPECTIVE TRANSFORMATION

The next step in the graphics pipeline applies the perspective transformation to every vertex inside the view frustum. Vertices inside will be projected onto the view plane window and vertices in any object outside the frustum can be disregarded because the object is not visible. Objects that are only partially inside will have to be broken up into visible and nonvisible parts in a process called *clipping*. Thinking ahead, once we have applied the perspective transformation, we will still need to determine whether one object obscures or partially obscures another. To do this requires knowing how far the object is from the camera, and since the camera looks down the z-axis, we need to keep track of the z coordinates.

The perspective transformation we developed earlier required homogeneous coordinates, used the xy plane as the view plane, and placed the camera at position e on the z-axis. We formed a 4×4 matrix to represent the transformation.

$$M_{per} = \begin{bmatrix} 1 & 0 & 0 & 0 \\ 0 & 1 & 0 & 0 \\ 0 & 0 & 0 & 0 \\ 0 & 0 & -\frac{1}{e} & 1 \end{bmatrix}$$

The matrix sends the point $(x, y, z, 1)$ with homogeneous coordinates to the point $(x, y, 0, (e - 1)/e)$ with the z coordinate equal to zero, reminding us that we are in the xy plane for the final image. Although this transformation captures the idea of perspective, we can customize it for the view frustum. We can also be a little more careful in our treatment of the z coordinate to make subsequent operations on the graphics pipeline more efficient. There are various ways we can proceed with a customized transformation, but as graphics systems have developed, one or two forms for the perspective transformation have emerged as particularly useful, so we will use one of these.

If we apply the generic perspective transformation, all vertices in the view frustum will end up on the view plane window. If we also preserve the original z coordinate, we will end up with a rectangular box instead of a truncated pyramid. Then, if we normalize all the coordinates to fit in the range -1 to 1, we will turn the box into a cube centered at the origin. Points in the cube are called *normalized device coordinates* and they can be transformed in various ways to appropriately fit other display screens. Notice, however, that we will have to recall the original aspect ratio of the view window if we wish to display the image with its original proportions. Normalized device coordinates are just a convenient state for the projected image in preparation for display (Figure 8.2).

Our current orientation of the view frustum respects the camera coordinate system, placing the camera at the origin and setting the view plane to coincide with the near plane ($z = z_n$). Consequently, the perspective transformation should send a point (x, y, z) to a point (x_p, y_p, z_p) on the view plane. We know $z_p = z_n$ and we construct similar triangles to find $\frac{|x|}{|x_p|} = \frac{|z|}{|z_n|}$. The geometry gives ratios of distances, but note in the current orientation of the z-axis, $|z| = -z$ and $|z_n| = -z_n$. Since the sign of x and x_p should match, we get the following perspective equations for points in the view frustum (Figure 8.3):

$$x_p = \frac{x \cdot (-z_n)}{-z} \quad y_p = \frac{y \cdot (-z_n)}{-z} \quad z_p = z_n$$

To construct a matrix for the perspective transformation, we use homogeneous coordinates for our points. For any vertex with Cartesian coordinates (x, y, z), we can take the homogeneous coordinates to be $(x, y, z, 1)$. After the perspective transformation is applied, the fourth homogeneous coordinate may no longer be 1. The point becomes (ux_p, uy_p, uz_p, u), and since both formulas for x_p and y_p divide by $-z$, we will construct the transformation matrix so that $u = -z$. For an arbitrary point

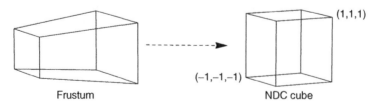

Figure 8.2 View frustum transformation

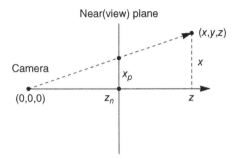

Figure 8.3   Perspective similar triangles

$P = (x, y, z, 1)$, we have a first draft of the transformation matrix.

$$T_{per}(P) = M_{per}P = \begin{bmatrix} -z_n & 0 & 0 & 0 \\ 0 & -z_n & 0 & 0 \\ 0 & 0 & 1 & 0 \\ 0 & 0 & -1 & 0 \end{bmatrix} \begin{bmatrix} x \\ y \\ z \\ 1 \end{bmatrix} = \begin{bmatrix} z_n x_p \\ z_n y_p \\ z \\ -z \end{bmatrix}$$

In this first draft, we are simply preserving the z coordinate. It is still unclear how we should normalize it. The x_p coordinate of any point in the view window satisfies $-\frac{w}{2} \leq x_p \leq \frac{w}{2}$. To scale it so that it falls between -1 and 1, we multiply by $\frac{2}{w}$. Similarly, to scale the y_p coordinate, we multiply by $\frac{2}{h}$. The z coordinate also needs to be scaled and translated, but for the second draft of the matrix we include a scale factor S and a translation amount T_z. This draft of the perspective matrix looks like the following:

$$M_{per} = \begin{bmatrix} -\dfrac{2z_n}{w} & 0 & 0 & 0 \\ 0 & -\dfrac{2z_n}{h} & 0 & 0 \\ 0 & 0 & S & T_z \\ 0 & 0 & -1 & 0 \end{bmatrix}$$

To settle on the S and T_z, we recall that the normalized coordinates we seek fall between -1 and 1. It is also conventional to arrange the transformed z coordinates so that larger values represent points farther from the camera than those with smaller values. This essentially flips the direction of the z-axis. When $z = z_n$, we want the transformed three-dimensional coordinate, designated z^*, to be -1, and when $z = z_f$ we want $z^* = 1$. Following the matrix multiplication gives us the transformed homogeneous coordinate, and division by $-z$ gives z^*.

$$z^* = \frac{Sz + T_z}{-z} \implies -1 = -S - \frac{T_z}{z_n}, \qquad 1 = -S - \frac{T_z}{z_f}$$

Solving for S and T_z gives the customized perspective matrix:

$$
M_{per} = \begin{bmatrix} -\dfrac{2z_n}{w} & 0 & 0 & 0 \\ 0 & -\dfrac{2z_n}{h} & 0 & 0 \\ 0 & 0 & \dfrac{z_n + z_f}{z_n - z_f} & -\dfrac{2z_n z_f}{z_n - z_f} \\ 0 & 0 & -1 & 0 \end{bmatrix}
\tag{8.1}
$$

Remember that the z_n and z_f coordinates are negative; we could have decided to use their absolute value, but then some of the signs in the matrix would change. Applying this transformation turns a symmetric view frustum into a cube of side two centered at the origin. It is noteworthy that, since we essentially flipped the z-axis, the coordinate system of the cube is left-handed while the camera coordinate system is right-handed.

There is one more step we can take to make our transformation a little more flexible. Instead of insisting that the window in the view plane is centered on the z-axis, we can position it off center. If the window is defined by $w_l \le x \le w_r$ and $w_b \le y \le w_t$, then to center the window we need a translation of $-\frac{1}{2}(w_r + w_l)$ in the x direction and $-\frac{1}{2}(w_t + w_b)$ in the y direction. These translation amounts must be multiplied by the scale factors for x and y ($2/(w_r - w_l)$) and they need to be multiplied by $-z$, because conversion from homogeneous to Cartesian coordinates will divide by $-z$. Positioning the translations in the third column guarantees that they will be multiplied by z, so we finish with the -1 multiple. The resulting more general perspective transformation matrix becomes

$$
M_{per} = \begin{bmatrix} \dfrac{-2z_n}{w_r - w_l} & 0 & \dfrac{w_r + w_l}{w_r - w_l} & 0 \\ 0 & \dfrac{-2z_n}{w_t - w_b} & \dfrac{w_t + w_b}{w_t - w_b} & 0 \\ 0 & 0 & \dfrac{z_n + z_f}{z_n - z_f} & -\dfrac{2z_n z_f}{z_n - z_f} \\ 0 & 0 & -1 & 0 \end{bmatrix}
\tag{8.2}
$$

Notice that, if the view window is centered, then $w_r = -w_l$ and $w_b = -w_t$, turning the general matrix into the matrix for the symmetric case. We can also let the far plane move to infinity by letting z_f go to $-\infty$. The resulting matrix is

$$
M_{per} = \begin{bmatrix}
\dfrac{-2z_n}{w_r - w_l} & 0 & \dfrac{w_r + w_l}{w_r - w_l} & 0 \\[2ex]
0 & \dfrac{-2z_n}{w_t - w_b} & \dfrac{w_t + w_b}{w_t - w_b} & 0 \\[2ex]
0 & 0 & -1 & 2z_n \\[1ex]
0 & 0 & -1 & 0
\end{bmatrix}
\tag{8.3}
$$

8.2.1 Clipping

Processing the whole scene is usually computationally expensive, so we try to apply the perspective transformation only to the vertices of objects that have a chance of being seen. Earlier, we may be able to tell that a group of vertices is obviously outside the view frustum by noting perhaps that they are on the wrong side of one of the bounding planes. However, it is also possible that one of the two vertices bounding some edge is inside the viewing volume and one is outside. Then we need to determine the intersection of the edge with a bounding plane and add that intersection as a vertex to the object.

Example 8.1 (Clipping a Line Segment). Consider a symmetric view frustum with near plane $z = -4$ and far plane $z = -10$. The window on the view plane is centered on the z-axis with width 5 and height 3. The two vertices $P_1 = (-1, 8, -5)$ and $P_2 = (1, 1, -7)$ are endpoints for an edge in some object.

Substituting the appropriate values into the matrix given in Equation 8.1 results in the following perspective matrix:

$$
M_{per} = \begin{bmatrix}
\frac{8}{5} & 0 & 0 & 0 \\[1ex]
0 & \frac{8}{3} & 0 & 0 \\[1ex]
0 & 0 & -\frac{7}{3} & -\frac{40}{3} \\[1ex]
0 & 0 & -1 & 0
\end{bmatrix}
$$

Multiplying this matrix by each of the vertices (represented in homogeneous coordinates) gives the transformed vertices. (We place the points as columns in a single matrix to consolidate the computations.)

$$
M_{per} \begin{bmatrix}
-1 & 1 \\
8 & 1 \\
-5 & -7 \\
1 & 1
\end{bmatrix} = \begin{bmatrix}
-1.6 & 1.6 \\
21.33 & 2.67 \\
-1.67 & 3 \\
5 & 7
\end{bmatrix}
$$

Dividing by the fourth homogeneous coordinate converts the transformed vertices back into Cartesian coordinates, giving $P_1^* = (-0.32, 4.27, -0.33)$ and $P_2^* = (0.23, 0.38, 0.43)$. If the original vertices were in the view frustum, these final points should be inside the cube representing normalized device coordinates. Yet, the y coordinate of P_1^* is not in the range -1 to 1; it is too large. We conclude that P_1 is above the top plane of the frustum and therefore the line segment from P_1 to P_2 intersects this plane. (The six planes of the frustum or the cube divide space into 27 sections, and deciding where a point is requires an algorithm. However, in this case, only one coordinate is out of bounds, so the decision is easy.)

Before continuing the calculations to find the intersection between the line segment and the top plane of the frustum, we go back to the homogeneous coordinates. The transformed points became $P_1^{h*} = (-1.6, 21.33, -1.67, 5)$ and $P_2^{h*} = (1.6, 2.67, 3, 7)$. At this stage of the game, without dividing by the fourth coordinate, we can tell that P_1^{h*} is outside the cube for normalized coordinates because $21.33 > 5$. Moreover, we can also determine the point of intersection.

The points P_1^{h*} and P_2^{h*} can be thought of as vectors on lines through the origin in four-dimensional space. Any linear combination of these vectors is on a plane and corresponds to a three-dimensional line through P_1^* and P_2^*. Since any multiple of a homogeneous point is the same point, we can take $P_1^{h*} + kP_2^{h*}$ as an arbitrary point on the line. The top plane of the cube for normalized device coordinates has y coordinate equal to 1, so we find k to give a y coordinate of 1.

$$\frac{21.33 + k(2.67)}{5 + k(7)} = 1 \implies k = 3.77$$

The intersection point R with the top plane is

$$P_1^{h*} + (3.77)P_2^{h*} = (4.43, 31.39, 9.64, 31.39) \implies R = (0.14, 1, 0.31)$$

The line segment $P_2 R$ is the clipped segment, and we found it using homogeneous coordinates alone.

We can verify the result by using the original two points P_1 and P_2. To determine where the segment $P_1 P_2$ intersects the top face, we know that $(1 - t)P_1 + tP_2$ describes the segment and the unit normal to the top plane (pointing inside the frustum) is $\frac{2}{\sqrt{73}}(0, -4, -1.5)$

Letting $\vec{v} = P_2 - P_1$, $\vec{n} = (0, -4, -1.5)$ (no need for the unit normal), and $Q_0 = (0, 1.5, -4)$ as a point on the top plane, we can utilize the formula developed earlier for the intersection of a line and a plane.

$$t = \frac{-\vec{n} \cdot (P_1 - Q_0)}{\vec{n} \cdot \vec{v}}$$
$$= \frac{(0, -4, -1.5) \cdot ((-1, 8, -5) - (0, 1.5, -4))}{(0, -4, -1.5) \cdot (2, -7, -2)} = 0.79$$

This gives the intersection point as $(0.58, 2.47, -6.58)$, and after the perspective transformation we get the homogeneous coordinates $(0.93, 6.58, 2.02, 6.58)$ which convert to the normalized device coordinates $(0.14, 1.0, 0.31)$.   □

The key steps in this last example began with writing the vertices in the homogeneous form. Then we applied the perspective transform. Staying with homogeneous coordinates, we can determine if any point is outside the frustum, and if so, we can clip the appropriate line segment. Of course, we could convert to Cartesian coordinates immediately and proceed with calculations, but saving any computation steps always helps. The clipping step is extended when we need to clip polygons instead of just line segments; then a more complete algorithm is needed.

8.2.2   Interpolating the z Coordinate

It may not be immediately obvious why the transformed z coordinate is particularly useful. After performing the homogeneous divide to reach normalized coordinates, the z coordinate can certainly be used to determine which of the two vertices is further from the camera, but there is more we can do. First, we need to review the effect of the z coordinate on the projected image.

Example 8.2 (Effect of Depth on the Perspective Image).   Refer to the setup in Example 8.1. This time, take three vertices on a line: $P_1 = (-1, 0, -4)$, $P_2 = (0, 0, -7)$, and $P_3 = (1, 0, -10)$. The points P_1 and P_3 form a line segment in the xz plane, P_1 is on the near plane, and P_3 is on the far plane. P_2 is the midpoint of this segment. We can transform each of the points with the perspective matrix. (All three points are arranged as columns in a 4×3 matrix and matrix multiplication transforms all three.)

$$
\begin{bmatrix}
\frac{8}{5} & 0 & 0 & 0 \\
0 & \frac{8}{3} & 0 & 0 \\
0 & 0 & -\frac{7}{3} & -\frac{40}{3} \\
0 & 0 & -1 & 0
\end{bmatrix}
\begin{bmatrix}
-1 & 0 & 1 \\
0 & 0 & 0 \\
-4 & -7 & -10 \\
1 & 1 & 1
\end{bmatrix}
=
\begin{bmatrix}
-1.6 & 0 & 1.6 \\
0 & 0 & 0 \\
-4 & 3 & 10 \\
4 & 7 & 10
\end{bmatrix}
$$

We can check that all three points are in the view frustum by comparing the first three coordinates to the fourth. For P_1, the first three are in the range -4 to 4 so the point is in view. After dividing by the fourth homogeneous coordinate, we have $P_1^* = (-0.4, 0, -1)$, $P_2^* = (0, 0, 0.43)$, and $P_3^* = (0.16, 0, 1)$. These are normalized coordinates, and when displaying on a screen we drop the z coordinate and plot the (x, y) points (possibly scaled): $(-0.4, 0)$, $(0, 0)$, $(0.16, 0)$. It is clear that the projected image of P_2 is not the midpoint of the line segment. The ratio of the interval between the projected images of P_1 and P_2 to the interval between the images of P_2 and P_3 is $\frac{0.4}{0.16} = 2.5$. Larger z coordinates project to smaller intervals on the screen.

The ratio 2.5 is not the same as the ratio of the intervals between the original z coordinates. That ratio is 1.0 because P_2 is the midpoint. However, the ratio of intervals between the normalized z coordinates is $\frac{0.43-(-1)}{1-0.43} \approx 2.5$. Although this seems like a surprise, it does follow because the normalized coordinates are linear functions of the reciprocals of the original z coordinates. The ratio of the intervals between the reciprocals $\left[\frac{(1/4)-(1/7)}{(1/7)-(1/10)}\right]$ is 2.5.   □

The goal currently is to understand how the ratios of intervals between coordinates change when we project onto the display screen. Each of the edges of a triangle in space projects to a line segment on the screen and one common problem is to decide how to color pixels on the segments correctly. We often know the color of the triangle's vertices and consequently the color of line segment endpoints on the screen. However, the colors of points in between the endpoints are unknown. Even if the midpoint of a triangle edge has a color shade that is the average of the colors of the endpoint, the point does not necessarily project to the midpoint on the screen. Simple linear interpolation of colors on the screen will not be correct. By using information about the z coordinates, we can more correctly determine how to interpolate colors.

After multiplying by the perspective transformation matrix, a transformed point holds $-z$ as the fourth coordinate. The third coordinate is the transformed z coordinate, denoted as z^*.

$$z^* = \frac{1}{-z}\left(\frac{z_n + z_f}{z_n - z_f}z - \frac{2z_n z_f}{z_n - z_f}\right) = -S + T_z \cdot \frac{1}{z}$$

Since S and T_z are just constants, we have a linear function of the reciprocal of z.

The first and second coordinates of the transformed point are x^* and y^*. By considering how the perspective matrix acts, we have

$$x^* = \frac{2z_n x}{w(-z)} = k_x \frac{x}{z} \quad \text{and} \quad y^* = \frac{2z_n y}{h(-z)} = k_y \frac{y}{z} \tag{8.4}$$

Let the two points P_1 and P_3 form a line segment. An arbitrary point on that segment is $P_2 = (1-t)P_1 + tP_3 = P_1 + t(P_3 - P_1)$. Following both the x and z coordinates of P_2, we have

$$\frac{x_2 - x_1}{x_3 - x_1} = t = \frac{z_2 - z_1}{z_3 - z_1} \implies x_2 = az_2 + b \tag{8.5}$$

where a and b depend on the coordinates of P_1 and P_3, but are otherwise constant. This is a rather intuitive result because it says that, on a line, the coordinates are linear functions of each other.

When P_1, P_2, and P_3 are projected onto the view window via the perspective transformation, we get the points P_1^*, P_2^*, and P_3^*. The x coordinate of P_2^* satisfies $x_2^* = (1-s)x_1^* + sx_3^*$ and the y coordinate satisfies a similar relation. The problem is that the s parameter here does not necessarily have the same value as the t parameter above. The perspective projection changes the ratios on the line segment.

Since $x_2^* = (1 - s)x_1^* + sx_3^*$, we can use Equation 8.4 and substitute for each x_i^*.

$$k\frac{x_2}{z_2} = (1 - s)k\frac{x_1}{z_1} + sk\frac{x_3}{z_3}$$

$$\implies \frac{x_2}{z_2} = (1 - s)\frac{x_1}{z_1} + s\frac{x_3}{z_3} \tag{8.6}$$

This says that the quantities $\frac{x_i}{z_i}$ are interpolated linearly across a line segment on the screen. In other words, at the midpoint, the ratio of the x to the z coordinate is the average of the ratios at the two endpoints.

According to Equation 8.5 , the x coordinate of any point on a line is a linear function of the z coordinate. Making this substitution gives the following:

$$x^* = k\frac{x}{z} = k\frac{az + b}{z} = k\left(a + b\frac{1}{z}\right) \tag{8.7}$$

Now, if we use this result to replace x_i^* in the relation $x_2^* = (1 - s)x_1^* + sx_3^*$, we have

$$k\left(a + b\frac{1}{z_2}\right) = (1 - s)k\left(a + b\frac{1}{z_1}\right) + sk\left(a + b\frac{1}{z_3}\right)$$

$$\implies \frac{1}{z_2} = (1 - s)\frac{1}{z_1} + s\frac{1}{z_3} \tag{8.8}$$

Both Equations 8.6 and 8.8 show that, on the screen, the ratio of x to z and the reciprocals of z interpolate linearly. Actually, we can generalize to any quantity, like color, that interpolates linearly across a line segment before the perspective transformation is applied.

Suppose that the previous points P_1 and P_3 are vertices with colors c_1 and c_3, respectively. If colors change linearly across the segment, the color c_2 of point P_2 satisfies

$$\frac{c_2 - c_1}{c_3 - c_1} = \frac{z_2 - z_1}{z_3 - z_1}$$

This mimics Equation 8.5, and we can follow the previous derivation to get

$$\frac{c_2}{z_2} = (1 - s)\frac{c_1}{z_1} + s\frac{c_3}{z_3} \tag{8.9}$$

Example 8.3   Continuing with Example 8.2, the projected images of the point P_1 and P_3 are $P_1^* = (-0.4, 0, -1)$ and $P_3^* = (0.16, 0, 1)$. The point P_2 was the midpoint of the original segment, but it did not project to the midpoint of the line on the screen. Using two-dimensional coordinates, that line has endpoints $(-0.4, 0)$ and $(0.16, 0)$.

To determine what point, call it Q, does project to the midpoint, we first interpolate the reciprocals of the z coordinates:

$$\frac{1}{z_Q} = \frac{1}{2} \cdot \frac{1}{z_1} + \frac{1}{2} \cdot \frac{1}{z_3} = \frac{1}{2(-4)} + \frac{1}{2(-10)} = -0.175$$

Taking the reciprocal gives $z_Q = -5.71$; the point with this z coordinate projects to the midpoint of the screen segment. Now, $Q = (1 - t)P_1 + tP_3$, so the z coordinates satisfy

$$-5.71 = (1 - t)(-4) + t(-10)$$

Solving for t gives $t = 0.285$, and using this value to find the other coordinates we get $Q = (-0.43, 0, -5.71)$. The projected value is $Q = (-0.12, 0, -0.01)$, which coincides with the midpoint on the screen.

Imagine that P_1 is colored red with intensity 0.5 (on a scale 0–1.0), and let P_3 be colored with intensity 0.75. Then to find the color of the midpoint on the screen, we interpolate the ratios of intensity to the z coordinate. (Recall that the value of $-z$ is saved as the fourth homogeneous coordinate for both P_1 and P_2.)

$$\frac{c_Q}{z_Q} = \frac{1}{2} \cdot \frac{c_1}{z_1} + \frac{1}{2} \cdot \frac{c_3}{z_3} = \frac{0.5}{-8} + \frac{0.75}{-20} = -0.1$$

Using the value of z_Q found earlier, we get $c_Q \approx 0.57$.   □

8.3   HIDDEN SURFACES

Displaying a scene on the screen requires projecting vertices, drawing edges, and filling in triangles with appropriate shades of color. As we have already noted, the only triangles we are really interested in are those that fall completely or partially inside the view frustum, but there is an additional problem. Some triangles may occlude others because they are closer to the camera and the resulting occluded triangles may be totally hidden or just partially hidden.

Theoretically, we can begin to sort all of this out by first checking every triangle in the scene to see if it is partially in the frustum. Then we could check every triangle to see if it is partially or fully hidden by any other triangle, although it is not immediately clear how we would do this. Yet, this theoretical solution is not practically feasible. There are often on the order of a hundred thousand triangles or more in a complex scene and the computation time starts to get out of hand particularly if we need real-time images. So the solution to the problem hinges on finding efficient ways of structuring the data and efficient mathematical methods for analyzing the geometry.

In determining visibility, the key mathematical question is to decide whether a vertex is on one side of a plane or the other. Recall the equation of a plane,

$\vec{n} \cdot (P - P_0) = 0$, where $\vec{n}$ is a normal to the plane, P_0 is a given point on the plane, and P is an arbitrary point on the plane. The direction of the normal vector $\vec{n}$ distinguishes one side of the plane from the other. If we have $\vec{n} \cdot (P - P_0) > 0$, then the angle between the normal $\vec{n}$ and $\vec{v} = (P - P_0)$ is less than $\pi/2$, and P is on the "positive" side of the plane. Conversely, $\vec{n} \cdot (P - P_0) < 0$ implies that P is on the "negative" side of the plane. If all three vertices of a triangle are on the same side of a plane, then we know the triangle does not intersect the plane.

Earlier we noted how to calculate the inward-pointing normal for each of the six bounding planes of the view frustum. Using the equation of each plane, we can determine on which side of the plane each vertex of a triangle lies. Putting the results together tells us whether the triangle intersects the frustum. We did see earlier that, if we apply the perspective transform, then to determine whether a vertex is inside the frustum we simply determine whether the projected vertex is in the normalized coordinate cube. This is a little easier because the planes are all positioned ± 1 from the origin. The computational cost of the perspective transform, however, complicates this second approach.

If we could determine that a cluster of triangles is not in the frustum before doing much work on the vertices, then we could save the cost of the perspective transform and any incidental calculations that follow. This is the idea behind a *bounding volume*. For example, if we can find a sphere that completely contains some object in our scene, then we could check to see whether the sphere intersects the view frustum. If not, then all the triangles in the object can be disregarded in rendering the scene on the display screen. Finding a bounding sphere is perhaps a little tricky, but once we have it we can determine whether the center of the sphere is closer to the frustum than the radius of the sphere.

Example 8.4 (Triangle Visiblity). We continue with the view frustum described earlier in Example 8.1. Let triangle T have the following vertices:

$$V_0 = (-2, -1, -6)$$
$$V_1 = (-1, 4, -8)$$
$$V_2 = (-4, 1, -5)$$

First, we list the inward-pointing normals for the view frustum. (For simplicity of calculation, the normals are not unit normals.)

Near:	$(0, 0, -1)$	Far:	$(0, 0, 1)$
Top:	$(0, -4, -1.5)$	Bottom:	$(0, 4, -1.5)$
Left:	$(4, 0, -2.5)$	Right:	$(-4, 0, -2.5)$

To calculate $\vec{n} \cdot (P - P_0)$ for each vertex and each plane, we need a P_0 on each bounding plane. The points $(0, 0, -4)$ and $(0, 0, -10)$ will work for the near and far planes, the corner vertex of the view window $(-2.5, 1.5, -4)$ will work for the top and

TABLE 8.1 Values of $\vec{n} \cdot \vec{v}$

	Near	Far	Top	Bottom	Left	Right
V_0	+2	+4	+13	+5	+7	+23
V_1	+4	+2	−4	+28	+16	+24
V_2	+1	+5	+3.5	+11.5	−3.5	+28.5

left planes, and the corner vertex $(2.5, -1.5, -4)$ will work for the right and bottom planes. So the dot product using V_1 and the near plane is $(0, 0, -1) \cdot ((-2, -1, -6) - (0, 0, -4)) = 2 > 0$. V_0 is on the positive side of the near plane, which is consistent with being in the view frustum. Before we know for sure that it is in the frustum, we have to check the other planes. The results for all three vertices are presented in Table 8.1.

Reading the table, all positive values for V_0 means it is inside the view frustum. V_1 is outside by being on the negative side of the top plane, and V_2 is outside by being on the negative side of the left plane. At this stage, we need to clip the triangle down to a smaller triangle just fitting in the frustum.

Suppose we have a bounding sphere containing a cluster of triangles from some set of objects in our scene. The sphere has radius 4 and center $C = (9, 0, -6)$. Finding the dot product of the normal to the right plane with the center of the sphere gives

$$(-4, 0, -2.5) \cdot (9, 0, -6) = -21 < 0$$

The center of the sphere is on the negative side of the right plane and therefore not in the view frustum. Calculating the distance from the center of the sphere to the right plane gives

$$d = \frac{|((9, 0, -6) - (2.5, -1.5, -4)) \cdot (-4, 0, -2.5)|}{|(-4, 0, -2.5)|} \approx 4.45$$

The distance is larger than the radius, implying the sphere is entirely on the negative side of the right plane. We conclude that the sphere does not intersect the view frustum and consequently none of the triangles inside the sphere needs to be processed for viewing. The sphere's center is on the positive side of the bottom plane, but all we need is for it to be completely on the negative side of some bounding plane before we disregard any triangles inside it.   □

In this last example, the visibility tests were conducted before we applied the perspective transform; we were still in what we call camera space. In previous examples, we checked vertices after the perspective transform to see whether they fell in the view frustum. Which of these two approaches is the most efficient really depends on the design of the particular application. In general, it is desirable to eliminate as many triangles as possible before expending computation time on the perspective transformation.

It may be convenient to cull large sections of the scene based only on the bounding planes of the view frustum, or it may be possible to determine bounding volumes that can be easily checked for intersection with the frustum. Bounding spheres are not the only canonical geometric object that can work here. Bounding boxes, bounding ellipsoids, and bounding cylinders are appropriate and useful. When we consider ray tracing, we will look closer at the details of using these bounding volumes to speed up the rendering process.

8.3.1 Back Face Culling

Once we have determined which triangles intersect the view frustum, we may need to clip those that are only partially inside. When that is done, we have a collection of triangles (or polygons) completely in view. Yet, one might be occluding another completely or partially. The image on the screen should not display any part of a triangle that is blocked by a triangle closer to the camera. There are many situations here that have to be addressed, but if we have opaque polyhedral objects with triangular faces, any of those triangles facing away from the camera, *back faces*, are hidden. We can cull the back faces and avoid displaying them on the screen.

To distinguish front faces from back faces, we need a normal for each face. If the normal points toward the camera, we have a front face; otherwise it is a back face. More specifically, the angle between the normal vector and a vector from the face to the camera is greater than $\pi/2$ for back faces; the dot product is negative. It is important in this test that the normal points out of the object, and to guarantee this we orient the vertices in counterclockwise order. If, when looking at a face from outside the object, the vertices V_0, V_1, V_2 are in counterclockwise order, then the normal formed by the cross product, $\vec{n} = (V_1 - V_0) \times (V_2 - V_0)$, is pointing out of the face. Constructing the object where face vertices are ordered consistently in the counterclockwise direction guarantees that we can easily calculate normals pointing out of the face. (Clearly, we could order vertices in the clockwise order as long as we are consistent, and then select $-\vec{n}$.)

It is important to note that while we cannot see a back face of an opaque object, we may also not see a front face. If the object is convex, then front faces are visible, but if it is not, then other faces can partially or completely obscure a front face (Figure 8.4).

Example 8.5 (Determining a Back Face). Once again, consider the view frustum orientation in Example 8.1. A tetrahedral shape has the following vertices:

$$V_0 = (0, 2, -7)$$
$$V_1 = (2, -1, -8)$$
$$V_2 = (-1, -2, -9)$$
$$V_3 = (0, -1, -5)$$

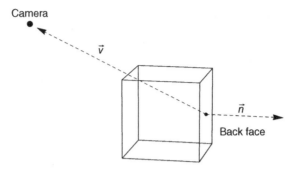

Figure 8.4 Back face

There are four triangular faces (A, B, C, D) in this shape and we can list the vertices for each face in counterclockwise order.

$$
\begin{array}{llll}
A: & V_0 & V_1 & V_2 \\
B: & V_0 & V_3 & V_1 \\
C: & V_0 & V_2 & V_3 \\
D: & V_1 & V_3 & V_2
\end{array}
$$

Normals for each face are calculated using the vertex order. For face A, the normal is $\vec{n} = (V_1 - V_0) \times (V_2 - V_0)$, and for face B it is $\vec{n} = (V_3 - V_0) \times (V_1 - V_0)$. After calculating all four normals, we also find vectors $\vec{v}$ from the faces to the camera position (the origin). Since this vector starts from any point on the face (the face is flat), the vertices are convenient to use; we use vertex V_0 for faces A, B, C, and vertex V_1 for D. Finally, we calculate the dot products.

Only the signs of the dot product matter in this test. Since faces B and C have positive dot products, they are visible; faces A and D are not visible (Table 8.2).

The calculations we have done so far have taken place in camera space, but we could see what happens in screen space by transforming each vertex with the perspective transformation. The four vertices transform as follows:

$$
\begin{aligned}
V_0^* &= (0, 0.76, 0.43) \\
V_1^* &= (0.4, -0.33, 0.67) \\
V_2^* &= (-0.18, -0.59, 0.85) \\
V_3^* &= (0, -0.53, -0.33)
\end{aligned}
$$

These are normalized device coordinates, and by looking at the z coordinate we can tell the relative position of the vertices. Vertex V_3 and V_0 are closest to the camera. (Remember that the more positive z coordinates are farther from the camera.) It is not definitive, but from this positioning alone we might guess that faces B and C hide the other two.

TABLE 8.2 Determining Back Faces in a Tetrahedron

Face	$\vec{n}$	$\vec{v}$	$\vec{n} \cdot \vec{v}$
A	$(2, 5, -11)$	$(0, -2, 7)$	-87
B	$(9, 4, 6)$	$(0, -2, 7)$	$+34$
C	$(-14, 2, 3)$	$(0, -2, 7)$	$+17$
D	$(3, -11, 2)$	$(-2, 1, 8)$	-1

Considering only face A, we get actual screen coordinates by scaling $(0, 0, 76)$, $(0.4, -0.33)$, and $(-0.18, -0.59)$ to fit a particular display screen. If we consider these points as all having the same z coordinates (they are all on the screen) and then calculate a normal to the triangle respecting the order of the vertices, we get $(0, 0, -0.74)$. This normal points away from the camera, indicating that face A is hidden. For screen coordinates, we always get a normal of the form $(0, 0, a)$, and the visibility test reduces to determining whether a is positive or negative. □

8.3.2 Painter's Algorithm

After eliminating as many triangles as possible, those that are left may still overlap in various ways when projected onto the view plane. If two triangles overlap, then one will hide part of the other and the hidden section should not be visible on the screen. One way to ensure that the triangles are displayed correctly is to use the *painter's algorithm* which simply draws the partially hidden triangles first. Then, when the triangle in front is drawn, it will hide the section of the first where they overlap. If we can order the triangles according to decreasing distance from the camera, drawing them in that order will display visible portions of the triangles correctly. (One way to find an order is to use the average z coordinate of the three vertices.)

This sounds straightforward until we realize that there can be some awkward arrangements of triangles like the one shown in Figure 8.5. The triangles are shown

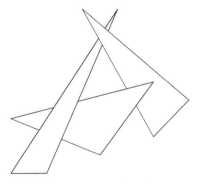

Figure 8.5 Overlapping triangles

projected onto the display screen, but the original spatial orientation should be clear. Each triangle overlaps one of the others, so there is no order among the triangles that will make the painter's algorithm work. Instead, splitting one of the triangles into smaller triangles is the only choice.

To phrase the problem more geometrically, consider just two triangles T_1 and T_2, along with the plane containing T_1 (called $\mathscr{P}_1$). If the three vertices of triangle T_2 are all on one side of plane $\mathscr{P}_1$, then we can decide how to draw the two triangles by determining where the camera is in relation to the plane. Assuming the triangles are actually in the view frustum, there are two cases:

1. If the camera is looking at the triangles from the opposite side of the plane from triangle T_2, then draw T_2 first, followed by T_1. In this positioning, triangle T_2 cannot hide any part of T_1.

2. If the camera is looking at the triangles from the same side of the plane as T_2, then draw T_1 first, followed by T_2. Triangle T_1 cannot hide any part of T_2.

The details of determining on which side of a plane the camera or a vertex lies follow the same procedure we used before. Find the normal to the plane by taking the cross product of vectors formed by the vertices of T_1. The dot product between the normal and a vector from the plane to the camera (or vertex) determines which side of the plane the camera is on, and a similar dot product with vectors to the vertices of T_2 establishes which side the vertices are on (Figure 8.6).

This method for ordering the two triangles assumes that the vertices of T_2 are all on one side of the plane containing T_1. If this is not true, we could reverse the role of the two triangles to see if it then works. If neither triangle is completely on one side of the plane containing the other, then a plane splits a triangle so that one vertex is on one side and the other two vertices are on the other side.

The plane divides the triangle into a triangle and a quadrilateral. Using the methods for finding the intersection of a line and a plane, we can find the vertices of the triangular and quadrilateral pieces; the quadrilateral is easily divided two triangles. Replacing the original triangle with the three smaller triangles changes the situation so that the plane cleanly divides the triangles. They are completely on one side or the

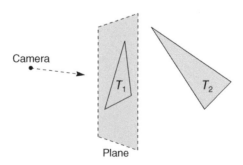

Figure 8.6 Triangles and camera

other, but we have increased the number of triangles and hence extended computation time. The smart thing to do is to minimize the number of triangles we have to split in a quest for planes that completely separate groups of triangles.

Consider now all the triangles in our scene, and imagine that we do have a plane that separates them cleanly into two groups. Position the camera somewhere and orient the view frustum so that it crosses the plane. Then we argue just as before. The group of triangles on the opposite side of the plane from the camera should all be drawn before any on the same side as the camera. None of those on the opposite side can occlude any on the same side. We have taken the first step in finding an appropriate order for drawing the triangles. Of course, we still have to order all the triangles on one side of the plane, but we do so by proceeding recursively.

We are about to build a data structure called a *BSP tree* where the acronym stands for "binary space partition." The tree starts with the root node holding the plane $\mathcal{P}_1$ and its triangle T_1. There are two branches out of this node, one leading to triangles on one side of $\mathcal{P}_1$, and the other leading to those on the other side. Focusing on those triangles on one side, we can search for another plane containing one of the triangles in hope of dividing this group into two smaller groups. If we are unlucky, more triangles will have to be split; searching for a plane that minimizes the splitting makes sense. This procedure is continued again and again until we have single triangles in every group. These triangles are stored in the leaves of the tree data structure. All of this processing can occur before we consider the camera and its associated view frustum.

Once we have built the BSP tree, then we position the camera and check the plane in the root node of the tree. All those triangles on the opposite side of the plane from the camera will be drawn first, but we now check the plane that divides these into two groups. Those again on the opposite side of this second plane from the camera are drawn before those on the same side. Following the tree in this manner (called a *depth-first search*) ascribes an order to the triangles that we can use when drawing on the screen. Figure 8.7 shows the tree, a small example of triangles, and a camera position. The triangles (and planes) are drawn edge on to improve the clarity of the diagram.

In the figure, plane $\mathcal{P}_1$ containing T_1 divides the triangles into two groups $\{T_2, T_4, T_5\}$ and $\{T_3, T_6, T_7\}$. The second group is drawn first. Plane $\mathcal{P}_3$ containing

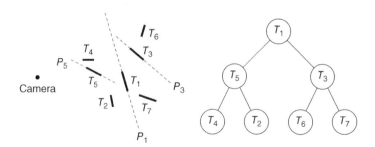

Figure 8.7   Example ordering and tree

T_3 divides this second group further into the two groups $\{T_7\}$ and $\{T_6\}$. These are singleton groups and hence are leaves in the BSP tree. At this stage, we can order some of the triangles: T_6, T_3, T_7, T_1. Now we order those on the same side of $\mathcal{P}_1$ as the camera. The final order becomes $T_6, T_3, T_7, T_1, T_2, T_5, T_4$.

With seven triangles in the small example, there are seven total nodes in the BSP tree; four of the nodes are leaves. This particular tree is balanced, meaning that the two branches out of each node hold the same number of triangles. The depth of the tree is the maximum number of branches on a path from the root node to a leaf node, and in the example case the depth is 2. In a perfectly balanced tree of depth d, there are $2^{d+1} - 1$ triangles. If we start with n triangles, we will have a tree of depth at least $\lfloor \log_2 n \rfloor$, where the brackets denote the floor function (greatest integer less than or equal to $\log_2 n$). Finding a balanced tree is desirable because unbalanced trees can have great depth and require more computation to find the correct triangle ordering.

8.3.3   Z-Buffer

The painter's algorithm deals with triangles and works in the camera space. Another similar approach works on pixels in screen space using a hardware device called the *z-buffer* (or *depth buffer*). To actually draw an opaque triangle on the screen, the graphics processor breaks the triangle into a series of horizontal scan lines. Each line is a set of pixels with integer coordinates and one pixel is drawn at a time. If the triangle is a solid color, then each pixel is set to the same color; otherwise, the color is chosen to produce shading.

If one triangle overlaps another on the view plane, then any point in the overlap region is the projection of a point P_1 on one triangle and a point P_2 on the other triangle. The point closest to the camera should determine the actual color of the screen pixel. As the triangles are processed, colors are chosen for pixels on the screen. Point P_1 may require one color and P_2 may require another. Checking the z coordinates, the graphics processor can determine which point is closer to the camera.

The z-buffer is used to store z coordinates as a triangle is scan-converted to determine the colors of relevant pixels and is an additional memory area of the same size as the screen. The three vertices of a triangle are first transformed with the perspective transform to normalized device coordinates. The transformed (x, y) pair identifies a pixel and the z coordinate is compared with the value in the (x, y) location of the z-buffer. If there is no previously stored value in the buffer, then the current z is stored and the pixel on the screen takes the color of the corresponding point on the triangle. If there is a value in the buffer, then the current z is compared with it to determine which is smaller (i.e., closer to the camera). The smaller z is stored and the pixel takes the corresponding color. This guarantees that the closest point to the camera determines the pixel color. In this way, the triangle vertices are turned into pixels (Figure 8.8).

Once the three vertices are transformed, there are algorithms (see Bresenham's algorithm in a later chapter) that find the correct pixels on the edges of the triangle. Then line by line, individual pixels and their accompanying z coordinates are found

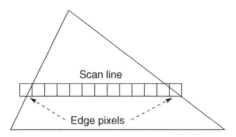

Figure 8.8   Triangle scan lines

by interpolation. Normalized z coordinates are compared with the current values in the z-buffer to determine whether the pixel should overlay the current one. Scan line by scan line the triangle takes shape, and overlapping regions are drawn correctly without any global geometric calculations.

8.4 RAY TRACING

So far we have treated visibility purely as a problem of positioning. Is a particular triangle in the view frustum and, if so, is there another triangle in front of it closer to the camera? We have temporarily left light out of the scene. There are no light sources and no shadows cast by objects nearer to the source than other objects. An approach to the whole visibility question that puts light back into the scene is called *ray tracing*. It turns out to be computationally intensive, but it has the ability to cope with some of the complex light interactions in a scene.

Light rays are an abstraction that helps turn the difficult physics of light into a approachable geometric problem. A light source sends light rays into the scene where they bounce off objects and, in some cases, end up entering the camera. Only those rays that are reflected into the camera finally determine the image. The computational difficulty is that the vast majority of rays do not enter the camera, so keeping track of them is irrelevant. The counterintuitive approach in ray tracing is to follow the rays backward, starting at the camera and moving into the scene. It is not physically realistic, but it keeps us from wasting computation on rays that end up reflected in a direction that completely misses the camera.

Tracing a ray from the camera to the scene means that it passes through the viewing window on the view plane. Points in the viewing window will get scaled appropriately to end up as pixels on the display screen, so we imagine targeting a pixel and backing up to find the ray going from the camera through the associated point in the view window. There will be a ray for each point in the viewing window which corresponds to the center of a pixel on the display screen.

Continuing into the view frustum, the ray enters the scene and may intersect an object. With the camera at the origin, the ray has the form $t\vec{v}$, where $\vec{v}$ is the vector from the origin (camera position) to a point in the view plane window. We are then looking for the smallest positive value of t such that the point $P = (0, 0, 0) + t\vec{v}$ is a point on some object. Assuming that the point is illuminated by a light source, P is visible because no other object in the frustum is in front of it (Figure 8.9).

The first object that a ray strikes is potentially visible, but unless it is directly illuminated by a light source it is in shadow and the corresponding pixel should not be so bright. So we can take a ray from the intersection point to a light source and see if it intersects any other object. Once we know whether it is in shadow, we can use various lighting models (Chapter 9) to determine the intensity of the pixel. From the visibility perspective, we know that the point is potentially visible as soon as we know it is the first point of intersection on a ray from the camera. By systematically finding rays through each pixel, we construct the entire image. This first attempt at a ray tracing algorithm is often referred to as *ray casting* and the only advantage over the previous visibility techniques is that it includes slightly more subtle lighting effects.

More can be done. From the first intersection point P, we can follow a ray to the various light sources (*shadow rays*), or we can follow the reflected ray (where the angle of incidence equals the angle of reflection), or in the case of a transparent object we can follow the transmitted ray (taking into account refraction). If the reflected ray from P hits an object at a point with a particular shading, then we mix this shading with any other illumination we find for P. The process can continue recursively for several levels, keeping in mind that the computation time will continue to grow exponentially with the number of levels. The result is an algorithm that captures some of the complexity of light interactions in a scene.

Ray Tracing Algorithm

For each pixel on the display screen:

1. Determine a point in the viewing window corresponding to the pixel center.
2. Find a ray from the camera to the point on the viewing window.
3. For each object, determine the parameter t for an intersection (if any) with the ray.
4. Save the minimum t value and the corresponding point P.

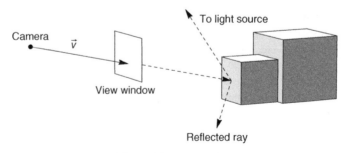

Figure 8.9 Ray tracing

5. Find the vector from point P to the light source and determine if its corresponding line intersects any object.

6. Calculate the intensity of the pixel and store it.

The algorithm relies on systematically checking objects for intersection with a light ray. An efficient way of organizing the objects to reduce the number of tests is essential.

8.4.1 Bounding Volumes

Ray tracing is computationally expensive because there is one ray (sometimes more) for each pixel on the screen and for each ray there are tests with various objects to look for the closest intersection. The goal, then, is to eliminate any objects we do not need to consider as we trace a ray and to hone our intersection algorithms, making them as efficient as possible. One way to do this is to find bounding volumes that enclose several objects. Then a single intersection test determines relatively quickly whether the ray needs to be tested against any of the enclosed objects. If the ray does not intersect the bounding volume, then it does not intersect any of the enclosed objects.

8.4.2 Bounding Boxes

Although there are other possibilities, it is convenient to make bounding boxes rectangular prisms: that is, opposite faces are parallel and adjacent faces are perpendicular. If the box is aligned so that faces are parallel to the xy, xz, or yz plane, we say it is an axis-aligned bounding box (AABB). If the box is not axis-aligned, then it is an oriented bounding box (OBB). One key characteristic of bounding volumes in general is that they should be as small as possible. For a large box, a ray may intersect it without intersecting any object inside. An intersection test in this case is not as definitive as it would be if the box were smaller.

To find the smallest AABB containing a collection of objects, it is relatively easy to read through the set of vertices and record the maximum and minimum of each coordinate. Then $x = x_{min}$ and $x = x_{max}$ are the equations of two planes containing opposite faces of the box. In an analogous manner, the other coordinates describe planes for the other faces of the box.

For a ray to intersect the box, it must enter one face and exit another. The volume between two planes containing opposite faces is a slab, and as long as the ray is not parallel to the slab it intersects it by entering through one plane and exiting through the other. With a ray of the form $P_0 + t\vec{v}$, the values of the parameter where it enters and exits the slab parallel to the yz plane are $t_x(in)$ and $t_x(out)$, where the first is less than (or equal to) the second. We can determine which of the two planes is intersected first, but we really just need to know the interval $[t_x(in), t_x(out)]$. The other two intervals, $[t_y(in), t_y(out)]$ and $[t_z(in), t_z(out)]$, are calculated and all three are compared. If the ray hits the box, there must be some values of t for which the ray is simultaneously inside all three slabs. If the intersection of all three intervals is non-empty, then the ray intersects the box (Figure 8.10). (It is possible that the ray just touches the box without entering.)

Example 8.6 (Bounding Boxes: AABB). Suppose we have two triangles with the following vertices:

$$V_0 = (0, 0, -4) \quad V_1 = (2, -1, -5) \quad V_3 = (1, 4, -7)$$
$$W_0 = (3, -1, -6) \quad W_1 = (-1, 2, -7) \quad W_2 = (0, -1, -10)$$

A quick scan finds the minimum and maximum for each coordinate, and the planes bounding the box are

$$x = -1 \quad y = -1 \quad z = -10$$
$$x = 3 \quad y = 4 \quad z = -4$$

Assume we pick a ray from the camera $(0, 0, 0)$ to the viewing window position $(-1, -2, -4)$. The technique developed earlier for finding the intersection of a line with a plane uses the following formula:

$$t = \frac{-\vec{n} \cdot (PQ_0)}{\vec{n} \cdot \vec{v}}$$

In the current case, $P = (0, 0, 0)$ and $\vec{v} = (-1, -2, -4)$. The values for t on entry and exit from each slab give the following intervals:

$$[-1.5, 1] \quad [-2, 0.5] \quad [1, 2.5]$$

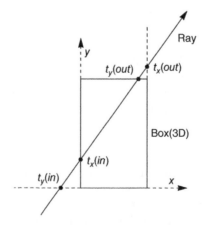

Figure 8.10 Bounding box intersection

The intersection of all three intervals is empty, so the ray misses the box and we can eliminate the two triangles from consideration.

Notice that the values of some interval endpoints are negative. This is fine, but we are considering a ray that begins at the camera and moves into the scene with positive t values. In this example, negative values mean that the ray started in the middle of a slab.   □

Finding a good OBB that is not axis-aligned is a little trickier. It depends on finding a good orthonormal coordinate system and then finding an axis-aligned box in the new system. A transformation that changes coordinates turns the OBB into an AABB. The technique for determining whether the ray intersects the box works the same in either coordinate system. We find intervals when t is inside each slab and then check for a nonzero intersection. The real problem with an OBB is finding a good set of axes, and one way is detailed in Section 8.5.

8.4.3 Bounding Spheres

Again, the goal is to find a sphere as small as possible that contains the objects we are trying to group together. One good algorithm looks at the set of vertices for all the objects and finds the six vertices with minimum and maximum x, y, and z coordinates, respectively. Then determine which pair of the six has the largest distance between them. Take a sphere centered at the midpoint between the two vertices with radius equal to half the distance between them. Let C be the center of the sphere and r be its radius (Figure 8.11).

This sphere may not contain all the vertices. If not, pick a vertex P outside the sphere. The line through P and C intersects the sphere in two points. Let Q be the intersection between P and C. Update to a new sphere by finding a new radius r' and a new center C'.

$$D = |P - C| \qquad Q = C + r\frac{(P - C)}{D}$$

$$r' = r + \frac{D}{2} \qquad C' = C + \frac{1}{2}(P - Q) \tag{8.10}$$

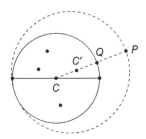

Figure 8.11 Bounding sphere

The sphere is adjusted slightly by increasing the radius and moving the center, so the new sphere contains P and the entire original sphere. This procedure is repeated by selecting vertices outside the updated sphere. Usually, a few passes through the loop will suffice to include all points.

Example 8.7 (Building Spheres). Suppose that the objects in a region have many vertices but the two that have maximum or minimum components in their coordinates and are the greatest distance apart are $(1, 0, -4)$ and $(2.3, 0, -5)$. The midpoint is the center of the sphere.

$$C = (1.65, 0, -4.5) \qquad r = 0.65$$

One more point $P = (1.5, 1, -4.5)$ is outside the initial sphere because the distance $D = |P - C| = 1.02 > r$. To adjust the sphere, first calculate Q.

$$Q = (1.65, 0, -4.5) + \frac{0.65}{1.02}(-0.15, 1, 0) \approx (1.55, 0.64, -4.5)$$

Finally, we can calculate the updated sphere.

$$r' = \frac{1}{2}(0.65 + 1.02) \approx 0.84$$

$$C' = (1.65, 0, -4.5) + \frac{1}{2}(-0.05, 0.36, 0) \approx (1.63, 0.18, -4.5)$$

Assuming this is the final sphere, suppose we use the same ray as in the previous example, $t\vec{v}$, where $\vec{v} = (-1, -2, -4)$. We need to find the distance between the sphere and the line containing the ray. If the distance is less than the radius $r' = 0.84$, then the ray intersects the sphere. We do not actually have to find the intersection, because it is sufficient at this stage to discover whether there is an intersection. If the ray intersects the sphere, then we must check intersections with each object in the sphere.

To find the distance between the line and the sphere, note that $(0, 0, 0)$ is the initial point of the ray. Vector $\vec{a} = (C' - (0, 0, 0)) = (1.63, 0.18, -4.5)$ is projected onto $\vec{v}$. The projection is one leg of a right triangle, while $\vec{a}$ forms the hypotenuse. We are looking for the length d of the second leg.

$$d^2 = |\vec{a}|^2 - \left(\frac{\vec{a} \cdot \vec{v}}{|\vec{v}|}\right)^2 = 22.94 - 16.01 = 6.93$$

Hence, $d \approx 2.63$, and the distance is greater than the radius of the sphere. We conclude that we can avoid checking objects in the sphere for ray intersections. □

Other bounding volumes can be useful, but clearly the simplicity and symmetry of spheres and bounding boxes help the calculations. Usually, the bounding volumes can be precalculated and used throughout ray-tracing procedures.

8.5   COMPLEMENTS AND DETAILS

8.5.1   Frustum Planes

In Section 8.2.1, we clipped a line segment that was only partially inside the view frustum. To do that, we can work in homogeneous coordinates, in normalized device coordinates, or in the original three-dimensional coordinates. In any case, we need the normals to the bounding planes in order to apply vector techniques to find the intersection between a point and a line. Characteristics of the perspective transformation matrix lead to useful relationships between normals before and after the perspective transformation is applied.

In normalized coordinates, after the perspective transformation, the view frustum is a cube centered at the origin with edge length 2. The top bounding plane, for example, has the equation $y = 1$, with the normal $(0, -1, 0)$ pointing into the cube. Remembering that the homogeneous representation of a plane $ax + by + cz + d = 0$ is (a, b, c, d), the top bounding plane for the cube has homogeneous representation $(0, -1, 0, 1)$. This vector is normal to any homogeneous point on the plane.

The perspective transform is given by the homogeneous matrix M_{per} and converts camera coordinates to normalized coordinates. The version of M_{per} given in this chapter has nonzero determinant, and so an inverse, M_{per}^{-1}, exists. The inverse converts normalized coordinates back to camera coordinates.

From our earlier study of transformations, if matrix M transforms an object, then $(M^{-1})^T$ transforms the normals. Since M_{per}^{-1} transforms the cube in normalized coordinates, the transpose, M_{per}^T, will transform the normals correctly. Using the perspective transform in Example 8.1, we can transform the top bounding plane for the cube (which is a normal) to the top bounding plane for the frustum in camera coordinates.

$$
M_{per}^T \begin{bmatrix} 0 \\ -1 \\ 0 \\ 1 \end{bmatrix} = \begin{bmatrix} \frac{8}{5} & 0 & 0 & 0 \\ 0 & \frac{8}{3} & 0 & 0 \\ 0 & 0 & -\frac{7}{3} & -1 \\ 0 & 0 & -\frac{40}{3} & 0 \end{bmatrix} \begin{bmatrix} 0 \\ -1 \\ 0 \\ 1 \end{bmatrix} = \begin{bmatrix} 0 \\ -\frac{8}{3} \\ -1 \\ 0 \end{bmatrix}
$$

The resulting plane is $-\frac{8}{3}y - z = 0$, and this is the top bounding plane of the viewing frustum in camera coordinates.

Since the transpose of a matrix just replaces the columns with rows, we can give formulas for the various bounding planes by referencing rows in the perspective matrix M_{per}. Multiplying the transpose times $(0, -1, 0, 1)$ just takes -1 times the second row of M_{per} and adds the fourth row. All of the bounding planes in normalized coordinates are represented as vectors with 1's, -1's, or 0's, so we can give simple formulas for the bounding planes in camera coordinates. Use the notation M_i to indicate the ith row in M_{per} where $0 \leq i \leq 3$ (Table 8.3):

TABLE 8.3   Bounding Planes (Homogeneous Coordinates)

	Normalized	Camera
Near	$(0, 0, 1, 1)$	$M_2 + M_3$
Far	$(0, 0, -1, 1)$	$-M_2 + M_3$
Top	$(0, -1, 0, 1)$	$-M_1 + M_3$
Bottom	$(0, 1, 0, 1)$	$M_1 + M_3$
Left	$(1, 0, 0, 1)$	$M_0 + M_3$
Right	$(-1, 0, 0, 1)$	$-M_0 + M_3$

8.5.2   Axes for Bounding Volumes

The purpose of a bounding volume is to allow a single test to possibly eliminate a group of objects from further consideration. If the bounding volume does not overlap the view frustum, nothing inside it can be visible. If a ray does not intersect the volume, then it cannot strike any object inside and the ray tracer can move on to other objects. A larger volume potentially contains more objects and is therefore desirable, but if it does not "fit" the objects very well, then the larger volume is a liability because a ray, for example, may well intersect it without intersecting anything inside. So constructing bounding volumes is an exercise in trying to match the shape of a set of vertices (from all the objects in a group) as efficiently as possible.

Usually, we are looking for three-dimensional volumes, but the ideas behind finding good orientations for the volumes can more easily be visualized in two dimensions. Figure 8.12 shows a small set of two-dimensional vertices along with an AABB and an OBB. The difference is that the OBB matches the shape of the vertices a little better than the AABB. An axis that represents the direction of the vertices looks like a good choice for a bounding box axis. We might also argue that such an axis could be used as a diameter in a bounding sphere. In fact, finding an axis that is a good fit for the data goes a long way in orienting an efficient bounding box.

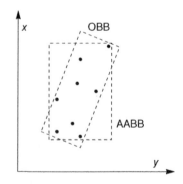

Figure 8.12   Dispersion of vertices

Actually, the problem of fitting an axis to data comes directly from statistics, where the resulting techniques are called *principal component analysis*. The following example shows how linear algebra can help find the best axis for the vertex data.

Example 8.8 (Finding the Best Axes). Start with the following set of vertices (the coordinates are all integers to help with visualization and calculation).

$$
\begin{aligned}
V_0 &= (1,2) & V_5 &= (5,4) \\
V_1 &= (2,1) & V_6 &= (6,1) \\
V_2 &= (3,3) & V_7 &= (7,3) \\
V_3 &= (4,2) &
\end{aligned}
$$

□

The average x coordinate is 4, and the average y coordinate is 2.29. The point $M = (4, 2.29)$ is marked in Figure 8.13 and serves as the origin of a new coordinate system (dotted lines). In that new system, the average of the new x coordinates is zero; similarly, the average of the new y coordinates is zero. There is a trend in the vertices which can be described as a slope up to the right; larger x coordinates give larger y coordinates.

To reframe this problem in terms of matrices, first form a (7×2) matrix V with all the vertices in the new coordinates (e.g., $(1, 2)$ becomes $(-3, -0.29)$).

$$
V = \begin{bmatrix}
-3 & -0.29 \\
-2 & -1.29 \\
-1 & 0.71 \\
0 & -0.29 \\
1 & 1.71 \\
2 & -1.29 \\
3 & 0.71
\end{bmatrix}
$$

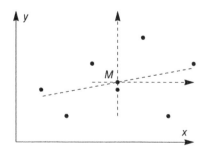

Figure 8.13 Example vertices

Then the 2×2 matrix $V^T V$ contains diagonal entries $\sum_{i=0}^{6} x_i^2$ and $\sum_{i=0}^{6} y_i^2$.

$$V^T V = \begin{bmatrix} 28 & 4 \\ 4 & 7.43 \end{bmatrix}$$

The matrix is symmetric, and the two off diagonal entries are both $\sum_{i=0}^{6} x_i y_i = 4$. If we divide this value by one less than the number of vertices, we get $4/6 \approx 0.67$. This is what statisticians call the covariance. A positive covariance indicates that, as one variable increases, so does the other. For an axis that matches the trend in the vertices, the covariance of the new coordinates (relative to the axis) would be closer to zero. The key idea now is to find a rotation of the dotted axes in the figure that will place an axis right along the trend of the vertices.

In the study of linear algebra, matrices can have special vectors called *eigenvectors*. For a matrix A, the vector $\vec{x}$ is an eigenvector if $A\vec{x} = \lambda\vec{x}$ for some constant λ called an *eigenvalue*. There are standard routines for finding the eigenvectors, and it turns out that the eigenvectors for $V^T V$ are good axes for a bounding volume, in particular a bounding box.

$$\vec{v}_1 = (0.98, 0.18) \qquad \vec{v}_2 = (-0.18, 0.98)$$

Vector $\vec{v}_1$ matches the trend well and is the major axis (or first principal component). The second vector $\vec{v}_2$ is perpendicular to the first and marks the second dimension in the bounding box.

To rotate the dotted axes into these new positions, use the matrix formed by putting the eigenvalues in the columns.

$$P = \begin{bmatrix} 0.98 & -0.18 \\ 0.18 & 0.98 \end{bmatrix}$$

Rotating the axis in one direction means that the vertices are rotated in the opposite direction. P is an orthogonal matrix so its inverse is P^T. Because of the way we stacked the vertices in V, the new rotated coordinates are given by $P^T V^T$. Call the rotated coordinate matrix W.

$$W^T = P^T V^T \implies W = VP \tag{8.11}$$

The new covariance between the two rotated coordinates is

$$W^T W = P^T V^T VP = \begin{bmatrix} 28.75 & 0 \\ 0 & 6.68 \end{bmatrix}$$

Now the covariance (off-diagonal value) is zero. This just verifies that the vectors $\vec{v}_1$ and $\vec{v}_2$ were chosen to minimize the covariance, and this property makes them good choices for bounding volumes.

8.6 EXERCISES

1. Position the camera at the origin and place the near and far planes at $z_n = -5$ and $z_f = -12$. With the view window of width 8 and height 5 centered on the z-axis, find the inward pointing normals for each bounding plane of the view frustum.

2. Construct the appropriate perspective transformation matrix for the setup in Exercise 1.

3. The perspective transformation sends camera space coordinates to normalized device coordinates. Determine where the camera space z coordinates which are between the near plane and the camera are sent. Also determine where z coordinates beyond the far plane and those behind the camera are sent. Which z coordinates are sent to the interval $[0, 1]$?

4. If in the perspective matrix we used the actual distance to the near and far planes rather than z_n and z_f, how would the matrix change?

5. Using the setup in Exercise 1, project the points $P_1 = (-4, 2, -6)$ and $P_2 = (9, -1, -8)$ onto the view plane. Find the normalized device coordinates. If clipping of the edge between the points needs to be done, find the point of intersection with the appropriate bounding plane.

6. In Example 8.1, use the normalized device coordinates to clip the line segment and verify that the answer is consistent with the other two methods used.

7. In Example 8.4, verify that the normals for the bounding planes are correct.

8. If two endpoints are both outside the view frustum, the line segment may be totally outside the frustum or it may need to be clipped. Develop an algorithm for determining the correct case.

9. Show that, if P_1^h and P_2^h are homogeneous points representing the three-dimensional points P_1 and P_2, the point $aP_1^h + bP_2^h$ is on the line determined by P_1 and P_2. If $a = b$, is the point at the midpoint of the line segment $P_1 P_2$?

10. With the setup in Exercise 1, a line with endpoints $(-3, 1, -6)$ and $(1, -1, -9)$ is projected onto the view plane. If the first point is blue with intensity 0.8 and second is blue with intensity 0.1 and if color is interpolated linearly across the segment, what is the color of the pixel at the midpoint of the segment on the view plane?

11. A unit cube is centered at the origin with sides parallel to the coordinate planes. The camera is at position $(10, -9, 4)$. Determine which faces are back faces.

12. What is the least depth of a BSP tree with 1000 triangles? How many planes have to be tested to see what side the camera is on before ordering the triangles?

13. In the method presented for determining whether a ray intersects a bounding box (Section 8.4.2), let t_{min} be the maximum of $t_x(in)$, $t_y(in)$, and $t_z(in)$. Let t_{max} be the minimum of $t_x(out)$, $t_y(out)$, and $t_z(out)$. Show that the ray intersects the box if and only if $t_{min} \leq t_{max}$.

14. An AABB is bounded by the xz plane and the planes $y = 2$, $x = 1$, $x = 3$, $z = 0$, $z = 4$. A ray originates at $(10, 12, 7)$ with direction vector $(-2, -2, -1)$. Use the method in Section 8.4.1 to determine whether the ray intersects the box.

8.6.1 Programming Exercises

1. Write a program that inputs a list of three-dimensional points and use the method given in Section 8.4.3 to find a bounding sphere. Optionally, display the projections of the sphere and points on each of the three coordinate planes.

9

LIGHTING

Lighting is complex. Physics explains the fundamental properties, but in a scene there are many reflections, refractions, diffractions, and absorptions taking place everywhere, and it is this complicated set of interactions that gives us the visual experience.

Of course, there are various levels of realism we can aim for in rendering a given scene. Wireframe images, where we only draw the outlines of triangles, can give a rudimentary sense of the scene, but coloring the interiors of the triangles at least with single colors can begin to flesh it out. Simple shadows and elementary shading are enough to give a three-dimensional cast to a scene, but even animated films demand much more on the realism front.

To approach the photo-realistic look, we need to add shading from various light sources, shadows overlapping each other, and the subtleties of reflections from various surface materials. The details of these interactions remain an area of research, but more and more sophisticated lighting models can ensure that brushed aluminum furniture in a scene looks decidedly different from plastic furniture. With some care, we can approximate the fundamentals of light interactions to develop lighting models that give satisfyingly good results.

9.1 COLOR COORDINATES

Cartesian coordinates are ideal for locating pixels on the screen, but in addition to a location, pixels have a color, and unlike location, color really depends on an individual's perception. Light is electromagnetic radiation, and the mix of wavelengths

Mathematical Structures for Computer Graphics, First Edition. Steven J. Janke.
© 2015 John Wiley & Sons, Inc. Published 2015 by John Wiley & Sons, Inc.

determines the color we perceive. General waveforms are difficult to characterize, and although we can define the color red as a light wave with wavelength 700 nm, the red in a rose petal is the result of a far more complicated waveform. The entire set of waveforms that humans perceive as various colors is ambiguous and indeed differs from person to person. Experiments with many people have resulted in a decent map of all the colors humans can perceive, but the set does not have much obvious symmetry, so designing a coordinate system to locate colors is difficult. Work by the Commission Internationale de L'Éclairage (CIE) has established some reasonable standards to ground coordinate systems in order to ensure that colors can be reproduced reliably.

RGB Color Space One obvious way to designate colors is to take a cue from the computer monitor itself. The technology is based on three primary colors (red, green, blue), and specifying the intensity of each component gives a color on the screen. Using a scale from zero to one, a color is then a triple of values (r, g, b) where each component falls between 0 and 1. This is the *RGB color space*, and because of the three components we can visualize it as a cube (Figure 9.1).

The color $(0, 0, 0)$ is black, and the color $(1, 1, 1)$ is white. Interpreting coordinates as a color is tricky, but at least we know that $(1, 0.3, 0)$ is made up of red with a little green, and the fact that one component is at the maximum value 1 means the color is fairly bright. All colors along the cube's diagonal from $(0, 0, 0)$ to $(1, 1, 1)$, are shades of gray from black to white.

To store colors, three bytes can be used, with each byte holding a value for a single component. Since a byte can hold 256 different values, instead of a scale from 0 to 1 for a component, often programming languages allow a scale from 0 to 255. Consequently, with three bytes (or 24 bits) we can store $256 \times 256 \times 256$ different colors. This does not cover all possible colors humans can perceive and it is not always the case that humans can distinguish the difference between two colors produced by this system.

The minute we set up three coordinates and call our space a cube, we tend to think of the geometric distance between points. Yet distance between colors is another

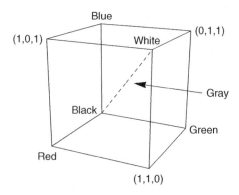

Figure 9.1 RGB color space

matter entirely. Distance along the diagonal does indicate brightness, but otherwise it is difficult to tell what we are measuring. Nevertheless, we often set about linearly interpolating between colors to fill in the shading of an object. The nonlinearities in our perception and in the display electronics will undoubtedly affect how we see the final image.

HSV Color Space   One awkward problem with the RGB color space is that it does not often match our intuitive idea of color. How do we change the three components to make a color brighter or a little more orange? It is more convenient to describe colors by, for example, attributes like tint and brightness. One set of useful attributes suggested by Alvy Ray Smith in 1978 includes hue (H), saturation (S), and value (V) as the key attributes. Hue measures the dominant wavelength of the color (red, orange, yellow, green, etc.), saturation determines how dominant the hue is, and value specifies how bright the color is. Again, we have three components now forming the *HSV color space*.

With three components, we do have a three-dimensional space of colors, but to align it with our perception, imagine looking at the RGB cube from the point $(1, 1, 1)$ down the diagonal toward $(0, 0, 0)$. Some (but not all) cross sections of the cube from this direction look like hexagons. This suggests arranging colors in what we might call a hexcone, a cone emanating from $(0, 0, 0)$ with hexagonal cross sections; this is the HSV color space. The axis down the middle of the cone goes from the origin up to the hexagonal end and again represents shades of gray from black up to white; it coincides with the diagonal in the RGB cube. To specify a color in this hexcone, start with the distance up the axis which is brightness; this is the value component V and is a number between 0 and 1 (Figure 9.2).

Next take the hexagonal cross section which is perpendicular to the axis. This cross section is smaller near the origin than it is at the maximum distance along the

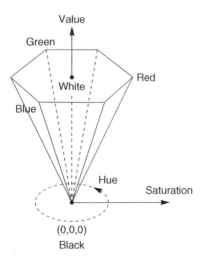

Figure 9.2   HSV color space

TABLE 9.1   Examples of RGB and HSV Coordinates

Color	RGB	HSV
Bright red	$(1, 0, 0)$	$(0, 1, 1)$
Muted red	$(1, 0, 0)$	$(0, 1, 0.6)$
Washed red	$(1, 0, 0)$	$(0, 0.5, 1)$
Yellow	$(1, 1, 0)$	$(60, 1, 1)$
Cyan	$(0, 1, 1)$	$(180, 1, 1)$
Blue	$(0, 0, 1)$	$(240, 1, 1)$
Blue tinted red	$(0.3, 0, 1)$	$(258, 1, 1)$

axis ($V = 1$). The hue is the angle around the axis in the hexagonal cross section; its value ranges from $0°$ to $360°$. We agree that $0°$ coincides with a vertex of the hexagon that corresponds to red. Angles are measured in the counterclockwise direction and the vertices of the hexagon in counterclockwise order correspond to red, yellow, green, cyan, blue, and magenta. Finally, saturation is the distance from the axis and is measured on a scale from 0 to 1. On the axis, saturation is 0 and we have a shade of gray; at the boundary of the hexagon, saturation is 1 and we have a pure color. The three components, namely hue, saturation, and value, form the coordinates (H, S, V) of a color in the HSV coordinate system (Table 9.1).

The HSV hexcone is just another way to organize colors. It is not geometrically equivalent to the RGB cube; rather it is a distortion of the cube. Since colors are perceptual concepts, they do not adhere to a strict geometry, and the distance between colors is most often meaningless. Nevertheless, proportional distances often can prove useful in shading an object and do offer a way to convert between the RGB and HSV systems (see Section 9.5 for details).

The HSV color space offers a more intuitive approach to choosing colors, but it is not perfect. For example, the saturation and value components are not really independent; changing saturation can affect our perception of the value. Yet, both the RGB and HSV systems have proved themselves very useful, and there are other systems tailored for specific purposes (like controlling printers) that also serve to approximate the human perception of color.

The Alpha Component   One more attribute (also introduced by Alvy Ray Smith) affects the way a pixel's color is displayed on the screen. Traditionally, a fourth color component called *alpha* (α) is included to specify pixel transparency; in the RGB color space we now have the coordinates (r, g, b, α). Again, the scale is from 0 to 1 and now the value determines whether the pixel is entirely transparent ($\alpha = 0$), entirely opaque ($\alpha = 1$), or something in between. To render fog, for example, we need to account for the fog's color and the colored objects we can see through the fog. If a pixel has color (r_0, g_0, b_0) and the color of fog is (r_f, g_f, b_f), then using α for fog allows a combination of the two colors.

$$(r, g, b) = \alpha(r_f, g_f, b_f) + (1 - \alpha)(r_0, g_0, b_0) \tag{9.1}$$

This is an affine combination of the two colors and is just one way the alpha value can be used to compose two images. When $\alpha = 1$, the underlying image is covered up and we see only the fog's color. We can go one step further and compose several images by either repeating the affine combination approach or trying some other operation based on combining alpha values (see Chapter 10 for more details).

9.2 ELEMENTARY LIGHTING MODELS

Both the shape and the color of an object are important in properly rendering the scene. Of course, the shape depends on the geometry, but the color depends on a large number of factors including the often complicated interaction of light with various materials. A totally realistic analysis of color requires the deeper results in the physics of light and materials, but a useful strategy for approximating lighting effects is to try simple light models first and then to increase their complexity if necessary until the screen images are satisfactory. There will always be a balance between realism and the speed of rendering.

A good elementary model starts by considering light traveling in rays. Of course, this is a simplification, albeit a reasonable one, of the modern understanding of light as photons that act both like particles and waves. The rays can be thought of as tracing points on an expanding wavefront. Very early on, Euclid postulated that light traveled in straight lines and he proceeded to develop the geometry of reflection. He, however, was skeptical of a prevailing theory that light rays emanated from the eyes and traveled to the object rather than reflecting off of objects and traveling to the eyes. It is often convenient in graphics to consider light rays as traveling in either direction, either to or from the eyes.

There can be several light sources in a scene, and the elementary model assumes that each source is a point emitting light in all directions. If the point source is far away from the center of the scene, then the light rays from the source are nearly parallel. During daylight hours, the light in a room comes from all the windows and can be reflected many times before illuminating a given object. To account for this more general lighting, the elementary model assumes that there is also *ambient* light, which has no source location.

As light strikes a surface, some of it is absorbed, some is reflected, and, if the surface is transparent, some is transmitted. In elementary models, we concentrate on the reflected light, disregard secondary reflections, and assume there are two cases. First, the light could be reflected in all directions equally. This is *diffuse* reflection and the argument is that small imperfections in the surface material reflect light in a wide range of directions. In the second case, the surface is sufficiently smooth and reflective to cause light from a point source to reflect predominantly in one direction; from that direction, the object appears to have a bright area called a *specular reflection*. Putting the various forms of reflection together, we have the following formula for the intensity (I) of light at any pixel.

$$I = I_{ambient} + I_{diffuse} + I_{specular} \tag{9.2}$$

Intensity refers to how bright the light is, and in a very elementary model we could consider only white light. On a display using red, green, and blue light to form colors, we can also consider the intensity of each primary color in turn. A blue colored surface, for example, would reflect more blue light than red or green light. The intensity equation is replicated three times, once each for red, green, and blue. Usually, the intensity scale for each color (often 0–1) is linear in the elementary model, although we know the eye does not respond equally to all intensities of all colors.

Ambient Light The ambient light in the model is considered constant, say I_a, but some surfaces are more highly reflective than others, so introducing a coefficient k_a allows the ambient light to be adjusted for individual surfaces. The contribution from ambient light is then $k_a I_a$.

Diffuse Reflection For diffuse reflection, the surface is assumed to reflect light in all directions equally; such surfaces are often called *Lambertian*, after the eighteenth century mathematician and physicist Johann Lambert who studied reflected light.

From a point on the surface, there is a normal vector $\vec{n}$ and a vector $\vec{L}$ to a point light source. The light rays hitting the surface close to the point are nearly parallel to $\vec{L}$. Using the angle θ between $\vec{n}$ and $\vec{L}$, the cross section E of a beam of light strikes the surface in an area proportional to the cosine of θ. This argues that the intensity of the reflected light is reduced according to how far the vector $\vec{L}$ is from being perpendicular to the surface. Light perpendicular to the surface will appear brighter than that at a low angle. More precisely, the intensity of the reflected light is proportional to $\cos\theta$ or, equivalently, proportional to the dot product of $\vec{n}$ and $\vec{L}$. This is Lambert's law of reflection (Figure 9.3).

The diffuse component in the model is $k_d I_d(\vec{n} \cdot \vec{L})$, where k_d is another coefficient controlling for the properties of the surface, the vectors are unit vectors, and I_d is the intensity of the point source. However, intensity of the point source decreases as the source is moved farther away; in fact, it falls off as the square of the distance. We could replace I_d with I_d/D^2, where D is the distance to the light. In practice, this is a slight problem because when D is rather small, the intensity becomes quite large. To mediate this, D^2 is often replaced with $a_2 D^2 + a_1 D + a_0$, where the a_i's are constants.

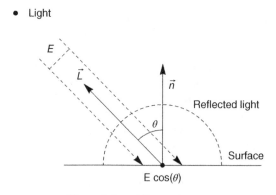

Figure 9.3 Diffuse reflection

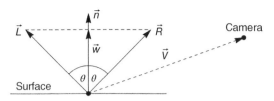

Figure 9.4   Reflected ray

Specular Reflection   Specular reflection results when the light source is actually reflected toward the viewer and not just reflected in all directions equally. Consequently, two rays are key: the reflected light ray, and the ray to the camera. The closer these are, the more the specular reflection we see in the object. The ray to the camera is easy to find, but the reflected ray requires a little geometric analysis. Since $\vec{L}$ points toward the light source, the vector $-\vec{L}$ is the incoming ray and the corresponding reflected ray is $\vec{R}$. Both the vectors $\vec{n}$ and $\vec{L}$ can be taken to be unit vectors. In Figure 9.4, $\vec{n}$ is the normal vector to the surface, and because of the way light reflects (angle of incidence equals angle of reflection), the angles between $\vec{n}$ and each of $\vec{L}$ and $\vec{R}$ are equal.

Vector $\vec{w}$ is the projection of $\vec{L}$ onto $\vec{n}$, so $\vec{w} = (\vec{n} \cdot \vec{L})\vec{n}$. Because of the symmetry of the vector positions, $\vec{R} - \vec{w} = \vec{w} - \vec{L}$. Rearranging gives a formula for the reflected ray.

$$\vec{R} = 2\vec{w} - \vec{L} = 2(\vec{n} \cdot \vec{L})\vec{n} - \vec{L} \qquad (9.3)$$

From the figure, it is also apparent that the lengths of $\vec{R}$ and $\vec{L}$ are equal, and since $\vec{L}$ is a unit vector, so is $\vec{R}$.

For the intensity of the specular reflection, we take the cosine of the angle between the unit vector $\vec{V}$ from the surface point to the camera and the reflected vector $\vec{R}$. Some surfaces are shinier than others, and with mirror-like surfaces the specular reflection can only be seen if the camera's angle with the reflected ray is small. This is incorporated into the expression for the specular intensity by introducing a power (p) of the cosine. The expression for specular intensity is then $k_s I_s (\vec{R} \cdot \vec{V})^p$. The coefficient k_s regulates the fraction of light the surface reflects, and the exponent p determines how much is reflected at various viewing angles. For a very shiny surface, p is large, meaning that $(\cos \theta)^p$ is close to 1 only for angles very close to zero. Only for camera positions in a small cone is the specular reflection very intense.

The final light intensity formula combines the ambient, diffuse, and specular components.

$$\boxed{\text{Elementary Model: } I = k_a I_a + k_d I_d (\vec{n} \cdot \vec{L}) + k_s I_s (\vec{R} \cdot \vec{V})^p} \qquad (9.4)$$

Example 9.1 (Intensity Calculation).   The elementary model applies to objects in camera space because the relations between camera, light sources, and triangles are key. As usual, the camera is placed at the origin looking down the z-axis at a triangle. The triangle's vertices are

$$V_0 = (1, 1, -6)$$
$$V_1 = (2, -1, -8)$$
$$V_2 = (-1, 0.5, -5)$$

There should be an order to the vertices so that we can determine how to calculate the normal coming out of the object. In this example, the order is clockwise, so we take $(V_2 - V_0) \times (V_1 - V_0)$ and normalize to find the unit normal $\vec{n} = (0.49, -0.49, 0.73)$. (We will round off calculations and expect some error to creep in.)

Next, focus on a point P in the interior of the triangle. Suppose the barycentric coordinates for P are $(0.5, 0.4, 0.1)$. Then the Cartesian coordinates will be

$$P = 0.5V_0 + 0.4V_1 + 0.1V_2 = (1.2, 0.15, -6.7)$$

The camera is positioned at the origin, so the vector from P to the camera is $(-1.2, -0.15, 6.7)$, and normalizing gives the vector $\vec{V} = (-0.18, -0.02, 0.98)$. Since $\vec{n} \cdot \vec{V} = 0.64 > 0$, the triangle is visible (assuming no other objects are in front of it) and the normal we found is pointing in the general direction of the camera.

Now position a point light source at $P_s = (9, 4, 2)$, which is behind the camera, up a little, and to the left. The vector $P_s - P$ will point from P on the triangle to the light source. Normalizing gives the unit vector $\vec{L} = (0.63, 0.31, 0.71)$. Calculating $\vec{n} \cdot \vec{L} = 0.68$ gives us the main factor in the diffuse reflection. To find the reflected ray, we use the formula derived above.

$$\vec{R} = 2(\vec{n} \cdot \vec{L})\vec{n} - \vec{L}$$
$$\approx 2(0.68)(0.49, -0.49, 0.73) - (0.63, 0.31, 0.71)$$
$$\approx (0.03, -0.97, 0.28)$$

The dot product with the vector to the camera gives $\vec{R} \cdot \vec{V} = 0.29$. If the surface is not very reflective, then the specular reflection is spread out a bit and we might argue for $p = 2$ in the illumination equation. Then the specular component is proportional to $(0.29)^2$. The illumination for the point P is now given by $I = k_a I_a + k_d I_d(0.68) + k_s I_s(0.29)^2$.

At this stage, we need to set the intensities and coefficients. The total intensity I depends on the scale we are using and probably differs between the wavelengths of light. In this example, suppose the scene is lit with white light and that all reflections are shades of gray. Let the color of the light range from 0 (black) to 1.0 (white); in the RGB color model, we are taking all three components to be equal.

The intensity I should have a maximum value of 1.0 and a minimum value of 0. It also makes some sense to interpret the coefficients k_a, k_d, and k_s as fractions of the light that is reflected in each mode. This implies that $I_a + I_d + I_s$ is at most 1.0 and at least 0. All three intensities are interrelated because a light source contributes to all three. However, practically, the ambient light is somewhat independent of the others and the point source light is divided between the diffuse and specular reflections. There are several reasonable ways to set these intensities.

Suppose we let $I_a = 0.3$, $I_d = 0.4$, and $I_s = 0.3$. If the triangle is made of material that is not very reflective and does have a roughness that encourages diffuse reflection, then perhaps $k_a = 0.7$, $k_d = 0.8$, and $k_s = 0.5$. The final intensity for P is the combination of the three reflective components.

$$I = I = (0.7)(0.3) + (0.8)(0.4)(0.67) + (0.5)(0.5)(0.30)^2 = 0.45$$

The lighting model we applied here is a rough approximation to the actual complex interaction between light and the scene. Most likely, further adjustment of the intensities and coefficients will be necessary to reach a satisfactory image.   □

The elementary model we have just outlined came out of Bui Tuong Phong's Ph.D. work published in 1975 [7] and is commonly referred to as the *Phong lighting model*. Note that, if there are several light sources in the scene, the intensity can be summed over all sources. If they are widely scattered light sources, then we may include attenuation due to distance by dividing by $D^* = a_2 D^2 + a_1 D + a_0$, where D is the distance to the light source.

$$I = k_a I_a + \sum_{i=1}^{n} (k_{(d,i)} I_{(d,i)} (\vec{n} \cdot \vec{L}) + k_{(s,i)} I_{(s,i)} (\vec{R} \cdot \vec{V})_i^p) \left(\frac{1}{D_i^*} \right) \qquad (9.5)$$

Since the coefficients and intensities are dependent on the wavelength of the light, we should repeat the intensity calculation for each primary color (red, green, blue) and combine the results to determine the shade of each point.

One of the several improvements that can be made to the model is to include different sorts of light sources like spot lights and non-point sources. At some point, the computational tradeoffs take too great a toll. Clearly, approximations and assumptions limit the accuracy of the elementary model, but the results are often quite satisfactory and the computation time is bearable.

9.2.1   Gouraud and Phong Shading

Drawing on the elementary model to determine the shading of an object made from flat triangular faces results in what is called *flat shading*. On a triangle, the normal vector is constant, and if the light source is relatively distant or the triangle is small, the vector $\vec{L}$ is nearly the same for every point on the triangle. Similarly, $\vec{V}$ is also nearly constant across the triangle (unless the camera is very close). Ambient, diffuse, and specular intensities are then fairly similar on a single triangular face, and the resulting flat shading accentuates edges between faces.

Intensities change abruptly from one triangle to an adjacent one because the normal usually changes abruptly. This might be fine for lighting a cube where each face is starkly different under a single light, but it is not fine for lighting a gently curved car body where it should not appear to be made of individual flat triangles. The problem is twofold. The flat triangles only approximate the surface, and the elementary model does not include more complex light interactions that might serve to soften edges in some cases.

One key idea to resolving this problem is to use interpolation to determine shading rather than relying on the fixed normal to a triangular face. Rather than using the normal for the plane containing the triangle, a normal is calculated at each vertex to better approximate the larger surface made of many triangles. If we actually knew the equation of the curved surface of an object, we could calculate the true normal at any point using calculus. Instead, with a large number of triangles approximating the curved surface, several triangles meet at a vertex. At that vertex, a reasonable approximation to a normal for the true curved surface is the average (component by component) of the normals for each triangle meeting the vertex. In this way, an averaged normal can be assigned to each vertex of a single triangle, and most likely those three normals will not be equal.

Using the elementary light model, we apply the intensity formula to determine the appropriate shade for each vertex. Then we interpolate to find the shading for each interior point of the triangle. For example, if a point on the edge of a triangle is $P(t) = (1 - t)V_0 + tV_1$, then the shade of this point is $S(t) = (1 - t)S_0 + tS_1$, where S_0 and S_1 are the shades of V_0 and V_1. In general, barycentric coordinates serve to interpolate the three vertices in order to shade any interior point. This technique was first suggested by the French computer scientist Henri Gouraud and is referred to as *Gouraud shading*. Instead of shading all points on a triangle nearly the same, it shades as though the underlying surface was curved. It softens the edges between triangles, but its simplicity causes other problems. An obvious one is that, because the shading of points is interpolated, specular reflections cannot be accurately rendered across a face. Only the values at the vertices are accurate, so the specular reflection tends to be smeared on the face.

A second approach to this interpolation technique is to interpolate the normals rather than the shade intensities. In other words, given the three normals at the vertices of a triangle, we interpolate to find the normal at any arbitrary point in the triangle. Then we revisit the intensity formula to find the appropriate shade for the point. This type of interpolation was suggested by B.T. Phong and is called *Phong shading*. It requires more computation, but does a better job of approximating specular reflections. Let $\vec{N}_0$ and $\vec{N}_1$ be normals calculated by averaging the normals around each of the vertices V_0 and V_1. At the point $P(t) = (1 - t)V_0 + tV_1$, the interpolated normal is $(1 - t)\vec{N}_0 + t\vec{N}_1$. Yet, this normal is not necessarily a unit normal, so dividing by the length gives

$$\vec{N}(t) = \frac{(1 - t)\vec{N}_0 + t\vec{N}_1}{|(1 - t)\vec{N}_0 + t\vec{N}_1|}$$

The values $\vec{N}(t) \cdot \vec{L}$ and $\vec{N}(t) \cdot \vec{V}$ along with the intensity formula determine the shading for the interior point.

Example 9.2 (Shading: Flat, Gouraud, Phong).   Consider a triangle with the following vertices:

$$V_0 = (1, -2, 6)$$
$$V_1 = (5, 2, 1)$$
$$V_2 = (-1, 4, 0)$$

A light source is at position $(10, 12, 8)$ and we are interested in shading the centroid of the triangle.

$$P = \frac{1}{3}(V_0 + V_1 + V_2) = \frac{1}{3}(5, 4, 7)$$

The unit vector from P to the light source is $\vec{L} = (0.57, 0.73, 0.39)$. Assume that the vertices were given in counterclockwise order (looking from the outside of the object) and therefore the normal to the triangle is $(V_1 - V_0) \times (V_2 - V_0) = (6, 34, 32)$. The unit normal is then $\vec{n} = (0.13, 0.72, 0.68)$. For flat shading, the diffuse reflection component (which depends on the dot product $\vec{n} \cdot \vec{L}$) is

$$I(F)_{\text{diffuse}} = k_d I_d (\vec{n} \cdot \vec{L}) = k_d I_d (0.86)$$

The ambient and specular components can be calculated, but we will compare the diffuse component among the three shading techniques.

Suppose that there are three triangles meeting at vertex V_2 and the three normals are

$$\vec{n}_{20} = \vec{n} = (0.13, 0.72, 0.68)$$
$$\vec{n}_{21} = (0, 0.71, 0.71)$$
$$\vec{n}_{22} = (-0.70, 0.66, 0.27)$$

The average of the three normals is $(-0.19, 0.70, 0.55)$. However, this vector does not have unit length; the length of the average is always less than or equal to 1. Normalizing gives a unit normal $\vec{n}_2 = (-0.21, 0.77, 0.60)$. Suppose similar calculations are done for the other two vertices in the triangle giving three unit normals. In addition, the vectors $\vec{L}_i$ are vectors from the vertices to the light source.

$$\vec{n}_0 = (-0.16, -0.31, 0.94) \qquad \vec{L}_0 = (0.54, 0.84, 0.12)$$
$$\vec{n}_1 = (0.89, 0.09, -0.45) \qquad \vec{L}_1 = (0.38, 0.76, 0.53)$$
$$\vec{n}_2 = (-0.21, 0.77, 0.60) \qquad \vec{L}_2 = (0.70, 0.51, 0.51)$$

The dot product of each normal with the vector to the light source gives the intensity of the diffuse component at each vertex.

$$\vec{n}_0 \cdot \vec{L}_0 = -0.23$$

$$\vec{n}_1 \cdot \vec{L}_1 = 0.17$$

$$\vec{n}_2 \cdot \vec{L}_2 = 0.55$$

For point P, the average of these three intensities gives the diffuse component, but notice that the intensity at V_0 is negative. Technically, this means that the vertex should be colored $(0, 0, 0)$, which is black. If we take it as intensity 0 and average, we get the Gouraud shade.

$$I(G)_{\text{diffuse}} = k_d I_d (0.24)$$

For Phong shading, interpolating the normals at P and renormalizing gives the unit normal $\vec{n}_p$.

$$\frac{1}{3}(\vec{n}_0 + \vec{n}_1 + \vec{n}_2) = (0.17, 0.18, 0.36) \implies \vec{n}_p = (0.39, 0.41, 0.82)$$

The dot product with $\vec{L}$ gives the diffuse component for the Phong model.

$$I(P)_{\text{diffuse}} = k_d I_d (0.84)$$

Keep in mind that both the Gouraud and Phong shading techniques are approximations to the actual light shading. To find normals at the vertices, we averaged face normals component by component and, this may not be the best way to find a vertex normal. It should approximate the ideal surface of the object, so it may be that a weighted normal, for example, would be a better choice.   □

To theoretically compare Gouraud and Phong interpolation techniques, focus on the diffuse component of the lighting model and consider interpolation along an edge between two vertices. For Gouraud shading, we interpolate shades S_i.

$$\begin{aligned} S_G(t) &= (1 - t)S_0 + tS_1 \\ &= k((1 - t)(\vec{N}_0 \cdot \vec{L}) + t(\vec{N}_1 \cdot \vec{L})) \end{aligned} \tag{9.6}$$

For Phong shading, the interpolation of the normals is followed by the dot product, giving the following formula.

$$\begin{aligned} S_P(t) = k\vec{N}(t) \cdot \vec{L} &= k\frac{((1 - t)\vec{N}_0 + t\vec{N}_1)}{|((1 - t)\vec{N}_0 + t\vec{N}_1)|} \cdot L \\ &= k\frac{((1 - t)(\vec{N}_0 \cdot \vec{L}) + t(\vec{N}_1 \cdot \vec{L}))}{|((1 - t)\vec{N}_0 + t\vec{N}_1)|} \end{aligned} \tag{9.7}$$

The denominator in the Phong case is less than 1. To see this, form a triangle with vectors $(1 - t)\vec{N}_0$ and $t\vec{N}_1$. The normals are unit normal, so the sum of the lengths of these two sides is 1. The length of the third side of the triangle is the Phong denominator; it must be less than or equal to 1.

$$\frac{S_G}{S_P} = |((1 - t)\vec{N}_0 + t\vec{N}_1| \leq 1 \tag{9.8}$$

The Phong diffuse component will be brighter than the Gouraud component. The ratio of the specular components does not simplify as nicely, but we can still tell that the Phong shading is brighter in some areas.

Both these shading techniques can be applied before a perspective transformation projects the object onto the screen. However, to possibly avoid unnecessary computations, we can wait until after the transformation. Referring to the object in camera space helps us to find all the normals, and then we use the perspective-correct interpolation to get appropriate shades for pixels on the screen.

9.2.2   Shadows

Shadows are a little difficult. The central idea is simple: the rays from a light source are obstructed, preventing them from illuminating some points in the scene. If the line segment from point P in the scene back to the point light source L intersects an object in between, then P is in the shadow and the intensity of light at P is diminished. With several light sources in the scene and not all of them point sources, the problem remains conceptually reasonable but practically a lot messier. If we further complicate the situation by requiring fast calculations for real-time shadows, the problem becomes very demanding (Figure 9.5).

Planar Shadows   For some scenes, the shadow problem is tractable. Take the situation where a cube is positioned above a ground plane and a light source somewhere

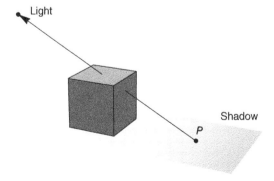

Figure 9.5   Casting shadows

higher than the cube casts a shadow of the cube on the ground. This is a straightforward case of projecting the vertices of the cube onto the ground plane; a perspective
transformation using the light source as the center of projection does the trick. Actually, the shadow is the convex hull of the projections of the eight vertices; we do not
need any vertices inside this silhouette. To this end, notice that basically we only need
to project vertices from faces (triangles) that are visible to the light source. By placing the camera at the light source position and using the visibility test we developed
before (dot product of normals with the vector to the camera), hidden triangles can be
ignored. Since the projected vertices we want are on the edge of the shadow, we only
need to project vertices from visible triangles that are adjacent to hidden triangles.
(Nonconvex objects become a little complicated.)

Example 9.3 (A Shadow on the Ground). Suppose we have a cube centered at the
origin in a local coordinate system. The vertices are $(\pm 1, \pm 1, \pm 1)$. Translate the local
coordinate system 4 units up (y direction), so the cube's center has world coordinates $(0, 4, 0)$ and the ground plane is the xz plane from the world coordinate system.
Position a point light source in the world system at $(-10, 8, 2)$.

A vector $\vec{v}$ from the light course to the cube vertex $(1, 5, 1)$ determines the direction
of the light ray, $\vec{v} = (11, -3, -1)$. The ray is given by $(-10, 8, 2) + t\vec{v}$, and it hits the
ground plane when the y coordinate is zero to give the projected vertex V^*.

$$8 + t(-3) = 0 \implies t = \frac{8}{3} \implies V^* \approx (19.33, 0, -0.67)$$

More generally, with a light source at (L_x, L_y, L_z) and a vertex at (V_x, V_y, V_z), the
expression for V_x^*, the x coordinate for the projection, is easy to calculate because
the ground plane in this example has a simple description ($y = 0$).

$$t = \frac{-L_y}{V_y - L_y} \implies V_x^* = L_x + t(V_x - L_x) = \frac{L_x V_y - L_y V_x}{V_y - L_y}$$

Using homogeneous coordinates gives a matrix M_s for the shadow projection:

$$M_s = \begin{bmatrix} -L_y & L_x & 0 & 0 \\ 0 & 0 & 0 & 0 \\ 0 & L_z & -L_y & 0 \\ 0 & 1 & 0 & -L_y \end{bmatrix} \implies M_s = \begin{bmatrix} -8 & -10 & 0 & 0 \\ 0 & 0 & 0 & 0 \\ 0 & 2 & -8 & 0 \\ 0 & 1 & 0 & -8 \end{bmatrix}$$

The matrix sends the vertex $(1, 5, 1, 1)$ in homogeneous coordinates to the point
$(-58, 0, 2, -3)$, which verifies the original calculation.

We can test to see which faces are visible from the light source by checking the
dot product between normals to the faces and a vector to the light source. The vector
to the light source from vertex $(-1, 5, 1)$ is $\vec{w} = (-9, 3, 1)$, and the dot products with
the face normals $(0, 1, 0)$, $(0, 0, 1)$, and $(-1, 0, 0)$ are all positive, indicating visibility.

The faces are naturally squares for the cube instead of triangles, but triangulating the faces does not add vertices, so we can deal just with the square faces. Since vertex $(-1, 5, 1)$ is not adjacent to a hidden face and vertex $(1, 3, -1)$ is itself hidden, these two are not vertices of the shadow; all other vertices are.

Vertex	Projection
$(1, 5, -1)$	$(19.33, 0, -6)$
$(1, 5, 1)$	$(19.33, 0, -0.67)$
$(1, 3, 1)$	$(7.6, 0, 0.4)$
$(-1, 5, -1)$	$(14, 0, -6)$
$(-1, 3, -1)$	$(4.4, 0, -2.8)$
$(-1, 3, 1)$	$(4.4, 0, 0.4)$

If we move the light source farther away from the cube, the rays are close to being parallel. If we position the light at $k(L_x, L_y, L_z)$, where k is a larger and larger positive number, it moves away along the vector (L_x, L_y, L_z). The formula for V_x changes as follows:

$$V_x^* = \frac{(kL_x)V_y - (kL_y)V_x}{V_y - kL_y} = \frac{(L_x)V_y - (L_y)V_x}{\left(\dfrac{V_y}{k}\right) - L_y}$$

As k goes to infinity, the V_y term in the denominator goes to zero and the 1 in the last row of the matrix M_s becomes zero. This is a parallel projection, where the light source is infinitely far away and the rays are parallel. It is easy to check that the vertex $(1, 5, 1)$ is projected to $(7.25, 0, -0.25)$ under this projection.   □

The algorithm in this example shifted the camera to the light source, determined visible faces, and then projected the appropriate vertices to the ground plane. The ground plane was the xz plane in the example, but it could easily be an arbitrary plane. We are using a projection, and the derivation in Chapter 8 using homogeneous coordinates will work here as well (see Section 9.5 for details of projection on an arbitrary plane).

Of course, there are complications. The object itself might obscure some of the shadow as, for example, when the cube rests on the ground rather than hovering above. It also happens that the shadow could be cast partially on the ground but continues by wrapping up a side of a nearby building. Again, these are conceptually tractable from the geometric point of view but practically are more involved.

Soft Shadows Notice that the simple shadow on a plane has a sharp edge. The shadow edge is the edge of a polygon, and there is a sharp division between the

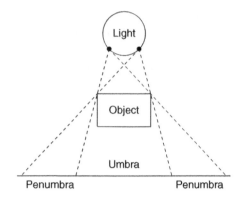

Figure 9.6   Soft shadows

brighter illumination outside the polygon and the darker interior. This is unrealistic and results from assuming that the light soueces are point sources. If the light has an area, then rays of light emanate from several points rather than a single point. Figure 9.6 shows that some of these rays may be obscured by an object while others are not. This gives rise to two regions in the shadow, the penumbra and the umbra. By picking several points on the light source and projecting vertices from these points, it becomes clear that the umbra is dark and the penumbra has varying intensity. This means the shadow edges will appear soft rather than hard and we call the result a *soft shadow*.

Once again, all the reflections (and some diffraction) of the light are not incorporated in this approximation of how soft shadows are formed. We can calculate hard shadows from a sampling of points in the light source and then superimpose them. The resulting approximation gives a soft shadow, but the result is not always satisfactory, so there needs to be various enhancements to this basic algorithm.

Shadow Maps   Our approach to shadows has been geometric, seeking to find polygons that approximate the shadow. Another, more often successful, approach systematically moves from point to point in the scene asking whether it is in the shadow or not. One way to do this is to move the camera to the light source (as we did in the geometric approach) and proceed to render the scene using something like the painter's algorithm. From the point of view of the light source, points in the scene project onto the view plane, but the closest point (to the light source) is visible from the light source and is therefore not in shadow. By saving the z coordinates of these closest points, we build what is called a *shadow map*.

Once the camera is returned to its original position and we start rendering the scene on the display, we can check each point to see if it is visible in the shadow map. To do this, transform the point's z coordinate to the coordinate system used by the shadow map and compare to the z coordinate of the map. If the current point is further from the light source, then it is in the shadow and needs a diminished intensity. Otherwise, it is rendered normally.

Shadow Volumes Another technique starts with the observation that each triangle, for example, when positioned in the path of a light source forms a volume behind it in the shape of a truncated pyramid before it casts the shadow on the ground plane. Any point in this volume is shaded by the triangle so the volume is a *shadow volume*.

To determine the triangle's shadow in the scene, points are checked to see if they fall in the shadow volume. Relative to each light source in a scene, there are a series of shadow volumes. To determine if a particular point is in one of them, we follow a ray from the camera to the point in the scene, recording along the way whether we entered or exited a shadow volume. If the ray both enters and exits a volume, then the point is not in that particular shadow. There is a lot of computation here, but the algorithm identifies overlapping shadows and can set the light intensity at points more appropriately. This technique is well suited for the ray tracing algorithm which we consider below.

9.2.3   BRDFs in Lighting Models

In the elementary lighting model, ambient light is an approximation for all the extraneous light that results from secondary reflections in the scene. It is an example of what we will call *global illumination*. Diffuse reflection and specular reflections from discrete light sources determine the *local illumination*. The assumption in the elementary model is that diffuse reflection is independent of direction; it is equal in all directions. On the other hand, specular reflection is concentrated around a single direction.

For a more general description of how surfaces might reflect light, we need to explain how much light coming from some arbitrary direction reflects in any other arbitrary direction. To say, as is done in the elementary model, that some light reflects equally in all directions and some reflects close to a single direction is just one possibility of how a surface might behave. Plastic surfaces behave differently from brushed nickel which behaves differently from polished marble. Lighting models one step up from the elementary model introduce a function first defined in 1977 [8] called the *bidirectional reflectance distribution function* (or BRDF for short) which gives a more detailed account of reflected light from a particular type of surface.

Let $\vec{v}_i$ be the direction to the light source. This light strikes the surface and some of it reflects in direction $\vec{v}_o$. (This is not necessarily a mirror reflection; $\vec{v}_o$ can be any direction.) The BRDF is a function denoted $\rho_r(\vec{v}_i, \vec{v}_o)$, which gives the ratio of the change in reflected light in direction $\vec{v}_o$ to the change in incoming light from the direction $\vec{v}_i$. If we know how intense the incoming light is from some direction, the BRDF allows us to calculate the reflected light in any outgoing direction. Before we can make complete sense of this, we need to be more careful about measuring quantities of light.

Measuring Light As light is emitted from a source, it transfers energy, and measuring this energy transfer is the key to measuring light. If we switch to the quantum view of light, energy transfer is the number of photons passing through a particular volume of space in a particular unit of time. Since light travels in all directions from a source much like the surface of an expanding sphere, a light beam in a given direction expands from the source into a cone. Conversely, a detector gathers light arriving at a surface from a particular direction by measuring energy transfer through the wide end of a cone. To measure light in a given direction, we need to quantify the energy transfer per unit time, adjust for the area of the source, and adjust for the solid angle of the cone. Energy transfer per time is measured in watts, and solid angles are measured in steradians (Appendix A). We measure light from a direction as *radiance* with units of watts per square meter per steradian.

In the science of radiometry, there are several carefully defined quantities that characterize light falling on a surface or reflected from it, but to focus on the aspects important for graphics we will consider radiance either incoming from a light source or outgoing from surface reflectance. As the incoming radiance changes, the outgoing reflectance changes. The BRDF details the ratio of the changes for the directions $\vec{v}_i$ (incoming) and $\vec{v}_o$ (reflected).

To analyze the light at a particular point P on a surface, place a hemisphere of radius 1 over the surface centered at P. Then, any vector direction from which the light strikes P or leaves P can be described by giving the spherical coordinates of the intersection of the ray with the hemisphere. The spherical coordinates $(1, \theta, \phi)$ are sufficient to determine a direction by giving the angle around the normal and the angle from the normal to the intersection. With this coordinate system, the BRDF becomes a function of four angles, $\rho_r(\theta_i, \phi_i, \theta_o, \phi_o)$, where the unit vector $\vec{v}_i$ is determined by the angles θ_i, ϕ_i and v_o is determined by θ_o, ϕ_o.

Let $L_i(\vec{v}_i)$ be the radiance of the incoming light from direction $\vec{v}_i$ and let $L_o(\vec{v}_o)$ be the radiance of light reflected from the surface in direction $\vec{v}_o$. The quantity $L_o(\vec{v}_o)$ is the result of reflecting light coming from all possible directions, so $L_i(\vec{v}_i)$ only determines a change $\Delta L_o(\vec{v}_o)$ in the reflected light.

The radiance $L_i(\vec{v}_i)$ of the incoming light passes through a small patch on the surface of the imagined hemisphere before striking the surface (Figure 9.7). The patch determines a solid angle emanating from P, and the measure of the solid angle is the area of the patch (since the radius of the hemisphere is 1). We call the area of the patch $\Delta\omega$ and adjust the total light coming in as $L_i(\vec{v}_i)\Delta\omega_i$. Since this light arrives at an angle ϕ with the normal, Lambert's law claims that the light is spread out at P and reduced by the cosine. Hence, the radiance falling at P from the direction $\vec{v}_i$ is $L_i(\vec{v}_i) \cos \phi_i \Delta\omega_i$.

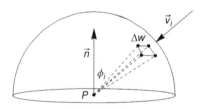

Figure 9.7   Incoming light

Definition 9.1 (BRDF). *If $L_i(\vec{v}_i)$ and $L_o(\vec{v}_o)$ are the incoming and reflected radiances from directions $\vec{v}_i$ and $\vec{v}_o$, respectively, then the BRDF is*

$$\rho_r(\vec{v}_i, \vec{v}_o) = \frac{\Delta L_o(\vec{v}_o)}{L_i(\vec{v}_i)(\vec{n} \cdot \vec{v}_i)\Delta\omega_i} \tag{9.9}$$

To be completely careful about the BRDF, note that it is undoubtedly dependent on the wavelength of light and may also vary with position on the surface. However, we will take the practical stance that calculating the BRDF at representative red, green, and blue wavelengths will be sufficient, and that it depends only on the material, not on the surface position.

For the total radiance L_o reflected in direction $(\vec{v}_o)$, we add up the incoming contributions from all the patches on the hemisphere. This means that we integrate L_i over the hemisphere. The small angle $\Delta\omega$ becomes the differential $d\omega$ and we consider this differential angle as a small rectangle on the hemisphere. Writing it in terms of small changes in the two direction angles gives $d\omega_i = \sin\phi_i d\phi_i d\theta_i$.

$$L_o(\vec{v}_o) = \int_0^{2\pi} \int_0^{\frac{\pi}{2}} \rho_r(\vec{v}_i, \vec{v}_o) L_i(\vec{v}_i)(\vec{n} \cdot \vec{v}_i)\sin\varphi_i d\varphi_i d\theta_i \tag{9.10}$$

With this integral, it is starting to look possible to compute the amount of light reflected off a surface in a given direction. We need the BRDF of course, but research groups have experimentally determined values for the function in many directions.

Properties of the BRDF There are a few properties inherent to the definition of the BRDF (including Equation 9.10), but there also others that should be imposed in order to ensure the BRDF satisfies the laws of physics.

1. Because of the cosine in the denominator of the BRDF, the value of the BRDF may be greater than 1.
2. Owing to the solid angle $\Delta\omega_i$ in the denominator, the BRDF has units of reciprocal steradians.
3. Physically, it makes sense that, if we reverse the incoming and outgoing directions, we should have the same ratio of radiances. Consequently, reasonable BRDF's should satisfy

$$\rho_r(\vec{L}_i, \vec{L}_o) = \rho_r(\vec{L}_o, \vec{L}_i)$$

   The BRDF should be bidirectional.
4. The laws of physics require the conservation of energy, so the total incoming radiance at a point should be greater than or equal to the total outgoing radiance at a point. In other words, the integral over the hemisphere of $L_i(\vec{v}_i)$ should be greater than or equal to the integral over the hemisphere of $L_o(\vec{v}_o)$.

Although Equation 9.10 may appear a little daunting, if the scene has a finite number of point sources or spot lights, the integral can be approximated by a sum over the various light sources.

$$L_o(\vec{v}_o) = \sum_{i=1}^{n} \rho_r(\vec{v}_i, \vec{v}_o) L_i(\vec{v}_i)(\vec{n} \cdot \vec{v}_i)\Delta\omega_i \qquad (9.11)$$

Here, $\Delta\omega_i$ may all be the same or may need to be adjusted for an appropriate balance between types of light sources. The light value we use to shade a pixel on the screen should be proportional to the radiance $L_o(\vec{v}_o)$.

BRDF Examples We can temporarily rethink the elementary lighting model in terms of a BRDF. The diffuse and specular reflection in that model are given by

$$k_d I_d(\vec{n} \cdot \vec{L}) + k_s I_s(\vec{R} \cdot \vec{V})^p$$

The vector to the light source $\vec{L}$ becomes $\vec{v}_i$ in the more refined model and $\vec{V}$ becomes $\vec{v}_o$. The quantities I_d and I_s denote incoming light, and the total of these two corresponds to the incoming intensity $L_i(\vec{v}_i)$. In effect, for some fraction λ, we have

$$I_d = \lambda L_i(\vec{v}_i) \qquad I_s = (1 - \lambda)L_i(\vec{v}_i)$$

Now we can define a BRDF that gives the elementary model.

$$\rho_r(\vec{v}_i, \vec{v}_o) = \lambda k_d + (1 - \lambda)\frac{k_s(\vec{R} \cdot \vec{v}_o)^p}{\vec{n} \cdot \vec{v}_i} \qquad (9.12)$$

With a single point source, we can calculate reflected light by simply multiplying by the intensity of incoming light reduced by the cosine law, $L(\vec{v}_i)(\vec{n} \cdot \vec{v}_i)$.

The idea here is just to understand the earlier lighting model in terms of a BRDF. Indeed, if we look more closely at this particular BRDF, we note that it is not bidirectional and it also does not satisfy conservation of energy. It comes, after all, from a lighting model designed to only approximate the physics and to be simple to calculate.

The BRDF allows us to model materials between two extremes. On one hand, we have materials that reflect light equally in all directions around the normal. That is, the BRDF is independent of the angle θ_o and is called *isotropic*. On the other hand, we have *anisotropic* BRDFs which do depend on θ_o. Diffuse reflection in the elementary lighting model was isotropic and specular reflection was anisotropic. An appropriate choice of a BRDF can produce a mixture of these two extremes. However, there are other complex interactions between light and material that are not captured by a BRDF. For example, when light strikes marble, it travels and reflects under the surface to a certain degree, giving marble a translucent look. Other approaches to lighting models try to deal with this effect.

The Cook–Torrance lighting model is an early model that improved on the elementary lighting model by considering the surface to be composed of micro-facets (small flat surfaces) distributed with random orientations. The resulting model effectively used a BRDF of the following form:

$$\rho_r(\vec{v}_i, \vec{v}_o) = F(\vec{v}_i, \vec{v}_o) \frac{D(\vec{v}_i, \vec{v}_o) G(\vec{v}_i, \vec{v}_o)}{\pi(\vec{n} \cdot \vec{v}_o)(\vec{n} \cdot \vec{v}_i)} \tag{9.13}$$

The function F describes reflection (amount and color) from a micro-facet, D gives the fraction of micro-facets in a particular orientation, and G quantifies how much shadowing goes on between facets. The Cook–Torrance model results in a significant difference, for example, between the look of plastic and the look of metal surfaces. (For a more complete description of the model, see [9].)

Researchers have experimentally measured BRDFs for a variety of surfaces, and by fitting curves to the resulting data graphics programmers can incorporate the functions to render objects much more realistically. The computational cost is rather high, so there is a constant search for reasonable approximations to the full theory.

9.3 GLOBAL ILLUMINATION

The lighting models developed so far are local models considering only the direct effect of light sources in illuminating a specified point. Yet, there are many complex lighting interactions in a scene and a physically correct global illumination model is generally computationally intractable. Instead, we move up one more step from the local models and try to incorporate a little more of light interaction in the scene. Ray tracing, which was introduced in an earlier chapter, takes a geometric approach to this goal and systematically follows light rays in the scene trying to track sources of illumination for each point. A more physics-oriented method, radiosity, focuses on light energy and attempts to balance that energy across all the object faces in a scene. Both of these methods are incremental improvements on the local models.

9.3.1 Ray Tracing

Ray tracing follows light rays as if they travel from the eye into the scene. We could stop at the first intersection with an object, say point P_1, and use the elementary lighting model to calculate the color at P_1. If we did this, then ray tracing simply becomes a visibility test and we gain nothing over some of the other elementary lighting models. However, some of the light sources may not reach P_1, or light reflected from other faces may reach P_1. In both cases, the elementary lighting model could be augmented with these slightly more complex interactions. Ray tracing can make these enhancements by following three types of rays from P_1 further into the scene.

Shadow Rays These are really test rays that we follow from the point P_1 to the various light sources in the scene. If one of these test rays strikes an object before the light source, the source does not illuminate P_1 and it is in a shadow. To calculate the color at P_1, we start with either the elementary model (Equation 9.5) or the BRDF model appropriate for the surface material (Equation 9.11). Since the point is in a shadow relative to one of the lights, the summations in either model are taken over a reduced set of light sources. Ray tracing then produces shadows, although they can appear rather sharp.

Reflected Rays   The light ray from the eye to P_1 can be reflected using the formula in Equation 9.3. The reflected ray starting at P_1 travels further into the scene perhaps intersecting an object at P_2. This just means that light could travel from P_2 to P_1 and then to the eye. In short, the color at point P_1 is influenced by the color at P_2. We add P_2 as a light source when determining the intensity at P_1.

Refracted Rays   Some materials, like water or glass, are transparent and light travels through them. Yet, when this happens, rays are bent as they move into a material where the speed of light suddenly changes. Figure 9.8(a) shows a light ray from P hitting the surface of a new material and bending slightly as it travels through the new material to the point R. If we knew where the ray intersected the surface (Q), then we could find the angles that determine how the light bends. The key concept here that helps pin down the position of Q is called *Fermat's principle*, which simply says that light finds the path that minimizes the time to get from P to R.

Suppose that the speed of light in the first medium (maybe air) is c_1 and the speed of light in the second medium (perhaps glass) is c_2. Then the length of PQ divided by c_1 is the time light spends going from P to Q. Similarly, the length of QR divided by c_2 gives the time for the second traversal. Since points P and R are fixed, the distances d, e_1, and e_2 are all constants. The time T for the light to go from P to R is dependent on Q and is therefore a function of distance x.

$$T(x) = \frac{\sqrt{x^2 + e_1^2}}{c_1} + \frac{\sqrt{(d-x)^2 + e_2^2}}{c_2}$$

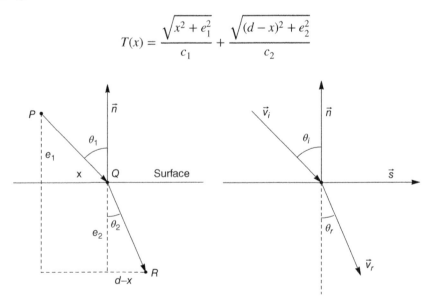

Figure 9.8(a,b)   Refraction

To find the value of x that minimizes the time, we take the derivative and set it to zero. (A check of the second derivative shows this is a minimum.)

$$T'(x) = \frac{x}{c_1 \sqrt{x^2 + e_1^2}} - \frac{d - x}{c_2 \sqrt{(d - x)^2 + e_2^2}} = 0$$

$$\implies \frac{\sin \theta_1}{\sin \theta_2} = \frac{c_1}{c_2}$$

The angles are between the rays and the normal to the surface, and the ratio of their sines turns out to be equal to the ratio of the speeds. By defining the *refractive index*, denoted by η, as the ratio of the speed of light in a vacuum to the speed of light in a particular medium, the ratio of the speeds is just the inverse ratio of the refractive indices.

$$\text{Snell's Law:} \quad \frac{\sin \theta_1}{\sin \theta_2} = \frac{\eta_2}{\eta_1} \qquad (9.14)$$

Figure 9.8(b) shows an incoming ray $\vec{v}_i$ and a refracted ray $\vec{v}_r$; we will take these vectors to be unit vectors. In addition, there is a unit normal $\vec{n}$ to the surface and a perpendicular unit vector $\vec{s}$ along the surface. By projecting the vector $\vec{v}_i$ onto $\vec{n}$ and then onto $\vec{s}$, it can be written as a combination of $\vec{n}$ and $\vec{s}$. The same is true for $\vec{v}_r$. (Notice how the direction of the vectors affects the signs.)

$$\vec{v}_i = -(\sin \theta_i)\vec{s} - (\cos \theta_i)\vec{n}$$

$$\vec{v}_r = -(\sin \theta_r)\vec{s} - (\cos \theta_r)\vec{n}$$

The problem is to find $\vec{v}_r$ once we know $\vec{v}_i$ and Snell's law helps immediately in finding $\sin \theta_r$.

$$\sin \theta_r = \frac{\eta_i}{\eta_r} \sin \theta_i$$

Just a little more work gives $\cos \theta_r$.

$$\eta_i^2 \sin^2 \theta_i = \eta_r^2 \sin^2 \theta_r = \eta_r^2 (1 - \cos^2 \theta_r)$$

$$\implies \cos^2 \theta_r = 1 - \frac{\eta_i^2}{\eta_r^2}(1 - \cos^2 \theta_i)$$

We can now write $\vec{v}_r$ in terms of the sine and cosine of θ_i, but it is even more convenient to write it in terms of v_i. To that end, we get the following equalities because the vectors are unit vectors.

$$-\cos \theta_i = \vec{v}_i \cdot \vec{n}$$

$$-(\sin \theta_i)\vec{s} = \vec{v}_i - (\vec{v}_i \cdot \vec{n})\vec{n}$$

Putting all these together gives an expression for the refracted ray.

$$\vec{v}_r = \frac{\eta_i}{\eta_r}(\vec{v}_i - (\vec{v}_i \cdot \vec{n})\,\vec{n}) - \left(1 - \frac{\eta_i^2}{\eta_r^2}(1 - (\vec{v}_i \cdot \vec{n})^2)\right)^{\frac{1}{2}}\vec{n} \qquad (9.15)$$

There is a square root in this formula, and if the quantity inside is negative, then there is no refracted ray. Instead, the incident ray is totally reflected. In a more complete model of light striking a transparent surface, some of the light is reflected and some of the light is refracted. The amount of each is determined by the Fresnel equations.

Example 9.4   A ray in the direction $(1, -2, 1)$ travels through air and hits a glass plate at $P_1 = (2, 0, 4)$. The plate has thickness 0.5 and normal $\vec{n} = (-1, 0, 0)$. Air has a refractive index of approximately 1.0 and the glass plate has an index of 1.5 (Figure 9.9).

To determine the direction of the refractive ray v_r, first normalize the incoming vector to get $\vec{v}_i = (0.41, -0.82, 0.41)$ and then use Equation 9.15.

$$\vec{v}_r = \frac{1.0}{1.5}((0.41, -0.82, 0.41) - (-0.41)(-1, 0, 0)) - (0.79)(-1, 0, 0)$$
$$= (0.79, -0.55, 0.27)$$

The refractive ray starts at P_1 and moves through the glass plate. Assuming parallel surfaces, the back surface of the plate contains the point $Q = (2.5, 0, 4)$. The ray intersects the back surface when

$$\vec{n} \cdot (P_1 + t(0.79, -0.55, 0.27) - Q) = 0 \implies t = 0.63$$

Using this value of t, we can determine that the refracted ray leaves the glass through the back surface at $P_2 = (2.5, -0.35, 4.17)$. As it leaves, it is refracted again on

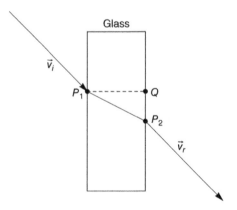

Figure 9.9   Refraction through a glass plate

moving from glass to air. Thinking of $\vec{v}_r$ as a new $\vec{v}_i$ and reversing the refractive indices, we can calculate the new refracted ray and discover that it is in the same direction as the initial $\vec{v}_i$. The exiting light ray is parallel to the original incident ray but displaced by passing through the glass plate. $\qquad\qquad\qquad\qquad\qquad\qquad\qquad\square$

Following a refracted ray further into the scene can enhance the lighting model just like reflected rays do. If it hits another object, the intersection point acts as an additional light source.

Full Ray Tracing   The ray tracing algorithm (first outlined by Whitted in [10]) is a recursive algorithm that continues following the rays until they pass entirely through the scene or until we reach a predetermined level of recursion. We began with rays from the camera (or eye) through points on the screen corresponding to pixels. At each intersection with an object in the scene, each of the possible three types of rays is followed deeper into the scene, building an entire tree of light rays and corresponding intersections. Each intersection generates a color and acts as a light source for points earlier in the tree. Once all these colors are combined as we back up the tree, we have a color for the pixel on the screen that defined the original ray. In this way, complexity is added to the elementary lighting models.

There are two problems that emerge from this approach. First, following a reflected or refracted ray does identify other sources of light, but rays close to these also will indicate possible paths of light. Probably, these other rays will not make huge contributions to the final illumination of point P_1, but there could be subtle effects that do contribute to the overall realism of the image. The BRDFs of materials in the scene will help predict just how much of a contribution a ray might make, but the main conclusion is that the straightforward ray tracing algorithm is an approximation, again, to the full complexity of light interactions in the scene. Of course, we can choose to follow additional rays, but the increasing computation cost starts to become a limiting constraint.

The second problem is that a ray-traced image can have a blocky or jagged look. Selecting one light ray per pixel on the screen means one ray determines the color of an entire pixel. Since adjacent rays may end up widely spaced in the scene, adjacent pixels on the screen may have significant differences in color, giving rise to an image that appears to be made of blocks; this is the common aliasing problem. To improve the image, additional rays can be taken through subpixels by perhaps dividing each pixel into four smaller ones. The four resulting rays give four colors that are then averaged to determine the color for the entire pixel. This distributive ray tracing produces better images, but there is, of course, a high computational cost.

9.3.2   Radiosity

The radiosity method approaches the problem of global illumination by focusing on the fact that surfaces in the scene are illuminated not only by direct light sources but also by light reflected off of other surfaces. As long as a point can be seen from another, it is possible that light reflecting from either of the two points can illuminate the other.

Trying to compute the connection between all pairs of points is a computational nightmare, so the immediate simplification is to consider only triangular surfaces that make up the scene; more specifically, selecting key surfaces often gives a satisfactory approximation. Assuming that the triangles are diffuse reflectors reduces the complexity even further and moves the solution within reach.

With light reflecting equally in all directions from a triangle (i.e., a Lambertian surface), the BRDF is constant. Light from direction $\vec{v}_i$ is reflected equally in all directions. Moreover, the fraction of light reflected is independent of $\vec{v}_i$ and we call this fraction diffuse reflectance, designated by $\rho(d)$.

Two triangular surfaces that can "see" each other possibly reflect light to each other. The amount of light illuminating one triangle from the other depends on their geometric orientation and we use F_{ij} to denote that relationship. Of the light that does strike triangle j, the fraction reflected in all directions is $\rho_j(d)$. The total light per area reflected off a triangle is called *radiosity* and for triangle i it is represented by B_i. In the event that triangle i is actually part of some light source, we let E_i be the intensity of that light; otherwise, $E_i = 0$. Putting these interactions together gives the radiosity equation.

$$\text{Radiosity Equation: } B_i = E_i + \rho_i(d) \sum_{j=1}^{N} B_j F_{ij} \qquad (9.16)$$

We can determine $\rho_i(d)$ based on the material composition of triangle i and the F_{ij} can all be calculated based solely on the geometry of the triangle orientation. This leaves the B_i as unknowns in the system of equations. (For a more complete derivation of the radiosity equation, see Section 9.5.)

Since the equations are linear in the unknowns, we can use matrices to describe the system and find a solution. First, put all the B_i variables in a column vector $\vec{B}$ and put all the emitted light radiosities (E_i) in a column vector $\vec{E}$; note that most of the E_i will be zero. Using the notation ρ_i instead of $\rho_i(d)$, define the matrix M as follows:

$$M = \begin{bmatrix} \rho_1 F_{11} & \rho_1 F_{12} & \cdots & \rho_2 F_{1N} \\ \rho_2 F_{21} & \rho_2 F_{22} & \cdots & \rho_2 F_{2N} \\ \vdots & & \ddots & \vdots \\ \rho_N F_{N1} & \rho_1 F_{N2} & \cdots & \rho_N F_{NN} \end{bmatrix}$$

The radiosity equation can be rephrased as follows:

$$B = E + MB \implies B = (I - M)^{-1} E \qquad (9.17)$$

The matrix formulation leads naturally to a solution, but these are large matrices and if $(I - M)$ does have an inverse, it usually is computationally expensive to find it.

Various numerical techniques can be brought to bear on this matrix equation and, in particular, because of the characteristics of M, iterative techniques that calculate successively better approximations work well but still require a reasonable amount of computation time. Once we have the radiosities, we shade pixels proportional to the corresponding B_i. The radiosity approach combined with ray tracing can produce some strikingly realistic images.

9.4 TEXTURES

Various shading models and the right BRDF can turn the flat faces of an object into a range of surfaces, from those with matte finishes and blurred bright spots to shiny finishes with mirror-like reflections of other objects in the scene. Changing color is also an easy matter in the rendering process, but adding details like the surface irregularities of a plaster wall or the periodic pattern of a brick wall requires a different approach.

Since modeling all the details of surface patterns and imperfections is usually computationally prohibitive, it makes sense, especially in time-sensitive animation, to simply paste a photo of a brick or stone wall, for example, onto the flat faces of an object. It even sometimes makes sense to use an image of a window to add interest to the wall. This is texture mapping and it basically takes an existing image and maps it onto a triangular face. The image (or map) can be an actual photo (like that of shingles on a roof), a color pattern (like patterns on fabric), or any other details (like varying normals to the surface) that alter the lighting model used to determine color shading.

9.4.1 Mapping

Suppose the texture map is two dimensional like a photo. In this case, it is a simple matter to select perpendicular axes, u and v, so that any point in the map has (u, v) coordinates. If the texture map has some other shape (perhaps circular), then another coordinate system may be more natural. In all cases, we find two parameters u and v that give a two-dimensional description for any point in the map. For convenience, normalize the coordinates so that u and v each take values between zero and 1 over the map. This is the texture coordinate system, or *texture space*.

Using a texture map involves stages at the beginning and end of the rendering process:

1. Connect the texture map to an object with an appropriate function.
2. Normal rendering—repositioning the object, converting to camera coordinates, and projecting onto the view window.
3. While converting to pixels, find the correct texture coordinates for points corresponding to the center of pixels. These coordinates determine the appropriate alteration of the shading model.

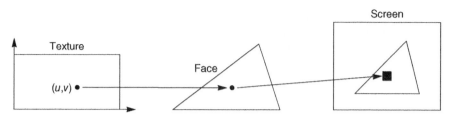

Figure 9.10 From texture map to screen

If the connection between the texture map and object is made by assigning texture coordinates (u, v) to the vertices of an object face, then as a face is converted to pixels at the end of the rendering pipeline, we could reference the texture map in order to select the correct color, shade, or other detail for enhancing the shading process (Figure 9.10).

The first step is to pick an appropriate function that sends points in the texture map to a triangular face, or vice versa. The texture map can be multidimensional, but start by thinking of it as a two-dimensional rectangle with normalized coordinates (u, v). A triangular face is also two dimensional, although it is positioned in three dimensions. Any type of two-dimensional parameterization of the face makes the connection with the texture map simpler. An xy coordinate system on the plane of the face will work, or even barycentric coordinates; the first two barycentric coordinates $(\alpha_0, \alpha 1)$ suffice because the sum of all three is 1. A mapping can now be thought of as a function of two variables mapping texture coordinates to coordinates (s, t) on the triangular face. If we are lucky, the mapping is one to one and there is an inverse.

$$f(u, v) = (s, t) \implies f^{-1}(s, t) = (u, v)$$

The texture source is usually a rectangular image, and there are many ways to map to the triangle. We can distort the source to fit the triangle, or simply cut a region out of the texture to fit the triangle; stretching, shrinking, tiling, or other manipulations are all possible functions that may be appropriate in certain situations. Whether the function or the inverse is easier to describe depends on the application and the amount of distortion that goes on in covering the triangular face. The end result is that we assign texture coordinates to each point on the face. After transformations, including the perspective transformation that brings the face to the view plane, we need some function to recover the texture coordinates of any point on the projected triangle.

Affine Mappings There are many possibilities for the function f, but if it is linear in some sense, then we can use linear interpolation to extend values at the vertices of the triangular face to any point inside the triangle. This means we only have to assign texture coordinates to the vertices of a face; the interior points follow by interpolation. So affine transformations are a good choice. Then, the function f can be expressed as multiplication by a homogeneous matrix M, and if the matrix has an inverse, f^{-1} is also easily represented by M^{-1}. By using the perspective-correct interpolation detailed in an earlier chapter, it is then easy to find the texture coordinates for the projected face vertices.

An affine transformation is determined by where it sends the three vertices of a triangle, so once we identify where the three points in the texture space are sent, we have the matrix M. (Notice that with homogeneous coordinates, the last row of the 3×3 matrix M can be taken as $(0, 0, 1)$. Then there are only six elements in the matrix to determine; knowing where the transformation sends three points gives us six equations to determine the unknowns.)

Once the triangle is projected onto the view plane, the texture coordinates associated with each vertex can be used along with interpolation to find the texture coordinates of any point inside the projected face. Instead of a color c_i for each vertex, we have texture coordinates (u_i, v_i); applying equation 8.9 then gives the correct interpolated coordinates.

The vertices of a triangular face have three-dimensional coordinates that are converted under the perspective transformation to normalized coordinates. For example, the first two vertices may end up with normalized coordinates $P_1 = (x_1, y_1, z_1)$ and $P_2 = (x_2, y_2, z_2)$. If we need the texture coordinates of point P between these two vertices, first find the z coordinate of $P = (1 - \alpha)P_1 + \alpha P_2$ by interpolating the reciprocals.

$$\frac{1}{z} = (1 - \alpha)\frac{1}{z_1} + \alpha\frac{1}{z_2}$$

Then interpolate the texture u coordinate.

$$\frac{u}{z} = (1 - \alpha)\frac{u_1}{z_1} + \alpha\frac{u_2}{z_2}$$

Finally, divide the two ($\frac{u}{z}$ by $\frac{1}{z}$) to find u. This procedure is consistent with using barycentric coordinates to find the texture coordinates of any point in the triangle.

Example 9.5 (Finding Texture Coordinates).   If we use perpendicular axes on a texture map and normalize the coordinates to stay within the interval [0,1], then the texture map is a unit square with vertices $(0, 0)$, $(1, 0)$, $(1, 1)$, and $(0, 1)$. Let a triangular face have the following vertices:

$$P_0 = (1, 4, -1)$$
$$P_1 = (-2, 5, 3)$$
$$P_2 = (4, 0, 1)$$

Suppose we decide to map the texture triangle with coordinates $(0, 0)$, $(1, 0)$, and $(0, 1)$ to the face vertices P_0, P_1, P_2 respecting the order. If we choose an affine function for the mapping, then knowing the values at the vertices is enough and we can find

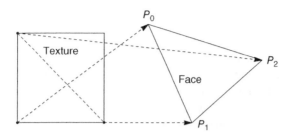

Figure 9.11 Affine map for texture coordinates

other values with interpolation. Yet, it is useful to actually describe the function and its inverse. Using homogeneous coordinates gives the following:

$$f(u, v, 1) = M \begin{bmatrix} u \\ v \\ 1 \end{bmatrix} = \begin{bmatrix} s \\ t \\ w \end{bmatrix}$$

For a parametrization of the triangular face, use the first two barycentric coordinates (α_0, α_1). Then $P_0 = (1, 0)$, $P_1 = (0, 1)$, and $P_2 = (0, 0)$. Putting all three texture map vertices in a matrix and all three face vertices in a matrix gives an equation for M. The matrix is homogeneous, so we can take the last row to be $(0, 0, 1)$ (Figure 9.11).

$$M \begin{bmatrix} 0 & 1 & 0 \\ 0 & 0 & 1 \\ 1 & 1 & 1 \end{bmatrix} = \begin{bmatrix} 1 & 0 & 0 \\ 0 & 1 & 0 \\ 1 & 1 & 1 \end{bmatrix} \implies M = \begin{bmatrix} -1 & -1 & 1 \\ 1 & 0 & 0 \\ 0 & 0 & 1 \end{bmatrix}$$

The function from texture coordinates to barycentric coordinates is an affine function represented by matrix M. The inverse M^{-1} sends barycentric coordinates to texture coordinates. In particular, the point $(0.25, 3.50, 1.50)$ is on the triangular face and has barycentric coordinates $(0.25, 0.50, 0.25)$. Using just the first two coordinates in a homogeneous form gives $(0.25, 0.50, 1)$.

$$f^{-1}(0.25, 0.50, 1) = M^{-1} \begin{bmatrix} 0.25 \\ 0.50 \\ 1 \end{bmatrix} = \begin{bmatrix} 0 & 1 & 0 \\ -1 & -1 & 1 \\ 0 & 0 & 1 \end{bmatrix} \begin{bmatrix} 0.25 \\ 0.50 \\ 1 \end{bmatrix} = \begin{bmatrix} 0.50 \\ 0.25 \\ 1 \end{bmatrix}$$

The point $(0.25, 3.50, 1.50)$ has texture coordinates $(0.50, 0.25)$.

The function f sends texture coordinates to barycentric coordinates (both in homogeneous form), but we can continue the conversions to find Cartesian coordinates of the point on the triangle.

$$(u, v, 1) \rightarrow (\alpha_0, \alpha_1, 1) \rightarrow (\alpha_0, \alpha_1, \alpha_2) \rightarrow (x, y, z)$$

The first conversion is accomplished with the matrix M. The second and third conversions are also matrices, R and C. Recalling that the barycentric coordinates give the equation $P = \alpha_0 P_0 + \alpha_1 P_1 + \alpha_2 P_2$, we can find the two matrices. The columns are just the vertices of the triangular face.

$$
R = \begin{bmatrix} 1 & 0 & 0 \\ 0 & 1 & 0 \\ -1 & -1 & 1 \end{bmatrix} \qquad C = \begin{bmatrix} 1 & -2 & 4 \\ 4 & 5 & 0 \\ -1 & 3 & 1 \end{bmatrix}
$$

If g is a function that takes texture coordinates to Cartesian coordinates, then g is just multiplication by the matrix $M_{total} = CRM$. Consequently, g^{-1} is multiplication by $M_{total}^{-1} = M^{-1}R^{-1}C^{-1}$.

$$
M_{total}^{-1} = \begin{bmatrix} 0 & 1 & 0 \\ -1 & -1 & 1 \\ 0 & 0 & 1 \end{bmatrix} \begin{bmatrix} 1 & 0 & 0 \\ 0 & 1 & 0 \\ 1 & 1 & 1 \end{bmatrix} \begin{bmatrix} 5 & 14 & -20 \\ -4 & 5 & 16 \\ 17 & -1 & 13 \end{bmatrix}
$$

$$
= \begin{bmatrix} -0.05 & 0.06 & 0.20 \\ 0.21 & -0.01 & 0.16 \\ 0.22 & 0.22 & 0.11 \end{bmatrix}
$$

Multiplying the Cartesian coordinates of a point on the face gives the corresponding texture coordinates.

$$
M_{total}^{-1} \begin{bmatrix} 0.25 \\ 3.50 \\ 1.50 \end{bmatrix} = \begin{bmatrix} 0.50 \\ 0.25 \\ 1 \end{bmatrix}
$$

Of course, the mapping we defined is affine, so interpolation works to give texture coordinates and it can naturally fit into the procedure for converting view window points to pixels.

Looking only at the function f (or g) and their corresponding matrices, it is a little hard to tell whether the texture is distorted or not as it is pasted onto the face. Certainly, only part of the entire map in this example is used, but by examining the correspondence between texture map vertices and face vertices it is clear here that although lines are sent to lines, the texture does get distorted in order to fit into the triangular face.   □

Bilinear Mappings Functions between texture maps and faces of objects need not be affine. The closer they are to linear, the easier it is to use some form of linear interpolation to fill in values of the function once we know the values at the vertices. Bilinear functions are not affine and do not preserve all lines, but they are linear in some ways and are convenient for mapping a square texture map onto an arbitrary convex quadrilateral.

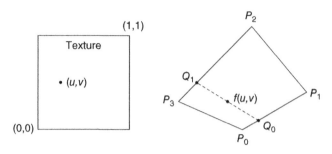

Figure 9.12   Bilinear map

The vertices of the texture map [using the normalized coordinates (u, v)] are sent to the vertices of the quadrilateral. In Figure 9.12, the vertices are ordered counterclockwise and are mapped as follows:

$$f(0,0) = P_0 \quad f(1,0) = P_1$$
$$f(1,1) = P_2 \quad f(0,1) = P_3$$

To determine where an arbitrary point (u, v) in the texture map is sent, we interpolate between the points P_0 and P_1 to find Q_0 and then between P_3 and P_2 to find Q_1.

$$Q_0 = (1 - u)P_0 + uP_1$$
$$Q_1 = (1 - u)P_3 + uP_2$$

Finally, we linearly interpolate between Q_0 and Q_1.

$$
\begin{aligned}
f(u, v) &= (1 - v)Q_0 + vQ_1 \\
&= (1 - v)(1 - u)P_0 + (1 - v)uP_1 + v(1 - u)P_3 + uvP_2
\end{aligned}
\tag{9.18}
$$

The order of the vertices P_i is important here because two opposite edges of the quadrilateral match two opposite edges of the texture map rectangle. This function is *bilinear*, because if either u or v is held fixed, the function becomes linear in the other variable. With $u = 1/4, f$ reduces to

$$f\left(\frac{1}{4}, v\right) = (1 - v)\left(\frac{1}{4}P_0 + \frac{3}{4}P_1\right) + v\left(\frac{3}{4}P_3 + \frac{1}{4}P_2\right)$$

This shows that the points $(1/4, v)$, which form a vertical line in the texture map, get sent to an affine combination of two points on opposite sides of the quadrilateral; this forms a line through the points. Similarly, horizontal lines in the texture map also are sent to lines through opposite sides of the quadrilateral.

The function is a one-to-one mapping and relatively easy to calculate, but perhaps, unfortunately, it does not preserve all lines. For example, if lines were preserved, the diagonal line segment $u = v$ in the texture map should get sent to the line segment between P_0 and P_2 in the quadrilateral. It is not hard to check that the point $(0.5, 0.5)$ is not on P_0P_2 unless P_1 and P_3 are well placed (see Exercises). The image of $u = v$ ends up curved, as do the images of other diagonal lines; this fact may or may not seriously compromise the effectiveness of this texture mapping.

The inverse function f^{-1} is not hard to find, but we need to be careful because two different points in texture space can map to the same point inside the quadrilateral. The function f is still one to one on the texture map itself, so picking the correct inverse point is not hard as the next example shows.

Example 9.6 (Inverse of a Bilinear Mapping). Suppose the texture map is sent to a planar quadrilateral, and for convenience assume the vertices of the quadrilateral are given in a standard two-dimensional Cartesian coordinate system. Then, $f(u, v) = (x, y)$.

$$(x, y) = (1 - v)(1 - u)P_0 + (1 - v)uP_1 + v(1 - u)P_3 + uvP_2$$
$$= P_0 + v(-P_0 + P_3) + u(-P_0 + P_1) + uv(P_0 - P_1 - P_3 + P_2)$$

Let the vertices of the quadrilateral be

$$P_0 = (1, 1) \quad P_1 = (5, 2)$$
$$P_2 = (6, 6) \quad P_3 = (3, 4)$$

The point $P = (2, 2)$ is inside the quadrilateral, and if we start with this point, we get the following equations:

$$2 = 1 + 2v + 4u - uv$$
$$2 = 1 + 3v + u + uv$$

Solving for v in the first equation and substituting into the second gives

$$5u^2 + 8u - 1 = 0$$

This quadratic has two solutions, $u = 0.117$ and $u = -1.717$. Only the first value is inside the texture map; remember the coordinates u and v are normalized to be between zero and 1. Substituting values for u in the equations gives the values for v. The point $(0.117, 0.283)$ maps to the point $(2, 2)$ in the quadrilateral. The second point $(-1.717, 2.117)$ also maps to $(2, 2)$, but it is clearly outside the actual texture map.

Rather than relying on algebra to find the relevant quadratic equation, we can also argue from the vector geometry point of view. The point P inside the quadrilateral is on the line segment Q_0Q_1 which is determined by u. If we form $\triangle Q_0PQ_1$, then P is on the line segment if and only if the triangle has area zero. Letting $\vec{v}_0 = Q_0 - P$ and

$\vec{v}_1 = Q_1 - P$, the area of the triangle is just the cross product of these two vectors (sign of the area is irrelevant here). The equation $v_0 \times v_1 = 0$ produces the same quadratic equation we found before (see Exercises).   □

In three-dimensional space, vectors along two adjacent sides of a quadrilateral can be found by constructing coordinates (s, t) for any interior point. Then the bilinear mapping and its inverse can be calculated just as in two dimensions. A quadrilateral can naturally arise from two adjacent triangular faces of some object, but there is no guarantee that the four vertices are planar. Nevertheless, the procedure for calculating the bilinear function still works although the two faces are not flat. This observation can prove useful in wrapping texture maps around surfaces.

Spherical Mappings A mapping from texture space to object space sends texture coordinates (u, v) to coordinates on the object (s, t). Various sorts of object coordinate systems will work as long as they have two parameters. If we concentrate on flat triangular faces, then barycentric coordinates work, as do the two parameters of bilinear functions. Instead of flat faces, we may have bicubic patches where the two parameters (s, t) give a coordinate system for the surface. Any function from one set of coordinates to the other serves as a mapping that effectively applies the texture to the object surface.

One common application of this is the mapping that wraps a texture around a sphere. Spherical coordinates (ρ, θ, ϕ) give positions on a sphere of radius ρ, and by using just the last two coordinates θ and ϕ we have two parameters defining the position. To map the texture once around the sphere, θ is determined by multiplying u by 2π.

$$f(u, v) = (2\pi u, \pi(1 - v)) = (\theta, \phi)$$

$$f^{-1}(\theta, \phi) = \left(\frac{\theta}{2\pi}, \left(1 - \frac{\phi}{\pi}\right) \right) = (u, v) \tag{9.19}$$

The texture map is stretched and shrunk to fit around the sphere, with the entire top edge of the map, for example, shrunk to a single point on top of the sphere. Similarly, the bottom edge is sent to a single point at the bottom of the sphere. This is just one of several different ways to distort the map to cover the entire sphere.

9.4.2 Resolution

Stretching the texture map or placing the camera close to the object results in magnifying the original texture. Yet, the texture map no doubt has some fixed resolution, so there are a fixed number of pixels forming the image. If we magnify it, the pixels appear larger and there is a distinct blocky appearance to the texture. To partially remedy the situation, we smooth the transition between pixels by blending adjacent pixels together. One approach is to find the texture coordinates and then bilinearly interpolate the four closet pixels to arrive at a blended shade (Figure 9.13).

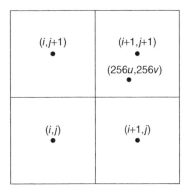

Figure 9.13 Pixel interpolation

Suppose the texture map is composed of an array of 256×256 square pixels centered on integer coordinates. The coordinates (u, v) indicate position $(256u, 256v)$ in the pixel array, but since they are not necessarily integers the position is inside a pixel but not at its center. Round down to the center of a pixel.

$$(i,j) = (\lfloor 256u \rfloor, \lfloor 256v \rfloor)$$

Then consider the four pixels $(i,j),(i+1,j),(i,j+1),(i,j)$. We can bilinearly interpolate the colors of these four pixels and assign them to the coordinates $(256u, 256v)$. To do this, let $u^* = 256u - \lfloor 256u \rfloor$ be the fractional part of $256u$, and calculate the fractional part v^* of $256v$ similarly. Use $c_{(i,j)}$ to designate the color of pixel (i,j). Then the bilinear interpolation gives the color (C) of point $(256u, 256v)$.

$$C = (1 - v^*)(1 - u^*)c_{(i,j)} + (1 - v^*)u^* c_{(i+1,j)}$$
$$+ v^*(1 - u^*)c_{(i,j+1)} + u^* v^* c_{(i+1,j+1)}$$

This is one of several anti-aliasing techniques that strive to smooth the blocky character of an image. For texture maps that are used at various magnifications throughout the rendering process, usually one of several preprocessed versions (called *mipmaps*) at various resolutions is selected rather than relying on interpolation alone.

9.4.3 Procedural Textures

A texture map can be an image of something like a wood surface, and the individual pixels, of course, store various shades of colors in patterns matching the grain of wood. Rather than relying on actual images, it is also possible to generate texture maps with an algorithm. For example, the function $\sin(k_1 u) + \cos(k_2 v)$ can be scaled to represent a periodically fluctuating shade of color in two dimensions. The resulting generated map is a *procedural* texture, and by altering the parameters it can be adjusted to give some modest visual effects. With more carefully selected functions, the maps can be useful in mimicking more realistic patterns.

Color is only one of the attributes a texture map can store. In particular, since most lighting effects rely on a normal to the surface, the texture map could hold information about how to adjust normals to achieve various lighting changes. In 1978, Jim Blinn (whose contributions to computer graphics are legendary) introduced the idea of a *bump map* that holds information on altering the look of a surface by perturbing the normals (Figure 9.14).

Without actually altering the surface, a bump map just changes the normals so the lighting effects (e.g., Phong shading) change giving the appearance of regular or random bumps. Surfaces can look like plaster or even like some heavy fabric. The idea is to start with a displacement function which alters the length of the normals at any point. A flat surface, for example, has equal normals at every point, but a displacement changes their length; the actual surface is left untouched. New normals are calculated based on the virtually changing heights of the normals. These altered normals are used instead of the original ones.

Start with a bump map with displacements stored for coordinates (u, v). The surface of an object is parameterized by s and t, so that each point is a function $P(s, t)$. (Think of the function as supplying x, y, and z coordinates.) Then on a face of an object, the inverse of a texture mapping gives the displacement $d(s, t)$ associated with the point $P(s, t)$. So the displaced normal is $d(s, t)\vec{n}(s, t)$, where $\vec{n}(s, t)$ is a unit normal to the surface at point P. A point on the (virtual) displaced surface is then

$$P^*(s, t) = P(s, t) + d(s, t)\vec{n}(s, t) \qquad (9.20)$$

With this expression for points on an altered surface, we can take partial derivatives to find tangent vectors and then use the cross product to find a new normal.

$$\frac{\partial P^*}{\partial s} = \frac{\partial P^*}{\partial s} + \frac{\partial d}{\partial s}\vec{n} + d\frac{\partial \vec{n}}{\partial s} \qquad \text{and} \qquad \frac{\partial P^*}{\partial t} = \frac{\partial P^*}{\partial t} + \frac{\partial d}{\partial t}\vec{n} + d\frac{\partial \vec{n}}{\partial t}$$

If the displacements are relatively small, then the last term in each equation can be ignored. The resulting approximation to the new normal to the surface is

$$\vec{n}_{new} \approx \left(\frac{\partial P^*}{\partial s} + \frac{\partial d}{\partial s}\vec{n}\right) \times \left(\frac{\partial P^*}{\partial t} + \frac{\partial d}{\partial t}\vec{n}\right) \qquad (9.21)$$

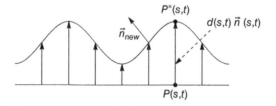

Figure 9.14 Bump map

Normalizing n_{new} gives the new unit vector. Notice here that the partial derivatives of P^* are vectors, so we are indeed taking the cross product of two vectors. The cross product can be simplified somewhat, and the partial derivatives can in practice be approximated by using ratios of differences in heights in the horizontal and vertical directions to approximate slopes. Lastly, notice that the expression for the new normal never needs the actual values of $d(s,t)$; it only needs the partial derivatives. These could replace the actual values in the texture map.

Using texture maps in this procedural way, where we algorithmically determine values that alter a surface, opens up many possibilities. Assuming we can find appropriate algorithms for producing displacement maps, color maps, or other types of texture maps, we can turn flat faces into a variety of materials. One last observation: there is no reason to restrict texture maps to two dimensions. Using three dimensions, we could make objects look as if they are carved out of wood or marble or other materials.

9.5   COMPLEMENTS AND DETAILS

9.5.1   Conversion between RGB and HSV

The RGB and HSV coordinate systems for representing color give a geometric shape to the color space. However, the absolute distance between colors is almost meaningless. Yet, proportional distances do make some intuitive sense and allow us to convert from RGB coordinates to HSV coordinates. Remembering that the RGB coordinates (R, G, B) are between 0 and 1 inclusive, the following algorithm converts the RGB coordinates to HSV coordinates:

1. Let $Min = \min\{R, G, B\}$ and $Max = \max\{R, G, B\}$.
2. Set $V = Max$. (This sets the brightness.)
3. If $Min = Max = 0$, then $H = S = V = 0$. (The color is black.)
4. If $Min = Max \neq 0$, then $S = 0$ and H is arbitrary. (The color is a shade of gray.)
5. If $Min \neq Max$, then $S = \frac{Max-Min}{Max}$. (This is the proportional distance from the axis.)
   (a) If $R = Max$, then $H = 60 * (G - B)/(Max - Min)$. If $H < 0$, then $H = H + 360$. (This sets the hue to within $\pm 60°$ of the red direction ($0°$).)
   (b) If $G = Max$, then $H = 120 + 60 * (B - R)/(Max - Min)$. (This sets the hue to within $\pm 60°$ of the green direction ($120°$).)
   (c) If $B = Max$, then $H = 240 + 60 * (R - G)/(Max - Min)$. (This sets the hue to within $\pm 60°$ of the blue direction ($240°$).)

This conversion algorithm is convenient and approximates the equivalence between colors in the two systems. To convert back from HSV coordinates to RGB coordinates, we effectively undo what the algorithm does.

9.5.2 Shadows on Arbitrary Planes

In Example 9.3, shadows were cast on the ground plane, which was simply the xz plane. To form the shadow, object vertices are projected from the light source onto the ground plane. The same general derivation can be used to project shadows onto any arbitrary plane like the side of a building. Projections like this are easily done in homogeneous coordinates and are derived in Example 4.12 from an earlier chapter. However, we can also derive the correct transformation matrix by following light rays as we did for the shadow on the xz plane.

The light source sits at point L and we select an object vertex V. Then the light ray emanates in the direction from the light source to the vertex and is described by $L + t\vec{v}$. Further, suppose that the ground plane is described by the equation $\vec{n} \cdot (P - Q)$ where Q is a fixed point on the plane and P is an arbitrary point on the plane.

Drawing on the previous analysis of intersections between lines and planes, the value of t when the ray hits the plane is

$$t = \frac{-\vec{n} \cdot (L - Q)}{\vec{n} \cdot (V - L)}$$

The corresponding point of intersection V^* is given by

$$V^* = L + \frac{-\vec{n} \cdot (L - Q)}{\vec{n} \cdot (V - L)}(V - L)$$

$$= \frac{(\vec{n} \cdot V)L - (\vec{n} \cdot Q)L + (\vec{n} \cdot Q)V - (\vec{n} \cdot L)V}{\vec{n} \cdot V - \vec{n} \cdot L}$$

Notice that we treat L, V, and Q as vectors to write the dot products in the expanded formula for V^*. To represent this projection by a matrix, set $A = \vec{n} \cdot L$ and $B = \vec{n} \cdot Q$ just to simplify the notation.

$$M_s = \begin{bmatrix} L_x n_x - A + B & L_x n_y & L_x n_z & -L_x B \\ L_y n_x & L_y n_y - A + B & L_y n_z & -L_y B \\ L_z n_x & L_z n_y & L_z n_z - A + B & -L_z B \\ n_x & n_y & n_z & -A \end{bmatrix} \tag{9.22}$$

Using the xz plane as the projection plane gives $\vec{n} = (0, 1, 0)$ and we can take $Q = (0, 0, 0)$. Then $A = L_y$ and $B = 0$, turning the matrix M_s into the one from Example 9.3.

The transformation matrix M_s is the same as the matrix developed using homogeneous coordinates in Example 4.12. However, there is a difference in notation, because in the current derivation we took L, V, and $\vec{n}$ as three-dimensional instead of as four-dimensional homogeneous coordinates. There is an advantage to the homogeneous approach when moving the light source out to infinity as we did earlier. With homogeneous coordinates, a zero fourth coordinate indicates a point at infinity, so if we take the light source to be positioned at $(L_x, L_y, L_z, 0)$, then the transformation matrix represents a parallel projection where the direction of the parallel rays is (L_x, L_y, L_z).

9.5.3   Derivation of the Radiosity Equation

Recall Equation 9.10 giving the radiance at a point. We need to add two details to this equation for the radiosity model. First, we add a term on the right representing the light emitted at the point to account for the possibility that the point is actually on a light source. Second, since we will be tracing light reflected by one surface and incident on another, we include a location (x) in the expressions.

$$L_o(x, \vec{v}_o) = L_s(x, \vec{v}_o) + \int_\Omega \rho_r(\vec{v}_i, \vec{v}_o) L_i(x, \vec{v}_i)(\vec{n} \cdot \vec{v}_i) d\omega \qquad (9.23)$$

This is called the *rendering equation*, and the integral is taken over Ω, that is, all directions in the hemisphere. (We use $d\omega$ here instead of $\sin\phi_i d\phi_i d\theta_i$ to make the expression a little more compact.) The quantity L_s is zero unless the point x is on a light source.

If we are dealing with a diffuse surface where light reflects equally in all directions, then the BRDF is constant (ρ). For these surfaces, it is useful to calculate the diffuse reflectance $(\rho(d))$, which we define as the fraction of incoming light that is reflected. This means that, since it is relative to the quantities $L_i(x, \vec{v}_i)$, we can calculate the diffuse reflectance as follows:

$$\rho(d) = \int_\Omega \rho(\vec{n} \cdot \vec{v}_i) d\omega = \rho \int_\Omega \cos\theta d\omega = \rho\pi \qquad (9.24)$$

We conclude that when the BRDF is constant, we can express it as $\rho(d)/\pi$ (Figure 9.15).

Light coming from a particular direction illuminates a patch on the hemisphere and determines the differential solid angle $d\omega$. Now, we want the source of light to be another triangle. We trace light from position x_1 on one triangle to position x_2 on another triangle. The triangles have normals $\vec{n}_1$ and $\vec{n}_2$, and the direction of incoming light is $\vec{v}_i$ which is the vector from x_1 to x_2.

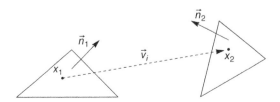

Figure 9.15   Radiance between triangles

The differential solid angle $d\omega$ is area dA_1 from the first triangle projected onto the hemisphere around x_2. To correct for the orientation of the two triangles, we multiply by the cosines of the angles between the ray and the normals. To measure the projection in terms of steradians, we divide by the square of the distance between the two points.

$$d\omega = \frac{(\vec{n}_1 \cdot \vec{v}_i)(\vec{n}_2 \cdot \vec{v}_i)dA_1}{|x_1 - x_2|^2} = \frac{\cos\phi_1 \cos\phi_2 dA_1}{|x_1 - x_2|^2} = G(x_1, x_2)dA_1$$

The quantity $G(x_1, x_2)$ represents the geometric relationship between the two triangles. To keep the reformed rendering equation compact, we also introduce the quantity $V(x_1, x_2)$, a visibility factor, which is 1 if the point x_2 can be seen from x_1 and zero otherwise. Now we have an updated rendering equation describing the light interaction between two triangles. (The integral is taken over the triangle T_1.)

$$L_o(x_2, \vec{v}_o) = L_s(x_2, \vec{v}_o) + \int_{T_1} \rho_r(\vec{v}_i, \vec{v}_o)L_i(x_1, \vec{v}_i)G(x_1, x_2)V(x_1, x_2)dA_1 \qquad (9.25)$$

The integral in this revised equation is taken over a surface (the first triangle) instead of over the hemisphere.

The radiosity method makes the assumption that light is reflected equally in all directions, so the BRDF is constant and equals ρ_d/π. Moreover, the L_o, L_s, and L_i terms are radiances coming from a diffuse surface, so they are independent of the direction.

$$L_o(x_2) = L_s(x_2) + \frac{\rho_2(d)}{\pi} \int_{T_1} L_i(x_1)G(x_1, x_2)V(x_1, x_2)dA_1$$

Recall the relationship between radiance and radiosity; radiosity is the integral of radiance in all directions. If the radiance is constant, the radiosity is proportional to radiance. In fact, radiosity equals π times radiance (since it is the integral over the hemisphere). Replacing radiance with the corresponding radiosity $B(x)$ gives us the following:

$$B(x_2) = E(x_2) + \frac{\rho_2(d)}{\pi} \int_{T_1} B(x_1)G(x_1, x_2)V(x_1, x_2)dA_1 \qquad (9.26)$$

The term $E(x_2)$ is the radiosity emitted if x_2 is on a light source. What we would like to do now is to assume that the radiosity B is constant over a small triangle. Then, for example, $B(x_1) = B_1$ for every point on the first triangle. Unfortunately, there is no guarantee that $B(x_2)$ will be constant for every x_2 because it depends on the integral. So we need to average the radiosity over all points in the second triangle.

$$B_2 = \frac{1}{A_2} \int_{T_2} B(x_2)dx_2$$

Now replacing $B(x_2)$ with Equation 9.26 gives us a good approximation to the interaction between triangles.

$$B_2 = E_2 + \rho_2(d)B_1 \frac{1}{A_2} \int_{T_2} \int_{T_1} \frac{1}{\pi} G(x_1, x_2) V(x_1, x_2) dA_1 dA_2 \qquad (9.27)$$

The double integral in Equation 9.27 is called a *form factor* (denoted F_{12}) and summarizes the geometric relation between the two triangles. It is the fraction of the total energy leaving T_1 that is incident on T_2. The symmetry of the definition implies that $A_i F_{ij} = A_j F_{ji}$, and the interpretation in terms of energy gives $\sum_j^n F_{ij} = 1$.

The scene is filled with triangles, and the radiosity of triangle T_2 depends not only T_1 but also on all the other triangles. The result is that the radiosity of triangle i a sum over all other triangles and gives us the *radiosity equation*.

$$\text{Radiosity Equation: } B_i = E_i + \rho_i(d) \sum_{j=1}^{N} B_j F_{ij} \qquad (9.28)$$

9.6 EXERCISES

1. What are the HSV coordinates for the RGB color $(0, 0, 0.5)$?

2. A ray from a light source at position $(10, 8, 6)$ in the direction $(-3, -3, -2)$ hits the plane containing the points $(2, 0, 0), (0, 1, 0)$, and $(0, 0, 1)$. Determine the point of intersection and a unit vector in the direction of the reflected ray.

3. A triangle has vertices $(1, 1, 2)$, $(1, 2, 4)$, and $(2, 0, -3)$. There is a light source at $(1, 10, -5)$ and the triangle surface is mildly shiny making $p = 3$. Using the elementary lighting model, determine the light intensity at the centroid of the triangle. (Assume $k_a I_a$, $k_d I$, d, and $k_s I_s$ are known.)

4. Specular lighting involves calculating the reflected vector $\vec{R}$ and using $(\vec{R} \cdot \vec{V})^p$ to determine intensity. In order to reduce the computations, one method uses the vector $\vec{H}$, the halfway vector, which is equal to $\vec{L} + \vec{V}$ divided by its length. This is a vector halfway between the vector to the camera and the one to the light. If this vector is close to the normal, then the specular intensity is high; we use $(\vec{H} \cdot \vec{n})^p$ to determine the intensity. Compare both these specular methods for a light source at $(8, 6, 4)$ shining on the xz plane at the origin with the camera at position $(-5, 3, -1)$.

5. When adjusting for the attenuation of light due to the distance to the light source, practically we use $a_2 D^2 + a_1 D + a_0$ instead of D^2. Show that this substitution means that there is a maximum of light intensity.

6. A tetrahedron has vertices $(0, 0, 0)$, $(3, -1, 4)$, $(-1, 1, 6)$, and $(0, 5, -1)$. There is a light source at position $(12, 10, 4)$. Determine the diffuse shading of the centroid of each face using both Gouraud and Phong shading.

7. A cube is sitting on the xz plane with one vertex at $(0,0,0)$ and the diagonally opposite vertex at $(1,1,1)$. A light source at position $(-5,5,0)$ casts a shadow of the cube on the plane. Determine the vertices of the shadow.

8. Suppose a material has a grain running in one direction, which means light is preferentially reflected in the direction of the grain (plus or minus direction). Construct a possible BRDF for this type of material.

9. In Example 9.4, the light ray enters the glass plate and is refracted. Calculate the direction of the ray when it leaves the glass plate and show that it is parallel to the incoming ray.

10. Using an affine transformation, map the texture triangle with vertices $(0,0)$, $(1,0)$, and $(0.5,1)$ to the triangle $(1.5,2,1)$, $(4,1.5,6)$,$(7,1,-2)$. Determine the texture coordinates of the centroid of the triangle.

11. Let a quadrilateral have coordinates $(1,0)$, $(2,-4)$, $(6,1)$, and $(3,5)$. Use a bilinear map to send the square texture map to the quadrilateral. Determine the texture coordinates of the point $(2.25,-1.75)$.

12. In Example 9.6, use the vector approach to find the texture coordinates for the point $(2,2)$ in the quadrilateral.

13. For a bilinear map of the square texture, show that the diagonal line in the texture map from $(0,0)$ to $(1,1)$ is not generally mapped to a straight line in the quadrilateral by determining where $(0.5,0.5)$ is mapped.

14. When doing bilinear interpolation of pixel colors to improve resolution of a texture map, show that the method given weights the pixel containing the point $(256u, 256v)$ the highest.

15. Verify Equation 9.24 by replacing $d\omega$ with $\sin \phi_i d\phi_i d\theta_i$ and evaluating the integral.

9.6.1 Programming Exercises

1. Implement the elementary lighting model with flat shading to produce a shaded cube on the screen. Allow rotations of the cube and repositioning of the light source.

2. Build an elementary ray tracer that can render a scene full of cubes and produce simple shadows. Input the number, size, and position of cubes along with the position of a single light source.

10

OTHER PARADIGMS

The core mathematics in computer graphics is based on vector geometry. From object modeling to shading techniques, vectors play a significant role and offer a very useful paradigm for constructing images. Yet, there are corners of the image gallery that cannot be reached conveniently with the standard geometric approaches. Gradually, other mathematical tools, structures, and methods have surfaced to solve particular graphics problems and to expand image generation possibilities. This chapter highlights three of those approaches that fall outside the main flow of vectors, transformations, and geometric optics. It is reasonable to consider these techniques as separate paradigms.

The first category of graphics problems focuses on the fact that all modeling and rendering efforts end with an array of pixels on the display screen. Resolutions continue to increase, but the pixel still is more a block of color than a colored point. Jagged edges in images are a common result of this coarseness. Coping with this and other artifacts requires a different take on the mathematics of images.

Nature is not particularly fond of Euclidean geometry, so a major challenge is to generate more natural organic forms. One approach here involves introducing noise into the process. It is a little odd that adding randomness expands the set of image-generating tools, but properly handled, noise produces many of the natural patterns we encounter.

A more structured approach to organic forms leads to the third paradigm. In an effort to construct images of plants, a technique borrowed from the theory of computation turns descriptions of plants into a process of selecting grammars and constructing words. The resulting L-systems have been successful in producing landscapes and fractal forms.

Mathematical Structures for Computer Graphics, First Edition. Steven J. Janke.
© 2015 John Wiley & Sons, Inc. Published 2015 by John Wiley & Sons, Inc.

All the above three alternative paradigms are well-established approaches in computer graphics and bring a wider array of mathematical tools to bear on some key graphics problems.

10.1 PIXELS

Pixels have nonzero area, and consequently drawing on the display screen is a matter of drawing with blocks of color. Theoretically, a line is an infinitely thin, continuous set of points, but on the screen it is a finite number of blocks arranged in a regular array. Higher screen resolutions generally mean more pixels per unit distance and therefore finer image detail, but the discrete nature of pixels causes two key problems.

First, an algorithm is necessary to decide which pixels to use in representing a line or a curve segment. Since the screen is an array of pixels centered at integer coordinates, there will be small jumps between some pixels on a line segment. Determining quickly where these discontinuities should occur is the key to decent graphics performance. Second, there are various unintended artifacts that appear in an image as a result of the array-centered pixels. In the case of a line segment, the image looks jagged instead of smoothly straight. In more complicated images, ghost patterns appear showing, for example, circular rings where the original image had no such curves. Coping with both these problems requires mathematical analysis of the pixel array.

10.1.1 Bresenham Line Algorithm

A line can be described in several ways, but since we are focused on its representation in terms of integer coordinates, the explicit form $y = mx + b$ is probably the most helpful. Assume that we have converted the original line segment in some scene into normalized device coordinates and then into actual coordinates for a particular display screen. By possibly rounding coordinates up or down, we have integer coordinates for both end points of the segment: (x_0, y_0) and (x_n, y_n).

The task is to find integer coordinates (x_i, y_i) for $0 < i < n$, where $x_{i+1} = x_i + 1$. In other words, there should be a pixel in each column on the screen between the first and last endpoints. The x coordinates for pixels on the line segment are then easy to determine. For the y coordinates, their position will depend on the slope m of the line, which can be positive or negative. Compare the line $y = mx + b$ with $y = -mx + b$; the point (x, y) is on the first line if and only if $(-x, y)$ is on the second. If we find the pixels for the line with a positive slope, then we can easily find the pixels for the other line. So, assume $m > 0$. (Note that $m = 0$ is a trivial case.)

If the slope is nonnegative, then we have either $m \leq 1$ or $m > 1$. In the second case, rearrange the line equation to get $x = \frac{1}{m}y - \frac{b}{m}$. Now we have a line with positive slope less than 1. If we interchange x and y in Figure 10.1 and in our analysis, we will find the appropriate pixels for the original line.

The end result of considering slopes is that we have reduced the problem of finding pixels for an arbitrary line to finding pixels for a line with slope $0 \leq m \leq 1$.

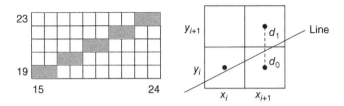

Figure 10.1   Screen pixels for a line segment

With this assumption, if pixel (x_i, y_i) is on the line, then the next pixel is one of the following:

$$(x_{i+1}, y_{i+1}) = (x_i + 1, y_i)$$

$$(x_{i+1}, y_{i+1}) = (x_i + 1, y_i + 1) \tag{10.1}$$

The next y coordinate can be the same as the current one or it can move up by 1. There are no other choices because the slope of the line is assumed to be less than or equal to 1.

To decide between these two choices, compare the distances between the true line and either of these pixels. We have drawn the pixels as squares in the figure, and we assume their centers are in the middle of the square. When the x coordinate is $x_{i+1} = x_i + 1$, the y coordinate for the point on the line is $y = m(x_i + 1) + b$. The distance between each pixel choice and the point on the line is just the difference in y coordinates. Let $d_{(0,i)}$ be the distance to the lower pixel and $d_{(1,i)}$ the distance to the upper pixel.

$$d_{(0,i)} = y - y_i = m(x_i + 1) + b - y_i$$

$$d_{(1,i)} = (y_i + 1) - y = y_i + 1 - m(x_i + 1) - b \tag{10.2}$$

Selecting the next pixel is simply a matter of comparing $d_{(0,i)}$ to $d_{(1,i)}$. If $d_{(0,i)} < d_{(1,i)}$, then the next pixel should be $(x_i + 1, y_i)$, and if $d_{(0,i)} \geq d_{(1,i)}$, it should be $(x_i + 1, y_i + 1)$. ($d_{(0,i)} = d_{(0,i)}$ is really a judgment call.)

Before continuing with the development of the algorithm, there is one further property that is desirable. If all the arithmetic operations are integer (as opposed to floating-point) operations, then implementations of the algorithm will run faster. With integer endpoints already established, the slope is

$$m = \frac{\Delta y}{\Delta x} = \frac{y_n - y_0}{x_n - x_0}$$

The division here probably results in a floating-point value for m, so it would be nice if we can avoid the division as we look for a decision process for each new pixel.

With this design approach in mind, we revise our decision criteria by defining a quantity D_i.

$$D_i = \Delta x(d_{(0,i)} - d_{(1,i)})$$

$$= \Delta x(m(x_i + 1) + b - y_i - y_i - 1 + m(x_i + 1) + b)$$

$$= 2\Delta y \cdot x_i - 2\Delta x \cdot y_i + b^* \qquad (10.3)$$

The quantity b^* is just a constant. By multiplying by Δx, references to m are removed and the resulting D_i only requires integer multiplication and addition (includes subtraction). Moreover, $D_i < 0$ implies that $d_{(0,i)} < d_{(1,i)}$ because $\Delta x > 0$. Comparing D_i to zero decides between the next two possible pixels.

Computing D_i for each i is made easier by the following recursion:

$$D_{i+1} - D_i = 2\Delta y \cdot (x_{i+1} - x_i) - 2\Delta x \cdot (y_{i+1} - y_i) + (b^* - b^*)$$

$$= 2\Delta y \cdot (x_i + 1 - x_i) - 2\Delta x \cdot (y_{i+1} - y_i)$$

$$\implies D_{i+1} = D_i + 2\Delta y - 2\Delta x \cdot (y_{i+1} - y_i) \qquad (10.4)$$

The endpoints of the segment are assumed correct, implying that $y_0 = mx_0 + b$. Using this in Equation 10.2 to find $d_{(0,0)}$ and $d_{(1,0)}$ gives $D_0 = \Delta x(m - (1 - m)) = 2\Delta y - \Delta x$. All the arithmetic operations in the recursion 10.4 are integer operations. The complete line algorithm patterned after Jack Bresenham's 1965 algorithm [11] now proceeds as follows:

1. Input (x_0, y_0) and (x_n, y_n). Set the first pixel to (x_0, y_0).
2. Calculate $\Delta x = (x_n - x_0)$ and $\Delta y = (y_n - y_0)$.
3. Calculate $D_0 = 2\Delta y - \Delta x$. Set $i = 0$.
   - If $D_i < 0$, the next pixel is $(x_i + 1, y_i)$. Set $D_{i+1} = D_i + 2\Delta y$.
   - If $D_i \geq 0$, the next pixel is $(x_i + 1, y_i + 1)$. Set $D_{i+1} = D_i + 2\Delta y - 2\Delta x$.
4. Repeat step 3 while $i < n$.

Example 10.1 (Bresenham's Line Algorithm). The algorithm for finding the pixels on a line from $(15, 19)$ to $(24, 23)$ proceeds by setting pixel $(15, 19)$ and then calculating the initial quantities:

$$\Delta x = (24 - 15) = 9$$

$$\Delta y = (23 - 19) = 4 \implies 2\Delta y = 8$$

$$2\Delta y - 2\Delta x = -10$$

$$D_0 = 2\Delta y - \Delta x = -1$$

i	D_i	Next Pixel
0	-1	$(16, 19)$
1	7	$(17, 20)$
2	-3	$(18, 20)$
3	5	$(19, 21)$
4	-5	$(20, 21)$
5	3	$(21, 22)$
6	-7	$(22, 22)$
7	1	$(23, 23)$
8	-9	$(24, 23)$

Then the steps selecting next pixels can be summarized in a table. Since the last line in the table gives a point which matches the second endpoint, the last calculation is not strictly necessary. □

Bresenham's line algorithm is an enhanced version of a *digital differential analyzer* or DDA. These form a class of algorithms that take unit steps through one coordinate and compute the change in the other coordinate. For a line, the change is connected to the slope, so both Δx and Δy play a role. The advantage of Bresenham's algorithm is that only integer calculations are necessary. Using the same techniques, Bresenham devised another algorithm for drawing circles, and with a little effort the DDA approach can work for a variety of curves.

10.1.2 Anti-Aliasing

The line algorithm by necessity produces a jagged line, and the effects of these somewhat abrupt jumps are called *aliases* in signal processing theory. The theoretical line is continuous, but when it is sampled at discrete positions, spurious patterns emerge.

On the simplest one-dimensional level, imagine sampling a single sine wave at some periodic rate. The resulting samples could always hit the peak of the wave or they might fluctuate with a frequency far different from the sine wave. In both cases, they exhibit a pattern that did not originally exist. If now we consider a two-dimensional signal, it is not hard to see that the patterns might disturb the image in a variety of ways. The study of signal processing includes a vast mathematical theory which helps considerably in designing anti-aliasing algorithms.

For the jagged line problem, the intensity of the two-dimensional image at any point, $I(x, y)$, forms a signal, and the pixels selected are samples from this signal. If the image changes intensity quickly as when we move from the line to the background, then this adds a high-frequency component to the signal. The signal is a sum of many frequencies, and sampling from it at discrete locations is an attempt to adequately capture all these frequencies. The jagged line is a result of not adequately capturing the signal detail and, at the same time, introducing spurious detail. With this in mind, there are two immediately accessible *anti-aliasing* techniques that minimize the jagged appearance.

First, increase the sampling rate. Pixels on the screen are a fixed size, but we could imagine that they are much smaller. In fact, referring to the pixel array analyzed in Bresenham's algorithm, divide each square pixel into four smaller pixels (Figure 10.2).

Apply Bresenham's algorithm as before on this higher resolution array. It is possible that of the 2×2 array of subpixels, 0, 1, or 2 are selected by the algorithm. Now, instead of an all-or-nothing decision, we have three levels and can color the pixel according to the level. Using gray levels, 0 denotes white, 1 is a middle gray, and 2 is black. This coloring mitigates some of the sudden jumps from one level to another by shading a pixel gray instead of just black or white. Of course, the procedure is more effective if we increase the subpixel array to a 3×3 array and add one more level of gray.

The *supersample* technique is effective, but human vision is complicated and different supersample schemes can improve things further. Thinking of the theoretical line as 2 pixels wide or using sampling patterns within the subpixel array can give some encouraging results. The major idea, however, in all these techniques is to introduce additional shading to the original notion of picking a pixel or not.

A second technique uses shading in a slightly different way. In Bresenham's algorithm, think of the line as a function, $f(x) = mx + b$. Then the pixel we pick is $\lfloor f(x_i) + 0.5 \rfloor$, where the notation $\lfloor \cdot \rfloor$ indicates the floor function (rounding down). This is the result of using a criterion that simply determines which pixel's center is closest to the line. Yet, there are other criteria that may better fit human visual perception.

Bresenham's algorithm results in a series of pixels that form an intensity function $I_B(x, y)$, which is I_0 over a selected pixel and zero elsewhere. The sharp jumps from one location to another are analogous to square waves that can be thought of as a sum of many sine waves of increasing frequency. In signal processing, applying what is called a *low-pass filter* eliminates some of the high frequencies and smooths the signal. Mathematically, the signal is averaged by integrating the signal over local regions. (This is called a *convolution*.)

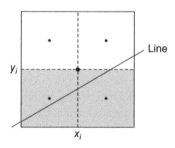

Figure 10.2   Supersampling a pixel

More practically, Bresenham's line algorithm picks between y_i and $y_i + 1$ when the true value of $f(x)$ is most often somewhere in between. So the idea is to shade both pixels $P_0 = (x_{i+1}, y_i)$ and $P_1 = (x_{i+1}, y_i + 1)$ in such a way that the center of intensity falls right at $y = f(x_i)$. We are effectively averaging a pixel over its immediate neighbors. To achieve this, recall that $d_{(0,i)}$ and $d_{(1,i)}$ are the distances from the line to the lower (P_0) and upper (P_1) pixels, respectively.

$$d_{(0,i)} = f(x_{i+1}) - y_i = f(x_{i+1}) - \lfloor f(x_{i+1}) \rfloor$$
$$d_{(1,i)} = y_i + 1 - f(x_{i+1}) = \lceil f(x_{i+1}) \rceil - f(x_{i+1})$$
$$d_{(0,i)} + d_{(1,i)} = 1$$

Use $d_{(0,i)}$ and $d_{(1,i)}$ as weights for the intensities of the two pixels. Specifically, to have an overall intensity of I_L at each position on the line, set the intensity of P_0 to $d_{(1,i)}I_L$ and the intensity of P_1 to $d_{(0,i)}I_L$. If the line is closer to P_0, then $d_{(1,i)} > d_{(0,i)}$ and we make P_0 more intense (brighter or darker depending on the background) than P_1. The center of gravity of the two intensities is just the affine combination of the two positions.

$$d_{(1,i)}P_0 + d_{(0,i)}P_1 = (y_i + 1 - f(x_{i+1}))(x_{i+1}, y_i)$$
$$+ (f(x_{i+1}) - y_i)(x_{i+1}, y_i + 1)$$
$$= (x_{i+1}, f(x_{i+1})) \tag{10.5}$$

Assuming that human perception integrates this combination of two intensities, the line should appear in its correct position and the sharp changes in intensity from one position to the next should be softened. The result is a respectable anti-aliasing algorithm (see [12] for more details).

10.1.3 Compositing

The color of an individual pixel is stored in the frame buffer (part of memory). One of the most common color models is the RGB model, which stores red, green, and blue color components often with one byte for each component; the pixel is then a vector (r, g, b) with each component between 0 and 1. Early in the development of graphics (late 1970s as a result of work by Alvy Ray Smith), a fourth component called the *alpha channel* was added to the mix. Pixels now could be considered as a vector (r, g, b, α), where the α component indicated how opaque the pixel was. With $\alpha = 1$, the pixel is fully opaque and with $\alpha = 0$ it is fully transparent.

Representing pixels as vectors hints at the possibility of a pixel arithmetic. Are there vector-like operations on pixels that have significant useful effects on an image? Scalar multiplication makes some sense: $s(r, g, b, \alpha) = (sr, sg, sb, s\alpha)$; if, for example, s decreases to zero, the pixel fades away as the color gradually reaches black and the pixel becomes transparent. We have to keep in mind that the color components are constrained between 0 and 1, so it is not entirely obvious how either scalar multiplication or pixel addition should work in general.

Earlier, while investigating shading, our technique was to find the appropriate colors at the vertices of a triangle and then interpolate the colors throughout the interior of the triangle. Since the coordinates sum to 1, an interpolation using barycentric coordinates certainly chooses colors in some sense between the vertex colors. (It should be noted that it is not totally clear how human visual perception of linear changes in color affects the sense of the scene.) The alpha channel, however, adds a little complexity, and it is not immediately clear whether interpolating the α component gives reasonable results.

One advantage of α is the possibility of placing one image over another where the foreground could obscure the background or perhaps where the background shows through slightly. This is one way to *composite* two images, and the operation historically is referred to as the *over operator*. Consider just the color components of two pixels, $F = (r_f, g_f, b_f)$ from the foreground image and $B = (r_B, g_B, b_B)$ from the background image, and let the notation $F \triangleright B$ represent the over operation. The task, then, is to define this operator in terms of the arithmetic of pixel components (Figure 10.3).

The over operation should produce a new pixel which will replace the current one at the given location in the frame buffer. If both F and B are completely opaque ($\alpha = 1$), then $P = F \triangleright B = F$. If B is opaque and F has α as the alpha channel value, then

$$P = \alpha F + (1 - \alpha)B \qquad (10.6)$$

The case where B is not fully opaque may not seem to make practical sense, but if we compose three images together, then it does make sense for the two foreground images.

If there are two foreground images and hence two pixels F_1 and F_2, then compositing the second over the first and then over the background gives $P = (F_2 \triangleright F_1) \triangleright B$. If this is to be a coherent operation, we may insist that it is associative.

$$P = (F_2 \triangleright F_1) \triangleright B = F_2 \triangleright (F_1 \triangleright B)$$

In this expression, we do not yet know how to define $(F_2 \triangleright F_1)$ because here F_1 may not be completely opaque. Designate the alpha value of $(F_2 \triangleright F_1)$ temporarily as α^*.

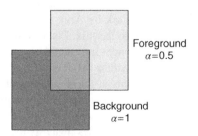

Figure 10.3   Over operation

Calling on a little algebra gives the following derivation:

$$(F_2 \triangleright F_1) \triangleright B) = \alpha^*(F_2 \triangleright F_1) + (1 - \alpha^*)B$$

$$= [\alpha^*(F_2 \triangleright F_1)] + [1 - \alpha^*]B$$

$$F_2 \triangleright (F_1 \triangleright B) = \alpha_2 F_2 + (1 - \alpha_2)(\alpha_1 F_1 + (1 - \alpha_1)B)$$

$$= [\alpha_2 F_2 + (1 - \alpha_2)\alpha_1 F_1] + [1 - \alpha_2 - \alpha_1 + \alpha_2\alpha_1]B \qquad (10.7)$$

The expressions in 10.7 must be equal to ensure associativity. For this to be true for any B, the coefficients (in brackets) in front of B in both equations must be equal. For it to be true for any F_1 and F_2, the remaining two expressions must be equal.

$$(1 - \alpha^*) = 1 - \alpha_2 - \alpha_1 + \alpha_2\alpha_1$$

$$\alpha^*(F_2 \triangleright F_1) = \alpha_2 F_2 + (1 - \alpha_2)\alpha_1 F_1 \qquad (10.8)$$

Pulling this together gives the correct pixel arithmetic for compositing two pixels when each has an arbitrary alpha value.

$$\alpha^* = \alpha_2 + (1 - \alpha_2)\alpha_1$$

$$F_2 \triangleright F_1 = \frac{\alpha_2}{\alpha^*} F_2 + \left(1 - \frac{\alpha_2}{\alpha^*}\right) F_1 \qquad (10.9)$$

Checking to see that this formula is consistent with our earlier assumption, we set $\alpha_1 = 1$, which makes F_1 fully opaque. Then, $\alpha^* = 1$ and we get Equation 10.6 which we initially developed for compositing a foreground over an opaque background. When $\alpha_2 = 1$, $F_2 \triangleright F_1 = F_2$, which is what we might expect when an opaque image is placed over another image.

Up to now, F_1 and F_2 were three-dimensional vectors representing the three color components. But suppose we represent pixels as $(\alpha r, \alpha g, \alpha b, \alpha)$, where the color components have already been multiplied by the alpha value. This is the *premultiplied alpha* form. The advantage is that we can bring further symmetry to the compositing formulas.

Let $\overline{F}_1$ and $\overline{F}_2$ be the premultiplied alpha forms for the pixels; they are now four dimensional vectors. Then

$$\overline{F}_2 \triangleright \overline{F}_1 = \overline{F}_2 + (1 - \alpha_2)\overline{F}_1 \qquad (10.10)$$

Some algebra verifies that this last formula encapsulates both the formulas in Equation 10.9. Now, the fourth component of the vector holds the correct value for alpha. The convenience of this expression argues for storing pixels in the premultiplied form; as one might expect, there are reasons to use either pixel form.

There are many compositing operations in addition to the over operation (see [13] for the original exposition of several operations). Some have tried to add and subtract pixels in various ways to combine images, and in particular situations the effects are useful. Yet, there does not seem to be a consistent theory of a universal pixel arithmetic.

10.2   NOISE

Organic objects like plants, mountains, and clouds are not simple cubes or spheres, and it is not even apparent how they can be formed from many polygons or polyhedra. Even if the basic shape of a mountain is captured with a multifaceted pyramid, the texture of each face is far from smooth and reflective. These modeling problems are indicative of many problems in graphics and also in mathematics where a deterministic approach to a solution seems elusive. Since plants, mountains, and clouds appear to have elements of randomness when viewed at any distance, it might be that a random perturbation here or there can turn a sphere into a rock or a pyramid into a mountain.

10.2.1   Random Number Generation

It all starts with random numbers, and most programming languages offer methods or functions for producing a sequence that appears to be random. Actually, unless we have a quantum computer or some way to sense electronic noise, the processes are all deterministic and the string of random numbers is really *pseudo-random*. That is, there is some algorithm which starts with a number (called the *seed*) and manipulates it to get the first pseudo-random number. Then, generally, the algorithm uses the first number to get the second number and continues indefinitely. One common and simple algorithm referred to as a *linear congruential generator* uses the following recurrence:

$$x_{n+1} \equiv ax_n + b \;(\text{mod } m) \tag{10.11}$$

The constants a, b, and m must be selected carefully, but then the sequence $\{x_n\}$ appears to be random. Notice that the recurrence uses arithmetic modulo m, meaning that all the x_n are remainders after dividing by m. That is, $0 \le x_n \le m - 1$. Certainly, m should be large to ensure plenty of possible numbers; once a number repeats, the sequence starts to cycle. There is some significant number theory behind choosing all three constants to give a good pseudo-random generator.

Example 10.2 (Simple Linear Congruential Generator).   Consider the recurrence $x_{n+1} \equiv 3x_n + 2 \;(\text{mod } 7)$. Starting with the seed $x_0 = 3$, the sequence proceeds as follows:

$$x_0 = 3, \quad x_1 = 4, \quad x_2 = 0, \quad x_3 = 2, \quad x_4 = 1, \quad x_5 = 5, \quad x_6 = 3$$

Once 3 appears for the second time, the sequence starts repeating. Clearly, m should be large and chosen so that a large number of possible remainders appear before repeating. Primes are good choices, and $m = 2^{31} - 1$ has proved desirable.   □

With a sequence of positive integers modulo m, the numbers $\frac{x_n}{m}$ are all rational (floating point) numbers between 0 and 1. A programming language might use the function name rand() to return one of these rational numbers, and they can then be used in a variety of ways to choose other sorts of random numbers. For example, $\lfloor 3 \cdot \text{rand}() \rfloor + 1$ selects one of the numbers 1, 2, or 3, pseudo-randomly.

From a long sequence of 1's, 2's, and 3's, the fraction of 1's should be close to $p_3 = 1/3$. If we consider adjacent pairs of numbers, the fraction of pairs that are two 1's should be close to $1/9$. These sorts of patterns should appear with frequencies indicative of equally likely chances of any of the three numbers. In particular, $p_1 = p_2 = p_3 = 1/3$ is the probability of each number appearing. Pseudo-random sequences that pass all these statistical tests are usually sufficiently random that if we use them in a graphics setting, no unintended patterns will arise in the image.

10.2.2   Distributions

Usually, the sequence generated above by rand() is uniform in that the fraction of numbers appearing in any small subinterval of $[0, 1)$ depends only on the width of the interval. So one-fourth of the numbers should appear in each of the intervals $[0, 0.25)$, $[0.25, 0.5), [0.5, 0.75)$, and $[0.75, 1)$. Of course, the numbers are pseudo-random, so the exact fraction in an interval may vary, but it approaches one-fourth as more numbers are generated. If rand() generates a uniform sequence, then $\lfloor 3 \cdot \text{rand}() \rfloor + 1$ generates the numbers 1, 2, 3 equally often.

Characterizing the distribution of these random (understood to be pseudo-random) numbers requires some ideas from probability theory. The probability that a number appears in a sequence is the fraction of the time it appears. If we only generate numbers 1, 2, and 3, we say we have a discrete sequence and to describe it we list the probability of getting each of the numbers. So the probabilities p_1, p_2, and p_3 where $p_1 + p_2 + p_3 = 1$ describe the possible sequences that may be produced by the generator. These probabilities depend on how we designed the generator. If we actually generate a sequence of 100 numbers, it may or may not exactly match the theoretical probabilities, but as we generate a longer and longer sequence, the match should become closer.

For a discrete generator, we put the probabilities together into a mass function, $f(k) = p_k$, giving the probabilities for each possible value k. A histogram showing bars whose heights are the probabilities p_i visually summarizes the distribution. With more possible values, there are more bars in the histogram, but the sum of all the probabilities is always 1 (Figure 10.4).

On the other hand, if the generator can produce any fraction, say between zero and 1, then the sequences generated are more continuous than discrete. Instead of focusing on a single value, we find the fraction of the time that the generated numbers appear in some interval $[a, b)$. As the sequence grows longer, this fraction gets closer to the theoretical probability of that interval. Instead of a histogram, we use a curve, $f(x)$, to describe the distribution's shape. The area under the curve between a and b is now the probability of that interval. This curve is called a *density function* for the distribution, and analogous to the bars in the histogram, the total area under the density curve is 1.

In probability theory, numbers in a random sequence are thought of as values for a random variable, denoted by X. A generator produces values of X, and theoretically

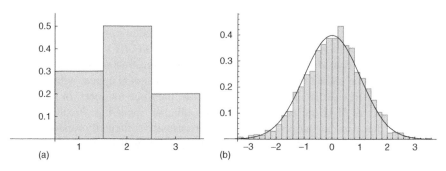

Figure 10.4   Distribution histogram (a) and curve (b)

the average of all those values should be what we call the *expected value* denoted as
EX. The expected value depends on the design of the generator, and in any particular
sequence produced the actual average may be a little different. Yet, as the sequence
grows, the average should get close to *EX*.

Definition 10.1 (Expected Value).   *For a discrete distribution of k distinct values x_i*
with probabilities p_i, the expected value is a sum.

$$EX = \sum_{i=1}^{k} p_i x_i$$

For a continuous distribution with density function f(x) and values ranging between
s_1 and s_2, the expected value is an integral.

$$EX = \int_{s_1}^{s_2} xf(x)dx$$

The variance (denoted σ^2) measures the spread of a distribution. Any particular
value of the random variable *X* may be close to or far from the expected value *EX*.
Variance measures how far away it is by calculating the square of the distance to *EX*
and then finding the average over all possible values.

Definition 10.2 (Variance).   *For a discrete distribution of k distinct values x_i with*
probabilities p_i, the variance is a sum.

$$\sigma^2 = \sum_{i=1}^{k} p_i (x_i - EX)^2$$

For a continuous distribution with density function f(x) and values ranging between
s_1 and s_2, the variance is an integral.

$$\sigma^2 = \int_{i=1}^{k} (x_i - EX)^2 f(x)dx$$

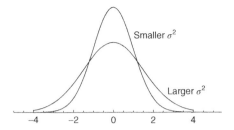

Figure 10.5   Variances of a normal distribution

The expected value and variance of a distribution summarize the key features of the distribution's shape. Expected value is the center, and the variance measures how spread out the curve is. In the case of the normal distribution which looks like a bell-shaped curve, the expected value marks the peak of the curve and hence indicates the values in the sequence that occur most often. With high probability, the numbers will be near the expected value. A high variance implies that the curve is flat and spread out, meaning that there is a larger probability that numbers will be far from EX, whereas a low variance indicates a curve with a sharper peak and a low probability of numbers straying far from EX (Figure 10.5).

10.2.3   Sequences of Random Numbers

Distributions are described theoretically, but once we have an actual sequence of random numbers (called a *sample*), we can summarize it by finding an average and measuring how spread out it is. If there are n numbers (a_i), then $\bar{a}$ is the sample mean.

$$\bar{a} = \frac{1}{n} \sum_{i=1}^{n} a_i$$

Most likely, $\bar{a}$ will be close to the theoretical expected value EX. To measure the spread of the sequence, we calculate the squared of the distance between each number and the average. The average of all these squared distances is the sample variance S^2.

$$S_a^2 = \frac{1}{n} \sum_{i=1}^{n} (a_i - \bar{a})^2$$

It is often necessary to determine whether two sequences are independent of each other or rather they rise and fall somewhat together. When generating an image using random sequences, we may want the effects in the horizontal direction to be independent of those in the vertical direction. To detect dependence, we calculate the *sample covariance* between two sequences $\{a_i\}$ and $\{b_i\}$.

$$c_{(a,b)} = \frac{1}{n} \sum_{i=1}^{n} (a_i - \bar{a}_i)(b_i - \bar{b}_i) \tag{10.12}$$

This quantity measures how the two sequences vary together. If at some position in the sequence they are both above their mean (or below their mean), then the product in the sum is positive. Otherwise, it is negative. So the sum is positive if the two sequences tend to rise and fall together. It is negative if they tend to move in opposite directions, and it is near zero if they do not seem to behave together in any way. (One quick aside: for both sample variance and sample covariance, there are good reasons to divide by $n - 1$ instead of n. This has to do with methods of statistical inference.)

Finally, by dividing by the square root of the sample variances of each sequence, the covariance is normalized to be a number between -1 and 1.

Definition 10.3 (Sample Correlation Coefficient). *The sample correlation coefficient is*

$$r = \frac{c_{(a,b)}}{S_a S_b}$$

In working with random sequences in graphics, we look mostly for evidence of correlation between sequences. This means that r is significantly nonzero.

Example 10.3 (Statistical Summary of Sequences). Suppose the $\{a_i\}$ sequence is $\{2, 0, 1, 5, 4\}$ and the $\{b_i\}$ sequence is $\{11, 7, 5, 2, 8\}$.

$$\bar{a} = \frac{1}{5}(2 + 0 + 1 + 5 + 4) = 2.4$$

$$\bar{b} = \frac{1}{5}(11 + 7 + 5 + 2 + 8) = 6.6$$

$$S_a^2 = \frac{1}{4} \sum_{i=1}^{5} (a_i - 2.4)^2 = 4.3$$

$$S_b^2 = \frac{1}{4} \sum_{i=1}^{5} (b_i - 6.6)^2 = 11.3$$

$$r = \frac{c_{(a,b)}}{S_a S_b} = \frac{-3.67}{\sqrt{4.3}\sqrt{11.3}} \approx -0.53$$

The correlation coefficient is always between -1 and 1, so the 0.53 value indicates a positive correlation between the sequences. There is some evidence that they move in opposite directions. Of course, we have very little data here. The key observation is that they appear correlated. Usually, we are looking for sequences that are uncorrelated and hence have a correlation coefficient close to zero. □

10.2.4 Uniform and Normal Distributions

Two distributions stand out in computer generation of random sequences: the *uniform* distribution and the *normal* (or Gaussian) distribution. The rand() function will produce a uniform distribution if the underlying linear congruential generator (or other algorithm) is tuned appropriately to produce numbers with equal probabilities. Then the distribution of $\frac{x_n}{m}$ can be considered continuous with density $f(x) = 1$ for $0 \leq x \leq 1$. Using the definition of expected value and variance, we discover that $EX = 1/2$ and $\sigma^2 = 1/12$.

The normal distribution has a density that is bell-shaped. Many measurements in nature like the height of pine trees or the density of vegetation tend to follow this shape. (If not normal, the quantities are often log-normal, which is related). This argues that the normal distribution is useful in producing natural-looking images. The actual shape of the bell curve (and hence of the normal density) is characterized by the expected value and the variance. The distribution with $EX = 0$ and $\sigma^2 = 1$ is called the *standard normal distribution* and its density function is as follows:

$$f(x) = \frac{1}{2\pi} e^{\frac{x^2}{2}} \text{ for } -\infty < x < \infty \tag{10.13}$$

To produce a sequence of numbers with a normal distribution, one approach is to start with the ubiquitous rand(). Perhaps the most important theorem in probability theory, the Central Limit Theorem, says that if we add up numbers from almost any distribution, the sum has a normal distribution.

Result 10.1 (Generating a Normal Distribution). *If the values $x_1, x_2, \ldots, x_k$ come from a uniform distribution on $[0, 1)$, then*

$$Z = \frac{\sum_{i=1}^{k} x_k - (k/2)}{\sqrt{k/12}}$$

is a value from an approximate normal distribution with $EX = 0$ and $\sigma^2 = 1$. As k gets larger, the approximation gets better.

Assuming rand() produces values from a uniform distribution (between 0 and 1), we generate k numbers and add them up. Then subtract $k/2$, which we recognize as k times the expected value of the uniform distribution. Finally, divide by the square root of k times the variance of the uniform distribution. The subtraction and division serves to normalize the value to fit the standard normal distribution. A histogram of the Z values will have a bell shape. (A slightly deeper study of probability theory verifies why these are the correct quantities to use for normalizing.)

Result 10.2 (Generating an Arbitrary Normal Distribution). *If the values Z form an approximate standard normal distribution, the values $aZ + b$ form an approximate normal distribution with $EX = b$ and $\sigma^2 = a^2$.*

Using the technique just outlined, we can produce a sequence from any normal distribution we wish. There are other more efficient techniques for doing this, but even with $k = 4$ [taking a sum of four values from *rand()*], the current technique gives a reasonable pseudo-random sequence with a normal distribution.

10.2.5   Terrain Generation

A raw form of a landscape is just a compilation of rocky hills and valleys. To produce a graphics simulation of such a terrain, one simple way is to start with a triangulation of a planar region. For each vertex in the triangulation, generate a random number representing the height (positive or negative) of the vertex. Reconnecting all the vertices forms a surface made up of triangular faces. The resulting terrain looks reasonable, although probably a little blocky. There are two reasons for this look: the resolution is fixed by the original triangulation, and the distribution of heights can drastically affect the overall shape of the terrain. If the variance of the random sequence is large, the terrain might look quite spikey, and if the variance is small it may be overly smooth. Moreover, if we choose a uniform distribution over a normal distribution, it may look as though changes in height are too sudden or too sharp (Figure 10.6).

There are many custom algorithms for generating terrains and all of them need to cope with two main criteria.

1. The distribution of random numbers should result in natural looking changes in height.
2. There should be detail at all scales. As we zoom in, the detail should look just as random as it did originally.

A general class of algorithms uses a midpoint displacement technique to improve on the primitive algorithm above by adding detail and improving resolution. One of these algorithms is called the *diamond-square* algorithm and begins with a square grid of points (Figure 10.7).

Diamond-Square Algorithm

1. *Initialization.* Assign heights to the grid points using a standard normal distribution. ($EX = 0$ and $\sigma_0^2 = 1$.)
2. *Update Distribution.* Reduce the variance by half ($\sigma_{n+1}^2 = \frac{1}{2}\sigma_n^2$).
3. *Square Midpoint.* Find the midpoint of each grid square and assign a height equal to the average of the four corner points plus an additional random amount (positive or negative).

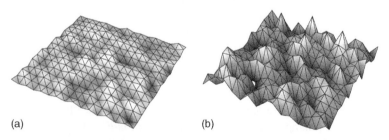

(a)   (b)

Figure 10.6   Terrains: low variance (a), high variance (b)

Figure 10.7 Diamond-square algorithm

4. *Diamond Midpoint.* The midpoints of two adjacent squares and the two common corner points of those squares form a diamond shape (a rotated square). Set the height of the center of the diamond shape to the average of the four corners of the diamond plus an additional random amount.

5. *Increased Resolution.* Now the original points together with the new points form a square grid with edge length one-half the original grid. Repeat steps 2 through 5 until the grid size becomes sufficiently small.

The algorithm continues looping until the grid size is small enough to look decent on the display. Adding diagonals to the squares produces triangular faces which can then be shaded and displayed. The use of randomly perturbed midpoints in this algorithm ensures that the terrain detail looks equally random at many scales. Reducing the variance on each pass through the loop keeps the distribution of peaks looking statistically the same as we enlarge the terrain. (More theoretically, the midpoint construction approximates a two-dimensional Brownian motion which is an example of a stochastic process.)

Without the diamond midpoint step in the algorithm, the resulting terrain can have faint remnants of the underlying rectangular grid. This is a common problem in random algorithms that begin with some geometrically uniform structure. Mathematically, there is a correlation between two lines of heights in the grid. Other correlations between sequences of heights may appear and add unwanted artifacts. It is sometimes more of an art than a science to adjust the algorithm appropriately to minimize correlations.

Finally, instead of changing the height of points on a grid, the algorithm could change the color of the points, perhaps on a gray scale. The result is a cloud-like image. Random image algorithms like the one above generally benefit from a wide range of input parameters, allowing the graphics programmer to alter details to match the type of terrain or cloud appropriate for the scene. In particular, different distributions of random numbers have a significant effect on the image.

10.2.6 Noise Generation

A terrain is an example of a two-dimensional random signal. At any point in the grid plane, the height of the terrain is a value from a signal that spatially changes randomly. We are most familiar with random signals in the context of sound waves where we call such signals noise and the random changes are in time and not in space. A simple sine wave is a pure musical tone, but if we add random perturbations to it we get noise. The key idea in Fourier analysis is that these noise signals can be decomposed in to a sum of sine waves with differing frequencies and amplitudes. Random perturbations tend to add additional frequencies to the mix, particularly high frequencies.

The field of signal processing studies various attributes of noise and catalogs random signals according to various properties of the decomposition into sine waves. For example, if the power in a sine wave is the same for all frequencies, then the signal is called *white noise*. Based on the power spectrum, noise signals can have widely different characters.

The coloring in a piece of granite can be thought of as a noisy perturbation of an underlying pattern (flecks of various minerals). Producing a texture map to simulate granite is then a matter of starting with an appropriate pattern and adding noise in various ways. It would be convenient if we had a noise function that returns a value from a random signal which could then be used to either add color to a texture or perturb the original texture pattern. In this way, the graphics programmer could generate textures algorithmically. Bump maps from an earlier chapter are examples of using noise to procedurally produce textures.

In 1983, Ken Perlin recognized the usefulness of noise in graphics and designed a noise function with many desirable properties. He was interested in constructing textures, so the function had to be used in a variety of ways to integrate randomness into other sorts of patterns. Simply calling on a random number generator would not do because it is too wildly fluctuating; more control is needed. Starting with a grid, Perlin built a surface that could be sampled at any point to get a noise value. The following criteria were the key in his design.

1. The function should be relatively controlled. Intuitively, it should not be widely fluctuating, but the programmer should be able to use it to produce more widely fluctuating textures. Technically, it should not have very high frequencies (small details) or very low frequencies (larger structural details). "Controlled" also means that it does not have discontinuities and that the average height is zero, allowing the programmer to scale and translate as needed.
2. Rotating or translating the surface should maintain all statistical characteristics. Basically, it should look random from any direction.
3. There should not be any correlations that are visually obvious.
4. It should be easy and efficient to calculate a value at any point.

We will focus on a two-dimensional noise function which gives a surface, but Perlin's methods work in any dimension and we could construct a three-dimensional function.corresponding to a random volume. One key criterion for Perlin is calculation efficiency. Part of the surface structure can be precomputed, but for any point the final calculations need to be fast.

Perlin's Method [Defining the function $\text{Noise}(x, y)$.]

1. Begin with a grid of points with integer coordinates.

2. Pick a random normal for each grid point to determine a plane through that grid point.

3. Compute the height of the plane at a given point (x, y).

4. Compute the weight of the grid point using a weight function which falls off with distance from the grid point.

5. Multiply the height by the weight to get the influence from the grid point.

6. Add up the influences at the four grid points, marking corners of a square containing (x, y). Return the sum as the quantity Noise(x, y).

Step 2 involves several details. For random normals, we really want vectors distributed on the surface of a sphere. These can be picked by selecting each of the three coordinates for a vector using a uniform distribution on $[0, 1)$. This gives vectors in a unit cube; simply discard any vector with length greater than 1. The resulting vectors are distributed throughout the sphere and can be normalized if needed.

Yet, we only want one normal per grid point; any time we have the same integer coordinates, we want the same normal. To guarantee this uniqueness, put all the normals in a table and use the grid point coordinates to find a position in the table. Perlin precomputes a random permutation and uses it to locate a normal in the table.

Example 10.4 (Computing Perlin Noise).   To find the value of Noise$(1.2, 0.6)$, first notice that it is in the square defined by the grid points $G_1 = (1, 0)$, $G_2 = (2, 0)$, $G_3 = (2, 1)$, and $G_4 = (1, 1)$.

Now use the grid point coordinates to find the associated random normals. Suppose that these normals are $\vec{n}_1 = (0.2, 0.1, 0.5)$, $\vec{n}_2 = (0.1, 0.3, -0.1)$, $\vec{n}_3 = (0.5, -0.1, 0.1)$, and $\vec{n}_4 = (0.1, 0.2, -0.2)$ (Figure 10.8).

Using three-dimensional coordinates for $G_1 = (1, 0, 0)$, this point is on a plane with normal $\vec{n}_1$, and point $P = (1.2, 0.6, h)$ is also on the plane where h is the height above (or below) the grid. Vector $(P - G_1)$ is parallel to the plane, and consequently

$$\vec{n}_1 \cdot (P - G_1) = 0 \implies 0.04 + 0.06 + 0.5h = 0 \implies h = -0.2$$

This is the height from step 3 of Perlin's method. To calculate the weight in step 4, we use the cubic polynomial $1 - 6t^5 + 15t^4 - 10t^3$. This function falls off in an S-shape

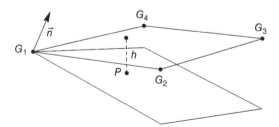

Figure 10.8   Perlin noise calculation

manner as we get farther from a grid point. The two-dimensional vector from G_1 to $(1.2, 0.6)$ is $(0.2, 0.6)$. The weight is then

$$(1 - 6|0.2|^5 + 15|0.2|^4 - 10|0.2|^3) = 0.942$$

$$(1 - 6|0.6|^5 + 15|0.6|^4 - 10|0.6|^3) = 0.317$$

$$\text{Weight} = (0.942)(0.317) \approx 0.3$$

The influence from grid point G_1 is then $Height \times Weight = -0.2 \times 0.3 = -0.06$. The same type of calculation gives the influence from each grid point.

	Height	Weight	Influence
G_1	−0.2	0.3	−0.06
G_2	1.0	0.018	0.018
G_3	−4.4	0.04	−0.176
G_4	−0.3	0.64	−0.192

In step 6, we find the sum of the influences to get $\text{noise}(1.2, 0.6) = -0.41$. □

Perlin's noise has proven very flexible and useful in constructing realistic textures. At first, the weight function was not quite right and the function $1 - 6t^5 - 15t^4 + 10t^3$ was substituted to guarantee smoothness (the first derivative is zero at the endpoints 0 and 1). The method for computing random normals presented here allows normals close to the direction of the grid lines and this can cause some artifacts. Perlin's revised algorithm deletes those normals in the direction of the lines. All these adjustments come from building textures using the noise function and then noting any visual flaws.

The distribution of heights in the noise function is not easy to calculate, but notice that the last step of Perlin's method adds four random quantities together. The Central Limit Theorem suggests that this introduces a hint of a normal distribution. To add higher frequencies to the noise and hopefully change the distribution in interesting ways, one approach is to sum up values of the noise function. Consider the following sum:

$$\text{noise}(x, y) + \frac{1}{2}\text{noise}(2(x, y)) + \frac{1}{4}\text{noise}(4(x, y)) \tag{10.14}$$

The sum could continue by adding more terms, but effectively it is adding higher and higher frequencies into the mix and making the surface less smooth. Dampening the higher frequencies with coefficients that get smaller and smaller controls the effects.

This sort of manipulation is indicative of the flexibility available when working with the noise function.

10.3   L-SYSTEMS

One characteristic of many organic forms is self-similarity. A single branch of a pine tree when scaled up looks much like the entire pine tree; a part of the tree is similar to the entire tree. Clouds behave in much the same way, where chunks of the cloud, on close examination, look like the entire cloud. The phenomenon can continue down in scale because pieces of pieces can also have the same form as the whole.

Sometimes the self-similarity is quite geometric, and we have *fractal* structures which were first thoroughly investigated by Benoit Mandelbrot. The snowflake curve introduced in an earlier chapter is an example of this deterministic self-similarity. To construct these shapes, basic parts of the image, such as line segments, are replaced recursively by some generating shape that determines the final image. In the case of the snowflake curve, line segments are replaced by four smaller segments forming a triangle. The process continues at smaller and smaller scales theoretically without limit. The mathematical characteristics of fractal curves are just as interesting as the visual image. Unlike simple curves with dimension one, the wiggly nature of fractal curves means they have fractional dimension, often between 1 and 2 (Figure 10.9).

Rather than being completely deterministic, plants and other natural forms have a stochastic component as well. Trees grow in uniform ways, but are perturbed by environmental events. Overall, tree growth displays self-similarity because a branch is made from smaller branches all with similar structure. In 1968, Aristid Lindenmayer, a theoretical biologist (University of Utrecht), devised a system for describing the recursive nature of plant growth in order to more carefully study multicellular organisms. His system borrowed from the use of grammars in the study of natural and artificial languages. Effectively, his grammar rules were growth rules, and rather than constructing sentences he was constructing plants.

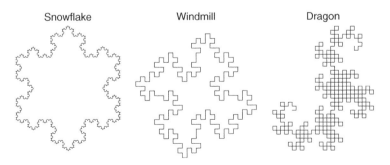

Snowflake   Windmill   Dragon

Figure 10.9   Fractal curves

10.3.1   Grammars

Grammars have been used for a long time in an attempt to describe how we generate good sentences. They also grew out of the study of logic, when computers were first conceived, to help describe the nature of computation. If we think of digital computers as devices that turn strings of characters (the input) into new strings of characters (the output), then we can imagine the computation process as starting with a string of symbols and applying grammar rules to produce other strings. Once the strings are interpreted as numbers or other forms of data, we understand the process as computation.

Grammars have different formal structures depending on the context, but all have some form of the following characteristics:

1. There is a finite set of possible symbols called the *alphabet* and denoted by Σ.
2. Each finite string of symbols (like *aaba*) is called a *word*.
3. A set of words is called a *language*.
4. A rule, or *production*, describes how to replace one string with another. For example, $a \rightarrow ab$ is a production that allows a to be replaced with ab.
5. There is an initial word called an *axiom*.

Many of the grammars used in studying natural language or the theory of computation allow the application of one production at a time to generate a new word. Starting with the axiom word, a series of productions derives a new word. The collection of all these words is called the *language of the grammar*; if G is the grammar, then $L(G)$ is the language of the grammar. When Lindenmayer designed the grammars now called *L-systems* (after Lindenmayer), he wanted to mimic the growth of living systems where all cells are participating in growth at the same time. So for L-systems, all possible productions are applied at the same time.

Example 10.5   Let G be a grammar with alphabet $\Sigma = \{a, b\}$. There are two productions in G: $a \rightarrow a, b \rightarrow ab$. The axiom is ab. Then we can successively derive the following words:

$$ab \rightarrow aab \rightarrow aaab$$

Notice that in the first step, the axiom ab becomes the word aab. Here, both productions were applied because a was replaced with a and b was replaced with ab.

It is not hard to see that we can continually produce words, an infinite number, and they all are a series of a's followed by a single b.

$$L(G) = \{a^n b | n \geq 1\}$$

Continuing with the biological analogy, we might consider that the symbol a represents a mature cell and the symbol b represents a cell that is ready to divide.   □

In the last example, the productions each allowed one symbol to be replaced. This is the key, and each symbol in the alphabet should have a corresponding production. If not, we assume there is an identity production that replaces a symbol with itself. With exactly one production for each symbol, the grammar is deterministic in that there is no choice involved when moving from one word to the next.

Definition 10.4 (DOL-system). *An L-system is a grammar where all possible productions are applied at once. If all productions have the form $\lambda \to W$, where λ is a symbol and W is a word, and if there is exactly one production for each symbol in the alphabet, then the system is called a* DOL-system *(deterministic context-free L-system).*

This definition hints at further extensions of L-systems. First, a DOL is context-free, which means all the productions have just one symbol on the left-hand side. For the production $a \to b$, it does not matter what other symbols are next to a; any a can be replaced with a b. On the other hand, a production like $ab \to abab$ can be applied only when b follows a in the string. This is a context-sensitive production. Extending L-systems to allow context-sensitive productions offers yet more descriptive power.

Moreover, if there were two productions like $a \to b$ and $a \to c$, then we have to make a decision as to which one to apply and this adds an element of randomness to the grammar. In addition to extending the form of productions, other avenues, like adding special symbols, can make the basic grammars more and more complex. Yet, the DOL-systems alone prove remarkably expressive in building graphics images.

10.3.2   Turtle Interpretation

A DOL-system describes words (more generally a language), but to turn those words into images we need a method for transcribing words into geometry. A useful approach is what has historically been called *turtle geometry*. Several research projects in the late 1960s sought to teach programming skills using a robot (referred to as a *turtle*) to draw simple two-dimensional geometric images as it rolled over paper on the floor. Writing programs for the turtle involved issuing commands to turn right or left, to go forward a certain amount, and to raise or lower the pen. These commands can be encoded as symbols in a grammar. A word in the resulting language is then a sequence of commands that can direct the construction of an image on the display screen instead of the floor. A somewhat common encoding is the following:

F	Move forward one step while drawing a line segment.
$+$	Turn left by angle θ.
$-$	Turn right by angle θ.

With $\theta = \pi/2$, the word $F + F + F + F$ means take one step while drawing, turn left $\pi/2$, take another step, turn left $\pi/2$, and so on. The end result is a

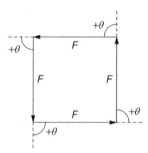

Figure 10.10   Turtle graphics

square traced counterclockwise. To step and turn, we need to keep track of where the turtle is and which direction it is headed. Suppose it is currently at position (x, y) heading in direction α, where horizontally to the right is $\alpha = 0$ and positive angles are counterclockwise. To go forward one step, a line is drawn from (x, y) to $(x + d \cos \alpha, y + d \sin \alpha)$. A left turn updates the heading to $\alpha + \theta$ (Figure 10.10).

To describe a DOL-system, we start with the alphabet $\Sigma = \{F, +, -\}$, specify the length of a step (d) and the turn angle (θ), give the initial axiom, and list the productions. To capture the recursive nature of some images, we devise a production rule that replaces a move forward F with some other pattern.

Example 10.6 (Snowflake Curve).   Let the DOL-system have the alphabet $\Sigma = \{F, +, -\}$ and axiom $F + +F + +F$. There is an identity production for each symbol except F.

$$F \to F - F + +F - F$$

Set the step size to d and let $\theta = \pi/3$. Then the production replaces an edge F with an edge of four segments forming a small equilateral triangle on the original edge. This is the way a snowflake curve is built.

Applying the productions starting from the axiom gives a new word.

$$F + +F + +F \to$$

$$F - F + +F - F + +F - F + +F - F + +F - F + +F - F$$

New words grow quickly in length, so the step size might need to be scaled appropriately to make sure the image fits on the display screen (see the curve on the left in Figure 10.9).   □

A useful addition to the alphabet for the DOL-system is a pair of brackets ([and]). The left bracket causes the turtle to save its current position and direction. (In programming terms, we push the position and direction onto a stack.) The right bracket causes the turtle to retrieve a position and direction from the stack (pop from the stack) and reposition itself accordingly. With these new symbols, additional image structures are possible.

Example 10.7 (Bracketed DOL-System). The *bracketed* DOL-system has alphabet $\Sigma = \{F, +, -, [,]\}$. The axiom is just F. Aside from the identity productions, there is one other production.

$$F \rightarrow F[+F]F[-F]F$$

Set $\theta = \pi/6$. The first few words derived are the following:

$$F \rightarrow F[+F]F[-F]F$$
$$\rightarrow F[+F]F[-F]F[+F[+F]F[-F]F]F[+F]F[-F]$$
$$F[-F[+F]F[-F]F]F[+F]F[-F]F$$

The brackets add a branching character to the image, which begins to resemble a plant or even a tree. It is not too hard to add a leaf symbol and adjust the productions so that leaves appear at the end of branches (Figure 10.11).   □

There is nothing prohibiting a three-dimensional version of these images. A forward step F is still a line segment on the screen, but now we need the position and direction to be adapted to three dimensions. The position is no problem; simply add a coordinate (x, y, z). The direction, however, requires not only a heading but also an up direction and a left (or right) direction. Actually, we need a right-handed coordinate system with an up vector, a forward vector, and a left vector. All three vectors need to be saved as the direction. In order to indicate various turns, we need more symbols in the alphabet to encode turns around each of the three axes. The resulting image should be rendered in perspective to preserve the three-dimensional quality.

10.3.3   Analysis of Grammars

The mathematical analysis of grammars can take several directions depending on the context. For the theory of computation, the main question is which grammars correspond to particular types of abstract machines (finite automata, push-down automata,

Figure 10.11   Branching plant (two and four iterations)

Turing machines). For the more general study of abstract languages (sets of words), an important question is to determine whether two grammars generate the same languages.

For graphics purposes, the main question is to infer the structure of a grammar that could generate a particular type of image. In the original study of L-systems, mimicking plant growth was the key goal. One interesting aspect of this is to determine how fast words grow in length under a particular grammar; this is analogous to how fast plants grow. Since this question can arise in various contexts in the study of grammars, it is useful to dig deeper.

Consider the DOL-system in Example 10.5. There were two productions $a \to a$ and $b \to ab$. Keeping track of how many of each symbol are in a derived word is a matter of looking at the productions and counting how each symbol gets replaced. For example, according to the productions, each a in the initial string leads to one a in the derived word, and each b in the initial string leads to one a in the derived word. So the number of a's in the derived word is the sum of the a's and b's in the initial string. Let $n_i(a)$ be the number of a's in the ith word and let $n_i(b)$ be the number of b's. The sum of these two quantities gives the total number of symbols in the word and is called the *growth function, $f(i)$*.

$$C = \begin{bmatrix} 1 & 1 \\ 0 & 1 \end{bmatrix} \implies C \begin{bmatrix} n_i(a) \\ n_i(b) \end{bmatrix} = \begin{bmatrix} 1 & 1 \\ 0 & 1 \end{bmatrix} \begin{bmatrix} n_i(a) \\ n_i(b) \end{bmatrix} = \begin{bmatrix} n_{i+1}(a) \\ n_{i+1}(b) \end{bmatrix} \tag{10.15}$$

The matrix C represents the effect of the grammar productions, and multiplication by C updates the symbol counts in the derived word. The total number of symbols in the derived word is $f(i + 1) = n_{i+1}(a) + n_{i+1}(b)$. Starting with the axiom ab, the growth function $f(k)$ is determined by the kth power of C.

$$C^k = \begin{bmatrix} 1 & k \\ 0 & 1 \end{bmatrix} \implies C^k \begin{bmatrix} 1 \\ 1 \end{bmatrix} = \begin{bmatrix} k + 1 \\ 1 \end{bmatrix} \tag{10.16}$$

There are $k + 1$ symbols a and one symbol b in the kth derived word, so $f(k) = k + 2$. This is not a surprise because it is rather simple to see how the symbols accumulate in this grammar.

Replace the first production with $a \to b$. Then the matrix C is slightly different, but the powers of C are very different.

$$C = \begin{bmatrix} 0 & 1 \\ 1 & 1 \end{bmatrix} \quad C^2 = \begin{bmatrix} 1 & 1 \\ 1 & 2 \end{bmatrix} \quad C^3 = \begin{bmatrix} 1 & 2 \\ 2 & 3 \end{bmatrix}$$

The corresponding growth function increases as follows: $f(0) = 2, f(1) = 3, f(2) = 5, f(3) = 8$. It follows the Fibonacci numbers and in fact grows exponentially. (The growth is determined by the eigenvalues of the matrix C. These are values λ such that $C\vec{v} = \lambda \vec{v}$ for some vector $\vec{v}$. The theory of eigenvalues is developed in linear algebra, but in this example the eigenvalues are $\frac{1 \pm \sqrt{5}}{2}$ and powers of these determine the growth function.)

The grammar in Example 10.6 has only one production that is not the identity: $F \rightarrow F - F + +F - F$, and it is rather straightforward to count symbols as they accumulate. However, the same matrix technique can work here. Suppose we divide the symbols into two categories: F's and all the others. The correct matrix C is again easy to construct.

$$C = \begin{bmatrix} 4 & 0 \\ 4 & 1 \end{bmatrix} \quad C^2 = \begin{bmatrix} 16 & 0 \\ 20 & 1 \end{bmatrix} \quad C^3 = \begin{bmatrix} 64 & 0 \\ 84 & 1 \end{bmatrix}$$

The growth function grows exponentially, and powers of 4 govern how rapidly it grows.

Grammars with many productions have complicated growth functions, but nevertheless, they all have a common structure [14].

Result 10.3 (Growth Functions for DOL-Systems). *For a DOL-system, the growth function has the following form:*

$$f(k) = \sum_{j=1}^{m} P_j(k) \lambda_j^k$$

The P_j's are polynomials and the λ_j's are nonnegative integers.

Unfortunately for those interested in modeling plants with L-systems, plant growth usually levels off (logistic growth). This means that the basic DOL-system has to be altered to adjust growth rates. Yet, this did not prove to be a major problem and the modeling of plants with L-systems has proved very successful.

10.3.4 Extending L-Systems

To give just a hint of further extensions that can lead to more interesting images, the next example makes two simple alterations: adding an additional symbol, and allowing a random choice of productions.

Example 10.8 (Recursive Tree). Replace the symbol F with two new symbols F_0 and F_1. Both new symbols cause a line segment to be drawn on the screen. The axiom for the system will be F_1, and the productions are:

$$F_1 \rightarrow F_0[++F_1] - F_1$$
$$F_1 \rightarrow F_0[+F_1] - F_1$$
$$F_1 \rightarrow F_0[+F_1] - F_1$$
$$F_1 \rightarrow F_0[++F_1] - F_1$$
$$F_0 \rightarrow F_0$$

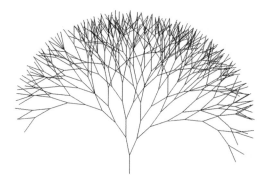

Figure 10.12   Recursive tree

All other symbols have an identity production. The four productions with F_1 on the left offer a choice, so each will be selected with probability one-fourth. Notice that the difference between these productions is the angle of a turn. In some, it is twice what it is in others. This adds a stochastic quality to the image, which may mimic the random perturbations in nature (Figure 10.12).

The production with F_0 simply designates a mature branch that no longer produces two new branches. For further realism, the production could be $F_0 \rightarrow F_0 F_0$, indicating that the mature branches grow longer and longer relative to new branches.   □

More elaborate L-systems actually track the ways in which varieties of plants grow. By introducing parametric L-systems, where symbols like F become functions $F(x)$, graphics programmers can simulate plant signals that prompt leaf or flower growth. In a parametric system, $F(x)$ can represent a line segment of length x. This type of control can simulate the way trees grow to avoid shading from other trees (see [15] for a more in-depth exposition).

10.4   EXERCISES

1. Use Bresenham's line algorithm to find the correct pixels on the line between $(6, 2)$ and $(20, 8)$.

2. Use Bresenham's line algorithm to find the correct pixels on the line between $(8, 4)$ and $(18, 16)$.

3. Design an improvement to Bresenham's line algorithm that looks ahead two pixels to decide which next two to include.

4. Design an algorithm analogous to Bresenham's line algorithm to draw a circle of radius r centered at the origin. (Hint: Consider the part of the circle in the first or second octant.)

5. Let pixels $P_0 = (0.2, 0.35, 0.7, 0.4)$ and $P_1 = (0.5, 0.5, 0.4, 0.3)$ be two pixels where the alpha is not premultiplied. Calculate the value of the pixel $P_0 \triangleright P_1$. Repeat the calculation using the premultiplied alpha form.

6. Suppose the boundary of a polygon (possibly concave) has already been converted to pixels. Design an algorithm which, when given the coordinates of any pixel inside the polygon, will fill the entire interior with a fixed color.

7. Algebraically verify that Equations 10.9 and 10.10 are correctly derived from the previous compositing results.

8. Starting with $x = 2$, find the sequence of numbers coming from the linear congruential generator $x_{n+1} = 3x_n + 5$ (mod 17). Do all the possible remainders show up in the sequence?

9. Using the definitions of expected value and variance of a continuous distribution, verify that for a uniform distribution between 0 and 1, $EX = 1/2$ and $\sigma^2 = 1/12$.

10. Calculate the covariance of the two sequences $2, 5, 4, 4, 3$ and $1, 1, 3, 2, 1$.

11. Evaluate Perlin's noise function at $(1.1, 2.7)$.

12. Find two different DOL-system grammars that produce the same language (set of words).

13. Determine how the growth function for the bracketed L-system in Example 10.7 behaves. Give the appropriate matrix C.

10.4.1 Programming Exercises

1. Implement Bresenham's line algorithm. Input the integer coordinates of two pixels on the screen and draw the line segment between them.

2. Experiment with compositing one solid color rectangle on top of another where the overlap is a smaller rectangle.

3. One common image processing task is to blur an image slightly. Read in an image and replace each pixel with the average of its four (or eight) neighbors. (Be careful not to overwrite previously blurred pixels.)

4. Using the technique given, write a method (function) for generating a sequence from a normal distribution where EX and σ^2 are the input. Produce a histogram (from any program or code) of the sequence and verify the bell shape.

5. Generate a terrain by simply selecting heights at grid points from a normal distribution. Experiment with changing the variance of the normal distribution. Compare the result with a terrain constructed using the diamond-square algorithm.

6. Write code to implement an L-system with the alphabet $\Sigma = \{F, +, -, [,]\}$. Input the axiom and productions from the examples and output the image.

APPENDIX A

GEOMETRY AND TRIGONOMETRY

A.1 TRIANGLES

Two triangles that share the same three interior angles are said to be *similar* (Figure A.1). The three ratios of corresponding sides for similar triangles are all equal. That is, letting $|AB|$ denote the length of the edge from vertex A to vertex B, the following ratios are equal:

$$\frac{|AB|}{|DE|} = \frac{|BC|}{|EC|} = \frac{|CA|}{|CD|} \tag{A.1}$$

A line segment passing through a vertex and perpendicular to the opposite side of a triangle is called an *altitude* (Figure A.2). There are three altitudes in a triangle and they all intersect in a single point called the *orthocenter*. Any side of the triangle can be considered the *base* and the area of the triangle is one-half of the length of the base (b) times the length of the altitude (h) that is perpendicular to the base

$$\text{Area of Triangle} = \frac{1}{2}bh \tag{A.2}$$

Mathematical Structures for Computer Graphics, First Edition. Steven J. Janke.
© 2015 John Wiley & Sons, Inc. Published 2015 by John Wiley & Sons, Inc.

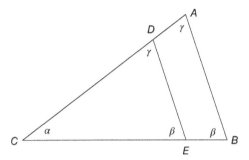

Figure A.1 Similar triangles

Another formula, known as *Heron's formula*, uses the lengths of the three sides of the triangle a, b, and c, along with one-half the perimeter $s = \frac{1}{2}(a + b + c)$.

$$\text{Area of Triangle} = \sqrt{s(s - a)(s - b)(s - c)} \qquad (A.3)$$

A line segment passing through a vertex and the midpoint of the opposite side is called a *median*. Again, the three medians of the triangle intersect in a single point called the *centroid*. This point divides each median in the ratio of 2 : 1; in other words, the intersection point is one-third of the way from a side to the opposite vertex along a median (Figure A.2).

A line segment passing through a vertex and bisecting the vertex angle is simply called an *angle bisector*. The three angle bisectors of a triangle meet in a single point called the *incenter*. A circle centered at the incenter that just touches (tangent to) one side of the triangle also touches the other two sides. This circle is the inscribed circle for the triangle and is called the *incircle*.

A perpendicular bisector for the side of a triangle is a line that intersects the side at its midpoint and is perpendicular to the side. The three perpendicular bisectors for a triangle all meet in a single point called the *circumcenter*. Any point on a perpendicular bisector is equidistant from the two vertices bounding the triangle's side.

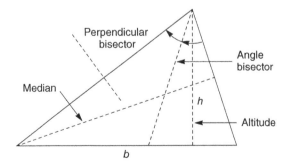

Figure A.2 Altitudes, bisectors, medians

Consequently, the circumcenter is equidistant from all three vertices and is the center of a circle that passes through the three vertices. This circle is the circumscribed circle for the triangle and is called the *circumcircle*.

A.2 ANGLES

Angles are measured by how much arc they cut from a circle. In Figure A.3, $\angle BAC$, positioned at the center of the circle, cuts the arc BC from the circle. A full circle has 360° or, in the *radian* measuring system, 2π radians. The circumference of a unit circle is 2π, so radian measure is measuring the length of the arc cut from a unit circle by an angle whose vertex is at the center of the circle. A right angle is 90°, which is $\frac{\pi}{2}$ radians.

The sum of the three interior angles for a triangle is 180° or π radians. Using this fact and by considering the triangles ΔDAB and ΔDAC in Figure A.3, it follows that $\angle BAC = 2 \times \angle BDC$. An angle inscribed in a semicircle with vertex on the circle cuts exactly half the circle and is therefore a right angle ($\frac{\pi}{2}$ radians or 90°).

A *dihedral* angle is the angle between two planes. If the planes are not parallel, they intersect in a line. Any plane perpendicular to this line cuts both planes in lines. The angle between these two lines of intersection is the dihedral angle. (There are actually four such angles with opposite angles equal. The sum of two adjacent angles is 180°.) The dihedral angle is equal to the angle between the normals to the plans.

Three-dimensional angles, called *solid angles*, can be formed by cones emanating from a vertex point. (A cone is formed by drawing straight lines from a vertex to the perimeter of Figure A.4.) The cone cuts the surface of a unit sphere just like an angle cuts the unit circle. The unit sphere has a total surface area of 4π, and the area cut by the cone is the size of the angle. The unit of measure is the *steradian*. A cone formed by the three perpendicular coordinate planes cuts one-eighth of the sphere and hence $\pi/2$ steradians.

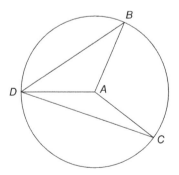

Figure A.3 Angle in circle

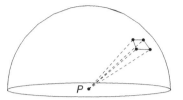

Figure A.4   Solid angle

A.3   TRIGONOMETRIC FUNCTIONS

Figure A.5(a): There is a large and small right triangle with one angle labeled α. Looking first at the larger triangle, define the basic trigonometric functions by

$$\sin \alpha = \frac{a}{c} \qquad \cos \alpha = \frac{b}{c} \qquad \tan \alpha = \frac{a}{b} \tag{A.4}$$

The smaller right triangle is a reduced version of the larger and therefore similar; the ratios of the sides stay the same, so our definition of sine, cosine, and tangent are consistent. Now suppose we scale the larger triangle until the hypotenuse is exactly equal to 1. Let the vertex of angle α be the center of a unit circle and let this center also be the origin of a Cartesian coordinate system. One side of the angle is placed along the positive x-axis and we move counterclockwise to indicate a positive angle. We can reinterpret the trigonometric functions in terms of the coordinates of the point where the angle's side intersects the circle.

Figure A.5(b): Since the length of the hypotenuse is 1, the point of intersection has coordinates $(\frac{b}{c}, \frac{a}{c})$, so the x coordinate is the cosine and the y coordinate is the sine. This definition allows us to find the sine and cosine of angles larger than $\pi/2$ radians. It is then possible that the coordinates are negative. Hence, using radian measure, $\sin(\frac{2\pi}{3}) = \frac{\sqrt{3}}{2}$ and $\cos(\frac{2\pi}{3}) = -\frac{1}{2}$.

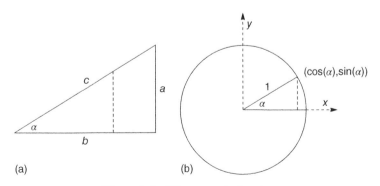

Figure A.5   Trigonometric functions

This definition of sine and cosine using the unit circle leads to several relations among the trigonometric functions:

$$\sin^2(\alpha) + \cos^2(\alpha) = 1$$

$$\sin(-\alpha) = -\sin(\alpha) \qquad \cos(-\alpha) = \cos(\alpha)$$

$$\sin(\pi - \alpha) = \sin(\alpha) \qquad \cos(\pi - \alpha) = -\cos(\alpha) \qquad \text{(A.5)}$$

$$\sin(\alpha + 2\pi) = \sin(\alpha) \qquad \cos(\alpha + 2\pi) = \cos(\alpha)$$

It is convenient to define other trigonometric functions in terms of sine and cosine.

$$\text{Tangent:} \qquad \tan(\alpha) = \frac{\sin(\alpha)}{\cos(\alpha)}$$

$$\text{Secant:} \qquad \sec(\alpha) = \frac{1}{\cos(\alpha)}$$

$$\text{Cosecant:} \qquad \csc(\alpha) = \frac{1}{\sin(\alpha)} \qquad \text{(A.6)}$$

$$\text{Cotangent:} \qquad \cot(\alpha) = \frac{\cos(\alpha)}{\sin(\alpha)}$$

Using the law of cosines establishes two addition formulas. Corresponding subtraction formulas can be found by substituting $-\beta$ for β.

$$\sin(\alpha + \beta) = \sin(\alpha)\cos(\beta) + \sin(\beta)\cos(\alpha)$$

$$\cos(\alpha + \beta) = \cos(\alpha)\cos(\beta) - \sin(\alpha)\sin(\beta) \qquad \text{(A.7)}$$

Setting $\beta = \alpha$ and using $\sin^2(\alpha) + \cos^2(\alpha) = 1$ gives

$$\cos(2\alpha) = \cos^2(\alpha) - \sin^2(\alpha) = 2\cos^2(\alpha) - 1$$

$$\implies \cos^2(\alpha) = \frac{1 + \cos(2\alpha)}{2} \qquad \text{(A.8)}$$

Similarly, we can also establish

$$\sin^2(\alpha) = \frac{1 - \cos(2\alpha)}{2}$$

Table A.1 gives a sampling of values derived from the previous relations:

The sine function takes an angle and returns a number between -1 and 1. There is an inverse sine function, denoted $\sin^{-1}(x)$, which takes a number between -1 and 1 and returns the angle. (The function is also called *arcsine*, and in some programming languages it is named *asin*). Several angles have the same sine, but the inverse function can return only one, so we have to be clear about the domain and range

TABLE A.1 Values of Trigonometric Functions

Degrees	Radians	Sine	Cosine	Tangent
0	0	0	1	0
22.5	$\pi/8$	$\frac{\sqrt{2-\sqrt{2}}}{2}$	$\frac{\sqrt{2+\sqrt{2}}}{2}$	$\sqrt{2}-1$
30	$\pi/6$	$\frac{1}{2}$	$\frac{\sqrt{3}}{2}$	$\frac{1}{\sqrt{3}}$
45	$\pi/4$	$\frac{\sqrt{2}}{2}$	$\frac{\sqrt{2}}{2}$	1
60	$\pi/3$	$\frac{\sqrt{3}}{2}$	$\frac{1}{2}$	$\sqrt{3}$
90	$\pi/2$	1	0	∞

of the inverse functions. For the inverse sine function, the domain is $[-1, 1]$ and the range is $[-\pi/2, \pi/2]$. The following gives the domain and range for the three main trigonometric inverse functions:

$$\sin^{-1} : [-1, 1] \rightarrow [-\pi/2, \pi/2]$$

$$\cos^{-1} : [-1, 1] \rightarrow [0, \pi]$$

$$\tan^{-1} : (-\infty, \infty) \rightarrow (-\pi/2, \pi/2) \tag{A.9}$$

APPENDIX B

LINEAR ALGEBRA

B.1 SYSTEMS OF LINEAR EQUATIONS

A system of m linear equations in n unknowns looks like this:

$$a_{11}x_1 + a_{12}x_2 + \cdots + a_{1n} = b_1$$

$$a_{21}x_1 + a_{22}x_2 + \cdots + a_{2n} = b_2$$

$$\vdots$$

$$a_{m1}x_1 + a_{m2}x_2 + \cdots + a_{mn} = b_m \qquad \text{(B.1)}$$

The x_i's are unknowns and a_{ij} and b_i are constants. To put this in simpler form, we form matrices and define matrix multiplication.

$$M = \begin{bmatrix} a_{11} & a_{12} & \cdots & a_{1n} \\ a_{21} & a_{22} & \cdots & a_{2n} \\ \vdots & \vdots & \ddots & \vdots \\ a_{m1} & a_{m2} & \cdots & a_{mn} \end{bmatrix} \qquad X = \begin{bmatrix} x_1 \\ x_2 \\ \vdots \\ x_n \end{bmatrix} \qquad B = \begin{bmatrix} b_1 \\ b_2 \\ \vdots \\ b_m \end{bmatrix} \qquad \text{(B.2)}$$

Mathematical Structures for Computer Graphics, First Edition. Steven J. Janke.
© 2015 John Wiley & Sons, Inc. Published 2015 by John Wiley & Sons, Inc.

Notice that matrix M has m rows and n columns; its size is denoted as $m \times n$. Matrix X is a column matrix and has size $n \times 1$. Matrix B is also a column matrix with size $m \times 1$.

To multiply two matrices, the rows of the first matrix are lined up with the columns of the second matrix and corresponding entries are multiplied. The resulting products are then added. In order for this to work, the number of columns in the first matrix must equal the number of rows in the second matrix. For example,

$$\begin{bmatrix} 1 & -1 & 2 \\ 0 & 3 & 2 \end{bmatrix} \begin{bmatrix} 8 & -4 \\ 1 & -2 \\ 6 & 1 \end{bmatrix} = \begin{bmatrix} 19 & 0 \\ 15 & -4 \end{bmatrix}$$

The first entry in the first row of the product is $1 \times 8 + (-1) \times 1 + 2 \times 6 = 19$. In general, when an $m \times n$ matrix is multiplied by an $n \times p$ matrix, the result is an $m \times p$ matrix. If the entries in the first matrix are $\{a_{ij}\}$ and the entries in the second are $\{c_{ij}\}$, the entry in the ith row and jth column of the product is $\sum_{k=1}^{n} a_{ik}c_{kj}$.

The identity matrix I is a square matrix of any size with 1's down the diagonal and zeroes elsewhere. When multiplied by any square matrix M, the product is just M.

Matrix multiplication is not necessarily commutative. In fact, only if the matrices are square can you actually multiply in either direction because the number of columns of the first matrix must match the number of rows in the second. Even then, however, the products often differ.

$$\begin{bmatrix} 2 & -1 \\ 3 & 3 \end{bmatrix} \begin{bmatrix} 4 & 2 \\ 1 & -5 \end{bmatrix} = \begin{bmatrix} 7 & 9 \\ 15 & -9 \end{bmatrix}$$

$$\begin{bmatrix} 4 & 2 \\ 1 & -5 \end{bmatrix} \begin{bmatrix} 2 & -1 \\ 3 & 3 \end{bmatrix} = \begin{bmatrix} 14 & 2 \\ -13 & -16 \end{bmatrix}$$

The original system of linear equations in (B.1) can be written as a product of matrices. Matrix M $(m \times n)$ and X $(n \times 1)$ are multiplied to give B $(m \times 1)$.

$$MX = B \tag{B.3}$$

The system does not necessarily have a unique solution. Geometrically, each equation is the equation of a plane in n-dimensional space. If the planes have a common point (or points) of intersection, then there is a solution to the system.

B.1.1   Solving the System

There are several approaches to solving the system of linear equations.

- *Gaussian Elimination.* By systematically using algebra to add multiples of one equation to another, unknowns can be removed one by one until there is either a unique value for one unknown or a range of possible values. Substituting back into the other equations yields values for the other unknowns. A well-defined algorithm keeps this process in order.

- *Inverses.* If the matrix M is a square matrix, then it possibly has an inverse, M^{-1}. This is a matrix such that when multiplied on either side of M, the product is the identity matrix.

$$M^{-1}M = MM^{-1} = I$$

In this case,

$$MX = B \implies M^{-1}MX = M^{-1}B$$
$$\implies X = IX = M^{-1}B \tag{B.4}$$

This gives the values of all the unknowns as a product of matrices. Again, only if M is square and satisfies certain properties does it have an inverse.

- *Determinants and Cramer's Rule.* For a 2×2 matrix, the determinant is defined as follows:

$$\begin{vmatrix} a_{11} & a_{12} \\ a_{21} & a_{22} \end{vmatrix} = a_{11}a_{22} - a_{12}a_{21}$$

Vertical lines indicate the determinant. For a 3×3 matrix, the determinant is defined in terms of the determinants of 2×2 submatrices.

$$\begin{vmatrix} a_{11} & a_{12} & a_{13} \\ a_{21} & a_{22} & a_{23} \\ a_{31} & a_{32} & a_{33} \end{vmatrix} = a_{11}\begin{vmatrix} a_{22} & a_{23} \\ a_{32} & a_{33} \end{vmatrix} - a_{12}\begin{vmatrix} a_{21} & a_{23} \\ a_{31} & a_{33} \end{vmatrix} + a_{13}\begin{vmatrix} a_{21} & a_{22} \\ a_{31} & a_{32} \end{vmatrix}$$

Notice the negative sign in front of the second term on the right. For $n \times n$ matrices, the determinant is defined recursively in terms of determinants of $(n-1) \times (n-1)$ submatrices. The signs of the terms alternate, starting with a plus sign in front of a_{11}. The determinant of a square matrix M is denoted $\det(M)$. If M is an $n \times n$ matrix, define $M(i,j)$ to be the submatrix equal to matrix M with the ith row and jth column deleted. Then the following formula gives one way to calculate the determinant of M.

$$\det(M) = \sum_{j=1}^{n} (-1)^{j+1} a_{1j} \det(M(1,j)) \tag{B.5}$$

Result B.1 *A square matrix has an inverse if and only if the determinant is nonzero.*

There is a method for solving a system of linear equations using determinants. To describe the method, first imagine replacing the ith column of the square $n \times n$ matrix M with the $n \times 1$ column matrix B to get a new $n \times n$ matrix $M_i(B)$.

Result B.2 (Cramer's Rule). *If M is an $n \times n$ matrix with an inverse and B is any $n \times 1$ matrix, then the unique solution of the system $MX = B$ is X, where the entries $\{x_i\}$ are*

$$x_i = \frac{\det(M_i(B))}{\det(M)} \text{ for } i = 1, 2, \ldots, n$$

Cramer's rule is usually more useful theoretically than it is practically, but with only a few unknowns it gives a reasonable algorithm for finding a solution.

B.2 MATRIX PROPERTIES

- *Algebra.* Two matrices of the same size can be added or subtracted component-wise. Any matrix can be multiplied by a scalar, again component-wise:

$$\begin{bmatrix} c_{11} & c_{12} & c_{13} \\ c_{21} & c_{22} & c_{23} \end{bmatrix} + \begin{bmatrix} d_{11} & d_{12} & d_{13} \\ d_{21} & d_{22} & d_{23} \end{bmatrix} = \begin{bmatrix} c_{11} + d_{11} & c_{12} + d_{12} & c_{13} + d_{13} \\ c_{21} + c_{21} & c_{22} + d_{22} & c_{23} + d_{23} \end{bmatrix}$$

$$k \begin{bmatrix} c_{11} & c_{12} & c_{13} \\ c_{21} & c_{22} & c_{23} \end{bmatrix} = \begin{bmatrix} kc_{11} & kc_{12} & kc_{13} \\ kc_{21} & kc_{22} & kc_{23} \end{bmatrix}$$

- *Transpose.* The transpose of a matrix M is denoted M^T and is defined by inter-changing the rows and columns.

$$C = \begin{bmatrix} c_{11} & c_{12} & c_{13} \\ c_{21} & c_{22} & c_{23} \end{bmatrix} \implies C^T = \begin{bmatrix} c_{11} & c_{21} \\ c_{12} & c_{22} \\ c_{13} & c_{23} \end{bmatrix}$$

- *Finding the Matrix Inverse.* Assuming that the determinant is nonzero (Result B.1), the inverse of a 2×2 matrix can be described as follows:

$$M = \begin{bmatrix} a_{11} & a_{12} \\ a_{21} & a_{22} \end{bmatrix} \implies M^{-1} = \frac{1}{\det(M)} \begin{bmatrix} a_{22} & -a_{12} \\ -a_{21} & a_{11} \end{bmatrix} \tag{B.6}$$

The inverse of an arbitrary square matrix can be described by first using the matrix $M(i, j)$ (obtained from M by deleting the ith row and the jth column). Let $C_{ij} = (-1)^{i+j} \det(M(i, j))$. If $\{C_{ij}\}$ are the entries of matrix C, then define the *adjugate* of M to be the transpose of C; that is, $\text{adj}(M) = C^T$. Finally,

$$M^{-1} = \frac{1}{\det(M)} \text{adj}(M) \tag{B.7}$$

- *Calculation Properties.*

  1. For matrices A and B with appropriate sizes,

$$(A + B)^T = A^T + B^T$$
$$(AB)^T = B^T A^T \tag{B.8}$$

  2. If A and B have inverses,

$$(AB)^{-1} = B^{-1} A^{-1}$$
$$(A^T)^{-1} = (A^{-1})^T \tag{B.9}$$

  3. For square matrices A and B,

$$\det(A^T) = \det(A)$$
$$\det(AB) = \det(A)\det(B) \tag{B.10}$$

- *Eigenvalues and Eigenvectors.* For square $(n \times n)$ matrices M, it is possible that there exist vectors $\vec{v}$ and scalars λ such that $M\vec{v} = \lambda\vec{v}$. In this case, λ is an *eigenvalue* and $\vec{v}$ is an *eigenvector*.
  To find eigenvalues, notice that

$$M\vec{v} = \lambda\vec{v} \implies (M - \lambda I)\vec{v} = 0$$

  If the matrix $(M - \lambda I)$ has an inverse, then only the trivial vector $\vec{v} = \vec{0}$ will work. So, in order to have nontrivial eigenvalues and eigenvectors, we must have

$$\det(M - \lambda I) = 0$$

Example B.1 (Finding Eigenvalues).

$$M = \begin{bmatrix} 4 & 1 \\ 3 & 6 \end{bmatrix} \implies \det(M - \lambda I) = \lambda^2 - 10\lambda + 21 = 0$$
$$\implies \lambda = 3, \qquad \lambda = 7$$

Using these values of λ, it is easy to find two eigenvectors:

$$M\vec{v}_1 = \begin{bmatrix} 4 & 1 \\ 3 & 6 \end{bmatrix} \begin{bmatrix} 1 \\ -1 \end{bmatrix} = 3 \begin{bmatrix} 1 \\ -1 \end{bmatrix}$$

$$M\vec{v}_2 = \begin{bmatrix} 4 & 1 \\ 3 & 6 \end{bmatrix} \begin{bmatrix} 1 \\ 3 \end{bmatrix} = 7 \begin{bmatrix} 1 \\ 3 \end{bmatrix}$$

Let V be a matrix with the eigenvectors as columns. Then M factors as $M = CDC^{-1}$, where D is a diagonal matrix with eigenvalues on the diagonal.

$$\begin{bmatrix} 4 & 1 \\ 3 & 6 \end{bmatrix} = \begin{bmatrix} 1 & 1 \\ -1 & 3 \end{bmatrix} \begin{bmatrix} 3 & 0 \\ 0 & 7 \end{bmatrix} \frac{1}{4} \begin{bmatrix} 3 & -1 \\ 1 & 1 \end{bmatrix}$$

Not all square matrices can be diagonalized like this one, but the eigenvalues and eigenvectors indicate the key characteristics of square matrices and their associated linear transformations. □

B.3 VECTOR SPACES

A set V is a *vector space* if there is an addition and scalar multiplication defined and the following axioms hold for all elements $\vec{u}, \vec{v}, \vec{w}$ in V:

1. $\vec{u} + \vec{v}$ is in V, and $\vec{u} + \vec{v} = \vec{v} + \vec{u}$.
2. $(\vec{u} + \vec{v}) + \vec{w} = \vec{u} + (\vec{v} + \vec{w})$.
3. There is a zero vector $\vec{0}$ in V such that $\vec{u} + \vec{0} = \vec{u}$.
4. For each $\vec{u}$, there is $-\vec{u}$ such that $\vec{u} + (-\vec{u}) = \vec{0}$.
5. For each real number a, $a\vec{u}$ is in V and $1\vec{u} = \vec{u}$.
6. For real numbers a and b, $a(b\vec{u}) = (ab)\vec{u}$.
7. $a(\vec{u} + \vec{v}) = a\vec{u} + a\vec{v}$ and $(a + b)\vec{u} = a\vec{u} + b\vec{u}$.

The set of column matrices can be considered a vector space, and consequently vectors (as defined in an early chapter) form a vector space.

A *subspace* of a vector space V is a subset of vectors such that the addition of any two is in the subset, the scalar multiplication of any element is in the subset, and the zero vector is in the subset. For example, the set of all three-dimensional vectors (3×1 matrices) with all three entries equal forms a subspace.

Given a set of vectors $\{\vec{v}_1, \vec{v}_2, \ldots, \vec{v}_n\}$, a linear combination of them is a vector $a_1\vec{v}_1 + a_2\vec{v}_2 + \cdots + a_n\vec{v}_n$ for real numbers a_i. The set of all linear combinations of the given vectors forms a subspace called the *span* of $\{\vec{v}_1, \vec{v}_2, \ldots, \vec{v}_n\}$.

The set of nonzero vectors $\{\vec{v}_1, \vec{v}_2, \ldots, \vec{v}_n\}$ is said to be linearly independent if the only scalar values that satisfy $a_1\vec{v}_1 + a_2\vec{v}_2 + \cdots + a_n\vec{v}_n = \vec{0}$ are $a_i = 0$ for $i = 1, 2, \ldots, n$. A linearly independent set of vectors whose span is the subspace W is said to be a *basis* for W, and the number of vectors in the basis is the *dimension* of W.

Multiplication by an $n \times m$ matrix is a linear transformation; it sends an $n \times 1$ vector ($\vec{v}$) to the $m \times 1$ vector $M\vec{v}$. All vectors $\vec{v}$ such that $M\vec{v} = \vec{0}$ form a subspace called the *null space* of M. The columns of M are vectors and their span is called the *column space* of M.

Return to the system of linear equations $MX = B$ and view the left-hand side as a linear transformation of the vector X. The system has a solution if the transformed vector equals B. In the case where the matrix M is $n \times n$, the system has a unique solution for every B if and only if M has an inverse M^{-1}. In the language of vector spaces, there is an inverse if and only if the null space contains only the zero vector; its dimension is zero. Continuing in this vein, the following fundamental theorem is the first part of a larger fundamental theorem for linear algebra.

Theorem B.1 (Fundamental Theorem of Linear Algebra). *Let M be an $m \times n$ matrix. Then the dimension of the null space for M plus the dimension of the column space for M equals n. Moreover, if M is a square matrix, it has an inverse if and only if the dimension of the null space is zero.*

REFERENCES

1. Maor E. *The Pythagorean Theorem*. Princeton University Press, Princeton; 2007.

2. Cromwell PR. *Polyhedra*. Cambridge University Press, New York; 1997.

3. Meyer M, Lee H, Barr A, Desbrun M. Generalized barycentric coordinates on irregular polygons. *J Graph Tools* 2002;7(1):13–22.

4. Floater M, Hormann K, Kos G. A general construction of barycentric coordinates over convex polygons. *Adv Comput Math* 2006;24:311–331.

5. Piegl L, Tiller W. *The NURBS Book*. 2nd ed. Springer-Verlag, New York; 1997.

6. Rogers DF. *An Introduction to NURBS with Historical Perspective*. Academic Press, San Francisco; 2001.

7. Phong BT. Illumination for computer generated pictures. *Commun ACM* 1975;18(6): 311–317.

8. Nicodemus F, Richmond J, Hsia J. *Geometrical Considerations and Nomenclature for Reflectance*. National Bureau of Standards; 1977.

9. Cook RL, Torrance KE. A reflectance model for computer graphics. *ACM Trans Graph* 1985;1(1):7–24.

10. Whitted T. An improved illumination model for shaded display. *Commun ACM* 1980;23(6):343–349.

11. Bresenham J. Algorithm for computer control of digital plotter. *IBM Syst J* 1965;4(1): 25–30.

12. Wu X. An efficient antialiasing technique. *Comput Graph* 1991;25(4):143–152.

13. Porter T, Duff T. Compositing digital images. *Comput Graph* 1984;18(3):253–259.

Mathematical Structures for Computer Graphics, First Edition. Steven J. Janke.
© 2015 John Wiley & Sons, Inc. Published 2015 by John Wiley & Sons, Inc.

14. Rozenberg G, Salomaa A. *The Mathematical Theory of L-Systems*. Academic Press, New York; 1980.

15. Przemysloaw P, Lindenmayer A. *The Algorithmic Beauty of Plants*. Springer-Verlag New York, Inc. New York; 1990.

16. Akenine-Möller T, Haines E. *Real-Time Rendering*. 2nd ed. A K Peters, Ltd., Natick, MA; 2002.

17. Arvo J, editor. *Graphics Gems II*. Academic Press, Inc. Boston; 1991.

18. Baumgart B. Winged Edge Polyhedron Representation, Advanced Research Projects Agency, 1972.

19. Beach RC. *An Introduction to Curves and Surfaces of Computer-Aided Design*. Van Nostrand Reinhold, New York; 1991.

20. Blinn JF. *Dirty Pixels*. Morgan Kaufmann Publishers, San Francisco; 1998.

21. Blinn JF, Newell ME. Clipping using homogeneous coordinates. SIGGRAPH Proceedings, 1978.

22. Blinn J. Simulation of wrinkled surfaces. SIGGRAPH Proceedings, 1978.

23. Buss SR. *3-D Computer Graphics: A Mathematical Introduction with OpenGL*. Cambridge University Press, New York; 2003.

24. Cohen M, Wallace J. *Radiosity and Realistic Image Synthesis*. Academic Press, Boston; 1993.

25. Coexeter H, Greitzer S. *Geometry Revisited*. The Mathematics Association of America, Washington, D.C.; 1967.

26. Crowe MJ. *A History of Vector Analysis*. University of Notre Dame Press, Notre Dame; London; 1967. (Dover reprint edition, 2011).

27. de Berg M, van Kreveld M, Overmars M, Schwarzkopf O. *Computational Geometry*. Springer-Verlag, Berlin; New York; 1997.

28. Devadoss S, O'Rourke J. *Discrete and Computational Geometry*. Princeton University Press, Princeton; 2011.

29. Ebert D, Musgrave F, Peachey D, Perlin K, Worley S. *Texturing & Modeling, A Procedural Approach*. 3rd ed. Morgan Kaufmann, San Francisco; 2003.

30. Ericson C. *Real-Time Collision Detection*. Morgan Kaufmann Publishers, San Francisco; 2005.

31. Farin G. *Curves and Surfaces for Computer Aided Geometric Design*. Academic Press, Boston; 1988.

32. Farin G. *Nurb Curves and Surfaces from Projective Geometry to Practical Use*. A.K.Peters, Ltd. Wellesley, MA; 1995.

33. Farin G, Hansford D. *Practical Linear Algebra: A Geometry Toolbox*. A.K.Peters, Ltd. Wellesley, MA; 2005.

34. Field JV. *The Invention of Infinity: Mathematics and Art in the Renaissance*. Oxford University Press, New York; 1997.

35. Glassner A., editor. *Graphics Gems*. Academic Press, Inc. Boston; 1990.

36. Goldman R. On the algebraic and geometric foundations of computer graphics. *ACM Trans Graph* 2002;21(1):52–86.

37. Gortler SJ. *Foundations of 3D Computer Graphics*. MIT Press, Cambridge; 2012.

38. Hearn D, Baker MP, Carithers W. *Computer Graphics with OpenGL*. 4th ed. Prentice Hall Upper Saddle River, NJ; 2011.

39. Heckbert P, editor. *Graphics Gems IV*. Academic Press, Inc. San Diego; 1994.

40. Henle M. *Modern Geometries, The Analytic Approach*. Prentice Hall Upper Saddle River, NJ; 1997.

41. Jensen H. *Realistic Image Synthesis Using Photon Mapping*. A K Peters, Ltd. Wellesley, MA; 2001.

42. Kirk D, editor. *Graphics Gems III*. Academic Press, Inc. San Diego; 1992.

43. Lay DC. *Linear Algebra and its Applications*. 4th ed. Addison-Wesley; Boston; 2012.

44. Lengyel E. *Mathematics for 3D Game Programming and Computer Graphics*. 3rd ed. Course Technology, Boston; 2012.

45. Luebke D, Reddy M, Cohen J, Varshney A, Watson B, Huebner R. *Level of Detail for 3D Graphics*. Morgan Kaufmann; San Francisco; 2003.

46. Marsh D. *Applied Geometry for Computer Graphics and CAD*. Springer-Verlag, London; 2000.

47. McConnell JJ. *Computer Graphics: Theory into Practice*. Jones and Barlett Pulishers, Inc. Boston; 2006.

48. Palais B, Palais R, Rodi S. A disorienting look at Euler's theorem on the axis of rotation. *Am Math Monthly* 2009;116(10):892.

49. Perlin K. An image synthesizer. SIGGRAPH Proceedings, 1985.

50. Perlin K. Improving noise. SIGGRAPH Proceedings, 2002.

51. Salomon D. *Curves and Surfaces for Computer Graphics*. Springer Science+Business Media, Inc. New York; 2006.

52. Schoenberg I. Contributions to the problem of approximation of equidistant data by analytic functions. *Q. Appl. Math.* 1946;4:44–99, 112–141.

53. Shirley P. *Fundamentals of Computer Graphics*. A.K.Peters, Ltd. Natick, MA; 2002.

54. Shoemake K. Animating rotation with quaternion curves. SIGGRAPH '85 Proceedings, Volume 19(3); 1985.

55. Shreiner D, Sellers G, Kessenich J, Licea-Kane B. *OpenGL Programming Guide*. 8th ed. Addison-Wesley; Upper Saddle River, NJ; 2013.

56. Sillion F, Peuch C. *Radiosity and Global Illumination*. Morgan Kaufmann Publishers, San Francisco; 1994.

57. Stillwell J. *The Four Pillars of Geometry*. Springer, New York; 2005.

58. Watt A. *3D Computer Graphics*. 3rd ed. Addison-Wesley; Harlow, England; New York; 2000.

59. Wu X, Rokne J. Double-step incremental generation of lines and circles. *Comput Vision Graph Image Process Volley* 1987;37(3):331–344.

INDEX

Mathematical Structures for Computer Graphics, First Edition. Steven J. Janke.
© 2015 John Wiley & Sons, Inc. Published 2015 by John Wiley & Sons, Inc.

Printed and bound by CPI Group (UK) Ltd, Croydon, CR0 4YY

22/11/2022

03165057-0002